D0883559

808.87   Untermeyer
U61tg   Great humor

CHRISTIAN HERITAGE COLLEGE
2100 Greenfield Dr.
El Cajon, CA 92021

808.87
U.61t

TREASURY OF Great Humor

TREASURY OF

Great Humor

INCLUDING WIT, WHIMSY, AND SATIRE FROM THE REMOTE PAST TO THE PRESENT

Edited, with a Running Commentary, by

LOUIS UNTERMEYER 1885-

comp.

McGraw-Hill Book Company

New York   St. Louis   San Francisco
Düsseldorf   London   Mexico   Sydney   Toronto

Book design by Elaine Gongora

Copyright © 1972 by McGraw-Hill Book Company.
All rights reserved. Printed in the United States of America. No part of this publication may be reproduced, stored in a retrieval system, or transmitted, in any form or
by any means, electronic, mechanical, photocopying, recording, or otherwise,
without the prior written permission of the publisher.

Untermeyer, Louis   comp.
    Great humor.
        1. Wit and humor.   I. Title.
PN6151.U5   808.87   79-37529
ISBN 0-07-065939-7

ACKNOWLEDGMENTS

The editor thanks the following authors, publishers, and agents for permission to
reprint the copyright material included in this volume. In the event of any error or
omission, he will be pleased to make the necessary correction in future editions of
this book.

BRANDT & BRANDT for "A. V. Laider," from *Seven Men,* by Max Beerbohm.
    Alfred A. Knopf, Inc. Copyright 1920, 1948 by Max Beerbohm. Reprinted by
    permission of Brandt & Brandt.

JONATHAN CAPE LTD. for "Cockadoodledoo," from *The Seance and Other
    Stories,* by Isaac Bashevis Singer, and for part of Chapter V from *Catch-22,*
    by Joseph Heller.

DOUBLEDAY & COMPANY, INC. for "The Colonel's Lady," by W. Somerset
    Maugham. Copyright 1946 by W. Somerset Maugham. From *Creatures of
    Circumstance,* by W. Somerset Maugham. Reprinted by permission of Double-
    day & Company, Inc.

FARRAR, STRAUS & GIROUX, INC. for "Cockadoodledoo," from *The Seance
    and Other Stories,* by Isaac Bashevis Singer; copyright © 1964, 1968 by Isaac
    Bashevis Singer. Reprinted with the permission of Farrar, Straus & Giroux, Inc.

RAOUL LIONEL FELDER for "The Hottest Guy in the World," from Damon Run-
    yon's *Guys and Dolls.* Copyright renewed 1957 by Damon Runyon, Jr., and
    Mary Runyon McCann.

HAMISH HAMILTON LTD. for "The Secret Life of Walter Mitty" and "File and
    Forget," by James Thurber. From *Vintage Thurber,* by James Thurber. Copy-
    right © 1963 by Hamish Hamilton Ltd.

HARCOURT BRACE JOVANOVICH, INC. for "On with the Dance!" "A Lingering
    Adieu," "Horace Loses His Temper," and "The Reconciliation," from *Including
    Horace,* by Louis Untermeyer, copyright 1919 by Harcourt Brace Jovanovich,
    Inc.; copyright 1947 by Louis Untermeyer. Also pages 5–9 from Molière's *The
    Misanthrope,* translated by Richard Wilbur, copyright 1954, 1955 by Richard
    Wilbur. Reprinted by permission of Harcourt Brace Jovanovich, Inc.

HARPER & ROW, PUBLISHERS, INC. for "The Murder Without Interest," from *No
    Poems, or Around the World Backwards and Sideways,* by Robert Benchley.
    Copyright 1932 by Robert Benchley; copyright renewed 1960 by Gertrude
    Benchley. Reprinted by permission of Harper & Row, Publishers, Inc.

WILLIAM HEINEMANN LTD. for "Insert Flap 'A' and Throw Away," from *The Most
    of S. J. Perelman.* Copyright 1958 by S. J. Perelman.

DAVID MCKAY COMPANY, INC. for "The Reeve's Tale" and "The Merchant's Tale," from Chaucer's *The Canterbury Tales* translated by Frank Ernest Hill. Copyright © 1935 by Longmans, Green & Co., Inc. Copyright © renewed 1963 by Frank Ernest Hill. Reprinted by permission of the publisher, David McKay Company, Inc.

LAURENCE POLLINGER LIMITED for "Cockadoodledoo," from *The Seance and Other Stories*, by Isaac Bashevis Singer, and for part of Chapter V from *Catch-22*, by Joseph Heller.

PRINCETON UNIVERSITY PRESS for the selection from Desiderius Erasmus, *The Praise of Folly*, translated by Hoyt Hopewell Hudson, copyright 1941 by Princeton University Press; Princeton Paperback 1970. Reprinted by permission of Princeton University Press.

ROUTLEDGE & KEGAN PAUL LTD. for the selections (numbers 31, 57, 64, 100, 112) from *Jest Upon Jest*, by John Wardroper. Reprinted by permission of Routledge & Kegan Paul Ltd.

SIMON & SCHUSTER, INC. for part of Chapter V from *Catch-22*, by Joseph Heller, copyright © 1955 by Joseph Heller; and for "Insert Flap 'A' and Throw Away," from *The Most of S. J. Perelman*, copyright © 1930, 1931, 1932, 1935, 1936, 1953, 1955, 1957, 1958 by S. J. Perelman.

THE SOCIETY OF AUTHORS for the selections from *A Shropshire Lad*, by A. E. Housman. Reprinted by permission of The Society of Authors as the literary representative of the estate of A. E. Housman and Jonathan Cape Ltd., publishers of A. E. Housman's *Complete Poems*.

MRS. JAMES THURBER for "The Secret Life of Walter Mitty," copyright © 1942 by James Thurber; copyright © 1970 by Helen Thurber, from *My World—and Welcome to It*, published by Harcourt Brace Jovanovich, Inc. Originally printed in *The New Yorker*. For "File and Forget," by James Thurber, copyright © 1953 by James Thurber. From *Thurber Country*, published by Simon & Schuster, Inc. Originally printed in *The New Yorker*.

UNIVERSITY OF MICHIGAN PRESS for the selection from *The Satyricon of Petronius* translated by William Arrowsmith. Copyright © 1959 by William Arrowsmith.

LOUIS UNTERMEYER for the adaptations from Aesop, the *Panchatantra*, *The Greek Anthology*, Martial, Lucian, *Reynard the Fox*, and La Fontaine, as well as the excerpts from *The Wonderful Adventures of Paul Bunyan* (Heritage Press), copyright by Louis Untermeyer.

THE VANGUARD PRESS, INC. for pages 185–197 of "Portrait of a Learned Lady," from *English Eccentrics*, by Edith Sitwell. Copyright 1957 by Edith Sitwell. Reprinted by permission of the publisher, The Vanguard Press, Inc.

THE VIKING PRESS, INC. for "The Waltz," from *The Portable Dorothy Parker*. Copyright 1933; copyright © renewed 1961 by Dorothy Parker. Reprinted by permission of The Viking Press, Inc. For "The Open Window" and "The Reticence of Lady Anne," from *The Short Stories of Saki*, by H. H. Munro. Reprinted by permission of The Viking Press, Inc.

A. P. WATT & SON for "The Colonel's Lady," by W. Somerset Maugham, from *Creatures of Circumstance*. Copyright 1946 by W. Somerset Maugham. Reprinted by permission of the literary executor of W. Somerset Maugham and William Heinemann Ltd.

P. G. WODEHOUSE for "Strychnine in the Soup," from *Mulliner Nights*, by P. G. Wodehouse (Doubleday Doran, 1933), and from *The Most of P. G. Wodehouse* (Simon & Schuster, 1960). Reprinted by permission of P. G. Wodehouse.

22876

22876

Contents

A Foreword

Nations are torn apart by wars; ideologies rise and empires fall. Man has his private as well as public tragedies. Laughter, his frail but unassailable refuge, survives them all.

Hell had its terrors, but men learned to face them with a grin. They carved the archfiend in stone above the sanctified grandeur of Notre Dame and let him loom comically over the rooftops of Paris. In England devils were a popular feature of medieval miracle plays, and demons with pitchforks, associated with stage imps, became too familiar to be frightening. The paintings of Hieronymus Bosch and Pieter Brueghel were animated by grotesque inventions, and the murkiest of their nightmares were enlivened with high-spirited if macabre mirth.

It is both a platitude and a paradox that though humor is ageless, nothing ages so quickly as a piece of humor. Laughter never dies, but the art of achieving a laugh varies not only with the teller but also with the listener. The scene in *The Frogs* in which the Greek tragedians lampoon each other's works must have been uproariously funny to those who knew their Aeschylus and Euripides, but few today are convulsed at Aristophanes' parody of his betters, and the famous chorus of frogs— *co-ax, co-ax, co-ax, brekekekex co-ax*—persists only in a college football cheer. The sadistic mockery of Juvenal amuses us because of the way John Dryden translated it into nimble couplets. Modern audiences seldom smile at the puns of Shakespeare's antic clowns.

If humor is volatile and viable, it is also indefinable. It includes the leap of fancy, the momentary whim, and the sidespring of caprice, as well as Milton's "light fantastic toe" with "Laughter holding both his sides." It is both confused with and distinguished from satire, wit, and burlesque. Humor can be either gentle or rough, supple or sophisticated, but it need not be critical. Satire, on the other hand, is essentially a form of criticism; it may even be so savage, so insulting, as to be wholly without humor. Wit is intellectual, sharp, and swift; it pierces, and its point is often barbed and tipped with poison. Satire goes further. It not only pierces but also probes; it claims that its incisions cure, but they are often so corrosive as to kill. Burlesque pounds with a buffoon's bludgeon, while humor is generally sympathetic. Opposed to the envenomed dart of wit and the pitiless scalpel of satire, humor is wholesome and often healing.

"Humor," wrote William Hazlitt, "is the describing of the ludicrous as it is in itself; wit is the exposing of it by comparing or contrasting it with something else. Humor is, as it were, the growth of nature and accident; wit is the product of art and skill." Humor, therefore, has about it an air of aimlessness, of genial purposelessness; it asks little of anyone. Satire, on the contrary, demands the concentration of alert and detached intelligence; it is never casual or careless, for it achieves its end with deliberation, and at someone's expense.

Hazlitt's remark that humor is "the growth of nature" suggests that humor is close to the soil and that wit is the product of the city, which considers itself superior to the country. That sophisticated maxim-maker, François Duc de La Rochefoucauld, made it plain that wit was a currency manufactured and circulated only in the town. Mark Twain felt that the essence of American humor was a rustic ability to string incongruous and absurd things together in a wandering and sometimes purposeless way and "to seem innocently unaware that they are absurdities." The word "humor" has meant incongruously different things to different people at different times. The Greeks believed that the body contained four "humors" that conditioned one's health and disposition: blood, phlegm, yellow bile (choler), and black bile (melancholy). In the sixteenth century humor was defined as a disorder of the blood.

In *The World Upside-Down* (1971) Ian Donaldson introduces the comic spirit with an appropriate quotation from *Measure for Measure:*

> *. . . Liberty plucks Justice by the nose*
> *The baby beats the nurse, and quite athwart*
> *Goes all decorum.*

Donaldson goes on to say that the comedy of inversion is "a satisfying act of comic revenge against those whose authority we habitually respect and fear." The writer of comedy, and especially the satirist, is "a social saboteur"; he not only mocks but also topples images of "the lunatic governor, the incompetent judge, the mock doctor, the equivocating priest, the henpecked husband—the familiar and recurrent figures in the comedy of a society which gives a general assent to the necessity of entrusting power to its governors, judges, doctors, priests, and husbands."

Analyzing the pages of this book, the reader may well conclude that much of the humor is far from merry. Lighthearted laughs were none too frequent in the comedies of the past. Usually the playfulness was anything but funny; all too often it was sardonic, grim, and even cruel. In this it is akin to the sick jokes, the theater of the absurd, and the black comedy of our own times. To pervert the proverb, the more humor changes the more it remains the same, and there are no features more flexible yet more immediately recognizable than those behind the comic mask.

The Bible

The Bible would seem to be the last place where one might expect to find humor of any kind. Nevertheless, the Old Testament is not without ironical wit. The parables cover their thrust with metaphors and symbols, but they are sharply pointed. Jotham's Parable of the Trees and the Bramble in the Book of Judges is a satirical fable that contains a sly rebuke. The Book of Job is part folk tale, part philosophical drama in which the dialogues mount to cosmic irony. Eliphaz the Temanite, for example, seasons his questions with heavy sarcasm.

ELIPHAZ TAUNTS JOB

Should a wise man make answer with vain knowledge,
And fill his belly with the east wind?
Should he reason with unprofitable talk,
Or with speeches wherewith he can do good? . . .
Art thou the first man that was born?
Or wast thou brought forth before the hills?
Hast thou heard the secret counsel of God?
And dost thou restrain wisdom to thyself?

But no human irony can contend with God's. Out of the whirlwind the voice of the Almighty issues in a blast of searing interrogation. After Job's comforters have failed, God suc-

ceeds, not by comforting Job, nor even by answering his
accusations and appeals, but by withering humor. Job's despair is overcome by God's universal riddles. Candidly, and with
relentless persistence, God rebukes Job with overwhelming
poetry, with enigmas beyond his penetration, and with questions that are unanswerable.

GOD QUESTIONS JOB

Who is this that darkeneth counsel
By words without knowledge?
Gird up now thy loins like a man;
For I will demand of thee, and answer thou me.
Where wast thou when I laid the foundations of the earth?
Whereupon were the foundations fastened?
Or who laid the cornerstone thereof
When the morning stars sang together
And all the sons of God shouted for joy?
Or who shut up the sea with doors
When it broke forth, as if it had issued from the womb;
When I made the cloud the garment thereof
And thick darkness a swaddling-band for it,
And prescribed for it my decree,
And set bars and doors,
And said "Hitherto shalt thou come, but no further,
And here shall thy proud waves be stayed?"
Hast thou commanded the morning since thy days began
And caused the dayspring to know its place? . . .

Declare, if thou knowest it all.
Where is the way to the dwelling of light,
And as for darkness, where is the place thereof? . . .
Doubtless thou knowest, for thou wast then born
And the number of thy days is great!
Hast thou entered the treasuries of the snow,
Or hast thou seen the treasuries of the hail? . . .

By what way is the light parted,
Or the east wind scattered upon the earth?
Who hath cleft a channel for the waterflood,
Or a way for the lightning of the thunder

To cause it to rain on a land where no man is? . . .
Hath the rain a father?
Or who has begotten the drops of dew?
Out of whose womb came the ice?
And the hoary frost of heaven, who hath gendered it?
Canst thou bind the sweet influences of the Pleiades,
Or loose the bands of Orion? . . .

Hast thou given the horse his might?
Hast thou clothed his neck with thunder?
Canst thou make him afraid as a grasshopper?
The glory of his nostrils is terrible.
He paweth in the valley and rejoiceth in his strength.
He goeth out to meet the armed men.
He mocketh at fear and is not affrighted,
Neither turneth he back from the sword.
The quiver rattleth against him,
The glittering spear and the javelin.
He swalloweth the ground with fierceness and rage;
Neither believeth he that it is the sound of the trumpet.
He saith among the trumpets "Ha! Ha!"
And he smelleth the battle afar off,
The thunder of the captains and the shouting . . .

Shall he that cavilleth contend with the Almighty?
He that argueth with God, let him answer it.

"In this drama of skepticism," wrote G. K. Chesterton, "God
Himself takes on the role of skeptic. He seems to say that if it
comes to asking questions, He can ask some questions which
will fling down and flatten out all conceivable human ques-
tioners. . . . The first question which he asks of Job is the
question that any criminal accused by Job would be most
entitled to ask. He asks Job who he is. And Job, being a man
of candid intellect, comes to the conclusion that he does not
know."

Aesop

The legends that have grown about Aesop are as fabulous as any of his fables. It is thought that his birthplace was in Asia Minor and that he was probably a Phrygian born about twenty-five hundred years ago. Herodotus mentions that Aesop was a slave, presumably black; the name "Aesop" may have meant simply "Aethiopian." He is usually portrayed as a ready-witted servant who found his way to Croesus and carried on the king's business in various provinces. It is said that he often achieved his ends by telling little parables with significantly concluding "morals." For example, when he heard the Athenians complain about the rule of Pisistratus, Aesop chided them with the fable of the frogs who asked for a king. When the citizens of Delphi demanded more money than Aesop had brought to distribute, he related the fable of the goose and the golden eggs.

The beast fable has always been a favorite method of pointing a moral and adorning a tale. It penetrated the East, enlivened the Middle Ages with *Reynard the Fox,* seeped through *The Canterbury Tales*, and acquired a new accent in the folk tales of Brer Rabbit. Whatever form Aesop's fables have taken, they have lost none of their wit and wisdom.

THE FROGS WHO ASKED FOR A KING

Some frogs who lived in a lake grew tired of their way of life. They asked Jupiter to send them a ruler. The great god smiled and threw a log into the lake. The frogs were greatly impressed by the splash it made. They clustered around the log and worshiped it.

However, it did not take them long to find out that they could do whatever they liked with the log. They ceased to be afraid of it. Again they petitioned Jupiter. This time they asked for a powerful king, one which inspired fear.

Jupiter sent down a stork. Its favorite food happened to be frogs. Soon there were no frogs left to complain.

Moral: Be content with what you have.

THE GOOSE AND THE GOLDEN EGGS

A man had the good fortune to own a remarkable goose. Every day it laid an egg of pure gold. The man grew rich, but the richer he grew the greedier he got. A gold egg a day was not enough for him—he wanted an immense treasure in a hurry. He killed the goose. However, when he cut her open, instead of finding a horde of golden eggs, he found she was just like any other goose.

Moral: He who wants everything gets nothing.

THE FOX AND THE GRAPES

The fox had gone without breakfast, lunch, and dinner. When he came to a vineyard his mouth watered. There was one particularly luscious-looking bunch of grapes hanging on a trellis. The fox leaped to pull it down, but it was a little beyond his reach. He went back a few steps, took a running start, and jumped again. Again he missed. Once more he tried, and once more he failed to get the tempting prize. At last, weary and worn out, he shrugged and left the vineyard. "I wasn't really hungry," he said. "Besides, I'm sure those grapes were sour."

Moral: Comfort yourself by pretending that what you can't get isn't worth having.

THE FOX AND THE CROW[1]

A crow had stolen a large piece of cheese and had flown with it into a tall tree. A fox who had seen it happen said to himself, "With a little cunning I should be able to get that cheese for my supper." He thought for a moment, and then addressed the bird.

"Good afternoon, Miss Crow," he began. "You look really beautiful today. I've never seen your feathers so radiant. Your neck is as graceful as a swan's, and your wings are as mighty as an eagle's. As for your voice, everyone knows it is as sweet as a nightingale's. Won't you do me a favor and sing something?"

Pleased with such praise, the gullible crow started to caw. As soon as she opened her mouth, the cheese fell to the ground, and the fox snapped it up.

Trotting off with the food, the fox made things worse by calling back to the crow. "I may have overestimated your voice and your beauty, but I said nothing about your brains."

Moral: Beware of flattery.

THE LIONESS AND THE VIXEN

All the animals were boasting of their large families. Only the lioness kept silent. She did not utter a word even when the vixen paraded her many offspring in front of the lioness.

"Look!" said the vixen. "Look at my litter of red foxes—seven of them! Tell me, how many did you just bear?"

"Only one," replied the lioness quietly. "But that one is a lion."

Moral: It's quality, not quantity, that counts.

THE ANT AND THE GRASSHOPPER[2]

One day in winter an ant dragged out some grains of food she had gathered during the summer. Seeing the seeds drying in the

[1]See the rhymed version by Jean de La Fontaine on page 213; also "The Sycophantic Fox and the Gullible Raven," by Guy Wetmore Carryl, on page 549.
[2]See the rhymed version, "The Grasshopper and the Ant," by Jean de La Fontaine on page 212.

sun, a grasshopper asked the ant to give him some.

"Why do you come to me now to be fed?" asked the ant. "What did you do during the summer?"

"Oh," answered the grasshopper, "during the summer I sang."

"Well," said the ant, "since you sang during the summer, during the winter you can dance."

Moral: When there's work to be done, don't play.

THE LION AND THE MOUSE

A mouse happened to run over the paw of a drowsing lion. Roused from his rest, the huge beast seized the small offender. He was about to devour the tiny animal when the mouse cried out.

"O mighty monarch, spare me. I would be scarcely a mouthful, and I doubt that you would like the taste. Besides, if I live I may be able to help you some day. You never can tell."

The idea that this insignificant creature might ever help his majesty amused the lion. He let the mouse go. "Off with you," he said. "And watch yourself."

Some time later the lion, roaming through the forest for food, was caught in a hunter's net. The more he struggled, the more he became entangled. His roar echoed throughout the forest. The mouse heard the sound, ran to the trap, and began to gnaw the ropes that bound the lion. It was not long before he had severed the last cord with his little teeth, and the lion was free.

"Now," he said, "now we are even."

Moral: Never belittle little things.

THE BULLFROG AND THE BULL

A bullfrog lived in a little bog. He considered himself the biggest thing in the pond, but he wanted to be the biggest bullfrog in the world.

"I am not like any other frog," he said to anyone who would listen. "I am the biggest thing of its kind. That's why they call me a bullfrog. I am to other frogs what a bull is to little calves."

Although he had heard about bulls, he had never seen one. However, one day a bull came to the pond for a drink. For a moment the bullfrog was startled, but only for a moment. His conceit was as great as ever.

"You think you're big, don't you?" he said to the bull. "Well, I can make myself as big as you."

The bull said nothing. He ignored the croaking creature.

"You don't believe it?" said the bullfrog. "Just watch!"

He blew himself up to twice his size. The bull paid no attention.

"Not big enough?" croaked the bullfrog. "I can make myself as big as I want. See!"

The bull made a scornful sound and turned away.

This was too much for the bullfrog. He took a huge breath and blew, and blew, and blew himself up until he burst.

Moral: Don't be a blowhard. Don't try to make yourself bigger than you are.

THE HARE AND THE TORTOISE

The hares always boasted about their speed. One of them made fun of a tortoise because he was so slow. For a while the tortoise stayed silent. But one day he tired of the teasing.

"I may be slow," he said to the hare, "but if we ever had a race I would win."

"Ridiculous!" said the hare.

"Is it?" said the tortoise. "We shall see. Right now. Are you ready?"

They started immediately, and the hare quickly outran the tortoise. He was, in fact, so far ahead that he treated the whole thing as a joke and lay down on the grass. "I'll take a little nap," he said to himself, "and when I wake up I'll finish the race far ahead of the crawler."

However, the hare overslept. When he arrived at the finish line, the tortoise, who had plodded steadily along, was there ahead of him.

Moral: The race is not always to the swift. Slow and steady is bound to win.

The Panchatantra

Differing from the Vedas, the religious mythology of the Hindus, and the Mahabharata, the Hindu heroic epic, the *Panchatantra*, collected about A.D. 500, is a compilation of folk fables. Written in Sanskrit, it is related to the animal tales of the West; it is obvious that many Occidental narratives originated in the Orient. As instructive as Aesop, the beasts in the *Panchatantra* illustrate human conduct, and the suggested morals are sharpened with native irony.

THE LOUSE AND THE FLEA

A louse had made her home in the bed of a certain king. Every night while the king slept, she feasted on the king's blood. The blood was as rich as it was royal, and the louse grew plump and proud. One day a flea blown by the wind dropped on the bed. Never had he encountered anything so soft, so perfumed, so luxurious. He started to make himself at home when the louse stopped him.

"Where have you come from, and what do you think you are doing?" she said. "Can't you see that I am in charge here, and that a king's bed is no place for a commoner like you?"

"Madam," said the flea, "I am no ordinary flea. I have tasted the blood of warriors and wise men, of priests and princes, but I have not yet sampled a king. A king nourishes himself on the choicest foods, meats seasoned with pomegranates and peppers, saffron and ginger, and every kind of stimulating spice. His sweets are the sweetest and his cakes the richest. His blood, therefore, must be free of bile or bitterness, fresh and fragrant as honey and nectar. I cannot wait to taste it."

"What impertinence!" said the louse. "It is out of the question! Remember that the fool who does not know his place will be accepted nowhere. Leave this bed!"

"It is you who should remember that Brahma said there is a place for everyone," rejoined the flea, "and that a guest is never to be spurned."

"Very well," said the louse grudgingly. "You may stay. But on one condition. You are not to touch the king until I have had my full dinner. And then you may suck only the smallest sip from his littlest toe. Never presume you can share what belongs to me and me alone."

The flea agreed. But as soon as the king came to bed and even before he fell asleep, the flea could not restrain himself. While the louse was creeping toward her dinner, the flea leaped fifty times his length and fastened his saw-toothed beak in the tenderest part of the king's back. The king jumped from the bed as though he had been burned by a firebrand.

"Help!" he cried. "Some monster has stung me! Find the assassin!"

The flea sprang again and hid himself in a crevice of the bed. The king's servants entered and explored the sheets. They found the louse crouched in the folds of the fabric and crushed her to death.

"That," said the flea to himself, "is what happens to those who do not show true hospitality."

THE MICE THAT ATE IRON

A merchant had had a bad year and was forced to go abroad to recoup his losses. He owned a valuable iron balance-beam which he had inherited and which weighed several hundred pounds. Afraid that thieves might break into his house during his absence and steal the iron beam, he asked his neighbor to take care of it. This the neighbor agreed to do, and the merchant departed.

It was many months before he could transact his business profitably. When he returned he thanked his neighbor for taking care of his property and asked for the iron beam.

"Alas," said the neighbor, "I cannot give it back to you. It has been eaten by mice."

"I understand," said the merchant. "You are in no way to blame because mice have eaten up the iron beam." He shrugged. "Like human beings, animals have strange appetites. Besides, nothing in the world lasts forever. Such is life. I am going to the river to wash away my sins. Will you lend me your fifteen-year-old boy to carry my bathing things?"

"Certainly," said the neighbor. "Take good care of him."

After the merchant had taken his bath, he took the boy and thrust him into a cave. He blocked the entrance with heavy rocks and returned to the neighbor's house.

"I assume you have had your bath," said the neighbor. "But where is my son?"

"Alas," said the merchant. "A hawk came along and carried him off."

"That is impossible! You are lying," cried the neighbor. "You have done a terrible thing and I will have you punished!"

Calling upon his friends, the neighbor dragged the merchant to a magistrate. When he was questioned, the merchant repeated what he had told the neighbor.

"But," said the magistrate, "how can a hawk carry off a fifteen-year-old boy?"

The merchant smiled. "It is as easy for a hawk to carry off a fifteen-year-old boy—or, for that matter, an elephant—as it is for mice to eat iron. If my neighbor wants me to believe his story, he will have to believe mine."

The Greek Anthology

As though to balance the doom-filled tragedies of Aeschylus, Euripides, and Sophocles, the Greek poets wrote thousands of lyrics delicate in design and delightful in effect. Their poems ranged from the sportive to the elegiac; they included teasing fragments of wit, compact images, and conceits that were alternately lightly erotic and downright bawdy. They were brief (few were more than eight lines in length), and most of them had the thrust of an epigram or the finality of an epitaph. Composed by known as well as unknown writers, they ran from the fifth century B.C. to the sixth century A.D.

Meleager of Gadara was the first to collect some of the scattered pieces in 60 B.C. From the more than one thousand poems, forty-six were selected for *The Garland of Meleager*, so called because Meleager introduced each poet by comparing him to a different flower. The *Garland* gave rise to the anthology, literally a flower-gathering. Meleager's collection was supplemented by many others, until in the fourteenth century *The Greek Anthology* encompassed more than forty-five hundred contributions.

The transcriptions that follow are a few of the more caustic examples paraphrased by the editor.

A RECORD

Marcus, the world's worst runner, ran so slow
He finished seventh in a race for six. How so?
Among the crowd a friend came out to greet him.
Running along with Marcus, lo—he beat him!

AS FOR DOCTORS

I had no need for drugs, was never ill.
But one unlucky day I had a chill
With just a little twitching in my side,
And, merely *thinking* of a doctor, died.

A STATUE

The sculptor carved Menodotis with love.
    It is—how very odd it is—
A noble, speaking likeness. But not of
    Menodotis.

LIGHTWEIGHT

Artemidora is so thin she needs
To hold fast to her amulet of beads
While her slave fans—fans carefully, lest he
Blow Artemidora off the balcony.

THE DEAD

Happy the dead. They do not ask applause,
    Or groan with each uneasy breath.
They are the happier because
    They have no fear of death.

THE LOOKING GLASS

Now that I'm grown old, alas,
And the sports of youth must pass,
Venus, take my looking glass.
What from now on I shall be
Never, never let me see.
Venus, take the glass from me.

UNFAIR EXCHANGE

A thief once stole a fortune; in its place
He left a rope. The victim, in disgrace,
Half in despair and half in hopeless grief,
Used the same rope left by the careless thief.

THIRSTY SOUL

Crudely carved, this drinking cup
Marks one who loved to lap it up.
She passed her life, the lucky lass,
With nose half-buried in her glass.
She mourns, not for her children pale,
Nor friends, but only for her ale.
Deep in her dusty grave, methinks,
She calls for drinks and still more drinks.

ON A PROFESSOR

This pedagogue deserves the highest heaven;
　He never diced or drank or went with wenches.
His listeners are a small but loyal seven:
　The four walls of his school and three old benches.

ON A MISANTHROPE

A bitter man one summer day
   Was bitten by a snake; it pierced his hide.
He merely winced and went his way.
   The snake it was that died.

ON LOVE

"Mockery murders love," they say—and she
   Laughed in my face last night and slammed the door.
I swore to go and stay away. But see,
   That was last night. And here I am once more.

ON STUDYING

Lifting my eyes from Hesiod's great book,
   I saw young Pyrrha pass and nod,
Linger, and give another look . . .
   Good-by to dull old Hesiod!

ON A FALSE FRIEND

O Earth, lie lightly upon Nearchus, please—
So that the dogs may dig him up with ease.

ON A FORMER MISTRESS

Some say you dye your hair, but I deny it.
The hair you wear *is* black. I saw you buy it.

ON LIFE

My name is Dion. Here I lie,
   Beaten by life, a silly game.
I had no wife nor child. And I
   Wish that my father had said the same.

Anacreon

In its inception satire was little more than the expression of animus. Homer's portrait of Thersites is a brutal gibe. But Homer had also a lighter sense of comedy. The adventures of Ulysses and his crew are fabulous, but as in the account of the escape from Polyphemus and the situation of Penelope's suitors, they are also farcical.

With the growth of an urban culture, the comic spirit grew more artful and sophisticated. It attained a relish as well as a refinement in what was characterized as "the delicious wantonness" of Anacreon, sometimes called the honey-poet, whose credo seemed to be "enjoy thy life, and if any hour slip away without mirth, account it misspent."

Anacreon was born in the Ionian city of Teos sometime during the latter half of the sixth century B.C. He was forced into exile when Cyrus the Great attacked the Greek cities of Asia Minor. Attaching himself to various rulers in Samos and Thessaly, he became court poet and produced lyrics that suggest a life of almost continual amorous festivities. If the legend is to be trusted, Anacreon's death was a piece of poetic injustice. The poet who celebrated wine, woman, and song (especially wine) choked on a grape pit.

It is difficult to separate Anacreon's own words from those of his imitators and translators. The best English adaptations were made in the seventeenth century by Abraham Cowley, who called his versions Anacreontics, versions that the critic

Hazlitt said "brim over with the spirit of wine and joy, with fresh impulses of eager and inexhaustible delight." Four of them follow.

DRINKING

The thirsty earth soaks up the rain,
And drinks, and gapes for drink again;
The plants suck in the earth and are
With constant drinking fresh and fair.
The sea itself, which one would think
Should have but little need of drink,
Drinks ten thousand rivers up,
So fill'd that they o'erflow the cup.
The busy sun (and one should guess
By's drunken fiery face no less)
Drinks up the sea, and when h'as done,
The moon and stars drink up the sun.
They drink and dance by their own light,
They drink and revel all the night,
Nothing in nature's sober found,
But an eternal health goes round.
Fill up the bowl then, fill it high,
Fill all the glasses there; for why
Should every creature drink but I.
Why, men of morals, tell me why?

THE DRUNKARD

Fill the bowl with rosy wine,
Around our temples roses twine,
And let us cheerfully a while,
Like the wine and roses smile.
Crown'd with roses we contemn
Gyges' wealthy diadem.
Today is ours, what do we fear;
Today is ours, we have it here.
Let's treat it kindly, that it may
Wish at least with us to stay.
Let's banish business, banish sorrow.
To the gods belongs tomorrow.

BEAUTY

Liberal nature did dispense
To all things arms for their defense;
And some she arms with sinewy force,
And some with swiftness in the course;
Some with hard hoofs or forkèd claws,
And some with horns or tuskèd jaws.
And some with scales and some with wings,
Some with teeth and some with stings.
Wisdom to man she did afford—
Wisdom for shield and wit for sword.

But what for beauteous womankind?
What arms, what armor was she assigned?
Beauty is both, for with the Fair
What arms, what armor can compare?
What gold, what steel, what diamond
More impassible is found?
And what flame, what lightning e'er
Such great and active force did bear?

These are all weapon, and they dart
Like porcupines from every part
Who can, alas, their strength express,
Armed when they themselves undress,
Cap-a-pie with nakedness.

THE BULL

This bull, my boy, sure is some Jove,
Who in disguise is making love.
Methinks through his gilt horns I spy,
The brightness of the deity.
His front does no curl'd fierceness wear,
All heav'n does in his looks appear,
His very looks speak him a god,
Who now has left the blest abode.
Nay whence I more of credit take,
Europa's mounted on his back.
Europa who outshines by far
All his beauteous harlots there,

Though each harlot's made a star.
Methinks I see him now convey
The nymph, through the wond'ring sea,
Whose crystal waves swell here and there,
Seemingly proud of what they bear.
He now like oars his feet does ply,
And rows through the wat'ry sky,
'Tis Jove I mean, for sure no beast
Half so happy, half so blest,
Wafted a virgin o'er the seas,
And left his loving mistresses.
Nay none of all the Gods above,
But he, nor he were't not for love.

Horace

The humor of the Greeks was rarely lighthearted. In *The Birds* Aristophanes peopled a world with winged creatures who resembled everyday Athenians—a device used more sardonically two thousand years later by Jonathan Swift, who created a nation governed by horses more humane than humans—and in *Lysistrata* he anticipated the feminist movement of the twentieth century when the Athenian women planned to deny their husbands their sexual pleasures. But for the most part, the play of laughter was restrained by ritual and checked by decorum.

The Latins were less reserved. Plautus rollicked in manipulated farces, and even Horace alternated between sophisticated town wit and broad country humor, between a flippant bawdiness and a philosophizing that was popular because it was playful. Horace relished the gossip of the taverns, the scandals that were enjoyed equally in Roman barber shops and on the Sabine farm. His protests against the corruption of his times were tempered with a shrugging *carpe diem;* he regarded vice as a passing and unimportant folly.

Son of a father who had been born a slave, Quintus Horatius Flaccus was born sixty-five years before the Christian era, near Venusia, a military colony in southern Italy. His father had become a collector of taxes and had saved enough money to buy a small estate and send his son to study in Rome. Completing his education in Athens when civil war followed the assassination of Caesar, Horace joined Brutus' army. After the Battle of Philippi he was given a clerkship in the Treasury. He began to write satires that were noticed by Virgil, who introduced him to Maecenas, a wealthy patron of the arts. Maecenas rescued Horace from the daily tedium of his work and presented him with a farm in the Sabine hills, where he composed odes, epodes, epistles, and satires.

Horace lived fifty-seven years and lived them fully. In spite of some avuncular sententiousness, his was a philosophy of the flesh. He ate rich food with the elite, indulged himself in a variety of wines and amours, and suffered from all of them. At fifty he began to feel the clutch of age. Virgil had died, and though Horace had the patronage of the Emperor Augustus, he was tired, especially tired of writing to order. When Maecenas died, Horace survived him by only a few weeks and was buried beside his protector.

A brilliant versifier, Horace was only occasionally the inspired poet. In spite of the Lydias, Lalages, Chloes, and other mistresses of his literary harem, he seldom strikes the note of genuine passion. He never lets an emotion overmaster him; he is more concerned with the distractions of love than with love itself. What keeps his poetry so alive is its essential liveliness, its alternation of solemn ridicule and frank burlesque, of good-humored mockery and companionable carnality. If Horace is not profound, he is provocative; his turns of phrase are surprising, and what he has to say is as diverting as it is delightful.

The versions that follow are by the editor.

A RUEFUL RONDEAU

Cum tu, Lydia, Telephi
cervicem roseam, cerea Telephi . . . Book I: Ode 13

Cum tu, Lydia . . . You know the rest —
Praising the waxen arms and breast
   Of Telephus you drove me mad.
   You made the sunniest moments sad,
While tortures racked my heaving chest.

Oh, I could see you loosely dressed,
Inciting him with amorous zest;

And hear you whisper low, "My lad,
    Come to Lydia."

Now you repent . . . Your arms protest
That they have been too roughly pressed.
    Oh gain your senses; leave the cad,
    And heed me as again I add:
Awake! Love is no giddy jest.
        Come to! Lydia!

"ON WITH THE DANCE!"

Quid bellicosus . . . Book II: Ode 11

Why all these questions that worry and weary us?
    Let's drop the serious role for a while.
Youth, with smooth cheeks, will be laughing behind us;
    Age will not mind us; the cynic—he'll smile.

Come, for the gray hairs already are fretting us;
    Girls are forgetting us. Lord, how we've got!
Come, let's convince them our blood is—well, red yet.
    We are not dead yet. Let's show them we're not!

Yes, we'll have cups till you can't keep a count of
        them;
    Any amount of them—hundreds, at least.
I'll have the table all tempting and tidy—
    And we'll get Lyde to come to the feast!

THE RECONCILIATION

Donec gratus eram tibi . . . Book III: Ode 9

HORACE
How fond, how fierce, your arms to me would cling
    Before your heart made various excursions;
Then I was happier than the happiest king
        Of all the Persians.

LYDIA
As long as I remained your constant flame,
  I was a proud and rather well-sung Lydia;
But now, in spite of all your precious fame,
      I'm glad I'm rid o' ye.

HORACE
Ah, well, I've Chloë for my present queen;
  Her voice would thrill the marble bust of Caesar.
And I would exit gladly from the scene
      If it would please her.

LYDIA
And as for me, with every burning breath
  I think of Calaïs, my handsome lover;
For him not only would I suffer death,
      But die twice over.

HORACE
What if the old love were to come once more
  With smiling face and understanding tacit,
Would you come in if I'd unbar the door?
      Or would you pass it?

LYDIA
Though he's a star that's constant, strong and true,
  And you're as light as cork or wild as fever,
With all your faults I'd live and die with you,
      You old deceiver.

A LINGERING ADIEU

Vixi puellis nuper idoneus . . . BOOK III: Ode 26

      As a militant lover
      I've taken to cover;
The lyrics of love—I have sung them all.
      My lutes and my armor
      Will charm not a charmer;
In the temple of Venus I've hung them all.

Though aging and hoary,
    Yet not without glory
I entered Love's lists when he 'sought me to;
    Each maid I enraptured,
    I came, saw and captured—
And lo, this is what it has brought me to.

    Here, then, lay the crow-bars;
    The door now needs no bars
That used to be fastened so tight to me.
    Lay down Cupid's arrows—
    The thought of them harrows
When girls are no sort of delight to me.

    Yet, Goddess, whose feelings
    Know not the congealings
Of Winter, the sting and the clutch of it,
    Come down where it's snowy,
    And give this cold Chloë
The lash—and a generous touch of it!

HORACE LOSES HIS TEMPER

Extremum Tanain si biberes . . . BOOK III: Ode 10

Your husband is stern and you're adamant, Lyce,
    Oh yes, there is not the least doubt of it.
But open the door, for the weather is icy;
        Let me in out of it.

Oh, cruel you are to behold me, unweeping,
    All huddled and drenched like a rabbit here;
Exposed to the pitiless snow and the sweeping
        Winds that inhabit here.

The blast, like the sharpest of knives, cuts between
        us—
    Ah, will you rejoice if I freeze to death?
Come, put off the pride that is hateful to Venus;
        Come, ere I sneeze to death!

Your sire was a Tuscan—may Hercules club me
 Or crush out my life like a mellow pea—
But who in Gehenna are you that you snub me?
        You're no Penelope!

Forgive me. I know that I rail like a peasant,
 But, won't you be more than a friend to me?
Won't tears and my prayers—and the costliest present—
        Make you unbend to me?

Once more I implore; give my pleadings a fresh hold;
 My soul in its torment still screams to you . . .
What? Think you I'll lie down and die on your
        threshold?
        Good Night! And bad dreams to you!

HORACE TEASES A FRIEND

Ne sit ancillae . . . BOOK II: Ode 4

You never need blush, since your love for a hand-maid,
 Friend Xanthias, is known to—well, more than a
        few.
Conceal it no more. Here's a girl who is planned, made
        And fashioned for you.

Briseis, the slave-girl, with tints like the lily's,
 Her body a mingling of fire and snow,
Enraptured the noble and haughty Achilles—
        A thing that you know.

And Ajax, the fearless and well-known defier,
 Was snared by Tecmessa, the modest and grave;
Though he was a lord who could surely look higher,
        And she was his slave.

And as for your Phyllis who scorns your sesterces,
 Her family tree may be broad as an oak's.
Her people, I'm sure, though upset by reverses,
        Were eminent folks.

A girl so devoted, unlike any other
  Your arm may have had the occasion to crush,
Could never, believe me, be born of a mother
      For whom you need blush.

Her arms and the turn of her ankles enthuse me;
  Her face has the glamour that all men adore.
What! Jealous? You mean it? Go on. You amuse
    me!
       I'm forty—and more.

Juvenal

We know little about Juvenal the man. He rarely confides in the reader. In this he is Horace's opposite: the personality of Horace comes through and almost overshadows his writings; Juvenal's subjects dominate and practically obliterate Juvenal. Lashing about him with the flail of invective, Juvenal drives mercilessly. "Horace is always on the amble," wrote Dryden, "Juvenal on the gallop. He goes with more impetuosity than Horace, but as securely; his swiftness adds a more lively agitation . . . his indignation against vice is more vehement."

The date of Juvenal's birth is uncertain, but authorities agree that it was about A.D. 60. The place of his birth was "probably" Aquinum, and legend has it that he had military service in Britain as well as Egypt, where he died at eighty. What is incontrovertible is that he was in constant conflict with the society of his times. "Why do I write satire?" asked Juvenal. "Say rather, how can I help it?"

Algernon Charles Swinburne suggested that Juvenal's power consisted in his hatred of despotism. But Juvenal is equally vituperative in all his ironies. He is grimly comic about the common people—as contemptuous of their simple pleasures as he is of the extravagance of the ruling class. He rages against casual adulteries more loudly than he inveighs against the most serious crimes.

The savagery of this first-century satirist was carried over into the seventeenth century when Dryden translated some of

Juvenal's satires. *The Sixth Satire*, a selection from which
follows, is a vicious diatribe against women, a poem with a bite
in almost every other line.

HOW TO CHOOSE A WIFE

(FROM THE SIXTH SATIRE)

Yet thou, they say, for marriage dost provide:
Is this an age to buckle with a bride?
They say thy hair the curling art is taught,
The wedding ring perhaps already bought:
A sober man like thee to change his life!
What fury would possess thee with a wife?
Art thou of ev'ry other death bereft,
No knife, no ratsbane, no kind halter left?
(For every noose compar'd to hers is cheap)
Is there no city bridge from whence to leap?
Wouldst thou become her drudge, who dost enjoy
A better sort of bedfellow, thy boy?
He keeps thee not awake with nightly brawls,
Nor with a begg'd reward thy pleasure palls;
Nor with insatiate heavings calls for more,
When all thy spirits were drain'd out before.
But still Ursidius courts the marriage bait,
Longs for a son to settle his estate,
And takes no gifts, tho' ev'ry gaping heir
Would gladly grease the rich old bachelor.
What revolution can appear so strange,
As such a lecher, such a life to change?
A rank, notorious whoremaster, to choose
To thrust his neck into the marriage noose!
He who so often in a dreadful fright
Had in a coffer scap'd the jealous cuckold's sight,
That he, to wedlock dotingly betray'd,
Should hope in this lewd town to find a maid!
The man's grown mad: to ease his frantic pain,
Run for the surgeon; breathe the middle vein:
But let a heifer with gilt horns be led
To Juno, regent of the marriage bed,
And let him every deity adore,

If his new bride prove not an arrant whore
In head and tail, and every other pore.
On Ceres' feast,[1] restrain'd from their delight,
Few matrons, there, but curse the tedious night;
Few whom their fathers dare salute, such lust
Their kisses have, and come with such a gust.
With ivy now adorn thy doors, and wed;
Such is thy bride, and such thy genial bed.

Think'st thou one man is for one woman meant?
She, sooner, with one eye would be content.
    And yet, 't is nois'd, a maid did once appear
In some small village, tho' fame says not where:
'T is possible; but sure no man she found;
'T was desert, all, about her father's ground:
And yet some lustful god might there make bold;
Are Jove and Mars[2] grown impotent and old?
Many a fair nymph has in a cave been spread,
And much good love without a feather bed.
Whither wouldst thou to choose a wife resort,
The Park, the Mall, the Playhouse, or the Court?
Which way soever thy adventures fall,
Secure alike of chastity in all.
    One sees a dancing master cap'ring high,
And raves, and pisses, with pure ecstasy;
Another does with all his motions move,
And gapes, and grins, as in the feat of love;
A third is charm'd with the new opera notes,
Admires the song, but on the singer dotes:
The country lady in the box appears,
Softly she warbles over all she hears;
And sucks in passion, both at eyes and ears.
    The rest, (when now the long vacation's come,
The noisy hall and theaters grown dumb,)
Their memories to refresh, and cheer their hearts,
In borrow'd breeches act the players' parts.
The poor, that scarce have wherewithal to eat,

---

[1] *Ceres' feast:* when the Roman women were forbidden to bed with their husbands
[2] *Jove and Mars:* of whom more fornicating stories were told than of any other gods

Will pinch, to make the singing-boy a treat:
The rich, to buy him, will refuse no price;
And stretch his quail-pipe, till they crack his voice.
Tragedians, acting love, for lust are sought:
(Tho' but the parrots of a poet's thought.)
The pleading lawyer, tho' for counsel us'd,
In chamber practice often is refus'd.
Still thou wilt have a wife, and father heirs;
(The product of concurring theaters.)
Perhaps a fencer did thy brows adorn,
And a young swordman to thy lands is born. . . .

    Lust is the smallest sin the sex can own;
Caesinia still, they say, is guiltless found
Of every vice, by her own lord renown'd:
And well she may, she brought ten thousand pound.
She brought him wherewithal to be call'd chaste;
His tongue is tied in golden fetters fast:
He sighs, adores, and courts her every hour;
Who would not do as much for such a dower?
She writes love letters to the youth in grace;
Nay, tips the wink before the cuckold's face;
And might do more; her portion makes it good;
Wealth has the privilege of widowhood.
    These truths with his example you disprove,
Who with his wife is monstrously in love:
But know him better; for I heard him swear,
'T is not that she's his wife, but that she's fair.
Let her but have three wrinkles in her face,
Let her eyes lessen, and her skin unbrace,
Soon you will hear the saucy steward say:
"Pack up with all your trinkets, and away;
You grow offensive both at bed and board:
Your betters must be had to please my lord."

    Meantime she's absolute upon the throne;
And, knowing time is precious, loses none:
She must have flocks of sheep, with wool more fine
Than silk, and vineyards of the noblest wine;
Whole droves of pages for her train she craves,
And sweeps the prisons for attending slaves.
In short, whatever in her eyes can come,

Or others have abroad, she wants at home.
When winter shuts the seas, and fleecy snows
Make houses white, she to the merchant goes;
Rich crystals of the rock she takes up there,
Huge agate vases, and old China ware:
Then Berenice's ring her finger proves,
More precious made by her incestuous loves,
And infamously dear; a brother's bribe,
Ev'n God's annointed, and of Judah's tribe;
Where barefoot they approach the sacred shrine,
And think it only sin to feed on swine.

But is none worthy to be made a wife
In all this town? Suppose her free from strife,
Rich, fair, and fruitful, of unblemish'd life;
Chaste as the Sabines, whose prevailing charms
Dismiss'd their husbands', and their brothers' arms:
Grant her, besides, of noble blood, that ran
In ancient veins ere heraldry began:
Suppose all these, and take a poet's word,
A black swan is not half so rare a bird. . . .

O what a midnight curse has he, whose side
Is pester'd with a mood and figure bride![3]
Let mine, ye gods, (if such must be my fate,)
No logic learn, nor history translate;
But rather be a quiet, humble fool:
I hate a wife to whom I go to school,
Who climbs the grammar tree, distinctly knows
Where noun, and verb, and participle grows;
Corrects her country neighbor; and, abed,
For breaking Priscian's,[4] breaks her husband's head.
The gaudy gossip, when she's set agog,
In jewels dress'd, and at each ear a bob,
Goes flaunting out, and, in her trim of pride,
Thinks all she says or does is justified.
When poor, she's scarce a tolerable evil;
But rich, and fine, a wife's a very devil.

---

[3] *mood and figure bride:* a woman who has learned logic
[4] *Priscian's:* a woman grammarian who corrects her husband for speaking bad
Latin, which is called breaking Priscian's head

She duly, once a month, renews her face;
Meantime, it lies in daub, and hid in grease:
Those are the husband's nights; she craves her due,
He takes fat kisses, and is stuck in glue.
But, to the lov'd adult'rer when she steers,
Fresh from the bath, in brightness she appears:
For him the rich Arabia sweats her gum,
And precious oils from distant Indies come,
How haggardly soe'er she looks at home.
Th' eclipse then vanishes; and all her face
Is open'd, and restor'd to ev'ry grace;
The crust remov'd, her cheeks, as smooth as silk,
Are polish'd with a wash of asses' milk;
And should she to the farthest North be sent,
A train of these attend her banishment.
But, hadst thou seen her plaister'd up before,
'T was so unlike a face, it seem'd a sore.

'T is worth our while to know what all the day
They do, and how they pass their time away;
For, if o'ernight the husband has been slack,
Or counterfeited sleep, and turn'd his back,
Next day, be sure, the servants go to wrack.
The chambermaid and dresser are call'd whores,
The page is stripp'd, and beaten out of doors;
The whole house suffers for the master's crime,
And he himself is warn'd to wake another time.
She hires tormentors by the year; she treats
Her visitors, and talks, but still she beats;
Beats while she paints her face, surveys her gown,
Casts up the day's account, and still beats on:
Tir'd out, at length, with an outrageous tone,
She bids 'em in the Devil's name be gone.
Compar'd with such a proud, insulting dame,
Sicilian tyrants may renounce their name.
For, if she hastes abroad to take the air,
Or goes to Isis' church, (the bawdyhouse of pray'r,)
She hurries all her handmaids to the task;
Her head, alone, will twenty dressers ask.
Psecas, the chief, with breast and shoulders bare,
Trembling, considers every sacred hair;
If any straggler from his rank be found,

A pinch must for the mortal sin compound.
Psecas is not in fault; but, in the glass,
The dame's offended at her own ill face.
That maid is banish'd; and another girl,
More dextrous, manages the comb and curl;
The rest are summon'd on a point so nice;
And first, the grave old woman gives advice.
The next is call'd, and so the turn goes round,
As each for age, or wisdom, is renown'd:
Such counsel, such delib'rate care they take,
As if her life and honor lay at stake:
With curls on curls, they build her head before,
And mount it with a formidable tow'r.
A giantess she seems; but, look behind,
And then she dwindles to the pigmy kind.
Duck-legg'd, short-waisted, such a dwarf she is,
That she must rise on tiptoes for a kiss.
Meanwhile her husband's whole estate is spent;
He may go bare, while she receives his rent.
She minds him not; she lives not as a wife,
But like a bawling neighbor, full of strife:
Near him in this alone, that she extends
Her hate to all his servants and his friends.

Ovid

Like Horace, Ovid is his own biographer. We know him, his life, his loves, and his works from his own exact accounts. Born of an upper-class family in 43 B.C. at Sulmo, a town in northern Italy, he was groomed for a public career. He became a Councilor of State but neglected law for literature. Horace was his good friend, but he was more facile and far more lubricous than Horace. Married three times, he was a prominent figure in the loose-living circle of Roman society. Even that sophisticated set was shocked by his *Art of Love,* one of the most carnal poems ever written. It is a satirical handbook of seduction; it shows young men how to get and hold mistresses, and it teaches girls how to keep lovers. Genuine passion is absent from the work, but it vibrates with the cold light of cynical observation and does not disdain pornography that is both hard core and humorous.

The scandal caused by *The Art of Love* delighted and disturbed the court. Determined to rid his regime of corrupt practices, the Emperor Augustus banished Ovid to the semi-barbaric town of Tomi on the Black Sea. It was hinted that the so-called offense against public morals was a flimsy excuse and that Ovid had become enmeshed in royal intrigues.

Ovid never gave up hope of a pardon and return to Rome. He wrote a series of abject and pathetic poems, *Triestia,* and continued his lamentations in *Epistles from Pontus* But the Emperor Tiberius was even more unforgiving than his predecessor, and at the age of sixty-one Ovid died in exile. The cause of his death was given as heartbreak.

It is a feverish world that Ovid pictures, voluptuous and almost as vicious as Juvenal's. His *Metamorphoses* are delicate and for the most part decorous. They assemble favorite myths that have acted as a source for poets and playwrights, including Shakespeare. But *The Art of Love* is his most persuasive if most perverse work. The selection that follows is from the first book of *The Art of Love* in Dryden's translation.

THE ART OF LOVE
THE TECHNIQUE OF SEDUCTION

All women are content that men should woo;
She who complains, and she who will not do.
Rest then secure, whate'er thy luck may prove,
Not to be hated for declaring love.
And yet how canst thou miss, since womankind
Is frail and vain, and still to change inclin'd?
Old husbands and stale gallants they despise,
And more another's than their own they prize.
A larger crop adorns our neighbor's field;
More milk his kine from swelling udders yield.

First gain the maid; by her thou shalt be sure
A free access and easy to procure:
Who knows what to her office does belong,
Is in the secret, and can hold her tongue.
Bribe her with gifts, with promises, and pray'rs;
For her good word goes far in love affairs.
The time and fit occasion leave to her,
When she most aptly can thy suit prefer.
The time for maids to fire their lady's blood,
Is, when they find her in a merry mood;
When all things at her wish and pleasure move:
Her heart is open then, and free to love.
Then mirth and wantonness to lust betray,
And smooth the passage to the lover's way.
Troy stood the siege, when fill'd with anxious care:

One merry fit concluded all the war.
   If some fair rival vex her jealous mind,
Offer thy service to revenge in kind.
Instruct the damsel, while she combs her hair,
To raise the choler of that injur'd fair;
And, sighing, make her mistress understand,
She has the means of vengeance in her hand:
Then, naming thee, thy humble suit prefer,
And swear thou languishest and di'st for her.
Then let her lose no time, but push at all;
For women soon are rais'd, and soon they fall.
Give their first fury leisure to relent,
They melt like ice, and suddenly repent.

   T' enjoy the maid, will that thy suit advance?
'T is a hard question and a doutful chance.
One maid, corrupted, bawds the better for 't;
Another for herself would keep the sport.
Thy bus'ness may be farther'd or delay'd.
But by my counsel, let alone the maid:
Ev'n tho' she should consent to do the feat,
The profit's little and the danger great.
I will not lead thee thro' a rugged road;
But where the way lies open, safe, and broad.
Yet if thou find'st her very much thy friend,
And her good face her diligence commend,
Let the fair mistress have thy first embrace,
And let the maid come after in her place.

   But this I will advise, and mark my words;
For 't is the best advice my skill affords:
If needs thou with the damsel wilt begin,
Before th' attempt is made, make sure to win;
For then the secret better will be kept;
And she can tell no tales when once she's dipp'd.
'T is for the fowler's interest to beware,
The bird intangled should not scape the snare.
The fish, once prick'd, avoids the bearded hook,
And spoils the sport of all the neighb'ring brook.
But if the wench be thine, she makes thy way,
And, for thy sake, her mistress will betray;

Tell all she knows, and all she hears her say.
Keep well the counsel of thy faithful spy:
So shalt thou learn whene'er she treads awry.

   All things the stations of their seasons keep;
And certain times there are to sow and reap.
Plowmen and sailors for the season stay,
One to plow land, and one to plow the sea:
So should the lover wait the lucky day.
Then stop thy suit, it hurts not thy design;
But think, another hour she may be thine.
And when she celebrates her birth at home,
Or when she views the public shows of Rome,
Know, all thy visits then are troublesome.
Defer thy work, and put not then to sea,
For that's a boding and a stormy day.
Else take thy time, and when thou canst, begin:
To break a Jewish Sabbath, think no sin;
Nor ev'n on superstitious days abstain;
Not when the Romans were at Allia slain.
Ill omens in her frowns are understood;
When she's in humor, ev'ry day is good.
But than her birthday seldom comes a worse;
When bribes and presents must be sent of course;
And that's a bloody day, that costs thy purse.
Be stanch; yet parsimony will be vain:
The craving sex will still the lover drain.
No skill can shift 'em off, nor art remove;
They will be begging, when they know we love.
The merchant comes upon th' appointed day,
Who shall before thy face his wares display.
To choose for her she craves thy kind advice;
Then begs again, to bargain for the price:
But when she has her purchase in her eye,
She hugs thee close, and kisses thee to buy:
"'T is what I want, and 't is a pen'orth too;
In many years I will not trouble you."
If you complain you have no ready coin;
No matter, 't is but writing of a line,
A little bill, not to be paid at sight;
(Now curse the time when thou wert taught to write.)

She keeps her birthday; you must send the cheer,
And she'll be born a hundred times a year!
With daily lies she dribs thee into cost;
That earring dropp'd a stone, that ring is lost.
They often borrow what they never pay;
Whate'er you lend her, think it thrown away.
Had I ten mouths and tongues to tell each art,
All would be wearied ere I told a part.
  By letters, not by words, thy love begin;
And ford the dangerous passage with thy pen.
If to her heart thou aim'st to find the way,
Extremely flatter, and extremely pray.
Priam by pray'rs did Hector's body gain;
Nor is an angry god invok'd in vain.
With promis'd gifts her easy mind bewitch;
For ev'n the poor in promise may be rich.
Vain hopes a while her appetite will stay;
'T is a deceitful but commodious way.
Who gives is mad, but make her still believe
'T will come, and that's the cheapest way to give.
Ev'n barren lands fair promises afford,
But the lean harvest cheats the starving lord.
Buy not thy first enjoyment, lest it prove
Of bad example to thy future love:
But get it *gratis;* and she'll give thee more,
For fear of losing what she gave before.
The losing gamester shakes the box in vain,
And bleeds, and loses on, in hopes to gain.
  Write then, and in thy letter, as I said,
Let her with mighty promises be fed.
Cydippe by a letter was betray'd,
Writ on an apple to th' unwary maid.
She read herself into a marriage vow;
(And ev'ry cheat in love the gods allow.)
Learn eloquence, ye noble youth of Rome;
It will not only at the bar o'ercome:
Sweet words the people and the senate move;
But the chief end of eloquence is love.
But in thy letter hide thy moving arts;
Affect not to be thought a man of parts.
None but vain fools to simple women preach:

A learned letter oft has made a breach.
In a familiar style your thoughts convey,
And write such things as present you would say;
Such words as from the heart may seem to move:
'T is wit enough to make her think you love.
If seal'd she sends it back, and will not read,
Yet hope, in time, the business may succeed.
In time the steer will to the yoke submit;
In time the restive horse will bear the bit.
Ev'n the hard plowshare use will wear away,
And stubborn steel in length of time decay.
Water is soft, and marble hard; and yet
We see soft water thro' hard marble eat.
Tho' late, yet Troy at length in flames expir'd;
And ten years more Penelope had tir'd.
Perhaps thy lines unanswer'd she retain'd;
No matter; there's a point already gain'd:
For she who reads, in time will answer too;
Things must be left by just degrees to grow.
Perhaps she writes, but answers with disdain,
And sharply bids you not to write again:
What she requires, she fears you should accord;
The jilt would not be taken at her word.

Meantime, if she be carried in her chair,
Approach, but do not seem to know she's there.
Speak softly, to delude the standers-by;
Or, if aloud, then speak ambiguously.
If saunt'ring in the portico she walk,
Move slowly too, for that's a time for talk;
And sometimes follow, sometimes be her guide;
But, when the crowd permits, go side by side.
Nor in the *playhouse* let her sit alone;
For she's the *playhouse* and the *play* in one.
There thou mayst ogle, or by signs advance
Thy suit, and seem to touch her hand by chance.
Admire the dancer who her liking gains,
And pity in the *play* the lover's pains;
For her sweet sake the loss of time despise;
Sit while she sits, and when she rises rise.
But dress not like a fop, nor curl your hair,

Nor with a pumice make your body bare.
Leave those effeminate and useless toys
To *eunuchs,* who can give no solid joys.
Neglect becomes a man: this Theseus found;
Uncurl'd, uncomb'd, the nymph his wishes crown'd.
The rough Hippolytus was Phaedra's care;
And Venus thought the rude Adonis fair.
Be not too finical; but yet be clean;
And wear well-fashion'd clothes, like other men.
Let not your teeth be yellow, or be foul;
Nor in wide shoes your feet too loosely roll.
Of a black muzzle and long beard beware;
And let a skillful barber cut your hair:
Your nails be pick'd from filth, and even par'd;
Nor let your nasty nostrils bud with beard.
Cure your unsav'ry breath, gargle your throat,
And free your armpits from the ram and goat.
Dress not, in short, too little or too much;
And be not wholly French nor wholly Dutch.

　　Now Bacchus calls me to his jolly rites:
Who would not follow, when a god invites?
He helps the poet, and his pen inspires,
Kind and indulgent to his former fires. . . .
　　But thou, when flowing cups in triumph ride,
And the lov'd nymph is seated by thy side;
Invoke the god, and all the mighty powers,
That wine may not defraud thy genial hours.
Then in ambiguous words thy suit prefer,
Which she may know were all address'd to her.
In liquid purple letters write her name,
Which she may read, and reading find thy flame.
Then may your eyes confess your mutual fires;
(For eyes have tongues, and glances tell desires.)
Whene'er she drinks, be first to take the cup;
And, where she laid her lips, the blessing sup.
When she to carving does her hand advance,
Put out thy own, and touch it as by chance.
Thy service ev'n her husband must attend:
(A husband is a most convenient friend.)
Seat the fool cuckold in the highest place,

And with thy garland his dull temples grace.
Whether below, or equal in degree,
Let him be lord of all the company,
And what he says be seconded by thee.
'T is common to deceive thro' friendship's name;
But, common tho' it be, 't is still to blame:
Thus factors frequently their trust betray,
And to themselves their masters' gains convey.
Drink to a certain pitch, and then give o'er;
Thy tongue and feet may stumble, drinking more.
Of drunken quarrels in her sight beware;
Pot-valor only serves to fright the fair.
Sing, if you have a voice; and show your parts
In dancing, if endued with dancing arts.
Do anything within your power to please;
Nay, ev'n affect a seeming drunkenness:
Clip every word; and if by chance you speak
Too home, or if too broad a jest you break,
In your excuse the company will join,
And lay the fault upon the force of wine.
True drunkenness is subject to offend;
But when 't is feign'd, 't is oft a lover's friend.
Then safely you may praise her beauteous face,
And call him happy, who is in her grace.
Her husband thinks himself the man design'd;
But curse the cuckold in your secret mind.
When all are risen and prepare to go,
Mix with the crowd, and tread upon her toe.

    This is the proper time to make thy court,
For now she's in the vein, and fit for sport.
Lay bashfulness, that rustic virtue, by;
To manly confidence thy thoughts apply.
On Fortune's foretop timely fix thy hold;
Now speak and speed, for Venus loves the bold.
No rules of rhetoric here I need afford;
Only begin, and trust the following word;
It will be witty of its own accord.
    Act well the lover; let thy speech abound
In dying words, that represent thy wound.
Distrust not her belief; she will be mov'd;

All women think they merit to be lov'd.
   Sometimes a man begins to love in jest,
And, after, feels the torments he profess'd.
For your own sakes be pitiful, ye fair;
For a feign'd passion may a true prepare.
By flatteries we prevail on womankind,
As hollow banks by streams are undermin'd.
Tell her, her face is fair, her eyes are sweet;
Her taper fingers praise, and little feet.
Such praises ev'n the chaste are pleas'd to hear;
Both maids and matrons hold their beauty dear. . . .

   Thus justly women suffer by deceit;
Their practice authorizes us to cheat.
Beg her, with tears, thy warm desires to grant;
For tears will pierce a heart of adamant.
If tears will not be squeez'd, then rub your eye,
Or noint the lids, and seem at least to cry.
Kiss, if you can: resistance if she make,
And will not give you kisses, let her take.
Fie, fie, you naughty man, are words of course;
She struggles, but to be subdued by force.
Kiss only soft, I charge you, and beware,
With your hard bristles not to brush the fair.
He who has gain'd a kiss, and gains no more,
Deserves to lose the bliss he got before.
If once she kiss, her meaning is express'd;
There wants but little pushing for the rest:
Which if thou dost not gain, by strength or art,
The name of clown then suits with thy desert;
'T is downright dulness, and a shameful part.
Perhaps, she calls it force; but, if she scape,
She will not thank you for th' omitted rape.
The sex is cunning to conceal their fires;
They would be forc'd ev'n to their own desires.
They seem t' accuse you, with a downcast sight,
But in their souls confess you did them right.

   Besides his longer works, Ovid wrote a series of short poems about his mistress, Corinna. That he was unfaithful to her—and was sometimes punished for his infidelity—is

evident in the following poem translated by Christopher
Marlowe.

AMORES

"LIE DOWN WITH SHAME"

Either she was foul, or her attire was bad,
Or she was not the wench I wished I had.
Idly I lay with her as if I loved not,
And like a burden grieved the bed that moved not.
Though both of us performed our true intent,
Yet I could not cast anchor where I meant.
She on my neck her ivory arms did throw,
Her arms far whiter than the Scythian snow,
And eagerly she kissed me with her tongue,
And under mine her wanton thigh she flung.
Yea, and she soothed me up, and called me "Sir,"
And used all speech that might provoke and stir.
Yet, like as if cold hemlock I had drunk,
It mocked me, and hung down the head, and sunk.
Like a dull cipher, or rude block I lay,
Or shade, or body was I, who can say?
What will my age do, age I cannot shun,
Seeing in my prime my force is spent and done?
I blush, that being youthful, hot, and lusty,
I prove neither youth nor man, but old and rusty.
Pure rose she, like a nun to sacrifice,
Or one that with her tender brother lies.
Yet boarded I the golden Chloe twice,
And Libas, and the white-cheeked Pitho thrice.
Corinna craved it in a summer's night,
And nine sweet bouts had we before daylight.
What, waste my limbs through some Thessalian charms?
May spells and drugs do silly souls such harms?
With virgin wax hath some abased my joints?
And pierced my liver with sharp needle-points?
Charms change corn to grass and make it die:
By charms are running springs and fountains dry.
By charms mast drops from oaks, from vines grapes fall,
And fruit from trees when there's no wind at all.

Why might not then my sinews be enchanted?
And I grow faint as with some spirit haunted?
To this, add shame: shame to perform it quailed me,
And was the second cause why vigor failed me.
My idle thoughts delighted her no more
Than did the robe or garment which she wore.
Yet might her touch make youthful Pylius fire
And Tithon livelier than his years require.
Even her I had, and she had me in vain,
What might I crave more, if I ask again?
I think the great gods grieved they had bestowed,
This benefit: which lewdly I foreslowed.
I wished to be received in, in I get me.
To kiss, I kiss; to lie with her, she let me.
Why was I blest? Why made king to refuse it?
Chuff-like had I not gold and could not use it?
So in a spring thrives he that told so much,
And looks upon the fruits he cannot touch.
Hath any rose so from a fresh young maid,
As she might straight have gone to church and prayed?
Well, I believe, she kissed not as she should,
Nor used the sleight and cunning which she could.
Huge oaks, hard adamants might she have moved,
And with sweet words caused deaf rocks to have loved.
Worthy she was to move both gods and men,
But neither was I man nor lived then.
What sweet thought is there but I had the same?
And one gave place still as another came.
Yet, notwithstanding, like one dead it lay,
Drooping more than a rose pulled yesterday.
Now, when he should not yet, he bolts upright,
And craves his task, and seeks to be at fight.
Lie down with shame, and see thou stir no more,
Seeing thou would'st deceive me as before.
Then cozenest me: by thee surprised am I,
And bide sore loss with endless infamy.
Nay more, the wench did not disdain a whit
To take it in her hand, and play with it.
But when she saw it would by no means stand,
But still drooped down, regarding not her hand,
"Why mock'st thou me," she cried, "or being ill,
Why bade thee lie down here against thy will?

Either thou art witched with blood of frogs new dead,
Or jaded cam'st thou from some other's bed."
With that, her loose gown on, from me she cast her,
In skipping out her naked feet much graced her.
And lest her maid should know of this disgrace,
To cover it, spilt water on the place.

Martial

Marcus Valerius Martialis was born at Bilbilis, in Spain, about
A.D. 40. In his early twenties he went to Rome and attached
himself to the Spanish house of the Senecas. He thought of
practicing law but lived chiefly on the bounty of his bene-
factors, one of whom presented him with a comfortable country estate. Nevertheless he continually complained of poverty.
To gain security he flattered his protectors and was especially
fulsome in his tributes to the Emperor Domitian, whom he
compared to the Supreme Being—to the disadvantage of the
latter. In his late fifties he returned to his native Spain and
died there.

Martial's verse reveals the gaudy life of Rome but does not
condemn it. Where Juvenal is vituperative about the wantonness of the period, Martial accepts it. His wit does not disdain
grossness, and many readers have found his humor distasteful.
Among his detractors was Byron, who wrote:

> *What proper person can be really partial*
> *To all those nauseous epigrams of Martial.*

Of the following poems, "A Hinted Wish" is translated by
Samuel Johnson: "On His Book," by Robert Herrick; "To Cloe,"
by Thomas Moore; "Praise for the Poet," by Byron. The other
five have been translated by the editor.

A HINTED WISH

You told me, Maro, whilst you live
You'd not a single penny give,
But that, whene'er you chanced to die,
You'd leave a handsome legacy.
You must be mad beyond redress,
If my next wish you cannot guess.

ON HIS BOOK

To read my book, the virgin shy
May blush while Brutus standeth by.
But when he's gone, read through what's writ,
And never stain a cheek for it.

TO CLOE

I could resign that eye of blue
　　Howe'er its splendor used to thrill me;
And even that cheek of roseate hue—
　　To lose it, Cloe, scarce would kill me.

That snowy neck I ne'er should miss,
　　However much I've raved about it;
And sweetly as your lip can kiss,
　　I *think* I could exist without it.

In short, so well I've learned to fast
　　That, sweet my love, I know not whether
I might not bring myself at last
　　To—do without you altogether.

PRAISE FOR THE POET

He unto whom thou art so partial,
O reader, is the well-known Martial,
The Epigrammatist. While living
Give him the fame thou wouldst be giving;

So he shall hear, and feel, and know it.
Post-obits rarely reach a poet.

NO, THANKS

They tell me, Paulus, when you dine,
You serve a very potent wine.
They also say, or so I've heard,
You poisoned your four wives. Absurd!
No one believes it. Still, I think
I'd just as soon *not* have a drink.

TO HIS GIRL

Your charms, alas, it's plain to see
   Are eminently salable.
Oh, be less beautiful, or be
   A little less available.

THE PROCRASTINATOR

You gape at my late hours, you recall
I talk and hate to go to bed at all.
You'd understand, my friend, if you could see
My wife who waits in bed for me.

THE ANTIQUE COLLECTOR

He asks you in to have a drink, and then
Brings out his cups dating from God-knows-when.
This one, he claims, before you get a swallow,
Came from the temple of the god Apollo.
Achilles, when he sat him down to dine,
Filled this same goblet to the brim with wine.
Look at this tankard! It's the one
From which Aeneas drank to Dido. . . . On
And on he goes, a glamorous catalogue.
Then offers what you wouldn't give a dog.

TO AN INJURED HUSBAND

You cut off the ears and the nose from his face
   Who treated your wife like a whore.
You did the right thing. But were I in your place,
   I'd have cut off considerably more.

Petronius

It has never been established where or when Petronius was born; it is thought that his work was written in the first century A.D. during the rule of Nero, but even this is uncertain. Juvenal and Martial do not mention him, and Tacitus, who described the man, says nothing about his writing. The name sometimes given to him, "Petronius Arbiter," indicates that he was, according to Tacitus, "one of the chosen circle of Nero's intimates and was looked upon as an absolute authority on questions of taste (*arbiter elegantiae*) in connection with the science of luxurious living. . . . He spent his days in sleep, his nights in attending to his official duties or in amusement; and by his dissolute life he had become as famous as other men by a life of energy." Legend has it that Petronius incurred the jealousy of another of Nero's favorites, Tigellinus, who brought about his ruin. Rather than be banished, Petronius committed suicide by opening his veins and then binding them up so that he bled to death slowly. Meanwhile he conversed with his friends, jested, and quoted playful verse. He dined, says Tacitus, and then "indulged himself in sleep so that death, although forced on him, might appear an accident."

Petronius' *Satyricon* (or the portion of it that has remained) has been characterized as the first novel. It is scarcely that. The earliest sustained work of Latin prose, it is a miscellany that develops into a wild farce which combines violent horseplay, casual obscenities, sexual deviations, puns, parodies, a magnificent set piece ("Dinner with Trimalchio"), and a favorite erotic story, "The Widow of Ephesus." The central figure of the *Satyricon* is Trimalchio, an ex-slave who has become a tremendously wealthy *parvenu*. The cast of characters includes Eumolpus, a pseudo philosopher; Encolpius, a sophisticated rascal; his unspeakable boy friend Giton; a runaway slave, Ascyltos; and a hurly-burly of thieves, ward heelers, pimps, poets, pederasts, soldier mercenaries, professional beggars, actors, jugglers, town ladies, tavern wenches, and perverts of both sexes, all of whom are brilliantly realized and uproariously comic.

The quality of the work is described by its most successful and most sensitive translator, William Arrowsmith:

> *One laughs with Petronius; the effect of the* Satyricon *is neither scorn nor indignation, but the laughter appropriate to good satire enlarged by the final gaiety of comedy. The comic completes the satire and gives the whole randy work that effortless rightness of natural gaiety that makes it so improbably wholesome. Thus Trimalchio may very well be a satirical portrait of the* nouveau riche, *but he is also, like Falstaff and Don Quixote, a comic creation in his own right, vulgarity at once so vast and so vivid that he easily survives his own satirical role.*

The *Satyricon* set the style for a long line of picaresque sagas, including the Spanish *Gil Blas*, Henry Fielding's *Tom Jones*, Tobias Smollett's *Roderick Random*, and Daniel Defoe's *Moll Flanders*. The translation that follows (part of one section of the work) is by William Arrowsmith.

THE SATYRICON
DINNER WITH TRIMALCHIO

We were just about to step into the dining room when suddenly a slave—clearly posted for this very job—shouted "Right feet first!" Well, needless to say, we froze. Who wants to bring down bad luck on his host by walking into his dining room in the wrong way? However, we synchronized our legs and were just stepping out, right feet first, when a slave, utterly naked, landed on the floor in front of us and implored us to save him from a whipping.

He was about to be flogged, he explained, for a trifling offense. He had let someone steal the steward's clothing, worthless stuff really, in the baths. Well, we pulled back our right feet, faced about and returned to the entry where we found the steward counting a stack of gold coins. We begged him to let the servant off. "Really, it's not the money I mind," he replied with enormous condescension, "so much as the idiot's carelessness. It was my dinner-suit he lost, a birthday present from one of my dependents. Expensive too, but then I've already had it washed. Well, it's a trifle. Do what you want with him." We thanked him for his gracious kindness, but when we entered the dining room up ran the same slave whom we'd just begged off. He overwhelmed us with his thanks and then, to our consternation, began to plaster us with kisses. "You'll soon see whom you've helped," he said. "The master's wine will prove the servant's gratitude."

At last we took our places. Immediately slaves from Alexandria came in and poured ice water over our hands. These were followed by other slaves who knelt at our feet and with extraordinary skill pedicured our toenails. Not for an instant, moreover, during the whole of this odious job, did one of them stop singing. This made me wonder whether the whole menage was given to bursts of song, so I put it to the test by calling for a drink. It was served immediately by a boy who trilled away as shrilly as the rest of them. In fact, anything you asked for was invariably served with a snatch of song, so that you would have thought you were eating in a concert-hall rather than a private dining room.

Now that the guests were all in their places, the *hors d'oeuvres* were served, and very sumptuous they were. Trimalchio alone was still absent, and the place of honor—reserved for the host in the modern fashion—stood empty. But I was speaking of the *hors d'oeuvres*. On a large tray stood a donkey made of rare Corinthian bronze; on the donkey's back were two panniers, one holding green olives, the other, black. Flanking the donkey were two side dishes, both engraved with Trimalchio's name and the weight of the silver, while in dishes shaped to resemble little bridges there were dormice, all dipped in honey and rolled in poppyseed. Nearby, on a silver grill, piping hot, lay small sausages, while beneath the grill black damsons and red pomegranates had been sliced up and arranged so as to give the effect of flames playing over charcoal.

We were nibbling at these splendid appetizers when suddenly the trumpets blared a fanfare and Trimalchio was carried in, propped up on piles of miniature pillows in such a comic way that some of us couldn't resist impolitely smiling. His head, cropped close in a recognizable slave cut, protruded from a cloak of blazing scarlet; his neck, heavily swathed already in bundles of clothing, was wrapped in a large napkin bounded by an incongruous senatorial purple stripe with little tassels dangling down here and there. On the little finger of his left hand he sported an immense gilt ring; the ring on the last joint of his fourth finger looked to be solid gold of the kind the lesser nobility wear, but was actually, I think, an imitation, pricked out with small steel stars. Nor does this exhaust the inventory of his trinkets. At last he rather ostentatiously bared his arm to show us a large gold bracelet and an ivory circlet with a shiny metal plate.

He was picking his teeth with a silver toothpick when he first addressed us. "My friends," he said, "I wasn't anxious to eat just yet, but I've ignored my own wishes so as not to keep you waiting. Still, perhaps you won't mind if I finish my game." At these words a slave jumped forward with a board of juniper wood and a pair of crystal dice. I noticed one other elegant novelty as well: in place of the usual black and white counters, Trimalchio had substituted gold and silver coins. His playing, I might add, was punctuated throughout with all sorts of vulgar exclamations.

We, meanwhile, were still occupied with the *hors d'oeuvres* when a tray was carried in and set down before us. On it lay a basket, and in it a hen, carved from wood, with wings outspread as though sitting on her eggs. Then two slaves came forward and, to a loud flourish from the orchestra, began rummaging in the straw and pulling out peahen's eggs which they divided among the guests. Trimalchio gave the whole performance his closest attention. "Friends," he said, "I ordered peahen eggs to be set under that hen, but I'm half afraid they may have hatched already. Still, let's see if we can suck them." We were handed spoons—weighing at least half a pound apiece—and cracked open the eggs, which turned out to be baked from rich pastry. To tell the truth, I had almost tossed my share away, thinking the eggs were really addled. But I heard one of the guests, obviously a veteran of these dinners, say, "I wonder what little surprise we've got in here." So I cracked the shell with my hand and found inside a fine fat oriole, nicely seasoned with pepper.

By this time Trimalchio had finished his game. He promptly sent for the same dishes we had had and with a great roaring voice offered a second cup of mead to anyone who wanted it.

Then the orchestra suddenly blared and the trays were snatched away from the tables by a troupe of warbling waiters. But in the confusion a silver side dish fell to the floor and a slave quickly stooped to retrieve it. Trimalchio, however, had observed the accident and gave orders that the boy's ears should be boxed and the dish tossed back on the floor. Immediately the servant in charge of the dishware came pattering up with a broom and swept the silver dish out the door with the rest of the rubbish. Two curly-haired Ethiopian slaves followed him as he swept, both carrying little skin bottles like the circus attendants who sprinkle the arena with perfume, and poured wine over our hands. No one was offered water.

We clapped enthusiastically for this fine display of extravagance. "The god of war," said Trimalchio, "is a real democrat. That's why I gave orders that each of us should have a table to himself. Besides, these stinking slaves will bother us less than if we were all packed in together."

Glass jars carefully sealed and coated were now brought in. Each bore this label:

GENUINE FALERNIAN WINE
GUARANTEED ONE HUNDRED YEARS
OLD!
BOTTLED
IN THE CONSULSHIP
OF
OPIMIUS.

While we were reading the labels, Trimalchio clapped his hands for attention. "Just think, friends, wine lasts longer than us poor suffering humans. So soak it up, it's the stuff of life. I give you, gentlemen, the genuine Opimian vintage. Yesterday I served much cheaper stuff and the guests were much more important." While we were commenting on it and savoring the luxury, a slave brought in a skeleton, cast of solid silver, and fastened in such a way that the joints could be twisted and bent in any direction. The servants threw it down on the table in front of us and pushed it into several suggestive postures by twisting its joints, while Trimalchio recited this verse of his own making:

Nothing but bones, that's what we are.
  Death hustles us humans away.
Today we're here and tomorrow we're not,
  so live and drink while you may!

The course that followed our applause failed, however, to measure up to our expectations of our host, but it was so unusual that it took everybody's attention. Spaced around a circular tray were the twelve signs of the zodiac, and over each sign the chef had put the most appropriate food. Thus, over the sign of Aries were chickpeas, over Taurus a slice of beef, a pair of testicles and kidneys over Gemini, a wreath of flowers over Cancer, over Leo an African fig, virgin sowbelly on Virgo, over Libra a pair of scales with a tartlet in one pan and a cheesecake in the other, over Scorpion a crawfish, a lobster on Capricorn, on Aquarius a goose, and two mullets over the sign of the Fishes. The centerpiece was a clod of turf with the grass still green on top and the whole thing surmounted by a fat honeycomb. Meanwhile, bread in a silver chafing dish was being handed around by a black slave with long hair who was shrilling in an atrocious voice some song from the pantomime called *Asafoetida*. With some reluctance we began to attack this wretched fare, but Trimalchio kept urging us, "Eat up, gentlemen, eat up!"

Suddenly the orchestra gave another flourish and four slaves came dancing in and whisked off the top of the tray. Underneath, in still another tray, lay fat capons and sowbellies and a hare tricked out with wings to look like a little Pegasus. At the corners of the tray stood four little gravy boats, all shaped like the satyr Marsyas, with phalluses for spouts and a spicy hot gravy dripping down over several large fish swimming about in the lagoon of the tray. The slaves burst out clapping, we clapped too and turned with gusto to these new delights. Trimalchio, enormously pleased with the success of his little *tour de force,* roared for a slave to come and carve. The carver appeared instantly and went to work, thrusting with his knife like a gladiator practicing to the accompaniment of a water-organ. But all the time Trimalchio kept mumbling in a low voice, "Carver, carver, carver, carver . . ." I suspected that this chant was somehow connected with a trick, so I asked my neighbor, an old hand at these party surprises. "Look," he said, "you see that slave who's carving? Well, he's called Carver, so every time Trimalchio says 'Carver,' he's also saying 'Carve 'er!' and giving him orders to carve."

This atrocious pun finished me: I couldn't touch a thing.

In no time at all the water had cleared the wine fumes from our heads, and we were taken into a second dining room where Fortunata had laid out some of her prize possessions. There was a number of curious lamps, but I particularly remember several figurines of fishermen in bronze and some tables of solid silver covered with gilded goblets into which fresh wine was being strained before our eyes. "My friends," said Trimalchio, apropos of nothing, "my pet slave is having his first shave today. He's a good boy and a model of thrift. So let's celebrate. We'll drink until dawn!"

Pat to these last words, a cock ominously crowed somewhere. Alarmed by the coincidence, Trimalchio superstitiously ordered the servants to pour some wine under the table and even to sprinkle the lamps with wine. Then he slipped his ring from his left hand to his right and said, "Buglers don't bugle for kicks, and that cockcrow means there's a fire nearby or somebody's died. Don't let it be bad luck for us, please heaven. Whoever fetches me that calamity-crowing rooster first, gets a fat reward." In half a minute, somebody had brought in the rooster from somewhere, and Trimalchio promptly ordered it cooked. The chef, Daedalus, that culinary genius who had whisked up birds and fish from the leg of pork, beheaded the bird and tossed it into a pot. And while the cook drew off the boiling broth, Fortunata ground up the pepper in a little wooden mill.

We were sampling this unexpected snack, when Trimalchio suddenly remembered that the servants had not yet eaten. "What?" he roared, "you haven't eaten yet? Then off with you. Go eat and send in another shift to take your places." So a fresh shift of slaves soon appeared at the door, all shouting, "Greetings, Gaius!" while the first shift went out with a cry of "Goodbye, Gaius!"

At this moment an incident occurred on which our little party almost foundered. Among the incoming slaves there was a remarkably pretty boy. Trimalchio literally launched himself upon him and, to Fortunata's extreme annoyance, began to cover him with rather prolonged kisses. Finally, Fortunata asserted her rights and began to abuse him. "You turd!" she shrieked, "you hunk of filth." At last she used the supreme insult: "Dog!" At this Trimalchio exploded with rage, reached for a wine cup and slammed it into her face. Fortunata let out a piercing scream and covered her face with trembling hands as though she'd just lost an eye. Scintilla, stunned and shocked, tried to comfort her sobbing friend in her arms, while a slave solicitously applied a glass of cold water to her livid cheek. Fortunata herself hunched over the glass heaving and sobbing.

But Trimalchio was still shaking with fury. "Doesn't that slut remember what she used to be? By god, *I* took her off the sale platform and made her an honest woman. But she blows herself up like a bullfrog. She's forgotten how lucky she is. She won't remember the whore she used to be. People in shacks shouldn't dream of palaces, I say. By god, if I don't tame that strutting Cassandra, my name isn't Trimalchio! And to think, sap that I was, that I could have married an heiress worth half a million. And that's no lie. Old Agatho, who sells perfume to the lady next door, slipped me the word: 'Don't let your line die out, old boy,' he said. But not me. Oh no, I was a good little boy, nothing fickle about me. And now I've gone and slammed the axe into my shins good and proper.—But someday, slut, you'll come scratching at my grave to get me back! And just so you understand what you've done, I'll remove your statue from my tomb. That's an order, Habinnas. No sir, I don't want any more domestic squabbles in my grave. And what's more, just to show her I can dish it out too, I won't have her kissing me on my deathbed."

After this last thunderbolt, Habinnas begged him to calm himself and forgive her. "None of us is perfect," he said, "we're men, not gods." Scintilla burst into tears, called him her dear dear Gaius and implored him by everything holy to forgive Fortunata. Finally, even Trimalchio began to blubber. "Habinnas," he whined, "as you hope to make a fortune, tell me the truth; if I've done anything wrong, spit right in my face. So I admit I kissed the boy, not because of his looks, but because he's a good boy, a thrifty boy, a boy of real character. He can divide up to ten, he reads at sight, he's saved his freedom price from his daily allowance and bought himself an armchair and two ladles out of his own pocket. Now doesn't a boy like that deserve his master's affection? But Fortunata says no.—Is that your idea, you high-stepping bitch? Take my advice, vulture, and keep your own nose clean. Don't make me show my teeth, sweetheart, or you'll feel my anger. You know me. Once I make up my mind, I'm as stubborn as a spike in wood.

"But the hell with her. Friends, make yourselves comfortable. Once I used to be like you, but I rose to the top by my ability. Guts are what make the man; the rest is garbage. I buy well, I sell well. Others have different notions. But I'm like to bust with good luck.—You slut, are you still blubbering? By god, I'll give you something to blubber about.

"But like I was saying, friends, it's through my business sense that I shot up. Why, when I came here from Asia, I stood no taller

than that candlestick there. In fact, I used to measure myself by
it every day; what's more, I used to rub my mouth with lamp oil
to make my beard sprout faster. Didn't do a bit of good, though.
For fourteen years I was my master's pet. But what's the shame in
doing what you're told to do? But all the same, if you know what
I mean, I managed to do my mistress a favor or two. But mum's
the word: I'm none of your ordinary blowhards.

"Well, then heaven gave me a push and I became master in the
house. I was my master's brains. So he made me joint heir with
the emperor to everything he had, and I came out of it with a
senator's fortune. But we never have enough, and I wanted to try
my hand at business. To cut it short, I had five ships built. Then
I stocked them with wine — worth its weight in gold at the time —
and shipped them off to Rome. I might as well have told them to
go sink themselves since that's what they did. Yup, all five of them
wrecked. No kidding. In one day old Neptune swallowed down a
cool million. Was I licked? Hell, no. That loss just whetted my
appetite as though nothing had happened at all. So I built some
more ships, bigger and better and a damn sight luckier. No one
could say I didn't have guts. But big ships make a man feel big
himself. I shipped a cargo of wine, bacon, beans, perfume and
slaves. And then Fortunata came through nicely in the nick of
time: sold her gold and the clothes off her back and put a hundred
gold coins in the palm of my hand. That was the yeast of my
wealth. Besides, when the gods want something done, it gets done
in a jiffy. On that one voyage alone, I cleared about five hundred
thousand. Right away I bought up all my old master's property.
I built a house, I went into slave-trading and cattle-buying. Everything I touched just grew and grew like a honeycomb. Once I was
worth more than all the people in my home town put together,
I picked up my winnings and pulled out. I retired from trade and
started lending money to ex-slaves. To tell the truth, I was tempted
to quit for keeps, but on the advice of an astrologer who'd just
come to town, I decided to keep my hand in. He was a Greek,
fellow by the name of Serapa, and clever enough to set up as con-
sultant to the gods. Well, he told me things I'd clean forgotten
and laid it right on the line from A to Z. Why, that man could have
peeked into my tummy and told me everything except what I'd
eaten the day before. You'd have thought he'd lived with me all
his life.

"Remember what he said, Habinnas? You were there, I think,
when he told my fortune. 'You have bought yourself a mistress

and a tyrant,' he said, 'out of your own profits. You are unlucky in your friends. No one is as grateful to you as he should be. You own vast estates. You nourish a viper in your bosom.' There's no reason why I shouldn't tell you, but according to him, I have thirty years, four months, and two days left to live. And soon, he said, I am going to receive an inheritance. Now if I could just add Apulia to the lands I own, I could die content.

"Meanwhile, with Mercury's help, I built this house. As you know, it used to be a shack; now it's a shrine. It has four dining rooms, twenty bedrooms, two marble porticoes, an upstairs dining room, the master bedroom where I sleep, the nest of that viper there, a fine porter's lodge, and guestrooms enough for all my guests. In fact, when Scaurus came down here from Rome, he wouldn't put up anywhere else, though his father has lots of friends down on the shore who would have been glad to have him. And there are lots of other things I'll show you in a bit. But take my word for it: money makes the man. No money and you're nobody. But big money, big man. That's how it was with yours truly: from mouse to millionaire.

"In the meantime, Stichus," he called to a slave, "go and fetch out the clothes I'm going to be buried in. And while you're at it, bring along some perfume and a sample of that wine I'm having poured on my bones."

Stichus hurried off and promptly returned with a white grave-garment and a very splendid robe with a broad purple stripe. Trimalchio told us to inspect them and see if we approved of the material. Then he added with a smile, "See to it, Stichus, that no mice or moths get into them, or I'll have you burned alive. Yes sir, I'm going to be buried in such splendor that everybody in town will go out and pray for me." He then unstoppered a jar of fabulously expensive spikenard and had us all anointed with it. "I hope," he chuckled, "I like this perfume as much after I'm dead as I do now." Finally he ordered the slaves to pour the wine into the bowl and said, "Imagine that you're all present at my funeral feast."

The whole business had by now become absolutely revolting. Trimalchio was obviously completely drunk, but suddenly he had a hankering for funeral music too and ordered a brass band sent into the dining room. Then he propped himself on piles of cushions and stretched out full length along the couch. "Pretend I'm dead," he said, "say something nice about me." The band blared a dead march, but one of the slaves belonging to Habinnas

— who was, incidentally, one of the most respectable people present — blew so loudly that he woke up the entire neighborhood. Immediately the firemen assigned to that quarter of town, thinking that Trimalchio's house was on fire, smashed down the door and rushed in with buckets and axes to do their job. Utter confusion followed, of course, and we took advantage of the heaven-sent opportunity, gave Agamemnon the slip, and rushed out of there as though the place were really in flames.

Lucian

The most brilliant as well as the most blasphemous satirist in the Roman empire, Lucian (Loukianos) was a Syrian who wrote in Greek. Born near Antioch during the second century A.D., he earned his living as a lawyer and as a writer of scripts for public performances. He enlivened literature with a new departure: the colloquial humorous dialogue. His *Dialogues of the Dead* is a tongue-in-cheek parody of mythology; his *Dialogues of the Gods* exposes the hypocrisies and venalities of mankind by lampooning the gods. The romantic fantasies of his time were burlesqued in Lucian's *True History,* an account of imaginary journeys that foreshadows *Gulliver's Travels.*

Lucian has been characterized by Edgar Johnson as the Anatole France of the ancient world. "He never attacks outright; he never preaches, denounces, or loses his control. He simply coaxes his victims into the position in which their weaknesses are ludicrously clear, and then mischievously shows them to the world." The estimate is just, for while Lucian delights to strip away any illusion about man's egotism and unwavering self-interest, he does not overwhelm his misanthropy with lugubriousness. On the contrary, his ridicule is always gay, and his blithe travesties are a kind of offhand farewell to the old faiths and old philosophies of the Greco-Roman world.

This debonair cynicism is immediately apparent in one of the *Dialogues of the Gods* that follows. Because she had not been invited to the wedding of the sea goddess Thetis and the hero Peleus, Eris, the goddess of discord, has thrown a golden apple into the Olympian gathering. It bears the inscription "For the Fairest." What ensues is told in Lucian's man-of-the-world manner transcribed by the editor.

THE GOLDEN APPLE

ZEUS: Take this apple, Hermes, and go with it to Phrygia. You will find Paris, a shepherd, on the slope of Mount Ida. Say this to him: "You are not only handsome but also wise. Therefore Zeus has commanded you to be a judge in a contest. Three goddesses will appear, and you will give this golden apple to the one who is the most beautiful". . . . Now *(turning to the goddesses)* you three, don't dally. Away with you and get yourself judged. Don't look to me for a judgment. You are all lovely and I love you all; I wish all three of you could win the award. But that is impossible, and if I were to give the apple to one of you, the others would, of course, hate me. This young fellow to whom you're going happens to be a prince—he's Priam's son—and for some reason or other, he has become a shepherd. You can trust him.

APHRODITE: As far as I'm concerned, that old fault-finding god, Momus, could be my judge. He couldn't find a blemish in me. But the other two must agree to play fair.

HERA: Don't worry yourself about me, dear Aphrodite. I'd take a chance even if your lover, Mars, were to do the judging. Paris will do, whoever he may be.

ZEUS: My little Athene, do you approve? Don't blush or cover your face. Well, young girls can't help being shy. Anyway, you nod consent. That's a good girl. Now away with the three of you. And mind, don't be hard on the judge. I won't have the poor fellow humiliated.

HERMES: Come along; I'll show you the way. Follow me, ladies, and don't be nervous. Paris is a connoisseur of beauty, a real ladies' man. You'll find him charming. He'll make a proper decision.

APHRODITE: I'm glad to hear it. By the way, Hermes, has he a wife? Or is he single?

HERMES: Well, not exactly single.

APHRODITE: What do you mean by "not exactly"?

HERMES: I believe there's a sort of wife somewhere. Decent and all that—nothing spectacular—a country girl. Why do you ask?

APHRODITE: Oh, I'm just curious.

ATHENE: Hermes, stop whispering with Aphrodite. It's not fair.

HERMES: We weren't talking about you. She only wanted to know whether Paris was married or single.

ATHENE: That's none of her business. Is it?

HERMES: Actually it isn't. It was an idle question. She just wanted to find out.

ATHENE: Well—*is* he single?

HERMES: No.

ATHENE: Then answer *my* questions. Is he really a shepherd? Does he have ambitions? Would he like to be a military hero?

HERMES: It's hard to say. But he's a man, and he's young. I'd assume he'd be glad to win glory on the field of battle.

APHRODITE: Who's doing the whispering now? I'm not complaining. Aphrodite isn't as fussy as some people I might mention.

HERMES: No harm is done by answering a plain question or two. Anyway, we're almost over Phrygia now. There is Mount Ida. I think I can see Paris himself.

HERA: I don't see him—or his herd.

HERMES: Look. Not on the top, but there to the left. Between the rocks, that's the herd. And the man keeping them together—do you see him?

HERA: I see him now, if that's the man we're looking for.

HERMES: That's Paris all right. Let's descend a little further away. If we were to drop down on him suddenly he might be frightened. Let's walk.

HERA: Very well. Now that we are on earth, you might guide us, Aphrodite. You know the lay of the land, having come here frequently to meet Anchises whenever he could get away from his wife. Or so they say.

APHRODITE: Spare me your sarcasm, Hera.

HERMES: No more quarreling! I'll guide you myself. I got to know this place during the time when Zeus was courting Ganymede. I remember how often Zeus made me keep watch over that beautiful boy. I was here to help the god when he swooped down disguised as an eagle. I remember it was at this very rock where it happened. Ganymede was playing something on his pipe when the great bird circled overhead, plunged, and lifted the boy—oh, so tenderly—in his claws and carried him off. Of course the lad was terrified. He strained to see his captor, but he was unharmed. I picked up the pipe, which he had dropped in his fright, and—but here is the one we're looking for. Let us speak to him. Good morning, shepherd.

PARIS: Good morning. And who may you be? And where do you come from? And who are these ladies? They do not seem to be dressed for mountain-climbing.

HERMES: These ladies, my dear Paris, happen to be goddesses. They are Hera, Athene, and Aphrodite. And I am Hermes, messenger of the gods. You don't have to tremble and turn pale. There's nothing to be afraid of. On the contrary, you've been honored. Zeus has decided that because you are not only handsome but also wise, you are fit to be an impartial judge. There's to be a contest, and a golden apple is the prize. Here it is—with an inscription.

PARIS: I don't understand what it's all about. Let me see the inscription. It says "For the Fairest." You mean I'm to judge three goddesses? And such dazzling immortals? How can a mere man, and a country man at that, dare to judge such unparalleled beauty? Bring me two goats and I can tell you which is the fairer. And I can point out the difference between one heifer and another. But what can I say when I'm confronted with such radiant splendor? No man could stop looking at one to gaze at either of the others. I make my eyes move, and what do they see? Beauty, and again beauty, and still more beauty. I am surrounded by beauty. I am besieged by beauty. Oh, why wasn't I made of nothing but eyes, like Argus, who had eyes all over his body! If I could only give the apple to all three! One is the wife and sister of Zeus. One is his magnificent martial daughter, and the other daughter is the eternal goddess of love. How can I dare to judge?

HERMES: It will be hard, Paris. But judge you must. It is Zeus's command.

PARIS: If I must, I must. But, Hermes, please make it plain to them that I can't get out of it, and that the losers must not think the worse of me. Let them blame only my poor eyes.

HERMES: They will understand. Now get busy.

PARIS: Well, since it's got to be done, I'll do the best I can. Before I begin there's something I'd like to know. Do I appraise them dressed the way they are? Or do I examine them—er—more closely.

HERMES: That's up to you, my boy. You are the judge; you give the orders.

PARIS: I give the orders? In that case, I'll want a thorough examination.

HERMES: Ladies, you have heard. Get yourselves ready. You first, Hera.

HERA: You are quite right, Paris, to require a complete scrutiny. Since I am first in rank, I will be the first to be inspected. You will notice that, unlike someone who boasts of her beauty, there is more to me than big eyes and a couple of white arms. All of me is beautiful.

PARIS: How about you, Aphrodite? Are you ready to show yourself?

ATHENE: Paris, she's keeping on her girdle. Make her take it off. It happens to be a magic girdle. It bewitches men, and that's not playing fair. Besides, she ought not to come here made up with rouge and lipstick like a call girl.

PARIS: Athene is right. Remove the girdle, madam.

APHRODITE: All right. But, Athene, if I take off my girdle, you must take off your helmet. Show your head without that gaudy ornament designed to take the judge's mind off your lackluster eyes.

ATHENE: Very well. There goes my helmet.

APHRODITE: And there goes my girdle.

HERA: So, Paris, here we are.

PARIS: Wonder of wonders! What indescribable beauty! The eyes cannot believe what they behold! How exquisite the youthful body of Athene! How marvelous the majesty of Olympus' queen! How delightful, how enticing the warm, slow smile of Aphrodite! It is much too much! How can I choose? My eyes wander from one enchantment to the other. Perhaps there *is* a way. Perhaps if I might examine the three of them separately—and in detail.

APHRODITE: That seems an excellent idea.

PARIS: Then, Aphrodite, you and Athene withdraw. Let Hera stay.

HERA: Here I am, Paris. Gaze on me now, and after you have scrutinized every part of me, think of what you would like as a gift. Give me the golden apple and I will give you unlimited power. You will become ruler of all of Asia.

PARIS: Thank you, but I accept no gifts. Retire. I must judge without presents or prejudice. Athene, you're next.

ATHENE: Paris, all you have to do is to say I am the fairest, and young though you are, you will be not only a man among men, but an unbeatable warrior. You will always conquer, for you will win every battle.

PARIS: I have no desire to be a fighter, Athene. At the moment there is peace throughout Phrygia, and I would be the last person to disturb it. I won't accept your gift on any terms; I will continue to play fair. Put on your helmet and the rest of your clothes. I have seen all I need to see. Now, Aphrodite, it's your turn.

APHRODITE: Here I am. Look me all over. Don't miss an inch. You have appreciative eyes, you handsome boy. You must be the best-looking lad in all Phrygia—I've had my eyes on you for a long time. What a pity that you must waste your attractiveness on this desert. You were not made to live in mountain pastures and be admired by cows! You should live in a town full of lovely women. You should be married—not to one of the country wenches around here—but to some high-class Greek girl, let's say an Argive or a Corinthian or even a Spartan. Yes, that's it, a Spartan like Helen, a really pretty girl—every bit as pretty as I'm supposed to be. And oh, *so* susceptible! If she ever saw you she'd follow you to the ends of the earth. And what a devoted wife she'd be! Of course you've heard of Helen.

PARIS: No, I don't think I have. Tell me about her.

APHRODITE: To begin with, she is the beautiful daughter of a beautiful woman, Leda. Leda, you know, was loved by Zeus and was ravished by him when he came to her in the guise of a swan.

PARIS: That scarcely describes Helen. What is *she* like?

APHRODITE: As might be expected of the daughter of a swan, she is both gorgeous and graceful. And soft!—soft as down—don't forget that she was hatched from a very precious egg. She had so great a reputation for beauty that Theseus carried her off when she was still a child. Even before she was in her teens, every important man in Greece was after her. Menelaus was the lucky one. He married her. Say the word, and she will be your wife.

PARIS: But—she is already married, isn't she?

APHRODITE: Don't worry about that. I'm the one who can arrange things.

PARIS: I don't understand.

APHRODITE: You don't have to. All you have to do is to go to Greece on some sort of tour. You will visit Sparta. Helen will see you. She will fall in love with you. Leave the rest to me.

PARIS: I can't believe it. I can't believe she will leave her husband to go overseas with a stranger, a foreigner.

APHRODITE: I said leave it to me. I have two children: Love and Desire. They will help. Love will weave a spell that no woman could withstand. Desire will make you utterly desirable. I will also be on hand. Helen will be unable to resist you. She will *want* to be taken.

PARIS: How will it all end? I don't understand anything. I don't understand myself. I am already in love with Helen. I can see her beside me—sailing away to Greece—on a homeward journey! Can it ever possibly come true?

APHRODITE: It certainly can't come true until I say so. And I won't say so until I have a certain award. There will be no union without my particular presence. Your triumph will be mine. Think—

beauty, love, the joys of marriage—all will be yours for a little apple.

PARIS: Maybe after you've won the prize you'll forget about me.

APHRODITE: Would you like me to take an oath?

PARIS: N-no. But you might make a solemn promise.

APHRODITE: So be it. I hereby promise that you shall have Helen, that she shall be your wife, that she shall follow you to Troy, that she shall make your home her home, and that I will be there to help in everything.

PARIS: And you will bring Love and Desire with you.

APHRODITE: Unquestionably. And Passion and Hymen as well.

PARIS: Here's the apple. It's yours.

Gesta Romanorum

The humor of the Middle Ages was energetic and anything but fastidious. Mischievous in impulse, malicious in practice, it knew almost no limitations. Court clowns tickled their patrons with rough badinage and licensed scurrility. Stone carvers decorated the holiest edifices with impious beasts and grinning gargoyles. Traveling tinkers regaled the peasantry with bawdry, and itinerant ballad makers entertained courtiers as well as country folk with scandals of the day in lusty rhymes. Pilgrims carried jokes as well as blessings from county to county; the journey to Canterbury, as Chaucer showed, was anything but a sanctimonious processional. Mimes and mummers interlarded the miracle plays with homely and often farcical episodes. In the Chester cycle of medieval English mystery plays the threat of the Flood is relieved—or intensified—by a domestic dispute between Noah and his shrewish wife, who insists that her good friends accompany them:

> They loved me full well, by Christ!
> And, but thou let them in thy chest,
> Row now, Noah, where'er thou list,
> And get thyself another wife!

Thomas Aquinas was not too sanctified for humorous anecdotes. One of them pictured him hurrying along the corridor of the monastery to vespers, and as the saint passed the statue of the Blessed Virgin, the image shook its head and spoke. "Thomas," admonished the statue, "you are late."

"Hush, Mary," reproved the saint, "this is the hour of silence."

Slapstick was the order (or disorder) of the day when the Lord of Misrule took command. The rollicking monarch (called the Abbot of Unreason in Scotland) assumed his office on Allhallow Eve and held it through the Christmas holidays until the Feast of Purification. Our Halloween frivolities are a timid echo of the liberties allowed, actually enforced, by the unhallowed Lord of Misrule.

Itinerant song makers devoted themselves to the triple pleasures of wine, woman, and song. Free-ranging, free-thinking hedonists, serious scholars, and vagabond priests called themselves Goliards, after the apocalyptic, disreputable Bishop Golias. Their songs were blithely blasphemous in exposures of clerical hypocrisy and churchly materialism. Religion to them was a subject for derision.

The churchmen struck back, and the battle between righteous sobriety and licentious merrymaking developed into a series of skirmishes in which both sides gave ground. Every spring the traditional merry month of May revived festivals that had once been fertility rites, but the Maypole was so swathed in decorous ribbons that its phallic origin was forgotten. Humor defied suppression; it raised its unregenerate head in the holiest places. Dante called his triptych of Hell, Purgatory, and Heaven a Divine Comedy, even though it is a comedy of retributions and few rewards, a comedy without laughter.

The most popular book of the Middle Ages was the *Gesta Romanorum*, a collection of one hundred eighty ingenious, ridiculous, and often reprehensible tales that ranged from the mocking to the melodramatic, from the diabolic to the bawdy. Compiled during the thirteenth century, it became a source for countless stories, poems, and plays. Boccaccio and Chaucer availed themselves of several spicy incidents; Shakespeare picked up suggestions in the tales for *Macbeth, King Lear*, and the plot of *The Rape of Lucrece*.

At the height of its vogue the churchmen attempted to dull the ribaldry and refine the satire of the *Gesta*. They edited the work with missionary zeal and insisted on treating the imaginative narratives as allegories and parables. They added prolix and generally inappropriate morals—morals that in their far-fetched applications made the stories more lurid than they actually were. Nevertheless, the zealous annotators never lost sight of the fact that the stories were originally told for enjoyment; even the censorious English editor the Reverend Charles Swan referred to them as "Entertaining Moral Stories," adding a subtitle: "Invented by the Monks as a Fireside Recreation and commonly applied in the Discourses from the Pulpit."

The following tales from the *Gesta Romanorum* are presented without their appended and irrelevant "applications."

OF HANGING

Valerius tells us that a man named Paletinus one day burst into a flood of tears, and calling his son and his neighbours around him, said, "Alas! alas! I have now growing in my garden a fatal tree, on which my first poor wife hung herself, then my second, and after that my third. Have I not therefore cause for the wretchedness I exhibit?" "Truly," said one who was called Arrius, "I marvel that you should weep at such an unusual instance of good fortune! Give me, I pray you, two or three sprigs of that gentle tree, which I will divide with my neighbours, and thereby afford every man an opportunity of indulging the laudable wishes of his spouse." Paletinus complied with his friend's request, and ever after found this remarkable tree the most productive part of his estate.

OF MAINTAINING TRUTH TO THE LAST

In the reign of Gordian, there was a certain noble soldier who had a fair but vicious wife. It happened that her husband having occasion to travel, the lady sent for her gallant. Now, one of her handmaids, it seems, was skilful in interpreting the song of birds; and in the court of the castle there were three cocks. During the night, while the gallant was with his mistress, the first cock began to crow. The lady heard it, and said to her servant, "Dear friend, what says yonder cock?" She replied, "That you are grossly injuring your husband." "Then," said the lady, "kill that cock without delay." They did so; but soon after the second cock crew, and the lady repeated her question. "Madam," said the handmaid, "he says 'My companion died for revealing the truth, and for the

same cause, I am prepared to die.'" "Kill him," cried the lady,—
which they did. After this, the third cock crew. "What says he?"
asked she again. "Hear, see, and say nothing, if you would live in
peace." "Oh, oh!" said the lady, *don't* kill *him!*" And her orders
were obeyed.

OF ABSENCE OF PARENTAL RESTRAINT

A soldier, going into a far country, intrusted his wife to the
care of her mother. But some time after her husband's departure
the wife fell in love with a young man, and communicated her
wishes to the mother. She approved of the connection, and without delay sent for the object of her daughter's criminal attachment. But while they feasted, the soldier unexpectedly returned
and beat at his gate. The wife, in great tremor, concealed the
lover in her bed, and then opened the door for her husband. Being
weary with travel, he commanded his bed to be got ready; and the
wife, more and more disturbed, knew not what she should do.
The mother observing her daughter's perplexity, said, "Before
you go, my child, let us show your husband the fair sheet which
we have made." Then standing up, she gave one corner of the
sheet to her daughter and held the other herself, extending it
before him so as to favour the departure of the lover, who took
the hint and escaped. When he had got clearly off, "Now," said
the mother, "spread the sheet upon the bed with your own hands
—we have done our parts in *weaving* it."

OF WOMEN, WHO NOT ONLY BETRAY
SECRETS BUT LIE FEARFULLY

There were two brothers, of whom one was a layman and the
other a parson. The former had often heard his brother declare
that there never was a woman who could keep a secret. He had
a mind to put this maxim to the test in the person of his own
wife, and one night he addressed her in the following manner:
"My dear wife, I have a secret to communicate to you, if I were
certain that you would reveal it to nobody. Should you divulge
it, it would cause me the greatest uneasiness and vexation." "My
lord," answered his wife, "fear not; we are one body, and your
advantage is mine. In like manner, your injury must deeply affect

me." "Well, then," said he, "know that, my bowels being oppressed
to an extraordinary degree, I fell very sick. My dear wife, what
will you think? I actually voided a huge black crow, which instantly took wing, and left me in the greatest trepidation and confusion of mind." "Is it possible?" asked the innocent lady; "but,
husband, why should this trouble you? You ought rather to rejoice
that you are freed from such a pestilent tenant." Here the conversation closed; in the morning, the wife hurried off to the house
of a neighbour. "My best friend," said she, "may I tell you a
secret?" "As safely as to your own soul," answered the fair auditor.
"Why," replied the other, "a marvellous thing has happened to my
poor husband. Being last night extremely sick, he voided two
prodigious black crows, feathers and all, which immediately flew
away. I am much concerned." The other promised very faithfully
—and immediately told her neighbour that *three* black crows had
taken this most alarming flight. The next edition of the story
made it *four;* and in this way it spread, until it was very credibly
reported that *sixty* black crows had been evacuated by one unfortunate varlet. But the joke had gone further than he dreamt of;
he became much disturbed, and assembling his busy neighbours,
explained to them that having wished to prove whether or not his
wife could keep a secret, he had made such a communication.
Soon after this, his wife dying, he ended his days in a cloister.

OF CONFESSION

A certain king, named Asmodeus, established an ordinance,
by which every malefactor taken and brought before the judge
should, if he distinctly declared three truths, against which no
exception could be taken, obtain his life and property. It chanced
that a certain soldier transgressed the law and fled. He hid himself in a forest, and there committed many atrocities, despoiling
and slaying whomsoever he could lay his hands upon. When the
judge of the district ascertained his haunt, he ordered the forest
to be surrounded, and the soldier to be seized and brought bound
to the seat of judgment. "You know the law," said the judge. "I
do," returned the other: "if I declare three unquestionable truths,
I shall be free; but if not, I must die." "True," replied the judge:
"take then advantage of the law's clemency, or this very day you
shall not taste food until you are hanged." "Cause silence to be
kept," said the soldier. His wish being complied with, he pro-

ceeded in the following manner:—"The first truth is this: I protest before ye all, that from my youth up I have been a bad man." The judge, hearing this, said to the bystanders, "He says true?" They answered, "Else, he had not now been in this situation." "Go on, then," said the judge; "what is the second truth?" "I like not," exclaimed he, "the dangerous situation in which I stand." "Certainly," said the judge, "we may credit thee. Now then for the third truth, and thou hast saved thy life." "Why," he replied, "if I once get out of this confounded place, I will never willingly re-enter it." "Amen," said the judge, "thy wit hath preserved thee; go in peace." And thus he was saved.

OF THE DECEITS OF THE DEVIL

There were once three friends, who agreed to make a pilgrimage together. It happened that their provisions fell short, and having but one loaf between them, they were nearly famished. "Should this loaf," they said to each other, "be divided amongst us, there will not be enough for any one. Let us then take counsel together, and consider how the bread is to be disposed of." "Suppose we sleep upon the way," replied one of them; "and whosoever hath the most wonderful dream shall possess the loaf?" The other two acquiesced, and settled themselves to sleep. But he who gave the advice arose while they were sleeping and ate up the bread, not leaving a single crumb for his companions. When he had finished he awoke them. "Get up quickly," said he, "and tell us your dreams." "My friends," answered the first, "I have had a very marvellous vision. A golden ladder reached up to heaven, by which angels ascended and descended. They took my soul from my body, and conveyed it to that blessed place, where I beheld the Holy Trinity, and where I experienced such an overflow of joy as eye hath not seen nor ear heard. This is my dream." "And I," said the second, "beheld the devils with iron instruments, by which they dragged my soul from the body, and plunging it into hell flames, most grievously tormented me, saying, 'As long as God reigns in heaven this will be your portion,'" "Now then," said the third, who had eaten the bread, "hear my dream. It appeared as if an angel came and addressed me in the following manner:— 'My friend, would you see what is become of your companions?' I answered, 'Yes, Lord. We have but one loaf between us, and I fear that they have run off with it.' 'You are mistaken,' he rejoined, 'it lies beside us: follow me.' He immediately led me to the gate of heaven, and by his command I put in my head and saw you; and I thought that you were snatched up into heaven and sat upon a throne of gold, while rich wines and delicate meats stood around you. Then said the angel, 'Your companion, you see, has an abundance of good things, and dwells in all pleasures. There he will remain for ever; for he has entered the celestial kingdom, and cannot return. Come now where your other associate is placed.' I followed, and he led me to hell-gates, where I beheld you in torment, as you just now said. Yet they furnished you, even there, with bread and wine in abundance. I expressed my sorrow at seeing you in misery, and you replied, 'As long as God reigns in heaven here I must remain, for I have merited it. Do you then rise up quickly and eat up all the bread, since you will see neither me nor my companion again.' I complied with your wishes, arose, and ate the bread."

Giovanni Boccaccio

The illegitimate son of an Italian merchant and a French-woman, Giovanni Boccaccio was born in 1313. He referred to himself as a Florentine, but it is uncertain whether he meant that Florence was his birthplace or the city he loved most. His father started him on a commercial career, but he soon abandoned it. As a child he had written poetry, and at twenty he composed stories in prose and verse. At twenty-eight he met Maria, natural daughter of King Robert of Naples, and fell in love with her. His passion was returned, and she became to Boccaccio the inspiration that Laura was to Petrarch and Beatrice was to Dante. Celebrating her under the name of Fiammetta, he wrote novels, elaborate acrostics, and even epic poems in her honor.

At forty Boccaccio published *The Decameron,* a book that earned him the title "Father of Italian prose" and that became one of the most famous works in all literature. It brings together a group of seven young ladies and three young men who, escaping the plague in Florence, take refuge for ten days in a country villa near Fiesole. There they while away the time matching stories. One hundred tales are assembled, including fabliaux, folklore, remnants of classical romances, and contemporary anecdotes. The tone is frank, the narration fluent, the manner outspoken, irreverent, and lightly licentious. All life is reflected in the pages of *The Decameron,* its grimness as well as its gaiety. Transmuted by Boccaccio, the give-and-

take narratives grew into a treasury ransacked by poets and
playwrights. Dryden, Keats, Tennyson, Longfellow, and Swinburne were among those who made memorable adaptations.
The plot of Shakespeare's *All's Well That Ends Well* is almost
identical to the ninth story of the third day; Chaucer's "The
Reeve's Tale" parallels the pornography of the sixth story of
the ninth day; Keats's "Isabella, or the Pot of Basil" frankly ac-
knowledges its indebtedness to the fifth story of the fourth day.

At fifty Boccaccio turned away from the pleasures of the
world, devoted himself to scientific works, and thought of
entering into holy orders. At sixty he lectured on Dante and
analyzed the *Divine Comedy*. He survived a terrible illness and
the death of his dearest friend, Petrarch, by little more than a
year. He died December 21, 1375.

THE DECAMERON

THE QUEEN'S HORSEKEEPER
(THE SECOND STORY OF THE THIRD DAY)

Agilulf, King of the Lombards, as his predecessors had done,
fixed the seat of his kingship at Pavia, a city of Lombardy, and
took to wife Theodolinda the widow of Autari, likewise King of
the Lombards, a very fair lady and exceeding discreet and virtuous, but ill fortuned in a lover. The affairs of the Lombards having,
thanks to the valour and judgment of King Agilulf, been for some
time prosperous and in quiet, it befell that one of the said queen's
horsekeepers, a man of very low condition, in respect of birth, but
otherwise of worth far above so mean a station, and comely of person and tall as he were the king, became beyond measure enamoured of his mistress. His mean estate hindered him not from being sensible that this love of his was out of all reason, wherefore,
like a discreet man as he was, he discovered it unto none, nor
dared he make it known to her even with his eyes. But, albeit he
lived without any hope of ever winning her favour, yet inwardly he
gloried in that he had bestowed his thoughts in such high place,
and being all aflame with amorous fire, he studied, beyond every
other of his fellows, to do whatsoever he deemed might pleasure
the queen; whereby it befell that, whenas she had occasion to ride
abroad, she liefer mounted the palfrey of which he had charge
than any other; and when this happened, he reckoned it a passing

great favour to himself nor ever stirred from her stirrup, accounting himself happy what time he might but touch her clothes. But,
as often enough we see it happen that, even as hope groweth less,
so love waxeth greater, so did it betide this poor groom, insomuch
that sore uneath it was to him to avail to brook his great desire,
keeping it, as he did, hidden and being upheld by no hope; and
many a time, unable to rid himself of that his love, he determined
in himself to die. And considering inwardly of the manner, he
resolved to seek his death on such wise that it should be manifest
he died for the love he bore the queen, to which end he bethought
himself to try his fortune in an enterprise of such a sort as should
afford him a chance of having or all or part of his desire. He set
not himself to seek to say aught to the queen nor to make her
sensible of his love by letters, knowing he should speak and write
in vain, but chose rather to essay an he might by practice avail to
lie with her; nor was there any other shift for it but to find a
means how he might, in the person of the king, who, he knew, lay
not with her continually, contrive to make his way to her and
enter her bedchamber.

Accordingly, that he might see on what wise and in what habit
the king went, whenas he visited her, he hid himself several times
by night in a great saloon of the palace, which lay between the
king's bedchamber and that of the queen, and one night, amongst
others, he saw the king come forth of his chamber, wrapped in
a great mantle, with a lighted taper in one hand and a little wand
in the other, and making for the queen's chamber, strike once or
twice upon the door with the wand, without saying aught, whereupon it was incontinent opened to him and the taper taken from
his hand. Noting this and having seen the king return after the
same fashion, he bethought himself to do likewise. Accordingly,
finding means to have a cloak like that which he had seen the king
wear, together with a taper and a wand, and having first well
washed himself in a bagnio, lest haply the smell of the muck
should offend the queen or cause her smoke the cheat, he hid
himself in the great saloon, as of wont. Whenas he knew that all
were asleep and it seemed to him time either to give effect to his
desire or to make his way by high emprise to the wished-for death,
he struck a light with a flint and steel he had brought with him and
kindling the taper, wrapped himself fast in the mantle, then, going
up to the chamber door, smote twice upon it with the wand. The
door was opened by a bedchamberwoman, all sleepy-eyed, who
took the light and covered it; whereupon, without saying aught,

he passed within the curtain, put off his mantle and entered the bed where the queen slept. Then, taking her desirefully in his arms and feigning himself troubled (for that he knew the king's wont to be that, when as he was troubled, he cared not to hear aught), without speaking or being spoken to, he several times carnally knew the queen; after which, grievous as it seemed to him to depart, yet, fearing lest his too long stay should be the occasion of turning the gotten delight into dolour, he arose and taking up the mantle and the light, withdrew, without word said, and returned, as quickliest he might, to his own bed.

He could scarce yet have been therein when the king arose and repaired to the queen's chamber, whereat she marvelled exceedingly; and as he entered the bed and greeted her blithely, she took courage by his cheerfulness and said, "O my lord, what new fashion is this of to-night? You left me but now, after having taken pleasure of me beyond your wont, and do you return so soon? Have a care what you do." The king, hearing these words, at once concluded that the queen had been deceived by likeness of manners and person, but, like a wise man, bethought himself forthright, seeing that neither she nor any else had perceived the cheat, not to make her aware thereof; which many simpletons would not have done, but would have said, "I have not been here, I. Who is it hath been here? How did it happen? Who came hither?" Whence many things might have arisen, whereby he would needlessly have afflicted the lady and given her ground for desiring another time that which she had already tasted; more by token that, an he kept silence of the matter, no shame might revert to him, whereas, by speaking he would have brought dishonour upon himself. The king, then, more troubled at heart than in looks or speech, answered, saying, "Wife, seem I not to you man enough to have been here a first time and to come yet again after that?" "Ay, my lord," answered she. "Nevertheless, I beseech you have regard to your health." Quoth Agilulf, "And it pleaseth me to follow your counsel, wherefore for the nonce I will get me gone again, without giving you more annoy."

This said, taking up his mantle, he departed the chamber, with a heart full of wrath and despite for the affront that he saw had been done him, and bethought himself quietly to seek to discover the culprit, concluding that he must be of the household and could not, whoever he might be, have issued forth of the palace. Accordingly, taking a very small light in a little lantern, he betook himself to a very long gallery that was over the stables of his palace and where all his household slept in different beds, and judging that, whoever he might be that had done what the queen said, his pulse and the beating of his heart for the swink endured could not yet have had time to abate, he silently, beginning at one end of the gallery, fell to feeling each one's breast, to know if his heart beat high. Although every other slept fast, he who had been with the queen was not yet asleep, but, seeing the king come and guessing what he went seeking, fell into such a fright that to the beating of the heart caused by the late exertions, fear added yet a greater and he doubted not but the king, if he became aware of this, would put him to death without delay, and many things passed through his thought that he should do. However, seeing him all unarmed, he resolved to feign sleep and await what he should do. Agilulf, then, having examined many and found none whom he judged to be he of whom he was in quest, came presently to the horse-keeper and feeling his heart beat high, said in himself, "This is the man." Nevertheless, as he would have nought be known of that which he purposed to do, he did nought to him but cut, with a pair of scissors he had brought with him, somewhat on one side of his hair, which they then wore very long, so by that token he might know him again on the morrow; and this done, he withdrew and returned to his own chamber.

The culprit, who had felt all this, like a shrewd fellow as he was, understood plainly enough why he had been thus marked; wherefore he arose without delay and finding a pair of shears, whereof it chanced there were several about the stables for the service of the horses, went softly up to all who lay in the gallery and clipped each one's hair on like wise over the ear; which having done without being observed, he returned to sleep. When the king arose in the morning, he commanded that all his household should present themselves before him, or ever the palace-doors were opened; and it was done as he said. Then, as they all stood before him with uncovered heads, he began to look that he might know him whom he had polled; but, seeing the most part of them with their hair clipped after one and the same fashion, he marvelled and said in himself, "He whom I seek, for all he may be of mean estate, showeth right well he is of no mean wit." Then, seeing that he could not, without making a stir, avail to have him whom he sought, and having no mind to incur a great shame for the sake of a paltry revenge, it pleased him with one sole word to admonish the culprit and show him that he was ware of the matter; wherefore, turning to all who were present, he said, "Let him who did

it do it no more and get you gone in peace." Another would have
been for giving them the strappado, for torturing, examining
and questioning, and doing this, would have published that which
every one should go about to conceal; and having thus discovered
himself, though he should have taken entire revenge for the affront suffered, his shame had not been minished, nay, were
rather much enhanced therefor and his lady's honour sullied.
Those who heard the king's words marvelled and long debated
amongst themselves what he meant by this speech; but none
understood it, save he whom it concerned, and he, like a wise
man, never, during Agilulf's lifetime, discovered the matter nor
ever again committed his life to the hazard of such a venture.

THE NIGHTINGALE
(THE FOURTH STORY OF THE FIFTH DAY)

It is, then, noble ladies, no great while ago since there lived in
Romagna a gentleman of great worth and good breeding, called
Messer Lizio da Valbona, to whom, well nigh in his old age, it
chanced there was born of his wife, Madam Giacomina by name,
a daughter, who grew up fair and agreeable beyond any other
of the country; and for that she was the only child that remained
to her father and mother, they loved and tendered her exceeding
dear and guarded her with marvellous diligence, looking to make
some great alliance by her. Now there was a young man of the
Manardi of Brettinoro, comely and lusty of his person, by name
Ricciardo, who much frequented Messer Lizio's house and conversed amain with him and of whom the latter and his lady took
no more account than they would have taken of a son of theirs.
Now, this Ricciardo, looking once and again upon the young
lady and seeing her very fair and sprightly and commendable of
manners and fashions, fell desperately in love with her, but was
very careful to keep his love secret. The damsel presently became
aware thereof and without anywise seeking to shun the stroke,
began on like wise to love him; whereat Ricciardo was mightily
rejoiced. He had many a time a mind to speak to her, but kept
silence of misdoubtance; however, one day, taking courage and
opportunity, he said to her, "I prithee, Caterina, cause me not die
of love." To which she straightway made answer, "Would God
thou wouldst not cause *me* die!"

This answer added much courage and pleasure to Ricciardo and he said to her, "Never shall aught that may be agreeable to thee miscarry for me; but it resteth with thee to find a means of saving thy life and mine." "Ricciardo," answered she, "thou seest how straitly I am guarded; wherefore, for my part, I cannot see how thou mayest avail to come at me; but, if thou canst see aught that I may do without shame to myself, tell it me and I will do it." Ricciardo, having bethought himself of sundry things, answered promptly, "My sweet Caterina, I can see no way, except that thou lie or make shift to come upon the gallery that adjoineth thy father's garden, where an I knew that thou wouldst be anights, I would without fail contrive to come to thee, how high soever it may be." "If thou have the heart to come thither," rejoined Caterina, "methinketh I can well enough win to be there." Ricciardo assented and they kissed each other once only in haste and went their ways.

Next day, it being then near the end of May, the girl began to complain before her mother that she had not been able to sleep that night for the excessive heat. Quoth the lady, "Of what heat dost thou speak, daughter? Nay, it was nowise hot." "Mother mine," answered Caterina, "you should say 'To my seeming,' and belike you would say sooth; but you should consider how much hotter are young girls than ladies in years." "Daughter mine," rejoined the lady, "that is true; but I cannot make it cold and hot at my pleasure, as belike thou wouldst have me do. We must put up with the weather, such as the seasons make it; maybe this next night will be cooler and thou wilt sleep better." "God grant it may be so!" cried Caterina. "But it is not usual for the nights to go cooling, as it groweth towards summer." "Then what wouldst thou have done?" asked the mother; and she answered, "An it please my father and you, I would fain have a little bed made in the gallery, that is beside his chamber and over his garden, and there sleep. There I should hear the nightingale sing and having a cooler place to lie in, I should fare much better than in your chamber." Quoth the mother, "Daughter, comfort thyself; I will tell thy father, and as he will, so will we do."

Messer Lizio, hearing all this from his wife, said, for that he was an old man and maybe therefore somewhat cross-gained, "What nightingale is this to whose song she would sleep? I will yet make her sleep to the chirp of the crickets." Caterina, coming to know this, more of despite than for the heat, not only slept not that night, but suffered not her mother to sleep, still complaining of the great heat. Accordingly, next morning, the latter repaired to her husband and said to him, "Sir, you have little tenderness for yonder girl; what mattereth it to you if she lie in the gallery? She could get no rest all night for the heat. Besides, can you wonder at her having a mind to hear the nightingale sing, seeing she is but a child? Young folk are curious of things like themselves." Messer Lizio, hearing this, said, "Go to, make her a bed there, such as you think fit, and bind it about with some curtain or other, and there let her lie and hear the nightingale sing to her heart's content."

The girl, learning this, straightway let make a bed in the gallery and meaning to lie there that same night, watched till she saw Ricciardo and made him a signal appointed between them, by which he understood what was to be done. Messer Lizio, hearing the girl gone to bed, locked a door that led from his chamber into the gallery and betook himself likewise to sleep. As for Ricciardo, as soon as he heard all quiet on every hand, he mounted a wall, with the aid of a ladder, and thence, laying hold of certain toothings of another wall, he made his way, with great toil and danger, if he had fallen, up to the gallery, where he was quietly received by the girl with the utmost joy. Then, after many kisses, they went to bed together and took delight and pleasure one of another well nigh all that night, making the nightingale sing many a time. The nights being short and the delight great and it being now, though they thought it not, near day, they fell asleep without any covering, so overheated were they what with the weather and what with their sport, Caterina having her right arm entwined about Ricciardo's neck and holding him with the left hand by that thing which you ladies think most shame to name among men.

As they slept on this wise, without awaking, the day came on and Messer Lizio arose and remembering him that his daughter lay in the gallery, opened the door softly, saying in himself, "Let us see how the nightingale hath made Caterina sleep this night." Then, going in, he softly lifted up the serge, wherewith the bed was curtained about, and saw his daughter and Ricciardo lying asleep, naked and uncovered, embraced as it hath before been set out; whereupon, having recognized Ricciardo, he went out again and repairing to his wife's chamber, called to her, saying, "Quick, wife, get thee up and come see, for that thy daughter hath been so curious of the nightingale that she hath e'en taken it and hath it in hand." "How can that be?" quoth she; and he answered, "Thou shalt see it, an thou come quickly." Accordingly, she made haste to dress herself and quietly followed her husband to the bed, where, the curtain being drawn, Madam Giacomina might plainly see how her daughter had taken and held the nightingale, which she had so longed to hear sing; whereat the lady, holding herself sore deceived of Ricciardo, would have cried out and railed at him; but Messer Lizio said to her, "Wife, as thou holdest my love dear, look thou say not a word, for, verily, since she hath gotten it, it shall be hers. Ricciardo is young and rich and gently born; he cannot make us other than a good son-in-law. An he would part from me on good terms, needs must he first marry her, so it will be found that he hath put the nightingale in his own cage and not in that of another."

The lady was comforted to see that her husband was not angered at the matter and considering that her daughter had passed a good night and rested well and had caught the nightingale, to boot, she held her tongue. Nor had they abidden long after these words when Ricciardo awoke and seeing that it was broad day, gave himself over for lost and called Caterina, saying, "Alack, my soul, how shall we do, for the day is come and hath caught me here?" Whereupon Messer Lizio came forward and lifting the curtain, answered, "We shall do well." When Ricciardo saw him, himseemed the heart was torn out of his body and sitting up in bed, he said, "My lord, I crave your pardon for God's sake. I acknowledge to have deserved death, as a disloyal and wicked man; wherefore do you with me as best pleaseth you; but, I prithee, an it may be, have mercy on my life and let me not die." "Ricciardo," answered Messer Lizio, "the love that I bore thee and the faith I had in thee merited not this return; yet, since thus it is and youth hath carried thee away into such a fault, do thou, to save thyself from death and me from shame, take Caterina to thy lawful wife, so that, like as this night she hath been thine, she may e'en be thine so long as she shall live. On this wise thou mayst gain my pardon and thine own safety; but, an thou choose not to do this, commend thy soul to God."

Whilst these words were saying, Caterina let go the nightingale and covering herself, fell to weeping sore and beseeching her father to pardon Ricciardo, whilst on the other hand she entreated her lover to do as Messer Lizio wished, so they might long pass such nights together in security. But there needed not overmany prayers, for that, on the other hand, shame of the fault committed and desire to make amends for it, and on the other, the fear of death and the wish to escape, — to say nothing of his ardent love and longing to possess the thing beloved, — made Ricciardo freely and without hesitation avouch himself ready to do that which pleased Messer Lizio; whereupon the latter borrowed of Madam Giacomina one of her rings and there, without budging, Ricciardo in their presence took Caterina to his wife. This done, Messer Lizio and his lady departed, saying, "now rest yourselves, for belike you have more need thereof than of rising." They being gone, the young folk clipped each other anew and not having run more than half a dozen courses overnight, they ran another two ere they arose and so made an end of the first day's tilting.

Then they arose and Ricciardo having had more orderly conference with Messer Lizio, a few days after, as it beseemed, he married the damsel over again, in the presence of their friends and kinsfolk, and brought her with great pomp to his own house. There he held goodly and honourable nuptials and after went long nightingale-fowling with her to his heart's content, in peace and solace, both by night and by day.

THE ONE-LEGGED CRANE

(THE FOURTH STORY OF THE SIXTH DAY)

Currado Gianfigliazzi, as each of you ladies may have both heard and seen, hath still been a noble citizen of our city, liberal and magnificent, and leading a knightly life, hath ever, letting be for the present his weightier doings, taken delight in hawks and hounds. Having one day with a falcon of his brought down a crane and finding it young and fat, he sent it to a good cook he had, a Venetian hight Chichibio, bidding him roast it for supper and dress it well. Chichibio, who looked the new-caught gull he was, trussed the crane and setting it to the fire, proceeded to cook it diligently. When it was all but done and gave out a very savoury smell, it chanced that a wench of the neighbourhood, Brunetta by name, of whom Chichibio was sore enamoured, entered the kitchen and smelling the crane and seeing it, instantly besought him to give her a thigh thereof. He answered her, singing, and said, "Thou shalt not have it from me, Mistress Brunetta, thou shalt not have it from me." Whereat she, being vexed, said to him, "By God His faith, and thou give it me not, thou shalt never have of me aught that shall pleasure thee." In brief, many were the words between them and at last, Chichibio, not to anger his mistress, cut off one of the thighs of the crane and gave it her.

The bird being after set before Messer Currado and certain

stranger guests of his, lacking a thigh, and the former marvelling
thereat, he let call Chichibio and asked him what was come of the
other thigh; whereto the liar of a Venetian answered without hesitation, "Sir, cranes have but one thigh and one leg." "What a
devil?" cried Currado in a rage. "They have but one thigh and one
leg? Have I never seen a crane before?" "Sir," replied Chichibio,
"it is as I tell you, and whenas it pleaseth you, I will cause you see
it in the quick." Currado, out of regard for the strangers he had
with him, chose not to make more words of the matter, but said,
"Since thou sayst thou wilt cause me see it in the quick, a thing I
never yet saw or heard tell of, I desire to see it to-morrow morning, in which case I shall be content; but I swear to thee, by Christ
His body, that, an it be otherwise, I will have thee served on such
wise that thou shalt still have cause to remember my name to thy
sorrow so long as thou livest." There was an end of the talk for
that night; but, next morning, as soon as it was day, Currado,
whose anger was nothing abated for sleep, arose, still full of wrath,
and bade bring the horses; then, mounting Chichibio upon a
rouncy, he carried him off towards a watercourse, on whose
banks cranes were still to be seen at break of day, saying, "We
shall soon see who lied yestereve, thou or I."

Chichibio, seeing that his master's wrath yet endured and that
needs must he make good his lie and knowing not how he should
avail thereunto, rode after Currado in the greatest fright that
might be, and fain would he have fled, so but he might. But, seeing
no way of escape, he looked now before him and now behind and
now on either side and took all he saw for cranes standing on two
feet. Presently, coming near to the river, he chanced to catch
sight, before any other, of a round dozen of cranes on the bank, all
perched on one leg, as they use to do, when they sleep; whereupon
he straightway showed them to Currado, saying, "Now, sir, if you
look at those that stand yonder, you may very well see that I told
you the truth yesternight, to wit, that cranes have but one thigh
and one leg." Currado, seeing them, answered, "Wait and I will
show thee that they have two," and going somewhat nearer to
them, he cried out, "Ho! Ho!" At this the cranes, putting down the
other leg, all, after some steps, took to flight; whereupon Currado
said to him, "How sayst thou now, malapert knave that thou art?
Deemest thou they have two legs?" Chichibio, all confounded and
knowing not whether he stood on his head or his heels, answered,
"Ay, sir; but you did not cry, "Ho! Ho!" to yesternight's crane. Had
you cried thus, it would have put out the other thigh and the other
leg, even as did those yonder!"

THE CROWDED BEDCHAMBER[1]
(THE SIXTH STORY OF THE NINTH DAY)

In the plain of Mugnone there was not long since a good man
who gave wayfarers to eat and drink for their money, and although
he was poor and had but a small house, he bytimes at a pinch gave,
not every one, but sundry acquaintances, a night's lodging. He had
a wife, a very handsome woman, by whom he had two children,
whereof one was a fine buxom lass of some fifteen or sixteen years
of age, who was not yet married, and the other a little child, not
yet a year old, whom his mother herself suckled, Now a young
gentleman of our city, a sprightly and pleasant youth, who was
often in those parts, had cast his eyes on the girl and loved her
ardently; and she, who gloried greatly in being beloved of a youth
of his quality, whilst studying with pleasing fashions to maintain
him in her love, became no less enamoured of him, and more
than once, by mutual accord, this their love had had the desired
effect, but that Pinuccio (for such was the young man's name)
feared to bring reproach upon his mistress and himself. However,
his ardour waxing from day to day, he could no longer master
his desire to foregather with her and bethought himself to find
means of harbouring with her father, doubting not, from his
acquaintance with the ordinance of the latter's house, but he
might in that event contrive to pass the night in her company,
without any being the wiser; and no sooner had he conceived this
design than he proceeded without delay to carry it into execution.

Accordingly, in company with a trusty friend of his called
Adriano, who knew his love, he late one evening hired a couple of
hackneys and set thereon two pairs of saddle-bags, filled belike
with straw, with which they set out from Florence and fetching a
compass, rode till they came overagainst the plain of Mugnone, it
being by this night; then, turning about, as they were on their way
back from Romagna, they made for the good man's house and
knocked at the door. The host, being very familiar with both of
them, promptly opened the door and Pinuccio said to him, "Look
you, thou must needs harbour us this night. We thought to reach
Florence before dark, but have not availed to make such haste
but that we find ourselves here, as thou seest, as this hour." "Pinuccio," answered the host, "thou well knowest how little com-

---

[1] For Chaucer's treatment of this story see "The Reeve's Tale" on page 121.

modity I have to lodge such men as you are; however, since the night hath e'en overtaken you here and there is no time for you to go otherwhere, I will gladly harbour you as I may." The two young men accordingly alighted and entered the inn, where they first stabled their hackneys and after supper with the host, having taken good care to bring provision with them.

Now the good man had but one very small bed-chamber, wherein were three pallet-beds set as best he knew, two at one end of the room and the third overagainst them at the other end; nor for all that was there so much space left that one could go there otherwise than straitly. The least ill of the three the host let make ready for the two friends and put them to lie there; then, after a while, neither of the gentlemen being asleep, though both made a show thereof, he caused his daughter betake herself to bed in one of the two others and lay down himself in the third, with his wife, who set by the bedside the cradle wherein she had her little son. Things being ordered after this fashion and Pinuccio having seen everything, after a while, himseeming that every one was asleep, he arose softly and going to bed where slept the girl beloved of him, laid himself beside the latter, by whom, for all she did it timorously, he was joyfully received, and with her he proceeded to take of that pleasure which both most desired. Whilst Pinuccio abode thus with his mistress, it chanced that a cat caused certain things fall, which the good wife, awaking, heard; whereupon, fearing lest it were otherwhat, she arose, as she was, in the dark and betook herself whereas she had heard the noise.

Meanwhile, Adriano, without intent aforethought, arose by chance for some natural occasion and going to despatch this, came upon the cradle, wheras it had been set by the good wife, and unable to pass without moving it, took it up and set it down beside his own bed; then, having accomplished that for which he had arisen, he returned and betook himself to bed again, without recking of the cradle. The good wife, having searched and found that the thing which had fallen was not what she thought, never troubled herself to kindle a light, to see it, but, chiding the cat, returned to the chamber and groped her way to the bed where her husband lay. Finding the cradle not here, "Mercy o' me!" quoth she in herself. "See what I was about to do! As I am a Christian, I had well nigh gone straight to our guests bed." Then, going a little farther and finding the cradle, she entered the bed whereby it stood and laid herself down beside Adriano, thinking to couch with her husband. Adriano, who was not yet asleep, feeling this, received her well and joyously and laying her aboard in a trice, clapped on all sail, to the no small contentment of the lady.

Meanwhile, Pinuccio, fearing lest sleep should surprise him with his lass and having taken of her his fill of pleasure, arose from her, to return to his own bed, to sleep, and finding the cradle in his way, took the adjoining bed for that of his host; wherefore, going a little farther, he lay down with the latter, who awoke at his coming. Pinuccio, deeming himself beside Adriano said, "I tell thee there never was so sweet a creature as is Niccolosa. Cock's body, I have had with her the rarest sport ever man had with woman, more by token that I have gone upwards of six times into the country, since I left thee." The host, hearing this talk and being not overwell pleased therewith, said first in himself, "What a devil doth this fellow here?" Then, more angered than well-advised, "Pinuccio," quoth he, "this hath been a great piece of villainy of thine, and I know not why thou shouldst have used me thus; but, by the body of God, I will pay thee for it!" Pinuccio, who was not the wisest lad in the world, seeing his mistake, addressed not himself to mend it as best he might, but said, "Of what wilt thou pay me? What canst thou do to me?" Therewithal the hostess, who thought herself with her husband, said to Adriano, "Good lack, hark to our guests how they are at I know not what words together!" Quoth Adriano, laughing, "Leave them do, God land them in an ill year! They drank overmuch yesternight."

The good wife, herseeming she had heard her husband scold and hearing Adriano speak, incontinent perceived where and with whom she had been; whereupon, like a wise woman as she was, she arose forthright, without saying a word, and taking her little son's cradle, carried it at a guess, for that there was no jot of light to be seen in the chamber, to the side of the bed where her daughter slept and lay down with the latter; then, as if she had been aroused by her husband's clamour, she called him and enquired what was to be between himself and Pinuccio. He answered, "Hearest thou not what he saith he hath done this night unto Niccolosa?" "Marry," quoth she, "he lieth in his throat, for he was never abed with Niccolosa, seeing that I have lain here all night; more by token that I have not been able to sleep a wink; and thou art an ass to believe him. You men drink so much of an evening that you do nothing but dream all night and fare hither and thither, without knowing it, and fancy you do wonders. 'Tis a thousand pities you don't break your necks. But what doth Pinuccio yonder? Why bideth he not in his own bed?" Adriano, on his part, seeing how adroitly the good wife went about to cover her own shame and that of her daughter, chimed in with, "Pinuccio, I have told thee an hundred times not to go abroad, for that this thy trick of arising in thy sleep and telling for true the extravagances thou dreamest will bring thee into trouble some day or other. Come back here, God give thee an ill night!"

The host, hearing what his wife and Adriano said, began to believe in good earnest that Pinuccio was dreaming; and accordingly, taking him by the shoulders, he fell to shaking and calling him, saying, "Pinuccio, awake; return to thine own bed." Pinuccio, having apprehended all that had been said, began to wander off into other extravagances, after the fashion of a man a-dream; whereat the host set up the heartiest laughter in the world. At last, he made believe to awake for stress of shaking, and calling Adriano, said, "Is it already day, that thou callest me?" "Ay," answered the other; "come hither." Accordingly, Pinuccio, dissembling and making a show of being sleepy-eyed, arose at last from beside the host and went back to bed with Adriano.

The day come and they being risen, the host fell to laughing and mocking at Pinuccio and his dreams; and so they passed from one jest to another, till the young men, having saddled their nags and strapped on their valises, remounted to horse and rode away to Florence, no less content with the manner in which the thing had betided than with the effect itself thereof. Thereafter Pinuccio found other means of foregathering with Niccolosa, who vowed to her mother that he had certainly dreamt the thing; wherefore the goodwife, remembering her of Adriano's embracements, inwardly avouched herself alone to have waked.

Geoffrey Chaucer

Laughter stretched its lungs and drew hearty breaths throughout the Renaissance. The gamut of lustiness was expanded
in an idiom rich and variable by Geoffrey Chaucer, whom
Dryden called "father of English poetry and perhaps the
prince of it." Chaucer was born in London sometime during
1340. His family was upper middle class. His father was a
wine merchant and at one time deputy butler to the king; his
mother boasted of an uncle in the Royal Mint. At seventeen
he served the Countess of Ulster as a page; at nineteen he
fought in France; at twenty-seven he was Valet of the King's
Chamber and a few years later was sent abroad for diplomatic
conferences on the king's secret affairs. At thirty-three he
went on a mission to Florence and came upon Boccaccio's
The Decameron, which suggested not only the framework but
many stories for *The Canterbury Tales*. Upon his return to
England, he was successively appointed Comptroller of Customs, Member of Parliament, and Clerk of the King's Works.
He died on October 25, 1400, in his sixty-first year, and was
entombed in Westminster Abbey, the first person to be buried
in the part that became known as the Poets' Corner.

In his late forties Chaucer had made a pilgrimage to the
shrine of Thomas à Becket in Canterbury. Struck by the odd
mixture of his fellow travelers, he put them into a fourteenth-
century cavalcade, using the colloquial speech of the people
rather than the literary language that had been the tradition.

No summary can suggest the variety and vitality of *The Canterbury Tales*. Chaucer's pilgrims present a period in microcosm. They are gross and noble, candid yet compassionate, always with an immense appetite for the casual procedures and oddities of everyday life. Echoing the broad humor of Boccaccio, Chaucer gloried in the commonplace. He loved the lewd Wife of Bath, the thickset Miller who excelled at wrestling and coarse jokes, the large, rude host of the Tabard Inn, the Monk who preferred hunting to studying, as much as he did the daintily coy Prioress and the "verray parfit gentil Knight."

The humor is boisterous, sometimes obscene, but never less than honest. In tune with his day, Chaucer relished the boldest possible extension of the vocabulary. As a consequence his bawdiness is easy and natural, never sniggering or smirking. "The Miller's Tale," for example, is a combination of two ribald stories: one, about a cuckolded husband, is shameless; the other, about a rejected lover, is a scatological farce. "The Reeve's Tale," founded on the sixth story of the ninth day in *The Decameron* (see page 88), is rowdy and erotic in the widest sense. Both tales are hilarious.

It is, perhaps, Chaucer's portraiture that is his greatest triumph; every detail is a perfect piece of miniature painting. For example, in "The Miller's Tale" the smooth little body of Alison is described to the last fluttering ribbon and the smallest plucked eyebrow. Her paramour, Nicholas, is shown as a lad made for dalliance, perfuming his breath while singing seductively. Absalon is revealed as the village fop, his scarlet hose showing through openwork shoes and his tight jacket flounced at the waist. Every figure in Chaucer's crowded canvas is equally brilliant and three-dimensional.

The two tales that follow have been put into modern English by Frank Ernest Hill.

THE CANTERBURY TALES

THE MILLER'S TALE

At Oxford town there dwelt upon a day,
An artisan that took in guests for pay —
A wealthy wretch, a carpenter by trade.
And in his house a poor young student stayed —

One that had learned the arts, but busily
Was now devoted to astrology.
And there were certain problems and equations
That he could solve by means of calculations—
If men would ask of him at certain hours
As to a drought, or when there might be showers,
Or if they asked him what was like to fall
In other things; I cannot count them all.
   They called this student gentle Nicholas;
Skilled both in mirth and secret love he was;
And he was sly and subtle as could be,
And seemed a very maid for modesty.
There in that house he had a room alone—
None shared it with him, it was all his own—
Scented with pleasant herbs, and trim and neat;
And he himself as fragrant was and sweet
As licorice, or the odor of setwall.
His Almagest and books both great and small,
His Astrolabe, essential to his art,
His augrim-counters—all were set apart
Neatly on shelves that ran beside his bed.
He had a clothes press decked with cloth of red;
And over this there hung a psaltery
On which at night he made a melody
So sweet that all the chamber with it rang;
And *Angelus ad Virginem* he sang;
And after that he carolled the King's Note;
Often such singing blessed his merry throat.
Thus on his funds this clerk contrived to live,
With what from time to time his friends would give.
   This carpenter had newly wed a wife,
And her he loved more than he loved his life;
And she was only eighteen years of age.
Jealous he was, and kept her close in cage;
For he was old, and wild and young was she,
And much he feared a cuckold he might be.
He knew not Cato (for his wit was rude),
Who bade men wed in some similitude;
Men ought to mate with those of like condition,
For youth and age are oft in opposition;
But now, since he had fallen in the snare,
He must endure, like other men, his care.
   Fair to behold was this young wife of his,

And small and slender as a weasel is.
She wore a girdle made of stripèd silk;
And a trim apron, white as morning milk,
Over her loins, with many a cunning gore.
Of white, too, was the dainty smock she wore,
Embroidered at the collar all about
With coal-black silk, alike within and out.
On her white hood were tapes of the same hue,
And these were also silk. Her fillet, too,
Was silk, and it was broad, and worn full high.
And certainly she had a wanton eye.
Her brows were narrow — she had plucked them so —
And they were arched, and black as any sloe.
She was as gay and fair a sight to see
As any fresh young blossoming pear tree,
And soft to touch as wool of any wether.
And by her girdle hung a purse of leather,
Inlaid with bits of latten ornament,
With tassels wrought of silk. Although ye went
Through all the world, ye could not hope to meet
A darling half so gay, a wench so sweet;
She shone as clear, and had as bright a glint,
As any gold piece freshly from the mint.
And ye could hear her song as clearly ringing
As any swallow on a stable singing.
And she could be as sportive and as gay
As any suckling kid or calf at play.
Her breath was sweet as honeyed ale, or mead,
Or apples laid in hay for winter need.
Skittish she was, and frisky as a colt,
Slim as a mast, straight as a cross-bow's bolt.
Beneath her collar gleamed a brooch, as large
And bright as is the boss upon a targe.
Upon her legs her shoes were laced up high.
She was a primrose or a sweet pig's eye
For any lord that had the luck to bed her,
Or any honest yeoman who would wed her!
    Now sirs and gentlemen, it came to pass
That on a day this gentle Nicholas
Began to wanton with this wife, and play —
Her husband having gone to Oseney —
In ways these artful students can devise;

And caught her stealthily between the thighs,
And cried: "Unless I slake my hidden thirst
And hunger for thee, sweetheart, I shall burst!"
And gripped her flanks, and pressed them hard, and said:
"Come, sweetheart, love me now, or I am dead,
God save me!" As a colt, in being broke,
Leaps up and rears against the breaking-yoke,
She jumped at that, and writhed her head aside.
"I will not kiss thee, by my faith!" she cried.
"Stop it, I tell you; stop it, Nicholas!
Or I will cry, and call out, 'Help! Alas!'
Take off your hands for decency, I say!"
   This Nicholas at once began to pray
For mercy, and he wooed so well and fast
She granted him the love he asked at last,
And she would do for him, she gave her promise,
All that he craved, and swore it by St. Thomas,
As soon as such a thing could safely be.
"My husband is so full of jealousy,
Unless ye watch and wait your time," she said,
"I know too well I am as good as dead.
In this affair ye must be sly and prudent."
   "Nay, never worry over that! A student
Has badly used his time," he said to her,
"If he cannot deceive a carpenter."
So they agreed, and in this fashion swore
To wait a while, as I have said before.
And Nicholas, when he had done all this,
Began to stroke her thighs, and sweetly kiss
Her lips, and then he took his psaltery
And played it fast, and made sweet melody.
   Then to the parish church, as it befell,
To honor Christ, and do his works as well,
On holidays this wife would take her way.
Her forehead always shone as bright as day,
So would she scrub it when she stopped her work.
   Now at that church there was a parish clerk,
A young man by the name of Absalon.
His curly hair, shining like gold new-spun,
Like a great fan spread out to left and right;
The parting line showed even, straight, and white.
His cheeks were red; his eyes gray as a goose;

He had Paul's window carved upon his shoes;
His hose were red, and elegant to see.
And he was clad all tight and properly
In kirtle of the lightest watchel blue,
With laces set all fair, and thickly too;
And over this he wore a surplice gay,
As white as any bough that blooms in May.
A merry lad he was, so God me save!
And he could bleed a man, and clip and shave,
And make a deed, a charter, or a will.
And he could dance and trip with subtle skill
In twenty ways, all of the Oxford fashion,
And fling his legs out with a jolly passion;
And from the rebeck he could pluck a song,
And sing a treble as he went along,
And skilfully he played on his guitar.
In all the town was not a tavern bar
But he would give it entertainment fair
Were any lively barmaid serving there.
And yet indeed the man was far from daring
In breaking wind, and in his speech was sparing.
   This Absalon, this merry lad and gay,
Went with his censer of a holiday
Among the parish wives, and as he passed,
Full many a loving look about him cast,
And most upon this carpenter's young wife.
To look at her would be a merry life,
He thought, she was so wanton and so sweet!
If she had been a sleek mouse at his feet,
And he a cat, he would have made short work
Of seizing her!
               This Absalon, this clerk,
Hath in his heart so great a love-longing
That he would never take an offering
From any wife—he said he wanted none.
The moon at night in all its brightness shone,
And his guitar this Absalon hath taken,
With thought of lovers that his song would waken;
And forth he goes, with love and joy astir,
And reached the dwelling of this carpenter,
Just as the cocks had crowed across the land.
And by a casement window took his stand,

That in the moonlight showed against the wall.
He singeth in a gentle voice and small,
"Now lady dear, if it thy pleasure be,
I pray you well that ye will pity me,"
With music to his ditty sweetly ringing.
This carpenter awoke, and heard him singing,
And whispered to his wife, "What, Alison!
Dost thou not hear," he said, "how Absalon
Is chanting underneath our chamber wall?"
"Yes, John. God knows, indeed, I hear it all!"
Thus Alison replied when it befell.
    And thus it went. What will ye better than well?
From day to day this jolly Absalon
So wooeth her, that he is woe-begone.
He neither sleeps by night nor yet by day;
He combs his spreading locks, and dresseth gay;
He wooeth her by suit and embassage,
And swears that he will serve her as a page;
He sings with quaverings like a nightingale;
Sends her spiced wine, and mead, and honeyed ale;
And wafers from the oven, hot and brown,
And proffers money, since she lives in town.
For there are some that gold will win, and some
To boldness or to virtue will succumb.
    Sometimes, his grace and mastery to try,
He playeth Herod on a scaffold high.
But none of these will help him to succeed,
For it is Nicholas she loves, indeed,
And Absalon may go and blow the horn,
For all his labor earned him only scorn;
She makes a silly ape of Absalon,
And all his earnestness becomes her fun!
For the old proverb is a true if wry one:
"Always the nearer, if he be a sly one,
Leaveth a distant lover to be hated."
Though Absalon was madly agitated
Because he seemed but little in her sight;
This nearer Nicholas stood in his light.
    Now play it well, thou gentle Nicholas,
And Absalon may wail and sing "Alas!"
    And so it happened on a Saturday
This carpenter had gone to Oseney,

And gentle Nicholas and Alison
Agreed at last that thus it should be done:
That Nicholas a subtle plot should weave,
This simple, jealous husband to deceive,
And if the game should chance to go aright,
Then she would sleep within his arms all night,
For this was his desire and hers as well.
And soon, the story brief and straight to tell,
This Nicholas would neither wait nor tarry,
But quietly doth to his chamber carry
Both food and drink to last for several days,
And of this young wife Alison he prays
That if her husband asked for Nicholas,
She should reply she knew not where he was—
She had not seen him all that day, indeed.
She thought he must be sick; he would not heed
Her maid, though she had often gone to call;
He would not stir or answer her at all.
    So Nicholas for all that Saturday
Close and secluded in his chamber lay,
And ate or slept, or did what pleased him best,
Till Sunday, when the sun had gone to rest.
    This simple carpenter was full of wonder
At what this Nicholas might suffer under.
"St. Thomas! I am much afraid today
That something is not right with Nicholay!
Now God forbid he perish suddenly.
This world is full of instability!
Today I saw a corpse to burial borne
That I had seen at work last Monday morn.
Go up," he told his boy. "Stand there before
His room and shout, or pound upon the door;
Look in, and tell what thou canst hear or see."
    This boy obeyed. He went up sturdily,
And while he stood there, as his master bade,
He beat upon the door and cried like mad:
"What! How! What do ye, Master Nicholas!
What! Will ye sleep and let the whole day pass?"
    But all for nothing, there was not a word.
He found a hole, low down upon a board,
Through which the cat went in. There hard and fast
He set his eye and looked, and so at last

He saw the student lying there alone.
This Nicholas was staring, stretched out prone,
As if he gazed upon the crescent moon.
The boy went down, and told his master soon
In what condition he had seen the man.
"Saint Frideswide!" The carpenter began
To cross himself, a shudder running through him.
"A man knows little what may happen to him!
This man hath fallen, with all his astromy,
Into some madness or some agony.
I always guessed too well how it would be.
Men should know nothing of God's privacy.
An ignorant man is blest, that knows no more
Than his own faith. A young clerk once before
Got into trouble with his astromy.
For walking in the fields by night to see
The stars, and read the future things they tell,
Into a marble pit at last he fell.
He saw not *that*. Yet I am sad, I say,
That this should come to gentle Nicholay.
I will reprove him for his studying
If so I may, by Jesus, heaven's king.
    "Get me a staff to pry with from the floor,
While thou, good Robin, heavest up the door.
I guess he will not study longer there."
Then to the student's door the two repair.
His boy was strong; the chamber door he grasps,
And heaves it upward quickly by the hasps,
And soon upon the floor he sets it prone.
This Nicholas lay still as any stone,
Forever gazing upward into air.
This carpenter was now in great despair
And seized him by the shoulders, firm and strong,
And cried hard, as he shook him well and long,
"What! Nicholas! Stare not in such a fashion!
Awake, I say, remember Jesus' passion!
I cross thee now from spite of elves or men!"
And said the night-spell on the instant then,
In all four quarters of the house about,
And on the threshold of the door without:
Jesus Christ and holy Benedict,
Keep this house; let no ill thing afflict.

White pater-noster, *guard us till the dawn;*
St. Peter's sister, whither hast thou gone?
　　At last stirred gentle Nicholas, and sighed
A long and painful sigh. "Alas!" he cried,
"Shall all the world be lost so quickly now?"
　　This carpenter exclaimed: "What sayest thou?
What! Think on God, as do we working men."
　　"Fetch me a drink," this student answered then,
"And later will I speak in privacy
About a matter touching me and thee.
I cannot tell it unto other men."
　　This carpenter goes down, and comes again
And brings a jug of ale, a brimming quart;
And when at length each man has drunk his part,
And Nicholas has made his door all fast,
By him he sets this carpenter at last.
　　He said: "Now John, belovèd host and dear,
Upon thy troth I bid thee swear me here
That what I tell thou wilt betray to none,
For it is Christ's affair and his alone,
Which thou art lost indeed if thou betray;
For this would be thy punishment, I say:
Thou shouldst be struck with madness if thou did it!"
"Nay, Christ for his own sacred blood forbid it!"
This simple man declared. "I do not babble!
Nay, though I say it, I will never gabble.
Say what thou wilt; to no one will I tell
A word of it, by Him that harrowed hell!"
　　"John," he replied, "I will not lie to thee.
I have discovered by astrology
By gazing on the moon when it was bright,
That Monday next, a quarter through the night,
A rain shall fall, so mad and wild a spate
That Noah's flood was never half so great.
This world," he said, "beneath its hideous power,
Shall all be drowned in less time than an hour.
So shall mankind be drowned and lost to life!"
　　This carpenter replied, "Alas, my wife!
Alas, my Alison! And shall she drown?"
And with the thought he almost tumbled down,
And asked: "Is there no remedy for this?"

Said Nicholas: "Why yes, through God there is,
If by advice and learning thou be led;
Thou canst not hope to work by thine own head.
King Solomon the wise in words hath set it:
'Work by advice, and thou shalt not regret it!'
And if thou wilt submit from first to last
To good advice, with neither sail nor mast
I will save her along with thee and me.
Hast thou not heard how Noah rode the sea
Because God warned him, and he understood
How all the world should perish in the flood?"
   "Yes," said this carpenter, "long, long ago."
   "Dost thou," said Nicholas, "not also know
What trouble Noah had, and what discord,
Before he got his wife to come aboard?
I think he would have given his last black wether
If they had been apart, and not together,
She safely in her ship, and he in his!
And know'st thou then what best and needful is?
There must be haste, and with a hasty thing
There should be no delay or sermoning.
Go get for each of us a tub of wood
Or kneading trough, and let them all be good
In workmanship, and large enough to float,
So each of us can swim as in a boat;
And set in each some food and drink—a store
For one day only—we shall need no more;
The water shall subside and go away
About mid-morning of the second day.
But Robin thy boy must hear no word of this,
Nor Gill thy maid; nor ask me why it is,
For though thou ask I will not answer thee;
I cannot tell what God has told to me.
Thou shouldst be grateful, if thou art not mad,
To have as great a grace as Noah had.
And I will save thy wife, too, never doubt it.
Now to thy labor, and be quick about it;
And having got for her and thee and me
These kneading tubs I spoke of, all the three,
Then thou shalt hang them near the roof, up high,
Where no man may our preparation spy.

And when thou shalt have done these things I say,
And neatly stored our food and drink away,
And also put an axe in every boat,
That each of us may cut his rope, and float,
And made a hole high up within the gable,
Off toward the garden and above the stable,
That we may freely sail forth on that day
After the great rain shall have passed away,
Then shalt thou swim as merry, I undertake,
As any white duck following her drake.
Then shall I call, 'Ho! John! Ho! Alison!
Be of good cheer, the flood will soon be done!'
And thou shalt call: 'Hail, master Nicholay!
Hail! I can see thee well, for it is day.'
And then shall we be rulers all our life
Of all the world, like Noah and his wife.
    "But I give warning to thee of one thing:
Remember this—when on that evening
Each boards his vessel, then let none of us
Whisper or call out—any one of us—
Nor cry, but each in prayer on every hand
Be diligent, for this is God's command.
    "And thou must hang thy boat far from thy wife,
That thou shalt do no sin, upon thy life,
No more in thought or look than in the deed.
This is thy full commandment. Go! God speed!
Tomorrow night, when men are all asleep,
Into our kneading tubs we three will creep,
And sit, and wait God's mercy while we pray.
Now there is no more time, so go thy way.
I must not make a sermon, by my faith.
'Say naught, but send the wise,' the prophet saith;
Thou art so wise I have no need to teach thee;
Go, save our lives, is all that I beseech thee."
    This simple carpenter now goes his way,
And often cried "Alas!" and "Well-a-day!"
And told his wife of all this secrecy.
She knew it well; and knew far more than he
What all this curious tale betokeneth;
And yet she seemed afraid, as for her death:
"Alas! Go quickly, do thy work," she said,

"And help us to escape, or we are dead.
I am thy true and loyal wedded wife;
Go, husband, go, and help to save my life."
    Lo! What a power may lie in perturbation!
A man may die of his imagination,
So deep is the impression it may make!
This simple carpenter began to shake.
He thought he saw in actuality
The flood of Noah rolling like the sea
To drown his Alison, his honey dear.
He weepeth, waileth, shuddereth with fear,
And many a heavy sigh the man blows off.
He goes at last and gets a kneading trough,
And after that a tub and kimelin,
And secretly he sent them to his inn,
And hung them in the rafters secretly;
His own hand shaped the ladders, all the three,
Which by the rungs and shafts could be ascended
Up to the beams where the tubs hung suspended.
And he provisioned both the tubs and trough
With bread and cheese, and ale to finish off—
What for a day would be an ample ration.
But first, before he made this preparation,
He sent his maid and his apprentice down
On errands for him into London town.
And then on Monday, with the falling night,
He shut his door, and lit no candle light,
And saw that all was as it ought to be.
And soon they climbed the ladders, all the three,
And sat there still, a furlong's length away.
    "Now, *pater-noster*, mum!" said Nicholay;
And "Mum!" quoth John, and "Mum!" said Alison.
This carpenter hath his devotion done,
And lies in quiet now, and says his prayer,
And waits to hear the rain, if it be there.
    But dead sleep, after all his busyness,
Fell on this carpenter, as I should guess,
At curfew time, or later, it may be;
Disturbed of heart, he groaneth grievously,
And since his head was laid an awkward way,
He snored. Then down at once stole Nicholay,

And downward Alison as softly sped,
And with no further word they went to bed
There where the carpenter was wont to be.
Then came the revel and the melody!
And so lie Nicholas and Alison;
In mirth and pleasure there they play as one
Until the bell of lauds began to ring
And in the chancel monks commenced to sing.
   This parish clerk, this amorous Absalon,
That ever is for love so woe begone,
Upon this Monday was at Oseney
With company, for pleasure and for play;
And asked by accident a cloisterer
In private of this John the carpenter.
He drew him from the church, and in his ear
He said, "I have not seen him working here
Since Saturday, and I suppose he went
For timber somewhere, by our abbot sent,
For often this is what he has to do,
Remaining at the grange a day or two;
Or he is at his house, for certainty.
Truly, I cannot tell where he may be."
   This Absalon was gay, his heart was light,
He thought: "I shall not go to bed tonight;
For certainly I have not seen the man
About his door at all since day began.
As I may thrive, at crowing of the cock,
I shall in secret at his window knock,
The one low down upon the chamber wall.
Then shall I speak to Alison of all
My longing and my love; and shall not miss
At very least, that I shall get a kiss.
I shall have comfort in some kind of way!
I had an itching at my lips all day,
And that must signify a kiss, at least.
Also I dreamed that I was at a feast.
So I will go and sleep an hour or two,
Then will I wake and play the whole night through."
   When the first cock crowed, long before the dawn,
Up rose this jolly lover Absalon,
And dressed him gay, with every artifice,
But first chewed cardamon and licorice

Before he combed his hair, for their sweet smell,
And, with the hope to be acceptable,
A "true love" leaf beneath his tongue he laid.
So to the house with languid feet he strayed,
And by her chamber window stood at rest,
The sill of which was level with his breast,
And coughed, and half aloud his suit begun:
"What do ye, honey-comb, sweet Alison?
Sweet cinnamon, my lovely bride to be,
Sweetheart, awake, I say, and speak to me.
Little, alas! ye think upon my woe,
And how I sweat for passion as I go.
No wonder that I swoon and sweat, my sweet;
I suffer like a lamb that wants the teat!
Yea, I am so consumed with longing, love,
That I am sad as any turtle dove;
I cannot eat more than a maid," he sighed.
   "Go! Leave my window, jackass," she replied.
"It will not be 'Come kiss me,' by God's name;
I love another, or else I were to blame,
Better than thee, by Jesu, Absalon.
Be off, or I will stone thee. What! Have done!
And let me sleep, in the devil's name, I say!"
   "Alas!" cried Absalon. "Alackaday!
That true love ever had so hard a debtor!
Kiss me at least, if it may be no better,
For Jesu's love and mine, I beg of thee."
"Then wilt thou go thy way?" demanded she.
"Yea, of a truth, my dear; yea, sweetheart," said he.
"Then I will come at once," she called, "make ready!"
And whispered low to Nicholas, "Lie still
And make no sound, and thou shalt laugh thy fill!"
   This Absalon kneeled down. His heart was gay.
He said: "I am a lord in every way,
Of what shall come this kiss is but the savor;
Sweetheart, thy grace! O lovely bride, thy favor!"
   Now hastily the window she undid.
"Have done! Come up, and speed thee fast," she bid,
"For fear thou shouldst attract some neighbor's eye."
   This Absalon now wiped his mouth all dry;
Like a black coal, or pitch, the darkness there
Hung dense, and out she thrust her bottom bare,

And Absalon did nothing more nor less
Than with his lips to set a sweet caress
Upon her arse, before he knew of this.
He started back, for something seemed amiss;
He knew well that a woman has no beard.
He felt a thing all rough and thickly haired,
And "Fie!" he muttered. "What is this I do?"
"Te-hee!" cried she, and clapped the window to;
And Absalon goes wretchedly away.
"A beard, a beard!" cried gentle Nicholay.
"Now by God's *corpus,* this goes well and fair!"
    This simple Absalon, that still was there,
Heard all, and bit his lips until they bled.
"I shall repay thee!" to himself he said.
    Who rubbeth now, who scours and scrubs his lips
With dust and sand and straw, with cloth, with chips,
But Absalon, who often cries, "Alas!
Now will I sell my soul to Sathanas
If rather than to hold this town in fee
I would not be revenged for this," said he.
"Fool! Fool! I lacked the sense to turn aside!"
His burning love was quenched and satisfied,
For since he gave her buttocks that caress,
He rated love not worth a piece of cress;
He was clean purged of all his malady.
He cursed all wenches long and bitterly,
And like a whipped child often sobbed and wept.
Then quietly across the street he crept,
To where Gervase, a blacksmith, had his house,
That in his forge beat out the parts of plows;
Coulters and shares he sharpened busily.
This Absalon knocked softly. "Hist!" said he,
"Come out, Gervase; undo thy door at once."
    "Who art thou?" "Absalon," was the response.
"What, Absalon! By Christ upon his tree,
Why rise ye up so early, *ben'cite!*
What ails you, lad, I say? Some gay girl—what?—
Hath brought you out this morning at a trot;
By St. Note, boy, ye know well what I mean."
    This Absalon he did not care a bean
For joking, and he would not speak or laugh.

He had more tow to spin on his distaff
Than Gervase knew, and said, "Good friend and dear,
Lend me this red hot coulter lying here
For something that I have a mind to do,
And I will shortly bring it back to you."
    Gervase replied, "Of course. Why, were it gold,
Or a fat bag of nobles still untold,
It should be thine, or I be no true smith.
Eh! Foe of Christ! What will ye do therewith?"
    "Let that," said Absalon, "be as it may;
I shall inform thee well when it is day,"
And caught the coulter where the steel was cool,
And softly from the smithy door he stole,
And to the carpenter's returned again.
He coughed at first, and knocked a little then
Against the window, just as he had done
Before. "Who's there?" demanded Alison,
"Who knocks? I'll warrant that some thief is here!"
    "Why nay," said he, "God knows, my sweet and
        dear,
I am thine Absalon, my treasureling,
And I have brought thee here a golden ring—
My mother's, as I hope I shall be saved,
And it is fine, and cunningly engraved.
This will I give thee for another kiss."
    Now Nicholas had left the bed to piss,
And thought the joke a better one to tell
If Absalon should kiss his arse as well;
And raising up the window, backed into it,
And stealthily he thrust his own arse through it,
Out past the buttocks, half way up the thigh.
This clerk, this Absalon, began to cry:
"Speak, my sweet bird; I know not where thou art."
    At once this Nicholas let fly a fart,
That like a clap of thunder smote the quiet.
And Absalon was almost staggered by it,
But had the red hot iron in his hand,
And square upon the buttocks set his brand.
    Off goes the skin a hand's breadth with the blow,
The red hot coulter seared his bottom so;
It smarted till he thought that he should die.

Wild as a madman he began to cry:
"Help! Water! Water! Help me, for God's sake!"
   The screaming made this carpenter awake.
"Water!" was all he heard and understood.
He thought: "Alas! At last comes Noah's flood!"
He raised himself, and with no more ado
He seized his axe and cut the rope in two,
And down he went, and never stopped until
He came to rest at length beside the sill,
Upon the floor, and there aswoon he lay.
   Up started Alison and Nicholay,
And ran out shouting in their agitation.
The neighbors, both of great and lesser station,
Rushed in and stared upon this fallen man,
Where he lay swooning, very pale and wan,
For he had broke his arm in his descent.
But he must still digest his accident,
For hardly had he spoke, when Alison
And Nicholas both talked him down as one;
Telling all those who came that he was mad,
Such was this fear of "Noah's flood" he had
That he had bought these tubs and troughs, all three,
Through fantasy, and in his vanity,
And hung them to the roof-beams high above,
And prayed the both of them for God's sweet love
To sit there in the roof, *pour compagnie.*
   Everyone laughed at this strange fantasy,
And in the roof began to peer and poke,
And made his injury a kind of joke.
For anything this carpenter might say
Was useless, no one listened, anyway.
With mighty oaths so many swore him down
They thought him crazy all about the town.
For every student would support the other;
They said: "The man is mad, no doubt, dear
        brother;"
And everyone would laugh about this strife.
Thus bedded was this carpenter's young wife
In spite of all his guard and jealousy;
And Absalon hath kissed her under eye,
And Nicholas is branded for his fun
Upon the rump. God save you; I am done!

THE REEVE'S TALE[1]

Not far from Cambridge, close to Trumpington,
Beneath a bridge of stone, there used to run
A brook, and there a mill stood well in view;
And everything I tell you now is true.
Here dwelt a miller many a year and day,
As proud as any peacock, and as gay.
And he could pipe and fish, wrestle and shoot,
Mend nets, and make a well-turned cup to boot,
He wore a long knife belted at his side,
A sword that had a sharp blade and a wide,
And carried in his pouch a handsome dagger.
No man durst touch him, though he boast and
       swagger.
A Sheffield dirk was hidden in his hose.
His face was round; he had a broad pug nose;
Smooth as an ape's the skull above his face.
He was a bully in the market-place.
No man dared lay a little finger on him
But he would swear to be revenged upon him.
He was indeed a thief of corn and meal,
A sly one, and his habit was to steal;
And scornful Simkin was the name he carried.
A wife of noble kindred he had married:
Her father was the parson of the town!
Many good pans of brass this priest paid down
To win this Simkin to his family!
And she was fostered in a nunnery,
For Simkin would not have a wife, he said,
That was not gently nurtured, and a maid,
To match his standing as a proper yeoman.
As pert as any magpie was this woman.
It was a sight to see them take the road
On holidays. Before her Simkin strode,
His tippet proudly wrapped about his head;
And she came after in a smock of red,
With Simkin clad in stockings of the same.
None dared to call her anything but "dame,"

---

[1] *Reeve:* a steward or overseer. This reeve also happens to be a carpenter, and he is furious because the miller's tale ridiculed a carpenter-husband. In retaliation he tells a story in which the butt is a thieving miller.

And there was none that passed them on the way
So bold that he would romp with her or play,
Unless in truth he wished to lose his life
At Simkin's hand by dagger or by knife.
A jealous husband is a dangerous beast—
Or so he wants his wife to think, at least!
And since by birth a little smirched men thought her,
She was as sour of mien as stagnant water,
And haughty in her ways, and full of scorn.
She thought that, since her father was well born,
And she had got a convent education,
A distant air was suited to her station.
    A daughter had these two—a girl a score
Of years in age; and after her, no more,
Except a child a half year old they had,
Still in the cradle, and a proper lad.
This daughter was a stout and full-blown lass
With a pug nose and eyes as gray as glass,
And buttocks broad, and breasts shaped round and
        high,
And yet her hair was fair, I will not lie.
    The parson of the town, since she was fair,
Had it in mind that she should be his heir
Unto his house and goods and everything.
He was severe about her marrying.
He meant to place her in some family
Of worthy blood and lofty ancestry;
For holy church's goods must be expended
On those from holy church's blood descended;
His holy blood—he would do honor to it,
Though he devoured holy church to do it!
    This miller took great toll, ye need not doubt,
On wheat and malt from all the land about,
And from a certain college most of all,
At Cambridge, which was known there as King's Hall,
That brought their wheat and barley to his mill.
It happened once, the manciple lay ill,
And with his malady was kept a-bed,
And he was sure to die of it, men said.
Therefore this miller stole of corn and meal
A hundred times what he had dared to steal
Before; for then he took his toll discreetly,

But now the fellow was a thief completely,
Which made the warden fume and scold and swear,
Yet the bold miller did not give a tare;
But boasted loud, and swore it was not true.
   Among the Cambridge students there were two
In dwelling at the Hall of which I tell.
Headstrong they were, and quick and bold as well.
And all for lustihood and jollity
They begged the warden long and eagerly
For his permission to be gone until
They saw their grain ground at the miller's mill.
Each offered sturdily to lay his neck
The miller should not steal a half a peck
Whether by trickery or force, and so
At length the warden gave them leave to go.
One was named John, and Alan was the other;
Born in the same town both—a place called Strother—
Far to the north—I cannot tell you where.
   This Alan for the journey doth prepare,
And brought a horse to put their sack upon,
And off they go, this Alan and this John,
Each with a sword and buckler by his side.
John knew the way; they did not need a guide;
And at the mill at length the sack he lay'th.
Alan spoke first: "Hail, Simon, by my faith!
How fares thy daughter fair, and thy good wife?"
   Said Simkin: "Welcome, Alan, by my life!
And John the same! How now, what do ye here?"
   "Simon," said John, "By God, need has no peer.
Who hath no servant, as the clerks have said,
Unless a fool, must serve himself instead.
Our manciple, I fear, will soon be dead,
The poor man's jaws are waggling in his head;
So I am come, and Alan, with our sack,
To have our grain ground, and to bear it back.
I pray you, put it quickly through the mill."
   "Now by my faith," this Simkin said, "I will.
What will ye while I have the thing in hand?"
   "By God, right by the hopper will I stand,"
Said John, "and see the grain go down the maw;
For by my father's kin, I never saw
The way a hopper waggles to and fro."

Alan replied: "What, John, and wilt thou so?
Then I will stand beneath it, by my crown,
And I will watch the meal come falling down
Into the trough; so shall I have my fun.
For, John, in faith, when all is said and done,
I am as poor a miller as are ye."
   The miller smiled at their simplicity.
"All this is but a trick of theirs," he thought.
"They think they cannot be deceived or caught;
But I shall pull the wool across their eyes
However shrewdly they philosophize.
The more involved the strategems they make,
The more shall be the stealing when I take!
Instead of flour they shall be served with bran!
'The greatest clerk is not the wisest man,'
As the wolf heard the proverb from the mare.
I count this art of theirs not worth a tare!"
   Then when he saw his opportunity,
He slipped out through the doorway stealthily,
And looked about him when he stood outside,
And found the student's horse, which they had tied
Behind the mill, beneath an arbor there.
Then he approached it with a friendly air,
And straightway stripped the bridle from its head.
And when the horse found he was loose, he fled
Off toward the fen, where wild mares ran at play;
"We-hee!" Through thick and thin he streaked
         away.
   The miller then came back. No word he spoke,
But did his work, or sometimes cracked a joke,
Until the grain was well and fairly ground.
And when the meal at length was sacked and bound,
This John found that his horse had run away;
And "Help!" he shouted, and "Alackaday!
Our horse is gone! Alan, come out!" he cried,
"By God's bones, man, step lively! Come outside!
Alas! Our warden's palfrey hath been lost!"
All thought of meal and grain this Alan tossed
Into the wind, and all economy.
"What! Which way is he gone?" demanded he.
   The wife came leaping in among them then.
"Alas!" she said. "Your horse makes for the fen

With the wild mares, as fast as he can go!
Bad luck upon the hand that tied him so,
That should have bound him better with the rein!"
   "Alas!" cried John. "Now, Alan, for Christ's pain,
Off goes my sword; lay thine beside it here.
God knows I be as nimble as a deer;
He shall not get away from both of us.
Alan, thou wast a fool to tie him thus.
Why didst na' put the nag into the stable?"
   These students ran as fast as they were able
Off to the fen, this Alan and this John,
And when the miller saw that they were gone
He took a half a bushel of their flour
And bade his wife go knead it up that hour
Into a cake. "These students were a-feared!
A miller still can trim a student's beard
For all his art! Now let them go their way!
Look where they run! Yea, let the children play;
They will not get him quickly, by my crown!"
   These simple students scurried up and down
With "Whoa there, whoa!" "Hold hard!" "Look
         to the rear!"
"Go whistle to him while I keep him here!"
But, to be brief, until the edge of night
They could not, though they strove with all their
         might,
Capture their horse, he ran away so fast,
Till in a ditch they cornered him at last.
   Like cattle in the rain, wet through and through,
And wearied out, they plodded back, the two.
"Alas!" cried John, "the day that I was born!
Now we are brought to mockery and scorn!
Our grain is stolen; each will be called a fool
Both by the warden and our friends at school,
And by the miller most. Alackaday!"
   Thus John came back, complaining all the way,
With Bayard's rope in hand, through brush and mire.
He found the miller sitting by the fire,
For it was night. Return they did not dare,
And begged him he would give them lodging there,
For love of God, and they would pay their penny.
   The miller answered: "Yea, if there be any,

Such as it is, that will I share with you.
My house is small; but ye are schooled, ye two,
And by your arguments can make a place
A mile in breadth from twenty feet of space!
Let us see now if this will hold us all,
Or talk it larger, if it be too small!"
   "Now by St. Cuthbert, Simon, shrewdly spoke!"
This John replied. "Always thou hast thy joke!
They say a man must choose between two things:
Take what he finds, or do with what he brings.
But specially I pray thee, landlord dear,
Get us some meat and drink, and make good cheer,
And we will pay in full upon demand.
No one can lure a hawk with empty hand;
Lo!—here our silver ready to be spent."
   This miller to the town his daughter sent
For ale and bread, and roasted them a goose,
And tied their horse so it should not get loose—
And in his own room laid them out a bed
With sheets and blankets well and fairly spread,
Not more than ten or twelve feet from his own.
His daughter had one for herself alone,
In the same chamber, in its proper place.
Better it might not be—the little space
Within the house had made it necessary.
They sat and supped and talked and made them merry
And drank strong ale, and so the evening sped.
At midnight, or about, they went to bed.
   Well was this miller varnished in the head:
So pale with drink his face was drained of red.
He hiccoughs, and his voice comes through his nose
As if he had a cold. To bed he goes,
And by his side the good wife goes her way.
She was as light and saucy as a jay,
So well her merry whistle had been wet.
At the bed's foot the baby's crib they set,
To rock it, and to give the child the dug.
And when the ale was emptied from the jug
The daughter followed with no more ado;
And then to bed went John and Alan too.
No need of drugs to send them off to sleep;
This miller of the ale had drunk so deep

He snorted like a horse, nor had a mind
For any noises from his tail behind.
His wife sang with him—such a lusty singing
Two furlongs off ye might have heard it ringing;
The wench snored loudly, too, *pour compagnie.*
  Alan the student heard this melody,
And nudging John he whispered: "Sleepest thou?
Heardst ever such a song as this ere now?
Lo! what an evening liturgy they make!
May wild fire all their cursèd bodies take!
Who ever heard so weird a chant ascending?
Yea, they deserve the flower of all bad ending!
All this long night I shall not get my rest.
No matter—all shall happen for the best.
For John, as I have hope to thrive," he said,
"I shall go lay that wench in yonder bed.
The law allows some easement unto us:
For, John, there is a law that puts it thus:
That if a man in one point shall be grieved,
Then in another he shall be relieved!
Our grain is stolen—there is no saying nay,
Ill luck hath dogged us all this livelong day.
Now since for this I get no compensation,
I mean to salve my loss with consolation.
By God's soul, this shall be the way, I swear!"
  This John replied, "Nay, Alan, have a care.
This miller is a dangerous man," he said,
"And if ye wake him as he lies in bed,
He might do both of us an injury."
  Alan replied: "I count him not a fly,"
And rose, and to the wench's bed he crept.
The girl lay on her back and soundly slept.
Before she knew what Alan was about
It was too late for her to cry or shout,
And, to be brief, the two were soon as one.
Now, Alan, play! for I will speak of John.
  John lay in silence while a man might go
A furlong, and he moaned for very woe.
"Alas! This is a wicked jest," cried he.
"Plainly it makes a clumsy ape of me.
My comrade gets some pay for all his harms;
He holds the miller's daughter in his arms;

He hath adventured, and his quest hath sped,
And I lie like a sack of bran in bed.
And when this prank of ours is told at school,
I shall be held a milk-sop and a fool!
I will arise and risk it, by my faith!
'No pluck, no luck,' is what the proverb saith."
And up he rose, and with a noiseless tread
Stole to the cradle, and bore it to his bed,
And at the foot he set it on the flooring.
   Soon after this the wife left off her snoring,
Rose and relieved herself, and came again,
But by her bed she missed the cradle then,
And in the darkness groped about and sought.
"Alas! I almost went amiss," she thought,
"I would have climbed into the students' bed!
Eh, *ben'cite!* That would be bad!" she said.
And groped, and found the cradle, and went past
With hand outstretched, and reached the bed at last.
And had no thought but everything was good
Because the baby's cradle by it stood,
And in the dark she knew not where she went.
So she crept in, relieved and well content,
And there lay still, and would have gone to sleep.
But soon this John the student with a leap
Was on this wife, at work with all his might;
So merry she had not been for many a night;
He pricketh hard and deep, as he were mad.
And thus a jolly life these students had
Until at length the third cock started crowing.
   Alan, with dawn a little weary growing,
For all night he had labored hard and well:
"Sweetheart, dear Malin, I must say farewell.
Day comes; I cannot stay beyond this kiss;
But always, as my soul may win to bliss,
I am thy student, where I go or ride."
   "So then, dear love, farewell," the wench replied.
"But one thing, while thou lie beside me still—
When thou art going homeward by the mill—
Right at the entry door—look thou behind;
A loaf of half a bushel wilt thou find,
Kneaded and baked it was from thine own meal
Which yesterday I helped my father steal.

Now, sweetheart, may God save thee well, and keep."
And with that word almost began to weep.
   Alan arose. "Before the night shall end,
I will go creep in bed beside my friend,"
And touched the cradle as he groped along.
"By God," he muttered, "I am going wrong;
My head is dizzy from my work this night
And hath confused me, so I go not right,
For by the cradle I can surely tell;
Here lie the miller and his wife as well."
By twenty devils, forth he goes his way,
And found the bed in which the miller lay,
And crawled in softly where his comrade slept,
As he supposed, and to the miller crept,
And caught him by the neck, and softly spake,
Saying: "Thou, John, thou swine's head! What!
      Awake!
And hear, for Christ's soul, of this noble sport;
For by St. James, although this night was short,
Thrice have I laid the miller's daughter flat
Upon her back, and had her, and all that
While like a coward thou hast lain in bed."
   "Yea, hast thou, lecherous rogue?" the miller said.
"Ha! thou false student, traitor false!" cried he.
"Thou shalt be dead, yea, by God's dignity!
Who dare disgrace," he cried in fearful rage,
"My daughter, come of such a lineage?"
And caught this Alan by the Adam's apple,
And choked him as the two began to grapple,
And smote him with his fist full on the nose.
Down on his breast the warm blood spurting flows,
And on the floor; his nose and mouth were broke.
They wallow like two pigs tied in a poke,
And up they go, then down again are thrown,
Until the miller on a paving stone
Stumbled, and fell down backward on his wife,
That lay there dead to all this crazy strife,
For she began a little sleep to take
By John, that all night long had been awake,
And started from her slumber when he fell.
"Help, cross of Bromholm!" she began to yell.
"*In manus tuas!* Lord, I call on thee!

Simon, awake! The fiend hath fallen on me;
My heart is cracked! Help! I am all but dead!
One on my belly, one upon my head!
Help, Simon! for these lying students fight!"
    This John jumped up as quickly as he might,
And back and forth along the wall he flew
To find a staff, and she had jumped up too,
And knew the room much better than he knew it,
And where a staff was, and went quickly to it,
And saw a little shimmering of light,
For through a hole the moon was shining bright,
And by the light in struggle saw the two,
But did not know for certain who was who,
But saw a glimmer there of something white,
And with this white thing dancing in her sight,
She thought, because she could not see it clearer,
It was a student's night-cap, and drew nearer,
And would have hit this Alan, but instead
She struck the bald spot on the miller's head,
And down he went, and cried out: "Help, I die!"
These students beat him well and let him lie,
And dressed themselves, and got their horse and meal,
And on their homeward journey off they steal.
And at the mill they got the loaf of bread—
Of half a bushel—and away they sped.
    Thus was the haughty miller roundly beat,
And got no pay for grinding all their wheat,
And paid for supper ere the game was through
For Alan and John, that thrashed him soundly, too.
His wife and daughter are both of them disgraced;
So fares a miller that is double-faced
And false: the proverb tells the honest truth:
"Let him not look for good that evil do'th;"
He that deceives, himself deceived shall be.
And God, that sits aloft in majesty,
Save you, both great and humble, without fail!
Thus I pay off the miller with my tale!

François Villon

François Villon's autobiographical *Testament* asserts that he was born in 1431, but his birthplace has never been ascertained and his surname is a matter of conjecture. Legend has it that he had a high-sounding title, François de Montcorbier, and that he discarded it because he refused to identify himself with run-down aristocrats. At fifteen he entered the University of Paris and joined a group of reckless students who turned to robbery, mayhem, and murder. In his early twenties there was a brawl in which a priest was killed, and Villon was exiled from Paris. He returned as a member and possibly leader of a brotherhood of sneak thieves, picklocks, debauched nuns, and common prostitutes. In his thirty-second year he was arrested because of various crimes and tortured—he was forced to drink gallons of water, a beverage that Villon claimed was poison to him. He was found guilty and condemned to be hanged, but the sentence was commuted. Instead of being executed, Villon was banished again. He disappeared; nothing further is known about him.

Villon shares with Chaucer the gift of transmuting characteristics into character; like Chaucer, he relished the rough and unrelenting casualty of life. If his laughter is bitter, it is because it is directed against the pretension of manners and prankishness of his times. Although their popularity may have been due to their frank realism rather than to their technical skill, his poems were relished by all his contemporaries. Less than eighty years after his death, thirty-four editions of his works had been published.

Time does not blur the sharp colors nor dull the vigor of Villon's wit. His verses bristle with satirical bequests. He bequeaths long cloaks to thieves in order to conceal their booty, donates dissipation to monks and nuns, and gives prostitutes the right to hold school by night, where the teachers are taught by the pupils. His details are as gross and lovingly painted as those of Bruegel. No one has more knowingly and sympathetically pictured the crowded life of the streets, the loud pothouses, the dark alleys, the pretty wantons, the withered trulls. Villon's inherent compassion may be muffled by his rollicking manner, but it struggles through. Swinburne recognized this contradiction of mockery and misery when he hailed the poet as "bird of the bitter bright grey golden morn" with "poor splendid wings so frayed and soiled and torn."

"A Ballade of the Women of Paris" is translated by Algernon Charles Swinburne. "A Ballade of the Fair Helm-maker to the Light-o'-Loves" and "A Ballade of Villon and Muckle Meg" are translated by John Payne. The paraphrase in thieves' argot of *Toute aux tavernes et aux filles*—a slang version as strictly made as the original ballade—is by W. E. Henley.

A BALLADE OF THE WOMEN OF PARIS

Albeit the Venice girls get praise
    For their sweet speech and tender air,
And though the old women have wise ways
    Of chaffering for amorous ware,
    Yet at my peril dare I swear,
Search Rome, where God's grace mainly tarries,
    Florence and Savoy, everywhere,
There's no good girl's lip out of Paris.

The Naples women, as folk prattle,
    Are sweetly spoken and subtle enough:
German girls are good at tattle,
    And Prussians make their boast thereof;
    Take Egypt for the next remove,
Or that waste land the Tartar harries,
    Spain or Greece, for the matter of love,
There's no good girl's lip out of Paris.

Breton and Swiss know nought of the matter,
    Gascony girls or girls of Toulouse;
Two fishwomen with a half-hour's chatter
    Would shut them up by threes and twos;
Calais, Lorraine, and all their crews,
(Names enow the mad song marries)
    England and Picardy, search them and choose,
There's no good girl's lip out of Paris.

Prince, give praise to our French ladies
    For the sweet sound their speaking carries;
'T wixt Rome and Cadiz many a maid is,
    But no good girl's lip out of Paris.

A BALLADE OF THE FAIR HELM-MAKER
TO THE LIGHT-O'-LOVES

Now think on't, Nell, the glover fair,
    That wont my scholar once to be,
And you, Blanche Slippermaker there,
    Your case in mine I'd have you see:
    Look all to right and left take ye;
Forbear no man; for trulls that bin
    Old have nor course nor currency,
No more than money that's called in.

You, Sausage-huckstress debonair,
    That dance and trip it brisk and free,
And Guillemette Upholstress, there,
    Look you transgress not Love's decree:
    Soon must you shut up shop, perdie;
Soon old you'll grow, faded and thin,
    Worth, like some old priest's visnomy,
No more than money that's called in.

Jenny the hatter, have a care
    Lest some false lover hamper thee;
And Kitty Spurmaker, beware;
    Deny no man that proffers fee;
    For girls that are not bright o'blee
Men's scorn and not their service win:
    Foul eld gets neither love nor gree,

No more than money that's called in.
Wenches, give ear and list (quo' she)
    Wherefore I weep and make this din;
'Tis that there is no help for me,
    No more than money that's called in.

A BALLADE OF VILLON AND MUCKLE MEG

Because I love and serve a whore sans glose,
    Think not therefore or knave or fool am I:
She hath in her such goods as no man knows.
    For love of her target and dirk I ply:
    When clients come I hend a pot therenigh
And get me gone for wine, without word said:
Before them water, fruit, bread, cheese, I spread.
    If they pay well, I bid them "Well, God aid!
Come here again when you of lust are led,
    In this the brothel where we ply our trade."

But surely before long an ill wind blows
    When, coinless, Margot comes by me to lie.
I hate the sight of her, catch up her hose,
    Her gown, her surcoat and her girdle-tie,
    Swearing to pawn them, meat and drink to buy.
She grips me by the throat and cuffs my head,
Cries "Antichrist!" and swears by Jesus dead,
    It shall not be: till I, to quell the jade,
A potsherd seize and I score her nose with red,
    In this the brothel where we ply our trade.

Then she, peace made, to show we're no more foes,
    A hugeous crack of wind at me lets fly
And laughing sets her fist against my nose,
    Bids me "Go to" and claps me on the thigh;
    Then, drunk, like logs we sleep, till, by and by,
Awaking, when her womb is hungerèd,
To spare the child beneath her girdlestead,
    She mounts on me, flat as a pancake laid.
With wantoning she wears me to the thread,
    In this the brothel where we ply our trade.

Hail, rain, freeze, ready baked I hold my bread:
Well worth a lecher with a wanton wed!
Whether's the worse. They differ not a shred.
   Ill cat to ill rat; each for each was made.
We flee from honour; it from us hath fled:
Lewdness we love, that stands us well in stead,
   In this the brothel where we ply our trade.

A STRAIGHT TIP TO ALL CROSS COVES

Suppose you screeve? or go cheap-jack?
   Or fake the broads? or fig a nag?
Or thumble-rig? or knap a yack?
   Or pitch a snide? or smash a rag?
   Suppose you duff? or nose and lag?
Or get the straight, and land your pot
   How do you melt the multy swag?
Booze and the blowens cop the lot.

Fiddle or fence, or mace, or mack,
   Or moskeneer, or flash the drag;
Dead-lurk a crib, or do a crack,
   Pad with a slang, or chuck a fag;
   Bonnet, or tout, or mump and gag;
Rattle the tats, or mark the spot:
   You cannot bag a single stag—
Booze and the blowens cop the lot.

Suppose you try a different tack,
   And on the square you flash your flag?
At penny-a-lining make your whack,
   Or with the mummers mump and gag?
   For nix, for nix, the dibs you bag!
At any graft, no matter what,
   Your merry goblins soon stravag,—
Booze and the blowens cop the lot.

It's up the spout and Charly Wag
   With wipes and tickers and what not;
Until the squeezer nips your scrag,
   Booze and the blowens cop the lot.

Erasmus

Conformity was put to severe tests in the sixteenth century. It was questioned from within the church and challenged from without. Although they were in no way affiliated, both Erasmus and François Rabelais assailed sacrosanct doctrines with diverse and devastating types of humor.

A Dutch scholar, Desiderius Erasmus disseminated a spirit of liberalism throughout Europe at a time when bigotry and superstition were rampant. An illegitimate child, probably born in 1466 either at Rotterdam or Gouda, he was ordained a priest at the age of twenty-six, became Latin secretary to the Bishop of Bergen, and spent the rest of his life studying, teaching, editing, and writing. He traveled continually and in London formed a close friendship with Thomas More, to whom he dedicated *The Praise of Folly*.

Prior to this work, he had been a struggling scholar, dependent on the bounty of wealthy patrons; but with the appearance of this "declamation" his fame spread, and one high clerical position after another was offered to him. He refused them all, preferring to read and write as he wished. For years he poured out translations of religious classics and editions of sacred works, notably that of the Greek text of the New Testament, as well as pamphlets on timely topics. He was always industrious and never in robust health. He could drink only a little wine and no beer. Lent was an intolerable season, for he could not stand the smell of fish. "My heart," he said, "is Catholic, but my stomach is Lutheran."

Erasmus did not direct his satire against the church but against its oppressive dogmas and elaborate ritual ceremonies. He pitted tolerance against fanaticism and clear-eyed reason against blind belief. At Canterbury he saw pilgrims kissing Thomas à Beckett's shoe that glistened with jewels. The sight moved him to reproachful sarcasm. "We kiss the old shoes and dirty handkerchiefs of the saints," he expostulated, "and we neglect their books, which are the more holy relics. We lock up their shirts in cabinets adorned with gems, but we leave their writings to mouldiness and vermin." When he died at seventy he left no money for the customary Masses, and he was unattended by a confessor at his deathbed.

Erasmus wrote in a Latin that was not only a living but a lively language. The wit of *The Praise of Folly* is the wit of a scholar, but the speech is that of the man of letters who is also a man of the world. This book, which proved Erasmus a humorist as well as a humanist, troubled and profoundly influenced the thought of a century. It maintained that even the most drastic reform should be seasoned with a kind of pensive whimsicality and that folly often is needed to sweeten the bitterness of life.

The excerpt from *The Praise of Folly* is in the translation by Hoyt Hopewell Hudson.

THE PRAISE OF FOLLY

However mortal folk may commonly speak of me (for I am not ignorant how ill the name of Folly sounds, even to the greatest fools), I am she—the only she, I may say—whose divine influence makes gods and men rejoice. One great and sufficient proof of this is that the instant I stepped up to speak to this crowded assembly, all faces at once brightened with a fresh and unwonted cheerfulness, all of you suddenly unbent your brows, and with frolic and affectionate smiles you applauded; so that as I look upon all present about me, you seem flushed with nectar, like gods in Homer, not without some nepenthe, also; whereas a moment ago you were sitting moody and depressed, as if you had come out of the cave of Trophonius. Just as it commonly happens, when the sun first shows his splendid golden face to the earth or when, after a bitter winter, young spring breathes mild west winds, that a new face comes over everything, new color and a sort of youthfulness appear; so at the mere sight of me, you straightway take on another aspect. And thus what great orators elsewhere can hardly bring about in a long, carefully planned speech, I have done in a moment, with nothing but my looks.

As to why I appear today in this unaccustomed garb, you shall now hear, if only you will not begrudge lending your ears to my discourse—not those ears, to be sure, which you carry to sermons, but those which you are accustomed to prick up for mountebanks in the marketplace, for clowns and jesters, the ears which, in the old days, our friend Midas inclined to the god Pan. It is my pleasure for a little while to play the rhetorician before you, yet not one of the tribe of those who nowadays cram certain pedantic trifles into the heads of schoolboys, and teach a more than womanish obstinacy in disputing; no, I emulate those ancients who, to avoid the unpopular name of philosophers, preferred to be called Sophists. Their study was to celebrate in eulogies the virtues of gods and of heroic men. Such a eulogy, therefore, you shall hear, but not of Hercules or Solon; rather of my own self—to wit, Folly.

Nor do I have any use for those wiseacres who preach that it is most foolish and insolent for a person to praise himself. Yet let it be as foolish as they would have it, if only they will grant that it is proper: and what is more suitable than that Folly herself should be the trumpeter of her praises? "She is her own fluteplayer." Who, indeed, could portray me better than can I myself? Unless it could so happen that I am better known to some one else that I am to myself. On the whole, however, I deem that what I am doing is much more decent than what a host of our best people, and scholars even, do continually. With a certain perverse modesty they are wont to convey instructions to some sycophantic speaker or prattling poet whom they have engaged at a fee; and then they hear back from him their praises, that is to say, some pure fiction. The blushing listener, meanwhile, spreads his plumes like a peacock, and bridles, while the brazen adulator searches among the gods to find a parallel for this good-for-nothing, and proposes him as the complete exemplar of all virtues —from which the man himself knows that he is farther away than twice infinity. Thus the flatterer adorns a crow with other birds' feathers, washes the Ethiopian white, and, in sum, makes an elephant out of a gnat. Lastly, I follow the familiar proverb of the folk, to the effect that he rightly praises himself who never meets anyone else who will praise him. Here, by the way, I wonder at the ingratitude, or perhaps the negligence, of men: although all of them studiously cherish me and freely acknowledge my benefits, not a one has emerged so far in all the ages to celebrate the praises of Folly in a grateful oration. In the meantime, there has been no lack of those who at great expense of lamp-oil and of sleep have extolled, in elegant eulogies, Busiruses, Phalarises, quartan fevers, flies, baldness, and pests of that sort.

And now you shall hear from me an extemporaneous speech, unlabored, but so much the truer for all that. I should not want you to think it is made to show off my wit, as is done by the common run of orators. They, as you know so well, when they bring out a speech they have been working on for thirty whole years, and sometimes not their own at all, will swear it was written in three days, for pastime, or even that they merely dictated it. For my part, it has always been most satisfactory to speak "whatever pops into my head."

And let no one expect that, after the manner of these ordinary orators, I shall expound myself by definition, much less divide myself. For it is equally unlucky to circumscribe with a limit her whose nature extends so universally or to dissect her in whose worship every order of being is at one. Anyway, what end would be served in setting forth by definition a sketch and, as it were, a shadow of me, when you, present here, with your own eyes perceive me in your presence? I am as you see me, that true disposer of good things whom the Latins call *Stultitia* and the Greeks Μωρία.

Still, what need was there to tell you this, as if in my very face and front, so to speak, I do not sufficiently announce who I am? As if anyone who was claiming that I am Minerva or the Spirit of Wisdom could not immediately be refuted by one good look, even if I were not speaking—though speech is the least deceptive mirror of the mind. I have no use for cosmetics. I do not feign one thing in my face while I hold something else in my heart. I am in all points so like myself that even those who specially arrogate to themselves the part and name of wise men cannot conceal me, though they walk about "like apes in scarlet or asses in lion-skins." Let them carry it as cunningly as you could ask, the protruding ears will somewhere betray the Midas. An ungrateful class of men that, so help me! Although they are wholly of my party, in public they are so ashamed of my name that they toss it up at others as a great reproach! Wherefore, since in fact they are μωρότατοι, "most foolish," and yet are eager to seem wise men and

veritable Thaleses, shall we not with entire justice dub them
μωροσόφους, "foolosophers"? It has seemed well, you note, to imitate the rhetoricians of our time, who believe themselves absolutely to be gods if they can show themselves bilingual (like a
horse-leech), and account it a famous feat if they can weave a
few Greekish words, like inlay work, ever and anon into their
Latin orations, even if at the moment there is no place for them.
Then if they want exotic touches, they dig four or five obsolete
words out of decaying manuscripts, by which they spread darkness over the reader; with the idea, I warrant you, that those who
understand will be vastly pleased with themselves, and those who
do not understand will admire the more—and all the more the
less they understand. The fact is that there is a rather elegant
species of enjoyment among our sect, to fall into special love with
what is specially imported. Some who are a little more ambitious
laugh and applaud, and, by example of the ass, shake their ears,
so that in the eyes of the rest they will seem to comprehend:
"Quite so, quite so." Now I go back to my outline.

You have my name, gentlemen . . . gentlemen . . . what shall
I add by way of an epithet? What but "most foolish"? For by what
more honorable style could the Goddess of Folly address her de-
votees? But since it is not known to very many from what stock I
have sprung, I shall now attempt, with the Muses' kind help, to
set this forth. Not Chaos, or Orcus, or Saturn, or Iapetus, or any
other of that old-fashioned and musty set of gods, was my father
at all. It was Plutus, who only, in spite of Hesiod, Homer, and
Jove himself to boot, is "the father of gods and men." At a single
nod of Plutus, as of old so nowadays, all things sacred and profane
are turned topsy-turvy. At his pleasure, all war, peace, empires,
plans, judgments, assemblies, marriages, treaties, pacts, laws, arts,
sports, weighty matters (my breath is giving out)—in short, all
public and private affairs of mortal men, are governed. . . .

. . . The gods now play the fool much more freely and pleasantly,
"doing all things carelessly," as father Homer puts it; that is to say,
without a censor. For what merry pranks will not the ramshackle
god, Priapus, afford? What games will not Mercury play, with his
thefts and deceits? And is it not the custom for Vulcan to act as
jester at the banquets of the gods, and partly by his lameness,
partly by his taunts, partly by his silly sayings, to enliven the community drinking? Then there is also that old amorist, Silenus,
who is wont to dance the cancan, together with Polyphemus and
his lyre-twanging, and the nymphs with their barefoot ballet. The

half-goat satyrs act out interludes. Stupid Pan moves the laughter
of all by some ballad, which the gods prefer above hearing the
Muses themselves, especially when they begin to be drenched with
nectar. And why go on to rehearse what the drunken gods so fitly
do after the banquet? Such foolish things, so help me, that sometimes I, though I am Folly, cannot keep from laughing. Yet it is
better at this point to think of Harpocrates, for fear some spy
among the gods may overhear us telling those things which
Momus did not tell with impunity.

But now the time has come when, following the pattern of
Homer, we should turn our backs on the heavens and travel down
again to earth, where likewise we shall perceive nothing joyous
or fortunate except by my favor. First of all, you see with what
foresight nature, the source and artificer of the human race, has
made provision that this race shall never lack its seasoning of
folly. For since, by the Stoic definitions, wisdom is no other than
to be governed by reason, while folly is to be moved at the whim
of the passions, Jupiter, to the end, obviously, that the life of mankind should not be sad and harsh, put in—how much more of
passions than of reason? Well, the proportions run about one
pound to half an ounce. Besides, he imprisoned reason in a
cramped corner of the head, and turned over all the rest of the
body to the emotions. After that he instated two most violent
tyrants, as it were, in opposition to reason: anger, which holds the
citadel of the breast, and consequently the very spring of life,
the heart; and lust, which rules a broad empire lower down, even
to the privy parts. How much reason is good for, against these
twin forces, the ordinary life of men sufficiently reveals when
reason—and it is all she can do—shouts out her prohibitions
until she is hoarse and dictates formulas of virtue. But the passions simply bid their so-called king go hang himself, and more
brazenly roar down the opposition, until the man, tired out as
well, willingly yields and knuckles under.

But a tiny bit more than a grain of reason is vouchsafed to the
male, born as he is for handling affairs; and in order that he
might give and take counsel in manly fashion, he brought me into
the council chamber, as everywhere else. Right off I gave him
advice worthy of myself: namely, that he should form an alliance
with woman—a stupid animal, God wot, and a giddy one, yet
funny and sweet—so that in domestic familiarity her folly might
leaven the lumpishness of the male temperament. When Plato
shows himself in doubt whether to place woman in the class of

rational creatures or in that of brutes, he only wishes to point out how flagrant is the folly of the sex. For if by chance some woman wishes to be thought of as wise, she does nothing but show herself twice a fool. It is as if one took a bull to the masseuse, a thing quite "against the grain," as the phrase is. It is doubly a fault, you know, when against nature one assumes the color of a virtue, warping one's character in a direction not its own. Just as, according to the proverb of the Greeks, "an ape is always an ape, though dressed in scarlet," so a woman is always a woman—that is, a fool—whatever part she may have chosen to play.

And yet I do not suppose the female sex is so foolish as to become incensed at me for this, that I, a woman and Folly as well, attribute folly to women. For if they rightly consider the matter, they are bound to score up a credit to Folly for this, that in many respects they are better off than men. For one thing, they have the gift of beauty, which with good reason they prefer above all things else. Assisted by it, they wield a tyranny over tyrants themselves. Whence but from the malady of prudence comes that horrendous visage, rough as to skin, with an undergrowth of beard and a suggestion of senility, in men? Whereas the cheeks of women are always bare and smooth, their voice gentle, their skin soft, as if presenting a picture of perpetual youth. Furthermore, what else do they want in life but to be as attractive as possible to men? Do not all their trimmings and cosmetics have this end in view, and all their baths, fittings, creams, scents, as well—and all those arts of making up, painting, and fashioning the face, eyes, and skin? Just so. And by what other sponsor are they better recommended to men than by folly? What is there that men will not permit to women? But for what consideration, except pleasure? And women please by no other thing than their folly. The truth of this no one will deny who has considered what nonsense a man talks with a woman, and what quaint tricks he plays, as often as he has a mind to enjoy the delights of feminine society.

You have heard, then, about the source whence flows the first and sovereign solace of life. But there are some men, principally old ones, who are topers rather than womanizers, and decree that the highest pleasure lies in bouts of drinking. Whether there can be any genteel entertainment with no woman present, let others decide. This remains certain: without some relish of folly, no banquet is pleasing. Hence if someone is not present who creates laughter by his real or simulated folly, the revellers send out and get a comedian for hire, or bring in some other silly parasite, who by his jests—that is, foolish gibes—will drive silence and moroseness away from the company. For what avails it to load the belly with all those fine wines, savory dishes, and rare meats, if similarly our eyes and ears, our whole souls, do not batten on laughter, jests, and witticisms? I am the only confectioner of these desserts. Yes, and those other ceremonies of banquets, such as choosing a king by lot, playing at dice, drinking healths, sending the cups around, singing in rounds and relays, dancing, mimicking—the Seven Sages of Greece did not discover these for the solace of mankind; I did. The nature of all this sort of thing is such that the more of folly it has in it, the more it advantages the life of men, which surely ought not to be called life at all if it is unhappy. Yet unhappy it must needs be, unless by diversions of this kind you chase away ennui, the brother of unhappiness.

The Renaissance Parable

The Renaissance was literally a rebirth. Ancient legends, popular folklore, and favorite fables were refurbished and appeared in new forms. The animal parables of Aesop were revived and revitalized in the humorous villainies of *Reynard the Fox*, although, differing from Aesop, *Reynard* offered no comforting moral. On the contrary, Reynard is conscienceless, a killer as well as a clown, and the other participants in his outragèous episodes include the greedy Isengrim, a wolf in every sense of the word; Bruin, the blundering, universal bore; Tybert the Tomcat, who is not as clever as he thinks he is; and the gullible King Lion. When Goethe retold the twelfth-century *Roman de Renart* in *Reineke Fuchs*, he called it a World Bible, indicating that it mirrored the basic if not the base animal nature embedded in human nature.

Immensely popular in the Middle Ages in every European language—Thomas Carlyle said it was "a house-book and universal companion, lectured on in universities and kept on the toilette table of princesses"—the first English version was published by William Caxton in 1481. Cynical, rough, and full of comic devices, the *Reynard* saga bears a certain resemblance to the children's Brer Fox and Brer Rabbit stories, although in the latter tales it is the rabbit who outfoxes the fox. It is also related to the fourteenth century Tyll Eulenspiegel, who, like Reynard, is both scurrilous and unscrupulous, an incorrigible cheat and a practical joker who refuses to die, whose lusty pranks swagger through Richard Strauss's *Till Eulenspiegels Lustige Streiche*

The following group of episodes has been adapted by the editor.

REYNARD THE FOX

King Lion was holding court in the great forest. It was the time of year when the animals gathered to air their complaints, and if possible, settle their disputes. All the creatures had been summoned, and all had arrived except Reynard the Fox. He had good reason not to appear. There was not one animal that did not have a grievance against him. Isengrim the Wolf spoke first.

"Your majesty," he said, "there is no creature in your kingdom as faithless and treacherous as Reynard. He is a smooth-faced liar who has cheated me again and again. But I do not talk of that. It is because of my wife that I harbor the deepest resentment, for he did my wife a terrible injury, and I cry for justice."

"Tell your tale," said King Lion.

"Last winter," said the Wolf, "my wife was feeling poorly. She had lost her appetite; all she could eat was fish, and fish was hard to come by in winter. Reynard, who happens to be my neighbor, assured her that he had no trouble getting fish and there was an easy way to get all anyone might desire. This excited my wife, and when he suggested she come with him to the river, she followed him eagerly. The river was frozen and Reynard chopped a hole in the ice. 'Now,' he said to my wife, 'here is how you can catch fish to your heart's content. All you have to do is sit here above the hole and let your tail dangle in the water. As soon as you feel a bite — and you'll feel it very soon — pull up your tail. I would wait and watch you do it, but I must get home to my poor, ailing wife.'"

"What happened?" asked King Lion.

"Of course, that villain Reynard did not go home. Instead he ran to the village and cried out that a wolf had been trapped at the riverside. Since men have always warred against us wolves, the villagers took up clubs and pitchforks and ran to the river. Meanwhile the ice had frozen around the hole, and my wife's tail was caught as fast as though it were in a steel trap. She moaned bitterly, and when the villagers heard the sound of her lamenting, they knew exactly where to find her. They fell upon her and beat her almost to death. In her agony she managed to get away, but when she tore herself loose she tore off her tail. The wounds have partly healed, but she has never recovered from the shame. She will not leave the house, and sits weeping in her room. And so, your majesty, I cry for justice against Reynard. Let him, too, lose his tail, that plume which he flaunts so brazenly."

"I, too, cry out against Reynard the Fox," said Chanticleer the Cock, coming forward. "My grievance is greater than the Wolf's. See what I carry."

Everyone stared as the Cock opened a coffinlike box and displayed the body of a young chick.

"This," said Chanticleer, "was my dear daughter Pippet. She was one of fifteen children who lived with me and my wife in a clearing on the edge of the forest. A thick hedge with a wicket gate enclosed our yard, and when Reynard passed our way he peered hungrily through the hedge. A few days ago he walked up to the door and asked to be admitted. He looked somehow different than usual. 'You see a changed fox,' he said. 'I have become a vegetarian. Never again will I eat meat or fish or flesh of any kind. I will live on fruit and berries, on whatever grows on tree and bush, and an occasional piece of bread. If you have a crust or crumb I will be happy if you would let me share it with you.'

"I invited him in. He sat at the table while he told my wife and all the children the good news of his reformation. 'And now,' he said as he licked up a stray crumb, 'I must leave you. It is time for me to retire and say my prayers.' He waved good-by and the children waved back.

"Now that there was no longer a reason to be afraid, the children ran through the gate. They ran gleefully—and Reynard, who had concealed himself, pounced on them. He devoured a dozen of them and would have eaten Pippet had I not flown at him. As it was, she died of shock. I demand reparation as well as justice."

"You have a right to make such a demand," said King Lion. "If what you say is true—and I do not doubt you for a moment— then the scoundrel should be driven out of the forest. Are there any other complainants?"

"Yes," said Tybert the Tomcat. "I am a rather tough character and I am not easily deceived. But I almost lost my life because of a nasty trick Reynard played on me. One day he met me when I was feeling low. 'You seem down on your luck,' he said, with what sounded like sympathy.

"'You may say that,' I replied. 'I'm starving. I haven't had a thing to eat in days.'

"'Your lean days are over,' said Reynard. 'There's a barn half a mile from here that's crowded with fat mice.'

"'I know that barn,' I said. 'The door is always shut tight, and a huge, savage dog lies in front of it.'

"'Don't let that worry you,' said Reynard. 'If a fox wants to, he can lure any dog away from his post, and I know a way of opening that door.'

"He sounded so certain and so friendly that I not only trusted but thanked him. When we reached the barn, the dog happened to be sleeping. Reynard slunk around him, and working with teeth and claws, got the door open. No sooner was I in than Reynard snapped at the dog. Never in my life have I heard such snarling and barking! I tried to get out of the barn, but Reynard had shut the door and there was no hole to squirm through. I backed into the darkest corner I could find, but it did not help. The barking had roused the farmer, and he and his son rushed in looking for whatever animal they thought was stealing their grain. I was beaten until every bone in my body seemed broken, and when I was torn and bleeding, they let me go. When I recovered and reproached Reynard bitterly, he merely said, 'It was just a joke, a practical joke.'"

"It is the kind of joke," said King Lion, "that will not go unpunished. Reynard must be judged, and since he has not appeared, someone must bring him to court. Bruin, I appoint you to fetch the culprit. But beware—you have heard how sly Reynard can be. Don't let him trick you."

"Thank you, your majesty," said Bruin. "I am not worried. No one has ever got the better of a bear."

When Bruin reached Reynard's home and delivered the king's command, to his great surprise he was heartily welcomed.

"I am honored," said Reynard, "that the king has sent so distinguished an ambassador to convey his message. Of course I will be delighted to explain everything to his majesty and I am doubly happy that you will accompany me on the way to the court. Before we go I wish I could offer you the kind of food and drink to which you are accustomed. But I have forsworn the eating of flesh, and I appease my appetite with whatever can be found in the wilds.

Curiously enough, I have developed a taste for honey, something, I believe, of which you are fond and which is plentiful hereabouts. Would you, perhaps, care for any?"

Bruin's mouth began to water, although he tried to restrain his eagerness. "Well," he said, "I would not refuse a taste, especially when it is offered so graciously."

"I do not happen to have any honey in the house at the moment," said Reynard. "But there is a place nearby where there is plenty of it. Shall we go?"

Bruin did not wait to answer. He was out of the door almost before Reynard could open it. Dusk was beginning to fall, and they went through the forest to the yard of a woodcutter who was having his supper. Among the trees that had been felled there was a log that had been practically split by two wedges. The wedges had not been removed.

"There," said Reynard, "is your honey. All you have to do is put your paws in that crack and dig up as much as you please. I'll leave you to your feast."

Bruin thrust his forefeet into the crack. As he dug into the log, the wedges flew apart and the crack closed up. Bruin was not only trapped but in terrible pain. He knew he should keep quiet, but he could not help screaming. His roars brought out the woodcutter, and when he saw Bruin he called to the neighbors. At first they laughed to see so huge a creature so helpless. Then the sport grew cruel. They pounded and pummeled the poor beast until, losing several claws and quite a lot of skin, he tore himself free. As he limped away, sticks and stones were thrown at him, and when, after three miserable days, he reached the court he could scarcely speak. Somehow, he managed to tell what had happened before he broke down. As he finished, to everyone's astonishment, Reynard appeared. He was more nonchalant than ever.

"I hear," said Reynard, "that charges have been brought against me. And if what I hear is correct, I know what they are."

"If you know what they are," said the king, "and if you are as crafty as they say you are, I suppose you have an answer to the charges."

"Several answers, your majesty. First, the matter of the wolf's wife. Last winter I had caught quite a few fish by making a hole in the ice and dropping a line through it. I had lost my line, and when lady wolf showed so great a desire for fish, it seemed to me that a tail would serve as well as a line, and I told her so. It did not occur to me that ice would freeze so quickly around the hole. When I saw her plight I tried to rescue her, but I lacked the strength to do it. I ran for aid. While I was searching for help, some men came and maltreated her. Surely I am not to blame if men act as they always have acted when they spot a wolf."

For a minute or two the king said nothing. Then he said, "Go on."

"I know that Chanticleer holds me responsible for the death of his daughter. It was a death I never expected, a death for which I grieve. It is true that there were several dead chickens in the yard, but although the cock suspects me, I have no idea who, if anyone, may have killed them. Pippet was frightened, and I did my best to still her fears. Trying to calm her, I put my arms about her. She grew quiet, and I thought all was well. Then, much to my chagrin, she stopped breathing. That is the truth, your majesty. She was a sweet young thing, and no one could feel sorrier than I."

Again the king was silent. When it became evident that he was not going to speak, Reynard went on.

"As for Tybert, it is a cat's nature to appear clever rather than conscientious. Had he come to me asking advice in a straight-forward manner I would have told him that there were many places where not only fat mice but lazy rats could be found. But, no, he insisted on breaking into a barn, a barn that was well guarded at that. Perhaps I should have dissuaded him from his foolish plan. But my failure to have done so is surely not a criminal offense."

There was another pause as the king lifted his royal eyebrows. Then he motioned Reynard to continue.

"I hate to say anything against my old friend Bruin," Reynard resumed. "Besides being your ambassador, he is an upright being, a good soul, one of whom we are all fond. But—we may as well admit it—he is greedy. I suppose I should have warned him that gluttony can come to no good end. But, poor fellow, once he gets a sniff of honey, he cannot control himself. And who am I to control him? For what I have failed to do, I ask your majesty's mercy. But, more than mercy, I ask your understanding."

No animal could have looked more humble than Reynard. His attitude was contrite, his head was bowed, a few tears squeezed from his eyes. Finally King Lion spoke.

"You make quite a case for yourself," he said. "Some of the

things you say sound plausible enough. I shall have to reserve judgment until I have thought it over. Meanwhile, you can consider yourself on parole."

"Thank you, your majesty," said Reynard. "I knew I could depend on your wisdom." And with a flirt of his tail and just the suggestion of a smile, off he went into the cool retreat of the forest.

François Rabelais

François Rabelais did not merely join the train of Folly: he rioted with her, dominated her, and drove her to thitherto unimagined excesses. His beginnings are unknown. The derivation of his name is as uncertain as the date of his birth. He is said to have been born about 1494 on a farm in Touraine, and he was brought up by monks. He became a novice of the Franciscan order, entered a monastery, and not only acquired Greek, Latin, Hebrew, and Arabic, but also studied mathematics, medicine, botany, and astronomy. After courses at Montpellier, he went to Lyons, where he became a hospital physician.

In Lyons there appeared a work that attained immediate and immense popularity. It was called *The Great and Inestimable Chronicles of the Grand and Enormous Giant Gargantua*. It was not by Rabelais, although it is possible that he had a hand in it. This was in 1532. In the same year Rabelais wrote a sequel to the work, *Pantagruel*, a combination of thoughtful satire and the wildest nonsense, and in the following year he published a book completely his own, a new *Gargantua*. Both books were issued under a pseudonym and both were condemned by the Sorbonne.

From this time on Rabelais was in and out of difficulties. Involved in churchly irregularities, he received absolution from the Pope, but he was censured, accused of heresy, and hounded. Somehow, he escaped his persecutors. Poor health dogged him and he had to give up all work except, according to a persistent legend, teaching plainsong to little children. Equally apocryphal are his last words, "The farce is over," and the date of his death, usually given as April 9, 1553.

Rabelais flourished in an atmosphere of unbridled vigor. He fed on burlesque and fattened on exaggeration; his coarseness was an exultation of the whole man. Using the license of his day, Rabelais was a furious mocker; his humor is gross but healthy. His obscurity, the result of a concatenation of learned allusions and gutter talk, absurd puns and pedantry, is more likely to trouble the reader than his unperturbed indecencies. No other writer has matched his vast relish, his violent appetites, his contagious vitality, his scorn of sham and shame. His work is a grandiose catalogue of carnalities, and in his exuberant, bawdy, belching, and immensely robust pages we hear the earth heaving in irrepressible laughter.

The classic seventeenth-century translation, including Rabelais' invention of meaningless but mouth-filling words, is by Sir Thomas Urquhart.

THE BOOK OF GARGANTUA

HOW GARGANTUA WAS CARRIED ELEVEN MONTHS IN HIS MOTHER'S BELLY

Grangousier was a good fellow in his time, and notable jester; he loved to drink neat, as much as any man that then was in the world, and would willingly eat salt meat. To this intent he was ordinarily well furnished with gammons of bacon, both of Westphalia, Mayence and Bayonne, with store of dried neat's tongues, plenty of links, chitterlings and puddings in their season; together with salt beef and mustard, a good deal of hard roes of powdered mullet called botargos, great provision of sausages, not of Bolonia (for he feared the Lombard Boccone), but of Bigorre, Longaulnay, Brene, and Rouargue. In the vigor of his age he married Gargamelle, daughter to the King of the Parpaillons, a jolly pug, and well-mouthed wench. These two did oftentimes do the two-backed beast together, joyfully rubbing and frotting their bacon 'gainst one another in so far, that at last she became great with child of a fair son, and went with him unto the eleventh month; for so long, yea longer, may a woman carry her great belly, especially when it is some masterpiece of nature, and a person predestinated to the performance, in his due time, of great exploits. As Homer says, that the child, which Neptune begot upon the nymph, was born a whole year after the conception, that is, in the twelfth month. For, as Aulus Gellius saith, Lib. 3, this long time was suitable to the majesty of Neptune, that in it the child might receive his perfect form. For the like reason Jupiter made the night, wherein he lay with Alcmena, last forty-eight hours, a shorter time not being sufficient for the forging of Hercules, who cleansed the world of the monsters and tyrants wherewith it was suppressed. My masters, the ancient Pantagruelists, have confirmed that which I say, and withal declared it to be not only possible, but also maintained the lawful birth and legitimation of the infant born of a woman in the eleventh month after the decease of her husband.

According to ancient laws, the widows may, without danger, play at the close-buttock game with might and main, and as hard as they can for the space of the first two months after the decease of their husbands. I pray you, my good lusty springal lads, if you find any of these females, that are worth the pains of untying the codpiece point, get up, and bring them to me; for if they happen within the third month to conceive, the child shall be heir to the deceased, and the mother shall pass for an honest woman.

When she is known to have conceived, thrust forward boldly, spare her not, whatever betide you, seeing the paunch is full. As Julia, the daughter of the Emperor Octavian, never prostituted herself to her belly-bumpers, but when she found herself with child; after the manner of ships that receive not their steersman till they have their ballast and lading. And if any blame the women for that after pregnancy they still continue buxom, and push for more; whereas any beast, a cow or mare will kick and flounce, and admit no farther courtship from the bull or stallion: the answer will be, these are beasts and know no better: but the other are women, and understand the glorious right they have to the pretty perquisite of a superfoetation, as Populia heretofore answered, according to the relation of Macrobius, Lib. 2. Saturnal. If the devil will not have them to bagge, he must wring hard the spigot, and stop the bung-hole.

HOW GARGAMELLE, BEING BIG WITH GARGANTUA, DID EAT A HUGE DEAL OF TRIPES

The occasion and manner how Gargamelle was brought to bed, and delivered of her child, was thus: and if you do not believe it

I wish your bum-gut may fall out. Her bum-gut indeed, or fundament escaped her in an afternoon, on the third day of February,
with having eaten at dinner too many godebillios: godebillios are
the fat tripes of coiros; coiros are beeves fattened in the ox-stalls,
and guimo meadows: guimo meadows are those that may be
mowed twice a year; of those fat beeves they had killed three
hundred sixty-seven thousand and fourteen, to be salted at
Shrovetide; that in the entering of the spring they might have
plenty of powdered beef, wherewith to season their mouths at
the beginning of their meals, and to taste their wine the better.

They had abundance of tripes as you have heard, and they were
so delicious that every one licked his fingers. But, as the devil
would have it, there was no possibility of keeping them sweet, and
to let them stink was not so commendable or handsome; it was
therefore concluded, that they should be all of them gulched up,
without any waste. To this effect they invited all the burghers of
Sainais, of Suillé, of the Roche Clermaud, of Vaugaudry, without
omitting Coudray, Monpensier, the Gué de Vede, and other their
neighbours; all stiff drinkers, brave fellows, and good players at
nine-pins. The good man Grangousier took great pleasure in their
company, and commanded there should be no want nor pinching
for anything: nevertheless he bade his wife eat sparingly, because
she was near her time, and that these tripes were no very commendable meat; they would fain (said he) be at the chewing of
ordure, who eat the bag that contained it. Notwithstanding these
admonitions, she did eat sixteen quarters, two bushels, three
pecks, and a pipkin full. What a filthy deal of loblolly was here,
to swell and wamble in her guts?

After dinner they all went tag-rag together to the willow-grove,
where, on the green grass, to the sound of merry flutes and
pleasant bagpipes, they danced so gallantly that it was a sweet
and heavenly sport to see them so frolic.

HOW GARGANTUA WAS BORN IN A STRANGE MANNER

Whilst they were discoursing of drinking, Gargamelle began to
be a little unwell in her lower parts. Whereupon Grangousier
arose from the grass, and fell to comfort her very honestly and
kindly, suspecting that she was in travail, and told her that it was
best for her to sit down upon the grass, under the willows, because
she was like very shortly to see young feet; and that, therefore, it
was convenient she should pluck up her spirits, and take a good

heart at the new coming of her baby; saying to her withal, that although the pain was somewhat grievous to her, it would be but of
short continuance; and that the succeeding joy would quickly remove that sorrow, in such sort that she should not so much as remember it. "On with a sheep's courage," quoth he; "dispatch this
boy, and we will speedily fall to work for the making of another."
"Ha!" said she, "so well as you speak at your own ease, you that
are men: well, then, in the name of God, I'll do my best, seeing
you will have it so; but would to God that it were cut off from you."
"What?" said Grangousier. "Ha!" said she, "you are a good man
indeed—you understand it well enough." "What, my member?"
said he. "Udzookers, if it please you, that shall be done instantly;
bid 'em bring hither a knife." "Alas!" said she, "the Lord forbid;
I pray Jesus to forgive me; I did not say it from my heart: do it
not any kind of harm, neither more nor less, for my speaking:
but I am like to have work enough today, and all for your member;
yet God bless both you and it."

"Courage, courage," said he; "take you no care of the matter;
let the four foremost oxen do the work. I will yet go drink one
whiff more, and if, in the meantime, anything befall you, I will
be so near that, at the first whistling in your fist, I shall be with
you." A little while after, she began to groan, lament, and cry:
then suddenly came the midwives from all quarters, who, groping
her below, found some *peloderies* of a bad savor indeed: this they
thought had been the child; but it was her fundament that was
slipped out with the mollification of her *intestinum rectum,*
which you call the bum-gut, and that merely by eating of too
many tripes, as we have shewed you before. Whereupon an old,
ugly trot in the company, who was reputed a notable physician,
and was come from Brispaille, near to St. Gnou, threescore years
before, made her so horrible a restrictive and binding medicine,
whereby all her arsepipes were so oppilated, stopped, obstructed,
and contracted, that you could hardly have opened and enlarged
them with your teeth, which is a terrible thing to think upon,
seeing the devil at mass at St. Martin's was puzzled with the like
task, when with his teeth he lengthened out the parchment
whereon he wrote the tittle-tattle of two young mangy whores.

The effect of this was, that the *cotyledons* of her matrix were
all loosened above, through which the child sprung up and leaped,
and so entering into the hollow vein, did climb by the *diaphragm*
even above her shoulders (where that vein divides itself into two),
and, from thence taking his way towards the left side, issued forth
at her left ear. As soon as he was born, he cried, not as other

babes use to do, *"mies, mies, mies;"* but, with a high, sturdy, and big voice, shouted "Give us drink! Drink! Drink!" as though inviting the world to share it with him. The noise thereof was exceedingly great, so that it was heard at the same time in two counties, Beauce and Bibarois. I doubt me that you may not thoroughly believe the truth of this strange nativity. Though you believe it or not, I care not much; but an honest man, and one of good judgment, believeth what is told him and that which he finds written.

Is this beyond our law or our faith? Is it against reason or the Holy Scripture? For my part I find nothing in the sacred Bible that is against it. But tell me, if it had been the will of God, would you say that he could not do it? Ha, for favor sake, I beseech you, never emberlucock or inpulregafize your spirits with these vain thoughts and idle conceits; for I tell you, it is not impossible with God, and, if he pleased, all women henceforth should bring forth their children at the ear. Was not Bacchus engendered out of the very thigh of Jupiter? Did not Roquetaillade come out at his mother's heel, and Crocmoush from the slipper of his nurse? Was not Minerva born of the brain, even through the ear of Jove? Adonis, of the bark of a myrrh tree; and Castor and Pollux of the doupe of that egg which was laid and hatched by Leda? But you would wonder more, and with far greater amazement, if I should now present you with that chapter of Plinius, wherein he treateth of strange births, and contrary to nature, and yet am not I so impudent a liar as he was. Read the seventh book of his *Natural History,* Chap. 3, and trouble not my head any more about this.

HOW THEY APPARELED GARGANTUA

Being of this age, his father ordained to have clothes made for him in his own livery, which was white and blue. To work then went the tailors, and with great expedition were those clothes made, cut, and sewed, according to the fashion that was then in vogue. I find by the ancient records, to be seen in the chamber of accounts at Montsoreau, that he was accoutered in manner as followeth: To make one shirt of his there were taken up nine hundred ells of Chasteleraud linen, and two hundred for the gussets, in manner of cushions, which they put under his armpits; his shirt was not gathered nor plaited, for the plaiting of shirts was not found out till the seamstresses (when the point of their needles was broken) began to work and occupy with the tail.

There were taken up for his doublet eight hundred and thirteen ells of white satin, and for his codpiece points, fifteen hundred and nine dog skins and a half. Then was it that men began to tie their breeches to their doublets, and not their doublets to their breeches; for it is against nature, as hath most amply been shewed by Ockam.

For his breeches, were taken up eleven hundred and five ells and a third of white broadcloth. They were cut in form of pillars, chamfred, channeled, and pinked behind, that they might not overheat his reins; and were, within the panes, puffed out with the lining of as much blue damask as was needful; and remark, that he had very good knee-rollers, proportionable to the rest of his stature.

For his codpiece were used sixteen ells and a quarter of the same cloth, and it was fashioned on the top like unto a triumphant arch, most gallantly fastened with two enameled clasps, in each of which was set a great emerald as big as an orange; for, as says Orpheus, *Lib. de lapidibus,* and Pliny *Lib. ultimo,* it hath an erective virtue and comfortative of the natural member. The ject, or outstanding of his codpiece, was of the length of a yard, jagged and pinked, and withal bagging, and strutting out with the blue damask lining, after the manner of his breeches. But had you seen the fair embroidery of the small needlework purl, and the curiously interlaced knots, by the goldsmith's art, set out and trimmed with rich diamonds, precious rubies, fine turquoises, costly emeralds, and Persian pearls, you would have compared it to a fair cornucopia, or horn of abundance, such as you see in antiques, or as Rhea gave to the two nymphs, Amalthea and Ida, the nurses of Jupiter.

And like to that horn of abundance, it was still gallant, succulent, droppy, sappy, pithy, lively, always flourishing, always fructifying, full of juice, full of flower, full of fruit, and all manner of delight. Blessed lady! It would have done one good to have seen it: but I will tell you more of it in the book which I have made of the dignity of codpieces. One thing I will tell you, that as it was both long and large, so was it well furnished and provided within, nothing like unto the hypocritical codpieces of some fond wooers and wench-courters, which are stuffed only with wind, to the great prejudice of the female sex.

For his shoes, were taken up four hundred and six ells of blue crimson velvet, and were very neatly cut by parallel lines, joined in uniform cylinders: for the soling of them were made use of eleven hundred hides of brown cows, shapen like the tail of a keeling.

For his coat, were taken up eighteen hundred ells of blue velvet, dyed in grain, embroidered in its borders with fair gilliflowers, in the middle decked with silver purl, intermixed with plaits of gold, and store of pearls, hereby showing that in his time he would prove an especial good fellow, and singular whip-can.

His girdle was made of three hundred ells and a half of silken serge, half white and half blue, if I mistake it not. His sword was not of Valentia, nor his dagger of Saragosa, for his father could not endure these *Hidalgos borrachos maranisados como diablos;* but he had a fair sword made of wood, and the dagger of boiled leather, as well painted and gilded as any man could wish.

His purse was made of the cod of an elephant, which was given him by Her Pracontal, proconsul of Lybia.

For his gown, were employed nine thousand six hundred ells, wanting two-thirds, of blue velvet, as before, all so diagonally purled, that by true perspective issued thence an unnamed color, like that you see in the necks of turtle-doves or turkey-cocks, which wonderfully rejoiceth the eyes of the beholders. For his bonnet, or cap, were taken up three hundred two ells and a quarter of white velvet, and the form thereof was wide and round, of the bigness of his head; for his father said, that the caps of the Marrabaise fashion, made like the cover of a pasty, would, one time or other, bring a mischief on those that wore them. For his plume, he wore a fair great blue feather, plucked from an Onocrotal of the country of Hircania the Wild, very prettily hanging down over his right ear: for the jewel or broach, which in his cap he carried, he had in a cake of gold, weighing threescore and eight marks, a fair piece of enameled work, wherein were portrayed a man's body with two heads, looking towards one another; four arms, four feet, two arses, such as Plato, in Symposio, says was the mystical beginning of man's nature; and about it was written in Ionic letters, "Charity seeketh not her own."

To wear about his neck he had a golden chain, weighing twenty-five thousand and sixty-three marks of gold, the link thereof being made after the manner of great berries, amongst which were set in work green jaspers, engraven, and cut dragon-like, all environed with beams and sparks, as King Nicepsos of old was wont to wear them, and it reached down to the very bust of the rising of his belly, whereby he reaped great benefit all his life long.

THE BOOK OF PANTAGRUEL

HOW PANURGE, CARPALIM, EUSTHENES, AND EPISTEMON (THE GENTLEMEN ATTENDANTS OF PANTAGRUEL) VANQUISHED AND DISCOMFITED SIX HUNDRED AND THREESCORE HORSEMEN VERY CUNNINGLY

As he was speaking this, they perceived six hundred and threescore light horsemen, gallantly mounted, who came to discover what ship and company it was that was newly arrived in the harbour, and came in a full gallop to take them if they had been able. Then said Pantagruel, "My lads, retire yourselves into the ship; here are some of our enemies coming apace, but I will kill them here before you like beasts, although they were ten times so many: in the meantime withdraw yourselves, and take your sport at it." Then answered Panurge, "No, sir, there is no reason that you should do so; but on the contrary, retire you into the ship, both you and the rest; for I alone will here discomfit them: but we must not linger, come, set forward." Whereunto the others said, "It is well advised; sir, withdraw yourself, and we will help Panurge here, so shall you know what we are able to do." Then said Pantagruel, "Well, I am content; but if that you be too weak, I will not fail to come to your assistance."

With this, Panurge took two great cables of the ship, and tied them to the capstan which was on the deck towards the hatches, and fastened them in the ground, making a long circuit, the one further off, the other within that. Then said he to Epistemon, "Go aboard the ship, and, when I give you a call, turn about the capstan upon the orlop diligently, drawing unto you the two cable-ropes:" and said to Eusthenes and to Carpalim, "My bullies, stay you here, and offer yourselves freely to your enemies; do as they bid you, and make as if you would yield unto them: but take heed you come not within the compass of the ropes; be sure to keep yourselves free of them." And presently he went aboard the ship, and took a bundle of straw and a barrel of gunpowder, strewed it round about the compass of the cords, and stood by with a brand of fire, or match, lighted in his hand. Presently came the horsemen with great fury, and the foremost ran almost home to the ship; and by reason of the slipperiness of the bank they fell, they and their horses, to the number of four and forty:

which the rest seeing, came on, thinking that resistance had been made them at their arrival. But Panurge said unto them, "My masters, I believe that you have hurt yourselves: I pray you pardon us, for it is not our fault, but the slipperiness of the sea water that is always flowing: we submit ourselves to your good pleasure." So said likewise his two other fellows, and Epistemon, that was upon the deck. In the meantime, Panurge withdrew himself, and seeing that they were all within the compass of the cables, and that his two companions were retired, making room for all those horses which came in a crowd, thronging upon the neck of one another to see the ship and such as were in it, cried out on a sudden to Epistemon, "Draw, draw." Then began Epistemon to wind about the capstan, by doing whereof, the two cables so entangled and impestered the legs of the horses, that they were all of them thrown down to the ground easily, together with their riders. But they, seeing that, drew their swords, and would have cut them. Whereupon Panurge set fire to the train, and there burnt them up all like damned souls, both men and horses, not one escaping save one alone; who being mounted on a fleet Turkey courser, by mere speed in flight, got himself out of the circle of the ropes. But when Carpalim perceived him, he ran after him with such nimbleness and celerity, that he overtook him in less than a hundred paces: then, leaping close behind him upon the crupper of his horse, clasped him in his arms, and brought him back to the ship.

This exploit being ended, Pantagruel was very jovial, and wondrously commended the ingenuity of these gentlemen, whom he called his fellow soldiers, and made them refresh themselves, and feed well and merrily upon the sea-shore, and drink heartily with their bellies upon the ground, and their prisoner with them, whom they admitted to that familiarity; only that the poor devil was not well assured but that Pantagruel would have eat him up whole: which, considering the wideness of his mouth, and capacity of his throat, was no great matter for him to have done; for he could have done it as easily as you would eat a small comfit, he shewing no more in his throat than would a grain of millet seed in the mouth of an ass.

Miguel de Cervantes

Free speech and forthright criticism were almost nonexistent in sixteenth-century Spain. Comedy was confined to the lowest levels, and satire was clandestinely smuggled into picaresque romances. Cervantes' *Don Quixote* was an astounding departure. While Lope de Vega was at the height of his fame with one popular swashbuckling drama after another, Miguel de Cervantes, born at Alcalá de Henares in 1547, son of a poor apothecary, was an obscure soldier who lost the use of his left arm at the Battle of Lepanto. Captured by the Moors, he was enslaved in Algiers for five years and finally ransomed. Back in Spain Cervantes tried to earn a living as an author, but he was so unsuccessful that he re-enlisted and served in Portugal and the Azores. Working for the government, he was imprisoned because of a shortage in his accounts, although the books had been falsified by an associate.

It was not until Cervantes was in his late fifties that the first part of *Don Quixote* appeared. It was read by everyone in his own country, and translations into French and English were published almost immediately. It was a startling innovation in the field of fiction—a panoramic parody of romantic stereotypes, a synthesis of wry absurdities and roistering satire. It provoked a spurious *Second Part of Don Quixote*, which castigated the author of the original work. This so enraged Cervantes, then in his late sixties, that he turned out a genuine *Second Part*. Unlike most sequels, it was a literary wonder.

It astounded scholars because of its erudition and delighted all readers because of its fresh, unflagging humor and unshaken love of humanity. Although *Don Quixote* was so often pirated that it brought him little revenue, Cervantes rarely complained. Almost impoverished but not embittered, he died in his seventieth year.

Although he insisted that his prime object was to turn the local extravagances of romantic fiction into ridicule, Cervantes wrote more universally than he knew. His burlesque of more than three centuries ago has become a deathless parable. Medieval chivalry is dead; the courtly gentlemen and country wenches are stock figures in an old-fashioned farce. But Sancho Panza is still the symbol of the sententious, proverb-loving, perenially faithful servant, and something of the mad old Don is in every determined tilter at windmills.

DON QUIXOTE
THE ADVENTURE OF THE WIND-MILLS

As they were thus discoursing, they discovered some thirty or forty wind-mills that are in that plain; and, as soon as the knight had spied them, "Fortune," cried he, "directs our affairs better than we ourselves could have wished: look yonder, friend Sancho, there are at least thirty outrageous giants, whom I intend to encounter; and, having deprived them of life, we will begin to enrich ourselves with their spoils: for they are lawful prize, and the extirpation of that cursed brood will be an acceptable service to Heaven."

"What giants?" quoth Sancho Panza.

"Those whom thou seest yonder," answered Don Quixote, "with their long-extended arms; some of that detested race have arms of so immense a size that sometimes they reach two leagues in length."

"Pray, look better, sir," quoth Sancho; "those things yonder are no giants, but wind-mills, and the arms you fancy are their sails, which, being whirled about by the wind, make the mill go."

"It is a sign," cried Don Quixote, "thou art but little acquainted with adventures. I tell thee they are giants; and therefore, if thou art afraid, go aside and say thy prayers, for I am resolved to engage in a dreadful, unequal combat against them all."

This said, he clapped spurs to his horse Rozinante, without giving ear to his squire Sancho, who bawled out to him and assured him that they were wind-mills, and no giants. But he was so fully possessed with a strong conceit of the contrary that he did not so much as hear his squire's outcry, nor was he sensible of what they were although he was already very near them; far from that. "Stand, cowards," cried he as loud as he could; "stand your ground, ignoble creatures, and fly not basely from a single knight who dares encounter you all."

At the same time the wind rising, the mill-sails began to move, which, when Don Quixote spied, "Base miscreants," cried he, "though you move more arms than the giant Briareus, you shall pay for your arrogance." He most devoutly recommended himself to his lady Dulcinea, imploring her assistance in this perilous adventure; and so, covering himself with his shield, and couching his lance, he rushed with Rozinante's utmost speed upon the first wind-mill he could come at, and, running his lance into the sail, the wind whirled about with such swiftness that the rapidity of the motion presently broke the lance into shivers, and hurled away both Knight and horse along with it, till down he fell, rolling a good way off in the field.

Sancho Panza ran as fast as his ass could drive to help his master, whom he found lying, and not able to stir, such a blow he and Rozinante had received. "Mercy on me!" cried Sancho, "did I not give your worship fair warning? did not I tell you they were wind-mills, and that nobody could think otherwise unless he had also wind-mills in his head?"

"Peace, friend Sancho," replied Don Quixote: "there is nothing so subject to the inconstancy of fortune as war. I am verily persuaded that cursed necromancer Freston, who carried away my study and books, has transformed these giants into wind-mills to deprive me of the honor of the victory; such is his inveterate malice against me; but, in the end, all his pernicious wiles and stratagems shall prove ineffectual against the prevailing edge of my sword."

"Amen, say I," replied Sancho; and so heaving him up again upon his legs, once more the Knight mounted poor Rozinante, that was half shoulderslipped with his fall.

This adventure was the subject of their discourse as they made the best of their way towards the pass of Lapice; for Don Quixote took that road, believing he could not miss of adventures in one so mightily frequented. However, the loss of his lance was no

small affliction to him; and, as he was making his complaint about
it to his squire, "I have read," said he, "friend Sancho, that a
certain Spanish knight, whose name was Diego Perez de Vargas,
having broken his sword in the heat of an engagement, pulled
up by the roots a huge oak tree, or at least tore down a massy
branch, and did such wonderful execution, crushing and grinding
so many Moors with it that day, that he won himself and his posterity the surname of The Pounder or Bruiser. I tell thee this
because I intend to tear up the next oak or crab-tree we meet;
with the trunk whereof I hope to perform such wondrous deeds,
that thou wilt esteem thyself particularly happy in having had the
honor to behold them and been the ocular witness of achievements which posterity will scarce be able to believe."

"Heaven grant you may," cried Sancho. "I believe it all, because
your worship says it. But, if it please you, sit a little more upright
in your saddle; you ride sidelong, methinks; but that, I suppose,
proceeds from your being bruised by the fall."

"It does so," replied Don Quixote; "and, if I do not complain,
it is because a knight-errant must never complain of his wounds,
though his bowels were dropping out through them."

"Then I have no more to say," quoth Sancho; "and yet, heaven
knows my heart, I should be glad to hear your worship hone a
little now and then, when something ails you. For my part, I shall
not fail to bemoan myself when I suffer the smallest pain, unless
indeed it can be proved that the rule of not complaining extends
to the squires as well as knights."

Don Quixote could not forbear smiling at the simplicity of his
squire, and told him he gave him leave to complain not only when
he pleased, but as much as he pleased, whether he had any cause
or no; for he had never yet read anything to the contrary in any
books of chivalry. Sancho desired him, however, to consider that
it was high time to go to dinner; but his master answered him that
he might eat whenever he pleased; as for himself, he was not yet
disposed to do it. Sancho, having thus obtained leave, fixed himself as orderly as he could upon his ass, and, taking some victuals
out of his wallet, fell to munching lustily as he rode behind his
master, and ever and anon he lifted his bottle to his nose and
fetched such hearty pulls that it would have made the best-pam-
pered vintner in Malaga a-dry to have seen him. While he thus
went on stuffing and swilling, he did not think in the least of all
٬his master's great promises; and was so far from esteeming it a

trouble to travel in quest of adventures that he fancied it to be the greatest pleasure in the world though they were never so dreadful.

In fine, they passed that night under some trees, from one of which Don Quixote tore a withered branch, which in some sort was able to serve him for a lance, and to this he fixed the head or spear of his broken lance. But he did not sleep all that night, keeping his thoughts intent on his dear Dulcinea, in imitation of what he had read in books of chivalry, where the knights pass that time, without sleep, in forests and deserts, wholly taken up with the entertaining thoughts of their absent mistresses. As for Sancho, he did not spend the night at that idle rate; for, having his paunch well stuffed with something more substantial than dandelion-water, he made but one nap of it; and, had not his master waked him, neither the sprightly beams which the sun darted on his face, nor the melody of the birds, that cheerfully on every branch welcomed the smiling morn, would have been able to have made him stir. As he got up to clear his eyesight, he took two or three long-winded swigs at his friendly bottle for a morning's draught; but he found it somewhat lighter than it was the night before; which misfortune went to his very heart, for he shrewdly mistrusted that he was not in a way to cure it of that distemper as soon as he could have wished.

On the other side, Don Quixote would not break fast, having been feasting all night on the more delicate and savory thoughts of his mistress; and therefore they went on directly towards the pass of Lapice, which they discovered about three o'clock. When they came near it, "Here it is, brother Sancho," said Don Quixote, "that we may wanton, and as it were, thrust our arms up to the very elbows in that which we call adventures. But let me give thee one necessary caution; know that though thou shouldest see me in the greatest extremity of danger, thou must not offer to draw thy sword in my defense, unless thou findest me assaulted by base plebeians and vile scoundrels; for, in such a case, thou mayest assist thy master: but if those with whom I am fighting are knights, thou must not do it; for the laws of chivalry do not allow thee to encounter a knight till thou art one thyself."

"Never fear," quoth Sancho; "I will be sure to obey your worship in that, I warrant you; for I have ever loved peace and quietness, and never cared to thrust myself into frays and quarrels; and yet I do not care to take blows at anyone's hands neither; and should

any knight offer to set upon me first, I fancy I should hardly mind
your laws; for all laws, whether of God or man, allow one to stand
in his own defense, if any offer to do him a mischief."

"I agree to that," replied Don Quixote; "but, as for helping me
against any knights, thou must set bounds to thy natural impulses."

"I will be sure to do it," quoth Sancho; "never trust me if I do
not keep your commandment as well as I do the Sabbath."

As they were talking, they spied coming towards them two
monks of the order of St. Benedict, mounted on two dromedaries,
for the mules on which they rode were so high and stately that
they seemed little less. They wore riding-masks, with glasses at
the eyes, against the dust, and umbrellas to shelter them from the
sun. After them came a coach, with four or five men on horseback
and two muleteers on foot. There proved to be in the coach a
Biscayan lady, who was going to Seville to meet her husband, that
was there in order to embark for the Indies, to take possession of
a considerable post. Scarce had Don Quixote perceived the
monks, who were not of the same company, though they went
the same way, but he cried to his squire, "Either I am deceived,
or this will prove the most famous adventure that ever was known;
for, without question, those two black things that move towards
us must be some necromancers that are carrying away by force
some princess in that coach, and it is my duty to prevent so great
an injury."

"I fear me this will prove a worse job than the wind-mills,"
quoth Sancho. "'Slife, sir, do not you see these are Benedictine
friars, and it is likely the coach belongs to some travelers that
are in it; therefore once more take warning, and do not you be
led away by the devil."

"I have already told thee, Sancho," replied Don Quixote, "thou
art miserably ignorant in matters of adventures; what I say is true,
and thou shalt find it so presently." This said, he spurred on his
horse and posted himself just in the middle of the road where the
monks were to pass: and when they came within hearing, "Cursed
implements of hell," cried he in a loud and haughty tone, "immediately release those high-born princesses, whom you are violently
conveying away in the coach, or else prepare to meet with instant
death, as the just punishment of your pernicious deeds."

The monks stopped their mules, no less astonished at the figure,
than at the expressions of the speaker. "Sir Knight," cried they,
"we are no such persons as you are pleased to term us, but reli-

gious men of the order of St. Benedict, that travel about our affairs, and are wholly ignorant whether or no there are any princesses carried away by force in that coach."

"I am not to be deceived with fair words," replied Don Quixote;
"I know you well enough, perfidious caitiffs"; and immediately,
without expecting their reply, he set spurs to Rozinante and ran
so furiously, with his lance couched, against the first monk that,
if he had not prudently flung himself off to the ground, the Knight
would certainly have laid him either dead or grievously wounded.
The other, observing the discourteous usage of his companion,
clapped his heels to his over-grown mule's flanks, and scoured
over the plain as if he had been running a race with the wind.
Sancho Panza no sooner saw the monk fall, but he nimbly skipped
off his ass, and running to him, began to strip him immediately,
but then the two muleteers, who waited on the monks, came
up to him, and asked why he offered to strip him. Sancho told
them that this belonged to him as lawful plunder, being the spoils
won in battle by his lord and master Don Quixote. The fellows,
with whom there was no jesting, not knowing what he meant
by his spoils and battle, and seeing Don Quixote at a good distance in deep discourse by the side of the coach, fell both upon
poor Sancho, threw him down, tore his beard from his chin,
trampled on his stomach, thumped and mauled him in every
part of his carcass, and there left him sprawling without breath
or motion. In the meanwhile the monk, scared out of his wits,
and as pale as a ghost, got upon his mule again as fast as he could,
and spurred after his friend, who stayed for him at a distance,
expecting the issue of this strange adventure: but, being unwilling
to stay to see the end of it, they made the best of their way, making
more signs of the cross than if the devil had been posting after
them.

THE ADVENTURE OF THE TWO ARMIES

When Don Quixote, perceiving a thick cloud of dust arise right
before them in the road, "The day is come," said he, turning to
his squire, "the day is come, Sancho, that shall usher in the happiness which fortune has reserved for me: this day shall the strength
of my arm be signalized by such exploits as shall be transmitted
even to the latest posterity. See'st thou that cloud of dust, Sancho?
It is raised by a prodigious army marching this way, and composed of an infinite number of nations."

"Why then, at this rate," quoth Sancho, "there should be two armies; for yonder's as great a dust on t'other side."

With that Don Quixote looked, and was transported with joy at the sight, firmly believing that two vast armies were ready to engage each other in that plain: for his imagination was so crowded with those battles, enchantments, surprising adventures, amorous thoughts, and other whimsies which he had read of in romances, that his strong fancy changed everything he saw into what he desired to see; and thus he could not conceive that the dust was only raised by two large flocks of sheep that were going the same road from different parts, and could not be discerned till they were very near. He was so positive that they were two armies, that Sancho firmly believed him at last.

"Well, sir," quoth the squire, "what are we to do, I beseech you?"

"What should we do," replied Don Quixote, "but assist the weaker and the injured side? For know, Sancho, that the army which now moves towards us is commanded by the Great Alifanfaron, Emperor of the vast island of Taprobana. The other that advances behind us is his enemy, the King of the Garamantians, Pentapolin with the naked arm; so called, because he always enters into the battle with his right arm bare."

"Pray, sir," quoth Sancho, "why are these two great men going together by the ears?"

"The occasion of their quarrel is this," answered Don Quixote, "Alifanfaron, a strong pagan, is in love with Pentapolin's daughter, a very beautiful lady and a Christian. Now, her father refuses to give her in marriage to the heathen prince, unless he abjure his false belief and embrace the Christian religion."

"Burn my beard," said Sancho, "if Pentapolin ben't in the right on't; I'll stand by him, and help him all I may."

"I commend thy resolution," replied Don Quixote, "'tis not only lawful but requisite; for there's no need for being a knight to fight in such battles."

"I guessed as much," quoth Sancho. "But where shall we leave my ass in the meantime, that I may be sure to find him again after the battle; for I fancy you never heard of any man that ever charged upon such a beast."

"'Tis true," answered Don Quixote, "and therefore I would have thee turn him loose, though thou wert sure never to find him again; for we shall have so many horses after we have got the day, that even Rozinante himself will be in danger of being changed for another." Then mounting to the top of a hillock, whence they might have seen both the flocks, had not the dust obstructed their sight, "Look yonder, Sancho," cried Don Quixote, "that knight whom thou see'st in the gilded arms, bearing in his shield a crowned lion couchant at the feet of a lady, is the valiant Laurealco, lord of the silver bridge. He in the armor powdered with flowers of gold, bearing three crows argent in a field azure, is the formidable Micocolembo, great Duke of Quiracia. That other of a gigantic size that marches on his right is the undaunted Brandabarbaran of Boliche, sovereign of the three Arabias; he's arrayed in a serpent's skin, and carries instead of a shield a huge gate, which they say belonged to the Temple which Samson pulled down at his death, when he revenged himself upon his enemies. But cast thy eyes on this side, Sancho, and at the head of t'other army see the ever victorious Timonel of Carcaiona, Prince of New Biscay, whose armor is quartered azure, vert, or, and argent, and who bears in his shield a cat or, in a field gules, with these four letters, MIAU, for a motto, being the beginning of his mistress's name, the beautiful Miaulina, daughter to Alpheniquen, Duke of Algarva. That other monstrous load upon the back of yonder wild horse, with arms as white as snow, and a shield without any device, is a Frenchman, new-created knight, called Pierre Papin, Baron of Utrick. He whom you see pricking that pied courser's flanks with his armed heels, is the mighty Duke of Nervia, Espartafilardo of the wood, bearing in his shield a field of pure azure, powdered with asparagus (esparrago) with this motto in Castilian, *Rastrea mi suerte;* Thus trails, or drags my fortune."

And thus he went on, naming a great number of others in both armies, to every one of whom his fertile imagination assigned arms, colors, impresses and mottos, as readily as if they had really been that moment extant before his eyes.

Sancho listened to all this romantic muster roll as mute as a fish, with amazement; all that he could do was now and then to turn his head on this side and t'other side, to see if he could discern the knights and giants whom his master named. But at length not being able to discover any, "Why," cried he, "you had as good tell me it snows; the devil of any knight, giant, or man can I see, of all those you talk of now; who knows but all this may be witchcraft and spirits, like yesternight?"

"How!" replied Don Quixote. "Dost thou not hear their horses neigh, their trumpets sound, and their drums beat?"

"Not I," quoth Sancho. "I prick up my ears like a sow in the beans, and yet I can hear nothing but the bleating of sheep."

Sancho might justly say so indeed, for by this time the two flocks were got very near them.

"Thy fear disturbs thy senses," said Don Quixote, "and hinders thee from hearing and seeing right. But 'tis no matter; withdraw to some place of safety, since thou art so terrified; for I alone am sufficient to give the victory to that side which I shall favor with my assistance."

With that he couched his lance, slapped spurs to Rozinante, and rushed like a thunderbolt from the hillock into the plain. Sancho bawled after him as loud as he could. "Hold, sir," cried Sancho; "for heaven's sake come back. What do you mean? As sure as I am a sinner those you're going to maul are nothing but poor harmless sheep. Come back, I say. Woe be to him that begot me! Are you mad, sir? There are no giants, no knights, no cats, no asparagus gardens, no golden quarters, no what d'ye call 'ems. Does the Devil possess you? You're leaping over the hedge before you come at the stile. You're taking the wrong sow by the ear. Oh that I was ever born to see this day!"

But Don Quixote still riding on, deaf and lost to good advice, outroared his expostulating squire. "Courage, brave knights," cried he; "march up, fall on, all you who fight under the standard of the valiant Pentapolin with the naked arm: Follow me, and you shall see how easily I will revenge him on that infidel Alifanfaron of Taprobana"; and so saying, he charged the squadron of sheep with that gallantry and resolution that he pierced, broke, and put it to flight in an instant, charging through and through, not without a great slaughter of his mortal enemies, whom he laid at his feet, biting the ground and wallowing in their blood. The shepherds, seeing their sheep go to rack, called out to him; till finding fair means ineffectual, they unloosed their slings, and began to ply him with stones as big as their fists. But the champion disdaining such a distant war, spite of their showers of stones, rushed among the routed sheep, trampling both the living and the slain in a most terrible manner, impatient to meet the general of the enemy, and end the war at once.

"Where, where art thou," cried he, "proud Alifanfaron? Appear! See here a single knight who seeks thee everywhere, to try now, hand to hand, the boasted force of thy strenuous arm, and deprive thee of life, as a due punishment for the unjust war which thou hast audaciously waged with the valiant Pentapolin."

Just as he had said this, while the stones flew about his ears, one unluckily lit upon his small ribs, and had like to have buried two of the shortest deep in the middle of his body. The knight thought himself slain, or at least desperately wounded; and therefore calling to mind his precious balsam, and pulling out his earthen jug, he clapped it to his mouth. But before he had swallowed a sufficient dose, souse comes another of those bitter almonds that spoiled his draught, and hit him so pat upon the jug, hand and teeth, that it broke the first, maimed the second, and struck out three or four of the last. These two blows were so violent that the boisterous knight, falling from his horse, lay upon the ground as quiet as the slain; so that the shepherds, fearing he was killed, got their flock together with all speed, and carrying away their dead, which were no less than seven sheep, they made what haste they could out of harm's way, without looking any farther into the matter.

All this while Sancho stood upon the hill, where he was mortified upon the sight of this mad adventure. There he stamped and swore, and banned his master to the bottomless pit; he tore his beard for madness, and cursed the moment he first knew him. But seeing him at last knocked down, and settled, the shepherds being scampered, he thought he might venture to come down; and found him in a very ill plight, though not altogether senseless.

"Ah! Master," quoth he, "this comes of not taking my counsel. Did not I tell you 'twas a flock of sheep, and no army?"

"Friend Sancho," replied Don Quixote, "know 'tis any easy matter for necromancers to change the shapes of things as they please. Thus that malicious enchanter, who is my inveterate enemy, to deprive me of the glory which he saw me ready to acquire, while I was reaping a full harvest of laurels, transformed in a moment the routed squadrons into sheep. If thou wilt not believe me, Sancho, yet do one thing for my sake; do but take thy ass, and follow those supposed sheep at a distance, and I dare engage thou shalt soon see them resume their former shapes, and appear such as I described them."

Thomas Dekker

In pre-Elizabethan England nonconformism and broad comedy grew together. They flowered naturally and vigorously in the brisk and often ribald poems of John Skelton and in such rollicking plays as *Ralph Roister Doister* and *Gammer Gurton's Needle*. Shakespeare employed the purge of comedy as well as the catharsis of tragedy, and there was plenty of mischief in the Elizabethan songbooks, where the lyricists mocked the affected city sophisticates, the false rustics, the willful wives and henpecked husbands. Thomas Dekker particularly enjoyed painting derisive portraits of women who led wasteful lives, "dieted their faces" and brightened their eyes "with spiritualized distillations," highlighting their frivolities against a background of plague-stricken and frantically pleasure-seeking London.

A hack writer who spent some years in a debtors' prison, Dekker was born in London about 1570. He led a harassed existence preparing pamphlets, collaborating on work, most of which he detested, and occasionally writing plays of his own. Although he was born in want and reared in poverty, he was seldom morose. His sordid surroundings gave him an understanding of the hopelessly poor, a sympathy with the oppressed shines out of work. He did not attempt to escape the world of reality; he turned to it with love, even with liveliness, notably in *The Shoemaker's Holiday*.

Dekker's dramas are seldom performed, and his "moral

satires" are forgotten, but *The Gull's Hornbook* survives because of its sharp-edged delineation of young bloods and
boors. A "gull" was an affected and frivolous gallant; a "hornbook" was a single page, usually containing an alphabet and
a few simple words, protected by a transparent sheet of horn.
It was used as a child's primer, and Dekker's title is an out-and-
out irony. His advice to the Elizabethan man about town is a
patently burlesque primer, a manual devoted to unmanner-
liness.

HOW A GALLANT SHOULD BEHAVE HIMSELF IN A PLAYHOUSE

The theatre is your poets' Royal Exchange, upon which their
muses (that are now turned to merchants) meeting, barter away
that light commodity of words for a lighter ware than words,
plaudities, and the breath of the great beast; which, like the
threatenings of two cowards, vanish all into air. Players are their
factors, who put away the stuff, and make the best of it they
possibly can (as indeed 'tis their parts so to do). Your gallant,
your courtier, and your captain had wont to be the soundest
paymasters; and I think are still the surest chapmen; and these,
by means that their heads are well stocked, deal upon this comical
freight by the gross; when your groundling and gallery-commoner
buys his sport by the penny and, like a haggler, is glad to utter it
again by retailing.

Sithence then the place is so free in entertainment, allowing
a stool as well to the farmer's son as to your templar; that your
stinkard has the selfsame liberty to be there in his tobacco fumes,
which your sweet courtier hath; and that your carman and tinker
claim as strong a voice in their suffrage, and sit to give judgment
on the play's life and death, as well as the proudest momus among
the tribe of critic; it is fit that he, whom the most tailors' bills
do make room for, when he comes, should not be basely (like
a viol) cased up in a corner.

Whether therefore the gatherers of the public or private playhouse stand to receive the afternoon's rent, let our gallant (having
paid it) presently advance himself up to the throne of the stage.
I mean not into the lord's room, which is now but the stage's
suburbs; no, those boxes, by the iniquity of custom, conspiracy
of waiting women and gentlemen ushers, that there sweat to-

gether, and the covetousness of sharers, are contemptibly thrust into the rear, and much new satin is there damned by being smothered to death in darkness. But on the very rushes where the comedy is to dance, yea, and under the state of Cambises himself, must our feathered estridge,[1] like a piece of ordnance, be planted, valiantly (because impudently) beating down the mews and hisses of the opposed rascality.

For do but cast up a reckoning, what large comings-in are pursed up by sitting on the stage. First a conspicuous eminence is gotten; by which means the best and most essential parts of a gallant (good clothes, a proportionable leg, white hand, the Persian lock, and a tolerable beard) are perfectly revealed.

By sitting on the stage you have a signed patent to engross the whole commodity of censure; may lawfully presume to be a girder[2]; and stand at the helm to steer the passage of scenes; yet no man shall once offer to hinder you from obtaining the title of an insolent, overweening coxcomb.

By sitting on the stage, you may, without travelling for it, at the very next door ask whose play it is; and, by that quest of inquiry, the law warrants you to avoid much mistaking; if you know not the author, you may rail against him; and peradventure so behave yourself that you may enforce the author to know you.

By sitting on the stage, if you be a knight you may happily get you a mistress; if a mere Fleet-street gentleman, a wife; but assure yourself, by continual residence, you are the first and principal man in election to begin the number of We Three.

By spreading your body on the stage, and by being a justice in examining of plays, you shall put yourself into such true scenical authority that some poet shall not dare to present his muse rudely upon your eyes, without having first unmasked her, rifled her, and discovered all her bare and most mystical parts before you at a tavern, when you most knightly shall, for his pains, pay for both their suppers.

By sitting on the stage, you may (with small cost) purchase the dear acquaintance of the boys; have a good stool for sixpence; at any time know what particular part any of the infants present; get your match lighted, examine the play-suits' lace, and perhaps win wagers upon laying 'tis copper, etc. And to conclude, whether you be a fool or a justice of peace, a cuckold or a captain, a lord-

---

[1] *estridge:* ostrich
[2] *girder:* a sneering critic

mayor's son or a dawcock,[3] a knave or an under-sheriff; of what
stamp soever you be, current or counterfeit, the stage, like time,
will bring you to most perfect light and lay you open; neither are
you to be hunted from thence, though the scarecrows in the yard
hoot at you, hiss at you, spit at you, yea, throw dirt even in your
teeth; 'tis most gentlemanlike patience to endure all this and to
laugh at the silly animals; but if the rabble, with a full throat,
cry, "Away with the fool," you were worse than a madman to
tarry by it; for the gentleman and the fool should never sit on the
stage together.

Marry, let this observation go hand in hand with the rest; or
rather, like a country serving-man, some five yards before them.
Present not yourself on the stage (especially at a new play) until
the quaking Prologue hath (by rubbing) got colour into his cheeks,
and is ready to give the trumpets their cue that he's upon point
to enter; for then it is time, as though you were one of the properties or that you dropped out of the hangings, to creep from behind
the arras, with your tripos or three-footed stool in one hand and
a teston[4] mounted between a forefinger and a thumb in the
other; for if you should bestow your person upon the vulgar when
the belly of the house is but half full, your apparel is quite eaten
up, the fashion lost, and the proportion of your body in more
danger to be devoured than if it were served up in the Counter[5]
amongst the poultry; avoid that as you would the bastone. It shall
crown you with rich commendation to laugh aloud in the midst of
the most serious and saddest scene of the terriblest tragedy; and
to let that clapper, your tongue, be tossed so high that all the
house may ring of it. Your lords use it; your knights are apes to
the lords, and do so too; your Inn-a-Court-man is zany to the
knights, and (many, very scurvily) comes likewise limping after
it; be thou a beagle to them all, and never lin[6] snuffing, till you
have scented them; for by talking and laughing (like a ploughman
in a morris) you heap Pelion upon Ossa, glory upon glory; as first,
all the eyes in the galleries will leave walking after the players and
only follow you; the simplest dolt in the house snatches up your
name, and when he meets you in the streets, or that you fall into
his hands in the middle of a watch, his word shall be taken for you;
he'll cry "He's such a gallant," and you pass. Secondly, you publish

---

[3] *dawcock:* fool
[4] *teston:* a small coin
[5] *Counter:* a debtors' prison
[6] *lin:* stop

your temperance to the world, in that you seem not to resort thither to taste vain pleasures with a hungry appetite; but only as a gentleman to spend a foolish hour or two, because you can do nothing else; thirdly, you mightily disrelish the audience and disgrace the author; marry, you take up (though it be at the worst hand) a strong opinion of your own judgment, and enforce the poet to take pity of your weakness and, by some dedicated sonnet, to bring you into a better paradise only to stop your mouth.

If you can, either for love or money, provide yourself a lodging by the water side; for, above the convenience it brings to shun shoulder-clapping and to ship away your cockatrice[7] betimes in the morning, it adds a kind of state unto you to be carried from thence to the stairs of your play-house; hate a sculler (remember that) worse than to be acquainted with one o' the scullery. No, your oars are your only sea-crabs, board them, and take heed you never go twice together with one pair; often shifting is a great credit to gentlemen; and that dividing of your fare will make the poor watersnakes be ready to pull you in pieces to enjoy your custom; no matter whether upon landing you have money or no; you may swim in twenty of their boats over the river upon ticket; marry, when silver comes in, remember to pay treble their fare, and it will make your flounder-catchers to send more thanks after you when you do not draw than when you do; for they know it will be their own another day.

Before the play begins, fall to cards; you may win or lose (as fencers do in a prize) and beat one another by confederacy, yet share the money when you meet at supper; notwithstanding, to gull the ragamuffins that stand aloof gaping at you, throw the cards (having first torn four or five of them) round about the stage, just upon the third sound, as though you had lost; it skills not if the four knaves lie on their backs, and outface the audience; there's none such fools as dare take exceptions at them, because, ere the play go off, better knaves than they will fall into the company.

Now, sir, if the writer be a fellow that hath either epigrammed you, or hath had a flirt at your mistress, or hath brought either your feather, or your red beard, or your little legs, etc., on the stage, you shall disgrace him worse than by tossing him in a blanket or giving him the bastinado in a tavern, if, in the middle of his play (be it pastoral or comedy, moral or tragedy) you rise with a screwed and discontented face from your stool to be gone;

[7] *cockatrice:* mistress

no matter whether the scenes be good or no; the better they are, the worse do you distaste them; and, being on your feet, sneak not away like a coward, but salute all your gentle acquaintance that are spread either on the rushes or on stools about you, and draw what troop you can from the stage after you. The mimics are beholden to you for allowing them elbow-room; their poet cries, perhaps, "A pox go with you," but care not you for that, there's no music without frets.

Marry, if either the company or indisposition of the weather bind you to sit it out, my counsel is then that you turn plain ape, take up a rush, and tickle the earnest ears of your fellow gallants, to make other fools fall a-laughing; mew at passionate speeches, blare at merry, find fault with the music, whew at the children's action, whistle at the songs; and above all, curse the sharers, that whereas the same day you had bestowed forty shillings on an embroidered felt and feather (Scotch-fashion) for your mistress in the court or your punk in the city, within two hours after you encounter with the very same block on the stage, when the haberdasher swore to you the impression was extant but that morning.

To conclude, hoard up the finest play-scraps you can get, upon which your lean wit may most savourly feed, for want of other stuff, when the Arcadian and Euphuized gentlewomen have their tongues sharpened to set upon you; that quality (next to your shuttlecock) is the only furniture to a courtier that's but a new beginner, and is but in his A B C of compliment. The next places that are filled, after the play-houses be emptied, are (or ought to be) taverns. Into a tavern then let us next march, where the brains of one hogshead must be beaten out to make up another.

HOW A GALLANT SHOULD BEHAVE HIMSELF IN A TAVERN

Whosoever desires to be a man of good reckoning in the city, and (like your French lord) to have as many tables furnished as lackeys (who, when they keep least, keep none), whether he be a young quat[1] of the first year's revenue or some austere and sullen-faced steward who (in despite of a great beard, a satin suit, and a chain of gold wrapped in cypress) proclaims himself to any

---

[1] *quat:* fellow

(but to those to whom his lord owes money) for a rank coxcomb, or whether he be a country gentleman that brings his wife up to learn the fashion, see the tombs at Westminster, the lions in the Tower, or to take physic; or else is some young farmer, who many times makes his wife in the country believe he hath suits in law, because he will come up to his lechery; be he of what stamp he will that hath money in his purse, and a good conscience to spend it, my counsel is that he take his continual diet at a tavern, which (out of question) is the only *rendezvous* of boon company; and the drawers the most nimble, the most bold, and most sudden proclaimers of your largest bounty.

Having therefore thrust yourself into a case most in fashion (how coarse soever the stuff be, 'tis no matter so it hold fashion), your office is (if you mean to do your judgment right) to inquire out those taverns which are best customed, whose masters are oftenest drunk (for that confirms their taste, and that they choose wholesome wines), and such as stand furthest from the counters; where, landing yourself and your followers, your first compliment shall be to grow most inwardly acquainted with the drawers, to learn their names, as Jack, and Will, and Tom, to dive into their inclinations, as whether this fellow useth to the fencing school, this to the dancing school . . . and protest yourself to be extremely in love, and that you spend much money in a year, upon any one of those exercises which you perceive is followed by them. The use which you shall make of this familiarity is this: if you want money five or six days together, you may still pay the reckoning with this most gentleman-like language, "Boy, fetch me money from the bar," and keep yourself most providently from a hungry melancholy in your chamber. Besides, you shall be sure, if there be but one faucet that can betray neat wine to the bar, to have that arraigned before you sooner than a better and worthier person.

The first question you are to make (after the discharging of your pocket of tobacco and pipes, and the household stuff thereto belonging) shall be for an inventory of the kitchen; for it were more than most tailor-like, and to be suspected you were in league with some kitchen-wench, to descend yourself, to offend your stomach with the sight of the larder, and happily to grease your accoutrements. Having therefore received this bill, you shall (like a captain putting up dead pays) have many salads stand on your table, as it were for blanks to the other more serviceable dishes; and according to the time of the year, vary your fare, as capon is a stirring meat sometime, oysters are a swelling meat sometimes, trout a tickling meat sometimes, green goose and woodcock a delicate meat sometimes, especially in a tavern, where you shall sit in as great state as a church-warden amongst his poor parishioners at Pentecost or Christmas.

For your drink, let not your physician confine you to any one particular liquor; for as it is requisite that a gentleman should not always be plodding in one art, but rather be a general scholar (that is, to have a lick at all sorts of learning, and away), so 'tis not fitting a man should trouble his head with sucking at one grape, but that he may be able (now there is a general peace) to drink any stranger drunk in his own element of drink, or more properly in his own mist language.

Your discourse at the table must be such as that which you utter at your ordinary; your behaviour the same, but somewhat more careless; for where your expense is great, let your modesty be less; and though you should be mad in a tavern, the largeness of the items will bear with your incivility; you may, without prick to your conscience, set the want of your wit against the superfluity and sauciness of their reckonings.

If you desire not to be haunted with fiddlers (who by the statute have as much liberty as rogues to travel into any place, having the passport of the house about them) bring then no women along with you; but if you love the company of all the drawers, never sup without your cockatrice; for, having her there, you shall be sure of most officious attendance. Inquire what gallants sup in the next room, and if they be any of your acquaintance do not you (after the city fashion) send them in a pottle of wine, and your name, sweetened in two pitiful papers of sugar, with some filthy apology crammed into the mouth of a drawer; but rather keep a boy in fee, who underhand shall proclaim you in every room, what a gallant fellow you are, how much you spend yearly in taverns, what a great gamester, what custom you bring to the house, in what witty discourse you maintain a table, what gentle-women or citizens' wives you can with a wet finger[2] have at any time to sup with you, and such like. By which encomiastics of his, they that know you not shall admire you and think themselves to be brought into a paradise but to be meanly in your acquaintance; and if any of your endeared friends be in the house, and beat the same ivy bush that yourself does, you may join companies and be drunk together most publicly.

---

[2] *with a wet finger:* by making a gesture, a sign

But in such a deluge of drink, take heed that no man counterfeit himself drunk, to free his purse from the danger of the shot;
'tis a usual thing now among gentlemen; it had wont be the quality
of cockneys. I would advise you to leave so much brains in your
head as to prevent this. When the terrible reckoning (like an
indictment) bids you hold up your hand, and that you must
answer it at the bar, you must not abate one penny in any particular, no, though they reckon cheese to you when you have
neither eaten any, nor could ever abide it, raw or toasted; but
cast your eye only upon the *totalis*, and no further; for to traverse
the bill would betray you to be acquainted with the rates of the
market, nay more, it would make the vintners believe you were
pater-familias, and kept a house; which, I assure you, is not now
in fashion.

If you fall to dice after supper, let the drawers be as familiar
with you as your barber, and venture their silver amongst you;
no matter where they had it; you are to cherish the unthriftiness
of such young tame pigeons, if you be a right gentleman; for when
two are yolked together by the purse strings, and draw the chariot
of Madam Prodigality, when one faints in the way and slips his
horns let the other rejoice and laugh at him.

At your departure forth the house, to kiss mine hostess over the
bar, or to accept of the courtesy of the cellar when 'tis offered
you by the drawers (and you must know that kindness never
creeps upon them but when they see you almost cleft to the
shoulders),[3] or to bid any of the vintners good night, is as commendable as for a barber after trimming to lave your face with
sweet water.

To conclude, count it an honour either to invite or be invited
to any rifling[4]; for commonly, though you find much satin there,
yet you shall likewise find many citizens' sons, and heirs, and
younger brothers there, who smell out such feasts more greedily
than tailors hunt upon Sundays after weddings. And let any hook
draw you either to a fencer's supper or to a player's that acts such
a part for a wager; for by this means you shall get experience, by
being guilty to their abominable shaving.[5]

---

[3] *cleft to the shoulders:* thoroughly drunk
[4] *rifling:* gambling party
[5] *shaving:* crooked dealing

John Donne

Son of an ironmonger, John Donne was born in 1572 in London, was brought up as a Catholic, attended Cambridge and Oxford, and studied law. When he came of age he discarded Catholic doctrine, became private secretary to Thomas Egerton, Lord Keeper of the Great Seal, and secretly married Egerton's young niece Anne More. Lacking family consent, this was tantamount to abduction. Egerton not only dismissed Donne from his service, but had him arrested and kept in prison for several weeks. Facing a bleak future Donne summed up the situation in a grim pun: "John Donne—Anne Donne—Undone."

During the following decade, harassed by poverty and hounded by debtors, Donne did what he could to support a growing family. He wrote pamphlets against the Papists with one hand and pious epistles with the other. In his early forties he was persuaded by James I to enter sacred orders. At forty-eight, author of some of the most mocking as well as some of the most magnificent poetry of his times, he was made dean of St. Paul's. In his fifties he became seriously ill, collapsed in his fifty-seventh year, and died two years later.

Many of Donne's lightly mocking poems as well as his most probing ones were written before he was thirty. As early as his mid-twenties he was preoccupied with the uncertain balance of lust and love and his need to fuse these conflicting emotions. He rebelled against the prettified, romantic stereotypes of his contemporaries and employed an idiom that was deeply impassioned yet as intimate as conversation. It was a poetic speech that joined the physical with the metaphysical, the erotic with the satiric.

One of the strangest and most revealing of Donne's poems, "The Flea," is a grotesque reappraisal of the traditional love lyric in which the ardent lover is held off by the virtuous lady. The image is monstrous—the favorite setting of a couch in a blossomy bower is now the black body of a flea, whose "living walls of jet" serve as nuptial bed—but the sophistry is as persuasive as it is unprecedented.

No poet suffered more than Donne from the shifts in taste and vagaries of poetic fashion. His work was admired in his own day, furiously condemned in the eighteenth century, and enthusiastically rediscovered in the twentieth. Donne's bitter contradiction of desire and disgust, his battles between belief and disillusion, the constant civil war of flesh and spirit are as characteristic of our age as they were of Donne's.

THE FLEA

Mark but this flea, and mark in this,
How little that which thou deniest me is;
It sucked me first, and now sucks thee,
And in this flea our two bloods mingled be.
Thou know'st that this cannot be said
A sin, nor shame, nor loss of maidenhead;
    Yet this enjoys before it woo,
    And pampered swells with one blood made of two;
    And this, alas! is more than we would do.

Oh stay, three lives in one flea spare,
Where we almost, yea, more than married are.
This flea is you and I, and this
Our marriage bed, and marriage temple is.
Though parents grudge, and you, we're met,
And cloistered in these living walls of jet.
    Though use make you apt to kill me,
    Let not to that self-murder added be,
    And sacrilege, three sins in killing three.

Cruel and sudden, hast thou since
Purpled thy nail in blood of innocence?
Wherein could this flea guilty be,
Except in that drop which it sucked from thee?
Yet thou triumph'st, and sayest that thou
Find'st not thyself nor me the weaker now.
    'Tis true; then learn how false fears be;
    Just so much honor, when thou yieldest to me,
    Will waste, as this flea's death took life from thee.

THE CANONIZATION

For God's sake hold your tongue, and let me love;
    Or chide my palsy, or my gout,
My five grey hairs, or ruined fortune flout;
    With wealth your state, your mind with arts improve,
        Take you a course, get you a place,
        Observe his Honor, or his Grace,
Or the King's real, or his stamped face
    Contemplate; what you will, approve,
    So you will let me love.

Alas, alas, who's injured by my love?
    What merchant's ships have my sighs drowned?
Who says my tears have overflowed his ground?
    When did my colds a forward spring remove?
        When did the heats which my veins fill
        Add one more to the plaguy bill?
Soldiers find wars, and lawyers find out still
    Litigious men, which quarrels move,
    Though she and I do love.

Call us what you will, we are made such by love;
    Call her one, me another fly,
We're tapers too, and at our own cost die,
    And we in us find the Eagle and the Dove.
        The Phoenix riddle hath more wit
        By us; we two being one, are it.
So to one neutral thing both sexes fit,
    We die and rise the same, and prove
    Mysterious by this love.

We can die by it, if not live by love,
  And if unfit for tombs and hearse
Our legend be, it will be fit for verse;
  And if no piece of Chronicle we prove,
    We'll build in sonnets pretty rooms;
    As well a well-wrought urn becomes
The greatest ashes as half-acre tombs,
  And by these hymns, all shall approve
  Us canonized for Love:

And thus invoke us: You whom reverend love
  Made one another's hermitage;
You, to whom love was peace that now is rage;
  Who did the whole world's soul contract, and drove
    Into the glasses of your eyes
    (So much made mirrors and such spies
That they did all to you epitomize),
  Countries, towns, courts—beg from above
  A pattern of your love!

SONG: GO, AND CATCH A FALLING STAR

Go, and catch a falling star,
  Get with child a mandrake root,
Tell me, where all past years are,
  Or who cleft the devil's foot,
Teach me to hear mermaids singing,
  Or to keep off envy's stinging,
        And find
        What wind
Serves to advance an honest mind.

If thou be'st born to strange sights,
  Things invisible to see,
Ride ten thousand days and nights,
  Till age snow white hairs on thee,
Thou, when thou return'st, wilt tell me
All strange wonders that befell thee,
        And swear
        Nowhere
Lives a woman true, and fair.

If thou find'st one, let me know,
  Such a pilgrimage were sweet.
Yet do not; I would not go,
  Though at next door we might meet,
Though she were true, when you met her,
And last till you write your letter,
            Yet she
            Will be
False, ere I come, to two or three.

WOMAN'S CONSTANCY

Now thou hast loved me one whole day,
Tomorrow when thou leav'st, what wilt thou say?
Wilt thou then antedate some new-made vow?
        Or say that now
We are not just those persons, which we were?
Or that oaths made in reverential fear
Of Love, and his wrath, any may forswear?
Or, as true deaths true marriages untie,
So lovers' contracts, images of those,
Bind but till sleep, death's image, them unloose?
        Or, your own end to justify,
For having purposed change, and falsehood, you
Can have no way but falsehood to be true?
Vain lunatic, against these 'scapes I could
        Dispute, and conquer, if I would,
        Which I abstain to do;
For by tomorrow, I may think so too.

Ben Jonson

Born in 1572, stepson of a bricklayer in Charing Cross, Ben Jonson had little more than a common school education. For a while he followed his stepfather's trade, then served as a soldier in the Netherlands. By the time he was twenty he had become an actor, a husband, and a father. In his mid-twenties he turned playwright; one of the best English comedies, *Every Man in His Humor*, was written in Jonson's twenty-fifth year. It is said that Shakespeare, Jonson's good friend and senior by nearly nine years, acted in the play.

There followed a series of dramas, exuberant and witty comedies satirizing the affectations of the period, as well as tragedies adapted from classical sources. Jonson drew about him the poets and dramatists of the younger generation; the circle that met at the Mermaid Tavern boasted of belonging to "the tribe of Ben." He lived expansively and wrote voluminously. He was patronized by three monarchs. Elizabeth relished his comedies; James I offered him knighthood and urged him to forsake tragedy for the more profitable masques; Charles I made him poet laureate. In spite of royal pensions, Jonson was never financially secure. It is likely that he cared nothing about security: he preferred to rollick through life. Lustily entering his sixties, Jonson was overtaken by a stroke and died in his sixty-fourth year. He was buried at Westminster Abbey with a terse but significant tribute: "O rare Ben Jonson."

Jonson's most trenchant satire, *Volpone*, stems from *Rey-*

nard the Fox. (See page 146.) Here, however, the human beings are more beastly than the beasts. The unscrupulously covetous Fox is attended by his parasitic confederate, Mosca the Fly, and surrounded by a crowd of sycophants: the avaricious Carrion Crow, the hovering Vulture, and the debased Raven. Delineating their hypocritic greed, Jonson achieves a bitter satire surpassed only by Swift's.

Volpone is prefaced by an Argument, which Jonson, summarizing the plot of the play, framed into the following acrostic.

V olpone, childless, rich, feigns sick, despairs,
O ffers his state to hopes of several heirs,
L ies languishing: his parasite receives
P resents from all, assures, deludes, then weaves
O ther cross plots, which ope themselves, are told.
N ew tricks for safety are sought; they thrive; when bold
E ach tempts the other again, and all are sold!

VOLPONE

ACT 1, SCENE 1

A room in Volpone's house.
(Enter Volpone and Mosca.)

VOLPONE: Good morning to the day; and next, my gold!
Open the shrine, that I may see my saint.
(MOSCA *withdraws the curtain,*
and discovers piles of gold, plate,
jewels, &c.)
Hail the world's soul, and mine! more glad than is
The teeming earth to see the longed-for sun
Peep through the horns of the celestial Ram,
Am I, to view thy splendour darkening his;
That lying here, amongst my other hoards,
Show'st like a flame by night, or like the day
Struck out of chaos, when all darkness fled
Unto the centre. O thou son of Sol,
But brighter than thy father, let me kiss,
With adoration, thee, and every relic
Of sacred treasure in this blessed room.
Well did wise poets, by thy glorious name,

Title that age which they would have the best;
Thou being the best of things, and far transcending
All style of joy, in children, parents, friends,
Or any other waking dream on earth:
Thy looks when they to Venus did ascribe,
They should have given her twenty thousand Cupids;
Such are thy beauties and our loves! Dear saint,
Riches, the dumb god, that giv'st all men tongues,
That canst do nought, and yet mak'st men do all
    things;
The price of souls; even hell, with thee to boot,
Is made worth heaven. Thou art virtue, fame,
Honour, and all things else. Who can get thee,
He shall be noble, valiant, honest, wise —

Mosca: And what he will, sir. Riches are in fortune
A greater good than wisdom is in nature.

Volpone: True, my beloved Mosca. Yet I glory
More in the cunning purchase of my wealth,
Than in the glad possession, since I gain
No common way; I use no trade, no venture;
I wound no earth with ploughshares, fat no beasts
To feed the shambles; have no mills for iron,
Oil, corn, or men, to grind them into powder:
I blow no subtle glass, expose no ships
To threat'nings of the furrow-faced sea;
I turn no monies in the public bank,
No usurer private.

Mosca: No sir, nor devour
Soft prodigals. You shall have some will swallow
A melting heir as glibly as your Dutch
Will pills of butter, and ne'er purge for it;
Tear forth the fathers of poor families
Out of their beds, and coffin them alive
In some kind clasping prison, where their bones
May be forthcoming, when the flesh is rotten:
But your sweet nature doth abhor these courses;
You loathe the widow's or the orphan's tears
Should wash your pavements, or their piteous cries
Ring in your roofs, and beat the air for vengeance.

VOLPONE: Right, Mosca; I do loathe it.

MOSCA: And, besides, sir,
You are not like the thresher that doth stand
With a huge flail, watching a heap of corn,
And, hungry, dares not taste the smallest grain,
But feeds on mallows, and such bitter herbs;
Nor like the merchant, who hath filled his vaults
With Romagnia, and rich Candian wines,
Yet drinks the lees of Lombard's vinegar:
You will not lie in straw, whilst moths and worms
Feed on your sumptuous hangings and soft beds;
You know the use of riches, and dare give now
From that bright heap, to me, your poor observer,
Or to your dwarf, or your hermaphrodite,
Your eunuch, or what other household trifle
Your pleasure allows maintenance —

VOLPONE: Hold thee, Mosca,   *(Gives him money.)*
Take of my hand; thou strik'st on truth in all,
And they are envious term thee parasite.
Call forth my dwarf, my eunuch, and my fool,
And let them make me sport. (*Exit* MOSCA) What
        should I do,
But cocker up my genius, and live free
To all delights my fortune calls me to?
I have no wife, no parent, child, ally,
To give my substance to; but whom I make
Must be my heir; and this makes men observe me:
This draws new clients daily to my house,
Women and men of every sex and age,
That bring me presents, send me plate, coin, jewels
With hope that when I die (which they expect
Each greedy minute) it shall then return
Tenfold upon them; whilst some, covetous
Above the rest, seek to engross me whole,
And counter-work the one unto the other,
Contend in gifts, as they would seem in love:
All which I suffer, playing with their hopes,
And am content to coin them into profit,
And look upon their kindness, and take more,
And look on that; still bearing them in hand,

Letting the cherry knock against their lips,
And draw it by their mouths, and back again.

SONG: FOOLS, THEY ARE THE ONLY NATION

Fools, they are the only nation
Worth men's envy or admiration;
Free from care or sorrow-taking,
Selves and others merry making:
All they speak or do is sterling.
Your fool, he is your great man's darling,
And your ladies' sport and pleasure;
Tongue and bauble are his treasure.
E'en his face begetteth laughter,
And he speaks truth free from slaughter.
He's the gracc of every feast,
And some times the chiefest guest,
Hath his trencher and his stool
When wit waits upon the fool.
   O, who would not be
   He, he, he?

Sir John Suckling

The greatest gambler of his time, Sir John Suckling, born in 1609 in Middlesex, was also the greatest gallant. His father, who had been knighted by James I, died when his son was seventeen and left him the title and also a fortune, which permitted the youth to dazzle the court with one extravagance after another. When his play *Aglaura* was produced, he insisted that the actors wear real lace and pure gold embroidery instead of the usual tarlatan and tinsel. When Suckling accompanied Charles on an expedition to Scotland, he raised a troop of one hundred caparisoned horses at a cost of twelve thousand pounds. In a life of easy successes, he made one serious mistake. He conspired against the irresolute Charles, was discovered, and fled to France. There, at the age of thirty-three, he died, either by suicide or through the vengeance of a disgruntled servant.

Suckling's plays and masques have been forgotten, but his lyrics can never be pried loose from the anthologies. Their flippant attitude is so cavalier, their humor so spontaneous, and their lighthearted irony so irresistible that they never date.

THE BESIEGED HEART

'Tis now, since I sat down before
  That foolish fort, a heart,
(Time strangely spent) a year and more,
  And still I did my part.

Made my approaches; from her hand
  Unto her lip did rise,
And did already understand
  The language of her eyes;

Proceeded on with no less art,
  My tongue was engineer;
I thought to undermine the heart
  By whispering in the ear.

When this did nothing, I brought down
  Great cannon-oaths, and shot
A thousand thousand to the town;
  And still it yielded not.

I then resolved to starve the place
  By cutting off all kisses,
Praising and gazing on her face,
  And all such little blisses.

To draw her out and from her strength,
  I drew all batteries in,
And brought myself to lie at length
  As if no siege had been.

When I had done what man could do,
  And thought the place mine own,
The enemy lay quiet too,
  And smiled at all was done.

I sent to know from whence and where
  These hopes and this relief;
A spy informed, Honor was there,
  And did command in chief.

March, march, quoth I, the word straight give,
    Let's lose no time, but leave her;
That giant upon air will live,
    And hold it out forever.

To such a place our camp remove,
    As will no siege abide.
I hate a fool that starves her love,
    Only to feed her pride.

THE CONSTANT LOVER

Out upon it, I have loved
    Three whole days together!
And am like to love three more,
    If it prove fair weather.

Time shall moult away his wings
    Ere he shall discover
In the whole wide world again
    Such a constant lover.

But the spite on't is, no praise
    Is due at all to me:
Love with me had made no stays,
    Had it been but she.

Had it any been but she,
    And that very face,
There had been at least ere this
    A dozen in her place.

WHY SO PALE AND WAN?

Why so pale and wan, fond lover?
    Prithee why so pale?
Will, when looking well can't move her,
    Looking ill prevail?
    Prithee why so pale?

Why so dull and mute, young sinner?
   Prithee why so mute?
Will, when speaking well can't win her,
   Saying nothing do't?
   Prithee why so mute?

Quit, quit, for shame; this will not move,
   This cannot take her;
If of herself she will not love,
   Nothing can make her:
   The devil take her!

Samuel Butler

Variously compared to Cervantes and Juvenal, Samuel But-
ler was a little of both. Son of a small Worcestershire farmer,
he was born at Strensham in 1612. His schooling was brief.
He thought of studying law, but nothing came of it. He turned
to painting, but his pictures were used to stop up windows.
He remained a bachelor until he was fifty, when he married a
wealthy Mrs. Herbert, who soon afterward lost all her money.
Butler eked out a living as clerk and secretary, chiefly to Sir
Samuel Luke, who served as a model for the ridiculous knight
Hudibras, whom he pilloried in verse.

A mock-heroic poem that flagellated the Puritans, *Hudibras*
was a scandalous success. The dissolute court loved it; Charles
II carried it about in his pocket; everyone quoted from it. But
there was little financial reward. Butler died poverty-stricken
at sixty-eight. A bust was erected to his memory and an engraved epitaph commented wryly:

> *See him, when starved to death and turned to dust,*
> *Presented with a monumental bust.*
> *The poet's fate is here in emblem shown:*
> *He asked for bread, and he received a stone.*

Although *Hudibras* no longer interests us as an angry echo
of the conflict between Puritans and Cavaliers, its satire takes
on universal overtones. A cross between a rude epic and a
boisterous farce, it combines dryness and extravagance. In

an idiom that burlesques poetic diction in its very pomposity, Butler sends his comic hero out on a series of absurd adventures. Like Don Quixote, Hudibras rides a spavined nag and suffers similar downfalls; his is a rough-and-tumble set-to with greed, cant, and self-righteousness. The style is rambling, the manner sprawling, the rhymes are hit and miss. But even the doggerel has a kind of improvised brilliance, and it is sparked with an inventiveness that sometimes attains a grotesque grandeur. Rarely has Puritanism been more comically belabored than in Butler's raucous ridicule.

HUDIBRAS

When civil dudgeon first grew high,
And men fell out they knew not why;
When hard words, jealousies, and fears
Set folks together by the ears,
And made them fight, like mad or drunk,
For Dame Religion, as for punk,
Whose honesty they all durst swear for,
Though not a man of them knew wherefore;
When gospel-trumpeter, surrounded
With long-eared rout, to battle sounded;
And pulpit, drum ecclesiastic,
Was beat with fist, instead of a stick:
Then did Sir Knight abandon dwelling,
And out he rode a colonelling.
A wight he was whose very sight would
Entitle him, Mirror of Knighthood;
That never bowed his stubborn knee
To anything but chivalry;
Nor put up blow, but that which laid
Right Worshipful on shoulder-blade:
Chief of domestic knights and errant,
Either for chartel or for warrant:
Great on the bench, great in the saddle,
That could as well bind o'er as swaddle:
Mighty was he at both of these,
And styled of war as well as peace.
(So some rats, of amphibious nature,
Are either for the land or water.)

But here our authors make a doubt
Whether he were more wise or stout.
Some hold the one, and some the other;
But, howsoe'er they make a pother,
The difference was so small, his brain
Outweighed his rage but half a grain;
Which made some take him for a tool
That knaves do work with, called a Fool.
For't has been held by many, that
As Montaigne, playing with his cat,
Complains she thought him but an ass,
Much more she would Sir Hudibras,
(For that's the name our valiant Knight
To all his challenges did write):
But they're mistaken very much,
'Tis plain enough he was not such.
We grant, although he had much wit,
H' was very shy of using it;
As being loth to wear it out,
And therefore bore it not about,
Unless on holidays or so,
As men their best apparel do.
Besides, 'tis known he could speak Greek
As naturally as pigs squeak;
That Latin was no more difficile,
Than to a blackbird 'tis to whistle;
Being rich in both, he never scanted
His bounty unto such as wanted,
But much of either would afford
To many, that had not one word.
For Hebrew roots, although they're found
To flourish most in barren ground,
He has such plenty as sufficed
To make some think him circumcised:
And truly so he was, perhaps,
Not as a proselyte, but for claps.
    He was in logic a great critic,
Profoundly skilled in analytic:
He could distinguish and divide
A hair 'twixt south and south-west side;
On either which he would dispute,
Confute, change hands, and still confute:

He'd undertake to prove, by force
Of argument, a man's no horse;
He'd prove a buzzard is no fowl,
And that a lord may be an owl,
A calf an alderman, a goose a justice,
And rooks committee-men and trustees.
He'd run in debt by disputation,
And pay with ratiocination.
All this by syllogism, true
In mood and figure, he would do.

Beside he was a shrewd philosopher,
And had read every text and gloss over;
Whate'er the crabbed'st author hath,
He understood b' implicit faith;
Whatever skeptic could enquire for,
For every why he had a wherefore;
Knew more than forty of them do
As far as words and terms could go.
All which he understood by rote,
And, as occasion served, would quote;
No matter whether right or wrong,
They might be either said or sung.
His notions fitted things so well,
That which was which he could not tell,
But oftentimes mistook the one
For th'other, as great clerks have done. . . .

For his religion, it was fit
To match his learning and his wit:
'Twas Presbyterian true blue,
For he was of that stubborn crew
Of errant saints, whom all men grant
To be the true church militant;
Such as do build their faith upon
The holy text of pike and gun;
Decide all controversies by
Infallible artillery;
And prove their doctrine orthodox
By apostolic blows and knocks;
Call fire and sword and desolation,
A godly thorough reformation,

Which always must be carried on,
And still be doing, never done;
As if religion were intended
For nothing else but to be mended.
A sect whose chief devotion lies
In odd perverse antipathies;
In falling out with that or this,
And finding something still amiss:
More peevish, cross, and splenetic,
Than dog distract, or monkey sick.
That with more care keep holiday
The wrong, than others the right way:
Compound for sins they are inclined to,
By damning those they have no mind to.
Still so perverse and opposite,
As if they worshipped God for spite.
The self-same thing they will abhor
One way, and long another for.
Free-will they one way disavow,
Another, nothing else allow:
All piety consists therein
In them, in other men all sin.

Jean de La Fontaine

Half peasant, half patrician, and all poet, Jean de La Fontaine was born in July, 1621, at Château-Thierry. Prepared for the church, he quit the seminary and led a life of frivolity. Hoping to give him a sense of responsibility as well as an income, his father found him a wife with a large dowry. La Fontaine was twenty-six, his wife fifteen. The union was not successful. La Fontaine left his wife and spent most of his time in Paris. He seemed to need a mother far more than a young bride, and he did not lack patronesses happy to fulfill this role. The Dowager Duchess of Orléans was followed by the Duchess of Bouillon, who in turn was succeeded by the Duchess de la Sablière, with whom he lived twenty years.

La Fontaine continued to indulge in dissipation until he was seventy, when he was stricken by a serious illness. His amorality reflected the *laissez-faire* spirit of his times, but his lubricous tales, adapted from Boccaccio and Ariosto, had offended the church. Then he repented. He promised to discard any subject that was voluptuous; he destroyed a play on which he was at work, paraphrased a few psalms, and resumed the composition of fables. When he died in his seventy-fourth year, his end, according to an onlooker, "was as calm as the close of a summer day."

Although La Fontaine, who earned his sobriquet "the butterfly of Parnassus," was as versatile as he was prolific, he is remembered today as the author of fables that are versified

variations of Aesop's with added drolleries, and of rhymed
stories that range from the naughty and delicately indecent to
the downright bawdy—all of them accomplished with grace
and effortless skill.

The following are twentieth-century translations. The first
is by the editor, the next two are by Deems Taylor, and the
fourth, fifth, and sixth are by the editor.

THE SERVANT GIRL ABSOLVED

A pretty servant girl had caught the eye
Of her young master. Anything but shy,
Eager to live and learn, she was the sort
For fun and games, including amorous sport.

One morning, while his wife was still in bed,
Her husband rose and let himself be led
To seek the quietest of garden bowers
Where, just by chance, the maid was picking flowers.
He watched her while she made a gay bouquet
To give her mistress later in the day.
He praised her skill, her artless beauty, and
Approaching nearer, slyly slipped his hand
Inside her blouse. Coyly, she turned away—
And the blouse tore. Two buds peeped out. Then they,
Master and maid, laughing, began to play.
She flung the flowers at him. He returned
Them all with kisses. For a while she spurned
His hot demands, withdrew, but not too much.
Then, whispering warmly, answered touch for touch,
Grew limp within his arms, fainted, and fell. . . .
In point of fact, there is no need to tell
What happened but to say that all went well.

While they were thus engaged, a neighbor's eyes
Observed their frolicking with shocked surprise.
The husband saw she saw. He knew the fun
Was over. Somehow, something must be done
And done at once. His mind was suddenly rife
With schemes.

He ran inside and woke his wife.
"Today's your birthday. Don't lie there. Instead
Let's have a romp and celebrate," he said.
Puzzled but pleased, she followed where he led,
Which was, it seems, to the same flower bed
Where he had had his pleasure with the servant.
There he caressed his wife; and, growing fervent,
Cried, "Let's make love like lovers. Don't resist."
Delightedly she matched his mood. They kissed.
He loosed her petticoat. His fingers found
Their way. And soon he had her on the ground.

That afternoon the neighbor could not wait
To visit with the wife and to relate
What she had seen that morning. "You poor dear,
I hate to tell you this, but you must hear.
You have been wronged, most shamefully betrayed,
Here, by your faithless husband and your maid,
A brazen little wench, a wicked jade,
A common slut, a strumpet through and through.
I'd kick her out at once if I were you."

"Surely," replied the wife, "There's some mistake.
"She's just a girl; my husband's not a rake."

"Listen," went the neighbor. "There's no doubt
Of what I saw this morning. I looked out
And saw your husband and your precious maid
Throw flowers at each other. Then they played
A game too wanton to describe, while she—"

"I know," giggled the wife. "The girl was me."

NEIGHBOR
"Don't be absurd. Give me a moment, pray.
You've no idea what I am going to say.
What I observed was more than merely play.
The hussy gave more than I cared to see."

WIFE
"I know. I tell you once again, 'twas me."

NEIGHBOR
"Instead of blossoms he began to grasp
At bosoms. Soon he had a pair to clasp,
A round, ripe handful no one could deny."

WIFE
"Neighbor, I must repeat myself. 'Twas I.
Surely a husband has the right to try
A quaint way to amuse his wife."

NEIGHBOR
                              "She found
Herself placed gently on a grassy mound
Upon her back. You laugh?"

WIFE
                              "And so would you
If you knew that your news was scarcely new."

NEIGHBOR
"He loosed her petticoat . . ."

WIFE
                              "Such a to-do!
The silly petticoat was mine. So there!"

NEIGHBOR
"Upon your word of honor, could you swear
It was yourself who wore that underwear.
For, think, the game your husband played, my friend,
He played—and didn't stop—right to the end."

WIFE
"Once more I say, 'twas mine."

NEIGHBOR
                              "Well, I'm relieved,
Although it's hard to grant I've been deceived
And, for the first time, by my two sharp eyes.
Besides, I must admit I feel surprise
At what you tell me now. I could have sworn
I recognized the girl whose blouse was torn.

But I was wrong. Forgive me. I suppose
You'll keep her."

WIFE

                    "And be glad to. Goodness knows
A decent servant's hard to find these days."

NEIGHBOR
"You're right of course. A servant merits praise
Once you've become accustomed to her ways."

THE SADDLED ASS

A certain painter, leaving in the morning,
    Was jealous of his wife . . . and being deft,
    Painted a donkey, just before he left,
Upon her navel, as a sort of warning.

A friend of his, whose honor had small heft,
At once consoled the lady thus bereft;
And leaving of the donkey not a trace
Was quick to paint another in its place.

But through a lapse of memory, alas!
He put a saddle on the patient ass.

Our friend returned. "My dear," the lady sighed,
    "Regard this proof that I've not fiddle-faddled you."
"A pox on you!" the irate husband cried,
    "And on the proof, and whosoever saddled you!"

THE EXCHANGE

One day Guillot and Peronnelle were strolling, hand in hand,
    When a gentleman espied her, and was rooted to the spot.
    "Who gave you such a lovely wife? Do you know what you've
        got?
Would you kindly let me kiss her—fair exchange, you under-
        stand?"

Guillot enjoyed the compliment. "Why, certainly," he said,
  "The understanding being that I'm due to get one back."
  So the stranger sealed the bargain with a good, resounding
    smack—
And Peronnelle did not forget to turn a pretty red.

A week went by; the stranger and his wife were at the door;
Guillot received the same reward, and evened up the score.
But, having had a sample taste, he hankered after more.

"Now that I see, my friend," he said, "you keep your word so
    well,
  I'm filled with vain regrets, and blush to think, my honored
    sir,
That all you asked of me was just to kiss my Peronnelle,
  Instead of which, you might at least have gone to bed with
    her."

REPENTANCE

"Now that poor, wayward Jane is big with child,
She has repented and is reconciled
To lead a virtuous life in thought and deed."
So spoke her aunt, and all the girls agreed.

Then one of them, an artless, large-eyed one,
Murmured, "Repentance we would never shun—
But first let's learn to do what Jane has done."

THE GRASSHOPPER AND THE ANT[1]

A blithe and unconcerned grasshopper
Thought it was only good and proper
To hail the summer with a song.
In fact he sang all summer long.
Then came, alas, the wintertime
When he could find no easy rhyme

[1] See the prose version by Aesop on page 11.

And (that which made it ten times harder)
No food at all within the larder.

Starving but blandly confident,
Off to a neighboring ant he went.
"Give me," he said, "a little wheat
Or something else that I can eat.
Then, when the summer comes again.
I'll pay you back for every grain.
'Twill be a pleasure, not a task.
Surely that's not too much to ask."

The ant, a very prudent spender,
Was still more prudent as a lender.
"What did you do," she said, "last summer?"
"I sang," he said. "To each newcomer
I gave a taste of pure delight.
I sang all day and sang all night."

"You sang?" she said. "Well, now's your chance,
My fine and carefree friend, to dance."

THE FOX AND THE RAVEN[2]

A hungry raven, hidden by some trees,
Held in his beak a savory bit of cheese.
Its pleasant odor, borne upon the breeze,

Was wafted to a fox, who spied the bird,
And spoke in accents smooth as any curd:
"How brilliantly you shine! Upon my word,

"You make all other creatures in the wood
Seem dull and lifeless, coarse and crude.
Your voice, I'm sure, must match your pulchritude.

"I long to hear you sing, if but a phrase."

---

[2]See the prose version by Aesop on page 11; also the modernized elaboration by Guy Wetmore Carryl on page 549.

The foolish raven, flattered by the praise,
Opened his beak to show the various ways

He had of singing, and of singing well;
Forgot the precious cheese. And down it fell.
You know the rest. . . . What more is there to tell?

Licking his lips, the fox stole from the dell.

Molière

The *commedia dell' arte*, which had certain origins in ancient Roman farces, flourished in Italy, spread to France, fell into disrepute, and reappeared with a curiously acquired accent in the later English pantomimes. The plots were childishly simple and the characters a set of stock types: the slapstick clown, who is a serious fellow underneath—the prototype of Pagliacci; the comic doctor who survives his own medicine; the strutting hero; the pompous fool. The dramatists helped themselves to the situations, properties, and stock characters. Even Molière did not disdain the plots and patterns; glorifying them, he gloried in them. Molière's central subject was man in society, and he continually played variations on the theme. His genius for quick observation and complete deflation was consummate; his candor was implicit in his study of manners and characters. No one else wrote so accurately and yet so tolerantly, and it is not the least of Molière's distinctions that he widened the gamut of comedy from court ballets to aesthetic criticism, from howling but human farce to social satire.

Jean Baptiste Poquelin, born in Paris in 1623, son of an upholsterer to the king, worked for a while in his father's shop, but became associated with the theater before he was twenty-one. Under the influence of his "protectress," Madeleine Béjart, he took the stage name "Molière." Twenty years later he married Armande Béjart. Scandal-mongers had been busy before the event; now they circulated unspeakable rumors.

They hinted that Armande was not, as was claimed, the young
sister of Madeleine Béjart but her daughter, and that Molière
might well have been her father, for he had been intimate with
Madame Béjart since his youth. The marriage was hideously
unhappy. If not a hell, it was a long purgatory; Molière was
often identified with his much-cuckolded character, Sgana-
relle.

Before his marriage Molière was the head of the finest
theatrical company in France. Like Shakespeare, he began to
write plays for his own troupe of actors. Like Shakespeare's,
also, his early dramas were imitations of the classics and of
his contemporaries, but he soon experimented in works that
ranged from light farce to flailing satire. He exposed quackery
in medicine and religion in *Le Médecin Malgré Lui* and *Tartufe;*
snobbery and over-refinement in *Les Précieuses Ridicules;*
the absurd efforts of the *nouveau riche* to imitate the *haut
monde* in *Le Bourgeois Gentilhomme;* self-righteousness and
self-deception in *Le Misanthrope.* His influence spread while
he was still alive. He was echoed by Dryden, and imitated by
William Wycherley and William Congreve; Oliver Goldsmith
and Richard Sheridan could not have written as they did
without him; even the gentle essays of Joseph Addison reflect
their admiration for the caustic French dramatist.

Among his masterpieces, *Le Misanthrope* presents the
severest indictment of society's intrigues, deceptions, and
taken-for-granted dishonesties. Its central figure, the egotistic
Alceste, is (to quote from Richard Wilbur's introduction to the
play) "a victim, like all around him, of the moral enervation of
the times." His attitude is displayed in the following dialogue
from the first scene of the first act. The translation, by Wilbur,
brilliantly duplicates Molière's nimble rhymes and rhythms.

THE MISANTHROPE

ACT 1, SCENE 1

PHILINTE: Now, what's got into you?

ALCESTE *(seated):* Kindly leave me alone.

PHILINTE: Come, come, what is it? This lugubrious tone . . .

ALCESTE: Leave me, I said; you spoil my solitude.

PHILINTE: Oh, listen to me, now, and don't be rude.

ALCESTE: I choose to be rude, Sir, and to be hard of hearing.

PHILINTE: These ugly moods of yours are not endearing;
Friends though we are, I really must insist . . .

ALCESTE (abruptly rising): Friends? Friends, you say? Well,
cross me off your list.
I've been your friend till now, as you well know;
But after what I saw a moment ago
I tell you flatly that our ways must part.
I wish no place in a dishonest heart.

PHILINTE: Why, what have I done, Alceste? Is this quite just?

ALCESTE: My God, you ought to die of self-disgust.
I call your conduct inexcusable, Sir,
And every man of honor will concur.
I see you almost hug a man to death,
Exclaim for joy until you're out of breath,
And supplement these loving demonstrations
With endless offers, vows, and protestations;
Then when I ask you "Who was that?", I find
That you can barely bring his name to mind!
Once the man's back is turned, you cease to love him,
And speak with absolute indifference of him!
By God, I say it's base and scandalous
To falsify the heart's affections thus;
If I caught myself behaving in such a way,
I'd hang myself for shame, without delay.

PHILINTE: It hardly seems a hanging matter to me;
I hope that you will take it graciously
If I extend myself a slight reprieve,
And live a little longer, by your leave.

ALCESTE: How dare you joke about a crime so grave?

PHILINTE: What crime? How else are people to behave?

ALCESTE: I'd have them be sincere, and never part
With any word that isn't from the heart.

PHILINTE: When someone greets us with a show of pleasure,
It's but polite to give him equal measure,
Return his love the best that we know how,
And trade him offer for offer, vow for vow.

ALCESTE: No, no, this formula you'd have me follow,
However fashionable, is false and hollow,
And I despise the frenzied operations
Of all these barterers of protestations,
These lavishers of meaningless embraces,
These utterers of obliging commonplaces,
Who court and flatter everyone on earth
And praise the fool no less than the man of worth.
Should you rejoice that someone fondles you,
Offers his love and service, swears to be true,
And fills your ears with praises of your name,
When to the first damned fop he'll say the same?
No, no: no self-respecting heart would dream
Of prizing so promiscuous an esteem;
However high the praise, there's nothing worse
Than sharing honors with the universe.
Esteem is founded on comparison:
To honor all men is to honor none.
Since you embrace this indiscriminate vice,
Your friendship comes at far too cheap a price;
I spurn the easy tribute of a heart
Which will not set the worthy man apart:
I choose, Sir, to be chosen; and in fine,
The friend of mankind is no friend of mine.

PHILINTE: But in polite society, custom decrees
That we show certain outward courtesies. . . .

ALCESTE: Ah, no! we should condemn with all our force
Such false and artificial intercourse.
Let men behave like men; let them display
Their inmost hearts in everything they say;
Let the heart speak, and let our sentiments
Not mask themselves in silly compliments.

PHILINTE: In certain cases it would be uncouth
And most absurd to speak the naked truth;
With all respect for your exalted notions,
It's often best to veil one's true emotions.
Wouldn't the social fabric come undone
If we were wholly frank with everyone?
Suppose you met with someone you couldn't bear;
Would you inform him of it then and there?

ALCESTE: Yes.

PHILINTE: Then you'd tell old Emilie it's pathetic
The way she daubs her features with cosmetic
And plays the gay coquette at sixty-four?

ALCESTE: I would.

PHILINTE: And you'd call Dorilas a bore,
And tell him every ear at court is lame
From hearing him brag about his noble name?

ALCESTE: Precisely.

PHILINTE: Ah, you're joking.

ALCESTE: *Au contraire:*
In this regard there's none I'd choose to spare.
All are corrupt; there's nothing to be seen
In court or town but aggravates my spleen.
I fall into deep gloom and melancholy
When I survey the scene of human folly,
Finding on every hand base flattery,
Injustice, fraud, self-interest, treachery. . . .
Ah, it's too much; mankind has grown so base,
I mean to break with the whole human race.

PHILINTE: This philosophic rage is a bit extreme;
You've no idea how comical you seem;
Indeed, we're like those brothers in the play
Called *School for Husbands,* one of whom was
   prey . . .

ALCESTE: Enough, now! None of your stupid similes.

PHILINTE: Then let's have no more tirades, if you please.
The world won't change, whatever you say or do;
And since plain speaking means so much to you,
I'll tell you plainly that by being frank
You've earned the reputation of a crank,
And that you're thought ridiculous when you rage
And rant against the manners of the age.

ALCESTE: So much the better; just what I wish to hear.
No news could be more grateful to my ear.
All men are so detestable in my eyes,
I should be sorry if they thought me wise.

PHILINTE: Your hatred's very sweeping, is it not?

ALCESTE: Quite right: I hate the whole degraded lot.

PHILINTE: Must all poor human creatures be embraced,
Without distinction, by your vast distaste?
Even in these bad times, there are surely a few . . .

ALCESTE: No, I include all men in one dim view.

La Rochefoucauld

François Duc de La Rochefoucauld was born in 1613 in Paris. Because of his reckless involvements in political as well as amorous intrigues he was exiled for periods during his twenties. His liaisons led to disillusion, and disillusion is the keynote of the society that La Rochefoucauld delineated with malicious understanding. The prevailing dilettantism, self-deception, and self-interest provoked cynical reflections in his epigrams disguised as "moral maxims." A surreptitious *Memoirs*, which he wrote during his retirement, offended so many that it was withdrawn and La Rochefoucauld denied that he had anything to do with it.

Most of La Rochefoucauld's seven hundred maxims consist of a single sentence; only a few run to more than half a page. All of them are distinguished by their packed wit, penetration, clarity, and, opposed to the conventional platitudes, acutely independent conclusions.

TWENTY-FIVE APHORISMS

- Self-love is the greatest of flatterers.

- Usually we praise only to be praised.

- Those who give themselves to little things become incapable of anything great.

• Nothing stops our being natural as much as the desire to seem so.

• We would rather run ourselves down than not speak of ourselves at all.

• Bad people would be less dangerous if they had no good in them.

• It is as common for tastes to change as it is uncommon for traits of character to alter.

• Virtuous women, like prostitutes, often tire of their profession.

• It is not hard to find a woman who has never been guilty of an indiscretion; it is much harder to find a woman who has been guilty of only one.

• To do a favor for an ungrateful person is merely unpleasant; but to be indebted to a scoundrel is unbearable.

• An enemy's opinion of one's self often comes closer to the truth than one's own.

• Perfect love is like seeing a ghost. We talk about it but seldom see it.

• Jealousy is born with love, but it does not always die with it.

• Intellectual blemishes, like facial ones, grow more prominent with age.

• Our bodies may be lazy, but our minds are lazier.

• Old men like to give advice to comfort themselves for not being able to set a bad example.

• Passion often renders the most clever man a fool, and sometimes even renders the most foolish man clever.

• We all have sufficient strength to support the misfortunes of others.

• There is but one sort of love, but there are a thousand different copies.

• We often boast that we are never bored; yet we are so conceited that we do not perceive how often we bore others.

• As it is the mark of great minds to say things in a few words, so it is that of little minds to use many words to say nothing.

• However deceitful Hope may be, yet she carries us on pleasantly to the end of life.

• It would seem that Nature, which has so wisely ordered the organs of our body for our happiness, has also given us pride to spare us the mortification of knowing our imperfections.

• To establish ourselves in the world we do everything to appear as if we were established.

• Vanity, propriety, and other peculiarities of temperament account for most men's bravery and most women's chastity.

John Dryden

After the fall of Cromwell and the return of the Stuart dynasty in the person of the dissolute Charles II, there ensued a drastic reaction against the austerity of the Puritans. The Restoration was marked by a curious cultural phenomenon: its licentiousness was expressed in elegant conceits and polished epigrams, while its grossness was couched in the utmost delicacy. "There is no doubt," wrote Agnes Repplier *(In Pursuit of Laughter)*, "that the rakish society of the Restoration began by tolerating indecency for the sake of wit and ended by tolerating dullness for the sake of indecency. . . . The wits of the Restoration, indignant that they had been robbed of laughter for a matter of ten years, set it above price."

The exemplar of the period was John Dryden. Born in Northamptonshire in 1631, Dryden was both an encourager and a corrector of the Restoration spirit; a true poet and a political trimmer, he was called "both the glory and the shame of our literature." He was a supporter of Cromwell, but turned high Tory: a Puritan who became an Anglican, and finally a Roman Catholic. His vacillations coincided with the fashions of the day, and if he wrote a set of "Heroic Stanzas" in eulogy of Cromwell one year, and a "Panegyric" on the Restoration to Charles II another year, it was because Dryden's convictions changed with the changing times. The king appointed him poet laureate, and Dryden turned to the writing of plays.

At thirty-two Dryden married Lady Elizabeth Howard. The marriage was not congenial; rumor had it that the lady was no better than she should be and that the union had been forced by her brawny brothers. It is significant that Dryden rarely mentioned marriage without gibing at it. Before her death he wrote a savagely concise epitaph "On His Wife":

Here lies my wife; here let her lie.
Now she's at rest. And so am I.

As a dramatist Dryden had planned to write tragedies, but the public preferred comedies spiced with erotic lyrics, and though he detested the taste of his day, he did his best to please. He reserved his spleen for his poetry. He captured Juvenal's fierce bitterness and excelled in controversy. He held up the mirror of satire in such mock epics as *Absalom and Achitophel,* which exposed the politicos of the period (Achitophel being the conniving Earl of Shaftesbury), and *Mac Flecknoe,* a decapitating attack on Thomas Shadwell, the poet who succeeded him to the laureateship—a poet, according to Dryden, who never "deviates" into sense, and whom Dryden, using the customary device of initial letters followed by dashes, characterized as "loads of Sh—— which almost choked the way."

Dryden's style, a combination of clarity and innuendo, set the fashion for more than a century. As a classical reformist, he fought vagueness and affectation with constant zeal. He maintained that the satirist "is bound to give his reader some precept of moral virtue," and from a strictly literary standpoint, he held that "the nicest and most delicate touches of satire consist of fine raillery." But Dryden went far beyond mere raillery. Not since the Latins had any poet so firmly and flexibly used verse to rebuke, discomfit, and even to destroy the objects of his attack.

ABSALOM AND ACHITOPHEL

PORTRAIT OF THE EARL OF SHAFTESBURY

Of these the false Achitophel was first;
A name to all succeeding ages curst:

For close designs, and crooked counsels fit;
Sagacious, bold, and turbulent of wit;
Restless, unfixed in principles and place;
In power unpleased, impatient of disgrace;
A fiery soul, which, working out its way,
Fretted the pigmy-body to decay,
And o'er-informed the tenement of clay.
A daring pilot in extremity,
Pleased with the danger, when the waves went high,
He sought the storms; but for a calm unfit,
Would steer too nigh the sands, to boast his wit.
Great wits are sure to madness near allied,
And thin partitions do their bounds divide;
Else, why should he, with wealth and honour blest,
Refuse his age the needful hours of rest?
Punish a body which he could not please;
Bankrupt of life, yet prodigal of ease?
And all to leave what with his toil he won,
To that unfeathered two-legged thing, a son;
Got, while his soul did huddled notions try;
And born a shapeless lump, like anarchy.
In friendship false, implacable in hate;
Resolved to ruin, or to rule the state.
To compass this the triple bond he broke;
The pillars of the public safety shook;
And fitted Israel for a foreign yoke;
Then, seized with fear, yet still affecting fame,
Usurped a patriot's all-atoning name.
So easy still it proves in factious times,
With public zeal to cancel private crimes.
How safe is treason, and how sacred ill,
Where none can sin against the people's will,
Where crowds can wink, and no offence be known,
Since in another's guilt they find their own?
Yet fame deserved no enemy can grudge;
The statesman we abhor, but praise the judge.
In Israel's courts ne'er sat an Abbethdin
With more discerning eyes, or hands more clean,
Unbribed, unsought, the wretched to redress;
Swift of despatch, and easy of access.
Oh! had he been content to serve the crown,

With virtue only proper to the gown;
Or had the rankness of the soil been freed
From cockle, that oppressed the noble seed;
David for him his tuneful harp had strung,
And heaven had wanted one immortal song.
But wild ambition loves to slide, not stand,
And fortune's ice prefers to virtue's land.
Achitophel, grown weary to possess
A lawful fame, and lazy happiness,
Disdained the golden fruit to gather free,
And lent the crowd his arm to shake the tree.

MAC FLECKNOE

PORTRAIT OF SHADWELL

All human things are subject to decay,
And when fate summons, monarchs must obey.
This Flecknoe found, who, like Augustus, young
Was call'd to empire, and had govern'd long;
In prose and verse, was own'd, without dispute,
Thro' all the realms of *Nonsense,* absolute.
This aged prince, now flourishing in peace,
And blest with issue of a large increase;
Worn out with business, did at length debate
To settle the succession of the State;
And, pond'ring which of all his sons was fit
To reign, and wage immortal war with wit,
Cried: "'Tis resolv'd; for nature pleads, that he
Should only rule, who most resembles me.
Sh—— alone my perfect image bears,
Mature in dulness from his tender years:
Sh—— alone, of all my sons, is he
Who stands confirm'd in full stupidity.
The rest to some faint meaning make pretense,
But Sh—— never deviates into sense.
Some beams of wit on other souls may fall,
Strike thro', and make a lucid interval;
But Sh——'s genuine night admits no ray,
His rising fogs prevail upon the day.

Besides, his goodly fabric fills the eye,
And seems design'd for thoughtless majesty;
Thoughtless as monarch oaks that shade the plain,
And, spread in solemn state, supinely reign.
Heywood and Shirley were but types of thee,
Thou last great prophet of tautology!

Jonathan Swift

Blessed with a brilliant mind and cursed with a baffled spirit, Jonathan Swift gave satire a fresh vigor and sarcasm a new ferocity. Born in Dublin in 1667 a few months after the death of his father, he was brought up on the grudging charity of an uncle, which may account for much of his early bitterness. His unhappiness increased when at twenty-two he went to England to become secretary to a distant relative, Sir William Temple, his intellectual inferior, who demanded constant servility. In Temple's household he met Esther Johnson, a child who gossips insinuated was Temple's illegitimate daughter, and taught her to read and write. When after eleven submissive years with Temple Swift returned to Ireland, Esther, whom he had renamed "Stella," went with him.

Although Swift was linked with the Anglican church, preferment was slow; it was not until he was in his mid-forties that he was appointed Dean of St. Patrick's in Dublin. An Irishman, Swift was alien to the quick warmth of his countrymen. His thinking was unemotionally precise; even his rages were cold. Nevertheless, his sense of justice was outraged by the inhuman treatment meted out to the Irish by the absentee landlords and English lawmakers. He championed the cause of the Irish peasants in essays and pamphlets of such force that the poor came to regard Swift as their protector. *A Modest Proposal for Preventing the Children of Poor People in Ireland from Being a Burthen to Their Parents or Country* . . . is as brutal a mockery as has ever been written.

At the height of his fame Swift attracted the attention of Esther Van Homrigh, daughter of a Dublin merchant of Dutch origin. Like the other Esther, she became his pupil, even surpassing her predecessor in passionate admiration and unconcealed devotion. Flattered by this adulation, Swift termed her his "Vanessa," but he did not pursue the intimacy. He was already committed to Stella, who was accepted as Swift's mistress and may have been his wife by a secret marriage. However, Vanessa could not be dissuaded. Beside herself with jealousy, she wrote Stella demanding to know her relationship to Swift. When Swift saw the letter, he threw it at Vanessa's feet and flung himself out of the house. Stricken, Vanessa died a few weeks later. Stella followed Vanessa within five years. Swift survived both of them. What he wrote about women was never a tribute; on the contrary, it was usually steeped in misogyny.

In his sixties an ear affliction grew almost unbearable, and the power of his great mind began to wane. At seventy-five guardians had to be appointed. Aphasia followed paralysis, and he died at seventy-eight. His tombstone memorialized one of his last desperate thoughts: "Here lies Jonathan Swift . . . where savage indignation can no longer tear his heart." In a final thrust of bitterness he left his fortune to found a hospital for idiots.

It is an additional irony that his masterpiece, *Gulliver's Travels,* an unremitting denunciation of mankind, is enjoyed by youngsters as an adventure story. "I have ever hated all nations, professions, and communities," Swift wrote to Pope. "Although I love John, Peter, Thomas, etc., I hate and detest that animal called man." It has often been pointed out that *Gulliver's Travels* praises the Houyhnhnms, those splendid horses, in order to compare their nobility with the baseness of Yahoos, or men. However, it should be remembered that though Swift considered himself an unrelenting misanthrope, he wrote playfully under half a dozen pseudonyms, always in the hope that by reproving the race he might, somehow, improve it.

GULLIVER'S TRAVELS

(In the second chapter, which follows, Swift pictures the tininess of the Lilliputians, and by implication satirizes the insignificance of the people of his times.)

When I found myself on my feet, I looked about me, and must confess I never beheld a more entertaining prospect. The country round appeared like a continued garden, and the inclosed fields, which were generally forty foot square, resembled so many beds of flowers. These fields were intermingled with woods, and the tallest trees, as I could judge, appeared to be seven foot high. I viewed the town on my left hand, which looked like the painted scene of a city in a theatre.

I had been for some hours extremely pressed by the necessities of nature; which was no wonder, it being almost two days since I had last disburthened myself. I was under great difficulties between urgency and shame. The best expedient I could think on, was to creep into my house, which I accordingly did; and shutting the gate after me, I went as far as the length of my chain would suffer, and discharged my body of that uneasy load. But this was the only time I was ever guilty of so uncleanly an action; for which I cannot but hope the candid reader will give some allowance, after he hath maturely and impartially considered my case, and the distress I was in. From this time my constant practice was, as soon as I rose, to perform that business in open air, at the full extent of my chain, and due care was taken every morning before company came, that the offensive matter should be carried off in wheelbarrows, by two servants appointed for that purpose. I would not have dwelt so long upon a circumstance, that perhaps at first sight may appear not very momentous, if I had not thought it necessary to justify my character in point of cleanliness to the world; which I am told some of my maligners have been pleased, upon this and other occasions, to call in question.

When this adventure was at an end, I came back out of my house, having occasion for fresh air. The Emperor was already descended from the tower, and advancing on horseback towards me, which had like to have cost him dear; for the beast, though very well trained, yet wholly unused to such a sight, which appeared as if a mountain moved before him, reared up on his hinder feet: but that prince, who is an excellent horseman, kept his

seat, till his attendants ran in, and held the bridle, while his
Majesty had time to dismount. When he alighted, he surveyed
me round with great admiration, but kept beyond the length of
my chain. He ordered his cooks and butlers, who were already
prepared, to give me victuals and drink, which they pushed forward in a sort of vehicles upon wheels, till I could reach them.
I took these vehicles, and soon emptied them all; twenty of them
were filled with meat, and ten with liquor; each of the former'
afforded me two or three good mouthfuls, and I emptied the
liquor of ten vessels, which was contained in earthen vials, into
one vehicle, drinking it off at a draught; and so I did with the rest.
The Empress, and young Princes of the blood of both sexes, attended by many ladies, sat at some distance in their chairs; but
upon the accident that happened to the Emperor's horse, they
alighted, and came near his person, which I am now going to
describe. He is taller by almost the breadth of my nail, than any
of his court; which alone is enough to strike an awe into the beholders. His features are strong and masculine, with an Austrian
lip and arched nose, his complexion olive, his countenance erect,
his body and limbs well proportioned, all his motions graceful,
and his deportment majestic. He was then past his prime, being
twenty-eight years and three quarters old, of which he had reigned
about seven, in great felicity, and generally victorious. For the
better convenience of beholding him, I lay on my side, so that
my face was parallel to his, and he stood but three yards off:
however, I have had him since many times in my hand, and therefore cannot be deceived in the description. His dress was very
plain and simple, and the fashion of it between the Asiatic and
the European: but he had on his head a light helmet of gold,
adorned with jewels, and a plume on the crest. He held his sword
drawn in his hand, to defend himself, if I should happen to break
loose; it was almost three inches long, the hilt and scabbard were
gold enriched with diamonds. His voice was shrill, but very clear
and articulate, and I could distinctly hear it when I stood up.
The ladies and courtiers were all most magnificently clad, so that
the spot they stood upon seemed to resemble a petticoat spread
on the ground, embroidered with figures of gold and silver. His
Imperial Majesty spoke often to me, and I returned answers, but
neither of us could understand a syllable. There were several of
his priests and lawyers present (as I conjectured by their habits)
who were commanded to address themselves to me, and I spoke
to them in as many languages as I had the least smattering of,

which were High and Low Dutch, Latin, French, Spanish, Italian, and Lingua Franca; but all to no purpose. After about two hours the court retired, and I was left with a strong guard, to prevent the impertinence, and probably the malice of the rabble, who were very impatient to crowd about me as near as they durst, and some of them had the impudence to shoot their arrows at me as I sat on the ground by the door of my house, whereof one very narrowly missed my left eye. But the colonel ordered six of the ringleaders to be seized, and thought no punishment so proper as to deliver them bound into my hands, which some of his soldiers accordingly did, pushing them forwards with the butt-ends of their pikes into my reach; I took them all in my right hand, put five of them into my coat-pocket, and as to the sixth, I made a countenance as if I would eat him alive. The poor man squalled terribly, and the colonel and his officers were in much pain, especially when they saw me take out my penknife: but I soon put them out of fear: for, looking mildly, and immediately cutting the strings he was bound with, I set him gently on the ground, and away he ran. I treated the rest in the same manner, taking them one by one out of my pocket, and I observed both the soldiers and people were highly obliged at this mark of my clemency, which was represented very much to my advantage at court.

Towards night I got with some difficulty into my house, where I lay on the ground, and continued to do so about a fortnight; during which time the Emperor gave orders to have a bed prepared for me. Six hundred beds of the common measure were brought in carriages, and worked up in my house; an hundred and fifty of their beds sewn together made up the breadth and length, and these were four double, which however kept me but very indifferently from the hardness of the floor, that was of smooth stone. By the same computation they provided me with sheets, blankets, and coverlets, tolerable enough for one who had been so long inured to hardships as I.

As the news of my arrival spread through the kingdom, it brought prodigious numbers of rich, idle, and curious people to see me; so that the villages were almost emptied, and great neglect of tillage and household affairs must have ensued, if his Imperial Majesty had not provided, by several proclamations and orders of state, against this inconveniency. He directed that those who had already beheld me should return home, and not presume to come within fifty yards of my house without licence from court; whereby the secretaries of state got considerable fees.

In the meantime, the Emperor held frequent councils to debate
what course should be taken with me; and I was afterwards assured by a particular friend, a person of great quality, who was
looked upon to be as much in the secret as any, that the court was
under many difficulties concerning me. They apprehended my
breaking loose, that my diet would be very expensive, and might
cause a famine. Sometimes they determined to starve me, or at
least to shoot me in the face and hands with poisoned arrows,
which would soon dispatch me; but again they considered, that
the stench of so large a carcass might produce a plague in the
metropolis, and probably spread through the whole kingdom. In
the midst of these consultations, several officers of the army went
to the door of the great council-chamber; and two of them being
admitted, gave an account of my behaviour to the six criminals
above-mentioned, which made so favourable an impression in the
breast of his Majesty and the whole board, in my behalf, that an
Imperial Commission was issued out, obliging all the villages nine
hundred yards around the city, to deliver in every morning six
beeves, forty sheep, and other victuals for my sustenance; together with a proportionable quantity of bread, and wine, and
other liquors; for the due payment of which his Majesty gave
assignments upon his treasury. For this prince lives chiefly upon
his own demesnes, seldom, except upon great occasions, raising
any subsidies upon his subjects, who are bound to attend him in
his wars at their own expense. An establishment was also made of
six hundred persons to be my domestics, who had board-wages
allowed for their maintenance, and tents built for them very con-
veniently on each side of my door. It was likewise ordered, that
three hundred tailors should make me a suit of clothes after the
fashion of the country: that six of his Majesty's greatest scholars
should be employed to instruct me in their language: and, lastly,
that the Emperor's horses, and those of the nobility, and troops
of guards, should be frequently exercised in my sight, to accustom
themselves to me. All these orders were duly put in execution, and
in about three weeks I made a great progress in learning their
language; during which time, the Emperor frequently honoured
me with his visits, and was pleased to assist my masters in teaching me. We began already to converse together in some sort; and
the first words I learnt were to express my desire that he would
please to give me my liberty, which I every day repeated on my
knees. His answer, as I could comprehend it, was, that this must
be a work of time, not to be thought on without the advice of his
council, and that first I must *Lumos kelmin pesso desmar lon*

Emposo; that is, swear a peace with him and his kingdom. However, that I should be used with all kindness; and he advised me
to acquire, by my patience and discreet behaviour, the good opinion of himself and his subjects. He desired I would not take it ill,
if he gave orders to certain proper officers to search me; for probably I might carry about me several weapons, which must needs
be dangerous things, if they answered the bulk of so prodigious
a person. I said, his Majesty should be satisfied, for I was ready
to strip myself, and turn up my pockets before him. This I delivered part in words, and part in signs. He replied, that by the
laws of the kingdom I must be searched by two of his officers;
that he knew this could not be done without my consent and assistance; that he had so good an opinion of my generosity and
justice, as to trust their persons in my hands: that whatever they
took from me should be returned when I left the country, or paid
for at the rate which I would set upon them. I took up the two
officers in my hands, put them first into my coat-pockets, and
then into every other pocket about me, except my two fobs, and
another secret pocket which I had no mind should be searched,
wherein I had some little necessaries that were of no consequence
to any but myself. In one of my fobs there was a silver watch, and
in the other a small quantity of gold in a purse. These gentlemen,
having pen, ink, and paper about them, made an exact inventory
of every thing they saw; and when they had done, desired I would
set them down, that they might deliver it to the Emperor. This
inventory I afterwards translated into English, and is word for
word as follows:

Imprimis, In the right coat-pocket of the Great Man-Mountain
(for so I interpret the words *Quinbus Flestrin*) after the strictest
search, we found only one great piece of coarse cloth, large
enough to be a foot-cloth for your Majesty's chief room of state.
In the left pocket we saw a huge silver chest, with a cover of the
same metal, which we, the searchers, were not able to lift. We
desired it should be opened, and one of us stepping into it, found
himself up to the mid leg in a sort of dust, some part whereof
flying up to our faces, set us both a sneezing for several times
together. In his right waistcoat-pocket we found a prodigious
bundle of white thin substances, folded one over another, about
the bigness of three men, tied with a strong cable, and marked
with black figures; which we humbly conceive to be writings,
every letter almost half as large as the palm of our hands. In the
left there was a sort of engine, from the back of which were ex-

tended twenty long poles, resembling the pallisadoes before your Majesty's court; wherewith we conjecture the Man-Mountain combs his head; for we did not always trouble him with questions, because we found it a great difficulty to make him understand us. In the large pocket on the right side of his middle cover (so I translate the word *ranfu-lo,* by which they meant my breeches) we saw a hollow pillar of iron, about the length of a man, fastened to a strong piece of timber, larger than the pillar; and upon one side of the pillar were huge pieces of iron sticking out, cut into strange figures, which we know not what to make of. In the left pocket, another engine of the same kind. In the smaller pocket on the right side, were several round flat pieces of white and red metal, of different bulk; some of the white, which seemed to be silver, were so large and heavy, that my comrade and I could hardly lift them. In the left pocket were two black pillars irregularly shaped: we could not, without difficulty, reach the top of them as we stood at the bottom of his pocket. One of them was covered, and seemed all of a piece: but at the upper end of the other, there appeared a white round substance, about twice the bigness of our heads. Within each of these was enclosed a prodigious plate of steel; which, by our orders, we obliged him to show us, because we apprehended they might be dangerous engines. He took them out of their cases, and told us, that in his own country his practice was to shave his beard with one of these, and cut his meat with the other. There were two pockets which we could not enter: these he called his fobs; they were two large slits cut into the top of his middle cover, but squeezed close by the pressure of his belly. Out of the right fob hung a great silver chain, with a wonderful kind of engine at the bottom. We directed him to draw out whatever was fastened to that chain; which appeared to be a globe, half silver, and half of some transparent metal; for, on the transparent side, we saw certain strange figures circularly drawn, and thought we could touch them, till we found our fingers stopped by that lucid substance. He put this engine to our ears, which made an incessant noise like that of a water-mill. And we conjecture it is either some unknown animal, or the god that he worships; but we are more inclined to the latter opinion, because he assured us, (if we understood him right, for he expressed himself very imperfectly) that he seldom did any thing without consulting it. He called it his oracle, and said it pointed out the time for every action of his life. From the left fob he took out a net almost large enough for a fisherman, but contrived to open and shut like a purse, and served him for the same use: we found therein several massy pieces of yellow metal, which, if they be real gold, must be of immense value.

Having thus, in obedience to your Majesty's commands, diligently searched all his pockets, we observed a girdle about his waist made of the hide of some prodigious animal; from which, on the left side, hung a sword of the length of five men; and on the right, a bag or pouch divided into two cells, each capable of holding three of your Majesty's subjects. In one of these cells were several globes or balls of a most ponderous metal, about the bigness of our heads, and requiring a strong hand to lift them: the other cell contained a heap of certain black grains, but of no great bulk or weight, for we could hold about fifty of them in the palms of our hands.

This is an exact inventory of what we found about the body of the Man-Mountain, who used us with great civility, and due respect to your Majesty's Commission. Signed and sealed on the fourth day of the eighty-ninth moon of your Majesty's auspicious reign.

CLEFRIN FRELOCK, MARSI FRELOCK.

When this inventory was read over to the Emperor, he directed me, although in very gentle terms, to deliver up the several particulars. He first called for my scimitar, which I took out, scabbard and all. In the mean time he ordered three thousand of his choicest troops (who then attended him) to surround me at a distance, with their bows and arrows just ready to discharge: but I did not observe it, for my eyes were wholly fixed upon his Majesty. He then desired me to draw my scimitar, which, although it had got some rust by the seawater, was in most parts exceeding bright. I did so, and immediately all the troops gave a shout between terror and surprise; for the sun shone clear, and the reflection dazzled their eyes, as I waved the scimitar to and fro in my hand. His Majesty, who is a most magnanimous prince, was less daunted than I could expect; he ordered me to return it into the scabbard, and cast it on the ground as gently as I could, about six foot from the end of my chain. The next thing he demanded, was one of the hollow iron pillars, by which he meant my pocket-pistols. I drew it out, and at his desire, as well as I could, expressed to him the use of it; and charging it only with powder, which, by the closeness of my pouch, happened to escape wetting in the sea (an inconvenience against which all prudent mariners take special care to provide,) I first cautioned the Emperor not to be afraid, and then I let it off in the air. The astonishment here was much

greater than at the sight of my scimitar. Hundreds fell down as if
they had been struck dead; and even the Emperor, although he
stood his ground, could not recover himself in some time. I delivered up both my pistols in the same manner as I had done my
scimitar, and then my pouch of powder and bullets; begging him
that the former might be kept from fire, for it would kindle with
the smallest spark, and blow up his imperial palace into the air.
I likewise delivered up my watch, which the Emperor was very
curious to see, and commanded two of his tallest yeomen of the
guards to bear it on a pole upon their shoulders, as draymen in
England do a barrel of ale. He was amazed at the continual noise
it made, and the motion of the minute-hand, which he could easily
discern; for their sight is much more acute than ours: and asked
the opinions of his learned men about him, which were various
and remote, as the reader may well imagine without my repeating;
although indeed I could not very perfectly understand them. I
then gave up my silver and copper money, my purse, with nine
large pieces of gold, and some smaller ones; my knife and razor,
my comb and silver snuff-box, my handkerchief and journal-
book. My scimitar, pistols, and pouch, were conveyed in carriages
to his Majesty's stores; but the rest of my goods were returned
to me.

I had, as I before observed, one private pocket which escaped
their search, wherein there was a pair of spectacles, (which I
sometimes use for the weakness of my eyes) a pocket perspective,
and several other little conveniences; which being of no consequence to the Emperor, I did not think myself bound in honour
to discover, and I apprehended they might be lost or spoiled if
I ventured them out of my possession.

A MODEST PROPOSAL

FOR PREVENTING THE CHILDREN OF POOR PEOPLE IN IRELAND FROM BEING A BURTHEN TO THEIR PARENTS OR COUNTRY, AND FOR MAKING THEM BENEFICIAL TO THE PUBLIC

It is a melancholy object to those who walk through this great
town or travel in the country, when they see the streets, the roads,
and cabin-doors, crowded with beggars of the female sex, followed

by three, four, or six children, *all in rags*, and importuning every passenger for an alms. These mothers, instead of being able to work for their honest livelihood, are forced to employ all their time in strolling, to beg sustenance for their helpless infants, who, as they grow up, either turn thieves for want of work, or leave their dear native country to fight for the Pretender in Spain, or sell themselves to the Barbadoes.

I think it is agreed by all parties that this prodigious number of children, in the arms, or on the backs, or at the heels of their mothers, and frequently of their fathers, is in the present deplorable state of the kingdom a very great additional grievance; and therefore whoever could find out a fair, cheap, and easy method of making these children sound, useful members of the commonwealth, would deserve so well of the public as to have his statue set up for a preserver of the nation.

But my intention is very far from being confined to provide only for the children of professed beggars; it is of a much greater extent, and shall take in the whole number of infants at a certain age, who are born of parents in effect as little able to support them as those who demand our charity in the streets.

As to my own part, having turned my thoughts for many years upon this important subject, and maturely weighed the several schemes of other projectors, I have always found them grossly mistaken in their computation. It is true, a child, just dropped from its dam, may be supported by her milk for a solar year with little other nourishment, at most not above the value of two shillings, which the mother may certainly get, or the value in scraps, by her lawful occupation of begging; and it is exactly at one year old that I propose to provide for them in such a manner as instead of being a charge upon their parents or the parish, or wanting food and raiment for the rest of their lives, they shall, on the contrary, contribute to the feeding and partly to the clothing of many thousands.

There is likewise another great advantage in my scheme, that it will prevent those voluntary abortions, and that horrid practice of women murdering their bastard children, alas, too frequent among us, sacrificing the poor innocent babes, I doubt, more to avoid the expense than the shame, which would move tears and pity in the most savage and inhuman breast.

The number of souls in this kingdom being usually reckoned one million and a half, of these I calculate there may be about two hundred thousand couple whose wives are breeders; from which number I subtract thirty thousand couple who are able to maintain their own children, although I apprehend there cannot be so many under the present distresses of the kingdom; but this being granted, there will remain an hundred and seventy thousand breeders. I again subtract fifty thousand for those women who miscarry, or whose children die by accident or disease within the year. There only remain an hundred and twenty thousand children of poor parents annually born. The question therefore is, how this number shall be reared and provided for, which, as I have already said, under the present situation of affairs, is utterly impossible by all the methods hitherto proposed, for we can neither employ them in handicraft or agriculture; we neither build houses (I mean in the country) nor cultivate land; they can very seldom pick up a livelihood by stealing till they arrive at six years old, except where they are of towardly parts, although I confess they learn the rudiments much earlier, during which time, they can however be properly looked upon only as *probationers;* as I have been informed by a principal gentleman in the County of Cavan, who protested to me, that he never knew above one or two instances under the age of six, even in a part of the kingdom so renowned for the quickest proficiency in that art.

I am assured by our merchants that a boy or a girl before twelve years old is no saleable commodity, and even when they come to this age, they will not yield above three pounds, or three pounds and half-a-crown at most on the Exchange, which cannot turn to account either to the parents or kingdom, the charge of nutriment and rags having been at least four times that value.

I shall now therefore humbly propose my own thoughts, which I hope will not be liable to the least objection.

I have been assured by a very knowing American of my acquaintance in London, that a young healthy child well nursed is at a year old a most delicious, nourishing, and wholesome food, whether stewed, roasted, baked, or boiled, and I make no doubt that it will equally serve in a fricassee or a ragout.

I do therefore humbly offer it to public consideration that of the hundred and twenty thousand children already computed, twenty thousand may be reserved for breed, whereof only one fourth part to be males, which is more than we allow to sheep, black cattle, or swine; and my reason is that these children are seldom the fruits of marriage, a circumstance not much regarded by our savages. Therefore one male will be sufficient to serve four females. That the remaining hundred thousand may at a year old be offered in sale to the persons of quality and fortune through the kingdom, always advising the mother to let them suck plentifully in the last month, so as to render them plump and fat for a good table. A child will make two dishes at an entertainment for friends, and when the family dines alone, the fore or hind quarter will make a reasonable dish, and seasoned with a little pepper or salt will be very good boiled on the fourth day, especially in winter.

I have reckoned, upon a medium, that a child just born will weigh 12 pounds, and in a solar year if tolerably nursed will increase to 28 pounds.

I grant this food will be somewhat dear, and therefore very proper for landlords, who, as they have already devoured most of the parents, seem to have the best title to the children.

Infants' flesh will be in season throughout the year, but more plentiful in March, and a little before and after, for we are told by a grave author, an eminent French physician, that fish being a prolific diet, there are more children born in Roman Catholic countries about nine months after Lent, than at any other season; therefore reckoning a year after Lent, the markets will be more glutted than usual, because the number of Popish infants is at least three to one in this kingdom, and therefore it will have one other collateral advantage, by lessening the number of Papists among us.

I have already computed the charge of nursing a beggar's child (in which list I reckon all cottagers, labourers, and four-fifths of the farmers) to be about two shillings *per annum*, rags included, and I believe no gentleman would repine to give ten shillings for the carcass of a good fat child, which, as I have said, will make four dishes of excellent nutritive meat, when he has only some particular friend or his own family to dine with him. Thus the squire will learn to be a good landlord, and grow popular among his tenants, the mother will have eight shillings net profit, and be fit for work till she produces another child.

Those who are more thrifty (as I must confess the times require) may flay the carcass; the skin of which, artificially dressed, will make admirable gloves for ladies, and summer boots for fine gentlemen.

As to our city of Dublin, shambles may be appointed for this purpose in the most convenient parts of it, and butchers we may be assured will not be wanting, although I rather recommend buying the children alive, and dressing them hot from the knife, as we do roasting pigs.

A very worthy person, a true lover of his country, and whose virtues I highly esteem, was lately pleased, in discoursing on this matter, to offer a refinement upon my scheme. He said, that many gentlemen of this kingdom having of late destroyed their deer, he conceived that the want of venison might be well supplied by the bodies of young lads and maidens, not exceeding fourteen years of age, nor under twelve, so great a number of both sexes in every country being now ready to starve, for want of work and service, and these to be disposed of by their parents if alive, or otherwise by their nearest relations. But with due deference to so excellent a friend, and so deserving a patriot, I cannot be altogether in his sentiments; for as to the males, my American acquaintance assured me from frequent experience, that their flesh was generally tough and lean, like that of our schoolboys, by continual exercise, and their taste disagreeable, and to fatten them would not answer the charge. Then as to the females, it would, I think with humble submission, be a loss to the public, because they soon would become breeders themselves. And besides, it is not improbable that some scrupulous people might be apt to censure such a practice, (although indeed very unjustly) as a little bordering upon cruelty, which, I confess, has always been with me the strongest objection against any project, however so well intended.

But in order to justify my friend, he confessed that this expedient was put into his head by the famous Psalmanazar,[1] a native of the island Formosa, who came from thence to London, above twenty years ago, and in conversation told my friend, that in his country when any young person happened to be put to death, the executioner sold the carcass to persons of quality, as a prime dainty, and that, in his time, the body of a plump girl of fifteen, who was crucified for an attempt to poison the emperor, was sold to his Imperial Majesty's Prime Minister of State, and other great Mandarins of the Court, in joints from the gibbet, at four hundred crowns. Neither indeed can I deny, that if the same use were made of several plump young girls in this town, who, without one single groat to their fortunes, cannot stir abroad without a chair, and appear at the playhouse and assemblies in foreign fineries, which they never will pay for, the kingdom would not be the worse.

Some persons of a desponding spirit are in great concern about that vast number of poor people who are aged, diseased, or

[1] *Psalmanazar:* a Frenchman who published a fictitious account of Formosa

maimed, and I have been desired to employ my thoughts what course may be taken, to ease the nation of so grievous an encumbrance. But I am not in the least pain upon that matter, because it is very well known that they are every day dying and rotting, by cold, and famine, and filth, and vermin, as fast as can be reasonably expected. And as to the young labourers, they are now in as hopeful a condition. They cannot get work, and consequently pine away for want of nourishment, to a degree that if at any time they are accidentally hired to common labour, they have not strength to perform it; and thus the country and themselves are happily delivered from the evils to come.

I have too long digressed, and therefore shall return to my subject. I think the advantages by the proposal which I have made are obvious and many, as well as of the highest importance.

For first, as I have already observed, it would greatly lessen the number of Papists, with whom we are yearly over-run, being the principal breeders of the nation, as well as our most dangerous enemies, and who stay at home on purpose to deliver the kingdom to the Pretender, hoping to take their advantage by the absence of so many good Protestants, who have chosen rather to leave their country, than stay at home, and pay tithes against their conscience, to an Episcopal curate.

Secondly, The poor tenants will have something valuable of their own, which by law may be made liable to distress, and help to pay their landlord's rent, their corn and cattle being already seized, and *money a thing unknown.*

Thirdly, Whereas the maintenance of an hundred thousand children, from two years old and upward, cannot be computed at less than ten shillings a piece per annum, the nation's stock will be thereby increased fifty thousand pounds *per annum,* besides the profit of a new dish, introduced to the tables of all gentlemen of fortune in the kingdom who have any refinement in taste, and the money will circulate among ourselves, the goods being entirely of our own growth and manufacture.

Fourthly, The constant breeders, beside the gain of eight shillings sterling *per annum,* by the sale of their children, will be rid of the charge of maintaining them after the first year.

Fifthly, This food would likewise bring great custom to taverns, where the vintners will certainly be so prudent as to procure the best receipts for dressing it to perfection, and consequently have their houses frequented by all the fine gentlemen who justly value themselves upon their knowledge in good eating; and a skilful cook, who understands how to oblige his guests, will contrive to make it as expensive as they please.

Sixthly, This would be a great inducement to marriage, which all wise nations have either encouraged by rewards, or enforced by laws and penalties. It would increase the care and tenderness of mothers toward their children, when they were sure of a settlement for life, to the poor babes, provided in some sort by the public, to their annual profit instead of expense. We should see an honest emulation among the married women, which of them could bring the fattest child to the market. Men would become as fond of their wives, during the time of their pregnancy, as they are now of their mares in foal, their cows in calf, their sows when they are ready to farrow, nor offer to beat or kick them (as is too frequent a practice) for fear of a miscarriage.

Many other advantages might be enumerated. For instance, the addition of some thousand carcasses in our exportation of barrelled beef, the propagation of swine's flesh, and improvement in the art of making good bacon, so much wanted among us by the great destruction of pigs, too frequent at our table, which are no way comparable in taste, or magnificence, to a well-grown, fat yearling child, which roasted whole will make a considerable figure at a Lord Mayor's feast, or any other public entertainment. But this and many others I omit, being studious of brevity.

Supposing that one thousand families in this city would be constant customers for infants' flesh, beside others who might have it at merry-meetings, particularly at weddings and christenings, I compute that Dublin would take off annually about twenty thousand carcasses; and the rest of the kingdom (where probably they will be sold somewhat cheaper) the remaining eighty thousand.

I can think of no one objection, that will possibly be raised against this proposal, unless it should be urged that the number of people will be thereby much lessened in the kingdom. This I freely own, and it was indeed one principal design in offering it to the world. I desire the reader will observe, that I calculate my remedy *for this one individual kingdom of Ireland, and for no other that ever was, is, or, I think, ever can be upon earth.* Therefore let no man talk to me of other expedients: *Of taxing our absentees at five shillings a pound: Of using neither clothes, nor household furniture, except what is of our own growth and manufacture: Of utterly rejecting the materials and instruments that promote foreign luxury: Of curing the expensiveness of pride,*

*vanity, idleness, and gaming in our women: Of introducing a vein
of parsimony, prudence and temperance: Of learning to love our
Country, wherein we differ even from* Laplanders, *and the inhabitants of* Topinamboo:[2] *Of quitting our animosities and fac-
tions, nor act any longer like the Jews, who were murdering one
another at the very moment their city was taken: Of being a little
cautious not to sell our country and conscience for nothing: Of
teaching landlords to have at least one degree of mercy toward
their tenants. Lastly of putting a spirit of honesty, industry, and
skill into our shopkeepers, who, if a resolution could now be
taken to buy only our native goods, would immediately unite to
cheat and exact upon us in the price, the measure, and the goodness, nor could ever yet be brought to make one fair proposal of
just dealing, though often and earnestly invited to it.*

Therefore I repeat, let no man talk to me of these and the like
expedients till he hath at least some glimpse of hope that there
will ever be some hearty and sincere attempt to put them in practice.

But as to myself, having been wearied out for many years with
offering vain, idle, visionary thoughts, and at length utterly de-
spairing of success, I fortunately fell upon this proposal, which
as it is wholly new, so it hath something solid and real, of no expense and little trouble, full in our own power, and whereby we
can incur no danger in *disobliging* ENGLAND. For this kind of
commodity will not bear exportation, the flesh being of too tender
a consistence to admit a long continuance in salt, *although perhaps I could name a country which would be glad to eat up our
whole nation without it.*

After all, I am not so violently bent upon my own opinion as to
reject any offer, proposed by wise men, which shall be found
equally innocent, cheap, easy and effectual. But before something
of that kind shall be advanced in contradiction to my scheme,
and offering a better, I desire the author or authors will be pleased
maturely to consider two points. First, as things now stand, how
they will be able to find food and raiment for an hundred thousand
useless mouths and backs. And secondly, there being a round
million of creatures in human figure throughout this kingdom,
whose whole subsistence put into a common stock would leave
them in debt two million pounds sterling, adding those who are
beggars by profession to the bulk of farmers, cottagers and la-

---

[2] *Topinamboo:* a part of Brazil thought to be inhabited by savages

bourers, with their wives and children, who are beggars in effect, I desire those politicians, who dislike my overture, and may perhaps be so bold as to attempt an answer, that they will first ask the parents of these mortals, whether they would not at this day think it a great happiness to have been sold for food at a year old, in the manner I prescribe, and thereby have avoided such a perpetual scene of misfortunes as they have since gone through by the oppression of landlords, the impossibility of paying rent without money or trade, the want of cómmon sustenance, with neither house nor clothes to cover them from the inclemencies of the weather, and the most inevitable prospect of entailing the like or greater miseries upon their breed for ever.

I profess, in the sincerity of my heart, that I have not the least personal interest in endeavouring to promote this necessary work, having no other motive than the *public good of my country, by advancing our trade, providing for infants, relieving the poor, and giving some pleasure to the rich.* I have no children by which I can propose to get a single penny; the youngest being nine years old, and my wife past child-bearing.

A MEDITATION UPON A BROOMSTICK

This single stick, which you now behold ingloriously lying in that neglected corner, I once knew in a flourishing state in a forest: it was full of sap, full of leaves, and full of boughs: but now, in vain does the busy art of man pretend to vie with nature, by tying that withered bundle of twigs to its sapless trunk; it is now, at best, but the reverse of what it was, a tree turned upside down, the branches on the earth, and the root in the air; it is now handled by every dirty wench, condemned to do her drudgery, and by a capricious kind of fate, destined to make other things clean, and be nasty itself: at length, worn to the stumps in the service of the maids, it is either thrown out of doors, or condemned to the last use, of kindling a fire. When I beheld this, I sighed, and said within myself, *Surely Man is a Broomstick!* Nature sent him into the world strong and lusty, in a thriving condition, wearing his own hair on his head, the proper branches of this reasoning vegetable, until the axe of intemperance has lopped off his green boughs, and left him a withered trunk: he then flies to art, and puts on a periwig, valuing himself upon an unnatural bundle of hairs (all covered with powder) that never grew on his head; but now, should this our broomstick pretend to enter the scene, proud of those birchen spoils it never bore, and all covered with dust, though the sweepings of the finest lady's chamber, we should be apt to ridicule and despise its vanity. Partial judges that we are of our own excellencies, and other men's defaults!

But a broomstick, perhaps you will say, is an emblem of a tree standing on its head; and pray what is man, but a topsy-turvy creature, his animal faculties perpetually mounted on his rational, his head where his heels should be, groveling on the earth! And yet, with all his faults, he sets up to be a universal reformer and corrector of abuses, a remover of grievances, rakes into every slut's corner of nature, bringing hidden corruption to the light, and raises a mighty dust where there was none before; sharing deeply all the while in the very same pollutions he pretends to sweep away: his last days are spent in slavery to women, and generally the least deserving; till worn out to the stumps, like his brother's besom, he is either kicked out of doors, or made use of to kindle flames for others to warm themselves by.

THOUGHTS FROM SWIFT'S NOTE-BOOK

• We have just religion enough to make us hate, but not enough to make us love one another.

• No preacher is listened to but Time, which gives us the same train and turn of thought that elder people have in vain tried to put into our heads before.

• All fits of pleasure are balanced by an equal degree of pain or languor; 'tis like spending this year part of the next year's revenue.

• When a true genius appears in the world, you may know him by this sign, that the dunces are all in confederacy against him.

• The stoical scheme of supplying our wants by lopping off our desires, is like cutting off our feet when we want shoes.

• The reason why so few marriages are happy, is, because young ladies spend their time in making nets, not in making cages.

• An idle reason lessens the weight of the good ones you gave before.

• Some people take more care to hide their wisdom than their folly.

• The humor of exploding many things under the name of trifles,

fopperies, and only imaginary goods, is a very false proof either
of wisdom or magnanimity, and a great check to virtuous actions.
For instance, with regard to fame; there is in most people a
reluctance and unwillingness to be forgotten. We observe even
among the vulgar, how fond they are to have an inscription over
their grave. It requires but little philosophy to discover and
observe that there is no intrinsic value in all this; however, if it
be founded in our nature, as an incitement to virtue, it ought not
to be ridiculed.

• The common fluency of speech in many men, and most women,
is owing to a scarcity of matter, and a scarcity of words; for whoever is a master of language, and has a mind full of ideas, will be
apt, in speaking, to hesitate upon the choice of both; whereas
common speakers have only one set of ideas, and one set of words
to clothe them in; and these are always ready at the mouth; so
people come faster out of a church when it is almost empty, than
when a crowd is at the door.

• Love of flattery, in most men, proceeds from the mean opinion
they have of themselves; in women, from the contrary.

• A very little wit is valued in a woman, as we are pleased with
a few words spoken plain by a parrot.

• If a man makes me keep my distance, the comfort is, he keeps
his at the same time.

• That was excellently observed, say I, when I read a passage
in an author where his opinion agrees with mine. When we differ,
there I pronounce him to be mistaken.

A GENTLE ECHO ON WOMAN

SHEPHERD: Echo, I ween, will in the woods reply,
             And quaintly answer questions. Shall I try?
ECHO: *Try.*

SHEPHERD: What must we do our passion to express?
ECHO: *Press.*

SHEPHERD: How shall I please her, who ne'er loved
                                        before?
ECHO: *Be fore.*

SHEPHERD: What most moves women when we them
                                                  address?
ECHO: *A dress.*

SHEPHERD: Say, what can keep her chaste whom I
                                                  adore?
ECHO: *A door.*

SHEPHERD: If music softens rocks, love tunes my lyre.
ECHO: *Liar.*

SHEPHERD: Then teach me, Echo, how shall I come
                                                  by her?
ECHO: *Buy her.*

SHEPHERD: But what can glad me when she's laid
                                                  on bier?
ECHO: *Beer.*

SHEPHERD: What must I do when women will be
                                                  kind?
ECHO: *Be kind.*

SHEPHERD: What must I do when women will be
                                                  cross?
ECHO: *Be cross.*

SHEPHERD: Lord, what is she that can so turn and
                                                  wind?
ECHO: *Wind.*

SHEPHERD: If she be wind, what stills her when she
                                                  blows?
ECHO: *Blows.*

SHEPHERD: But if she bang again, still should I
                                                  bang her?
ECHO: *Bang her.*

SHEPHERD: Is there no way to moderate her anger?
ECHO: *Hang her.*

SHEPHERD: Thanks, gentle Echo! right thy answers tell
                   What woman is and how to guard her well.
ECHO: *Guard her well.*

Joseph Addison

Son and grandson of a clergyman, Joseph Addison was born in his father's rectory in Wiltshire in 1672. He attended several schools, notably Charterhouse and Oxford, where he spent ten years acquiring a Master of Arts degree and the skill in Latin versification that won him a pension of one hundred pounds a year. With this income Addison traveled on the Continent, mingled with high society, and composed a classical tragedy, *Cato*.

In accordance with the custom of the times, which was to give royal sinecures to university men willing to eulogize the royal family and other notables, Addison composed *The Campaign*, a stilted and lifeless panegyric to the Duke of Marlborough, victor of Blenheim. It was enthusiastically received and opened the door to a long line of government preferments.

At thirty-six Addison entered the most rewarding period of his life. While he was stationed in Dublin on a diplomatic mission, he began to contribute short essays to *The Tatler*, a literary periodical founded and edited by his friend Richard Steele. *The Tatler* and its successor, *The Spectator*, combined wit and rationalism as they featured the diversions of London and the gossip of the coffee houses. In their pages the town comes vividly alive. Beaux and belles parade through the streets, attend a rehearsal of a new play, or listen to the latest satirical poem by Alexander Pope; the fashionable world of the early eighteenth century is pictured from the widest periwig to the smallest shoe buckle. Steele was interested in reforming morals and improving social conditions; Addison, the inexhaustible reporter and clubman, was content to smile at the fopperies and peccadilloes of his day. As the uncommitted bystander, Addison pointed out his position in one of his little essays:

> I live in the world rather as a "Spectator" of mankind than as one of the species; by which means I have made myself a speculative statesman, soldier, merchant, and artisan, without ever meddling in any practical part in life I am very well versed in the theory of a husband or a father, and can discern the errors in the economy, business, and diversions of others, better than those who are engaged in them. In short, I have acted, in all the parts of my life, as a looker-on, which is the character I intend to preserve in this paper.

For most of his life, Addison was also a looker-on at the matrimonial state. It was not until three years before his death that he married the widowed Charlotte, Countess-dowager of Warwick. The union was stately but barren. Addison's health grew steadily worse. He suffered from asthma accompanied by painful dropsy. Yet he was serene and ready for death when it came, sustained and comforted by the diffident acceptance of the ways of the world, which he had expressed with such grace and urbanity.

"Ned Softly the Poet" is an excellent example of Addison's humor. Suggested by Molière's *Les Précieuses Ridicules (The Ridiculously Precious Ladies)*, it is a characteristically Addisonian portrait of the eternal dilettante who is avid for any listener, but who will listen to nothing resembling criticism. "Dissection of a Coquette's Heart" is a masculine but not a malicious piece of raillery.

NED SOFTLY THE POET

I yesterday came hither about two hours before the company generally make their appearance, with a design to read over all the newspapers; but upon my sitting down, I was accosted by

Ned Softly, who saw me from a corner in the other end of the room, where I found he had been writing something. "Mr. Bicker-staff," says he, "I observe by a late paper of yours that you and I are just of a humor; for you must know, of all impertinences, there is nothing which I so much hate as news. I never read a Gazette in my life, and never trouble my head about our armies, whether they win or lose, or in what part of the world they lie encamped." Without giving me time to reply, he drew a paper of verses out of his pocket, telling me that he had something which would entertain me more agreeably, and that he would desire my judgment upon every line, for that we had time enough before us till the company came in.

Ned Softly is a very pretty poet, and a great admirer of easy lines. Waller is his favorite; and as that admirable writer has the best and worst verses of any among our great English poets, Ned Softly has got all the bad ones without book, which he repeats upon occasion, to show his reading and garnish his conversation. Ned is indeed a true English reader, incapable of relishing the great and masterly strokes of this art, but wonderfully pleased with the little Gothic ornaments of epigrammatical conceits, turns, points, and quibbles, which are so frequent in the most admired of our English poets, and practised by those who want genius and strength to represent, after the manner of the ancients, simplicity in its natural beauty and perfection.

Finding myself unavoidably engaged in such a conversation, I was resolved to turn my pain into a pleasure, and to divert myself as well as I could with so very odd a fellow. "You must understand," says Ned, "that the sonnet I am going to read to you was written upon a lady, who showed me some verses of her own making, and is, perhaps, the best poet of our age. But you shall hear it."

Upon which he began to read as follows:

TO MIRA ON HER INCOMPARABLE POEMS

When dressed in laurel wreaths you shine,
  And tune your soft melodious notes,
You seem a sister of the Nine,
  Or Phœbus' self in petticoats.

I fancy, when your song you sing,
  (Your song you sing with so much art)

Your pen was plucked from Cupid's wing;
  For, ah! it wounds me like his dart.

"Why," says I, "this is a little nosegay of conceits, a very lump of salt: every verse has something in it that piques; and then the *dart* in the last line is certainly as pretty a sting in the tail of an epigram, for so I think you critics call it, as ever entered into the thought of a poet." "Dear Mr. Bickerstaff," says he, shaking me by the hand, "everybody knows you to be a judge of these things; and to tell you truly, I read over Roscommon's translation of 'Horace's Art of Poetry,' three several times, before I sat down to write the sonnet which I have shown you. But you shall hear it again, and pray observe every line of it; for not one of them shall pass without your approbation.

When dressed in laurel wreaths you shine.

"That is," says he, "when you have your garland on; when you are writing verses." To which I replied, "I know your meaning: a metaphor!" "The same," said he, and went on:

"And tune your soft melodious notes.

"Pray observe the gliding of that verse; there is scarce a consonant in it: I took care to make it run upon liquids. Give me your opinion of it." "Truly," said I, "I think it as good as the former." "I am very glad to hear you say so," says he; "but mind the next:

You seem a sister of the Nine.

"That is," says he, "you seem a sister of the Muses; for if you look into ancient authors, you will find it was their opinion that there were nine of them." "I remember it very well," said I; "but pray proceed."

"Or Phœbus' self in petticoats.

"Phœbus," says he, "was the God of Poetry. These little instances, Mr. Bickerstaff, show a gentleman's reading. Then to take off from the air of learning, which Phœbus and the Muses have given to this first stanza, you may observe how it falls all of a sudden into the familiar, 'in petticoats!'

Or Phœbus' self in petticoats."

"Let us now," says I, "enter upon the second stanza. I find the first line is still a continuation of the metaphor:

I fancy, when your song you sing."

"It is very right," says he; "but pray observe the turn of words in those two lines. I was a whole hour in adjusting of them, and have still a doubt upon me, whether in the second line it should be, 'Your song you sing'; or, 'You sing your song'? You shall hear them both:

"I fancy when your song you sing
  (Your song you sing with so much art).
Or,
I fancy, when your song you sing
  (You sing your song with so much art.)"

"Truly," said I, "the turn is so natural either way that you have made me almost giddy with it." "Dear sir," said he, grasping me by the hand, "you have a great deal of patience; but pray what do you think of the next verse:

Your pen was plucked from Cupid's wing?"

"Think!" says I; "I think you have made Cupid look like a little goose." "That was my meaning," says he; "I think the ridicule is well enough hit off. But we now come to the last, which sums up the whole matter:

For, ah! it wounds me like his dart.

"Pray, how do you like that 'Ah!' Does it not make a pretty figure in that place? *Ah!*——it looks as if I felt the dart, and cried out as being pricked with it!

For, ah! it wounds me like his dart.

"My friend Dick Easy," continued he, "assured me, he would rather have written that *Ah!* than to have been the author of the Æneid. He indeed objected, that I made Mira's pen like a quill in one of the lines, and like a dart in the other. But as to that——"
"Oh! as to that," says I, "it is but supposing Cupid to be like a porcupine, and his quills and darts will be the same thing." He was going to embrace me for the hint; but half a dozen critics coming into the room, whose faces he did not like, he conveyed the sonnet into his pocket, and whispered me in the ear, "he would show it me again as soon as his man had written it over fair."

DISSECTION OF A COQUETTE'S HEART

Having already given an account of the dissection of a beau's head, with the several discoveries made on that occasion, I shall here, according to my promise, enter upon the dissection of a coquette's heart and communicate to the public such particularities as we observed in that curious piece of anatomy.

I should, perhaps, have waived this undertaking, had not I been put in mind of my promise by several of my unknown correspondents, who are very importunate with me to make an example of the coquette, as I have already done of the beau. It is, therefore, in compliance with the request of friends, that I have looked over the minutes of my former dream, in order to give the public an exact relation of it, which I shall enter upon without further preface.

Our operator, before he engaged in this visionary dissection, told us, that there was nothing in his art more difficult, than to lay open the heart of a coquette, by reason of the many labyrinths and recesses which are to be found in it, and which do not appear in the heart of any other animal.

He desired us first of all to observe the *pericardium,* or outward case of the heart, which we did very attentively; and, by the help of our glasses, discerned in it millions of little scars, which seemed to have been occasioned by the points of innumerable darts and arrows, that from time to time had glanced upon the outward coat; though we could not discover the smallest orifice, by which any of them had entered and pierced the inward substance.

Every smatterer in anatomy knows that this *pericardium,* or case of the heart, contains in it a thin reddish liquor, supposed to be bred from the vapors which exhale out of the heart, and being stopped here, are condensed into this watery substance. Upon examining this liquor, we found that it had in it all the qualities of that spirit which is made use of in the thermometer to show the change of weather.

Nor must I here omit an experiment one of the company assured us he himself had made with this liquor, which he found in great quantity about the heart of a coquette whom he had formerly dissected. He affirmed to us, that he had actually enclosed it in a small tube made after the manner of a weatherglass; but that, instead of acquainting him with the variations of the atmosphere, it showed him the qualities of those persons who entered the room where it stood. He affirmed also, that it rose at the approach of a plume of feathers, an embroidered coat, or a pair of fringed gloves; and that it fell as soon as an ill-shaped periwig, a clumsy pair of shoes, or an unfashionable coat came into his house: nay, he proceeded so far as to assure us, that upon his laughing aloud when he stood by it, the liquor mounted very sensibly, and immediately sunk again upon his looking serious. In short, he told us that he knew very well by this invention whenever he had a man of sense or a coxcomb in his room.

Having cleared away the *pericardium,* or the case, and liquor above mentioned, we came to the heart itself. The outward surface of it was extremely slippery, and the *mucro,* or point, so very cold withal that, upon endeavoring to take hold of it, it glided through the fingers like a smooth piece of ice.

The fibres were turned and twisted in a more intricate and perplexed manner than they are usually found in other hearts; insomuch, that the whole heart was wound up together like a Gordian knot, and must have had very irregular and unequal motions, whilst it was employed in its vital function.

One thing we thought very observable, namely, that upon examining all the vessels which came into it or issued out of it, we could not discover any communication that it had with the tongue.

We could not but take notice, likewise, that several of those little nerves in the heart, which are affected by the sentiments of love, hatred, and other passions, did not descend to this before us from the brain, but from the muscles which lie about the eye.

Upon weighing the heart in my hand, I found it to be extremely light, and consequently very hollow; which I did not wonder at, when, upon looking into the inside of it, I saw multitudes of cells and cavities running one within another, as our historians describe the apartments of Rosamond's Bower.[1] Several of these little hollows were stuffed with innumerable sorts of trifles, which I shall forbear giving any particular account of, and shall therefore only take notice of what lay first and uppermost, which, upon our unfolding it and applying our microscope to it, appeared to be a flame-colored hood.

We were informed that the lady of this heart, when living, received the addresses of several who made love to her, and did

---

[1] *Rosamond's Bower:* a subterranean maze in Blenheim Park built by Henry II for his mistress, Rosamond Clifford

not only give each of them encouragement, but made everyone she conversed with believe that she regarded him with an eye of kindness; for which reason we expected to have seen the impression of multitudes of faces among the several plaits and foldings of the heart; but, to our great surprise, not a single print of this nature discovered itself, till we came into the very core and centre of it. We there observed a little figure, which, upon applying our glasses to it, appeared dressed in a very fantastic manner. The more I looked upon it, the more I thought I had seen the face before, but could not possibly recollect either the place or time; when at length one of the company, who had examined this figure more nicely than the rest, showed us plainly by the make of its face, and the several turns of its features, that the little idol that was thus lodged in the middle of the heart was the deceased beau, whose head I gave some account of in my last Tuesday's paper.

As soon as we had finished our dissection, we resolved to make an experiment of the heart, not being able to determine among ourselves the nature of its substance, which differed in so many particulars from that of the heart in other females. Accordingly we laid it into a pan of burning coals, when we observed in it a certain salamandrine quality, that made it capable of living in the midst of fire and flame, without being consumed, or so much as singed.

As we were admiring this strange phenomenon, and standing round the heart in a circle, it gave a most prodigious sigh, or rather crack, and dispersed all at once in smoke and vapor. This imaginary noise, which methought was louder than the burst of a cannon, produced such a violent shake in my brain, that it dissipated the fumes of sleep, and left me in an instant broad awake.

John Gay

Town humor was extended by John Gay in lighthearted poems and laugh-provoking plays. An urban wit who celebrated the country and a countryman who loved the city, he was born at Barnstaple in the west of England in 1685. His parents died while he was a child and he was apprenticed to a London silk merchant. Released by his master, he turned to poetry and in his twenties won the applause and friendship of Pope. *Trivia, or the Art of Walking the Streets of London* was aided by Swift, and *Poems on Several Occasions* brought him a thousand pounds, which he lost in the financial scandal of the day, the collapse of the South Sea Company. He died in his mid-forties and was buried in Westminster Abbey. His epitaph was written by Pope, but underneath was added Gay's much-quoted couplet:

Life is a jest and all things show it.
I thought so once, and now I know it.

Gay's *Fables* are the English reply to La Fontaine's. They go further in mockery and a little deeper in worldly wisdom; they are shrewd without being savage, amiable rather than acerb. Gay's most important as well as his most successful work is *The Beggar's Opera*, which, produced by John Rich, "made Rich gay and Gay rich." A pastoral turned upside down, *The Beggar's Opera* caricatures the corruption and chicanery of the period. The traditional nymphs have become hussies; the shepherds are thieves and brigands; the parents are procurers and receivers of stolen goods. The bouncing crew of highwaymen and cutpurses entertained Gay's audiences on two levels: as a rowdy farce and as an easily recognizable exposure of the governing classes. Bertolt Brecht and Kurt Weill gave it new life in their *Dreigroschenoper*, which became a prominent part of the repertoire of the English theater as *The Three Penny Opera*.

THE LION, THE FOX, AND THE GEESE

A Lion, tired with state affairs,
Quite sick of pomp, and worn with cares,
Resolved (remote from noise and strife)
In peace to pass his latter life.
    It was proclaim'd; the day was set;
Behold the gen'ral council met.
The Fox was Viceroy named. The crowd
To the new Regent humbly bow'd.
Wolves, bears, and mighty tigers bend,
And strive who most shall condescend.
He straight assumes a solemn grace,
Collects his wisdom in his face.
The crowd admire his wit, his sense:
Each word hath weight and consequence.
The flatt'rer all his art displays:
He who hath power, is sure of praise.
A Fox stept forth before the rest,
And thus the servile throng addrest:
    "How vast his talents, born to rule,
And train'd in virtue's honest school!
What clemency his temper sways!
How uncorrupt are all his ways!
Beneath his conduct and command,
Rapine shall cease to waste the land.
His brain hath stratagem and art;
Prudence and mercy rule his heart.
What blessings must attend the nation
Under this good administration!"
    He said. A Goose who distant stood,
Harangued apart the cackling brood:

"Whene'er I hear a knave commend,
He bids me shun his worthy friend.
What praise! what mighty commendation!
But 'twas a Fox who spoke th' oration.
Foxes this government may prize,
As gentle, plentiful, and wise;
If they enjoy these sweets, 'tis plain
We Geese must feel a tyrant reign.
What havoc now shall thin our race,
When ev'ry petty clerk in place,
To prove his taste, and seem polite,
Will feed on Geese both noon and night!"

THE LADY AND THE WASP

What whispers must the beauty bear!
What hourly nonsense haunts her ear!
Where'er her eycs dispense their charms,
Impertinence around her swarms.
Did not the tender nonsense strike,
Contempt and scorn might look dislike,
Forbidding airs might thin the place,
The slightest flap a fly can chase.
But who can drive the num'rous breed?
Chase one, another will succeed.
Who knows a fool, must know his brother;
One fop will recommend another:
And with this plague she's rightly curst,
Because she listen'd to the first.
    As Doris, at her toilet's duty,
Sat meditating on her beauty,
She now was pensive, now was gay,
And loll'd the sultry hours away.
    As thus in indolence she lies,
A giddy Wasp around her flies:
He now advances, now retires,
Now to her neck and cheek aspires.
Her fan in vain defends her charms;
Swift he returns, again alarms;
For by repulse he bolder grew,
Perch'd on her lip, and sipt the dew.

She frowns, she frets. "Good gods!" she cries,
"Protect me from these teasing flies!
Of all the plagues that heav'n hath sent,
A Wasp is most impertinent."
   The hov'ring insect thus complain'd:
"Am I then slighted, scorn'd, disdain'd?
Can such offence your anger wake?
'Twas beauty caused the bold mistake.
Those cherry lips that breathe perfume,
That cheek so ripe with youthful bloom,
Made me with strong desire pursue
The fairest peach that ever grew."
   "Strike him not, Jenny," Doris cries,
"Nor murder Wasps like vulgar flies:
For though he's free (to do him right),
The creature's civil and polite."
   In ecstasies away he posts;
Where'er he came, the favour boasts;
Brags how her sweetest tea he sips,
And shows the sugar on his lips.
   The hint alarm'd the forward crew.
Sure of success, away they flew.
They share the dainties of the day,
Round her with airy music play;
And now they flutter, now they rest,
Now soar again, and skim her breast.
Nor were they banish'd, till she found
That Wasps have stings, and felt the wound.

THE BUTTERFLY AND THE SNAIL

All upstarts insolent in place,
Remind us of their vulgar race.
   As, in the sunshine of the morn,
A Butterfly (but newly born)
Sat proudly perking on a rose,
With pert conceit his bosom glows;
His wings (all-glorious to behold)
Bedropt with azure, jet, and gold,
Wide he displays; the spangled dew
Reflects his eyes, and various hue.

His now-forgotten friend a Snail,
Beneath his house, with slimy trail
Crawls o'er the grass; whom when he spies,
In wrath he to the gard'ners cries:
    "What means yon peasant's daily toil,
From choking weeds to rid the soil?
Why wake you to the morning's care?
Why with new arts correct the year?
Why glows the peach with crimson hue?
And why the plums inviting blue?
Were they to feast his taste design'd,
That vermin of voracious kind?
Crush then the slow, the pilf'ring race;
So purge thy garden from disgrace."
    "What arrogance!" the Snail replied;
"How insolent is upstart pride!
Hadst thou not thus with insult vain,
Provoked my patience to complain,
I had conceal'd thy meaner birth,
Nor traced thee to the scum of earth.
For scarce nine suns have waked the hours,
To swell the fruit, and paint the flowers,
Since I thy humbler life survey'd.
In base, in sordid guise array'd;
A hideous insect, vile, unclean,
You dragg'd a slow and noisome train;
And from your spider-bowels drew
Foul film, and spun the dirty clue.
I own my humble life, good friend;
Snail was I born, and Snail shall end.
And what's a Butterfly? At best,
He's but a caterpillar, drest;
And all thy race (a numerous seed)
Shall prove of caterpillar breed."

THE POET AND THE ROSE

I hate the man who builds his name
On ruins of another's fame.
Thus scribblers, covetous of praise,
Think slander can transplant the bays.

Beauties and bards have equal pride—
With both all rivals are decried. . . .

As in the cool of early day,
A poet sought the sweets of May,
The garden's favorite breath ascends
And every stalk with odor bends.
A rose he plucked. He gazed, admired,
Thus singing, by the Muse inspired:

"Go, rose, my Chloe's bosom grace.
   How happy should I prove,
Might I supply that envied place
   With never-fading love!
There, phoenix-like, beneath her eye,
Involved in fragrance, burn, and die.
Know, hapless flower, that thou shalt find
   More fragrant perfume there;
I see thy withering head declined
   With envy and despair.
One common fate we both must prove:
You die with envy, I with love."

"Spare your comparisons!" replied
An angry rose who grew beside.
"Of all mankind you should not flout us.
What could a poet do without us?
In every love-song roses bloom;
We lend you color and perfume.
Does it to Chloe's charms conduce
To found her praise on our abuse?
Must we, to flatter her, be made
To wither, envy, pine, and fade?"

SONGS FROM THE BEGGAR'S OPERA

1
A fox may steal your hens, sir,
A whore your health and pence, sir,
Your daughter rob your chest, sir,
Your wife may steal your rest, sir,

A thief your goods and plate.
But this is all but picking;
With rest, peace, chest, and chicken,
It ever was decreed, sir,
If lawyer's hand is fee'd, sir,
    He steals your whole estate.

2

Fill ev'ry glass, for wine inspires us,
    And fires us,
With courage, love, and joy.
Women and wine should life employ.
    Is there aught else in life desirous?

3

Man may escape from rope and gun,
    Nay, some have outlived the doctor's pill,
But who takes a woman must be undone,
    That basilisk is sure to kill.
The fly that tastes treacle is lost in the sweets,
    So he that tastes woman, woman, woman,
He that tastes woman, ruin meets!

4

If you at an office solicit your due
    And would not have matters neglected,
You must quicken the clerk with the perquisite, too,
    To do what his duty directed.
Or would you the frowns of a lady prevent,
    She, too, has this palpable failing,
The perquisite softens her into consent:
    That reason with all is prevailing.

Alexander Pope

A hunchback who fashioned the shapeliest English verse, a malignant dwarf whose neatly turned phrases have become priceless proverbs, Alexander Pope was born in London on May 21, 1688. His life, he said, was "one long disease." He was handicapped not only by a deformed body but by his religion. As a cripple he could not take part in normal activities; as a Roman Catholic he was barred from universities and political preferment. In compensation, nature made him a prodigy. At ten he translated Greek and Latin; at seventeen he was recognized as a genius; at twenty-five he was a literary dictator. Men and women slighted him at their peril; they knew they would be impaled upon the barbs of his wit or dismembered for faults they did not possess. It was said that Pope could not sit down to tea without a stratagem.

Satire was his element as well as his livelihood. Pope claimed that he employed satire only for moral purposes; in "Epilogue to the Satires" he declared:

> O sacred weapon! left for Truth's defence,
> Sole dread of Folly, Vice, and Insolence!
> To all but Heaven-directed hands denied,
> The Muse may give thee, but the Gods must guide.
> Reverent I touch thee! but with honest zeal
> To rouse the watchman of the public weal.

Pope rarely lived up to these high-sounding sentiments and lofty lines. Unlike Dryden, who was scrupulous in attack, Pope was savage and unprincipled. *The Dunciad* broke minor versifiers, those ephemeral butterflies, upon a wheel of ridicule; the *Epistle to Dr. Arbuthnot,* a furious version of Dryden's *Mac Flecknoe,* is, unlike Dryden's fine-edged sword, a spiked bludgeon. Dryden's literary offspring, Pope surpassed his predecessor in technical performance. He brought to perfection the heroic couplet with its compressed thought, its clinched epigrammatic force, and its sharply emphasizing rhymes, little hammer-blows of sound and sense that were in themselves witticisms. If Jean de la Fontaine was "the butterfly of Parnassus," Pope was its gadfly. He "improved" the classics; he modernized Chaucer and gave the *Odyssey* a brisk English inflection. But "the high priest of an age of reason" was at his best, and, perversely enough, happiest when his pen was dipped in venom. His *Epistles* scarcely troubled to veil their calumnies and libels; *Imitations of Horace* served as a camouflage for unprovoked injuries added to unscrupulous insults.

The Rape of the Lock is a lighter satire; Pope's quick eye turned a foible of the day into a masterpiece of wit. A certain Lord Petre had clandestinely snipped a lock of hair from a Miss Arabella Fermor. The liberty was resented and grew into a scandal, a social tempest in China teacups. Pope expanded the subject and treated it as a mock epic. Dedicated to the lady, faintly disguised as Belinda, it is a teasing tribute to artifice and at the same time an acidulous parody of it, a pasquinade of style.

It is, however, neither his stylistic brilliance nor his nimble technique—chief desiderata of the eighteenth century—that insures Pope's permanent viability. Unaware of their source, unconscious of the rhymed dexterities, millions continue to quote his aphorisms: "To err is human, to forgive divine," "Hope springs eternal in the human breast," "Fools rush in where angels fear to tread," "A little learning is a dangerous thing," "An honest man's the noblest work of God," "Whatever is, is right," "Order is heaven's first law," "Damn with faint praise," "Guide, philosopher, and friend," "The proper study of mankind is man." The personal rancor is forgotten; the penetrating phrases remain.

EPISTLE TO DR. ARBUTHNOT
PORTRAIT OF ATTICUS

Peace to all such! but were there one whose fires
True genius kindles, and fair fame inspires;
Blest with each talent and each art to please,
And born to write, converse, and live with ease;
Should such a man, too fond to rule alone,
Bear, like the Turk, no brother near the throne,
View him with scornful, yet with jealous eyes,
And hate for arts that caused himself to rise;
Damn with faint praise, assent with civil leer,
And without sneering, teach the rest to sneer:
Willing to wound, and yet afraid to strike,
Just hint a fault, and hesitate dislike;
Alike reserved to blame, or to commend,
A timorous foe, and a suspicious friend;
Dreading ev'n fools, by flatt'rers besieged,
And so obliging, that he ne'er obliged;
Like Cato, give his little senate laws,
And sit attentive to his own applause;
While wits and templars every sentence raise,
And wonder with a foolish face of praise:—
Who but must laugh, if such a man there be?
Who would not weep, if Atticus[1] were he?

PORTRAIT OF SPORUS

Let Sporus[2] tremble—What? that Thing of silk,
Sporus, that mere white curd of ass's milk?
Satire, or sense alas! can Sporus feel?

---

[1] *Atticus:* a transparent disguise for Addison. Once a good friend of Pope's, Addison had praised two translations of Homer, one by Pope and one by Thomas Tickell, but he made the mistake of saying that Tickell's was closer to the original. Pope never forgave him. What begins as a tribute to Addison develops into censure and ends in scorn.
[2] *Sporus:* one of Nero's degenerate favorites whom Pope likens to Lord John Hervey. Pope does not actually accuse Hervey of homosexuality, but he implies that sexual ambivalence ("Now high, now low, now Master up, now Miss,/And he himself one vile antithesis") is the least of Hervey's indecencies. In this portrait Pope dispenses with his usual sly sarcasm in favor of unrestrained loathing.

Who breaks a butterfly upon a wheel?
Yet let me flap this Bug with gilded wings,
This painted Child of Dirt that stinks and stings;
Whose buzz the Witty and the Fair annoys,
Yet wit ne'er tastes, and beauty ne'er enjoys;
So well-bred spaniels civilly delight
In mumbling of the game they dare not bite.
Eternal smiles his emptiness betray,
As shallow streams run dimpling all the way.
Whether in florid impotence he speaks,
And, as the prompter breathes, the puppet squeaks;
Or at the ear of Eve, familiar toad,
Half froth, half venom, spits himself abroad,
In puns, or politics, or tales, or lies,
Or spite, or smut, or rhymes, or blasphemies.
His wit all see-saw between *that* and *this,*
Now high, now low, now Master up, now Miss,
And he himself one vile antithesis.
Amphibious Thing! that acting either part,
The trifling Head, or the corrupted Heart!
Fop at the toilet, flatt'rer at the board,
Now trips a Lady, and now struts a Lord.
Eve's Tempter thus the Rabbins have express'd,
A Cherub's face, a Reptile all the rest,
Beauty that shocks you, parts that none will trust,
Wit that can creep, and pride that licks the dust.

THE RAPE OF THE LOCK

CANTO I

What dire offence from amorous causes springs,
What mighty contests rise from trivial things,
I sing—This verse to CARYL,[1] Muse! is due:
This, even Belinda may vouchsafe to view:
Slight is the subject, but not so the praise,
If She inspire, and He approve my lays.
Say what strange motive, Goddess! could compel
A well-bred Lord to assault a gentle Belle?

---

[1] *Caryl:* John Caryl, common friend of Pope, Petre (the "Baron"), and Miss Fermor ("Belinda")

O say what stranger cause, yet unexplored,
Could make a gentle Belle reject a Lord?
In tasks so bold, can little men engage,
And in soft bosoms dwells such mighty Rage?
   Sol through white curtains shot a timorous ray,
And oped those eyes that must eclipse the day:
Now lap-dogs give themselves the rousing shake,
And sleepless lovers, just at twelve, awake:
Thrice rung the bell, the slipper knocked the ground,[2]
And the pressed watch returned a silver sound.
Belinda still her downy pillow prest,
Her guardian SYLPH prolonged the balmy rest:
'Twas He had summoned to her silent bed
The morning-dream that hovered o'er her head;
A Youth more glittering than a Birth-night Beau
(That even in slumber caused her cheek to glow),
Seemed to her ear his winning lips to lay,
And thus in whispers said, or seemed to say:
   "Fairest of mortals, thou distinguished care
Of thousand bright Inhabitants of Air!
If e'er one vision touched thy infant thought,
Of all the Nurse and all the Priest have taught;
Of airy Elves by moonlight shadows seen,
The silver token, and the circled green,
Or virgins visited by Angel-powers,
With golden crowns and wreaths of heavenly flowers;
Hear and believe! thy own importance know,
Nor bound thy narrow views to things below.
Some secret truths, from learned pride concealed,
To Maids alone and Children are revealed:
What though no credit doubting Wits may give?
The Fair and Innocent shall still believe.
Know, then, unnumbered Spirits round thee fly,
The light Militia of the lower sky:
These, though unseen, are ever on the wing,
Hang o'er the Box, and hover round the Ring.[3]
Think what an equipage thou hast in Air,
And view with scorn two Pages and a Chair.
As now your own, our beings were of old,

---

[2] *knocked the ground:* called the maid
[3] *Ring:* the riding ring in Hyde Park

And once inclosed in Woman's beauteous mould;
Thence, by a soft transition, we repair
From earthly Vehicles to these of air.
Think not, when Woman's transient breath is fled,
That all her vanities at once are dead.
For when the Fair in all their pride expire,
To their first Elements their Souls retire:
The Sprites of fiery Termagants in Flame
Mount up, and take a Salamander's name.
Soft yielding minds to Water glide away,
And sip, with Nymphs, their elemental Tea.
The graver Prude sinks downward to a Gnome,
In search of mischief still on Earth to roam.
The light Coquettes in Sylphs aloft repair,
And sport and flutter in the fields of Air.
   Know further yet: whoever fair and chaste
Rejects mankind, is by some Sylph embraced:
For Spirits, freed from mortal laws, with ease
Assume what sexes and what shapes they please.
What guards the purity of melting Maids,
In courtly balls, and midnight masquerades,
Safe from the treacherous friend, the daring spark,
The glance by day, the whisper in the dark,
When kind occasion prompts their warm desires,
When music softens, and when dancing fires?
'Tis but their Sylph, the wise Celestials know,
Though Honor is the word with Men below.
   Some nymphs there are, too conscious of their face,
For life predestined to the Gnomes' embrace.
These swell their prospects and exalt their pride,
When offers are disdained, and love denied:
Then gay Ideas crowd the vacant brain,
While Peers, and Dukes, and all their sweeping train,
And Garters, Stars, and Coronets appear,
And in soft sounds, Your Grace salutes their ear.
'Tis these that early taint the female soul,
Instruct the eyes of young Coquettes to roll,
Teach Infant-cheeks a bidden blush to know,
And little hearts to flutter at a Beau.
   Oft, when the world imagine women stray,
The Sylphs through mystic mazes guide their way;
Through all the giddy circle they pursue,
And old impertinence expel by new.

What tender maid but must a victim fall
To one man's treat, but for another's ball?
When Florio speaks what virgin could withstand,
If gentle Damon did not squeeze her hand?
With varying vanities, from every part,
They shift the moving Toyshop of their heart;
Where wigs with wigs, with sword-knots sword-knots strive,
Beaux banish beaux, and coaches coaches drive.
This erring mortals Levity may call;
Oh blind to truth! the Sylphs contrive it all.
    Of these am I, who thy protection claim,
A watchful sprite, and Ariel is my name.
Late, as I ranged the crystal wilds of air,
In the clear Mirror of thy ruling star
I saw, alas! some dread event impend,
Ere to the main this morning sun descend,
But heaven reveals not what, or how, or where:
Warned by the Sylph, oh pious maid, beware!
This to disclose is all thy guardian can:
Beware of all, but most beware of man!"
    He said; when Shock,⁴ who thought she slept too
        long,
Leaped up, and waked his mistress with his tongue.
'Twas then, Belinda, if report say true,
Thy eyes first opened on a Billet-doux;
Wounds, Charms, and Ardors were no sooner read,
But all the vision vanished from thy head.
    And now, unveiled, the Toilet stands displayed,
Each silver Vase in mystic order laid.
First, robed in white, the Nymph intent adores,
With head uncovered, the Cosmetic powers,
A heavenly image in the glass appears,
To that she bends, to that her eyes she rears;
Th' inferior Priestess,⁵ at her altar's side,
Trembling begins the sacred rites of Pride.
Unnumbered treasures ope at once, and here
The various offerings of the world appear;
From each she nicely culls with curious toil,
And decks the Goddess with the glittering spoil.
This casket India's glowing gems unlocks,

---

⁴ *Shock:* Belinda's dog
⁵ *Inferior Priestess:* the maid

And all Arabia breathes from yonder box.
The Tortoise here and Elephant unite,
Transformed to combs, the speckled and the white.
Here files of pins extend their shining rows,
Puffs, Powders, Patches, Bibles, Billet-doux.
Now awful Beauty puts on all its arms;
The Fair each moment rises in her charms,
Repairs her smiles, awakens every grace,
And calls forth all the wonders of her face;
Sees by degrees a purer blush arise,
And keener lightnings quicken in her eyes.
The busy Sylphs surround their darling care,
These set the head, and those divide the hair,
Some fold the sleeve, whilst others plait the gown;
And Betty's praised for labors not her own.

CANTO II

Not with more glories, in the ethereal plain,
The Sun first rises o'er the purpled main,
Than, issuing forth, the rival of his beams
Launched on the bosom of the silver Thames.
Fair Nymphs and well-drest Youths around her
    shone,
But every eye was fixed on her alone.
On her white breast a sparkling Cross she wore.
Which Jews might kiss, and Infidels adore.
Her lively looks a sprightly mind disclose,
Quick as her eyes, and as unfixed as those:
Favors to none, to all she smiles extends;
Oft she rejects, but never once offends.
Bright as the sun, her eyes the gazers strike,
And, like the sun, they shine on all alike.
Yet graceful ease, and sweetness void of pride,
Might hide her faults, if Belles had faults to hide:
If to her share some female errors fall,
Look on her face, and you'll forget 'em all.
    This Nymph, to the destruction of mankind,
Nourished two Locks, which graceful hung behind
In equal curls, and well conspired to deck
With shining ringlets the smooth ivory neck.

Love in these labyrinths his slaves detains,
And mighty hearts are held in slender chains.
With hairy springes⁶ we the birds betray,
Slight lines of hair surprise the finny prey,
Fair tresses man's imperial race ensnare,
And beauty draws us with a single hair.
   The adventurous Baron the bright locks admired;
He saw, he wished, and to the prize aspired.
Resolved to win, he meditates the way,
By force to ravish, or by fraud betray;
For when success a Lover's toil attends,
Few ask, if fraud or force attained his ends.
   For this, ere Phoebus rose, he had implored
Propitious heaven, and every power adored,
But chiefly Love—to Love an Altar built,
Of twelve vast French Romances, neatly gilt.
There lay three garters, half a pair of gloves;
And all the trophies of his former loves;
With tender Billet-doux he lights the pyre,
And breathes three amorous sighs to raise the fire.
Then prostrate falls, and begs with ardent eyes
Soon to obtain, and long possess the prize;
The powers gave ear, and granted half his prayer,
The rest, the winds dispersed in empty air.
   But now secure the painted vessel glides,
The sun-beams trembling on the floating tides:
While melting music steals upon the sky,
And softened sounds along the waters die;
Smooth flow the waves, the Zephyrs gently play,
Belinda smiled, and all the world was gay.
All but the Sylph—with careful thoughts opprest,
The impending woe sat heavy on his breast.
He summons straight his Denizens of air;
The lucid squadrons around the sails repair;
Soft o'er the shrouds aërial whispers breathe,
That seemed but Zephyrs to the train beneath.
Some to the sun their insect-wings unfold,
Waft on the breeze, or sink in clouds of gold;
Transparent forms, too fine for mortal sight,
Their fluid bodies half dissolved in light,

---

⁶*hairy springes:* snares made of horsehair

Loose to the wind their airy garments flew,
Thin glittering textures of the filmy dew,
Dipt in the richest tincture of the skies,
Where light disports in every-mingling dyes,
While every beam new transient colors flings,
Colors that change whene'er they wave their wings.
Amid the circle, on the gilded mast,
Superior by the head, was Ariel placed;
His purple pinions opening to the sun,
He raised his azure wand, and thus begun:

"Ye Sylphs and Sylphids, to your chief give ear!
Fays, Fairies, Genii, Elves, and Daemons, hear!
Ye know the spheres and various tasks assigned
By laws eternal to the aërial kind.
Some in the fields of purest Aether play,
And bask and whiten in the blaze of day.
Some guide the course of wandering orbs on high,
Or roll the planets through the boundless sky.
Some less refined, beneath the moon's pale light
Pursue the stars that shoot athwart the night,
Or suck the mists in grosser air below,
Or dip their pinions in the painted bow,
Or brew fierce tempests on the wintry main,
Or o'er the glebe distil the kindly rain.
Others on earth o'er human race preside,
Watch all their ways, and all their actions guide:
Of these the chief the care of Nations own,
And guard with Arms divine the British throne.
    Our humbler province is to tend the Fair,
Not a less pleasing, though less glorious care;
To save the powder from too rude a gale,
Nor let the imprisoned essences exhale;
To draw fresh colors from the vernal flowers;
To steal from rainbows ere they drop in showers
A brighter wash; to curl their waving hairs,
Assist their blushes, and inspire their airs;
Nay oft, in dreams, invention we bestow,
To change a Flounce, or add a Furbelow.
    This day, black Omens threat the brightest Fair
That e'er deserved a watchful spirit's care;
Some dire disaster, or by force, or slight;

But what, or where, the fates have wrapt in night.
Whether the nymph shall break Diana's law,
Or some frail China jar receive a flaw;
Or stain her honor or her new brocade;
Forget her prayers, or miss a masquerade;
Or lose her heart, or necklace, at a ball;
Or whether Heaven has doomed that Shock must fall.
Haste, then, ye spirits! to your charge repair:
The fluttering fan be Zephyretta's care;
The drops to thee, Brillante, we consign;
And, Momentilla, let the watch be thine;
Do thou, Crispissa, tend her favorite Lock;
Ariel himself shall be the guard of Shock.
   To fifty chosen Sylphs, of special note,
We trust the important charge, the Petticoat:
Oft have we known that seven-fold fence to fail,
Though stiff with hoops, and armed with ribs of whale;
Form a strong line about the silver bound,
And guard the wide circumference around."

   He spoke; the spirits from the sails descend;
Some, orb in orb, around the nymph extend;
Some thrid the mazy ringlets of her hair;
Some hang upon the pendants of her ear;
With beating hearts the dire event they wait,
Anxious, and trembling for the birth of Fate.

CANTO III

   Close by those meads, for ever crowned with
      flowers,
Where Thames with pride surveys his rising towers,
There stands a structure of majestic frame,
Which from the neighboring Hampton takes its name.
Here Britain's statesmen oft the fall foredoom
Of foreign tyrants and of nymphs at home;
Here thou, great ANNA! whom three realms obey,
Dost sometimes counsel take—and sometimes Tea.
   Hither the heroes and the nymphs resort,
To taste awhile the pleasures of a Court;
In various talk the instructive hours they past,
Who gave the ball, or paid the visit last;

One speaks the glory of the British Queen,
And one describes a charming Indian screen;
A third interprets motions, looks, and eyes;
At every word a reputation dies.
Snuff, or the fan, supply each pause of chat,
With singing, laughing, ogling, and all that.
    Meanwhile, declining from the noon of day,
The sun obliquely shoots his burning ray;
The hungry Judges soon the Sentence sign,
And wretches hang that jurymen may dine;
The merchant from the Exchange returns in peace,
And the long labors of the Toilet cease. . . .
    For lo! the board with cups and spoons is crowned,
The berries crackle, and the mill turns round;[7]
On shining Altars of Japan they raise
The silver lamp; the fiery spirits blaze:
From silver spouts the grateful liquors glide,
While China's earth receives the smoking tide:
At once they gratify their scent and taste,
And frequent cups prolong the rich repast.
Straight hover round the Fair her airy band;
Some, as she sipped, the fuming liquor fanned,
Some o'er her lap their careful plumes displayed,
Trembling, and conscious of the rich brocade.
Coffee (which makes the politician wise,
And see through all things with his half-shut eyes),
Sent up in vapors to the Baron's brain
New Stratagems, the radiant Lock to gain. . . .
    But when to mischief mortals bend their will,
How soon they find fit instruments of ill!
Just then, Clarissa drew with tempting grace
A two-edged weapon from her shining case:
So Ladies in Romance assist their Knight,
Present the spear, and arm him for the fight.
He takes the gift with reverence, and extends
The little engine on his fingers' ends;
This just behind Belinda's neck he spread,
As o'er the fragrant steams she bends her head.
Swift, to the Lock a thousand Sprites repair,

---

[7] berries . . . round: the berries (coffee beans) were ground on a sideboard by the ladies

A thousand wings, by turns, blow back the hair;
And thrice they twitched the diamond in her ear;
Thrice she looked back, and thrice the foe drew near.
Just in that instant, anxious Ariel sought
The close recesses of the Virgin's thought;
As on the nosegay in her breast reclined,
He watched the Ideas rising in her mind,
Sudden he viewed, in spite of all her art,
An earthy Lover lurking at her heart,
Amazed, confused, he found his power expired,
Resigned to fate, and with a sigh retired.
　　The Peer now spreads the glittering Forfex[8] wide,
To inclose the Lock; now joins it, to divide.
Even then, before the fatal engine closed,
A wretched Sylph too fondly interposed;
Fate urged the shears, and cut the Sylph in twain
(But airy substance soon unites again):
The meeting points the sacred hair dissever
From the fair head, for ever, and for ever!
　　Then flashed the living lightning from her eyes,
And screams of horror rend the affrighted skies.
Not louder shrieks to pitying Heaven are cast,
When husbands or when lap-dogs breathe their last;
Or when rich China vessels fallen from high,
In glittering dust and painted fragments lie!
　　"Let wreaths of triumph now my temples twine
(The victor cried); the glorious Prize is mine!
While fish in streams or birds delight in air,
Or in a coach and six the British Fair,
As long as *Atalantis*[9] shall be read,
Or the small pillow grace a Lady's bed,
While visits shall be paid on solemn days,
When numerous wax-lights in bright order blaze,
While nymphs take treats, or assignations give,
So long my honor, name, and praise shall live!
What Time would spare, from Steel receives its date,
And monuments, like men, submit to fate!
Steel could the labor of the Gods destroy,
And strike to dust the imperial towers of Troy;

---

[8] *Forfex:* scissors
[9] Atalantis: a popular book of scandal

Steel could the works of mortal pride confound,
And hew triumphal arches to the ground.
What wonder then, fair nymph! thy hairs should feel
The conquering force of unresisted steel?"

CANTO IV

But anxious cares the pensive nymph oppressed,
And secret passions labored in her breast.
Not youthful kings in battle seized alive,
Not scornful virgins who their charms survive,
Not ardent lovers robbed of all their bliss,
Not ancient ladies when refused a kiss,
Not tyrants fierce that unrepenting die,
Not Cynthia when her manteau's pinned awry,
E'er felt such rage, resentment, and despair,
As thou, sad Virgin! for thy ravished Hair.
For, that sad moment, when the Sylphs withdrew
And Ariel weeping from Belinda flew,
Umbriel, a dusky, melancholy sprite,
As ever sullied the fair face of light,
Down to the central earth, his proper scene,
Repaired to search the gloomy Cave of Spleen.
Swift on his sooty pinions flits the Gnome,
And in a vapor reached the dismal dome.
No cheerful breeze this sullen region knows,
The dreaded East is all the wind that blows.
Here in a grotto, sheltered close from air,
And screened in shades from day's detested glare,
She sighs for ever on her pensive bed,
Pain at her side, and Megrim[10] at her head.
Two handmaids wait the throne: alike in place,
But diff'ring far in figure and in face.
Here stood Ill-nature like an ancient maid,
Her wrinkled form in black and white arrayed;
With store of prayers, for mornings, nights, and noons,
Her hand is filled; her bosom with lampoons.
There Affectation, with a sickly mien,
Shows in her cheek the roses of eighteen,
Practised to lisp, and hang the head aside,

---

[10] *Megrim:* headache

Faints into airs, and languishes with pride,
On the rich quilt sinks with becoming woe,
Wrapt in a gown, for sickness, and for show.
The fair ones feel such maladies as these,
When each new night-dress gives a new disease.
    A constant Vapor o'er the palace flies;
Strange phantoms rising as the mists arise;
Dreadful, as hermit's dreams in haunted shades,
Or bright, as visions of expiring maids.
Now glaring fiends, and snakes on rolling spires,
Pale spectres, gaping tombs, and purple fires:
Now lakes of liquid gold, Elysian scenes,
And crystal domes, and angels in machines.
    Unnumbered throngs on every side are seen,
Of bodies changed to various forms by Spleen.
Here living Tea-pots stand, one arm held out,
One bent; the handle this, and that the spout:
A Pipkin there, like Homer's Tripod walks;
Here sighs a Jar, and there a Goose-pie talks;
Men prove with child, as powerful fancy works,
And maids turned bottles, call aloud for corks.
    Safe passed the Gnome through this fantastic band,
A branch of healing Spleenwort in his hand.
Then thus addressed the power: "Hail, wayward Queen!
Who rule the sex to fifty from fifteen:
Parent of vapors and of female wit,
Who give the hysteric or poetic fit,
On various tempers act by various ways,
Make some take physic, others scribble plays;
Who cause the proud their visits to delay,
And send the godly in a pet to pray.
A nymph there is, that all thy power disdains,
And thousands more in equal mirth maintains.
But oh! if e'er thy Gnome could spoil a grace,
Or raise a pimple on a beauteous face,
Like Citron-waters matrons' cheeks inflame,
Or change complexions at a losing game;
If e'er with airy horns I planted heads,
Or rumpled petticoats, or tumbled beds,
Or caused suspicion when no soul was rude,
Or discomposed the head-dress of a Prude,
Or e'er to costive lap-dog gave disease,

Which not the tears of brightest eyes could ease:
Hear me, and touch Belinda with chagrin,
That single act gives half the world the spleen."
   The Goddess with a discontented air
Seems to reject him, though she grants his prayer.
A wondrous Bag with both her hands she binds,
Like that where once Ulysses held the winds;
There she collects the force of female lungs,
Sighs, sobs, and passions, and the war of tongues.
A Vial next she fills with fainting fears,
Soft sorrows, melting griefs, and flowing tears.
The Gnome rejoicing bears her gifts away,
Spreads his black wings, and slowly mounts to day.
   Sunk in Thalestris' arms the nymph he found,
Her eyes dejected and her hair unbound.
Full o'er their heads the swelling bag he rent,
And all the Furies issued at the vent.
Belinda burns with more than mortal ire,
And fierce Thalestris fans the rising fire.
"O wretched maid!" she spread her hands, and cried
(While Hampton's echoes, "Wretched maid!" replied),
"Was it for this you took such constant care
The bodkin, comb, and essence to prepare?
For this your locks in paper durance bound,
For this with torturing irons wreathed around?
For this with fillets strained your tender head,
And bravely bore the double loads of lead?
Gods! shall the ravisher display your hair,
While the Fops envy, and the Ladies stare!
Honor forbid! at whose unrivalled shrine
Ease, pleasure, virtue, all our sex resign.
Methinks already I your tears survey,
Already hear the horrid things they say,
Already see you a degraded toast,
And all your honor in a whisper lost!
How shall I, then, your helpless fame defend?
'Twill then be infamy to seem your friend!
And shall this prize, the inestimable prize,
Exposed through crystal to the gazing eyes,
And heightened by the diamond's circling rays,
On that rapacious hand for ever blaze?
Sooner shall grass in Hyde-park Circus grow,

And wits take lodgings in the sound of Bow;[11]
Sooner let earth, air, sea, to Chaos fall,
Men, monkeys, lap-dogs, parrots, perish all!"

CANTO V

She said: the pitying audience melt in tears;
But Fate and Jove had stopped the Baron's ears.
In vain Thalestris with reproach assails,
For who can move when fair Belinda fails?
Not half so fixed the Trojan[12] could remain,
While Anna begged and Dido raged in vain.
Then grave Clarissa graceful waved her fan;
Silence ensued, and thus the nymph began:
"Say why are Beauties praised and honored most,
The wise man's passion, and the vain man's toast?
Why decked with all that land and sea afford,
Why Angels called, and Angel-like adored?
Why round our coaches crowd the white-gloved Beaux,
Why bows the side-box from its inmost rows;
How vain are all these glories, all our pains,
Unless good sense preserve what beauty gains:
That men may say, when we the front-box grace:
'Behold the first in virtue as in face!'
Oh! if to dance all night, and dress all day,
Charmed the small-pox, or chased old-age away;
Who would not scorn what housewife's cares produce,
Or who would learn one earthly thing of use?
To patch, nay ogle, might become a saint,
Nor could it sure be such a sin to paint.
But since, alas! frail beauty must decay,
Curled or uncurled, since locks will turn to grey;
Since painted, or not painted, all shall fade,
And she who scorns a man, must die a maid;
What then remains but well our power to use,
And keep good-humor still whate'er we lose?
And trust me, dear! good-humor can prevail,
When airs, and flights, and screams, and scolding fail.
Beauties in vain their pretty eyes may roll;

[11] *Bow:* the church bells of St. Mary-le-Bow, in a vulgar part of London
[12] *Trojan:* Aeneas, the Trojan wanderer

Charms strike the sight, but merit wins the soul."
   So spoke the Dame, but no applause ensued;
Belinda frowned, Thalestris called her Prude.
"To arms, to arms!" the fierce Virago cries,
And swift as lightning to the combat flies.
All side in parties, and begin the attack;
Fans clap, silks rustle, and tough whalebones crack;
Heroes' and Heroines' shouts confusedly rise,
And bass, and treble voices strike the skies.
No common weapons in their hands are found,
Like Gods they fight, nor dread a mortal wound.
   So when bold Homer makes the Gods engage,
And heavenly breasts with human passions rage;
'Gainst Pallas, Mars; Latona, Hermes arms;
And all Olympus rings with loud alarms:
Jove's thunder roars, heaven trembles all around,
Blue Neptune storms, the bellowing deeps resound,
Earth shakes her nodding towers, the ground gives way,
And the pale ghosts start at the flash of day!
   Triumphant Umbriel on a sconce's height
Clapped his glad wings, and sate to view the fight:
Propped on their bodkin spears, the Sprites survey
The growing combat, or assist the fray.
   While through the press enraged Thalestris flies,
And scatters death around from both her eyes,
A Beau and Witling perished in the throng,
One died in metaphor, and one in song.
"O cruel nymph! a living death I bear,"
Cried Dapperwit, and sunk beside his chair.
A mournful glance Sir Fopling upwards cast,
"Those eyes are made so killing"—was his last.
Thus on Maeander's flowery margin lies
The expiring Swan, and as he sings he dies.
   When bold Sir Plume had drawn Clarissa down,
Chloe stepped in, and killed him with a frown;
She smiled to see the doughty hero slain.
But, at her smile, the Beau revived again.
   Now Jove suspends his golden scales in air,
Weighs the Men's wits against the Lady's hair;
The doubtful beam long nods from side to side;
At length the wits mount up, the hairs subside.
   See, fierce Belinda on the Baron flies,

With more than usual lightning in her eyes:
Nor feared the Chief the unequal fight to try,
Who sought no more than on his foe to die.
But this bold Lord with manly strength endued,
She with one finger and a thumb subdued:
Just where the breath of life his nostrils drew,
A charge of snuff the wily virgin threw;
The Gnomes direct, to every atom just,
The pungent grains of titillating dust.
Sudden, with starting tears each eye o'erflows,
And the high dome re-echoes to his nose.
    "Now meet thy fate," incensed Belinda cried,
And drew a deadly bodkin from her side.
(The same, his ancient personage to deck,
Her great great grandsire wore about his neck,
In three seal-rings; which after, melted down,
Formed a vast buckle for his widow's gown:
Her infant grandame's whistle next it grew,
The bells she jingled, and the whistle blew;
Then in a bodkin graced her mother's hairs,
Which long she wore, and now Belinda wears.)
    "Boast not my fall" (he cried), "insulting foe!
Thou by some other shalt be laid as low,
Nor think, to die dejects my lofty mind:
All that I dread is leaving you behind!
Rather than so, ah let me still survive,
And burn in Cupid's flames—but burn alive."
    "Restore the Lock!" she cries; and all around
"Restore the Lock!" the vaulted roofs rebound.[13]
Not fierce Othello in so loud a strain
Roared for the handkerchief that caused his pain.
But see how oft ambitious aims are crossed,
And chiefs contend 'till all the prize is lost!
The Lock, obtained with guilt, and kept with pain,
In every place is sought, but sought in vain:
With such a prize no mortal must be blest,
So heaven decrees! with heaven who can contest?
    Some thought it mounted to the Lunar sphere,
Since all things lost on earth are treasured there.
There heroes' wits are kept in ponderous vases,

---

[13] "Restore . . . rebound": an echo of lines 31–32 in Dryden's "Alexander's Feast"

And beaux' in snuff-boxes and tweezer-cases.
There broken vows and death-bed alms are found,
And lovers' hearts with ends of riband bound,
The courtier's promises, and sick man's prayers,
The smiles of harlots, and the tears of heirs,
Cages for gnats, and chains to yoke a flea,
Dried butterflies, and tomes of casuistry.
　　But trust the Muse—she saw it upward rise,
Though marked by none but quick, poetic eyes
(So Rome's great founder to the heavens withdrew,
To Proculus alone confessed in view):
A sudden Star, it shot through liquid air,
And drew behind a radiant trail of hair,
Not Berenice's Locks[14] first rose so bright,
The heavens bespangling with dishevelled light.
The Sylphs behold it kindling as it flies,
And pleased pursue its progress through the skies.
　　This the Beau monde shall from the Mall survey,
And hail with music its propitious ray.
This the blest Lover shall for Venus take,
And send up vows from Rosamonda's lake.[15]
This Partridge[16] soon shall view in cloudless skies,
When next he looks through Galileo's eyes;[17]
And hence the egregious wizard shall foredoom
The fate of Louis, and the fall of Rome.
　　Then cease, bright Nymph! to mourn thy ravished hair,
Which adds new glory to the shining sphere!
Not all the tresses that fair head can boast,
Shall draw such envy as the Lock you lost.
For, after all the murders of your eye,
When, after millions slain, yourself shall die:
When those fair suns shall set, as set they must,
And all those tresses shall be laid in dust,
This Lock, the Muse shall consecrate to fame,
And 'midst the stars inscribe Belinda's name.

---

[14] *Berenice's Locks:* the constellation of seven stars
[15] *Rosamonda's lake:* pond in St. James's Park "consecrated to disastrous love and elegiac poetry"
[16] *Partridge:* a popular London astrologer and soothsayer
[17] *Galileo's eyes:* the telescope

Voltaire

In the eighteenth century every form of fanaticism, intolerance, and superstition was attacked by the militant wit of
François Marie Arouet, who wrote under the pen name of
Voltaire. Born in Paris in 1694, he was educated for the law
but decided to become a writer rather than argue dubious
cases. His godfather had introduced him to a circle of loose-
living littérateurs on the fringes of the court. From then on
Voltaire was continually involved in diplomatic cabals and
private troubles. At twenty-two, because of a lampoon on the
regent, he was banished from Paris, the first of several exiles.
At thirty-two, as the result of another altercation, he was
packed off to England, where he spent three years, read
Shakespeare and Milton, met the cognoscenti, and numbered
Pope, Dryden, and Gay among his friends.

In England his fortune took a turn for the better. Queen
Caroline accepted the dedication of his poem *La Henriade*,
and Voltaire sold the English edition for more than a thousand
pounds. The sale, a government lottery, and some lucky speculations gave him a considerable income. A few years later he
was again in difficulties. Two of his books were condemned
and burned. To save himself from arrest, Voltaire fled to Lorraine, where he was sheltered by the erratic but erudite
Marquise du Châtelet.

At the Marquise's Château de Cirey in Champagne he wrote

indefatigably and seemed anchored at last. However, some semiprivate utterances, as well as new publications, prompted another migration. For a long time Prussia's Frederick the Great had made tempting overtures. Finally accepting the invitation, Voltaire found himself in Berlin, housed in a royal palace, with a pension of twenty thousand francs.

He was no luckier nor more circumspect in Germany than elsewhere. He quarreled with Lessing, the much-esteemed German dramatist, suspected a rival in every writer, and was accused of forgery. Finally he alienated the king himself by a foolish attack on the ruler's character.

Voltaire was now sixty. France refused to allow him a permanent residence and he settled in Switzerland. He bought a large property a few miles from Geneva, where he became known as "the squire of Ferney." Here he achieved a measure of contentment and composed, among other challenging pieces, his masterpiece, *Candide*. At eighty-four he was accorded a triumphant welcome in Paris, a city he had not seen in almost thirty years. He was acclaimed by the Academy, and his last play, *Irene*, was produced in his honor. The excitement was too much for him. He died May 30, 1778, as he had lived— scoffing.

A prodigious author, there was no field he hesitated to enter. He projected himself in plays, poems, prose romances, historical writings, scientific examinations, philosophical speculations, and criticism, as well as inexhaustible correspondence. His *Philosophical Dictionary*, an alphabet of rapierlike wit, bristles with barbs aimed with unerring acuteness at the church, the literal interpretation of the Bible, ecclesiastical ritual, and anything resembling privileged orthodoxy. *Candide* is a two-edged travesty—a parody of all romantic attitudinizing and a long hilarious satire on the bland optimism of Wilhelm von Leibnitz, who contended that all things happened for the best—a belief echoed by Pope, who said that "whatever is, is right." Voltaire sends the guileless Candide, accompanied by his preceptor Pangloss, out on a series of adventures during which they encounter hideous wars, unspeakable outrages, casual rape, countless murders, drownings, plagues, and unremitting tortures in "the best of all possible worlds." Never has an author fought dogmatism and intolerance so fiercely, and never has satire been both so amusing and so exuberantly destructive.

CANDIDE
CHAPTER I

How Candide was brought up in a noble castle,
and how he was expelled from the same

In the castle of Baron Thunder-ten-tronckh in Westphalia there
lived a youth, endowed by Nature with the most gentle character.
His face was the expression of his soul. His judgment was quite
honest and he was extremely simple-minded; and this was the
reason, I think, that he was named Candide. Old servants in the
house suspected that he was the son of the Baron's sister and a
decent honest gentleman of the neighbourhood, whom this young
lady would never marry because he could only prove seventy-two
quarterings, and the rest of his genealogical tree was lost, owing
to the injuries of time.

The Baron was one of the most powerful lords in Westphalia,
for his castle possessed a door and windows. His Great Hall was
even decorated with a piece of tapestry. The dogs in his stable-
yards formed a pack of hounds when necessary; his grooms were
his huntsmen; the village curate was his Grand Almoner. They
all called him "My Lord," and laughed heartily at his stories.

The Baroness weighed about three hundred and fifty pounds,
was therefore greatly respected, and did the honours of the house
with a dignity which rendered her still more respectable. Her
daughter Cunegonde, aged seventeen, was rosy-cheeked, fresh,
plump and tempting. The Baron's son appeared in every respect
worthy of his father. The tutor Pangloss was the oracle of the
house, and little Candide followed his lessons with all the can-
dour of his age and character.

Pangloss taught metaphysico-theologo-cosmolo-nigology. He
proved admirably that there is no effect without a cause and that,
in this best of all possible worlds, My Lord the Baron's castle was
the best of castles and his wife the best of all possible Baronesses.

"'Tis demonstrated," said he, "that things cannot be otherwise;
for, since everything is made for an end, everything is necessarily
for the best end. Observe that noses were made to wear spectacles;
and so we have spectacles. Legs were visibly instituted to be
breeched, and we have breeches. Stones were formed to be quar-
ried and to build castles; and My Lord has a very noble castle;
the greatest Baron in the province should have the best house;

and as pigs were made to be eaten, we eat pork all the year round; consequently, those who have asserted that all is well, talk nonsense; they ought to have said that all is for the best."

Candide listened attentively and believed innocently; for he thought Miss Cunegonde extremely beautiful, although he was never bold enough to tell her so. He decided that after the happiness of being born Baron of Thunder-ten-tronckh, the second degree of happiness was to be Miss Cunegonde; the third, to see her every day; and the fourth to listen to Dr. Pangloss, the greatest philosopher of the province and therefore of the whole world.

One day when Cunegonde was walking near the castle, in a little wood which was called The Park, she observed Dr. Pangloss in the bushes, giving a lesson in experimental physics to her mother's waiting-maid, a very pretty and docile brunette. Miss Cunegonde had a great inclination for science and watched breathlessly the reiterated experiments she witnessed; she observed clearly the Doctor's sufficient reason, the effects and the causes, and returned home very much excited, pensive, filled with the desire of learning, reflecting that she might be the sufficient reason of young Candide and that he might be hers.

On her way back to the castle she met Candide and blushed; Candide also blushed. She bade him good-morning in a hesitating voice; Candide replied without knowing what he was saying. Next day, when they left the table after dinner, Cunegonde and Candide found themselves behind a screen; Cunegonde dropped her handkerchief, Candide picked it up; she innocently held his hand; the young man innocently kissed the young lady's hand with remarkable vivacity, tenderness and grace; their lips met, their eyes sparkled, their knees trembled, their hands wandered. Baron Thunder-ten-tronckh passed near the screen, and, observing this cause and effect, expelled Candide from the castle by kicking him in the backside frequently and hard. Cunegonde swooned; when she recovered her senses, the Baroness slapped her in the face; and all was in consternation in the noblest and most agreeable of all possible castles.

CHAPTER II

What happened to Candide among the Bulgarians

Candide, expelled from the earthly paradise, wandered for a long time without knowing where he was going, turning up his eyes to Heaven, gazing back frequently at the noblest of castles which held the most beautiful of young Baronesses; he lay down to sleep supperless between two furrows in the open fields; it snowed heavily in large flakes. The next morning the shivering Candide, penniless, dying of cold and exhaustion, dragged himself towards the neighbouring town, which was called Waldberghoff-trarbkdikdorff. He halted sadly at the door of an inn. Two men dressed in blue noticed him.

"Comrade," said one, "there's a well-built young man of the right height."

They went up to Candide and very civilly invited him to dinner.

"Gentlemen," said Candide with charming modesty, "you do me a great honour, but I have no money to pay my share."

"Ah, sir," said one of the men in blue, "persons of your figure and merit never pay anything; are you not five feet five tall?"

"Yes, gentlemen," said he, bowing, "that is my height."

"Ah, sir, come to table; we will not only pay your expenses, we will never allow a man like you to be short of money; men were only made to help each other."

"You are in the right," said Candide, "that is what Dr. Pangloss was always telling me, and I see that everything is for the best."

They begged him to accept a few crowns, he took them and wished to give them an IOU; they refused to take it and all sat down to table.

"Do you not love tenderly . . ."

"Oh, yes," said he. "I love Miss Cunegonde tenderly."

"No," said one of the gentlemen. "We were asking if you do not tenderly love the King of the Bulgarians."

"Not a bit," said he, "for I have never seen him."

"What! He is the most charming of kings, and you must drink his health."

"Oh, gladly, gentlemen."

And he drank.

"That is sufficient," he was told. "You are now the support, the aid, the defender, the hero of the Bulgarians; your fortune is made and your glory assured."

They immediately put irons on his legs and took him to a regiment. He was made to turn to the right and left, to raise the ramrod and return the ramrod, to take aim, to fire, to double up, and he was given thirty strokes with a stick; the next day he drilled not quite so badly, and received only twenty strokes; the day after, he only had ten and was looked on as a prodigy by his comrades.

Candide was completely mystified and could not make out how he was a hero. One fine spring day he thought he would take a walk, going straight ahead, in the belief that to use his legs as he pleased was a privilege of the human species as well as of animals. He had not gone two leagues when four other heroes, each six feet tall, fell upon him, bound him and dragged him back to a cell. He was asked by his judges whether he would rather be thrashed thirty-six times by the whole regiment or receive a dozen lead bullets at once in his brain. Although he protested that men's wills are free and that he wanted neither one nor the other, he had to make a choice; by virtue of that gift of God which is called *liberty,* he determined to run the gauntlet thirty-six times and actually did so twice. There were two thousand men in the regiment. That made four thousand strokes which laid bare the muscles and nerves from his neck to his backside. As they were about to proceed to a third turn, Candide, utterly exhausted, begged as a favour that they would be so kind as to smash his head; he obtained this favour; they bound his eyes and he was made to kneel down. At that moment the King of the Bulgarians came by and inquired the victim's crime; and as this King was possessed of a vast genius, he perceived from what he learned about Candide that he was a young metaphysician very ignorant in worldly matters, and therefore pardoned him with a clemency which will be praised in all newspapers and all ages. An honest surgeon healed Candide in three weeks with the ointments recommended by Dioscorides. He had already regained a little skin and could walk when the King of the Bulgarians went to war with the King of the Abares.

CHAPTER III

How Candide escaped from the Bulgarians and
what became of him

Nothing could be smarter, more splendid, more brilliant, better drawn up than the two armies. Trumpets, fifes, hautboys, drums, cannons formed a harmony such as has never been heard even in hell. The cannons first of all laid flat about six thousand men on each side; then the musketry removed from the best of worlds some nine or ten thousand blackguards who infested its surface. The bayonet also was the sufficient reason for the death of some thousands of men. The whole might amount to thirty thousand souls. Candide, who trembled like a philosopher, hid himself as well as he could during this heroic butchery.

At last, while the two kings each commanded a Te Deum in his camp, Candide decided to go elsewhere to reason about effects and causes. He clambered over heaps of dead and dying men and reached a neighbouring village, which was in ashes; it was an Abare village which the Bulgarians had burned in accordance with international law. Here, old men dazed with blows watched the dying agonies of their murdered wives who clutched their children to their bleeding breasts; there, disembowelled girls who had been made to satisfy the natural appetites of heroes gasped their last sighs; others, halfburned, begged to be put to death. Brains were scattered on the ground among dismembered arms and legs.

Candide fled to another village as fast as he could; it belonged to the Bulgarians, and Abarian heroes had treated it in the same way. Candide, stumbling over quivering limbs or across ruins, at last escaped from the theatre of war, carrying a little food in his knapsack, and never forgetting Miss Cunegonde. His provisions were all gone when he reached Holland; but, having heard that everyone in that country was rich and a Christian, he had no doubt at all but that he would be as well treated as he had been in the Baron's castle before he had been expelled on account of Miss Cunegonde's pretty eyes.

He asked an alms of several grave persons, who all replied that if he continued in that way he would be shut up in a house of correction to teach him how to live.

He then addressed himself to a man who had been discoursing on charity in a large assembly for an hour on end. This orator, glancing at him askance, said:

"What are you doing here? Are you for the good cause?"

"There is no effect without a cause," said Candide modestly. "Everything is necessarily linked up and arranged for the best. It was necessary that I should be expelled from the company of Miss Cunegonde, that I ran the gauntlet, and that I beg my bread until I can earn it; all this could not have happened differently."

"My friend," said the orator, "do you believe that the Pope is Anti-Christ?"

"I had never heard so before," said Candide, "but whether he is or isn't, I am starving."

"You don't deserve to eat," said the other. "Hence, rascal; hence, you wretch; and never come near me again."

The orator's wife thrust her head out of the window and seeing a man who did not believe that the Pope was Anti-Christ, she poured on his head a full . . . O Heavens! To what excess religious zeal is carried by ladies!

A man who had not been baptised, an honest Anabaptist named Jacques, saw the cruel and ignominious treatment of one of his brothers, a featherless two-legged creature with a soul; he took him home, cleaned him up, gave him bread and beer, presented him with two florins, and even offered to teach him to work at the manufacture of Persian stuffs which are made in Holland. Candide threw himself at the man's feet, exclaiming:

"Dr. Pangloss was right in telling me that all is for the best in this world, for I am vastly more touched by your extreme generosity than by the harshness of the gentleman in the black cloak and his good lady."

The next day when he walked out he met a beggar covered with sores, dull-eyed, with the end of his nose fallen away, his mouth awry, his teeth black, who talked huskily, was tormented with a violent cough and spat out a tooth at every cough.

CHAPTER IV

How Candide met his old master in philosophy,
Doctor Pangloss, and what happened

Candide, moved even more by compassion than by horror, gave this horrible beggar the two crowns he had received from the honest Anabaptist, Jacques. The phantom gazed fixedly at him, shed tears and threw its arms round his neck. Candide recoiled in terror.

"Alas!" said the wretch to the other wretch, "don't you recognise your dear Pangloss?"

"What do I hear? You, my dear master! You, in this horrible state! What misfortune has happened to you? Why are you no longer in the noblest of castles? What has become of Miss Cunegonde, the pearl of young ladies, the masterpiece of Nature?"

"I am exhausted," said Pangloss. Candide immediately took him to the Anabaptist's stable, where he gave him a little bread to eat; and when Pangloss had recovered:

"Well!" said he, "Cunegonde?"

"Dead," replied the other.

At this word Candide swooned; his friend restored him to his senses with a little bad vinegar which happened to be in the stable. Candide opened his eyes.

"Cunegonde dead! Ah! best of worlds, where are you! But what illness did she die of? Was it because she saw me kicked out of her father's noble castle?"

"No," said Pangloss. "She was disembowelled by Bulgarian soldiers, after having been raped to the limit of possibility; they broke the Baron's head when he tried to defend her; the Baroness was cut to pieces; my poor pupil was treated exactly like his sister; and as to the castle, there is not one stone standing on another, not a barn, not a sheep, not a duck, not a tree; but we were well avenged, for the Abares did exactly the same to a neighbouring barony which belonged to a Bulgarian Lord."

At this, Candide swooned again; but, having recovered and having said all that he ought to say, he inquired the cause and effect, the sufficient reason which had reduced Pangloss to so piteous a state.

"Alas!" said Pangloss, "'tis love; love, the consoler of the human race, the preserver of the universe, the soul of all tender creatures, gentle love."

"Alas!" said Candide, "I am acquainted with this love, this sovereign of hearts, this soul of our soul; it has never brought me anything but one kiss and twenty kicks in the backside. How could this beautiful cause produce in you so abominable an effect?"

Pangloss replied as follows:

"My dear Candide! You remember Paquette, the maid-servant of our august Baroness; in her arms I enjoyed the delights of Paradise which have produced the tortures of Hell by which you see I am devoured; she was infected and perhaps is dead. Paquette received this present from a most learned monk, who had it from the source; for he received it from an old countess, who had it from a cavalry captain, who owed it to a marchioness, who derived it from a page, who had received it from a Jesuit, who, when a novice, had it in a direct line from one of the companions of Christopher Columbus. For my part, I shall not give it to anyone, for I am dying."

"O Pangloss!" exclaimed Candide, "this is a strange genealogy! Wasn't the devil at the root of it?"

"Not at all," replied that great man. "It was something indis-

pensable in this best of worlds, a necessary ingredient; for, if
Columbus in an island of America had not caught this disease,
which poisons the source of generation, and often indeed prevents generation, we should not have chocolate and cochineal;
it must also be noticed that hitherto in our continent this disease
is peculiar to us, like theological disputes. The Turks, the Indians,
the Persians, the Chinese, the Siamese and the Japanese are not
yet familiar with it; but there is a sufficient reason why they in
their turn should become familiar with it in a few centuries.
Meanwhile, it has made marvellous progress among us, and especially in those large armies composed of honest, well-bred
stipendiaries who decide the destiny of States; it may be asserted
that when thirty thousand men fight a pitched battle against an
equal number of troops, there are about twenty thousand with the
pox on either side."

"Admirable!" said Candide. "But you must get cured."

"How can I!" said Pangloss. "I haven't a sou, my friend, and in
the whole extent of this globe, you cannot be bled or receive an
enema without paying or without someone paying for you."

This last speech determined Candide; he went and threw himself at the feet of his charitable Anabaptist, Jacques, and drew
so touching a picture of the state to which his friend was reduced
that the good easy man did not hesitate to succour Pangloss; he
had him cured at his own expense. In this cure Pangloss only
lost one eye and one ear. He could write well and knew arithmetic
perfectly. The Anabaptist made him his bookkeeper. At the end
of two months he was compelled to go to Lisbon on business and
took his two philosophers on the boat with him. Pangloss explained to him how everything was for the best. Jacques was not
of this opinion.

"Men," said he, "must have corrupted nature a little, for they
were not born wolves, and they have become wolves. God did not
give them twenty-four-pounder cannons or bayonets, and they
have made bayonets and cannons to destroy each other. I might
bring bankruptcies into the account and Justice which seizes the
goods of bankrupts in order to deprive the creditors of them."

"It was all indispensable," replied the one-eyed doctor, "and
private misfortunes make the public good, so that the more private
misfortunes there are, the more everything is well."

While he was reasoning, the air grew dark, the winds blew from
the four quarters of the globe and the ship was attacked by the
most horrible tempest in sight of the port of Lisbon.

CHAPTER V

Storm, shipwreck, earthquake, and what happened to
Dr. Pangloss, to Candide and the Anabaptist Jacques

Half the enfeebled passengers, suffering from that inconceivable anguish which the rolling of a ship causes in the nerves and in all the humours of bodies shaken in contrary directions, did not retain strength enough even to trouble about the danger. The other half screamed and prayed; the sails were torn, the masts broken, the vessel was leaking. Those worked who could, no one co-operated, no one commanded. The Anabaptist tried to help the crew a little; he was on the maindeck; a furious sailor struck him violently and stretched him on the deck; but the blow he delivered gave him so violent a shock that he fell head-first out of the ship. He remained hanging and clinging to part of the broken mast. The good Jacques ran to his aid, helped him to climb back, and from the effort he made was flung into the sea in full view of the sailor, who allowed him to drown without condescending even to look at him. Candide came up, saw his benefactor reappear for a moment and then be engulfed for ever. He tried to throw himself after him into the sea; he was prevented by the philosopher Pangloss, who proved to him that the Lisbon roads had been expressly created for the Anabaptist to be drowned in them. While he was proving this *a priori*, the vessel sank, and everyone perished except Pangloss, Candide and the brutal sailor who had drowned the virtuous Anabaptist; the blackguard swam successfully to the shore and Pangloss and Candide were carried there on a plank.

When they had recovered a little, they walked toward Lisbon; they had a little money by the help of which they hoped to be saved from hunger after having escaped the storm.

Weeping the death of their benefactor, they had scarcely set foot in the town when they felt the earth tremble under their feet; the sea rose in foaming masses in the port and smashed the ships which rode at anchor. Whirlwinds of flame and ashes covered the streets and squares; the houses collapsed, the roofs were thrown upon the foundations, and the foundations were scattered; thirty thousand inhabitants of every age and both sexes were crushed under the ruins. Whistling and swearing, the sailor said:

"There'll be something to pick up here."

"What can be the sufficient reason for this phenomenon?" said Pangloss.

"It is the last day!" cried Candide.

The sailor immediately ran among the debris, dared death to find money, found it, seized it, got drunk, and having slept off his wine, purchased the favours of the first woman of good-will he met on the ruins of the houses and among the dead and dying. Pangloss, however, pulled him by the sleeve.

"My friend," said he, "this is not well, you are disregarding universal reason, you choose the wrong time."

"Blood and 'ounds!" he retorted, "I am a sailor and I was born in Batavia; four times have I stamped on the crucifix during four voyages to Japan; you have found the right man for your universal reason!"

Candide had been hurt by some falling stones; he lay in the street covered with debris. He said to Pangloss:

"Alas! Get me a little wine and oil; I am dying."

"This earthquake is not a new thing," replied Pangloss. "The town of Lima felt the same shocks in America last year; similar causes produce similar effects; there must certainly be a train of sulphur underground from Lima to Lisbon."

"Nothing is more probable," replied Candide; "but, for God's sake, a little oil and wine."

"What do you mean, probable!" replied the philosopher; "I maintain that it is proved."

Candide lost consciousness, and Pangloss brought him a little water from a neighbouring fountain.

Next day they found a little food as they wandered among the ruins and regained a little strength. Afterwards they worked like others to help the inhabitants who had escaped death. Some citizens they had assisted gave them as good a dinner as could be expected in such a disaster; true, it was a dreary meal; the hosts watered their bread with their tears, but Pangloss consoled them by assuring them that things could not be otherwise.

"For," said he, "all this is for the best; for, if there is a volcano at Lisbon, it cannot be anywhere else; for it is impossible that things should not be where they are; for all is well."

A little, dark man, a familiar of the Inquisition, who sat beside him, politely took up the conversation, and said:

"Apparently you do not believe in original sin; for, if everything is for the best, there was neither fall nor punishment."

"I most humbly beg your excellency's pardon," replied Pangloss still more politely, "for the fall of man and the curse necessarily entered into the best of all possible worlds."

"Then you do not believe in free-will?" said the familiar.

"Your excellency will pardon me," said Pangloss; "free-will can exist with absolute necessity; for it was necessary that we should be free; for in short, limited will . . ."

Pangloss was in the middle of his phrase when the familiar nodded to his armed attendant who was pouring out port or Oporto wine for him.

CHAPTER XXIX

How Candide Found Cunegonde and the Old Woman Again

While Candide, the Baron, Pangloss, Martin and Cacambo were relating their adventures, reasoning upon contingent or non-contingent events of the universe, arguing about effects and causes, moral and physical evil, free will and necessity, and the consolations to be found in the Turkish galleys, they came to the house of the Transylvanian prince on the shores of Propontis. The first objects which met their sight were Cunegonde and the old woman hanging out towels to dry on the line. At this sight the Baron grew pale. Candide, that tender lover, seeing his fair Cunegonde sunburned, blear-eyed, flat-breasted, with wrinkles round her eyes and red, chapped arms, recoiled three paces in horror, and then advanced from mere politeness. She embraced Candide and her brother. They embraced the old woman; Candide bought them both.

In the neighborhood was a little farm; the old woman suggested that Candide should buy it, until some better fate befell the group. Cunegonde did not know that she had become ugly, for nobody had told her so; she reminded Candide of his promises in so peremptory a tone that the good Candide dared not refuse her. He therefore informed the Baron that he was about to marry his sister.

"Never," said the Baron, "will I endure such baseness on her part and such insolence on yours; nobody shall ever reproach me with this infamy; my sister's children could never enter the chapters of Germany. No, my sister shall never marry anyone but a Baron of the Empire."

Cunegonde threw herself at his feet and bathed them in tears; but he was inflexible.

"Madman," said Candide, "I rescued you from the galleys, I paid your ransom and your sister's; she was washing dishes here, she is ugly, I am so kind as to make her my wife, and you pretend to oppose me! I should kill you again if I listened to my anger."

"You may kill me again," said the Baron, "but you shall never marry my sister while I am alive."

CHAPTER XXX

Conclusion

At the bottom of his heart Candide had not the least wish to marry Cunegonde. But the Baron's extreme impertinence determined him to complete the marriage, and Cunegonde urged it so warmly that he could not retract. He consulted Pangloss, Martin and the faithful Cacambo. Pangloss wrote an excellent memorandum by which he proved that the Baron had no rights over his sister and that by all the laws of the empire she could make a left-handed marriage with Candide. Martin advised that the Baron should be thrown into the sea; Cacambo decided that he should be returned to the Levantine captain and sent back to the galleys, after which he would be returned by the first ship to the Vicar-General at Rome. This was thought to be very good advice; the old woman approved it; they said nothing to the sister.

The plan was carried out with the aid of a little money, and they had the pleasure of trapping a Jesuit and punishing the pride of a German baron. It would be natural to suppose that when, after many disasters, Candide was married to his mistress, and living with the philosopher Pangloss, the philosopher Martin, the prudent Cacambo and the old woman, having brought back so many diamonds from the country of the ancient Incas, he would lead the most pleasant life imaginable. . . .

The little farm yielded well. Cunegonde was indeed very ugly, but she became an excellent pastrycook; Paquette embroidered; the old woman took care of the linen. Even Friar Giroflée performed some service; he was a very good carpenter and even became a man of honor; and Pangloss sometimes said to Candide: "All events are linked up in this best of all possible worlds; for, if you had not been expelled from the noble castle by hard kicks in your backside for love of Mademoiselle Cunegonde, if you had not been clapped into the Inquisition, if you had not wandered about America on foot, if you had not stuck your sword in the Baron, if you had not lost all your sheep from the land of Eldorado, you would not be eating candied citrons and pistachios here."

"All that is very well," replied Candide, "but we must cultivate our gardens."

A PHILOSOPHICAL DICTIONARY
AUTHORS

Do you wish to be an author? Do you wish to make a book? Remember that it must be new and useful, or at least have great charm. Why from your provincial retreat should you slay me with another quarto, to teach me that a king ought to be just, and that Trajan was more virtuous than Caligula? You insist upon printing the sermons which have lulled your little obscure town to sleep, and you put all our histories under contributions to extract from them the life of a prince of whom you can say nothing new.

If you have written a history of your own time, doubt not but you will find some learned chronologist, or newspaper commentator, who will catch you up on a date, a Christian name, or a squadron which you have wrongly placed at the distance of three hundred paces from the place where it was really posted. Be grateful, and correct these important errors forthwith.

If an ignoramus, or an empty fool, pretend to criticize this thing or the other, you may properly confute him; but name him rarely, for fear of soiling your writings. If you are attacked on your style, never answer; your work alone should reply.

If you are said to be sick, content yourself that you are well, without wishing to prove to the people that you are in perfect health; and, above all, remember that the world cares very little whether you are well or ill.

A hundred authors compile to get their bread, and twenty fools extract, criticize, apologize, and satirize these compilations to get bread also, because they have no profession. All these people repair on Fridays to the lieutenant of the police at Paris to demand permission to sell their drugs. They have their audience immediately after the prostitutes, who pay no attention to them, because they know that they are poor customers.

They return with a tacit permission to sell and distribute throughout the kingdom their stories; their collection of bon-mots; the life of the blessed Regis; the translation of a German poem; new discoveries on eels; a new copy of verses; a treatise on the origin of bells, or on the loves of the toads. A bookseller buys their productions for ten crowns; they give five of them to a corner pamphleteer, on condition that he will speak well of them in his sheet. The scribbler takes their money and then says all the unpleasant things he can think of about their books.

NAKEDNESS

Why should we lock up a man or a woman who chooses to walk stark naked in the street? And why is no one shocked by absolutely nude statues, by pictures of the Madonna and of Jesus that may be seen in some churches?

It is quite probable that the human race lived for a long time without clothes. People unacquainted with clothing have been found in more than one island and on the American continent. The most civilized, however, hide the organs of generation with leaves, woven rushes, or feathers. Whence comes this form of modesty? Is it the instinct to arouse desire by hiding what gives pleasure when discovered?

Is it really true that among slightly more civilized nations, such as the Jews and half-Jews, there have been entire sects who would not worship God save by stripping themselves of all their clothes? Such, we are told, were the Adamites and the Abelians. They gathered quite naked to sing the praises of God: St. Epiphanius and St. Augustine say so. It is true that they were not contemporary, and that they were very far from these peoples' country. But, at all events, this madness is possible: it is no more extraordinary, no more mad than a hundred other follies which have traveled round the world one after the other.

We have said elsewhere that even today the Mohammedans still have saints who are madmen, and who go naked like monkeys. It is very possible that some fanatics thought it was better to present themselves to the Deity in the state in which He formed them, than in the disguise invented by man. It is possible that they showed all out of piety. There are so few well-made persons of both sexes, that nakedness might have inspired chastity, or rather disgust, instead of increasing desire.

It is said particularly that the Abelians renounced marriage. If there were any fine lads and pretty lasses among them, they were at least comparable to St. Adhelme and to blessed Robert d'Arbisselle, who slept with the most attractive girls, so that their continence might triumph the more.

But I admit that it must have been very entertaining to see a

hundred Helens and Parises singing anthems, giving each other
the kiss of peace, and making *agapae*.

All of which shows that there is no singularity, no extravagance,
no superstition which has not passed through the heads of mankind. Happy the day when these superstitions cease to trouble
society and make it a scene of disorder, hatred, and fury! It is
better, no doubt, to pray God stark naked than to stain His altars
and the public places with human blood.

SELF-LOVE

Nicole in his *Essais de Morale* — written on top of two or three
thousand other volumes of ethics — says that "by means of the
wheels and gibbets which people erect in common, the tyrannous
thoughts and designs of each individual's self-love are repressed."

I shall not inquire whether or not people have gibbets in common, as they have meadows and woods in common, and a common purse, or if one represses ideas with wheels; but it seems
very strange to me that Nicole should take highway robbery and
assassination for self-love. One should distinguish shades of difference a little better. The man who said that Nero had his mother
assassinated through self-love, and that Cartouche had an excess
of self-love, would not be expressing himself very correctly. Self-
love is not wickedness, it is a sentiment that is natural to all men;
it is much nearer vanity than crime.

A beggar in the suburbs of Madrid was nobly begging charity.
A passer-by said to him: "Are you not ashamed to practice this
infamous calling when you are able to work?"

"Sir," answered the beggar, "I ask for money, not advice." And
he turned on his heel with full Castilian dignity.

This gentleman was a proud beggar, his vanity was wounded
by a trifle. He asked charity out of love for himself, and could
not tolerate the reprimand out of further love for himself.

A missionary traveling in India met a fakir laden with chains,
naked as a monkey, lying on his stomach, who was having himself
whipped for the sins of his compatriots, the Indians, who gave
him a few farthings.

"What self-denial!" said one of the spectators.

"Self-denial!" answered the fakir. "I have myself flogged in this
world in order to give this flogging back to you in the next world,
when you will be horses and I a horseman."

Those who have said that love of ourselves is the basis of all our opinions and all our actions, have therefore been quite right in India, Spain, and all the habitable world: and as one does not write to prove to men that they have faces, it is not necessary to prove to them that they have self-love. Self-love is our instrument of preservation; it resembles the instrument which perpetuates the species. It is necessary, it is dear to us, it gives us pleasure, and it has to be hidden.

Benjamin Franklin

In eighteenth-century America the young republic found a philosopher whose wisdom was packed with wit, an astute politician who was also an ambassador of good will. Fifteenth of seventeen children, son of a candlemaker and soap boiler, Benjamin Franklin was born January 17, 1706, in Boston. Since he had to help his father at the age of ten, he never finished his schooling. Apprenticed to his half-brother, at seventeen he went to Philadelphia with a dollar in his pocket and became a printer. A year later he made his first visit abroad and remained for eighteen months, learning more than the demands of his trade.

Returning to America, he started in his mid-twenties one of the first circulating libraries, and under the name of Richard Saunders, he published the first of *Poor Richard's Almanacks*, which were to attain an annual sale of ten thousand copies for twenty-five years. Self-taught and insatiably learning, he served the community in the most diverse ways: postmaster in Philadelphia; organizer of the first fire company and police force in America; founder of an academy that became the University of Pennsylvania; instigator of debating clubs, the building of a hospital, and improvements in the method of street lighting. A few years later he invented the lightning rod and other devices as commonplace as a new type of stove, as novel as bifocal glasses, and as esoteric as the armonica, an instrument resembling a set of musical glasses. He was a framer of

the Declaration of Independence and a fund-raiser for the
Revolution, accumulating sixty million dollars in France,
where his reputation was as great as Voltaire's.

The latter portion of Franklin's life was spent as chief execu-
tive officer of Pennsylvania; his last official act was signing a
petition to Congress for the immediate abolition of slavery.
During his final illness Franklin was serene; he regarded the
hereafter as "a new ocean in which to swim," and he had always been a powerful swimmer. He was buried in Philadelphia
on April 18, 1790, beside his wife, whom despite his many ex-
tramarital interludes, he had loved wholeheartedly.

Early in life Franklin had written his own epitaph, but his
survivors thought it frivolous and marked his grave with a
simple stone. This was the intended inscription:

THE BODY OF
BENJAMIN FRANKLIN
PRINTER
(LIKE THE COVER OF AN OLD BOOK,
ITS CONTENTS TORN OUT
AND STRIPT OF ITS LETTERING AND GILDING)
LIES HERE, FOOD FOR WORMS.
BUT THE WORK SHALL NOT BE LOST,
FOR IT WILL (AS HE BELIEVED) APPEAR ONCE MORE,
IN A NEW AND MORE ELEGANT EDITION
REVISED AND CORRECTED
BY
THE AUTHOR

Poor Richard's Almanack is an accumulating set of maxims,
many of them borrowed, rephrased, and localized; in it the
sage and the satirist join hands. Franklin's whimsical humor
also led him to compose various "bagatelles," such as his "Advice on the Choice of a Mistress," "What Are the Poor Young
Women to Do?" and "Dialogue between Franklin and the
Gout," which was inspired by the thirty-six-year-old Mme.
Brillon, with whom the seventy-one-year-old Franklin was
in love and who had many things in common with her elderly
admirer, including gout. It is said that Mme. Brillon remained
faithful to her husband but comforted Franklin by assuring
him that she would become his wife in Paradise "on condition
that you do not eye too many of the maidens there while waiting for me."

ADVICE ON THE CHOICE OF A MISTRESS

My dear Friend:

I know of no medicine fit to diminish the violent natural inclinations you mention, and if I did, I think I should not communicate it to you. Marriage is the proper remedy. It is the most natural state of man, and therefore the state in which you are most likely to find solid happiness. Your reasons against entering into it at present appear to me not well founded. The circumstantial advantages you have in view by postponing it are not only uncertain, but they are small in comparison with that of the thing itself, the being married and settled. It is the man and woman united that make the complete human being. Separate, she wants his force of body and strength of reason; he, her softness, sensibility, and acute discernment. Together they are more likely to succeed in the world. A single man has not nearly the value he would have in the state of union. He is an incomplete animal. He resembles the odd half of a pair of scissors. If you get a prudent, healthy wife, your industry in your profession, with her good economy, will be a fortune sufficient.

But if you will *not* take this counsel and persist in thinking a commerce with the sex inevitable, then I repeat my former advice, that in all your amours you should perfer old women to young ones.

You call this a paradox and demand my reasons. They are these:

1. Because they have more knowledge of the world and their minds are better stored with observations, their conversation is more improving and more lastingly agreeable.

2. Because when women cease to be handsome they study to be good. To maintain their influence over men, they supply the diminution of beauty by an augmentation of utility. They learn to do a thousand services small and great, and are the most tender and useful of friends when you are sick. Thus they continue amiable. And hence there is hardly such a thing to be found as an old woman who is not a good woman.

3. Because there is no hazard of children, which irregularly produced may be attended with much inconvenience.

4. Because through more experience they are more prudent and discreet in conducting an intrigue to prevent suspicion. The commerce with them is therefore safer with regard to your reputation. And with regard to theirs, if the affair should happen to

be known, considerate people might be rather inclined to excuse an old woman, who would kindly take care of a young man, form his manners by her good counsels, and prevent his ruining his health and fortune among mercenary prostitutes.

5. Because in every animal that walks upright the deficiency of the fluids that fill the muscles appears first in the highest part. The face first grows lank and wrinkled; then the neck; then the breast and arms; the lower parts continuing to the last as plump as ever: so that covering all above with a basket, and regarding only what is below the girdle, it is impossible of two women to tell an old one from a young one. And as in the dark all cats are gray, the pleasure of corporal enjoyment with an old woman is at least equal, and frequently superior; every knack being, by practice, capable of improvement.

6. Because the sin is less. The debauching a virgin may be her ruin, and make her for life unhappy.

7. Because the compunction is less. The having made a young girl miserable may give you frequent bitter reflection; none of which can attend the making an old woman happy.

8th and lastly. They are so grateful!

Thus much for my paradox. But still I advise you to marry directly; being sincerely

Your affectionate friend,

Benjamin Franklin

WHAT ARE THE POOR YOUNG WOMEN TO DO?

The speech of Miss Polly Baker before a court of judicature, at Connecticut near Boston in New England; where she was prosecuted the fifth time for having a bastard child: Which influenced the court to dispense with her punishment, and which induced one of her judges to marry her the next day by whom she had fifteen children.

"May it please the honorable bench to indulge me in a few words: I am a poor, unhappy woman, who have no money to fee lawyers to plead for me, being hard put to it to get a living. I shall not trouble your honors with long speeches; for I have not the presumption to expect that you may, by any means, be prevailed on to deviate in your sentence from the law, in my favor. All I humbly hope is that your honors would charitably move the governor's goodness on my behalf, that my fine may be remitted. This is the fifth time, gentlemen, that I have been dragged before your court on the same account; twice I have paid heavy fines, and twice have been brought to public punishment, for want of money to pay those fines. This may have been agreeable to the laws, and I don't dispute it. But since laws are sometimes unreasonable in themselves, and therefore repealed; and others bear too hard on the subject in particular circumstances, and therefore there is left a power somewhere to dispense with the execution of them; I take the liberty to say that I think this law, by which I am punished, both unreasonable in itself, and particularly severe with regard to me, who have always lived an inoffensive life in the neighborhood where I was born, and defy my enemies (if I have any) to say I ever wronged any man, woman, or child. Abstracted from the law, I cannot conceive (may it please your honors) what the nature of my offense is. I have brought five fine children into the world, at the risk of my life; I have maintained them well by my own industry, without burdening the township, and would have done it better if it had not been for the heavy charges and fines I have paid. Can it be a crime (in the nature of things, I mean) to add to the King's subjects, in a new country, that really wants people? I own it, I should think it rather a praiseworthy than a punishable action. I have debauched no other woman's husband, nor enticed any other youth; these things I never was charged with; nor has anyone the least cause of complaint against me, unless, perhaps, the ministers of justice, because I have had children without being married, by which they have missed a wedding fee. But can this be a fault of mine? I appeal to your honors. You are pleased to allow I don't want sense; but I must be stupefied to the last degree, not to prefer the honorable state of wedlock to the condition I have lived in. I always was, and still am, willing to enter into it; and doubt not my behaving well in it, having all the industry, frugality, fertility, and skill in economy appertaining to a good wife's character. I defy anyone to say I ever refused an offer of the sort: on the contrary, I readily consented to the only proposal of marriage that ever was made me, which was when I was a virgin, but too easily confiding in the person's sincerity that made it, I unhappily lost my honor by trusting to his; for he got me with child, and then forsook me.

"That very person, you all know, he is now become a magistrate of this country; and I had hopes he would have appeared this day on the bench, and have endeavored to moderate the court in my favor; then I should have scorned to have mentioned it; but I must now complain of it, as unjust and unequal, that my betrayer and undoer, the first cause of all my faults and miscarriages (if they must be deemed such), should be advanced to honor and power in this government that punishes my misfortunes with stripes and infamy. I should be told, 'tis like, that were there no act of assembly in the case, the precepts of religion are violated by my transgressions. If mine is a religious offense, leave it to religious punishments. You have already excluded me from the comforts of your church communion. Is not that sufficient? You believe I have offended heaven, and must suffer eternal fire: Will not that be sufficient? What need is there then of your additional fines and whipping? I own I do not think as you do, for, if I thought what you call a sin was really such, I could not presumptuously commit it. But, how can it be believed that heaven is angry at my having children, when to the little done by me toward it, God has been pleased to add his divine skill and admirable workmanship in the formation of their bodies, and crowned the whole by furnishing them with rational and immortal souls?

"Forgive me, gentlemen, if I talk a little extravagantly on these matters; I am no divine, but if you, gentlemen, must be making laws, do not turn natural and useful actions into crimes by your prohibitions. But take into your wise consideration the great and growing number of bachelors in the country, many of whom, from the mean fear of the expenses of a family, have never sincerely and honorably courted a woman in their lives; and by their manner of living leave unproduced (which is little better than murder) hundreds of their posterity to the thousandth generation. Is not this a greater offense against the public good than mine? Compel them, then, by law, either to marriage, or to pay double the fine of fornication every year. What must poor young women do, whom customs and nature forbid to solicit the men, and who cannot force themselves upon husbands, when the laws take no care to provide them any, and yet severely punish them if they do their duty without them; the duty of the first and great command of nature and nature's God, *increase and multiply;* a duty, from the steady performance of which nothing has been able to deter me, but for its sake I have hazarded the loss of the public esteem, and have frequently endured public disgrace and punishment; and therefore ought, in my humble opinion, instead of a whipping, to have a statue erected to my memory."

DIALOGUE BETWEEN FRANKLIN AND THE GOUT

MIDNIGHT, *October 22, 1780*

FRANKLIN: Eh! Oh! Eh! What have I done to merit these cruel sufferings?

GOUT: Many things; you have ate and drank too freely, and too much indulged those legs of yours in their indolence.

FRANKLIN: Who is it that accuses me?

GOUT: It is I, even I, the Gout.

FRANKLIN: What! my enemy in person?

GOUT: No, not your enemy.

FRANKLIN: I repeat it; my enemy; for you would not only torment my body to death, but ruin my good name; you reproach me as a glutton and a tippler; now all the world, that knows me, will allow that I am neither the one nor the other.

GOUT: The world may think as it pleases; it is always very complaisant to itself, and sometimes to its friends; but I very well know that the quantity of meat and drink proper for a man, who takes a reasonable degree of exercise, would be too much for another, who never takes any.

FRANKLIN: I take—Eh! Oh!—as much exercise—Eh!—as I can, Madam Gout. You know my sedentary state, and on that account, it would seem, Madam Gout, as if you might spare me a little, seeing it is not altogether my own fault.

GOUT: Not a jot; your rhetoric and your politeness are thrown away; your apology avails nothing. If your situation in life is a sedentary one, your amusements, your recreations, at least, should be active. You ought to walk or ride; or, if the weather prevents that, play at billiards. But let us examine your course of life. While the mornings are long, and you have leisure to go abroad, what do you do? Why, instead of gaining an appetite for breakfast, by salutary exercise, you amuse yourself with books, pamphlets, or newspapers, which commonly are not worth the reading. Yet you eat an inordinate breakfast, four dishes of tea, with cream, and one or two buttered toasts, with slices of hung beef, which I fancy are not things the most easily digested. Immediately afterward you sit down to write at your desk, or converse with persons who apply to you on business. Thus the time passes till one, without any kind of bodily exercise. But all this I could pardon, in regard, as you say, to your sedentary condition. But what is your practice after dinner? Walking in the beautiful gardens of those friends, with whom you have dined, would be the choice of men of sense; yours is to be fixed down to chess, where you are found engaged for two or three hours! This is your perpetual recreation, which is the least eligible of any for a sedentary man, because, instead of accelerating the motion of the fluids, the rigid attention it requires helps to retard the circulation and obstruct internal secretions. Wrapt in the speculations of this wretched game, you destroy your constitution. What can be expected from such a course of living, but a body replete with stagnant humors, ready to fall a prey to all kinds of dangerous maladies, if I, the Gout, did not occasionally bring you relief by agitating those humors, and so purifying or dissipating them? If it was in some nook or alley in Paris, deprived of walks, that you played awhile at chess after dinner, this might be excusable; but the same taste prevails with you in Passy, Auteuil, Montmartre, or Sanoy, places where there are the finest gardens and walks, a pure air, beautiful women, and most agreeable and instructive conversation; all which you might enjoy by frequenting the walks. But these are rejected for this abominable game of chess. Fie, then, Mr. Franklin! But amidst my instructions, I had almost forgot to administer my wholesome corrections; so take that twinge, —and that.

FRANKLIN: Oh! Eh! Oh! Ohhh! As much instruction as you please, Madam Gout, and as many reproaches; but pray, Madam, a truce with your corrections!

GOUT: No, Sir, no,—I will not abate a particle of what is so much for your good,—therefore—

FRANKLIN: Oh! Ehhh!—It is not fair to say I take no exercise, when I do very often, going out to dine and returning in my carriage.

GOUT: That, of all imaginable exercises, is the most slight and insignificant, if you allude to the motion of a carriage suspended on springs. By observing the degree of heat obtained by different kinds of motion, we may form an estimate of the quantity of exercise given by each. Thus, for example, if you turn out to walk in winter with cold feet, in an hour's time you will be in a glow all over; ride on horseback, the same effect will scarcely be perceived by four hours' round trotting; but if you loll in a carriage, such as you have mentioned, you may travel all day, and gladly enter the last inn to warm your feet by a fire. Flatter yourself then no longer, that half an hour's airing in your carriage deserves the name of exercise. Providence has appointed few to roll in carriages, while he has given to all a pair of legs, which are machines infinitely more commodious and serviceable. Be grateful, then, and make a proper use of yours. Would you know how they forward the circulation of your fluids, in the very action of transporting you from place to place; observe when you walk, that all your weight is alternately thrown from one leg to the other; this occasions a great pressure on the vessels of the foot, and repels their contents; when relieved, by the weight being thrown on the other foot, the vessels of the first are allowed to replenish, and, by a return of this weight, this repulsion again succeeds; thus accelerating the circulation of the blood. The heat produced in any given time depends on the degree of this acceleration; the fluids are shaken, the humors attenuated, the secretions facilitated, and all goes well; the cheeks are ruddy, and health is established. Behold your fair friend at Auteuil [Madame Helvétius]; a lady who received from bounteous nature more really useful science that half a dozen such pretenders to philosophy as you have been able to extract from all your books. When she honors you with a visit, it is on foot. She walks all hours of the day, and leaves indolence, and its concomitant maladies, to be endured by her horses. In this see at once the preservative of her health and personal charms. But when you go to Auteuil, you must have your carriage, though it is no further from Passy to Auteuil than from Auteuil to Passy.

FRANKLIN: Your reasonings grow very tiresome.

GOUT: I stand corrected. I will be silent and continue my office; take that, and that.

FRANKLIN: Oh! Ohh! Talk on, I pray you!

GOUT: No, no; I have a good number of twinges for you tonight, and you may be sure of some more tomorrow.

FRANKLIN: What, with such a fever! I shall go distracted. Oh! Eh! Can no one bear it for me?

GOUT: Ask that of your horses; they have served you faithfully.

FRANKLIN: How can you so cruelly sport with my torments?

GOUT: Sport! I am very serious. I have here a list of offences against your own health distinctly written, and can justify every stroke inflicted on you.

FRANKLIN: Read it then.

GOUT: It is too long a detail; but I will briefly mention some particulars.

FRANKLIN: Proceed. I am all attention.

GOUT: Do you remember how often you have promised yourself, the following morning, a walk in the grove of Boulogne, in the garden de la Muette, or in your own garden, and have violated your promise, alleging, at one time, it was too cold, at another too warm, too windy, too moist, or what else you pleased; when in truth it was too nothing, but your insuperable love of ease?

FRANKLIN: That I confess may have happened occasionally, probably ten times in a year.

GOUT: Your confession is very far short of the truth; the gross amount is one hundred and ninety-nine times.

FRANKLIN: Is it possible?

GOUT: So possible, that it is fact; you may rely on the accuracy of my statement. You know M. Brillon's gardens, and what fine walks they contain; you know the handsome flight of an hundred steps, which lead from the terrace above to the lawn below. You have been in the practice of visiting this amiable family twice a week, after dinner, and it is a maxim of your own that "a man may take as much exercise in walking a mile, up and down stairs, as in ten on level ground." What an opportunity was here for you to have had exercise in both these ways! Did you embrace it, and how often?

FRANKLIN: I cannot immediately answer that question.

GOUT: I will do it for you; not once.

FRANKLIN: Not once?

GOUT: Even so. During the summer you went there at six o'clock. You found the charming lady, with her lovely children and friends, eager to walk with you, and entertain you with their agreeable conversation; and what has been your choice? Why to sit on the terrace, satisfying yourself with the fine prospect, and passing your eye over the beauties of the garden below, without taking one step to descend and walk about in them. On the contrary, you call for tea and the chessboard; and lo! you are occupied in your seat till nine o'clock, and that besides two hours' play after dinner; and then, instead of walking home, which would have bestirred you a little, you step into your carriage. How absurd to suppose that all this carelessness can be reconciled with health, without my interposition!

FRANKLIN: I am convinced now of the justness of poor Richard's remark, that "Our debts and our sins are always greater than we think for."

GOUT: So it is. You philosophers are sages in your maxims, and fools in your conduct.

FRANKLIN: But do you charge among my crimes that I return in a carriage from M. Brillon's?

GOUT: Certainly; for, having been seated all the while, you cannot object the fatigue of the day, and cannot want therefore the relief of a carriage.

FRANKLIN: What then would you have me do with my carriage?

GOUT: Burn it if you choose; you would at least get heat out of it once in this way; or, if you dislike that proposal, here's another for you; observe the poor peasants, who work in the vineyards and grounds about the villages of Passy, Auteuil, Chaillot, etc., you may find everyday, among these deserving creatures, four or five old men and women, bent and perhaps crippled by weight of years, and too long and too great labor. After a most fatiguing day, these people have to trudge a mile or two to their smoky huts. Order your coachman to set them down. This is an act that will be good for your soul; and, at the same time, after your visit to the Brillons, if you return on foot, that will be good for your body.

FRANKLIN: Ah! how tiresome you are!

GOUT: Well, then, to my office; it should not be forgotten that I am your physician. There.

FRANKLIN: Ohhh! what a devil of a physician!

GOUT: How ungrateful you are to say so! Is it not I who, in the character of your physician, have saved you from the palsy, dropsy, and apoplexy, one or other of which would have done for you long ago, but for me?

FRANKLIN: I submit, and thank you for the past, but entreat the discontinuance of your visits for the future; for in my mind, one had better die than be cured so dolefully. Permit me just to hint that I have also not been unfriendly to *you*. I never feed physician or quack of any kind, to enter the list against you; if then you do not leave me to my repose, it may be said you are ungrateful too.

GOUT: I can scarcely acknowledge that as any objection. As to quacks, I despise them; they may kill you indeed, but cannot injure me. And, as to regular physicians, they are at last convinced that the gout, in such a subject as you are, is no disease, but a remedy; and wherefore cure a remedy?—but to our business,—there.

FRANKLIN: Oh! oh!—for Heaven's sake leave me! and I promise faithfully never more to play at chess, but to take exercise daily, and live temperately.

GOUT: I know you too well. You promise fair; but, after a few months of good health, you will return to your old habits; your fine promises will be forgotten like the forms of last year's clouds. Let us then finish the account, and I will go. But I leave you with an assurance of visiting you again at a proper time and place; for my object is your good, and you are sensible now that I am your real friend.

POOR RICHARD'S MAXIMS

• To err is human, to forgive divine, but to persist in erring is devilish.

• Tart words make no friends; a spoonful of honey will catch more flies than a gallon of vinegar.

• A mob is a monster—many heads but no brains.

• To serve the public faithfully and please it entirely is impossible.

- Don't judge a man's wealth—or his piety—by his appearance on Sunday.

- Love your neighbor—but don't pull down your hedge.

- A countryman between two lawyers is like a fish between two cats.

- If you would lose a troublesome visitor, lend him money.

- God heals, and the doctor takes the fee.

- Men and melons are hard to know.

- After three days fish and guests smell.

- Let your maidservant be faithful, strong—and homely.

- Marry your son when you will, your daughter when you can.

- There is no ugly love, and no handsome prison.

- You cannot pluck roses without fear of thorns,
  Nor enjoy a fair wife without danger of horns.

- Blessed is the man who expects nothing; he shall never be disappointed.

Henry Fielding

It has been said that the world of Henry Fielding is Vanity
Fair on the largest scale and that he is its inexhaustible showman. Fielding was born in 1707 at Sharpham Park, near Glas-
tonbury. His was an aristocratic background. His father was
descended from the Earls of Denbigh and Desmond; his mother was the daughter of Sir Henry Gould. Among his school-
fellows at Eton were the future statesmen Henry Fox and the
elder Pitt. He studied literature at Leyden, and returning to
London at twenty-two, became an author-manager of a
theater in the Haymarket and wrote farces and burlesque,
including the uproarious *The Tragedy of Tragedies: or the Life
and Death of Tom Thumb the Great*. His work in this genre
led to the mocking parody of Samuel Richardson's shrewdly
chaste *Pamela*. Entitled *The History of Joseph Andrews and
of his Friend Mr. Abraham Adams*, it substituted an absurd
attempted male seduction for Pamela's virtuously resisted
temptations. The affronted Richardson never forgave Fielding.

Unperturbed, Fielding went on to make fun of prudery. Conventional morality was ridiculed in novels that pressed audacity to the furthest limits. His novels created a new type of English fiction; Fielding himself remarked that he had achieved
a "Comic Epos in Prose," an epic ludicrous instead of sublime.
His canvases were wide and crowded, Hogarthian in their
gusto. He exposed fashions in behavior as heartily as he condemned fatuousness and sentimentality. *The History of Tom*

Jones rollicks with improprieties—Tom has few scruples, but he captivates the reader with his frankness, generosity, and high spirits. *The Life of Mr. Jonathan Wild the Great* is a monstrous joke on polite society. Its hero is a scoundrel who becomes "great" by defying all the laws of decency—Fielding stresses the grim humor of his "greatness" by showing him picking the pocket of the parson just before his execution.

Like Hogarth, Fielding relished the rude rawness of life. He despised smugness and perfunctory twaddle. "His genius," wrote Thackeray, "had been nursed on sack posset, not on dishes of tea. His muse had sung the loudest in tavern choruses, had seen the daylight streaming in over thousands of emptied bowls, and had reeled home on the shoulders of the watchman."

THE LIFE OF MR. JONATHAN WILD THE GREAT

THE CHARACTER OF OUR HERO

We will now endeavour to draw the character of this great man; and, by bringing together those several features as it were of his mind which lie scattered up and down in this history, to present our readers with a perfect picture of greatness.

Jonathan Wild had every qualification necessary to form a great man. As his most powerful and predominant passion was ambition, so nature had, with consummate propriety, adapted all his faculties to the attaining those glorious ends to which this passion directed him. He was extremely ingenious in inventing designs, artful in contriving the means to accomplish his purposes, and resolute in executing them: for as the most exquisite cunning and most undaunted boldness qualified him for any undertaking, so was he not restrained by any of those weaknesses which disappoint the views of mean and vulgar souls, and which are comprehended in one general term of honesty, which is a corruption of HONOSTY, a word derived from what the Greeks call an ass. He was entirely free from those low vices of modesty and good-nature, which, as he said, implied a total negation of human greatness, and were the only qualities which absolutely rendered a man incapable of making a considerable figure in the world. His lust was inferior only to his ambition; but, as for what simple people call love, he knew not what it was. His avarice was immense, but

it was of the rapacious, not of the tenacious kind; his rapacious-
ness was indeed so violent that nothing ever contented him but
the whole; for, however considerable the share was which his
coadjutors allowed him of a booty, he was restless in inventing
means to make himself master of the smallest pittance reserved
by them. He said laws were made for the use of *prigs* only, and
to secure their property; they were never therefore more perverted than when their edge was turned against these; but that
this generally happened through their want of sufficient dexterity.
The character which he most valued himself upon, and which he
principally honoured in others, was that of hypocrisy. His opinion
was that no one could carry *priggism* very far without it; for which
reason, he said, there was little greatness to be expected in a man
who acknowledged his vices, but always much to be hoped from
him who professed great virtues: wherefore, though he would
always shun the person whom he discovered guilty of a good action, yet he was never deterred by a good character, which was
more commonly the effect of profession than of action; for which
reason, he himself was always very liberal of honest professions,
and had as much virtue and goodness in his mouth as a saint;
never in the least scrupling to swear by his honour, even to those
who knew him the best; nay, though he held good-nature and
modesty in the highest contempt, he constantly practiced the
affectation of both, and recommended this to others, whose welfare, on his own account, he wished well to. He laid down several
maxims as the certain methods of attaining greatness, to which,
in his own pursuit of it, he constantly adhered. As,

1. Never to do more mischief to another than was necessary
to the effecting his purpose; for that mischief was too precious a
thing to be thrown away.

2. To know no distinction of men from affection; but to sacrifice all with equal readiness to his interest.

3. Never to communicate more of an affair than was necessary
to the person who was to execute it.

4. Not to trust him who hath deceived you, nor who knows he
hath been deceived by you.

5. To forgive no enemy; but to be cautious and often dilatory in
revenge.

6. To shun poverty and distress, and to ally himself as close as
possible to power and riches.

7. To maintain a constant gravity in his countenance and behaviour, and to affect wisdom on all occasions.

8. To foment eternal jealousies in his gang, one of another.

9. Never to reward any one equal to his merit; but always to insinuate that the reward was above it.

10. That all men were knaves or fools, and much the greater number a composition of both.

11. That a good name, like money, must be parted with, or at least greatly risked, in order to bring the owner any advantage.

12. That virtues, like precious stones, were easily counterfeited; that the counterfeits in both cases adorned the wearer equally, and that very few had knowledge or discernment sufficient to distinguish the counterfeit jewel from the real.

13. That many men were undone by not going deep enough in roguery; as in gaming any man may be a loser who doth not play the whole game.

14. That men proclaim their own virtues, as shopkeepers expose their goods, in order to profit by them.

15. That the heart was the proper seat of hatred, and the countenance of affection and friendship.

He had many more of the same kind, all equally good with these, and which were after his decease found in his study, as the twelve excellent and celebrated rules were in that of King Charles the First; for he never promulgated them in his lifetime, not having them constantly in his mouth, as some grave persons have the rules of virtue and morality, without paying the least regard to them in their actions: whereas our hero, by a constant and steady adherence to his rules in conforming everything he did to them, acquired at length a settled habit of walking by them, till at last he was in no danger of inadvertently going out of the way; and by these means he arrived at that degree of greatness which few have equalled; none, we may say, have exceeded: for, though it must be allowed that there have been some few heroes who have done greater mischiefs to mankind, such as those who have betrayed the liberty of their country to others, or have undermined and overpowered it themselves; or conquerors who have impoverished, pillaged, sacked, burnt, and destroyed the countries and cities of their fellow-creatures, from no other provocation than that of glory, *i.e.* as the tragic poet calls it,

a privilege to kill,
A strong temptation to do bravely ill;

yet, if we consider it in the light wherein actions are placed in this line,

Lætius est, quoties magno tibi constat honestum;

when we see our hero, without the least assistance or pretence, setting himself at the head of a gang which he had not any shadow of right to govern; if we view him maintaining absolute power and exercising tyranny over a lawless crew, contrary to all law but that of his own will; if we consider him setting up an open trade publicly, in defiance not only of the laws of his country but of the common sense of his countrymen; if we see him first contriving the robbery of others, and again the defrauding the very robbers of that booty which they had ventured their necks to acquire, and which, without any hazard, they might have retained, here sure he must appear admirable, and we may challenge not only the truth of history, but almost the latitude of fiction, to equal his glory.

Nor had he any of those flaws in his character which, though they have been commended by weak writers, have (as I hinted in the beginning of this history) by the judicious reader been censured and despised. Such was the clemency of Alexander and Caesar, which nature had so grossly erred in giving them, as a painter would who should dress a peasant in robes of state, or give the nose or any other feature of a Venus to a satyr. What had the destroyers of mankind, that glorious pair, one of whom came into the world to usurp the dominion and abolish the constitution of his own country; the other to conquer, enslave, and rule over the whole world, at least as much as was well known to him, and the shortness of his life would give him leave to visit; what had, I say, such as these to do with clemency? Who cannot see the absurdity and contradiction of mixing such an ingredient with those noble and great qualities I have before mentioned? Now, in Wild everything was truly great, almost without alloy, as his imperfections (for surely some small ones he had) were only such as served to denominate him a human creature, of which kind none ever arrived at consummate excellence. But surely his whole behaviour to his friend Heartfree is a convincing proof that the true iron or steel greatness of his heart was not debased by any softer metal. Indeed, while greatness consists in power, pride, insolence, and doing mischief to mankind—to speak out—while a great man and a great rogue are synonymous terms, so long shall Wild stand unrivalled on the pinnacle of GREATNESS. Nor must we omit here, as the finishing of his character, what indeed ought to be remembered on his tomb or his statue, the conformity above mentioned of his death to his life; and that Jonathan Wild the Great, after all his mighty exploits, was, what so few GREAT men can accomplish—hanged by the neck till he was dead.

Laurence Sterne

Laurence Sterne was born in 1713 at Clonmel, County Tipperary, where his father's regiment happened to be stationed. Son of an infantry officer, he spent part of his youth in Ireland, moving from one barracks to another; at ten he was taken care of by relatives who sent him to school at Halifax and Cambridge. At twenty-five he was ordained a clergyman and three years later married Elizabeth Lumley, daughter of a minister.

The marriage was not successful. Sterne had various extra-marital attachments, including a "sentimental friendship" with Catherine de Fourmantelle ("dear, dear Kitty"), with the flirtatious Lady Percy, and with the exotic, olive-skinned Eliza Draper, child-bride of a merchant and more than thirty years younger than Sterne. After eighteen years of marriage his wife suffered a mental collapse and believed herself to be queen of Bohemia. Sterne did everything in his power to help her, even humoring her pathetic delusions.

Stern was forty-six when he wrote the first volume of *The Life and Opinions of Tristram Shandy*, a set of loosely assembled memoirs that is part novel, part essay, part philosophical satire. Its success was immediate and made its author the literary lion of London society. It also brought him a considerable sum of money—insufficient, however, to meet his ever-growing expenses. Although all London read his book and laughed at its covert suggestiveness and outspoken bawdiness, Sterne was angered by the attacks of such leading literary lights as Johnson and Goldsmith, who criticized him for its digressive style, its dubiousness, and its indecency.

Sterne entered with such abandon into the pleasure-loving life of the town—the elaborate dinner parties, the theater, the races at York—that his always delicate health was impaired. He was ordered to the south of France to rest. His wife, now recovered, and his beloved daughter Lydia remained with him at Toulouse. The sojourn did not help his serious lung condition, yet he continued to issue additions to the original *Tristram Shandy* until the work totaled nine volumes. The Continent yielded a further benefit: it provided the background for *A Sentimental Journey through France and Italy,* his last and gaiest work. Sterne returned to England knowing that death, which had always dogged his footsteps, was close upon him. He died, debt-ridden, on March 18, 1768, three weeks after the publication of *A Sentimental Journey.* His was a shabby funeral. A single coach accompanied the body to the grave. A few days later the corpse was exhumed and placed on a table to be used for a lesson in anatomy.

Sterne brought to English writing a fresh kind of humor, part knowingness, part impishness. *The Life and Opinions of Tristram Shandy* and *A Sentimental Journey* are unique performances; each is a tour de force of whimsicality in rococo prose. Sterne loosened the structure of the novel. His puckish mannerisms and eccentric digressions proceed with continual improvisations. He is unsurpassed in the naughty art of the *double-entendre.* Yet even when Sterne is friskiest, he whips his way through convention with a dry sarcasm that shames propriety and laughs sententiousness out of court. It is his capricious heart rather than his clerical head that wins us. An overburdened world will always be brightened by the apparition of the odd clergyman, forever eager, forever young, scattering his risqué innuendoes and accompanied by as lively a crew of characters as ever lightened literature.

A SENTIMENTAL JOURNEY
THE CASE OF DELICACY

The peasants had been all day at work removing the obstruction in the road; and, by the time my *voiturin* got to the place, it wanted

two full hours of completing before a passage could anyhow be
gained. There was nothing but to wait with patience;—'twas a wet
and tempestuous night; so that by the delay and that together, the
voiturin found himself obliged to put up five miles short of his
stage, at a little decent kind of an inn by the roadside.

I forthwith took possession of my bed-chamber, got a good fire,
ordered supper, and was thanking Heaven it was no worse,—when
a *voiturin* arrived with a lady in it, and her servant-maid.

As there was no other bed-chamber in the house, the hostess,
without much nicety, led them into mine, telling them, as she
ushered them in, that there was nobody in it but an English gentleman—that there were two good beds in it, and a closet within the
room which held another. The accent in which she spoke of this
third bed, did not say much for it—however, she said there were
three beds, and but three people—and she durst say the gentleman would do anything to accommodate matters. I left the lady not
a moment to make a conjecture about it, so instantly made a
declaration that I would do anything in my power.

As this did not amount to an absolute surrender of my bed-
chamber, I still felt myself so much the proprietor, as to have a
right to do the honours of it;—so I desired the lady to sit down,
pressed her into the warmest seat, called for more wood, desired
the hostess to enlarge the plan of the supper, and to favour us with
the very best wine.

The lady had scarce warmed herself five minutes at the fire before she began to turn her head back and to give a look at the beds:
and the oftener she cast her eyes that way, the more they returned
perplexed. I felt for her—and for myself; for in a few minutes,
what by her looks, and the case itself, I found myself as much
embarrassed as it was possible the lady could be herself.

That the beds we were to lie in were in one and the same room,
was enough simply by itself to have excited all this;—but the position of them (for they stood parallel, and so very close to each
other as only to allow a space for a small wicker-chair betwixt
them) rendered the affair still more oppressive to us;—they were
fixed up, moreover, near the fire, and the projection of the chimney on one side, and a large beam which crossed the room on the
other, formed a kind of recess for them that was no way favourable to the nicety of our sensations:—if anything could have added
to it, it was that the two beds were both of them so very small as
to cut us off from every idea of the lady and the maid lying together, which, in either of them, could it have been feasible, my
lying beside them, though a thing not to be wished, yet there was

nothing in it so terrible which the imagination might not have passed over without torment.

As for the little room within, it offered little or no consolation to us. 'Twas a damp, cold closet, with a half-dismantled window-shutter, and with a window which had neither glass nor oil-paper in it to keep out the tempest of the night. I did not endeavour to stifle my cough when the lady gave a peep into it; so it reduced the case in course to this alternative,—that the lady should sacrifice her health to her feelings, and take up with the closet herself, and abandon the bed next mine to her maid,—or, that the girl should take the closet, etc.

The lady was a Piedmontese of about thirty, with a glow of health in her cheeks. The maid was a Lyonoise of twenty, and as brisk and lively a French girl as ever moved. There were difficulties every way,—and the obstacle of the stone in the road, which brought us into the distress, great as it appeared whilst the peasants were removing it, was but a pebble to what lay in our way now—I have only to add that it did not lessen the weight which hung upon our spirits, that we were both too delicate to communicate what we felt to each other upon the occasion.

We sat down to supper; and, had we not had more generous wine to it than a little inn in Savoy could have furnished, our tongues had been tied up till Necessity herself had set them at liberty. But the lady having a few bottles of Burgundy in her *voiture,* sent down her *fille de chambre* for a couple of them; so that by the time supper was over and we were left alone, we felt ourselves inspired with a strength of mind sufficient to talk, at least, without reserve, upon our situation. We turned it every way, and debated and considered it in all kinds of lights in the course of a two hours' negotiation; at the end of which the articles were settled finally betwixt us, and stipulated for in form and manner of a treaty of peace,—and, I believe, with as much religion and good faith on both sides, as in any treaty which has yet had the honour of being handed down to posterity.

They were as follows:

First. As the right of the bed-chamber is in Monsieur,—and he thinking the bed next to the fire to be the warmest, he insists upon the concession on the lady's side of taking up with it.

Granted on the part of Madame; with a proviso that, as the curtains of that bed are of a flimsy transparent cotton, and appear likewise too scanty to draw close, that the *fille de chambre* shall fasten up the opening, either by corking-pins or needle and thread, in such a manner as shall be deemed a sufficient barrier on the side of Monsieur.

Second. It is required on the part of Madame, that Monsieur shall lie the whole night through in his *robe de chambre.*

Rejected: inasmuch as Monsieur is not worth a *robe de chambre;* he having nothing in his portmanteau but six shirts and a black silk pair of breeches.

The mentioning the silk pair of breeches made an entire change of the article, for the breeches were accepted as an equivalent for the *robe de chambre;* and so it was stipulated and agreed upon that I should lie in my black silk breeches all night.

Third. It was insisted upon, and stipulated for, by the lady, that after Monsieur was got to bed, and the candle and fire extinguished, Monsieur should not speak one single word the whole night.

Granted, provided Monsieur's saying his prayers might not be deemed an infraction of the treaty.

There was but one point forgot in this treaty, and that was the manner in which the lady and myself should be obliged to undress and get to bed;—there was one way of doing it, and that I leave to the reader to devise, protesting as I do it, that if it is not the most delicate in nature,—'tis the fault of his own imagination,—against which this is not my first complaint.

Now when we were got to bed, whether it was the novelty of the situation, or what it was, I know not; but so it was, I could not shut my eyes. I tried this side and that, and turned and turned again, till a full hour after midnight, when Nature and Patience both wearing out,—"O my God!" said I.

—"You have broken the treaty, Monsieur," said the lady, who had no more slept than myself. I begged a thousand pardons; but insisted it was no more than an ejaculation.—She maintained 'twas an entire infraction of the treaty.—I maintained it was provided for in the clause of the third article.

The lady would by no means give up the point, though she weakened her barrier by it; for, in the warmth of the dispute, I could hear two or three corking-pins fall out of the curtain to the ground.

—"Upon my word and honour, Madame," said I, stretching my arm out of bed by way of asseveration—

(I was going to have added, that I would not have trespassed against the remotest idea of decorum for the world)—

—But the *fille de chambre,* hearing there were words between us, and fearing that hostilities would ensue in course, had crept silently out of her closet; and, it being totally dark, had stolen so close to our beds that she had got herself into the narrow passage which separated them, and had advanced so far up as to be in a line betwixt her mistress and me.

So that, when I stretched out my hand, I caught hold of the *fille de chambre's—*

TRISTRAM SHANDY
HOW I WAS BEGOT

I wish either my father or my mother, or indeed both of them, as they were in duty both equally bound to it, had minded what they were about when they begot me; had they duly considered how much depended upon what they were then doing;—that not only the production of a rational Being was concerned in it, but that possibly the happy formation and temperature of his body perhaps his genius and the very cast of his mind;—and, for aught they knew to the contrary, even the fortunes of his whole house might take their turn from the humours and dispositions which were then uppermost;—had they duly weighed and considered all this, and proceeded accordingly,—I am verily persuaded I should have made a quite different figure in the world, from that in which the reader is likely to see me.—Believe me, good folks, this is not so inconsiderable a thing as many of you may think it;—you have all, I dare say, heard of the animal spirits, as how they are transfused from father to son, etc. etc.—and a great deal to that purpose:—Well, you may take my word, that nine parts in ten of a man's sense or his nonsense, his successes and mis-carriages in this world depend upon their motions and activity, and the different tracts and trains you put them into, so that when they are once set a-going, whether right or wrong, 'tis not a half-penny matter,—away they go cluttering like hey-go mad; and by treading the same steps over and over again, they presently make a road of it, as plain and as smooth as a garden-walk, which, when they are once used to, the devil himself sometimes shall not be able to drive them off it.

"Pray, my dear," quoth my mother, "have you not forgot to wind up the clock?"—"Good G—!" cried my father, making an ex-clamation, but taking care to moderate his voice at the same time.

"Did ever woman, since the creation of the world, interrupt a man with such a silly question?" Pray, what was your father saying?— Nothing.

— Then, positively, there is nothing in the question that I can see, either good or bad. — Then, let me tell you, sir, it was a very unseasonable question at least, — because it scattered and dispersed the animal spirits, whose business it was to have escorted and gone hand in hand with the Homunculus, and conducted him safe to the place destined for his reception.

The Homunculus, sir, in however low and ludicrous a light he may appear, in this age of levity, to the eye of folly or prejudice; — to the eye of reason in scientific research, he stands confessed — a Being guarded and circumscribed with rights. — The minutest philosophers who, by the bye, have the most enlarged understandings, (their souls being inversely as their enquiries) shew us incontestably, that the Homunculus is created by the same hand, — engendered in the same course of nature, — endowed with the same locomotive powers and faculties with us: — That he consists as we do, of skin, hair, fat, flesh, veins, arteries, ligaments, nerves, cartilages, bones, marrow, brains, glands, genitals, humours, and articulations; — is a Being of as much activity, — and, in all senses of the word, as much and as truly our fellow-creature as my Lord Chancellor of England. — He may be benefited, — he may be injured, — he may obtain redress; — in a word, he has all the claims and rights of humanity, which Tully, Puffendorf, or the best ethic writers allow to arise out of that state and relation.

Now, dear sir, what if any accident had befallen him in his way alone! — or that, through terror of it, natural to so young a traveller, my little Gentleman had got to his journey's end miserably spent; — his muscular strength and virility worn down to a thread; — his own animal spirits ruffled beyond description, — and that in this sad disordered state of nerves, he had lain down a prey to sudden starts, or a series of melancholy dreams and fancies, for nine long, long months together. — I tremble to think what a foundation had been laid for a thousand weaknesses both of body and mind, which no skill of the physician or the philosopher could ever afterwards have set thoroughly to rights.

To my uncle Mr. Toby Shandy do I stand indebted for the preceding anecdote, to whom my father, who was an excellent natural philosopher, and much given to close reasoning upon the smallest matters, had oft, and heavily complained of the injury; but once more particularly, as my uncle Toby well remembered, upon his observing a most unaccountable obliquity, (as he called it) in my manner of setting up my top, and justifying the principles upon which I had done it, — the old gentleman shook his head, and in a tone more expressive by half of sorrow than reproach, — he said his heart all along foreboded, and he saw it verified in this, and from a thousand other observations he had made upon me, That I should neither think nor act like any other man's child: — "But alas!" continued he, shaking his head a second time, and wiping away a tear which was trickling down his cheeks, "My Tristram's misfortunes began nine months before ever he came into the world."

— My mother, who was sitting by, looked up, — but she knew no more than her backside what my father meant, — but my uncle, Mr. Toby Shandy, who had been often informed of the affair, — understood him very well.

I was begot in the night, betwixt the first Sunday and the first Monday in the month of March, in the year of our Lord one thousand seven hundred and eighteen. I am positive I was, — But how I came to be so very particular in my account of a thing which happened before I was born, is owing to another small anecdote known only in our own family, but now made public for the better clearing up this point.

My father, you must know, who was originally a Turkey merchant, but had left off business for some years, in order to retire to, and die upon, his paternal estate in the county of ——, was, I believe, one of the most regular men in everything he did, whether 'twas matter of business, or matter of amusement, that ever lived. As a small specimen of this extreme exactness of his, to which he was in truth a slave, — he had made it a rule for many years of his life — on the first Sunday-night of every month throughout the whole year, — as certain as ever the Sunday-night came, — to wind up a large house-clock, which we had standing on the backstairs head, with his own hands: — And being somewhere between fifty and sixty years of age at the time I have been speaking of, — he had likewise gradually brought some other little family concernments to the same period, in order, as he would often say to my uncle Toby, to get them all out of the way at one time, and be no more plagued and pestered with them the rest of the month.

It was attended with but one misfortune, which, in a great measure, fell upon myself, and the effects of which I fear I shall carry with me to my grave; namely, that from an unhappy association of ideas, which have no connection in nature, it so fell out at length, that my poor mother could never hear the said clock wound up,—but the thoughts of some other things unavoidably popped into her head—and *vice versa:*—Which strange combination of ideas, the sagacious Locke, who certainly understood the nature of these things better than most men, affirms to have produced more wry actions than all other sources of prejudice whatsoever.

Robert Burns

Robert Burns has had two kinds of a reputation. He has been appraised as a failed farmer who wrote some remarkable (and remarkably uneven) verse, and he has been worshiped as an untutored, heaven-inspired plowman who became Caledonia's Bard, the Voice of Scotland. He was born January 25, 1759, in the county of Ayrshire, in a two-room thatch-and-plaster cottage that his father had built with his own hands. There were six other children; nine human beings, as well as several animals, were crowded in the two rooms. His mother could not write and was able to read only a bit of the Bible, but she had a store of folklore. Her cousin, who helped with the chores from time to time, had "the largest collection of tales and songs concerning devils, ghosts, fairies, brownies, witches, warlocks, spunkies, kelpies, wraiths, apparitions, enchanted towers, giants, dragons, and other trumpery," which, Burns averred, "cultivated the latent seeds of poetry."

Somehow he managed to get a little schooling. He discovered Pope and Shakespeare and began rhyming in the local dialect. Brought up among countrymen and complaisant girls, he fell in love at fourteen and never fell out of it. Although consistently a lover, he was an inconstant one. His many amours include Elizabeth Paton, who bore him the first of his illegitimate children; Jean Armour, to whom, after sporadic infidelities, he always returned; Mary Campbell, his "Highland Mary," whom he apparently promised to marry; Anne Park, who delivered Burns's child nine days before Jean bore Burns another son; and several others.

At twenty-nine Burns went to Edinburgh with a collection of poems printed on a provincial press. In the capital he became the fashion of the moment; he was sought after by the metropolitan society not because he was appreciated as a poet but because he was a rustic novelty. Nothing could have been worse for him.

The quick popularity was followed by equally sudden neglect and consequent poverty. He abandoned farming and began to drink heavily. Overcome by misfortunes, he died in delirium at thirty-seven, "a poor, damned, incautious, duped, unfortunate fool," as he called himself, "the sport, the miserable victim of rebellious pride and bedlam passions."

Most convivial of poets, Burns was at his best when he was most himself, in the simple love songs and country humors. He opposed the glitter of "style" with plain speaking and answered preciosity with vulgar nonchalance. His love of irresponsibility and native audacity are clinched with satire. It laughs aloud while it attacks the pretentions of all creeds and philosophies. His "Address to the Deil" treats the world of morality as though its existence were mythical and literally gives the devil his due. "Tam o' Shanter" is a madly galloping scherzo never slackening in pace and continually increasing in wildness. A Rabelaisian riot of witches and warlocks, brownies and bogies, it turns folklore into a frolic. "The Jolly Beggars" is a cantata that is an annihilating mockery. No one, from the country parson to the prime minister, is safe before Burns's brawling abandon. Instead of being offended by its bawdiness, the Victorian Matthew Arnold compared it to the cellar scene in Goethe's *Faust* and concluded that it had a breadth and power "which are matched only by Shakespeare and Aristophanes."

THE JOLLY BEGGARS

DRINKING SONG

See the smoking bowl before us;
　Mark our jovial, ragged ring.
Round and round take up the chorus,
　And in raptures let us sing.

Chorus
A fig for those by law protected!
  Liberty's a glorious feast!
Courts for cowards were erected,
  Churches built to please the priest.

What is title, what is treasure,
  What is reputation's care?
If we lead a life of pleasure,
  'Tis no matter how or where!
            A fig for, *etc.*

With the ready trick and fable,
  Round we wander all the day;
And at night in barn or stable,
  Hug our doxies on the hay.
            A fig for, *etc.*

Does the train-attended carriage
  Thro' the country lighter rove?
Does the sober bed of marriage
  Witness brighter scenes of love?
            A fig for, *etc.*

Life is all a variorum,
  We regard not how it goes;
Let them cant about decorum,
  Who have character to lose.
            A fig for, *etc.*

Here's to budgets, bags and wallets!
  Here's to all the wandering train.
Here's our ragged brats and callets,[1]
  One and all cry out: Amen!

Chorus
A fig for those by law protected!
  Liberty's a glorious feast!
Courts for cowards were erected,
  Churches built to please the priest.

---

[1]*callets:* wenches

I ONCE WAS A MAID

I once was a maid, tho' I cannot tell when,
An' still my delight is in proper young men;
Some one of a troop of dragoons was my daddie,
No wonder I'm fond of a sodger laddie.

The first of my loves was a swaggering blade,
To rattle the thundering drum was his trade;
His leg was so tight, and his cheek was so ruddy,
Transported I was with my sodger laddie.

But the godly old chaplain left him in the lurch,
The sword I forsook for the sake of the church,
He ventured the soul, and I risk'd the body,
'Twas then I proved false to my sodger laddie.

Full soon I grew sick of my sanctified sot.
The regiment at large for a husband I got;
From the gilded spontoon to the life I was ready,
I asked no more but a sodger laddie.

But the peace it reduced me to beg in despair,
Till I met my old boy at a Cunningham fair;
His rags regimental they fluttered so gaudy,
My heart it rejoiced at my sodger laddie.

An' now I have lived—I know not how long,
An' still I can join in a cup or a song;
But whilst with both hands I can hold the glass steady,
Here's to thee, my hero, my sodger laddie.

TAM O' SHANTER

When chapman billies[1] leave the street,
And drouthy neibors neibors meet;
As market days are wearing late,
And folk begin to tak the gate,

---

[1]*chapman billies:* peddlers

While we sit bousing at the nappy,[2]
An' getting fou and unco happy,
We think na on the lang Scots miles,
The mosses, waters, slaps[3] and stiles,
That lie between us and our hame,
Where sits our sulky, sullen dame,
Gathering her brows like gathering storm,
Nursing her wrath to keep it warm.

This truth fand honest Tam o' Shanter,
As he frae Ayr ae night did canter
(Auld Ayr, wham ne'er a town surpasses,
For honest men and bonie lasses).

O Tam! had'st thou but been sae wise,
As taen thy ain wife Kate's advice!
She tauld thee weel thou was a skellum,[4]
A blethering, blustering, drunken blellum;[5]
That frae November till October,
Ae market-day thou was no sober;
That ilka melder[6] wi' the Miller,
Thou sat as lang as thou had siller;[7]
That ev'ry nag was ca'd a shoe on[8]
The Smith and thee gat roarin fou on;
That at the Lord's house, ev'n on Sunday,
Thou drank wi' Kirkton Jean till Monday;
She prophesied that late or soon,
Thou wad be found, deep drowned in Doon,
Or catched wi' warlocks in the mirk,
By Alloway's auld, haunted kirk.

Ah, gentle dames! it gars me greet,[9]
To think how mony counsels sweet,
How mony lengthened, sage advices,
The husband frae the wife despises!

---

[2]*bousing at the nappy:* drinking ale
[3]*slaps:* hedge gaps
[4]*skellum:* rascal
[5]*blellum:* babbler
[6]*ilka melder:* every corn-grinding
[7]*siller:* silver, i.e., money
[8]*ca'd a shoe on:* called for another drink
[9]*gars me greet:* makes me weep

But to our tale:—Ae market night,
Tam had got planted unco right,
Fast by an ingle, bleezing finely,
Wi' reaming swats[10] that drank divinely;
And at his elbow, Souter[11] Johnie,
His ancient, trusty, drouthy crony:
Tam lo'ed him like a very brither;
They had been fou for weeks thegither.
The night drave on wi' sangs an' clatter;
And aye the ale was growing better:
The Landlady and Tam grew gracious,
Wi' favors secret, sweet and precious:
The Souter tauld his queerest stories;
The Landlord's laugh was ready chorus:
The storm without might rair and rustle,
Tam did na mind the storm a whistle.

Care, mad to see a man sae happy,
E'en drowned himsel amang the nappy.
As bees flee hame wi' lades[12] o' treasure,
The minutes winged their way wi' pleasure:
Kings may be blest, but Tam was glorious,
O'er a' the ills o' life victorious!

But pleasures are like poppies spread,
You seize the flow'r, its bloom is shed;
Or like the snow falls in the river,
A moment white—then melts for ever;
Or like the borealis race,
That flit ere you can point their place;
Or like the rainbow's lovely form
Evanishing amid the storm.
Nae man can tether time or tide;—
The hour approaches Tam maun ride;
That hour, o' night's black arch the key-stane,
That dreary hour he mounts his beast in;

---

[10] *reaming swats:* tankards of foaming ale
[11] *Souter:* cobbler
[12] *lades:* loads

And sic a night he taks the road in,
As ne'er poor sinner was abroad in.

The wind blew as 'twad blawn its last;
The rattling showers rose on the blast;
The speedy gleams the darkness swallowed;
Loud, deep, and lang, the thunder bellowed:
That night, a child might understand,
The Deil had business on his hand.

Weel mounted on his gray mare, Meg,
A better never lifted leg,
Tam skelpit[13] on through dub[14] and mire,
Despising wind, and rain, and fire;
Whiles holding fast his guid blue bonnet;
Whiles crooning o'er some auld Scots sonnet;
Whiles glowering round wi' prudent cares,
Lest bogles[15] catch him unawares;
Kirk Alloway was drawing nigh,
Whare ghaists and houlets[16] nightly cry.

By this time he was cross the ford,
Whare in the snaw the chapman smoored,[17]
And past the birks and meikle stane,[18]
Whare drunken Charlie brak's neckbane;
And through the whins,[19] and by the cairn,[20]
Whare hunters fand the murdered bairn:
And near the thorn, aboon the well,
Whare Mungo's mither hanged hersel.
Before him Doon pours all his floods;
The doubling storm roars through the woods;
The lightnings flash from pole to pole;
Near and more near the thunders roll:
When, glimmering through the groaning trees,

---

[13] *skelpit:* splashed
[14] *dub:* puddle
[15] *bogles:* goblins
[16] *houlets:* owls
[17] *smoored:* smothered
[18] *meikle stane:* huge stone
[19] *whins:* bushes
[20] *cairn:* stone pile

Kirk Alloway seemed in a bleeze;
Through ilka bore[21] the beams were glancing;
And loud resounded mirth and dancing.

   Inspiring bold John Barleycorn!
What dangers thou canst make us scorn!
Wi' tippenny,[22] we fear nae evil;
Wi' usquebae,[23] we'll face the Devil!
The swats sae reamed in Tammie's noddle,
Fair play, he cared na deils a boddle.[24]
But Maggie stood right sair astonished,
Till, by the heel and hand admonished,
She ventured forward on the light;
And, wow! Tam saw an unco sight!

Warlocks and witches in a dance;
Nae cotillion brent-new frae France,
But hornpipes, jigs, strathspeys, and reels,
Put life and mettle in their heels.
At winnock-bunker[25] in the east,
There sat auld Nick, in shape o' beast;
A towzie tyke,[26] black, grim, and large,
To gie them music was his charge:
He screwed the pipes and gart them skirl,[27]
Till roof and rafters a' did dirl. —[28]
Coffins stood round, like open presses,
That shawed the dead in their last dresses;
And by some devilish cantrip sleight,[29]
Each in its cauld hand held a light —
By which heroic Tam was able
To note upon the holy table
A murderer's banes in gibbet-airns;[30]
Two span-lang, wee, unchristened bairns;
A thief, new-cutted frae a rape,

---

[21] *bore:* chink
[22] *tippenny:* twopenny ale
[23] *usquebae:* whisky
[24] *cared na deils a boddle:* didn't care a farthing
[25] *winnock-bunker:* window seat
[26] *towzie tyke:* shaggy cur
[27] *gart them skirl:* made them squeal
[28] *dirl:* rattle
[29] *cantrip sleight:* magic trick
[30] *gibbet-airns:* gallows irons

Wi' his last gasp his gab did gape;
Five tomahawks wi' blude red-rusted;
Five scimitars wi' murder crusted;
A garter which a babe had strangled;
A knife a father's throat had mangled,
Whom his ain son of life bereft,
The gray hairs sticking to the heft;
Wi' mair of horrible and awfu',
Which even to name wad be unlawfu'.

As Tammie glowered, amazed and curious,
The mirth and fun grew fast and furious;
The Piper loud and louder blew,
The dancers quick and quicker flew,
They reeled, they set, they crossed, they cleekit,[31]
Till ilka carlin swat and reekit,[32]
And coost her duddies to the wark,[33]
And linkit at it in her sark![34]

But Tam kent what was what fu' brawlie:
There was ae winsome wench and waulie[35]
That night enlisted in the core
(Lang after kenned on Carrick shore
For mony a beast to dead she shot,
And perished mony a bonie boat,
And shook baith meikle corn and bear,[36]
And kept the country-side in fear);
Her cutty-sark,[37] o' Paisley harn,
That while a lassie she had worn,
In longitude though sorely scanty,
It was her best, and she was vauntie.[38]
Ah! little kenned thy reverend grannie,
That sark she coft[39] for her wee Nannie,

---

[31] *cleekit:* joined hands
[32] *ilka carlin swat and reekit:* every hag sweat and smoked
[33] *coost her duddies to the wark:* cast off her clothes for the work
[34] *linkit at it in her sark:* danced in her shirt
[35] *waulie:* jolly
[36] *bear:* barley
[37] *cutty-sark:* short shirt
[38] *vauntie:* proud
[39] *coft:* bought

Wi' twa pund Scots ('twas a' her riches),
Wad ever graced a dance of witches!

But here my Muse her wing maun cower,
Sic flights are far beyond her power;
To sing how Nannie lap and flang
(A souple jade she was and strang),
And how Tam stood, like ane bewitched,
And thought his very een enriched:
Even Satan glowered, and fidged fu' fain,
And hotched[40] and blew wi' might and main:
Till first ae caper, syne anither,
Tam tint[41] his reason a' thegither,
And roars out, "Weel done, Cutty-sark!"
And in an instant all was dark:
And scarcely had he Maggie rallied,
When out the hellish legion sallied.

As bees bizz out wi' angry fyke,[42]
When plundering herds assail their byke;[43]
As open pussie's[44] mortal foes,
When, pop! she starts before their nose;
As eager runs the market-crowd,
When "Catch the thief!" resounds aloud;
So Maggie runs, the witches follow,
Wi' mony an eldritch[45] skreich and hollo.

Ah, Tam! Ah, Tam! thou'll get thy fairin![46]
In hell they'll roast thee like a herrin!
In vain thy Kate awaits thy comin!
Kate soon will be a woefu' woman!
Now, do thy speedy utmost, Meg,
And win the key-stane o' the brig;[47]
There, at them thou thy tail may toss,
A running stream they dare na cross;

40 *hotched:* squirmed
41 *tint:* lost
42 *fyke:* fuss
43 *byke:* hive
44 *pussie's:* the hare's
45 *eldritch:* unearthly
46 *fairin:* reward
47 *brig:* bridge

But ere the key-stane she could make,
The fiend a tail she had to shake!
For Nannie, far before the rest,
Hard upon noble Maggie prest,
And flew at Tam wi' furious ettle;[48]
But little wist she Maggie's mettle!
Ae spring brought off her master hale,
But left behind her ain gray tail:
The carlin claught her by the rump,
And left poor Maggie scarce a stump.

   Now wha this tale o' truth shall read,
Ilk' man and mother's son, take heed:
Whene'er to drink you are inclined,
Or cutty-sarks run in your mind,
Think, ye may buy the joys o'er dear,
Remember Tam o' Shanter's mare!

---

[48] *ettle:* intent

Sydney Smith

Sydney Smith, born at Woodford, Essex, in 1771, was a wit who made the mistake of choosing the ministry as his livelihood. He was a popular, almost a professional, diner-out, who declared, "My idea of heaven is eating pâté de foie gras to the sound of trumpets." It can be understood why, with his exuberant drolleries coupled with a refusal to follow the rigors of orthodoxy, he failed to advance beyond his clerical status as a country parson. No matter how sound Smith's theology may have been, the eminence of bishop could never be offered to a man who could express the truth so lightly as to tell a wealthy brother, "Both of us illustrate contradictions in nature. You rise by your weight; I fall by my levity."

One of the founders of the *Edinburgh Review*, Smith wrote more than sixty articles on prison abuses, game laws, Catholic emancipation, and American repudiation. But it was the irreverent aphorisms that enlivened the articles and sharpened their thoughts.

FIFTEEN THOUGHTS

• As the French say, there are three sexes: men, women, and clergymen.

• So-and-so has not body enough to cover his mind decently with; his intellect is improperly exposed.

• Take short views, hope for the best, and trust in God.

• Among the smaller duties of life I hardly know any more important than that of not praising when praise is not due.

• Daniel Webster struck me much like a steam-engine in trousers.

• The country is a place with only one post a day. In the country I always fear that creation will expire before tea-time.

• I am going to pray for you at St. Paul's, but with no very lively hope of success.

• Poverty is no disgrace to a man, but it is confoundedly inconvenient.

• Macaulay has occasional flashes of silence that make his conversation perfectly delightful. . . . He is like a book in breeches.

• Children are horribly insecure—the life of a parent is the life of a gambler.

• Dame Partington was seen with mop and pattens vigorously pushing away the Atlantic ocean. The Atlantic ocean beat Mrs. Partington.

• I never could find any man who could think for two minutes together.

• No two ideas are more inseparable than Beer and Britain.

• What a pity it is that we have no amusements in England but vice and religion.

• Beginning with the best intentions, societies for the suppression of vice degenerate into a receptacle for every species of tittle-tattle, impertinence, and malice. Men whose trade is rat-catching love to catch rats; the bug-destroyer seizes on his bug with delight; and the suppressor is gratified by finding his vice. The last becomes a mere tradesman like the others.

RECIPE FOR A SALAD

To make this condiment, your poet begs
The pounded yellow of two hard-boiled eggs;
Two boiled potatoes, passed through kitchen sieve,
Smoothness and softness to the salad give;

Let onion atoms lurk within the bowl,
And, half-suspected, animate the whole.
Of mordant mustard add a single spoon,
Distrust the condiment that bites so soon;
But deem it not, thou man of herbs, a fault,
To add a double quantity of salt;
Four times the spoon with oil from Lucca drown,
And twice with vinegar procured from town;
And, lastly, o'er the flavored compound toss
A magic soupçon of anchovy sauce.
Oh, green and glorious! Oh, herbaceous treat!
'Twould tempt the dying anchorite to eat:
Back to the world he'd turn his fleeting soul,
And plunge his fingers in the salad-bowl!
Serenely full, the epicure would say,
Fate cannot harm me, I have dined to-day.

Charles Lamb

An essayist who surpassed Addison in both humor and tenderness, one of the most beloved of English writers, Charles Lamb was born in 1775 in London. His family was poor; a speech defect barred him from the ministry, which might have been his profession, and most of his life Lamb earned a living as a clerk. Like William Hogarth, whom he was to extoll in Leigh Hunt's *Reflector*, he loved the teeming streets of his native city, from the patricians and parvenus down to the chimney sweeps and beggars, all "part and parcel of London with-the-many-sins."

Lamb had fallen in love when a tragedy occurred that made him abandon all thoughts of marriage. His sister, Mary, ten years his senior, who had been doing needlework to eke out the family's pitifully small income, suddenly became deranged. After wounding her father, she stabbed her mother to death. John, the older brother, wanted Mary confined to Bethlehem, the city's insane asylum, but Charles managed to obtain her release on the assurance that he would be responsible for her. It was a never-ending burden, for although Mary was an affectionate companion and lucid most of the time, she was subject to recurring fits of insanity, and during these periods she had to be removed to a nursing home. Harassed by anxiety as well as poverty, the Lambs moved from one lodging to another.

Lamb's writings had yielded little in either money or reputation until he was commissioned to contribute to Godwin's Juvenile Library in 1832, when the now-famous *Tales from Shakespeare* by Charles and Mary Lamb were published. Inevitably it was Charles who retold the tragedies, and it is somewhat ironic that Mary did the comedies.

It was not until he was forty-five that Lamb came into his own with essays he wrote for the *London Magazine*. The first of these described the South Sea house, where he had worked so many years alongside a foreign clerk named Elia. For this as well as the subsequent essays Lamb chose the name as his pseudonym—*The Last Essays of Elia* were collected in 1833.

The Lambs had left London and had taken a cottage in the quiet countryside, but Mary's attacks became more frequent and more violent. Charles's health had also become impaired; in his fifty-ninth year he contracted erysipelas and died on December 27, 1834. Mary survived him by thirteen years.

Two years after his death Wordsworth composed a long memorial poem that evoked Lamb's spirit from its beginnings,

> *From the great city where he first drew breath,*
> *Was reared and taught, and humbly earned his bread,*
> *To the strict labors of the merchant's desk*
> *By duty chained . . .*

to a likening of Lamb's genius with the lightning that plays around mountaintops:

> *Thus innocently sported, breaking forth,*
> *As from a cloud of some grave sympathy,*
> *Humor and wild instinctive wit, and all*
> *The vivid flashes of his spoken words.*

DISSERTATION ON ROAST PIG

Mankind, says a Chinese manuscript which my friend was obliging enough to read and explain to me, for the first seventy thousand ages ate their meat raw, clawing or biting it from the living animal, just as they do in Abyssinia to this day. This period is not obscurely hinted at by their great Confucius in the second chapter of his Mundane Meditations, where he designates a kind of golden age by the term Cho-fang,—literally, the Cook's Holiday. The manuscript goes on to say that the art of roasting, or rather broiling (which I take to be the elder brother), was accidentally discovered in the manner following. The swineherd, Ho-ti, having gone out into the woods one morning, as his manner was, to collect mast for his hogs, left the cottage in the care of his eldest son, Bo-bo, a great lubberly boy, who, being fond of playing with fire, as younkers of his age commonly are, let some sparks escape into a bundle of straw, which, kindling quickly, spread the conflagration over every part of their poor mansion, till it was reduced to ashes. Together with the cottage (a sorry antediluvian makeshift of a building, you may think it), what was of much more importance, a fine litter of new-farrowed pigs, no less than nine in number, perished. China pigs have been esteemed a luxury all over the East from the remotest periods that we read of. Bo-bo was in the utmost consternation, as you may think, not so much for the sake of the tenement, which his father and he could easily build up again with the aid of a few dry branches, and the labor of an hour or two, at any time, as for the loss of the pigs. While he was thinking what he should say to his father, and wringing his hands over the smoking remnants of one of those untimely sufferers, an odor assailed his nostrils unlike any scent which he had before experienced. What could it proceed from?—not from the burnt cottage,—he had smelt that smell before: indeed, this was by no means the first accident of the kind which had occurred through the negligence of this unlucky young firebrand. Much less did it resemble that of any known herb, weed, or flower. A premonitory moistening at the same time overflowed his nether lip. He knew not what to think. He next stooped down to feel the pig, if there were any signs of life in it. He burnt his fingers, and to cool them he applied them, in his booby fashion, to his mouth. Some of the crumbs of the scorched skin had come away with his fingers, and for the first time in his life (in the world's life, indeed, for before him no man had known it) he tasted—*crackling!* Again he felt and fumbled at the pig. It did not burn him so much now; still he licked his fingers from a sort of habit. The truth at length broke into his slow understanding, that it was the pig that smelt so, and the pig that tasted so delicious; and, surrendering himself up to the new-born pleasure, he fell to tearing up whole handfuls of the scorched skin with the flesh next it, and was cramming it down his throat in his beastly fashion, when his sire entered amid the smoking rafters, armed with retributory cudgel, and, finding how affairs stood, began to rain blows upon the young rogue's shoulders as thick as hailstones, which Bo-bo heeded not any more than if they had been flies. The tickling pleasure which he experienced in his lower regions had rendered him quite callous to any inconveniences he might feel in these remote quarters. His father might lay on, but he could not beat him from his pig till he had fairly made an end of it, when, becoming a little more sensible of his situation, something like the following dialogue ensued.

"You graceless whelp, what have you got there devouring? Is it not enough that you have burnt me down three houses with your dog's tricks, and be hanged to you! but you must be eating fire, and I know not what?—What have you got there, I say?"

"Oh, father, the pig, the pig! do come and taste how nice the burnt pig eats!"

The ears of Ho-ti tingled with horror. He cursed his son, and cursed himself that ever he should beget a son that should eat burnt pig.

Bo-bo, whose scent was wonderfully sharpened since morning, soon raked out another pig, and, fairly rending it asunder, thrust the lesser half by main force into the fists of Ho-ti, shouting out, "Eat, eat, eat the burnt pig, father; only taste; O Lord!"—with such-like barbarous ejaculations, cramming all the while as if he would choke.

Ho-ti trembled in every joint while he grasped the abominable thing, wavering whether he should not put his son to death for an unnatural young monster, when, the crackling scorching his fingers, as it had done his son's, and applying the same remedy to them, he in his turn tasted some of its flavor, which, make what sour mouths he would for a pretence, proved not altogether displeasing to him. In conclusion (for the manuscript here is a little tedious), both father and son fairly sat down to the mess, and never left off till they had despatched all that remained of the litter.

Bo-bo was strictly enjoined not to let the secret escape, for the neighbors would certainly have stoned them for a couple of abominable wretches, who could think of improving upon the good meat which God had sent them. Nevertheless, strange stories got about. It was observed that Ho-ti's cottage was burnt down now more frequently than ever. Nothing but fires from this time forward. Some would break out in broad day, others in the night-time. As often as the sow farrowed, so sure was the house of Ho-ti to be in a blaze; and Ho-ti himself, which was the more remarkable, instead of chastising his son, seemed to grow more indulgent

to him than ever. At length they were watched, the terrible
mystery discovered, and father and son summoned to take their
trial at Pekin, then an inconsiderable assize town. Evidence was
given, the obnoxious food itself produced in court, and verdict
about to be pronounced, when the foreman of the jury begged
that some of the burnt pig, of which the culprits stood accused,
might be handed into the box. He handled it, and they all handled
it; and burning their fingers, as Bo-bo and his father had done
before them, and nature prompting to each of them the same
remedy,—against the face of all the facts, and the clearest charge
which judge had ever given,—to the surprise of the whole court,
townsfolk, strangers, reporters, and all present,—without leaving
the box, or any manner of consultation whatever, they brought in
a simultaneous verdict of Not Guilty.

The judge, who was a shrewd fellow, winked at the manifest
iniquity of the decision, and, when the court was dismissed, went
privily, and bought up all the pigs that could be had for love or
money. In a few days his lordship's town-house was observed to
be on fire. The thing took wing, and now there was nothing to be
seen but fire in every direction. Fuel and pigs grew enormously
dear all over the district. The insurance-offices one and all shut
up shop. People built slighter and slighter every day, until it was
feared that the very science of architecture would in no long time
be lost to the world. Thus this custom of firing houses continued,
till in process of time, says my manuscript, a sage arose, like our
Locke, who made a discovery that the flesh of swine, or indeed of
any other animal, might be cooked (*burnt*, as they called it) without the necessity of consuming a whole house to dress it. Then
first began the rude form of a grid-iron. Roasting by the string or
spit came in a century or two later,—I forget in whose dynasty.
By such slow degrees, concludes the manuscript, do the most useful, and seemingly the most obvious, arts make their way among
mankind.

Without placing too implicit faith in the account above given,
it must be agreed that if a worthy pretext for so dangerous an
experiment as setting houses on fire (especially in these days)
could be assigned in favor of any culinary object, that pretext and
excuse might be found in ROAST PIG.

Of all the delicacies in the whole *mundus edibilis,* I will maintain it to be the most delicate,—*princeps obsoniorum.*

I speak not of your grown porkers,—things between pig and
pork,—those hobbydehoys,—but a young and tender suckling,—

under a moon old,—guiltless as yet of the sty,—with no original speck of the *amor immunditiae*, the hereditary failing of the first parent, yet manifest,—his voice as yet not broken, but something between a childish treble and a grumble, the mild forerunner, or *praeludium*, of a grunt.

He must be roasted. I am not ignorant that our ancestors ate them seethed, or boiled; but what a sacrifice of the exterior tegument!

There is no flavor comparable, I will contend, to that of the crisp, tawny, well-watched, not over-roasted, *crackling*, as it is well called: the very teeth are invited to their share of the pleasure at this banquet, in overcoming the coy, brittle resistance,—with the adhesive oleaginous,—oh, call it not fat! but an indefinable sweetness growing up to it,—the tender blossoming of fat,—fat cropped in the bud,—taken in the shoot,—in the first innocence,—the cream and quintessence of the child-pig's yet pure food,—the lean, no lean, but a kind of animal manna,—or, rather, fat and lean (if it must be so) so blended and running into each other that both together make but one ambrosian result, or common substance.

Behold him while he is "doing:" it seemeth rather a refreshing warmth, than a scorching heat, that he is so passive to. How equably he twirleth round the string! Now he is just done. To see the extreme sensibility of that tender age! he hath wept out his pretty eyes,—radiant jellies,—shooting stars.

See him in the dish, his second cradle, how meek he lieth!— wouldst thou have had this innocent grow up to the grossness and indocility which too often accompany maturer swinehood? Ten to one he would have proved a glutton, a sloven, an obstinate, disagreeable animal, wallowing in all manner of filthy conversation: from these sins he is happily snatched away

Ere sin could blight, or sorrow fade,
Death came with timely care;

his memory is odoriferous; no clown curseth, while his stomach half rejecteth, the rank bacon; no coal-heaver bolteth him in reeking sausages; he hath a fair sepulchre in the grateful stomach of the judicious epicure, and for such a tomb might be content to die.

He is the best of sapors. Pine-apple is great. She is, indeed, almost too transcendent,—a delight, if not sinful, yet so like to sinning that really a tender-conscienced person would do well to pause; too ravishing for mortal taste, she woundeth and excoriateth the lips that approach her; like lovers' kisses, she biteth; she is a pleasure bordering on pain from the fierceness and insanity of her relish; but she stoppeth at the palate; she meddleth not with the appetite; and the coarsest hunger might barter her consistently for a mutton-chop.

Pig—let me speak his praise—is no less provocative of the appetite than he is satisfactory to the criticalness of the censorious palate. The strong man may batten on him, and the weakling refuseth not his mild juices.

Unlike to mankind's mixed characters, a bundle of virtues and vices, inexplicably intertwisted, and not to be unravelled without hazard, he is—good throughout. No part of him is better or worse than another. He helpeth, as far as his little means extend, all around. He is the least envious of banquets. He is all neighbor's fare.

I am one of those who freely and ungrudgingly impart a share of the good things of this life which fall to their lot (few as mine are in this kind) to a friend. I protest I take as great an interest in my friend's pleasures, his relishes and proper satisfactions, as in mine own. "Presents," I often say, "endear Absents." Hares, pheasants, partridges, snipes, barn-door chickens (those "tame villatic fowl"), capons, plovers, brawn, barrels of oysters, I dispense as freely as I receive them. I love to taste them, as it were, upon the tongue of my friend. But a stop must be put somewhere. One would not, like Lear, "give everything." I make my stand upon pig. Methinks it is an ingratitude to the Giver of all good flavors to extradomiciliate, or send out of the house, slightingly (under pretence of friendship, or I know not what), a blessing so particularly adapted, predestined, I may say, to my individual palate. It argues an insensibility.

POPULAR FALLACIES

That we should rise with the lark.—At what precise minute that airy little musician doffs his night gear and prepares to tune up his unseasonable matins, we are not naturalists enough to determine. But for a mere human gentleman—that has no orchestra business to call him from his warm bed to such preposterous exercise—we take ten, or half after ten (eleven, of course, during this Christmas solstice), to be the very earliest hour at which he can begin to think of abandoning his pillow. To think of it, we say; for to do it in earnest requires another half hour's good consideration. Not but there are pretty sunrisings, as we are told, and such like gawds, abroad in the world, in summer-time especially, some hours before what we have assigned, which a gentleman may see, as they say, only for getting up. But having been tempted once or twice, in earlier life, to assist at those ceremonies, we confess our curiosity abated. We are no longer ambitious of being the sun's courtiers, to attend at his morning levees. We hold the good hours of the dawn too sacred to waste them upon such observances; which have in them, besides, something Pagan and Persic. To say truth; we never anticipated our usual hour, or got up with the sun (as 'tis called), to go a journey, or upon a foolish whole day's pleasuring, but we suffered for it all the long hours after in listlessness and headaches; Nature herself sufficiently declaring her sense of our presumption in aspiring to regulate our frail waking courses by the measures of that celestial and sleepless traveler. We deny not that there is something sprightly and vigorous, at the outset especially, in these break-of-day excursions. It is flattering to get the start of a lazy world, to conquer death by proxy in his image. But the seeds of sleep and mortality are in us; and we pay usually, in strange qualms before night falls, the penalty of the unnatural inversion. Therefore, while the busy part of mankind are fast huddling on their clothes, or are already up and about their occupations, content to have swallowed their sleep by wholesale, we choose to linger abed, and digest our dreams. It is the very time to recombine the wandering images which night in a confused mass presented; to snatch them from forgetfulness; to shape and mould them. Some people have no good of their dreams. Like fast feeders, they gulp them too grossly to taste them curiously. We love to chew the cud of a foregone vision; to collect the scattered rays of a brighter phantasm, or act over again, with firmer nerves, the sadder nocturnal tragedies; to drag into daylight a struggling and half-vanishing nightmare; to handle and examine the terrors or the airy solaces. We have too much respect for these spiritual communications to let them go so lightly. We are not so stupid or so careless as that imperial forgetter of his dreams, that we should need a seer to remind us of the form of them. They seem to us to have as much significance as our waking concerns; or rather to import us more nearly, as more nearly we approach by years to the shadowy world whither we are hastening. We have shaken

hands with the world's business; we have done with it; we have
discharged ourself of it. Why should we get up? We have neither
suit to solicit, nor affairs to manage. The drama has shut in upon
us at the fourth act. We have nothing here to expect but in a short
time a sick-bed and a dismissal. We delight to anticipate death
by such shadows as night affords. We are already half acquainted
with ghosts. We were never much in the world. Disappointment
early struck a dark veil between us and its dazzling illusions. Our
spirits showed gray before our hairs. The mighty changes of the
world already appear as but the vain stuff out of which dramas
are composed. We have asked no more of life than what the mimic
images in playhouses present us with. Even those types have
waxed fainter. Our clock appears to have struck. We are SUPER-
ANNUATED. In this dearth of mundane satisfaction, we contract
politic alliances with shadows. It is good to have friends at court.
The abstracted media of dreams seem no ill introduction to that
spiritual presence, upon which, in no long time, we expect to be
thrown. We are trying to know a little of the usages of that colony;
to learn the language, and the faces we shall meet with there, that
we may be the less awkward at our first coming among them. We
willingly call a phantom our fellow, as knowing we shall soon be
of their dark companionship. Therefore we cherish dreams. We
try to spell in them the alphabet of the invisible world, and think
we know already how it shall be with us. Those uncouth shapes,
which, while we clung to flesh and blood, affrighted us, have become familiar. We feel attenuated into their meager essences,
and have given the hand of half-way approach to incorporeal being. We once thought life to be something, but it has unaccount-
ably fallen from us before its time. Therefore we choose to dally
with visions. The sun has no purposes of ours to light us to. Why
should we get up?

That we should lie down with the lamb. —We could never quite
understand the philosophy of this arrangement, or the wisdom
of our ancestors in sending us for instruction to these woolly
bedfellows. A sheep, when it is dark, has nothing to do but to shut
his silly eyes, and sleep if he can. Man found out long sixes. Hail,
candlelight! without disparagement to sun or moon, the kindliest
luminary of the three—if we may not rather style thee their radiant deputy, mild viceroy of the moon! We love to read, talk, sit
silent, eat, drink, sleep, by candlelight. They are everybody's sun
and moon. This is our peculiar and household planet. Wanting it,

what savage unsocial nights must our ancestors have spent, wintering in caves and unillumined fastnesses! They must have lain about and grumbled at one another in the dark. What repartees could have passed, when you must have felt about for a smile, and handled a neighbor's cheek to be sure that he understood it? This accounts for the seriousness of the elder poetry. It has a somber cast (try Hesiod or Ossian), derived from the tradition of those unlanterned nights. Jokes came in with candles. We wonder how they saw to pick up a pin, if they had any. How did they sup? What a mélange of chance carving they must have made of it! Here one had got a leg of a goat, when he wanted a horse's shoulder; there another had dipped his scooped palm in a kid-skin of wild honey, when he meditated right mare's milk.—There is neither good eating nor drinking in fresco. Who, even in these civilized times, has never experienced this, when at some economic table he has commenced dining after dusk, and waited for the flavor till the lights came? The senses absolutely give and take reciprocally. Can you tell pork from veal in the dark? or distinguish Sherris from pure Malaga? Take away the candle from the smoking man: by the glimmering of the left ashes, he knows that he is still smoking, but he knows it only by an inference; till the restored light, coming in aid of the olfactories, reveals to both senses the full aroma.

That the worst puns are the best.—If by worst be only meant the most far-fetched and startling, we agree to it. A pun is not bound by the laws which limit nicer wit. It is a pistol let off at the ear, not a feather to tickle the intellect. It is an antic which does not stand upon manners, but comes bounding into the presence, and does not show the less comic for being dragged in sometimes by the head and shoulders. What though it limp a little, or prove defective in one leg—all the better. A pun may easily be too curious and artificial. Who has not at one time or other been at a party of professors (himself perhaps an old offender in that line), where, after ringing a round of the most ingenious conceits, every man contributing his shot, and some there the most expert shooters of the day; after making a poor *word* run the gantlet till it is ready to drop; after hunting and winding it through all the possible ambages of similar sounds; after squeezing and hauling and tugging at it, till the very milk of it will not yield a drop further— suddenly some obscure, unthought-of fellow in a corner, who was never 'prentice to the trade, whom the company for very pity passed over, as we do by a known poor man when a money-sub-scription is going round, no one calling upon him for his quota, has all at once come out with something so whimsical, yet so pertinent—so brazen in its pretensions, yet so impossible to be denied—so exquisitely good, and so deplorably bad at the same time—that it has proved a Robin Hood's shot? Anything ulterior to that is despaired of; and the party breaks up, unanimously voting it to be the very worst (that is, best) pun of the evening. This species of wit is the better for not being perfect in all its parts. What it gains in completeness, it loses in naturalness. The more exactly it satisfies the critical, the less hold it has upon some other faculties. The puns which are most entertaining are those which will least bear an analysis. Of this kind is the following recorded with a sort of stigma in one of Swift's Miscellanies:

An Oxford scholar, meeting a porter who was carrying a hare through the streets, accosts him with this extraordinary question: "Prithee, friend, is that thy own hare, or a wig?"

There is no excusing this, and no resisting it. A man might blur ten sides of paper in attempting a defense of it against a critic who should be laughter-proof. The quibble in itself is not consid-erable. It is only a new turn given by a little false pronunciation to a very common, though not a very courteous inquiry. Put by one gentleman to another at a dinner-party, it would have been vapid; to the mistress of the house, it would have shown much less wit than rudeness. We must take in the totality of *time, place,* and *person:* the pert look of the inquiring scholar, the desponding looks of the puzzled porter; the one stopping at leisure, the other hurrying on with his burden; the innocent though rather abrupt tendency of the first member of the question, with the utter and inextricable irrelevancy of the second; the place—a public street—not favorable to frivolous investigations; the affrontive quality of the primitive inquiry (the common question) invidiously trans-ferred to the derivative (the new turn given to it) in the implied satire; namely, that few of that tribe are expected to eat of the good things which they carry, they being in most countries con-sidered rather as the temporary trustees than owners of such dainties—which the fellow was beginning to understand; but then the wig again comes in, and he can make nothing of it; all put together constitute a picture. Hogarth could have made it intel-ligible on canvas.

Washington Irving

A shy, self-conscious author who until he was fifty did not publish under his own name but under a set of odd pseudonyms —"Diedrich Knickerbocker," "Jonathan Oldstyle," "Anthony Evergreen," "Geoffrey Crayon," "Friar Antonio Agapida"— Washington Irving was born in 1783 in New York City. The eleventh child of stern Presbyterian parents, he was spoiled by his older brothers and sisters, not only because he was the youngest but because he was the most delicate. Irving never went to college; he studied law privately until at twenty-one he was threatened by tuberculosis and sent by his brothers for a two-year sojourn abroad. Most of this time was spent in Rome, where Irving was almost persuaded to become a painter.

Back in New York he passed his bar examinations more because of his ingratiating charm than because of any real legalistic knowledge. He practiced law rarely; his one interest was writing. His first work of any significance was a collection of sketches, *Salmagundi, or the Whim-Whams and Opinions of Launcelot Langstaff, Esq, and Others*, written in collaboration with one of his brothers and a well-known novelist. More important was the next miscellany, *A History of New York from the Beginning of the World to the End of the Dutch Dynasty by Diedrich Knickerbocker*. Although Irving was only twenty-six when this satirical memoir of the city of his birth was composed, many consider it his greatest achievement. It is a fabulous burlesque of fabulous figures, an improvisation in the grand manner.

In his early thirties he went to Liverpool as a silent partner in one of his brothers' enterprises. Irving was no businessman and the venture failed. Once again he was obliged to turn to his pen for revenue, and in 1819 the first number of *The Sketch Book* was published. This was a happy mélange of such English themes as the description of an English Christmas and such American subjects as "Rip Van Winkle" and "The Legend of Sleepy Hollow." Three years later *Bracebridge Hall,* Irving's commentary on English country life, appeared, followed by *Tales of a Traveler.* All won critical approval and financial reward. With Sir Walter Scott and Lord Byron, Irving had become the third of a triumvirate of internationally popular writers.

When Irving was fifty-nine, Daniel Webster and Henry Clay procured for him an ambassadorship to Madrid. But though he remained at this diplomatic post four years, he was anxious to return to his spacious estate, Sunnyside-on-the-Hudson. There was a monumental biography of George Washington to be completed and a life story of Mahomet as well as a biography of Oliver Goldsmith, one of his literary masters. The work was too much for him. Worn out, Irving died of a heart attack at seventy-six.

A HISTORY OF NEW YORK BY DIEDRICH KNICKERBOCKER

WOUTER VAN TWILLER

It was in the year of our Lord 1629, that Mynheer Wouter Van Twiller was appointed governor of the province of Nieuw Nederlandts under the commission and control of their High Mightinesses the Lords States-General of the United Netherlands, and the privileged West India Company.

This renowned old gentleman arrived at New Amsterdam in the merry month of June, the sweetest month in all the year; — when the robin, the thrush, and a thousand other wanton songsters, make the woods to resound with amorous ditties, and the luxurious little boblincon revels among the clover-blossoms of the meadows,—all which happy coincidence persuaded the old dames of New Amsterdam, who were skilled in the art of fore-telling events, that this was to be a happy and prosperous administration.

The renowned Wouter (or Walter) Van Twiller was descended from a long line of Dutch burgomasters, who had successively dozed away their lives and grown fat upon the bench of magistracy in Rotterdam; and who had comported themselves with such singular wisdom and propriety, that they were never either heard or talked of—which, next to being universally applauded, should be the object of ambition of all magistrates and rulers. There are two opposite ways by which some men make a figure in the world: one, by talking faster than they think, and the other, by holding their tongues and not thinking at all. By the first, many a smatterer acquires the reputation of a man of quick parts; by the other, many a dunderpate, like the owl, the stupidest of birds, comes to be considered the very type of wisdom. This, by the way, is a casual remark, which I would not, for the universe, have it thought I apply to Governor Van Twiller. It is true he was a man shut up within himself, like an oyster, and rarely spoke, except in monosyllables; but then it was allowed he seldom said a foolish thing. So invincible was his gravity that he was never known to laugh or even to smile through the whole course of a long and prosperous life. Nay, if a joke were uttered in his presence, that set light-minded hearers in a roar, it was observed to throw him into a state of perplexity. Sometimes he would deign to inquire into the matter, and when, after much explanation, the joke was made as plain as a pike-staff, he would continue to smoke his pipe in silence, and at length, knocking out the ashes, would exclaim, "Well! I see nothing in all that to laugh about."

With all his reflective habits, he never made up his mind on a subject. His adherents accounted for this by the astonishing magnitude of his ideas. He conceived every subject on so grand a scale that he had not room in his head to turn it over and examine both sides of it. Certain it is, that, if any matter were propounded to him on which ordinary mortals would rashly determine at first glance, he would put on a vague, mysterious look, shake his capacious head, smoke some time in profound silence, and at length observe, that "he had his doubts about the matter"; which gained him the reputation of a man slow of belief and not easily imposed upon. What is more, it gained him a lasting name; for to this habit of the mind has been attributed his surname of Twiller; which is said to be a corruption of the original Twijfler, or, in plain English, *Doubter*.

The person of this illustrious old gentleman was formed and proportioned, as though it had been moulded by the hands of some cunning Dutch statuary, as a model of majesty and lordly grandeur. He was exactly five feet six inches in height, and six feet five inches in circumference. His head was a perfect sphere, and of such stupendous dimensions, that Dame Nature, with all her sex's ingenuity, would have been puzzled to construct a neck capable of supporting it; wherefore she wisely declined the attempt, and settled it firmly on the top of his backbone, just between the shoulders. His body was oblong and particularly capacious at bottom; which was wisely ordered by Providence, seeing that he was a man of sedentary habits, and very averse to the idle labor of walking. His legs were short, but sturdy in proportion to the weight they had to sustain; so that when erect he had not a little the appearance of a beer-barrel on skids. His face, that infallible index of the mind, presented a vast expanse, unfurrowed by any of those lines and angles which disfigure the human countenance with what is termed expression. Two small gray eyes twinkled feebly in the midst, like two stars of lesser magnitude in a hazy firmament, and his full-fed cheeks, which seemed to have taken toll of everything that went into his mouth, were curiously mottled and streaked with dusky red, like a Spitzenberg apple.

His habits were as regular as his person. He daily took his four stated meals, appropriating exactly an hour to each; he smoked and doubted eight hours, and he slept the remaining twelve of the four-and-twenty. Such was the renowned Wouter Van Twiller, —a true philosopher, for his mind was either elevated above, or tranquilly settled below, the cares and perplexities of this world. He had lived in it for years, without feeling the least curiosity to know whether the sun revolved round it, or it round the sun; and he had watched, for at least half a century, the smoke curling from his pipe to the ceiling, without once troubling his head with any of those numerous theories by which a philosopher would have perplexed his brain, in accounting for its rising above the surrounding atmosphere.

In his council he presided with great state and solemnity. He sat in a huge chair of solid oak, hewn in the celebrated forest of the Hague, fabricated by an experienced timmerman of Amster-

dam, and curiously carved about the arms and feet, into exact
imitations of gigantic eagle's claws. Instead of a sceptre, he swayed
a long Turkish pipe, wrought with jasmin and amber, which had
been presented to a stadtholder of Holland at the conclusion of
a treaty with one of the petty Barbary powers. In this stately chair
would he sit, and this magnificent pipe would he smoke, shaking
his right knee with a constant motion, and fixing his eye for hours
together upon a little print of Amsterdam, which hung in a black
frame against the opposite wall of the council-chamber. Nay, it
has even been said, that when any deliberation of extraordinary
length and intricacy was on the carpet, the renowned Wouter
would shut his eyes for full two hours at a time, that he might
not be disturbed by external objects; and at such times the internal
commotion of his mind was evinced by certain regular guttural
sounds, which his admirers declared were merely the noise of
conflict, made by his contending doubts and opinions.

I have been the more anxious to delineate fully the person and
habits of Wouter Van Twiller, from the consideration that he
was not only the first, but also the best governor that ever presided over this ancient and respectable province; and so tranquil
and benevolent was his reign, that I do not find throughout the
whole of it a single instance of any offender being brought to
punishment,—a most indubitable sign of a merciful governor,
and a case unparalleled, excepting in the reign of the illustrious
King Log, from whom, it is hinted, the renowned Van Twiller was
a lineal descendant.

The very outset of the career of this excellent magistrate was
distinguished by an example of legal acumen, that gave flattering
presage of a wise and equitable administration. The morning
after he had been installed in office, and, at the moment that he
was making his breakfast from a prodigious earthen dish, filled
with milk and Indian pudding, he was interrupted by the appearance of Wandle Schoonhoven, a very important old burgher of
New Amsterdam, who complained bitterly of one Barent Bleecker,
inasmuch as he refused to come to a settlement of accounts, seeing that there was a heavy balance in favor of the said Wandle.
Governor Van Twiller, as I have already observed, was a man of
few words; he was likewise a mortal enemy to multiplying writings—or being disturbed at his breakfast. Having listened attentively to the statement of Wandle Schoonhoven, giving an occasional grunt, as he shovelled a spoonful of Indian pudding into
his mouth,—either as a sign that he relished the dish, or com-

prehended the story,—he called unto him his constable, and pulling out of his breeches-pocket a huge jackknife, despatched it after the defendant as a summons, accompanied by his tobacco-box as a warrant.

This summary process was as effectual in those simple days as was the seal-ring of the great Haroun-al-Raschid among the true believers. The two parties being confronted before him, each produced a book of accounts, written in a language and character that would have puzzled any but a High-Dutch commentator, or a learned decipherer of Egyptian obelisks. The sage Wouter took them one after the other, and having poised them in his hands, and attentively counted over the number of leaves, fell straightway into a very great doubt, and smoked for half an hour without saying a word; at length laying his finger beside his nose, and shutting his eyes for a moment, with the air of a man who has just caught a subtle idea by the tail, he slowly took his pipe from his mouth, puffed forth a column of tobacco-smoke, and with marvellous gravity and solemnity pronounced, that, having carefully counted over the leaves and weighed the books, it was found, that one was just as thick and as heavy as the other: therefore, it was the final opinion of the court that the accounts were equally balanced: therefore, Wandle should give Barent a receipt, and Barent should give Wandle a receipt, and the constable should pay the costs.

The decision, being straightway made known, diffused general joy throughout New Amsterdam, for the people immediately perceived that they had a very wise and equitable magistrate to rule over them. But its happiest effect was, that not another lawsuit took place throughout the whole of his administration; and the office of constable fell into such decay that there was not one of those losel scouts known in the province for many years. I am the more particular in dwelling on this transaction, not only because I deem it one of the most sage and righteous judgments on record, and well worthy the attention of modern magistrates, but because it was a miraculous event in the history of the renowned Wouter —being the only time he was ever known to come to a decision in the whole course of his life.

WILLIAM KIEFT

There was nothing in the whole range of moral offences against which the jurisprudence of William the Testy was more strenuously directed than the crying sin of poverty. He pronounced it the root of all evil, and determined to cut it up, root and branch, and extirpate it from the land. He had been struck, in the course of his travels in the old countries of Europe, with the wisdom of those notices posted up in country towns, that "any vagrant found begging there would be put in the stocks," and he had observed that no beggars were to be seen in these neighborhoods; having doubtless thrown off their rags and their poverty, and become rich under the terror of the law. He determined to improve upon this hint. In a little while a new machine, of his own invention, was erected hard by Dog's Misery. This was nothing more nor less than a gibbet, of a very strange, uncouth, and unmatchable construction, far more efficacious, as he boasted, than the stocks, for the punishment of poverty. It was for altitude not a whit inferior to that of Haman so renowned in Bible history; but the marvel of the contrivance was, that the culprit, instead of being suspended by the neck, according to venerable custom, was hoisted by the waistband, and kept dangling and sprawling between heaven and earth for an hour or two at a time—to the infinite entertainment and edification of the respectable citizens who usually attend exhibitions of the kind.

It is incredible how the little governor chuckled at beholding caitiff vagrants and sturdy beggars thus swinging by the crupper, and cutting antic gambols in the air. He had a thousand pleasantries and mirthful conceits to utter upon these occasions. He called them his dandelions—his wild-fowl—his high-fliers—his spread-eagles—his goshawks—his scarecrows—and finally, his *gallows-birds;* which ingenious appellation, though originally confined to worthies who had taken the air in this strange manner, has since grown to be a cant name given to all candidates for legal elevation. This punishment, moreover, if we may credit the assertions of certain grave etymologists, gave the first hint for a kind of harnessing, or strapping, by which our forefathers braced up their multifarious breeches, and which has of late years been revived, and continues to be worn at the present day.

Such was the punishment of all petty delinquents, vagrants, and beggars and others detected in being guilty of poverty in a small way; as to those who had offended on a great scale, who had been guilty of flagrant misfortunes and enormous backslidings of the purse, and who stood convicted of large debts, which they were unable to pay, William Kieft had them straightway inclosed within the stone walls of a prison, there to remain until they should reform and grow rich. This notable expedient, however, does not appear to have been more efficacious under William the Testy than in more modern days: it being found that the longer a poor devil was kept in prison the poorer he grew.

Next to his projects for the suppression of poverty may be classed those of William the Testy for increasing the wealth of New Amsterdam. Solomon, of whose character for wisdom the little governor was somewhat emulous, had made gold and silver as plenty as the stones in the streets of Jerusalem. William Kieft could not pretent to vie with him as to the precious metals, but he determined, as an equivalent, to flood the streets of New Amsterdam with Indian money. This was nothing more nor less than strings of beads wrought of clams, periwinkles, and other shellfish, and called seawant or wampum. These had formed a native currency among the simple savages, who were content to take them of the Dutchmen in exchange for peltries. In an unlucky moment, William the Testy, seeing this money of easy production, conceived the project of making it the current coin of the province. It is true it had an intrinsic value among the Indians, who used it to ornament their robes and moccasins, but among the honest burghers it had no more intrinsic value than those rags which form the paper currency of modern days. This consideration, however, had no weight with William Kieft. He began by paying all the servants of the company, and all the debts of government, in strings of wampum. He sent emissaries to sweep the shores of Long Island, which was the Ophir of this modern Solomon, and abounded in shell-fish. These were transported in loads to New Amsterdam, coined into Indian money, and launched into circulation.

And now, for a time, affairs went on swimmingly; money became as plentiful as in the modern days of paper currency, and, to use the popular phrase, "a wonderful impulse was given to public prosperity." Yankee traders poured into the province, buying everything they could lay their hands on, and paying the worthy Dutchmen their own price — in Indian money. If the latter, however, attempted to pay the Yankees in the same coin for their tin ware and wooden bowls, the case was altered; nothing would do but Dutch guilders and such like "metallic currency." What was worse, the Yankees introduced an inferior kind of wampum made of oyster-shells, with which they deluged the province, carrying off in exchange all the silver and gold, the Dutch herrings, and Dutch cheeses: thus early did the knowing men of the east manifest their skill in bargaining the New Amsterdammers out of the oyster, and leaving them the shell.

It was a long time before William the Testy was made sensible how completely his grand project of finance was turned against him by his eastern neighbors; nor would he probably have ever found it out, had not tidings been brought him that the Yankees had made a descent upon Long Island, and had established a kind of mint at Oyster Bay, where they were coining up all the oyster-banks.

Now this was making a vital attack upon the province in a double sense, financial and gastronomical. Ever since the council-dinner of Oloffe the Dreamer at the founding of New Amsterdam, at which banquet the oyster figured so conspicuously, this divine shell-fish has been held in a kind of superstitious reverence at the Manhattoes; as witness the temples erected to its cult in every street and lane and alley. In fact, it is the standard luxury of the place, as is the terrapin at Philadelphia, the soft crab at Baltimore, or the canvas-back at Washington.

The seizure of Oyster Bay, therefore, was an outrage not merely on the pockets, but the larders of the New Amsterdammers; the whole community was aroused, and an oyster crusade was immediately set on foot against the Yankees. Every stout trencherman hastened to the standard; nay, some of the most corpulent burgo-masters and schepens joined the expedition as a *corps de reserve,* only to be called into action when the sacking commenced.

The conduct of the expedition was intrusted to a valiant Dutch-man, who for size and weight might have matched with Colbrand the Danish champion, slain by Guy of Warwick. He was famous throughout the province for strength of arm and skill at quarter-staff, and hence was named Stoffel Brinkerhoff, or rather Brinker-hoofd, that is to say Stoffel, the head-breaker.

This sturdy commander, who was a man of few words but vigorous deeds, led his troops resolutely on through Nineveh, and Babylon, and Jericho, and Patch-hog, and other Long Island towns, without encountering any difficulty of note; though it is said that some of the burgomasters gave out at Hardscramble Hill and Hungry Hollow, and that others lost heart and turned back at Pusspanick. With the rest he made good his march until he arrived in the neighborhood of Oyster Bay.

Here he was encountered by a host of Yankee warriors, headed by Preserved Fish, and Habakkuk Nutter, and Return Strong, and Zerubbabel Fisk, and Determined Cock, at the sound of whose names Stoffel Brinkerhoff verily believed the whole parliament of Praise-God Barebones had been let loose upon him. He soon found, however, that they were merely the "selectmen" of the settlement, armed with no weapon but the tongue, and disposed only to meet him on the field of argument. Stoffel had but one mode of arguing, that was, with the cudgel; but he used it with such effect that he routed his antagonists, broke up the settlement, and would have driven the inhabitants into the sea if they had not managed to escape across the Sound to the mainland by the Devil's stepping-stones, which remain to this day monuments of this great Dutch victory over the Yankees.

Stoffel Brinkerhoff made great spoil of oysters and clams, coined and uncoined, and then set out on his return to the Manhattoes. A grand triumph, after the manner of the ancients, was prepared for him by William the Testy. He entered New Amsterdam as a conqueror, mounted on a Narragansett pacer. Five dried codfish on poles, standards taken from the enemy, were borne before him, and an immense store of oysters and clams, Weathersfield onions, and Yankee "notions" formed the *spolia opima;* while several coiners of oyster-shells were led captive to grace the hero's triumph.

The procession was accompanied by a full band of boys and negroes, performing on the popular instruments of rattle-bones and clam-shells, while Antony Van Corlear sounded his trumpet from the ramparts.

A great banquet was served up in the stadthouse from the clams and oysters taken from the enemy; while the governor sent the shells privately to the mint, and had them coined into Indian money, with which he paid his troops.

It is moreover said that the governor, calling to mind the practice among the ancients to honor their victorious general with public statutes, passed a magnanimous decree, by which every tavern-keeper was permitted to paint the head of Stoffel Brinkerhoff upon his sign!

Wilhelmus Kieft, as has already been observed, was a great legislator on a small scale, and had a microscopic eye in public affairs. He had been greatly annoyed by the factious meeting of the good people of New Amsterdam, but, observing that on these occasions the pipe was ever in their mouths, he began to think that the pipe was at the bottom of the affair, and that there was some mysterious affinity between politics and tobacco-smoke.

Determined to strike at the root of the evil, he began forthwith to
rail at tobacco, as a noxious, nauseous weed, filthy in all its uses;
and as to smoking, he denounced it as a heavy tax upon the public
pocket, — a vast consumer of time, a great encourager of idleness,
and a deadly bane to the prosperity and morals of the people.
Finally he issued an edict, prohibiting the smoking of tobacco
throughout the New Netherlands. Ill-fated Kieft. Had he lived in
the present age and attempted to check the unbounded license
of the press, he could not have struck more sorely upon the
sensibilities of the million. The pipe, in fact, was the greatest
organ of reflection and deliberation of the New Netherlander. It
was his constant companion and solace: was he gay, he smoked;
was he sad, he smoked; his pipe was never out of his mouth; it
was part of his physiognomy; without it his best friends would
not know him. Take away his pipe? You might as well take away
his nose!

The immediate effect of the edict of William the Testy was a
popular commotion. A vast multitude, armed with pipes and
tobacco-boxes, and an immense supply of ammunition, sat themselves down before the governor's house, and fell to smoking with
tremendous violence. The testy William issued forth like a wrathful spider, demanding the reason of this lawless fumigation. The
sturdy rioters replied by lolling back in their seats, and puffing
away with redoubled fury, raising such a murky cloud that the
governor was fain to take refuge in the interior of his castle.

A long negotiation ensued through the medium of Antony the
Trumpeter. The governor was at first wrathful and unyielding,
but was gradually smoked into terms. He concluded by permitting
the smoking of tobacco, but he abolished the fair long pipes used
in the days of Wouter Van Twiller, denoting ease, tranquillity,
and sobriety of deportment; these he condemned as incompatible
with the despatch of business, in place whereof he substituted
little captious short pipes, two inches in length, which, he observed, could be stuck in one corner of the mouth, or twisted in
the hatband, and would never be in the way. Thus ended this
alarming insurrection, which was long known by the name of The
Pipe-Plot, and which, it has been somewhat quaintly observed,
did end, like most plots and seditions, in mere smoke.

But mark, oh, reader! the deplorable evils which did afterwards result. The smoke of these villainous little pipes, continually ascending in a cloud about the nose, penetrated into and
befogged the cerebellum, dried up all the kindly moisture of the

brain, and rendered the people who used them as vaporous and testy as the governor himself. Nay, what is worse, from being goodly, burly, sleek-conditioned men, they became, like our Dutch yeomanry who smoke short pipes, a lantern-jawed, smoke-dried, leathern-hided race.

Nor was this all. From this fatal schism in tobacco-pipes we may date the rise of parties in the Nieuw Nederlandts. The rich and self-important burghers who had made their fortunes, and could afford to be lazy, adhered to the ancient fashion, and formed a kind of aristocracy known as the *Long Pipes;* while the lower order, adopting the reform of William Kieft as more convenient in their handicraft employments, were branded with the plebeian name of *Short Pipes.*

A third party sprang up, headed by the descendants of Robert Chewit, the companion of the great Hudson. These discarded pipes altogether and took to chewing tobacco; hence they were called *Quids,* — an appellation since given to those political mongrels which sometimes spring up between two great parties, as a mule is produced between a horse and an ass.

And here I would note the great benefit of party distinctions in saving the people at large the trouble of thinking. Hesiod divides mankind into three classes — those who think for themselves, those who think as others think, and those who do not think at all. The second class comprises the great mass of society; for most people require a set creed and a file-leader. Hence the origin of party: which means a large body of people, some few of whom think, and all the rest talk. The former take the lead and discipline the latter; prescribing what they must say, what they must approve, what they must hoot at, whom they must support, but, above all, whom they must hate; for no one can be a right good partisan, who is not a thorough-going hater.

The enlightened inhabitants of the Manhattoes, therefore, being divided into parties, were enabled to hate each other with great accuracy. And now the great business of politics went bravely on, the long pipes and short pipes assembling in separate beer-houses, and smoking at each other with implacable vehemence, to the great support of the State and profit of the tavern-keepers. Some, indeed, went so far as to bespatter their adversaries with those odoriferous little words which smell so strong in the Dutch language, believing, like true politicians, that they served their party, and glorified themselves in proportion as they bewrayed their neighbors. But, however they might differ among themselves, all parties agreed in abusing the governor, seeing that he was not a governor of their choice, but appointed by others to rule over them.

Unhappy William Kieft! exclaims the sage writer of the Stuyvesant manuscript, doomed to contend with enemies too knowing to be entrapped, and to reign over a people too wise to be governed. All his foreign expeditions were baffled and set at naught by the all-pervading Yankees; all his home measures were canvassed and condemned by "numerous and respectable meetings" of pot-house politicians.

In the multitude of counsellors, we are told, there is safety; but the multitude of counsellors was a continual source of perplexity to William Kieft. With a temperament as hot as an old radish, and a mind subject to perpetual whirlwinds and tornadoes, he never failed to get into a passion with every one who undertook to advise him. I have observed, however, that your passionate little men, like small boats with large sails, are easily upset or blown out of their course; so was it with William the Testy, who was prone to be carried away by the last piece of advice blown into his ear. The consequence was, that, though a projector of the first class, yet by continually changing his projects he gave none a fair trial; and by endeavoring to do everything, he in sober truth did nothing.

PETER STUYVESANT

Peter Stuyvesant was the last, and, like the renowned Wouter Van Twiller, the best of our ancient Dutch governors. Wouter having surpassed all who preceded him, and Peter, or Piet, as he was sociably called by the old Dutch burghers, who were ever prone to familiarize names, having never been equalled by any successor. He was in fact the very man fitted by nature to retrieve the desperate fortunes of her beloved province, had not the Fates, those most potent and unrelenting of all ancient spinsters, destined them to inextricable confusion.

To say merely that he was a hero, would be doing him great injustice: he was in truth a combination of heroes; for he was of a sturdy, raw-boned make, like Ajax Telamon, with a pair of round shoulders that Hercules would have given his hide for (meaning his lion's hide) when he undertook to ease old Atlas of his load. He was, moreover, as Plutarch describes Coriolanus, not only terrible for the force of his arm, but likewise of his voice, which

sounded as though it came out of a barrel; and, like the self-same
warrior, he possessed a sovereign contempt for the sovereign
people, and an iron aspect, which was enough of itself to make the
very bowels of his adversaries quake with terror and dismay.
All this martial excellency of appearance was inexpressibly
heightened by an accidental advantage, with which I am surprised
that neither Homer nor Virgil have graced any of their heroes.
This was nothing less than a wooden leg, which was the only
prize he had gained in bravely fighting the battles of his country,
but of which he was so proud, that he was often heard to declare
he valued it more than all his other limbs put together; indeed so
highly did he esteem it, that he had it gallantly enchased and
relieved with silver devices, which caused it to be related in
divers histories and legends that he wore a silver leg. . . .

The very first movements of the great Peter, on taking the reins
of government, displayed his magnanimity, though they occasioned not a little marvel and uneasiness among the people of the
Manhattoes. Finding himself constantly interrupted by the opposition, and annoyed by the advice of his privy council, the members
of which had acquired the unreasonable habit of thinking and
speaking for themselves during the preceding reign, he determined at once to put a stop to such grievous abominations.
Scarcely, therefore, had he entered upon his authority, than he
turned out of office all the meddlesome spirits of the factious
cabinet of William the Testy; in place of whom he chose unto himself counsellors from those fat, somniferous, respectable burghers
who had flourished and slumbered under the easy reign of Walter
the Doubter. All these he caused to be furnished with abundance
of fair long pipes, and to be regaled with frequent corporation
dinners, admonishing them to smoke, and eat, and sleep for the
good of the nation, while he took the burden of government upon
his own shoulders—an arrangement to which they all gave hearty
acquiescence.
Nor did he stop here, but made a hideous rout among the inventions and expedients of his learned predecessor,—rooting
up his patent gallows, where caitiff vagabonds were suspended
by the waistband,—demolishing his flagstaffs and wind-mills,
which, like mighty giants, guarded the ramparts of New Amsterdam,—pitching to the duyvel whole batteries of Quaker guns,—
and, in a word, turning topsy-turvy the whole philosophic, economic, and wind-mill system of the immortal sage of Saardam.

The honest folk of New Amsterdam began to quake now for the fate of their matchless champion, Antony the Trumpeter, who had acquired prodigious favor in the eyes of the women, by means of his whiskers and his trumpet. Him did Peter the Headstrong cause to be brought into his presence, and eying him a moment from head to foot, with a countenance that would have appalled anything else than a sounder of brass, — "Pr'ythee who and what art thou?" said he. "Sire," replied the other, in no wise dismayed, "for my name, it is Antony Van Corlear; for my parentage, I am the son of my mother; for my profession, I am champion and garrison of this great city of New Amsterdam." "I doubt me much," said Peter Stuyvesant, "that thou art some scurvy costard-monger knave. How didst thou acquire this paramount honor and dignity?" "Marry, sir," replied the other, "like many a great man before me, simply *by sounding my own trumpet.*" "Ay, is it so?" quoth the governor; "why, then let us have a relish of thy art." Whereupon the good Antony put his instrument to his lips, and sounded a charge with such a tremendous outset, such a delectable quaver, and such a triumphant cadence, that it was enough to make one's heart leap out of one's mouth only to be within a mile of it. Like as a war-worn charger, grazing in peaceful plains, starts at a strain of martial music, pricks up his ears, and snorts, and paws, and kindles at the noise, so did the heroic Peter joy to hear the clangor of the trumpet; for of him might truly be said, what was recorded of the renowned St. George of England, "there was nothing in all the world that more rejoiced his heart than to hear the pleasant sound of war, and see the soldiers brandish forth their steeled weapons." Casting his eye more kindly, therefore, upon the sturdy Van Corlear, and finding him to be a jovial varlet, shrewd in his discourse, yet of great discretion and immeasurable wind, he straightway conceived a vast kindness for him, and discharged him from the troublesome duty of garrisoning, defending, and alarming the city, ever after retained him about his person, as his chief favorite, confidential envoy, and trusty squire. Instead of disturbing the city with disastrous notes, he was instructed to play so as to delight the governor while at his repasts, as did the minstrels of yore in the days of glorious chivalry, — and on all public occasions to rejoice the ears of the people with warlike melody, — thereby keeping alive a noble and martial spirit.

But the measure of the valiant Peter which produced the greatest agitation in the community, was his laying his hand upon the currency. He had old-fashioned notions in favor of gold and silver, which he considered the true standards of wealth and mediums of commerce; and one of his first edicts was, that all duties to government should be paid in those precious metals, and that seawant, or wampum, should no longer be a legal tender.

Here was a blow at public prosperity! All those who speculated on the rise and fall of this fluctuating currency, found their calling at an end; those, too, who had hoarded Indian money by barrels-full, found their capital shrunk in amount; but, above all, the Yankee traders, who were accustomed to flood the market with newly coined oyster-shells, and to abstract Dutch merchandise in exchange, were loud-mouthed in decrying this "tampering with the currency." It was clipping the wings of commerce; it was checking the development of public prosperity; trade would be at an end; goods would moulder on the shelves; grain would rot in the granaries; grass would grow in the marketplace. In a word, no one who has not heard the outcries and howlings of a modern Tarshish, at any check upon "paper-money," can have any idea of the clamor against Peter the Headstrong, for checking the circulation of oyster-shells.

George Gordon, Lord Byron

George Gordon, Lord Byron, was his own most colorful creation. Flashing across the nineteenth century in the protean role
of flaming poet, impetuous lover, champion of liberty, and
reckless soldier, his name and temperament gave the Romantic movement its most popular adjective. If he was a showman
proudly exhibiting "the pageant of a bleeding heart," an actor
who regarded the world as so much stage scenery, he was
also the physically handicapped and psychologically maimed
youth who triumphed over every disadvantage.

Byron was a cynical aristocrat who wearied of his postur-
ings; self-indulgence and self-dramatization were part of his
inheritance. His great-uncle, from whom Byron inherited the
title, was known as the wicked lord—he had killed a man in a
duel in a locked room lighted only by a candle. His father, "Mad
Jack" Byron, a rakehell captain, had run off with a marquis'
wife, who after a divorce married him and bore him a daughter,
Augusta. Byron's mother, his father's second wife, was a descendant of James I and was vain, hysterical, and utterly incapable of dealing with a difficult child.

Born in 1788 in London, lame at birth, young Byron nevertheless devoted himself to sports. At Trinity College he rode,

boxed, and later became so powerful a swimmer that he dared the Hellespont. He literally lived in action, traveled sporadically, made love indiscriminately, and wrote continually.

A collection of poems, *Hours of Idleness*, published when he was nineteen, was cut to pieces by the *Edinburgh Review*. Two years later he retaliated with a savage Popelike satire, *English Bards and Scotch Reviewers*. During a tour of Europe he began *Childe Harold's Pilgrimage*, and when the first two cantos appeared in print Byron woke one morning to find himself famous. He was pursued by women—one of them, Lady Caroline Lamb, masqueraded as a boy to gain access to his rooms. There were many casual affairs and one serious attachment, which led to a national scandal. At twenty-seven Byron married an heiress, Anne Isabella Milbanke. The marriage was ill-fated and lasted less than a year. After the birth of a daughter, there was a separation when his wife charged him with cruelty and insanity and intimated that he was having incestuous relations with his half-sister.

His social life ruined, Byron left England never to return. In Switzerland he joined Percy Bysshe Shelley, his mistress, Mary Godwin, and her stepsister, Jane Clairmont. Jane was eager to be to Byron what Mary had become to Shelley. Byron did not like her; nevertheless he slept with her and she bore him a daughter. In Italy he composed his masterpiece, *Don Juan*, and had a succession of inamoratas, most important of whom was Teresa, Countess Guiccioli, whose husband was her senior by forty years.

At thirty-three Byron joined an abortive revolution in Italy. Two years later he threw in his lot with the Greeks who were revolting against Turkish rule. He sailed for Greece, ready to die on the battlefield. The heroic gesture was denied him. After arriving at Missolonghi, he contracted a fever, variously diagnosed as rheumatic inflammation, malaria, and typhus; struggling with delirium, he died ingloriously on a sickbed. He was thirty-six years old.

In spite of his countless amours, Byron's passion for himself was his greatest romance. He was his own multiple hero: the adventure-seeking Harold, the elegantly saturnine Lucifer, and the cynical, self-infatuated Don Juan. He was not, as he fancied himself, "the exiled pilgrim of eternity," but the flamboyantly spoiled child of his age.

THE VISION OF JUDGMENT[1]

The angels all were singing out of tune,
   And hoarse with having little else to do,
Excepting to wind up the sun and moon,
   Or curb a runaway young star or two,
Or wild colt of a comet, which too soon
   Broke out of bounds o'er th' ethereal blue,
Splitting some planet with its playful tail,
As boats are sometimes by a wanton whale.

The guardian seraphs had retired on high,
   Finding their charges past all care below;
Terrestrial business fill'd nought in the sky
   Save the recording angel's black bureau;
Who found, indeed, the facts to multiply
   With such rapidity of vice and woe,
That he had stripp'd off both his wings in quills,
And yet was in arrear of human ills.

His business so augmented of late years,
   That he was forced, against his will no doubt,
(Just like those cherubs, earthly ministers,)
   For some resource to turn himself about,
And claim the help of his celestial peers,
   To aid him ere he should be quite worn out
By the increased demand for his remarks:
Six angels and twelve saints were named his clerks.

This was a handsome board—at least for heaven;
   And yet they had even then enough to do,
So many conquerors' cars were daily driven,
   So many kingdoms fitted up anew;
Each day too slew its thousands six or seven,
   Till at the crowning carnage, Waterloo,
They threw their pens down in divine disgust—
The page was so besmear'd with blood and dust.

---

[1] A burlesque vision of George III stealing into heaven and also a parody of a similarly named poem by Robert Southey, whom Byron despised. See the opening of *Don Juan* on page 387.

This by the way; 't is not mine to record
   What angels shrink from: even the very devil
On this occasion his own work abhorr'd,
   So surfeited with the infernal revel:
Though he himself had sharpen'd every sword,
   It almost quench'd his innate thirst of evil.
(Here Satan's sole good work deserves insertion—
'T is, that he has both generals in reversion.)

Let's skip a few short years of hollow peace,
   Which peopled earth no better, hell as wont,
And heaven none—they form the tyrant's lease,
   With nothing but new names subscribed upon 't;
'T will one day finish: meantime they increase,
   "With seven heads and ten horns," and all in front,
Like Saint John's foretold beast; but ours are born
Less formidable in the head than horn.

In the first year of freedom's second dawn
   Died George the Third; although no tyrant, one
Who shielded tyrants, till each sense withdrawn
   Left him nor mental nor external sun:
A better farmer ne'er brush'd dew from lawn,
   A worse king never left a realm undone!
He died—but left his subjects still behind,
One half as mad—and t'other no less blind.

He died! his death made no great stir on earth:
   His burial made some pomp; there was profusion
Of velvet, gilding, brass, and no great dearth
   Of aught but tears—save those shed by collusion.
For these things may be bought at their true worth;
   Of elegy there was the due infusion—
Bought also; and the torches, cloaks, and banners
Heralds, and relics of old Gothic manners,

Form'd a sepulchral melodrame. Of all
   The fools who flock'd to swell or see the show,
Who cared about the corpse? The funeral
   Made the attraction, and the black the woe.
There throbb'd not there a thought which pierced the
      pall;

And when the gorgeous coffin was laid low,
It seem'd the mockery of hell to fold
The rottenness of eighty years in gold.

So mix his body with the dust! It might
   Return to what it *must* far sooner, were
The natural compound left alone to fight
   Its way back into earth, and fire, and air;
But the unnatural balsams merely blight
   What nature made him at his birth, as bare
As the mere million's base unmummied clay—
Yet all his spices but prolong decay.

He's dead—and upper earth with him has done;
   He's buried; save the undertaker's bill,
Or lapidary scrawl, the world is gone
   For him, unless he left a German will:
But where's the proctor who will ask his son?
   In whom his qualities are reigning still,
Except that household virtue, most uncommon,
Of constancy to a bad, ugly woman.

"God save the king!" It is a large economy
   In God to save the like; but if he will
Be saving, all the better: for not one am I
   Of those who think damnation better still:
I hardly know too if not quite alone am I
   In this small hope of bettering future ill
By circumscribing, with some slight restriction,
The eternity of hell's hot jurisdiction.

I know this is unpopular; I know
   'Tis blasphemous; I know one may be damn'd
For hoping no one else may e'er be so;
   I know my catechism; I know we're cramm'd
With the best doctrines till we quite o'erflow;
   I know that all save England's church have
       shamm'd,
And that the other twice two hundred churches
And synagogues have made a *damn'd* bad purchase.

God help us all! God help me too! I am,

God knows, as helpless as the devil can wish,
And not a whit more difficult to damn,
   Than is to bring to land a late-hook'd fish,
Or to the butcher to purvey the lamb;
   Not that I'm fit for such a noble dish,
As one day will be that immortal fry
Of almost everybody born to die.

Saint Peter sat by the celestial gate,
   And nodded o'er his keys; when, lo! there came
A wondrous noise he had not heard of late—
   A rushing sound of wind, and stream, and flame;
In short, a roar of things extremely great,
   Which would have made aught save a saint ex-
      claim;
But he, with first a start and then a wink,
Said, "There's another star gone out, I think!"

But ere he could return to his repose,
   A cherub flapp'd his right wing o'er his eyes—
At which St. Peter yawn'd, and rubb'd his nose:
   "Saint porter," said the angel, "prithee rise!"
Waving a goodly wing, which glow'd, as glows
   An earthly peacock's tail, with heavenly dyes:
To which the saint replied, "Well, what's the mat-
      ter?
Is Lucifer come back with all this clatter?"

"No," quoth the cherub; "George the Third is dead."
   "And who *is* George the Third?" replied the apos-
      tle:
"*What George! What Third?*" "The king of Eng-
      land," said
   The angel. "Well! he won't find kings to jostle
Him on his way; but does he wear his head?
   Because the last we saw here had a tustle,
And ne'er would have got into heaven's good graces,
Had he not flung his head in all our faces.

"He was, if I remember, king of France;
   That head of his, which could not keep a crown

On earth, yet ventured in my face to advance
   A claim to those of martyrs—like my own:
If I had had my sword, as I had once
   When I cut ears off, I had cut him down;
But having but my *keys,* and not my brand,
I only knock'd his head from out his hand.

"And then he set up such a headless howl,
   That all the saints came out and took him in;
And there he sits by St. Paul, cheek by jowl;
   That fellow Paul—the parvenù! The skin
Of St. Bartholomew, which mades his cowl
   In heaven, and upon earth redeem'd his sin,
So as to make a martyr, never sped
Better than did this weak and wooden head.

"But had it come up here upon its shoulders,
   There would have been a diffcrent tale to tell:
The fellow-fecling in the saints beholders
   Seems to have acted on them like a spell,
And so this very foolish head heaven solders
   Back on its trunk: it may be very well,
And seems the custom here to overthrow
Whatever has been wisely done below."

The angel answer'd, "Peter! do not pout:
   The king who comes has head and all entire,
And never knew much what it was about—
   He did as doth the puppet—by its wire,
And will be judged like all the rest, no doubt:
   My business and your own is not to inquire
Into such matters, but to mind our cue—
Which is to act as we are bid to do."

DON JUAN

Bob Southey! You're a poet—Poet laureate,
   And representative of all the race;
Although 'tis true that you turned out a Tory at
   Last—yours has lately been a common case;

And now, my Epic Renegade! what are ye at?
    With all the Lakers,[1] in and out of place?
A nest of tuneful persons, to my eye
Like "four and twenty Blackbirds in a pye;[2]

"Which pye being opened they began to sing"
    (This old song and new simile holds good),
"A dainty dish to set before the King,"
    Or Regent, who admires such kind of food;—
And Coleridge, too, has lately taken wing,
    But like a hawk encumbered with his hood—
Explaining metaphysics to the nation—
I wish he would explain his Explanation.

You, Bob! are rather insolent, you know,
    At being disappointed in your wish
To supersede all warblers here below,
    And be the only Blackbird in the dish;
And then you overstrain yourself, or so,
    And tumble downward like the flying fish
Gasping on deck, because you soar too high, Bob,
And fall for lack of moisture quite a-dry, Bob!

And Wordsworth, in a rather long "Excursion"
    (I think the quarto holds five hundred pages),
Has given a sample from the vasty version
    Of his new system to perplex the sages;
'Tis poetry—at least by his assertion,
    And may appear so when the dog-star rages—
And he who understands it would be able
To add a story to the Tower of Babel.

You—Gentlemen! by dint of long seclusion
    From better company, have kept your own
At Keswick, and through still continued fusion
    Of one another's minds, at last have grown
To deem as a most logical conclusion,

---

[1] *Lakers:* the Lake School of poets, Coleridge, Southey, and Wordsworth, who lived in the neighborhood of the English lakes
[2] *"four and twenty Blackbirds in a pye":* the pun here is directed against Henry James Pye, who became laureate in 1790 and was the target of contemporary derision

That poesy has wreaths for you alone;
There is a narrowness in such a notion,
Which makes me wish you'd change your lakes for ocean.

I would not imitate the petty thought,
　　Nor coin my self-love to so base a vice,
For all the glory your conversion brought,
　　Since gold alone should not have been its price,
You have your salary; was't for that you wrought?
　　And Wordsworth has his place in the Excise.
You're shabby fellows—true—but poets still,
And duly seated on the Immortal Hill.

William Makepeace Thackeray

William Makepeace Thackeray, who in moments of whimsy liked to sign himself "Michael Angelo Titmarsh" and "Charles J. Yellowplush," was born in 1811 in Calcutta, where his father was in the service of the East India Company. He was five years old when, after his father's death, he was sent home to England. His schooling was anything but happy; he always referred to the Charterhouse School as the Slaughterhouse, and he left Cambridge after little more than a year.

After Cambridge Thackeray traveled on the Continent—to Paris, where he was tormented by fleas; to Rotterdam, where he felt at home with the Dutch; and to Weimar, where he met Goethe. On his return he invested a considerable income in two journals, both of which failed. This misfortune, together with heavy losses at cards and an Indian bank failure, consumed what money he had inherited. His marriage was even more unfortunate. His wife became mentally unbalanced after the birth of her third child; remaining insane, she outlived her husband by thirty years.

For a while Thackeray thought of turning to art as a profession—he studied in Rome and Paris—but he was no more successful in this career than in gambling. In his late twenties he had become a journalist; contributions to *Fraser's Magazine* began to be noticed, and his essays in *Punch*, particularly the sly, sardonic drolleries of *The Book of Snobs*, attracted an amused public.

Thackeray was thirty-six when *Vanity Fair* was published. Conceded to be his masterpiece, it placed him in the forefront of English novelists, his only rival being Charles Dickens. With *Vanity Fair* his humor took a new turn; what was vivacious became incisive, and playfulness gave way to irony. This penetration characterized the books that followed: *Pendennis*, *The Newcomes*, *Henry Esmond*, and *The Virginians*. Unlike Dickens, who pictured the tribulations of the poor, Thackeray portrayed the doings of the affluent middle class. *The Book of Snobs* pokes fun at the ostentation of the caste system and exposes the toadyism prevalent in the "society" of his times. His aversion to all forms of pretentiousness breaks through the ridicule.

Had it not been for the ever-pressing need of money, Thackeray would have been content to be a clubman, a connoisseur of food, tobacco, and wine. But Thackeray disciplined himself to write until the end, although strenuous lecture tours in the United States and the arduous task of editing the *Cornhill Magazine* had affected his health. His was fifty-two when he died of a cerebral hemorrhage on Christmas Eve, 1863.

THE BOOK OF SNOBS
CONTINENTAL SNOBBERY

We are accustomed to laugh at the French for their braggadocio propensities, and intolerable vanity about "la France, la gloire, l'Empereur," and the like; and yet I think in my heart that the British Snob, for conceit and self-sufficiency and braggartism in his way, is without a parallel. There is always something uneasy in a Frenchman's conceit. He brags with so much fury, shrieking, and gesticulation — yells out so loudly that the Français is at the head of civilisation, the centre of thought, &c. — that one can't but see the poor fellow has a lurking doubt in his own mind that he is not the wonder he professes to be.

About the British Snob, on the contrary, there is commonly no noise, no bluster, but the calmness of profound conviction. We are better than all the world; we don't question the opinion at all: it's an axiom. And when a Frenchman bellows out, "La France, Monsieur, la France est à la tête du monde civilisé!" we laugh good-naturedly at the frantic poor devil. *We* are the first-chop of the world; we know the fact so well in our secret hearts, that a claim set up elsewhere is simply ludicrous. My dear brother reader, say, as a man of honour, if you are not of this opinion. Do you think a Frenchman your equal? You don't—you gallant British Snob—you know you don't; no more, perhaps, does the Snob your humble servant, brother.

And I am inclined to think it is this conviction, and the consequent bearing of the Englishman towards the foreigner whom he condescends to visit,—this confidence of superiority which holds up the head of the owner of every English hat-box from Sicily to St. Petersburg, that makes us so magnificently hated throughout Europe as we are; this—more than all our little victories, and of which many Frenchmen and Spaniards have never heard—this amazing and indomitable insular pride, which animates my Lord in his travelling-carriage as well as John in the rumble.

If you read the old Chronicles of the French wars, you find precisely the same character of the Englishman, and Henry V.'s people behaved with just the cool domineering manner of our gallant veterans of France and the Peninsula. Did you never hear Colonel Cutler and Major Slasher talking over the war after dinner? or Captain Boarder describing his action with the "Indomptable?" "Hang the fellows," says Boarder, "their practice was very good. I was beat off three times before I took her." "Cuss those carabineers of Milhaud's!" says Slasher, "what work they made of our light cavalry!" implying a sort of surprise that the Frenchmen should stand up against Britons at all; a good-natured wonder that the blind, mad, vain-glorious, brave poor devils should actually have the courage to resist an Englishman. Legions of such Englishmen are patronising Europe at this moment, being kind to the Pope, or good-natured to the King of Holland, or condescending to inspect the Prussian reviews. When Nicholas came here, who reviews a quarter of a million of pairs of moustaches to his breakfast every morning, we took him off to Windsor and showed him two whole regiments of six or eight hundred Britons apiece, with an air as much as to say,—"There, my boy, look at *that*. Those are *Englishmen*, those are, and your master whenever you please," as the nursery song says. The British Snob is long long past scepticism, and can afford to laugh quite good-humouredly at those conceited Yankees, or besotted little Frenchmen, who set up as models of mankind. *They* forsooth!

I have been led into these remarks by listening to an old fellow

at the Hotel du Nord, at Boulogne, and who is evidently of the
Slasher sort. He came down and seated himself at the breakfast-
table, with a surly scowl on his salmon-coloured bloodshot face,
strangling in a tight, cross-barred cravat; his linen and his ap-
pointments so perfectly stiff and spotless that everybody at once
recognised him as a dear countryman. Only our port-wine and
other admirable institutions could have produced a figure so
insolent, so stupid, so gentlemanlike. After a while our attention
was called to him by his roaring out, in a voice of plethoric fury,
"O!"

Everybody turned round at the "O," conceiving the Colonel
to be, as his countenance denoted him, in intense pain; but the
waiters knew better and, instead of being alarmed, brought the
Colonel the kettle. "O," it appears, is the French for hot-water.
The Colonel (though he despises it heartily) thinks he speaks the
language remarkably well. Whilst he was inhausting his smoking
tea, which went rolling and gurgling down his throat, and hissing
over the "hot coppers" of that respectable veteran, a friend joined
him, with a wizened face and very black wig, evidently a Colonel
too.

The two warriors, waggling their old heads at each other, presently joined breakfast, and fell into conversation, and we had the
advantage of hearing about the old war, and some pleasant con-
jectures as to the next, which they considered imminent. They
psha'd the French fleet; they pooh-pooh'd the French commercial
marine; they showed how, in a war, there would be a cordon
("cordong, by ———") of steamers along our coast, and "by
———," ready at a minute to land anywhere on the other shore,
to give the French as good a thrashing as they got in the last war,
"by ———." In fact, a rumbling cannonade of oaths was fired by
the two veterans during the whole of their conversation.

There was a Frenchman in the room, but as he had not been
above ten years in London, of course he did not speak the language, and lost the benefit of the conversation. "But, O my country!" said I to myself, "it's no wonder that you are so beloved! If
I were a Frenchman, how I would hate you!"

That brutal, ignorant, peevish bully of an Englishman is showing himself in every city of Europe. One of the dullest creatures
under heaven, he goes trampling Europe under foot, shouldering
his way into galleries and cathedrals, and bustling into palaces
with his buckram uniform. At church or theatre, gala or picture-
gallery, *his* face never varies. A thousand delightful sights pass

before his bloodshot eyes, and don't affect him. Countless brilliant scenes of life and manners are shown him, but never move him. He goes to church, and calls the practices there degrading and superstitious; as if *his* altar was the only one that was acceptable. He goes to picture-galleries, and is more ignorant about Art than a French shoeblack. Art, Nature pass, and there is no dot of admiration in his stupid eyes: nothing moves him, except when a very great man comes his way, and then the rigid, proud, self-confident, inflexible British Snob can be as humble as a flunkey and as supple as a harlequin.

A VISIT TO SOME COUNTRY SNOBS

Of the dinner to which we now sat down, I am not going to be a severe critic. The mahogany I hold to be inviolable; but this I will say, that I prefer sherry to Marsala when I can get it, and the latter was the wine of which I have no doubt I heard the "cloop" just before dinner. Nor was it particularly good of its kind; however, Mrs. Major Ponto did not evidently know the difference, for she called the liquor Amontillado during the whole of the repast, and drank but half a glass of it, leaving the rest for the Major and his guest.

Stripes was in the livery of the Ponto family—a thought shabby, but gorgeous in the extreme—lots of magnificent worsted lace, and livery buttons of a very notable size. The honest fellow's hands, I remarked, were very large and black; and a fine odour of the stable was wafted about the room as he moved to and fro in his ministration. I should have preferred a clean maid-servant, but the sensations of Londoners are too acute perhaps on these subjects; and a faithful John, after all, *is* more genteel.

From the circumstances of the dinner being composed of pig's head mock-turtle soup, of pig's fry and roast ribs of pork, I am led to imagine that one of Ponto's black Hampshires had been sacrificed a short time previous to my visit. It was an excellent and comfortable repast; only there *was* rather a sameness in it, certainly. I made a similar remark the next day.

During the dinner Mrs. Ponto asked me many questions regarding the nobility, my relatives. "When Lady Angelina Skeggs would come out? and if the countess her mamma" (this was said with much archness and he-he-ing) "still wore that extraordinary purple hair-dye?" "Whether my Lord Guttlebury kept, besides his French chef, and an English cordon-bleu for the roasts, an

Italian for the confectionery?" "Who attended at Lady Clapperclaw's conversazioni?" and "whether Sir John Champignon's
'Thursday Mornings' were pleasant?" "Was it true that Lady Carabas, wanting to pawn her diamonds, found that they were paste,
and that the Marquis had disposed of them before hand?" "How
was it that Snuffin, the great tobacco-merchant, broke off the
marriage which was on the tapis between him and their second
daughter; and was it true that a mulatto lady came over from the
Havannah and forbade the match?"

"Upon my word, Madam," I had begun, and was going on to say
that I didn't know one word about all these matters which seemed
so to interest Mrs. Major Ponto, when the Major, giving me a
tread or stamp with his large foot under the table, said—

"Come, come, Snob my boy, we are all titled, you know. We
know you're one of the fashionable people about town: *we* saw
your name at Lady Clapperclaw's *soirées*, and the Champignon
breakfasts; and as for the Rubadubs, of course, as relations———"

"Oh, of course, I dine there twice a week," I said; and then I
remembered that my cousin, Humphry Snob, of the Middle Temple, *is* a great frequenter of genteel societies, and to have seen
his name in the *Morning Post* at the tag-end of several party lists.
So, taking the hint, I am ashamed to say I indulged Mrs. Major
Ponto with a deal of information about the first families in England, such as would astonish those great personages if they knew
it. I described to her most accurately the three reigning beauties
of last season at Almack's: told her in confidence that his Grace
the D——— of W——— was going to be married the day after his
Statue was put up; that his Grace the D——— of D——— was
also about to lead the fourth daughter of the Archduke Stephen
to the hymeneal altar:—and talked to her, in a word, just in the
style of Mrs. Gore's last fashionable novel.

Mrs. Major was quite fascinated by this brilliant conversation.
She began to trot out scraps of French just for all the world as they
do in the novels; and kissed her hand to me quite graciously, telling me to come soon to caffy, *ung pu de Musick o salong*—with
which she tripped off like an elderly fairy.

"Shall I open a bottle of port, or do you ever drink such a thing
as hollands and water?" says Ponto, looking ruefully at me. This
was a very different style of thing to what I had been led to expect
from him at our smoking-room at the club: where he swaggers
about his horses and his cellar: and slapping me on the shoulder
used to say, "Come down to Mangelwurzelshire, Snob my boy,

and I'll give you as good a day's shooting and as good a glass of claret as any in the country."—"Well," I said, "I like hollands much better than port, and gin even better than hollands." This was lucky. It *was* gin; and Stripes brought in hot water on a splendid plated tray.

The jingling of a harp and piano soon announced that Mrs. Ponto's *ung pu de Musick* had commenced, and the smell of the stable again entering the dining-room, in the person of Stripes, summoned us to *caffy* and the little concert. She beckoned me with a winning smile to the sofa, on which she made room for me, and where we could command a fine view of the backs of the young ladies who were performing the musical entertainment. Very broad backs they were too, strictly according to the present mode, for crinoline or its substitutes is not an expensive luxury, and young people in the country can afford to be in the fashion at very trifling charges. Miss Emily Ponto at the piano, and her sister Maria at that somewhat exploded instrument the harp, were in light blue dresses that looked all flounce, and spread out like Mr. Green's balloon when inflated.

"Brilliant touch Emily has—what a fine arm Maria's is," Mrs. Ponto remarked good-naturedly, pointing out the merits of her daughters, and waving her own arm in such a way as to show that she was not a little satisfied with the beauty of that member. I observed she had about nine bracelets and bangles, consisting of chains and padlocks, the Major's miniature, and a variety of brass serpents with fiery ruby or tender turquoise eyes, writhing up to her elbow almost, in the most profuse contortions.

"You recognise those polkas? They were played at Devonshire House on the 23rd of July, the day of the grand fête." So I said yes—I know 'em quite intimately; and began wagging my head as if in acknowledgment of those old friends.

When the performance was concluded, I had the felicity of a presentation and conversation with the two tall and scraggy Miss Pontos; and Miss Wirt, the governess, sat down to entertain us with variations on "Sich a gettin' up Stairs." They were determined to be in the fashion.

For the performance of the "Gettin' up Stairs," I have no other name but that it was a *stunner*. First Miss Wirt, with great deliberation, played the original and beautiful melody, cutting it, as it were, out of the instrument, and firing off each note so loud, clear, and sharp, that I am sure Stripes must have heard it in the stable.

"What a finger!" says Mrs. Ponto; and indeed it was a finger, as knotted as a turkey's drumstick, and splaying all over the piano. When she had banged out the tune slowly, she began a different manner of "Gettin' up Stairs," and did so with a fury and swiftness quite incredible. She spun upstairs; she whirled upstairs; she galloped upstairs; she rattled upstairs; and then having got the tune to the top landing, as it were, she hurled it down again shrieking to the bottom floor, where it sank in a crash as if exhausted by the breathless rapidity of the descent. Then Miss Wirt played the "Gettin' up Stairs" with the most pathetic and ravishing solemnity; plaintive moans and sobs issued from the keys—you wept and trembled as you were gettin' up stairs. Miss Wirt's hands seemed to faint and wail and die in variations; again, and she went up with a savage clang and rush of trumpets, as if Miss Wirt was storming a breach; and although I knew nothing of music, as I sat and listened with my mouth open to this wonderful display, my *caffy* grew cold, and I wondered the windows did not crack and the chandelier start out of the beam at the sound of this earthquake of a piece of music.

"Glorious creature! Isn't she?" said Mrs. Ponto.—"Squirtz's favourite pupil—inestimable to have such a creature. Lady Carabas would give her eyes for her! A prodigy of accomplishments! Thank you, Miss Wirt!"—And the young ladies gave a heave and a gasp of admiration—a deep-breathing gushing sound, such as you hear at church when the sermon comes to a full stop.

Miss Wirt put her two great double-knuckled hands round a waist of her two pupils, and said, "My dear children, I hope you will be able to play it soon as well as your poor little governess. When I lived with the Dunsinanes, it was the dear Duchess's favourite, and Lady Barbara and Lady Jane Macbeth learned it. It was while hearing Jane play that, I remember, that dear Lord Castletoddy first fell in love with her; and though he is but an Irish Peer, with not more than fifteen thousand a year, I persuaded Jane to have him. Do you know Castletoddy, Mr. Snob?— round towers—sweet place—county Mayo. Old Lord Castletoddy (the present Lord was then Lord Inishowan) was a most eccentric old man—they say he was mad. I heard his Royal Highness the poor dear Duke of Sussex—(*such* a man, my dears, but, alas! addicted to smoking!)—I heard His Royal Highness say to the Marquis of Anglesey, 'I am sure Castletoddy is mad!' but Inishowan wasn't in marrying my sweet Jane, though the dear child had but her ten thousand pounds *pour tout potage!*"

"Most invaluable person," whispered Mrs. Major Ponto to me. "Has lived in the very highest society:" and I, who have been accustomed to see governesses bullied in the world, was delighted to find this one ruling the roost, and to think that even the majestic Mrs. Ponto bent before her.

As for *my* pipe, so to speak, it went out at once. I hadn't a word to say against a woman who was intimate with every Duchess in the Red Book. She wasn't the rosebud, but she had been near it. She had rubbed shoulders with the great, and about these we talked all the evening incessantly, and about the fashions, and about the Court until bed-time came.

SIMPLICITY[1]

DEAR Lucy, you know what my wish is, —
   I hate all your Frenchified fuss;
Your silly entrées and made dishes
   Were never intended for us.
No footman in lace and in ruffles
   Need dangle behind my arm-chair;
And never mind seeking for truffles,
   Although they be ever so rare.

But a plain leg of mutton, my Lucy,
   I prithee get ready at three:
Have it smoking, and tender and juicy,
   And what better meat can there be?
And when it has feasted the master,
   'Twill amply suffice for the maid;
Meanwhile I will smoke my canaster,
   And tipple my ale in the shade.

---

[1] Thackeray's modernization of Horace, Book I: Ode 38

Charles Dickens

The most popular novelist the world has ever known, a writer whose works have elicited a response as great as Shakespeare's, Charles Dickens was born in 1812 in Landport, a suburb of Portsmouth. His father, a petty clerk in the Navy Pay Office, was an unstable opportunist, the prototype of Micawber —Dickens referred to him as "the Prodigal Father"—who, after moving to London, was imprisoned for debt. Ten-year-old Charles was put in a blacking factory, where amid the most sordid surroundings he pasted labels on the blacking bottles. It was physically as well as symbolically the darkest period of his life; it is recalled in the quasi-autobiographical *David Copperfield*.

Somehow he managed to get three years of schooling. At fifteen he taught himself shorthand and spent what leisure he had in the reading room of the British Museum. At seventeen he picked up a kind of living as a reporter, and at twenty-two he was permanently employed on the staff of a London newspaper. Meanwhile, he had been composing light articles that were collected and published as *Sketches by Boz*, the nickname of a younger brother.

He was now twenty-four. He married Catherine Hogarth, who bore him ten children, and a year after his marriage his reputation was established with the appearance of *Pickwick Papers*. From that time on his industry and ingenuity never slackened. Thirty-eight major works breathed life into characters that are not only a permanent part of our literature but part of our lives. Their influence is incalculable. Dostoevski called himself a Dickens disciple; Turgenev said that his own development was due to Dickens; Kafka's *The Trial* owed much of its power to *Bleak House;* Joyce's Molly Bloom was anticipated to some extent by the interminable stream-of-consciousness absurdities of Flora Finching in *Little Dorrit.*

After twenty-two years of not-too-compatible domesticity, Dickens' marriage failed. He left his wife for a young actress, Ellen Ternan. He was forty-five and the greatest part of his work had been done, but there were more years of creativity and public appearances, for Dickens was an inveterate performer. There were private theatricals, lectures, readings from his novels, plays, and travel abroad. In his mid-fifties a final tour of the United States broke his health—Dickens survived the ordeal on a diet of cream, rum, champagne, and beef tea. His vitality had been sapped: he was unable to complete the darkly mysterious *Mystery of Edwin Drood.* He died at fifty-eight on June 9, 1870, of an apoplectic stroke and was buried in the Poet's Corner of Westminster Abbey. His obituary in *The New York Times* took up practically the entire front page.

Dickens continually attacked the prevailing injustices and heartless cruelties; he was the champion of London's oppressed and downtrodden. George Santayana declared that Dickens was "one of the best friends mankind has ever had." If Dickens could not destroy the evils he portrayed, he let the light of humor and truth pierce the darkness. Against the heavy murk he pitted the spirit of the genial Pickwick, the indomitably cheerful Mark Tapley, the inevitably optimistic Micawber, the effervescent Sam Weller. His characters are not dependent on their times. They breathe immortality.

His boundless ebullience, his inexhaustible narrative flow, which mingles farce and pathos, establish an endless communication that after a hundred years never passes from a reader's remembrance. Among the most typical although the least known are the amusing period pieces in "Sketches of Young Couples" and "Lively Turtle," a sardonic portrait of the complacent, self-indulgent conservative to whom the status quo is sacred. The excerpt from the chapter entitled "Containing the Whole Science of Government" in *Little Dorrit* is a brilliant piece of nonsense as well as a Kafkalike satire on bureaucracy, while Sam Weller's anecdote about the eccentric barber in *Master Humphrey's Clock* is a fragment of true Dickensian absurdity.

Whether Dickens is read as an entertainer or as a critic of communities, as a romantic storyteller or as a realistic analyst, he is inimitable and, on any level, irresistible.

LITTLE DORRIT
CONTAINING THE WHOLE SCIENCE OF GOVERNMENT

The Circumlocution Office was (as everybody knows without being told) the most important Department under government. No public business of any kind could possibly be done at any time, without the acquiescence of the Circumlocution Office. Its finger was in the largest public pie, and in the smallest public tart. It was equally impossible to do the plainest right and to undo the plainest wrong, without the express authority of the Circumlocution Office. If another Gunpowder Plot had been discovered half an hour before the lighting of the match, nobody would have been justified in saving the parliament until there had been half a score of boards, half a bushel of minutes, several sacks of official memoranda, and a family-vault-full of ungrammatical correspondence, on the part of the Circumlocution Office.

This glorious establishment had been early in the field, when the one sublime principle involving the difficult art of governing a country, was first distinctly revealed to statesmen. It had been foremost to study that bright revelation, and to carry its shining influence through the whole of the official proceedings. Whatever was required to be done, the Circumlocution Office was beforehand with all the public departments in the art of perceiving—HOW NOT TO DO IT.

Through this delicate perception, through the tact with which it invariably seized it, and through the genius with which it always acted on it, the Circumlocution Office had risen to overtop all the public departments; and the public condition had risen to be— what it was.

It is true that How Not To Do It was the great study and object of all public departments and professional politicians all round the Circumlocution Office. It is true that every new premier and every new government, coming in because they had upheld a certain thing as necessary to be done, were no sooner come in than they applied their utmost faculties to discovering, How not to do it. It is true that from the moment when a general election was over, every returned man who had been raving on hustings because it hadn't been done, and who had been asking the friends of the honorable gentleman in the opposite interest on pain of impeachment to tell him why it hadn't been done, and who had been asserting that it must be done, and who had been pledging himself that it should be done, began to devise, How it was not to be done. It is true that the debates of both Houses of Parliament, the whole session through, uniformly tended to the protracted deliberation, How not to do it. It is true that the royal speech at the opening of such session virtually said, My lords and gentlemen, you have a considerable stroke of work to do, and you will please to retire to your respective chambers, and discuss, How not to do it. It is true that the royal speech, at the close of such session, virtually said, My lords and gentlemen, you have through several laborious months been considering with great loyalty and patriotism, How not to do it, and you have found out; and with the blessing of Providence upon the harvest (natural, not political), I now dismiss you. All this is true, but the Circumlocution Office went beyond it.

Because the Circumlocution Office went on mechanically, every day, keeping this wonderful, all-sufficient wheel of statesmanship, How not to do it, in motion. Because the Circumlocution Office was down upon any ill-advised public servant who was going to do it, or who appeared to be by any surprising accident in remote danger of doing it, with a minute, and a memorandum, and a letter of instructions, that extinguished him. It was this spirit of national efficiency in the Circumlocution Office that had gradually led to its having something to do with everything. Mechanicians, natural philosophers, soldiers, sailors, petitioners, memorialists, people with grievances, people who wanted to prevent grievances, people who wanted to redress grievances, jobbing people, jobbed people, people who couldn't get rewarded for merit, and people who couldn't get punished for demerit, were all indiscriminately tucked up under the foolscap paper of the Circumlocution Office.

Numbers of people were lost in the Circumlocution Office. Unfortunates with wrongs, or with projects for the general welfare (and they had better have had wrongs at first, than have taken that bitter English recipe for certainly getting them), who in slow lapse of time and agony had passed safely through other public departments; who, according to rule, had been bullied in this, over-reached by that, and evaded by the other; got referred at last to the Circumlocution Office, and never reappeared in the light of day. Boards sat upon them, secretaries minuted upon them, commissioners gabbled about them, clerks registered, entered, checked, and ticked them off, and they melted away. In short, all the business of the country went through the Circumlocution Office, except business that never came out of it; and *its* name was Legion.

Sometimes, angry spirits attacked the Circumlocution Office. Sometimes, parliamentary questions were asked about it, and even parliamentary motions made or threatened about it, by demagogues so low and ignorant as to hold that the real recipe of government was, How to do it. Then would the noble lord, or right honorable gentleman, in whose department it was to defend the Circumlocution Office, put an orange in his pocket, and make a regular field-day of the occasion. Then would he come down to that House with a slap upon the table, and meet the honorable gentleman foot to foot. Then would he be there to tell that honorable gentleman that the Circumlocution Office not only was blameless in this matter, but was commendable in this matter, was extollable to the skies in this matter. Then would he be there to tell that honorable gentleman, that, although the Circumlocution Office was invariably right and wholly right, it never was so right as in this matter. Then would he be there to tell that honorable gentleman, that it would have been more to his honor, more to his credit, more to his good taste, more to his good sense, more to half the dictionary of commonplaces, if he had left the Circumlocution Office alone, and never approached this matter. Then would he keep one eye upon a coach or crammer from the Circumlocution Office sitting below the bar, and smash the honorable gentleman with the Circumlocution Office account of this matter. And although one of two things always happened; namely, either that the Circumlocution Office had nothing to say and said it, or that it had something to say of which the noble lord, or right honorable gentleman, blundered one half and forgot the other; the Circumlocution Office was always voted immaculate, by an accommodating majority.

Such a nursery of statesmen had the Department become in virtue of a long career of this nature, that several solemn lords had attained the reputation of being quite unearthly prodigies of business, solely from having practised, How not to do it, at the head of the Circumlocution Office. As to the minor priests and acolytes of that temple, the result of all this was that they stood divided into two classes, and, down to the junior messenger, either believed in the Circumlocution Office as a heaven-born institution, that had an absolute right to do whatever it liked; or took refuge in total infidelity, and considered it a flagrant nuisance.

MARTIN CHUZZLEWIT
PORTRAIT OF MRS. GAMP

Mrs. Gamp had a large bundle with her, a pair of pattens,[1] and a species of gig umbrella, — the latter article in color like a faded leaf, except where a circular patch of a lively blue had been dexterously let in at the top. She was much flurried by the haste she had made, and labored under the most erroneous views of cabriolets, which she appeared to confound with mail-coaches or stage-wagons, inasmuch as she was constantly endeavoring for the first half-mile to force her luggage through the little front window and clamoring to the driver to "put it in the boot." When she was disabused of this idea, her whole being resolved itself into an absorbing anxiety about her pattens, with which she played innumerable games at quoits on Mr. Pecksniff's legs. It was not until they were close upon the house of mourning that she had enough composure to observe, —

"And so the gentleman's dead, sir. Ah! The more's the pity." She didn't even know his name. "But it's what we must all come to. It's as certain as being born, except that we can't make our calculations as exact. Ah! Poor dear!"

She was a fat old woman, this Mrs. Gamp, with a husky voice and a moist eye, which she had a remarkable power of turning up and only showing the white of it. Having very little neck, it cost her some trouble to look over herself, if one may say so, at those to whom she talked. She wore a very rusty black gown, rather the worse for snuff, and a shawl and bonnet to correspond. In these dilapidated articles of dress she had, on principle, arrayed her-

---

[1] *pattens:* heavy shoes

self, time out of mind, on such occasions as the present; for this at once expressed a decent amount of veneration for the deceased, and invited the next of kin to present her with a fresher suit of weeds, — an appeal so frequently successful that the very fetch and ghost of Mrs. Gamp, bonnet and all, might be seen hanging up, any hour in the day, in at least a dozen of the second-hand clothes-shops about Holborn. The face of Mrs. Gamp—the nose in particular—was somewhat red and swollen, and it was difficult to enjoy her society without becoming conscious of a smell of spirits. Like most persons who have attained to great eminence in their profession, she took to hers very kindly, insomuch that, setting aside her natural predilections as a woman, she went to a lying-in or a laying-out with equal zest and relish.

"Ah!" repeated Mrs. Gamp; for it was always a safe sentiment in cases of mourning. "Ah, dear! When Gamp was summoned to his long home, and I see him a-lying in Guy's Hospital with a penny-piece on each eye, and his wooden leg under his left arm, I thought I should have fainted away. But I bore up."

If certain whispers current in the Kingsgate Street circles had any truth in them, she had indeed borne up surprisingly, and had exerted such uncommon fortitude as to dispose of Mr. Gamp's remains for the benefit of science. But it should be added, in fairness, that this had happened twenty years before, and that Mr. and Mrs. Gamp had long been separated, on the ground of incompatibility of temper in their drink.

"You have become indifferent since then, I suppose," said Mr. Pecksniff. "Use is second nature, Mrs. Gamp."

"You may well say second nater, sir," returned that lady. "One's first ways is to find sich things a trial to the feelings, and so is one's lasting custom. If it wasn't for the nerve a little sip of liquor gives me (I never was able to do more than taste it), I never could go through with what I sometimes has to do. 'Mrs. Harris,' I says, at the very last case as ever I acted in, which it was but a young person,—'Mrs. Harris,' I says, 'leave the bottle on the chimley-piece, and don't ask me to take none, but let me put my lips to it when I am so dispoged, and then I will do what I am engaged to do, according to the best of my ability.' 'Mrs. Gamp,' she says, in answer, 'if ever there was a sober creetur to be got at eighteen-pence a day for working-people and three-and-six for gentlefolks, —night watching,'" said Mrs. Gamp, with emphasis, "'being a extra charge,—you are that inwallable person.' 'Mrs. Harris,' I says to her, 'don't name the charge, fer if I could afford to lay all

my feller-creeturs out for nothink I would gladly do it, sich is the
love I bears 'em. But what I always says to them as has the manage-
ment of matters, Mrs. Harris,'" here she kept her eye on Mr. Pecksniff, "'be they gents or be they ladies, is, don't ask me whether
I won't take none, but leave the bottle on the chimley-piece, and
let me put my lips to it when I am so dispoged.'"

MASTER HUMPHREY'S CLOCK
SAM WELLER'S ANECDOTE

It seems that the housekeeper and the two Mr. Wellers were
no sooner left together on the occasion of their first becoming
acquainted, than the housekeeper called to her assistance Mr.
Slithers the barber, who had been lurking in the kitchen in expectation of her summons; and with many smiles and much sweetness introduced him as one who would assist her in the responsible office of entertaining her distinguished visitors.

"Indeed," said she, "without Mr. Slithers I should have been
placed in quite an awkward situation."

"There is no call for any hock'erdness, mum," said Mr. Weller
with the utmost politeness; "no call wotsumever. A lady," added
the old gentleman, looking about him with the air of one who es-
tablishes an incontrovertible position, — "a lady can't be hock'erd.
Natur' has otherwise purwided."

The housekeeper inclined her head and smiled yet more sweetly. The barber, who had been fluttering about Mr. Weller and
Sam in a state of great anxiety to improve their acquaintance,
rubbed his hands and cried, "Hear, hear! Very true, sir;" whereupon Sam turned about and steadily regarded him for some sec-
onds in silence.

"I never knew," said Sam, fixing his eyes in a ruminative manner upon the blushing barber, — "I never knew but vun o' your
trade, but *he* wos worth a dozen, and wos indeed dewoted to his
callin'!"

"Was he in the easy shaving way, sir," inquired Mr. Slithers;
"or in the cutting and curling line?"

"Both," replied Sam; "easy shavin' was his natur', and cuttin'
and curlin' was his pride and glory. His whole delight wos in his
trade. He spent all his money in bears and run in debt for 'em
besides, and there they wos a-growling away down in the front

cellar all day long, and ineffectooally gnashing their teeth, vile
the grease o' there relations and friends wos being re-tailed in
gallipots in the shop above, and the first-floor winder wos orna-
mented vith their heads; not to speak o' the dreadful aggrawation
it must have been to 'em to see a man alvays a-walkin' up and
down the pavement outside, vith the portrait of a bear in his last
agonies, and underneath in large letters, 'Another fine animal
wos slaughtered yesterday at Jinkinson's!' Hows'ever, there they
wos, and there Jinkinson wos, till he wos took wery ill with some
inn'ard disorder, lost the use of his legs, and wos confined to his
bed, vere he laid a wery long time, but sich wos his pride in his
profession, even then, that wenever he wos worse than usual the
doctor used to go down-stairs and say, 'Jinkinson's wery low this
mornin'; we must give the bears a stir;' and as sure as ever they
stirred 'em up a bit and made 'em roar, Jinkinson opens his eyes
if he wos ever so bad, calls out, 'There's the bears!' and rewives
agin."

"Astonishing!" cried the barber.

"Not a bit," said Sam, "human natur' neat as imported. Vun day
the doctor happenin' to say, 'I shall look in as usual to-morrow
mornin',' Jinkinson catches hold of his hand and says, 'Doctor,'
he says, 'will you grant me one favor?' 'I will, Jinkinson,' says the
doctor. 'Then doctor,' says Jinkinson, 'vill you come unshaved,
and let me shave you?' 'I will,' says the doctor. 'God bless you,'
says Jinkinson. Next day the doctor came, and arter he'd been
shaved all skilful and reg'lar, he says, 'Jinkinson,' he says, 'it's
wery plain this does you good. Now,' he says, 'I've got a coachman
as has got a beard that it 'ud warm your heart to work on, and
though the footman,' he says, 'hasn't got much of a beard, still
he's a-trying it on with a pair o' viskers to that extent that razors is
Christian charity. If they take it in turns to mind the carriage
when it's a-waitin' below,' he says, 'wot's to hinder you from oper-
atin' on both of 'em ev'ry day as well as upon me? you've got six
children,' he says, 'wot's to hinder you from shavin' all their heads
and keepin' 'em shaved? you've got two assistants in the shop
down-stairs, wot's to hinder you from cuttin' and curlin' them as
often as you like? Do this,' he says, 'and you're a man agin.' Jinkinson squeedged the doctor's hand and begun that wery day; he
kept his tools upon the bed, and wenever he felt hisself gettin'
worse, he turned to at vun o' the children who wos a runnin' about
the house vith heads like clean Dutch cheeses, and shaved him
agin. Vun day the lawyer come to make his vill; all the time he wos

a-takin' it down, Jinkinson was secretly a-clippin' avay at his hair vith a large pair of scissors. 'Wot's that 'ere snippin' noise?' says the lawyer every now and then; 'it's like a man havin' his hair cut.' —'It *is* wery like a man havin' his hair cut,' says poor Jinkinson, hidin' the scissors, and lookin' quite innocent. By the time the lawyer found it out, he wos wery nearly bald. Jinkinson wos kept alive in this vay for a long time, but at last vun day he has in all the children vun arter another, shaves each on 'em wery clean, and gives him vun kiss on the crown o' his head; then he has in the two assistants, and arter cuttin' and curlin' of 'em in the first style of elegance, says he should like to hear the woice o' the greasiest bear, vich rekvest is immedetly complied with; then he says that he feels wery happy in his mind and vishes to be left alone; and then he dies, prevously cuttin' his own hair and makin' one flat curl in the wery middle of his forehead."

THE YOUNG COUPLE

There is to be a wedding this morning at the corner house in the terrace. The pastry-cook's people have been there half-a-dozen times already; all day yesterday there was a great stir and bustle, and they were up this morning as soon as it was light. Miss Emma Fielding is going to be married to young Mr. Harvey.

Heaven alone can tell in what bright colours this marriage is painted upon the mind of the little housemaid at number six, who has hardly slept a wink all night with thinking of it, and now stands on the unswept door-steps leaning upon her broom, and looking wistfully towards the enchanted house. Nothing short of omniscience can divine what visions of the baker, or the green-grocer, or the smart and most insinuating butterman, are flitting across her mind—what thoughts of how she would dress on such an occasion, if she were a lady—of how she would dress, if she were only a bride—of how cook would dress, being bridesmaid, conjointly with her sister "in place" at Fulham, and how the clergyman, deeming them so many ladies, would be quite humbled and respectful. What day-dreams of hope and happiness—of life being one perpetual holiday, with no master and no mistress to grant or withhold it—of every Sunday being a Sunday out—of pure freedom as to curls and ringlets, and no obligation to hide fine heads of hair in caps—what pictures of happiness, vast and immense to her, but utterly ridiculous to us, bewilder the brain of the little housemaid at number six, all called into existence by the wedding at the corner!

We smile at such things, and so we should, though perhaps for a better reason than commonly presents itself. It should be pleasant to us to know that there are notions of happiness so moderate and limited, since upon those who entertain them, happiness and lightness of heart are very easily bestowed.

But the little housemaid is awakened from her reverie, for forth from the door of the magical corner house there runs towards her, all fluttering in smart new dress and streaming ribands, her friend Jane Adams, who comes all out of breath to redeem a solemn promise of taking her in, under cover of the confusion, to see the breakfast table spread forth in state, and —sight of sights!— her young mistress ready dressed for church.

And there, in good truth, when they have stolen upstairs on tiptoe and edged themselves in at the chamber-door—there is Miss Emma "looking like the sweetest picter," in a white chip bonnet and orange flowers, and all other elegancies becoming a bride (with the make, shape, and quality of every article of which the girl is perfectly familiar in one moment, and never forgets to her dying day)—and there is Miss Emma's mamma in tears, and Miss Emma's papa comforting her, and saying how that of course she has been long looking forward to this, and how happy she ought to be—and there, too, is Miss Emma's sister with her arms round her neck, and the other bridesmaid all smiles and tears, quieting the children, who would cry more but that they are so finely dressed, and yet sob for fear sister Emma should be taken away—and it is all so affecting, that the two servant-girls cry more than anybody; and Jane Adams, sitting down upon the stairs, when they have crept away, declares that her legs tremble so that she don't know what to do, and that she will say for Miss Emma, that she never had a hasty word from her, and that she does hope and pray she may be happy.

But Jane soon comes round again, and then surely there never was anything like the breakfast table, glittering with plate and china, and set out with flowers and sweets, and long-necked bottles, in the most sumptuous and dazzling manner. In the centre, too, is the mighty charm, the cake, glistening with frosted sugar, and garnished beautifully. They agree that there ought to be a little Cupid under one of the barley-sugar temples, or at least two hearts and an arrow; but, with this exception, there is nothing to wish for, and a table could not be handsomer. As they arrive at this conclusion, who should come in but Mr. John! to whom Jane says that it's only Anne from number six; and John says *he* knows, for he's often winked his eye down the area, which causes Anne to blush and look confused. She is going away, indeed; when Mr. John will have it that she must drink a glass of wine, and he says never mind it's being early in the morning, it won't hurt her: so they shut the door and pour out the wine; and Anne drinking Jane's health, and adding, "and here's wishing you yours, Mr. John," drinks it in a great many sips — Mr. John all the time making jokes appropriate to the occasion. At last Mr. John, who has waxed bolder by degrees, pleads the usage at weddings, and claims the privilege of a kiss, which he obtains after a great scuffle; and footsteps being now heard on the stairs, they disperse suddenly.

By this time a carriage has driven up to convey the bride to church, and Anne of number six prolonging the process of "cleaning her door," has the satisfaction of beholding the bride and bridesmaids, and the papa and mamma, hurry into the same and drive rapidly off. Nor is this all, for soon other carriages begin to arrive with a posse of company all beautifully dressed, at whom she could stand and gaze for ever; but having something else to do, is compelled to take one last long look and shut the street-door.

And now the company have gone down to breakfast, and tears have given place to smiles, for all the corks are out of the long-necked bottles, and their contents are disappearing rapidly. Miss Emma's papa is at the top of the table; Miss Emma's mamma at the bottom; and beside the latter are Miss Emma herself and her husband — admitted on all hands to be the handsomest and most interesting young couple ever known. All down both sides of the table, too, are various young ladies, beautiful to see, and various young gentlemen who seem to think so; and there, in a post of honour, is an unmarried aunt of Miss Emma's, reported to possess unheard of riches, and to have expressed vast testamentary intentions respecting her favourite niece and new nephew. This lady has been very liberal and generous already, as the jewels worn by the bride abundantly testify, but that is nothing to what she means to do, or even to what she has done, for she put herself in close communication with the dressmaker three months ago, and prepared a wardrobe (with some articles worked by her own hands) fit for a Princess. People may call her an old maid, and so she may be, but she is neither cross nor ugly for all that; on the contrary, she is very cheerful and pleasant-looking, and very kind and tender-hearted: which is no matter of surprise except to those who yield to popular prejudices without thinking why, and will never grow wiser and never know better.

Of all the company, though, none are more pleasant to behold or better pleased with themselves than two young children, who, in honour of the day, have seats among the guests. Of these, one is a little fellow of six or eight years old, brother to the bride—and the other a girl of the same age, or something younger, whom he calls "his wife." The real bride and bridegroom are not more devoted than they: he all love and attention, and she all blushes and fondness, toying with a little bouquet which he gave her this morning, and placing the scattered roseleaves in her bosom with nature's own coquettishness. They have dreamt of each other in their quiet dreams, these children, and their little hearts have been nearly broken when the absent one has been dispraised in jest. When will there come in after-life a passion so earnest, generous, and true as theirs; what, even in its gentlest realities, can have the grace and charm that hover round such fairy lovers!

By this time the merriment and happiness of the feast have gained their height; certain ominous looks begin to be exchanged between the bridesmaids, and somehow it gets whispered about that the carriage which is to take the young couple into the country has arrived. Such members of the party as are most disposed to prolong its enjoyments, affect to consider this a false alarm, but it turns out too true, being speedily confirmed, first by the retirement of the bride and a select file of intimates who are to prepare her for the journey, and secondly by the withdrawal of the ladies generally. To this there ensues a particularly awkward pause, in which everybody essays to be facetious, and nobody succeeds; at length the bridegroom makes a mysterious disappearance in obedience to some equally mysterious signal; and the table is deserted.

Now, for at least six weeks last past it has been solemnly devised and settled that the young couple should go away in secret; but they no sooner appear without the door than the drawing-room windows are blocked up with ladies waving their handkerchiefs and kissing their hands, and the dining-room panes with gentlemen's faces beaming farewell in every queer variety of its expression. The hall and steps are crowded with servants in white favours, mixed up with particular friends and relations who have darted out to say good-bye; and foremost in the group are the tiny lovers arm in arm, thinking, with fluttering hearts, what happiness it would be to dash away together in that gallant coach, and never part again.

The bride has barely time for one hurried glance at her old home, when the steps rattle, the door slams, the horses clatter on the pavement, and they have left it far away.

A knot of women servants still remain clustered in the hall, whispering among themselves, and there of course is Anne from number six, who has made another escape on some plea or other, and been an admiring witness of the departure. There are two points on which Anne expatiates over and over again, without the smallest appearance of fatigue or intending to leave off; one is, that she "never see in all her life such a—oh such a angel of a gentleman as Mr. Harvey"—and the other, that she "can't tell how it is, but it don't seem a bit like a work-a-day, or a Sunday neither—it's all so unsettled and unregular."

LIVELY TURTLE

I have a comfortable property. What I spend, I spend upon myself; and what I don't spend I save. Those are my principles. I am warmly attached to my principles, and stick to them on all occasions.

I am not, as some people have represented, a mean man. I never denied myself anything that I thought I should like to have. I may have said to myself "Snoady"—that is my name—"you will get those peaches cheaper if you wait till next week"; or, I may have said to myself, "Snoady, you will get that wine for nothing, if you wait till you are asked out to dine"; but I never deny myself anything. If I can't get what I want without buying it, and paying its price for it, I *do* buy it and pay its price for it. I have an appetite bestowed upon me; and, if I balked it, I should consider that I was flying in the face of Providence.

I have no near relation but a brother. If he wants anything of me, he don't get it. All men are my brothers; and I see no reason why I should make his, an exceptional case.

I live at a cathedral town where there is an old corporation. I am not in the Church, but it may be that I hold a little place of some sort. Never mind. It may be profitable. Perhaps yes, perhaps no. It may, or it may not, be a sinecure. I don't choose to say. I never enlightened my brother on these subjects, and I consider all men my brothers. The Negro is a man and a brother—should I hold myself accountable for my position in life, *to him?* Certainly not.

I often run up to London. I like London. The way I look at it, is this. London is not a cheap place, but, on the whole, you can get more of the real thing for your money there—I mean the best thing, whatever it is—than you can get in most places. Therefore, I say to the man who has got the money, and wants the thing, "Go to London for it, and treat yourself."

When *I* go, I do it in this manner. I go to Mrs. Skim's Private Hotel and Commercial Lodging House, near Aldersgate Street, City, (it is advertised in Bradshaw's Railway Guide, where I first found it), and there I pay, "for bed and breakfast, with meat, two and ninepence per day, including servants." Now, I have made a calculation, and I am satisfied that Mrs. Skim cannot possibly make much profit out of *me.* In fact, if all her patrons were like me, my opinion is, the woman would be in the *Gazette* next month.

Why do I go to Mrs. Skim's when I could go to the Clarendon, you may ask? Let us argue that point. If I went to the Clarendon I could get nothing in bed but sleep; could I? No. Now, sleep at the Clarendon is an expensive article; whereas sleep, at Mrs. Skim's, is decidedly cheap. I have made a calculation, and I don't hesitate to say, all things considered, that it's cheap. Is it an inferior article, as compared with the Clarendon sleep, or is it of the same quality? I am a heavy sleeper, and it is of the same quality. Then why should I go to the Clarendon?

But as to breakfast? you may say.—Very well. As to breakfast. I could get a variety of delicacies for breakfast at the Clarendon, that are out of the question at Mrs. Skim's. Granted. But I don't want to have them! My opinion is, that we are not entirely animal and sensual. Man has an intellect bestowed upon him. If he clogs that intellect by too good a breakfast, how can he properly exert that intellect in meditation, during the day, upon his dinner? That's the point. We are not to enchain the soul. We are to let it soar. It is expected of us.

At Mrs. Skim's, I get enough for breakfast (there is no limitation to the bread and butter, though there is to the meat) and not too much. I have all my faculties about me, to concentrate upon the object I have mentioned, and I can say to myself besides, "Snoady,

you have saved six, eight, ten, fifteen, shillings, already to-day.
If there is anything you fancy for your dinner, have it. Snoady,
you have earned your reward."

My objection to London, is, that it is the headquarters of the
worst radical sentiments that are broached in England. I consider that it has a great many dangerous people in it. I consider
the present publication (if it's "Household Words") very dangerous, and I write this with the view of neutralising some of its bad
effects. My political creed is, let us be comfortable. We are all
very comfortable as we are—*I* am very comfortable as I am—
leave us alone!

All mankind are my brothers, and I don't think it Christian—if
you come to that—to tell my brother that he is ignorant, or degraded, or dirty, or anything of the kind. I think it's abusive and
low. You meet me with the observation that I am required to love
my brother. I reply, "I do." I am sure I am always willing to say
to my brother, "My good fellow, I love you very much; go along
with you; keep to your own road; leave me to mine; whatever is,
is right; whatever isn't, is wrong; don't make a disturbance!" It
seems to me, that this is at once the whole duty of man, and the
only temper to go to dinner in.

Going to dinner in this temper in the City of London, one day
not long ago, after a bed at Mrs. Skim's, with meat-breakfast and
servants included, I was reminded of the observation which, if
my memory does not deceive me, was formerly made by somebody on some occasion, that man may learn wisdom from the
lower animals. It is a beautiful fact, in my opinion, that great
wisdom is to be learnt from that noble animal the Turtle.

I had made up my mind, in the course of the day I speak of, to
have a Turtle dinner. I mean a dinner mainly composed of Turtle.
Just a comfortable tureen of soup, with a pint of punch; and
nothing solid to follow, but a tender juicy steak. I like a tender
juicy steak. I generally say to myself when I order one, "Snoady,
you have done right."

When I make up my mind to have a delicacy, expense is no
consideration. The question resolves itself, then, into a question
of the very best. I went to a friend of mine who is a Member of
the Common Council, and with that friend I held the following
conversation.

Said I to him, "Mr. Groggles, the best Turtle is where?"

Says he, "If you want a basin for lunch, my opinion is, you can't
do better than drop into Birch's."

Said I, "Mr. Groggles, I thought you had known me better, than to suppose me capable of a basin. My intention is to dine. A tureen."

Says Mr. Groggles, without a moment's consideration, and in a determined voice, "Right opposite the India House, Leadenhall Street."

We parted. My mind was not inactive during the day, and at six in the afternoon I repaired to the house of Mr. Groggles's recommendation. At the end of the passage, leading from the street into the coffee-room, I observed a vast and solid chest, in which I then supposed that a Turtle of unusual size might be deposited. But, the correspondence between its bulk and that of the charge made for my dinner, afterwards satisfied me that it must be the till of the establishment.

I stated to the waiter what had brought me there, and I mentioned Mr. Groggles's name. He feelingly repeated after me, "A tureen of Turtle, and a tender juicy steak." His manner, added to the manner of Mr. Groggles in the morning, satisfied me that all was well. The atmosphere of the coffee-room was odoriferous with Turtle, and the steams of thousands of gallons, consumed within its walls, hung, in savoury grease, upon their surface. I could have inscribed my name with a penknife, if I had been so disposed, in the essence of innumerable Turtles. I preferred to fall into a hungry reverie, brought on by the warm breath of the place, and to think of the West Indies and the Island of Ascension.

My dinner came—and went. I will draw a veil over the meal, I will put the cover on the empty tureen, and merely say that it was wonderful—and that I paid for it.

I sat meditating, when all was over, on the imperfect nature of our present existence, in which we can eat only for a limited time, when the waiter roused me with these words.

Said he to me, as he brushed the crumbs off the table, "Would you like to see the Turtle, Sir?"

"To see what Turtle, waiter?" said I (calmly) to him.

"The tanks of Turtle below, Sir," said he to me.

Tanks of Turtle! Good Gracious! "Yes!"

The waiter lighted a candle, and conducted me downstairs to a range of vaulted apartments, cleanly whitewashed and illuminated with gas, where I saw a sight of the most astonishing and gratifying description, illustrative of the greatness of my native country. "Snoady," was my first observation to myself, "Rule Britannia, Britannia rules the waves!"

There were two or three hundred Turtle in the vaulted apartments — all alive. Some in tanks, and some taking the air in long dry walks littered down with straw. They were of all sizes; many of them enormous. Some of the enormous ones had entangled themselves with the smaller ones, and pushed and squeezed themselves into corners, with their fins over water-pipes, and their heads downwards, where they were apoplectically struggling and splashing, apparently in the last extremity. Others were calm at the bottom of the tanks; others languidly rising to the surface. The Turtle in the walks littered down with straw, were calm and motionless. It was a thrilling sight. I admire such a sight. It rouses my imagination. If you wish to try its effect on yours, make a call right opposite the India House any day you please — dine — pay — and ask to be taken below.

Two athletic young men, without coats, and with the sleeves of their shirts tucked up to the shoulders, were in attendance on these noble animals. One of them, wrestling with the most enormous Turtle in company, and dragging him up to the edge of the tank, for me to look at, presented an idea to me which I never had before. I ought to observe that I like an idea. I say, when I get a new one, "Snoady, book that!"

My idea, on the present occasion, was — Mr. Groggles! It was not a Turtle that I saw, but Mr. Groggles. It was the dead image of Mr. Groggles. He was dragged up to confront me, with his waistcoat — if I may be allowed the expression — towards me; and it was identically the waistcoat of Mr. Groggles. It was the same shape, very nearly the same colour, only wanted a gold watch-chain and a bunch of seals, to BE the waistcoat of Mr. Groggles. There was what I should call a bursting expression about him in general, which was accurately the expression of Mr. Groggles. I had never closely observed a Turtle's throat before. The folds of his loose cravat, I found to be precisely those of Mr. Groggles's cravat. Even the intelligent eye — I mean to say, intelligent enough for a person of correct principles, and not dangerously so — was the eye of Mr. Groggles. When the athletic young man let him go, and, with a roll of his head, he flopped heavily down into the tank, it was exactly the manner of Mr. Groggles as I have seen him ooze away into his seat, after opposing a sanitary motion in the Court of Common Council!

"Snoady," I couldn't help saying to myself, "you have done it. You have got an idea, Snoady, in which a great principle is involved. I congratulate you!" I followed the young man, who dragged up several Turtle to the brinks of the various tanks. I found them all the same — all varieties of Mr. Groggles — all extraordinarily like the gentlemen who usually eat them. "Now, Snoady," was my next remark, "what do you deduce from this?"

"Sir," said I, "what I deduce from this, is, confusion to those Radicals and other Revolutionists who talk about improvement. Sir," said I, "what I deduce from this, is, that there isn't this resemblance between the Turtles and the Groggleses for nothing. It's meant to show mankind that the proper model for a Groggles, is a Turtle; and that the liveliness we want in a Groggles, is the liveliness of a Turtle, and no more." "Snoady," was my reply to this, "you have hit it. You are right!"

I admired the idea very much, because, if I hate anything in the world, it's change. Change has evidently no business in the world, has nothing to do with it, and isn't intended. What we want is (as I think I have mentioned) to be comfortable. I look at it that way. Let us be comfortable, and leave us alone. Now, when the young man dragged a Groggles — I mean a Turtle — out of his tank, this was exactly what the noble animal expressed as he floundered back again.

I have several friends besides Mr. Groggles in the Common Council and it might be a week after this, when I said, "Snoady, if I was you, I would go to that court, and hear the debate to-day." I went. A good deal of it was what I call a sound, old English discussion. One eloquent speaker objected to the French as wearing wooden shoes; and a friend of his reminded him of another objection to that foreign people, namely, that they eat frogs. I had feared, for many years, I am sorry to say, that these wholesale principles were gone out. How delightful to find them still remaining among the great men of the City of London, in the year one thousand eight hundred and fifty! It made me think of the Lively Turtle.

But, I soon thought more of the Lively Turtle. Some Radicals and Revolutionists have penetrated even to the Common Council — which otherwise I regard as one of the last strongholds of our afflicted constitution; and speeches were made, about removing Smithfield Market — which I consider to be a part of that Constitution — and about appointing a Medical Officer for the City, and about preserving the public health; and other treasonable practices, opposed to Church and State. These proposals Mr. Groggles, as might have been expected of such a man, resisted; so warmly, that, as I afterwards understood from Mrs. Groggles, he had rather a sharp attack of blood to the head that night. All the Groggles party resisted them, too, and it was a fine constitutional sight to see waistcoat after waistcoat rise up in resistance of them and subside. But what struck me in the sight was this, "Snoady," said I, "here is your idea carried out, Sir! These Radicals and Revolutionists are the athletic young men in shirt sleeves, dragging the Lively Turtle to the edges of the tank. The Groggleses are the Turtle, looking out for a moment, and flopping down again. Honour to the Groggleses! Honour to the Court of Lively Turtle! The wisdom of the Turtle is the hope of England!"

There are three heads in the moral of what I had to say. First, Turtle and Groggles are identical; wonderfully alike externally, wonderfully alike mentally. Secondly, Turtle is a good thing every way, and the liveliness of the Turtle is intended as an example for the liveliness of man; you are not to go beyond that. Thirdly, we are all quite comfortable. Leave us alone!

Edward Lear

An ironic fate overtook Edward Lear: he tried hard to be a great painter, and without trying, he became a great humorist. Of Danish descent, one of a stockbroker's fifteen children, he was born in London in 1812. Cared for and educated by a sister twenty-one years his senior, he suffered from asthma and epilepsy from the age of seven until his death. At twenty he was an expert ornithologist. He was commissioned to make paintings of parrots in the zoological gardens; his drawings were favorably compared to John James Audubon's. Engaged to illustrate a book about the Earl of Derby's zoo, he was taken into the earl's family. It was for the Derby children that Lear spun many of the wonderfully absurd rhymes that made up his *Nonsense Songs* and *Laughable Lyrics*. A serious artist, he also gave drawing lessons to Queen Victoria.

From time to time Lear interrupted whatever he was doing to please himself by making variations on an odd five-line form of verse. This pastime stimulated a vogue for the light (and in other hands, the lewd) limerick. He composed more than two hundred of them. Once in a while he turned from random persiflage to ridiculous parody. "Incidents in the Life of My Uncle Arly" is a takeoff on Wordsworth's sententious "Resolution and Independence."

As a topographical painter, Lear traveled throughout Europe, painting countless canvasses and filling endless notebooks—one of his friends inherited more than two thousand designs. Most of the paintings are forgotten, but the droll fantasies are unforgettable. The teacher of a sovereign who was seldom amused has become childhood's madcap laureate and everybody's Merry Andrew.

INCIDENTS IN THE LIFE OF MY UNCLE ARLY

O my agéd Uncle Arly!
Sitting on a heap of Barley
  Through the silent hours of night—
Close beside a leafy thicket:—
On his nose there was a Cricket,
In his hat a Railway-Ticket;—
  (But his shoes were far too tight.)

Long ago, in youth, he squandered
All his goods away, and wandered
  To the Tiniskoop-hills afar.
There on golden sunsets blazing,
Every evening found him gazing—
Singing—"Orb! you're quite amazing!
  How I wonder what you are!"

Like the ancient Medes and Persians,
Always by his own exertions
  He subsisted on those hills;
Whiles—by teaching children spelling;
Or at times by merely yelling,
Or at intervals by selling
  "Propter's Nicodemus Pills."

Later, in his morning rambles
He perceived the moving brambles
  Something square and white disclose;
'Twas a First-class Railway-Ticket;
But, on stooping down to pick it
Off the ground, a pea-green Cricket
  Settled on my uncle's Nose.

Never—never more—oh! never
Did that Cricket leave him ever,

Dawn or evening, day or night;
Clinging as a constant treasure,
Chirping with a cheerious measure,
Wholly to my uncle's pleasure; —
    (Though his shoes were far too tight.)

So for three-and-forty winters,
Till his shoes were worn to splinters,
    All those hills he wandered o'er —
Sometimes silent, sometimes yelling —
Till he came to Borley Melling,
Near his old ancestral dwelling; —
    (But his shoes were far too tight.)

On a little heap of Barley
Died my agéd Uncle Arly,
    And they buried him one night —
Close beside the leafy thicket;
There — his hat and Railway Ticket;
There — his ever-faithful Cricket; —
    (But his shoes were far too tight.)

THE OWL AND THE PUSSY-CAT

The Owl and the Pussy-Cat went to sea
    In a beautiful pea-green boat:
They took some honey, and plenty of money
    Wrapped up in a five-pound note.
The Owl looked up to the stars above,
    And sang to a small guitar,
"O lovely Pussy! O Pussy, my love,
    What a beautiful Pussy you are,
        You are, you are!
    What a beautiful Pussy you are!"

Pussy said to the Owl, "You elegant fowl!
    How charmingly sweet you sing!
O let us be married! too long we have tarried!
    But what shall we do for a ring?"
They sailed away for a year and a day,
    To the land where the Bong tree grows,

And there in a wood a Piggy-wig stood,
  With a ring at the end of his nose,
    His nose, his nose,
  With a ring at the end of his nose.

"Dear Pig, are you willing to sell for one shilling
  Your ring?" Said the Piggy, "I will."
So they took it away, and were married next day
  By the Turkey who lives on the hill.
They dined on mince, and slices of quince,
  Which they ate with a runcible spoon;
And hand in hand, on the edge of the sand,
  They danced by the light of the moon,
    The moon, the moon,
  They danced by the light of the moon.

THE TWO OLD BACHELORS

Two old Bachelors were living in one house;
One caught a Muffin, the other caught a Mouse.
Said he who caught the Muffin to him who caught the Mouse,
"This happens just in time, for we've nothing in the house,
Save a tiny slice of lemon and a teaspoonful of honey,
And what to do for dinner—since we haven't any money?
And what can we expect if we haven't any dinner
But to lose our teeth and eyelashes and keep on growing
    thinner?"

Said he who caught the Mouse to him who caught the Muffin,
"We might cook this little Mouse if we only had some stuffin'!
If we had but Sage and Onions we could do extremely well,
But how to get that Stuffin' it is difficult to tell!"

And then those two old Bachelors ran quickly to the town
And asked for Sage and Onions as they wandered up and down;
They borrowed two large Onions, but no Sage was to be found
In the Shops or in the Market or in all the Gardens round.

But someone said, "A hill there is, a little to the north,
And to its purpledicular top a narrow way leads forth;
And there among the rugged rocks abides an ancient Sage—

An earnest Man, who reads all day a most perplexing page.
Climb up and seize him by the toes—all studious as he sits—
And pull him down, and chop him into endless little bits!
Then mix him with your Onion (cut up likewise into scraps),
And your Stuffin' will be ready, and very good—perhaps."

And then those two old Bachelors, without loss of time,
The nearly purpledicular crags at once began to climb;
And at the top among the rocks, all seated in a nook,
They saw that Sage a-reading of a most enormous book.

"You earnest Sage!" aloud they cried, "your book you've read
     enough in!
We wish to chop you into bits and mix you into Stuffin'!"
But that old Sage looked calmly up, and with his awful book
At those two Bachelors' bald heads a certain aim he took;
And over crag and precipice they rolled promiscuous down—
At once they rolled, and never stopped in lane or field or town;
And when they reached their house, they found (besides their
     want of Stuffin')
The Mouse had fled—and previously had eat up the Muffin.

They left their home in silence by the once convivial door;
And from that hour those Bachelors were never heard of more.

FIVE LIMERICKS

There was an old man with a beard,
Who said, "It is just as I feared.
     Two owls and a hen,
     Four larks and a wren,
Have all built their nests in my beard!"

There was an old man in a tree
Who was horribly bored by a bee.
     When they said, "Does it buzz?"
     He replied, "Yes, it does!
It's a regular brute of a bee!"

There was an old man who supposed
That the street door was partially closed.

But some very large rats
Ate his coats and his hats
While that futile old gentleman dozed.

There was an old man of Peru
Who watched his wife making a stew.
But once, by mistake,
In a stove she did bake
That unfortunate man of Peru.

There was an old man on some rocks
Who shut his wife up in a box.
When she said, "Let me out,"
He exclaimed, "Without doubt
You will spend your whole life in that box."

HOW PLEASANT TO KNOW MR. LEAR

How pleasant to know Mr. Lear!
Who has written such volumes of stuff!
Some think him ill-tempered and queer,
But a few think him pleasant enough.

His mind is concrete and fastidious,
His nose is remarkably big;
His visage is more or less hideous,
His beard it resembles a wig.

He has ears, and two eyes, and ten fingers,
Leastways if you reckon two thumbs;
Long ago he was one of the singers,
But now he is one of the dumbs.

He sits in a beautiful parlor,
With hundreds of books on the wall;
He drinks a great deal of Marsala,
But never gets tipsy at all.

He has many friends, laymen and clerical,
Old Foss is the name of his cat;

His body is perfectly spherical,
    He weareth a runcible hat.

When he walks in a waterproof white,
    The children run after him so!
Calling out, "He's come out in his night-
    gown, that crazy old Englishman, oh!"

He weeps by the side of the ocean,
    He weeps on the top of the hill;
He purchases pancakes and lotion,
    And chocolate shrimps from the mill.

He reads, but he cannot speak, Spanish,
    He cannot abide ginger beer:
Ere the days of his pilgrimage vanish,
    How pleasant to know Mr. Lear!

Charles Stuart Calverley

Endowed with so many talents that everything came easily, Charles Stuart Calverley was born in 1831 in Worcestershire. He was a musician, an athlete, a wit famous for his improvisations, a classicist who translated Virgil, Horace, and Theocritus into English, as well as "Lycidas" and many other English poems into Latin. A serious poet and a brilliant parodist, his was a lively and unsanctified intellect. Educated at Harrow, Oxford, and Cambridge, he romped through his courses casually breaking rules and just as casually winning prizes. After studying law, he was admitted to the bar, but a few months later a skating accident resulted in concussion of the brain and he was forced into semi-invalidism. He died of Bright's disease at fifty-three.

A donnish technician who performed adroit tricks with double rhyme, Calverley was a straight-faced ironist who was also a master of scintillating light verse.

FIRST LOVE

O my earliest love, who, ere I number'd
　　Ten sweet summers, made my bosom thrill!
Will a swallow—or a swift, or *some* bird—
　　Fly to her and say, I love her still?

Say my life's a desert drear and arid,
    To its one green spot I aye recur:
Never, never—although three times married—
    Have I cared a jot for aught but her.

No, mine own! though early forced to leave you,
    Still my heart was there where first we met;
In those "Lodgings with an ample sea-view,"
    Which were, forty years ago, "To Let."

There I saw her first, our landlord's oldest
    Little daughter. On a thing so fair
Thou, O Sun,—who (so they say) beholdest
    Everything,—hast gazed, I tell thee, ne'er.

There she sat—so near me, yet remoter
    Than a star—a blue-eyed bashful imp:
On her lap she held a happy bloater,
    'Twixt her lips a yet more happy shrimp.

And I loved her, and our troth we plighted
    On the morrow by the shingly shore:
In a fortnight to be disunited
    By a bitter fate for evermore.

O my own, my beautiful, my blue-eyed!
    To be young once more, and bite my thumb
At the world and all its cares with you, I'd
    Give no inconsiderable sum.

Hand in hand we tramp'd the golden seaweed,
    Soon as o'er the gray cliff peep'd the dawn:
Side by side, when came the hour for tea, we'd
    Crunch the mottled shrimp and hairy prawn:—

Has she wedded some gigantic shrimper,
    That sweet mite with whom I loved to play?
Is she girt with babes that whine and whimper,
    That bright being who was always gay?

Yes—she has at least a dozen wee things!
    Yes—I see her darning corduroys,

Scouring floors, and setting out the tea-things,
  For a howling herd of hungry boys,

In a home that reeks of tar and sperm-oil!
  But at intervals she thinks, I know,
Of those days which we, afar from turmoil,
  Spent together forty years ago.

O my earliest love, still unforgotten,
  With your downcast eyes of dreamy blue!
Never, somehow, could I seem to cotton
  To another as I did to you!

THE SCHOOLMASTER

ABROAD WITH HIS SON

O what harper could worthily harp it,
  Mine Edward! this wide-stretching wold
(Look out *wold*) with its wonderful carpet
  Of emerald, purple, and gold!
Look well at it—also look sharp, it
    Is getting so cold.

The purple is heather (*erica*);
  The yellow, gorse—call'd sometimes "whin."
Cruel boys on its prickles might spike a
  Green beetle as if on a pin.
You may roll in it, if you would like a
    Few holes in your skin.

You wouldn't? Then think of how kind you
  Should be to the insects who crave
Your compassion—and then, look behind you
  At yon barley-ears! Don't they look brave
As they undulate (*undulate,* mind you,
    From *unda, a wave*).

The noise of those sheep-bells, how faint it
  Sounds here—(on account of our height)!
And this hillock itself—who could paint it,

With its changes of shadow and light?
Is it not—(never, Eddy, say "ain't it")—
    A marvellous sight?

Then yon desolate eerie morasses,
    The haunts of the snipe and the hern—
(I shall question the two upper classes
    On *aquatiles,* when we return)—
Why, I see on them absolute masses
        Of *filix* or fern.

How it interests e'en a beginner
    (Or *tiro*) like dear little Ned!
Is he listening? As I am a sinner
    He's asleep—he is wagging his head.
Wake up! I'll go home to my dinner,
        And you to your bed.

The boundless ineffable prairie;
    The splendour of mountain and lake
With their hues that seem ever to vary;
    The mighty pine-forests which shake
In the wind, and in which the unwary
        May tread on a snake;

And this wold with its heathery garment
    Are themes undeniably great.
But—although there is not any harm in't—
    It's perhaps little good to dilate
On their charms to a dull little varmint
        Of seven or eight.

Charles Lutwidge Dodgson (Lewis Carroll)

A topsy-turvy Wonderland for children of all ages was discovered, explored, and charted to the last rabbit hole by a solemn mathematician who was also a deacon in holy orders. Born Charles Lutwidge Dodgson on January 27, 1832, in the Cheshire village of Daresbury, he published his first book, *A Syllabus of Plane Algebraical Geometry,* when he was twenty-eight. Seven years later, an ordained deacon who because of a pronounced stammer never preached, he issued an *Elementary Treatise on Determinants*.

In the meanwhile Dodgson, a lover of children, had gone on an excursion that was to exert a more profound influence on the world than any of his mathematical formulas. It was an idyllic and fateful day—the exact date was July 4, 1862—when he went boating with three little girls, Lorina, Edith, and Alice Liddell. It was Alice who became the heroine of a story told that afternoon, a story that has been translated into practically every foreign language as well as shorthand and Braille. More than sixty years later Alice Liddell, then a widow and the mother of three World War soldiers, sold the manuscript for sixty-two thousand dollars.

Carroll's Wonderland is a world of nonsense. The kings and queens are from a deck of cards; the footmen are frogs; croquet balls turn into hedgehogs; caterpillars give sage advice; mock turtles dance with mythical gryphons; dormice fall asleep in teacups; and smiling Cheshire cats dissolve until nothing is left but the grin without the cat. Yet the nonsense is plausible and even logical. The mathematical mind saw to that.

Although Dodgson tried to separate himself from his alter ego, he gave himself away in the very associations of his fiction. The disappearing feline is a Cheshire cat because Dodgson was born in Cheshire. "Dodo" is a pet name for Dodgson himself. Even his pseudonym is more revealing than at first appears. The names "Charles Lutwidge" reversed themselves into "Lewis Carroll" through a Latin-English transformation: "Charles" was changed to the Latin *Carolus* or *Carroll;* "Lutwidge" was shifted into "Ludovicus," then to "Louis," and so to "Lewis." However, Dodgson steadfastly refused to admit that he was Carroll. Still protesting, he died at Guildford in his sixty-sixth year.

Although they have been enjoyed by millions of children and uncritical readers, most of Carroll's rhymes are critical parodies of the didactic poems of the period. For example, "How Doth the Little Crocodile" is a burlesque of Isaac Watts's "How Doth the Little Busy Bee," and "Father William" is a mockery of the similarly named babbler in Southey's sanctimonious "The Old Man's Comforts." While *Sylvie and Bruno* contains some of the purest nonsense ever written, the nonsense vocabulary in "Jabberwocky" often makes sense. Carroll explained some of the "portmanteau" words. Telescoping "lithe" and "slimy," you get "slithy"; by trying to say "fretful," "furious," and "fuming" at the same time you get "frumious." Reversing the adage about pence and pounds, Carroll advised, "Take care of the sounds and the sense will take care of itself."

ALICE'S ADVENTURES IN WONDERLAND
FATHER WILLIAM

"You are old, Father William," the young man said,
    "And your hair has become very white;
And yet you incessantly stand on your head —
    Do you think at your age, it is right?"

"In my youth," Father William replied to his son,
    "I feared it might injure the brain;

But, now that I'm perfectly sure I have none,
    Why, I do it again and again."

"You are old," said the youth, "as I mentioned before,
    And have grown most uncommonly fat;
Yet you turned a back-somersault in at the door—
    Pray, what is the reason of that?"

"In my youth," said the sage, as he shook his gray locks,
    "I kept all my limbs very supple
By the use of this ointment—one shilling the box—
    Allow me to sell you a couple?"

"You are old," said the youth, "and your jaws are too weak
    For anything tougher than suet;
Yet you finished the goose, with the bones and the beak—
    Pray, how did you manage to do it?"

"In my youth," said his father, "I took to the law,
    And argued each case with my wife;
And the muscular strength which it gave to my jaw
    Has lasted the rest of my life."

"You are old," said the youth, "one would hardly suppose
    That your eye was as steady as ever;
Yet you balanced an eel on the end of your nose—
    What made you so awfully clever?"

"I have answered three questions, and that is enough,"
    Said his father. "Don't give yourself airs!
Do you think I can listen all day to such stuff?
    Be off, or I'll kick you down-stairs!"

HOW DOTH THE LITTLE CROCODILE

How doth the little crocodile
    Improve his shining tail,
And pour the waters of the Nile
    On every golden scale!

How cheerfully he seems to grin,
    How neatly spreads his claws,

And welcomes little fishes in,
    With gently smiling jaws!

THE WHITE RABBIT'S EVIDENCE

They told me you had been to her,
    And mentioned me to him:
She gave me a good character,
    But said I could not swim.

He sent them word I had not gone
    (We know it to be true):
If she should push the matter on,
    What would become of you?

I gave her one, they gave him two,
    You gave us three or more;
They all returned from him to you,
    Though they were mine before.

If I or she should chance to be
    Involved in this affair,
He trusts to you to set them free,
    Exactly as we were.

My notion was that you had been
    (Before she had this fit)
An obstacle that came between
    Him, and ourselves, and it.

Don't let him know she liked them best,
    For this must ever be
A secret, kept from all the rest,
    Between yourself and me.

THROUGH THE LOOKING-GLASS

JABBERWOCKY

'Twas brillig, and the slithy toves
    Did gyre and gimble in the wabe:

All mimsy were the borogoves,
    And the mome raths outgrabe.

"Beware the Jabberwock, my son!
    The jaws that bite, the claws that catch!
Beware the Jubjub bird, and shun
    The frumious Bandersnatch!"

He took his vorpal sword in hand;
    Long time the manxome foe he sought—
So rested he by the Tumtum tree,
    And stood awhile in thought.

And, as in uffish thought he stood,
    The Jabberwock, with eyes of flame,
Came whiffling through the tulgey wood,
    And burbled as it came!

One, two! One, two! And through and through
    The vorpal blade went snicker-snack!
He left it dead, and with its head
    He went galumphing back.

"And hast thou slain the Jabberwock?
    Come to my arms, my beamish boy!
O frabjous day! Callooh, Callay!"
    He chortled in his joy.

'Twas brillig, and the slithy toves
    Did gyre and gimble in the wabe:
All mimsy were the borogoves,
    And the mome raths outgrabe.

SYLVIE AND BRUNO

THE MAD GARDENER'S SONG

He thought he saw an Elephant
    That practised on a fife;
He looked again and found it was
    A letter from his wife.

"At length I realize," he said,
   "The bitterness of life."

He thought he saw a Buffalo
   Upon the chimney piece;
He looked again and found it was
   His Sister's Husband's Niece.
"Unless you leave this house," he said,
   "I'll send for the police."

He thought he saw a Rattlesnake
   That questioned him in Greek;
He looked again and found it was
   The Middle of Next Week.
"The one thing I regret," he said,
   "Is that it cannot speak."

He thought he saw a Banker's Clerk
   Descending from the bus;
He looked again and saw it was
   A Hippopotamus.
"If this should stay to dine," he said,
   "There won't be much for us."

He thought he saw an Albatross
   That fluttered round the lamp;
He looked again and found it was
   A Penny Postage Stamp.
"You'd best be getting home," he said,
   "The nights are very damp."

Samuel Langhorne Clemens (Mark Twain)

Nineteenth-century American humor was crude and raw. Most of it depended on exaggerated rural dialects, eccentricities of pronunciation, and absurd phonetic spellings. ("My naburs is mourn harf crazy on the new fangled idear about Sperrits." . . . "Yer mam had thuteen the old way, and ef this truck stays 'bout the house, you'se good for twenty-six.") The ridicule was fumbling, the aim was not only low but generally inaccurate, and the distortions were, to pervert Max Beerbohm's remark about Henry Irving's Hamlet, "vulgar without being funny." The frontier humor was particularly raucous, and while it was enjoyed by multitudes, its practitioners felt a little ashamed of it.

Almost all the professional fun-makers went to any length to get laughs and to even greater lengths to conceal themselves. The knockabout "phunny phellers" of the period hid behind fancy pseudonyms. Charles Farrar Browne achieved national popularity as "Artemus Ward." Melville D. Landon, a respectable cotton planter, transformed himself into the ridiculous "Eli Perkins." Benjamin P. Shillaber, who began as a journeyman printer, was the muddle-headed "Mrs. Partington," who rivaled Sheridan's Mrs. Malaprop. The industrious auctioneer Henry Wheeler Shaw turned into the cracker-barrel philosopher "Josh Billings," who "slewed spelling around" until it became "Joshbillingsgate." The serious, politically minded Robert Henry Newell adopted the pen name "Orpheus C.

Kerr," a brazen pun on "office seeker." Audience after audience applauded the jokesmith Sam Clemens; the world not
only laughed with him but loved him as "Mark Twain."

Son of an impractical speculator who in spite of every failure
believed he would make a fortune in land, Samuel Langhorne
Clemens was born in 1835 in Florida, Missouri. When he was
four the family moved to a town of less than five hundred people, Hannibal, Missouri, where he grew up under the influence
of his father's restless dream of wealth. The town had the
greatest influence on the future writer. His father died when
the boy was twelve and he had to leave school. Apprenticed to
a printer, Sam began writing for his brother Orion's newspaper. At eighteen he became a tramp printer in various parts
of the United States, then thought of seeking a fortune in South
America; but he succumbed to the lure of the Mississippi and
a little later became a steamboat pilot. It was a fascinating
experience, one that he dwelt upon with lifelong nostalgia.
The Civil War interrupted his piloting, and after two weeks
with a group of Confederate volunteers he went to Nevada,
where he became a luckless prospector, a reporter in Carson
City, and city editor of the Virginia City *Enterprise*.

He was twenty-seven when he adopted the pseudonym
"Mark Twain," a Mississippi river-calling meaning "two fathoms down," and began producing journalistic humor in the
traditional style. It was frontier fun—boisterous in tone, hi-
lariously exaggerated in accent and incident—a drawling out
of tall tales with a straight face and an air of deceptive innocence. Twain became an entertainer as popular as Artemus
Ward, a popularity that was enormously increased upon the
publication of "The Notorious Jumping Frog of Calaveras
County."

He traveled extensively. What he wrote about the Sandwich
Islands (Hawaii) enlarged his audience; instead of making him
cosmopolitan, his journeys to Europe and the Holy Land intensified his native predilections. He laughed at the Old World
in *Innocents Abroad*, and his countrymen rewarded him by
buying one hundred and fifty thousand copies of the book
that satirized guides and guidebooks.

While abroad Twain had fallen in love with a miniature
painting displayed by a fellow passenger; when he returned
he met the original, Olivia Langdon, and married her. It has
been contended that his well-to-do and ultraconservative wife

exerted an influence on Twain that was not only artificially "refining" but inhibiting. On the other hand, he shocked many of his readers by outright blasphemies and scarcely concealed attacks on the current mores.

Settling in Hartford, Connecticut, for twenty years, Twain wrote constantly. *Roughing It, A Connecticut Yankee at King Arthur's Court, The Adventures of Tom Sawyer, The Adventures of Huckleberry Finn, Life on the Mississippi* were some of the characteristically American works. He amassed a fortune and lost it in a variety of impractical schemes. He had, for example, invested almost a quarter of a million dollars in a typesetting machine that turned out to be worthless. To clear his debts Twain went on a world lecture tour, a tour that broke his health and made him bitter about lecturing—his account of the tour in *Following the Equator* has, unlike the other travel books, a gloomy overcast. From seventy on, Twain's life was a contradiction of public triumphs (including honorary degrees from Yale and Oxford) and private tragedies. Within a few years his brother, his wife, and his two favorite daughters died. These misfortunes deepened an inherent pessimism; much that he wrote was so morose that he instructed it should not be published until after his death. The posthumous *What Is Man?, The Mysterious Stranger*, and his *Autobiography* reveal an accumulating darkness, a bitter satisfaction that perhaps life is only a dream, although "a grotesque and foolish dream." "I have been reading the morning paper," he wrote to William Dean Howells, his friend and adviser. "I do it every morning, well knowing that I shall find in it the usual hypocrisies, depravities, and cruelties that make up civilization, and cause me to put in the rest of the day pleading for the damnation of the human race." His last years were spent in the richly furnished quiet of Stormfield in Redding, Connecticut, where, at the age of seventy-five, he died of angina pectoris.

The contrasting nature of Twain's greatly varied writings has given rise to critical controversy. It has been argued that even when he was earning his living as a humorist, Twain was an intimidated, repressed satirist, and that the books published after his death disclose his basic disbeliefs. Essentially Twain was a humorist who was also a liberator. Farcical at first, Twain's wit grew from slapstick and burlesque to an intolerance of sham and everything cheap; with the honest zest of a pioneering folklorist, he became a critical catalyst. He never wearied of showing up the difference between what man preaches and what he practices, between what he sanctimoniously murmurs on Sundays and what he actually does from Monday to Saturday. An irrepressible cynic, he was also the reproachful and responsible man. Like Walt Whitman's, his work presents a breakthrough in the democratizing of American literature.

THE NOTORIOUS JUMPING FROG OF CALAVERAS COUNTY

In compliance with the request of a friend of mine who wrote me from the East, I called on good-natured, garrulous old Simon Wheeler and inquired after my friend's friend, Leonidas W. Smiley, as requested to do, and I hereunto append the result. I have a lurking suspicion that *Leonidas W.* Smiley is a myth, that my friend never knew such a personage, and that he only conjectured that if I asked old Wheeler about him, it would remind him of his infamous *Jim* Smiley and he would go to work and bore me to death with some exasperating reminiscence of him as long and as tedious as it should be useless to me. If that was the design, it succeeded.

I found Simon Wheeler dozing comfortably by the barroom stove of the dilapidated tavern in the decayed mining camp of Angel's, and I noticed that he was fat and bald-headed and had an expression of winning gentleness and simplicity upon his tranquil countenance. He roused up and gave me good day. I told him that a friend of mine had commissioned me to make some inquiries about a cherished companion of his boyhood named *Leonidas W.* Smiley — *Rev. Leonidas W.* Smiley, a young minister of the Gospel, who he had heard was at one time a resident of Angel's Camp. I added that if Mr. Wheeler could tell me anything about this Rev. Leonidas W. Smiley, I would feel under many obligations to him.

Simon Wheeler backed me into a corner and blockaded me there with his chair, and then sat down and reeled off the monotonous narrative which follows this paragraph. He never smiled, he never frowned, he never changed his voice from the gentle-flowing key to which he tuned his initial sentence, he never betrayed the slightest suspicion of enthusiasm, but all through the interminable narrative there ran a vein of impressive earnestness and sincerity which showed me plainly that, so far from his imagining that there was anything ridiculous or funny about his story, he regarded it as a really important matter and admired its two heroes as men of transcendent genius in *finesse*. I let him go on in his own way and never interrupted him once.

"Rev. Leonidas W. H'm, Reverend Le— Well, there was a feller here once by the name of *Jim* Smiley, in the winter of '49—or maybe it was the spring of '50—I don't recollect exactly, somehow, though what makes me think it was one or the other is because I remember the big flume warn't finished when he first come to the camp; but anyway, he was the curiousest man about always betting on anything that turned up you ever see, if he could get anybody to bet on the other side, and if he couldn't he'd change sides. Any way that suited the other man would suit *him*—any way just so's he got a bet, *he* was satisfied. But still he was lucky, uncommon lucky; he most always come out winner. He was always ready and laying for a chance; there couldn't be no solit'ry thing mentioned but that feller'd offer to bet on it and take ary side you please, as I was just telling you. If there was a horse-race, you'd find him flush or you'd find him busted at the end of it; if there was a dog-fight, he'd bet on it; if there was a cat-fight, he'd bet on it; if there was a chicken-fight, he'd bet on it; why if there was two birds setting on a fence, he would bet you which one would fly first; or if there was a camp-meeting, he would be there reg'lar to bet on Parson Walker, which he judged to be the best exhorter about here, and so he was too, and a good man. If he even see a straddle-bug start to go anywheres, he would bet you how long it would take him to get to—to wherever he was going to, and if you took him up, he would foller that straddle-bug to Mexico but what he would find out where he was bound for and how long he was on the road. Lots of the boys here has seen that Smiley and can tell you about him. Why, it never made no difference to *him*—he'd bet on *any* thing—the dangdest feller. Parson Walker's wife laid very sick once for a good while, and it seemed as if they warn't going to save her; but one morning he come in and Smiley up and asked him how she was, and he said she was considerable better—thank the Lord for his inf'nite mercy—and coming on so smart that with the blessing of Prov'-dence she'd get well yet; and Smiley, before he thought, says, 'Well, I'll resk two-and-a-half she don't anyway.'

"Thish-yer Smiley had a mare—the boys called her the fifteen-

minute nag but that was only in fun, you know, because of
course she was faster than that—and he used to win money on
that horse, for all she was so slow and always had the asthma,
or the distemper, or the consumption, or something of that kind.
They used to give her two or three hundred yards' start and then
pass her under way, but always at the fag end of the race she'd
get excited and desperate like, and come cavorting and straddling
up and scattering her legs around limber, sometimes in the air
and sometimes out to one side among the fences, and kicking up
m-o-r-e dust and raising m-o-r-e racket with her coughing and
sneezing and blowing her nose—and *always* fetch up at the stand
just about a neck ahead, as near as you could cipher it down.

"And he had a little small bull-pup, that to look at him you'd
think he warn't worth a cent but to set around and look ornery and
lay for a chance to steal something. But as soon as money was up
on him he was a different dog; his under-jaw'd begin to stick out
like the fo'castle of a steamboat and his teeth would uncover and
shine like the furnaces. And a dog might tackle him and bully-
rag him, and bite him and throw him over his shoulder two or
three times, and Andrew Jackson—which was the name of the
pup—Andrew Jackson would never let on but what *he* was satisfied and hadn't expected nothing else—and the bets being doubled
and doubled on the other side all the time, till the money was
all up; and then all of a sudden he would grab that other dog jest
by the j'int of his hind leg and freeze to it—not chaw, you understand, but only just grip and hang on till they throwed up the
sponge, if it was a year. Smiley always come out winner on that
pup till he harnessed a dog once that didn't have no hind legs,
because they'd been sawed off in a circular saw, and when the
thing had gone along far enough and the money was all up and
he come to make a snatch for his pet holt, he see in a minute how
he's been imposed on and how the other dog had him in the door,
so to speak, and he 'peared surprised, and then he looked sorter
discouraged-like and didn't try no more to win the fight, and so he
got shucked out bad. He give Smiley a look, as much as to say his
heart was broke, and it was *his* fault for putting up a dog that
hadn't no hind legs for him to take holt of, which was his main
dependence in a fight, and then he limped off a piece and laid
down and died. It was a good pup, was that Andrew Jackson, and
would have made a name for hisself if he'd lived, for the stuff
was in him and he had genius—I know it, because he hadn't no

opportunities to speak of, and it don't stand to reason that a dog could make such a fight as he could under them circumstances if he hadn't no talent. It always makes me feel sorry when I think of that last fight of his'n and the way it turned out.

"Well, thish-yer Smiley had rat-tarriers, and chicken cocks, and tomcats and all them kind of things till you couldn't rest, and you couldn't fetch nothing for him to bet on but he'd match you. He ketched a frog one day and took him home, and said he cal'lated to educate him; and so he never done nothing for three months but set in his back yard and learn that frog to jump. And you bet you he *did* learn him, too. He'd give him a little punch behind, and the next minute you'd see that frog whirling in the air like a doughnut—see him turn one summerset, or maybe a couple if he got a good start, and come down flat-footed and all right, like a cat. He got him up so in the matter of ketching flies, and kep' him in practice so constant, that he'd nail a fly every time as fur as he could see him. Smiley said all a frog wanted was education and he could do 'most anything—and I believe him. Why, I've seen him set Dan'l Webster down here on this floor— Dan'l Webster was the name of the frog—and sing out, 'Flies, Dan'l, flies!' and quicker'n you could wink he'd spring straight up and snake a fly off'n the counter there, and flop down on the floor ag'in as solid as a gob of mud, and fall to scratching the side of his head with his hind foot as indifferent as if he hadn't no idea he'd been doin' any more'n any frog might do. You never see a frog so modest and straight-for'ard as he was, for all he was so gifted. And when it come to fair and square jumping on a dead level, he could get over more ground at one straddle than any animal of his breed you ever see. Jumping on a dead level was his strong suit, you understand; and when it come to that, Smiley would ante up money on him as long as he had a red. Smiley was monstrous proud of his frog, and well he might be for fellers that had traveled and been everywheres all said he laid over any frog that ever *they* see.

"Well, Smiley kep' the beast in a little lattice box, and he used to fetch him down-town sometimes and lay for a bet. One day a feller—a stranger in the camp, he was—come acrost him with his box and says:

"'What might it be that you've got in the box?'

"And Smiley says, sorter indifferent-like, 'It might be a parrot, or it might be a canary, maybe, but it ain't—it's only just a frog.'

"And the feller took it and looked at it careful, and turned it round this way and that, and says, 'H'm—so 'tis. Well, what's *he* good for?'

"'Well,' Smiley says, easy and careless, 'he's good enough for *one* thing, I should judge—he can outjump any frog in Calaveras County.'

"The feller took the box again and took another long, particular look, and give it back to Smiley and says, very deliberate, 'Well,' he says, 'I don't see no p'ints about that frog that's any better'n any other frog.'

"'Maybe you don't,' Smiley says. 'Maybe you understand frogs and maybe you don't understand 'em; maybe you've had experience and maybe you ain't only a amature, as it were. Anyways, I've got *my* opinion, and I'll resk forty dollars that he can outjump any frog in Calaveras County.'

"And the feller studied a minute and then says, kinder sadlike, 'Well, I'm only a stranger here and I ain't got no frog; but if I had a frog, I'd bet you.'

"And then Smiley says, 'That's all right—that's all right—if you'll hold my box a minute, I'll go and get you a frog.' And so the feller took the box and put up his forty dollars along with Smiley's, and set down to wait.

"So he set there a good while thinking and thinking to himself, and then he got the frog out and prized his mouth open and took a teaspoon and filled him full of quail-shot—filled him pretty near up to his chin—and set him on the floor. Smiley he went to the swamp and slopped around in the mud for a long time, and finally he ketched a frog and fetched him in and give him to this feller, and says:

"'Now, if you're ready, set him alongside of Dan'l, with his forepaws just even with Dan'l's, and I'll give the word.' Then he says, 'One—two—three—*git!*' and him and the feller touched up the frogs from behind, and the new frog hopped off lively, but Dan'l give a heave and hysted up his shoulders—so—like a Frenchman, but it warn't no use—he couldn't budge; he was planted as solid as a church, and he couldn't no more stir than if he was anchored out. Smiley was a good deal surprised, and he was disgusted too, but he didn't have no idea what the matter was, of course.

"The feller took the money and started away, and when he was going out the door, he sorter jerked his thumb over his shoulder—so—at Dan'l and says again, very deliberate, 'Well,' he says,

'*I* don't see no p'ints about that frog that's any better'n any other frog.'

"Smiley he stood scratching his head and looking down at Dan'l a long time, and at last he says, 'I do wonder what in the nation that frog throw'd off for—I wonder if there ain't something the matter with him—he 'pears to look mighty baggy, somehow.' And he ketched Dan'l by the nap of the neck and hefted him, and says, 'Why, blame my cats if he don't weigh five pound!' and turned him upside down and he belched out a double handful of shot. And then he see how it was, and he was the maddest man— he set the frog down and took out after that feller, but he never ketched him. And—"

[Here Simon Wheeler heard his name called from the front yard and got up to see what was wanted.] And turning to me as he moved away, he said: "Just set where you are, stranger, and rest easy—I ain't going to be gone a second."

But, by your leave, I did not think that a continuation of the history of the enterprising vagabond *Jim* Smiley would be likely to afford me much information concerning the Rev. *Leonidas W.* Smiley and so I started away.

At the door I met the sociable Wheeler returning, and he button-holed me and recommenced:

"Well, thish-yer Smiley had a yaller one-eyed cow that didn't have no tail, only just a short stump like a bannanner, and—"

However, lacking both time and inclination, I did not wait to hear about the afflicted cow but took my leave.

A TRAMP ABROAD

JIM BAKER'S BLUEJAY YARN

Animals talk to each other, of course. There can be no question about that, but I suppose there are very few people who can understand them. I never knew but one man who could. I knew he could, however, because he told me so himself. He was a middle-aged, simple-hearted miner who had lived in a lonely corner of California among the woods and mountains a good many years, and had studied the ways of his only neighbors, the beasts and the birds, until he believed he could accurately translate any remark which they made. This was Jim Baker. According to Jim Baker, some animals have only a limited education and use only very simple words, and scarcely ever a comparison or a flowery figure; whereas certain other animals have a large vocabulary, a fine command of language and a ready and fluent delivery; consequently these latter talk a great deal; they like it, they are conscious of their talent, and they enjoy "showing off." Baker said that after long and careful observation, he had come to the conclusion that the bluejays were the best talkers he had found among birds and beasts. Said he:

"There's more *to* a bluejay than any other creature. He has got more moods, and more different kinds of feelings than other creatures; and, mind you, whatever a bluejay feels, he can put into language. And no mere commonplace language, either, but rattling, out-and-out book-talk—and bristling with metaphor too—just bristling! And as for command of language—why *you* never see a bluejay get stuck for a word. No man ever did. They just boil out of him! And another thing: I've noticed a good deal and there's no bird, or cow, or anything that uses as good grammar as a bluejay. You may say a cat uses good grammar. Well, a cat does—but you let a cat get excited once; you let a cat get to pulling fur with another cat on a shed, nights, and you'll hear grammar that will give you the lockjaw. Ignorant people think it's the *noise* which fighting cats make that is so aggravating but it ain't so; it's the sickening grammar they use. Now I've never heard a jay use bad grammar but very seldom, and when they do, they are as ashamed as a human, they shut right down and leave.

"You may call a jay a bird. Well, so he is, in a measure—because he's got feathers on him, and don't belong to no church, perhaps, but otherwise he is just as much a human as you be. And I'll tell you for why. A jay's gifts and instincts and feelings and interests cover the whole ground. A jay hasn't got any more principle than a Congressman. A jay will lie, a jay will steal, a jay will deceive, a jay will betray; and four times out of five, a jay will go back on his solemnest promise. The sacredness of an obligation is a thing which you can't cram into no bluejay's head. Now on top of all this there's another thing, a jay can outswear any gentleman in the mines. You think a cat can swear. Well, a cat can, but you give a bluejay a subject that calls for his reserve-powers and where is your cat? Don't talk to *me*—I know too much about this thing. And there's yet another thing, in the one little particular of scolding—just good, clean, out-and-out scolding—a bluejay can lay over anything, human or divine. Yes, sir, a jay is everything that a man is. A jay can cry, a jay can laugh, a jay can feel shame, a jay can reason and plan and discuss, a jay likes gossip and scandal, a jay has got a sense of humor, a jay knows when he is an ass just as well as you do—maybe better. If a jay ain't human, he better take in his sign, that's all. Now I'm going to tell you a perfectly true fact about some bluejays.

"When I first begun to understand jay language correctly, there was a little incident happened here. Seven years ago, the last man in this region but me moved away. There stands his house—been empty ever since, a log house with a plank roof— just one big room and no more, no ceiling, nothing between the rafters and the floor. Well, one Sunday morning I was sitting out here in front of my cabin with my cat, taking the sun and looking at the blue hills and listening to the leaves rustling so lonely in the trees, and thinking of the home away yonder in the states that I hadn't heard from in thirteen years, when a blue-jay lit on that house, with an acorn in his mouth, and says, 'Hello, I reckon I've struck something.' When he spoke the acorn dropped out of his mouth and rolled down the roof, of course, but he didn't care; his mind was all on the thing he had struck. It was a knot-hole in the roof. He cocked his head to one side, shut one eye and put the other one to the hole, like a possum looking down a jug, then he glanced up with his bright eyes, gave a wink or two with his wings—which signifies gratification, you under-stand—and says, 'It looks like a hole, it's located like a hole— blamed if I don't believe it *is* a hole!'

"Then he cocked his head down and took another look; he glances up perfectly joyful this time, winks his wings and his tail both, and says, 'Oh, no, this ain't no fat thing, I reckon! If I ain't in luck!—why it's a perfectly elegant hole!' So he flew down and got that acorn and fetched it up and dropped it in, and was just tilting his head back with the heavenliest smile on his face, when all of a sudden he was paralyzed into a listening attitude and that smile faded gradually out of his countenance like breath off'n a razor, and the queerest look of surprise took its place. Then he says, 'Why, I didn't hear it fall!' He cocked his eye at the hole again and took a long look; raised up and shook his head; stepped around to the other side of the hole and took another look from that side; shook his head again. He studied a while, then he just went into the *de*tails—walked round and round the hole and spied into it from every point of the compass. No use. Now he took a thinking attitude on the comb of the roof and scratched the back of his head with his right foot a minute, and finally says, 'Well, it's too many for *me*, that's certain; must be a mighty long hole; however, I ain't got no time to fool around here, I got to 'tend to business; I reckon it's all right—chance it, anyway.'

"So he flew off and fetched another acorn and dropped it in, and tried to flirt his eye to the hole quick enough to see what become of it but he was too late. He held his eye there as much as a minute; then he raised up and sighed, and says, 'Confound it, I don't seem to understand this thing, no way; however, I'll tackle her again.' He fetched another acorn, and done his level best to see what become of it, but he couldn't. He says, 'Well, I never struck no such a hole as this before; I'm of the opinion it's a totally new kind of a hole.' Then he begun to get mad. He held in for a spell, walking up and down the comb of the roof and shaking his head and muttering to himself; but his feelings got the upper hand of him presently and he broke loose and cussed himself black in the face. I never see a bird take on so about a little thing. When he got through he walks to the hole and looks in again for half a minute; then he says, 'Well, you're a long hole, and a deep hole, and a mighty singular hole altogether— but I've started in to fill you and I'm d—d if I don't fill you, if it takes a hundred years!'

"And with that, away he went. You never see a bird work so since you was born. He laid into his work like a nigger and the way he hove acorns into that hole for about two hours and a half was one of the most exciting and astonishing spectacles I ever struck. He never stopped to take a look any more—he just hove 'em in and went for more. Well, at last he could hardly flop his wings, he was so tuckered out. He comes a-drooping down, once more, sweating like an ice-pitcher, drops his acorn in and says, 'Now I guess I've got the bulge on you by this time!' So he bent down for a look. If you'll believe me, when his head come up again he was just pale with rage. He says, 'I've shoveled acorns enough in there to keep the family thirty years, and if I can see a sign of one of 'em I wish I may land in a museum with a belly full of sawdust in two minutes!'

"He just had strength enough to crawl up on to the comb and lean his back agin the chimbly, and then he collected his impressions and begun to free his mind. I see in a second that what I had mistook for profanity in the mines was only just the rudiments, as you may say.

"Another jay was going by and heard him doing his devotions, and stops to inquire what was up. The sufferer told him the whole circumstance, and says, 'Now yonder's the hole, and if you don't believe me, go and look for yourself.' So this fellow went and looked, and comes back and says, 'How many did you say you put in there?' 'Not any less than two tons,' says the sufferer. The other jay went and looked again. He couldn't seem to make it out, so he raised a yell and three more jays come. They all examined the hole, they all made the sufferer tell it over again, then they all discussed it and got off as many leather-headed opinions about it as an average crowd of humans could have done.

"They called in more jays; then more and more, till pretty soon this whole region 'peared to have a blue flush about it. There must have been five thousand of them, and such another jawing and disputing and ripping and cussing, you never heard. Every jay in the whole lot put his eye to the hole and delivered a more chuckle-headed opinion about the mystery than the jay that went there before him. They examined the house all over, too. The door was standing half open and at last one old jay happened to go and light on it and look in. Of course, that knocked the mystery galley-west in a second. There lay the acorns, scattered all over the floor. He flopped his wings and raised a whoop. 'Come here!' he says, 'Come here, everybody; hang'd if this fool hasn't been trying to fill up a house with acorns!' They all came a-swooping down like a blue cloud, and as each fellow lit on the door and took a glance, the whole absurdity of the contract that that first jay had tackled hit him home and he fell over backward suffocating with laughter, and the next jay took his place and done the same.

"Well, sir, they roosted around here on the housetop and the trees for an hour, and guffawed over that thing like human beings. It ain't any use to tell me a bluejay hasn't got a sense of humor, because I know better. And memory, too. They brought jays here from all over the United States to look down that hole, every summer for three years. Other birds, too. And they could all see the point, except an owl that come from Nova Scotia to visit the Yosemite, and he took this thing in on his way back. He said he couldn't see anything funny in it. But then he was a good deal disappointed about Yosemite, too."

THE PRIVATE HISTORY OF A CAMPAIGN THAT FAILED

You have heard from a great many people who did something in the war, is it not fair and right that you listen a little

moment to one who started out to do something in it, but didn't?
Thousands entered the war, got just a taste of it, and then stepped
out again permanently. These, by their very numbers, are respectable and are therefore entitled to a sort of a voice—not a
loud one but a modest one, not a boastful one but an apologetic
one. They ought not to be allowed much space among better
people—people who did something. I grant that, but they ought at
least to be allowed to state why they didn't do anything and also
to explain the process by which they didn't do anything. Surely
this kind of light must have a sort of value.

Out West there was a good deal of confusion in men's minds
during the first months of the great trouble—a good deal of un-
settledness, of leaning first this way, then that, then the other way.
It was hard for us to get our bearings. I call to mind an instance of
this. I was piloting on the Mississippi when the news came that
South Carolina had gone out of the Union on the 20th of December, 1860. My pilot mate was a New Yorker. He was strong for the
Union; so was I. But he would not listen to me with any patience;
my loyalty was smirched, to his eye, because my father had owned
slaves. I said in palliation of this dark fact that I had heard my
father say, some years before he died, that slavery was a great
wrong and that he would free the solitary Negro he then owned
if he could think it right to give away the property of the family
when he was so straitened in means. My mate retorted that a mere
impulse was nothing—anybody could pretend to a good impulse,
and went on decrying my Unionism and libeling my ancestry. A
month later the secession atmosphere had considerably thick-
ened on the Lower Mississippi and I became a rebel; so did he.
We were together in New Orleans the 26th of January, when
Louisiana went out of the Union. He did his full share of the
rebel shouting but was bitterly opposed to letting me do mine.
He said that I came of bad stock—of a father who had been
willing to set slaves free. In the following summer he was piloting
a Federal gunboat and shouting for the Union again and I was
in the Confederate army. I held his note for some borrowed
money. He was one of the most upright men I ever knew but he
repudiated that note without hesitation because I was a rebel
and the son of a man who owned slaves.

THE ADVENTURES OF HUCKLEBERRY FINN
CHAPTER X

. . . Next morning I said it was getting slow and dull, and I wanted to get a stirring-up some way. I said I reckoned I would slip over the river and find out what was going on. Jim liked that notion, but he said I must go in the dark and look sharp. Then he studied it over and said, couldn't I put on some of them old things and dress up like a girl? That was a good notion, too. So we shortened up one of the calico gowns and I turned up my trouser-legs to my knees and got into it. Jim hitched it behind with the hooks and it was a fair fit. I put on the sunbonnet and tied it under my chin, and then for a body to look in and see my face was like looking down a joint of stove-pipe. Jim said nobody would know me, even in the daytime, hardly. I practised around all day to get the hang of the things, and by and by I could do pretty well in them, only Jim said I didn't walk like a girl, and he said I must quit pulling up my gown to get at my britches-pocket. I took notice and done better.

I started up the Illinois shore in the canoe just after dark.

I started across to the town from a little below the ferry-landing, and the drift of the current fetched me in at the bottom of the town. I tied up and started along the bank. There was a light burning in a little shanty that hadn't been lived in for a long time, and I wondered who had took up quarters there. I slipped up and peeped in at the window. There was a woman about forty year old in there knitting by a candle that was on a pine table. I didn't know her face; she was a stranger, for you couldn't start a face in that town that I didn't know. Now this was lucky, because I was weakening; I was getting afraid people might know my voice and find me out. But if this woman had been in such a little town two days she could tell me all I wanted to know; so I knocked at the door, and made up my mind I wouldn't forget I was a girl.

CHAPTER XI

"Come in," says the woman, and I did. She says: "Take a cheer."

I done it. She looked me all over with her little shiny eyes, and says:

"What might your name be?"

"Sarah Williams."

"Where'bouts do you live? In this neighborhood?"

"No'm. In Hookerville, seven mile below. I've walked all the way and I'm all tired out."

"Hungry, too, I reckon. I'll find you something."

"No'm, I ain't hungry. I was so hungry I had to stop two mile below here at a farm; so I ain't hungry no more. It's what makes me so late. My mother's down sick and out of money and everything, and I come to tell my uncle Abner Moore. He lives at the upper end of the town, she says. I hain't ever been here before. Do you know him?"

"No; but I don't know everybody yet. I haven't lived here quite two weeks. It's a considerable ways to the upper end of the town. You better stay here all night. Take off your bonnet."

"No," I says; "I'll rest awhile, I reckon, and go on. I ain't afeard of the dark."

She said she wouldn't let me go by myself, but her husband would be in by and by, maybe in a hour and a half, and she'd send him along with me. Then she got to talking about her husband, and about her relations up the river, and her relations down the river, and about how much better off they used to was, and how they didn't know but they'd made a mistake coming to our town, instead of letting well alone—and so on and so on, till I was afeard *I* had made a mistake coming to her to find out what was going on in the town; but by and by she dropped on to pap and the murder and then I was pretty willing to let her clatter right along. She told about me and Tom Sawyer finding the twelve thousand dollars (only she got it twenty) and all about pap and what a hard lot he was, and what a hard lot I was, and at last she got down to where I was murdered. I says:

"Who done it? We've heard considerable about these goings-on down in Hookerville, but we don't know who 'twas that killed Huck Finn."

"Well, I reckon there's a right smart chance of people *here* that 'd like to know who killed him. Some thinks old Finn done it himself."

"Most everybody thought it at first. He'll never know how nigh he come to getting lynched. But before night they changed around and judged it was done by a runaway nigger named Jim."

"Why *he*—"

I stopped. I reckoned I better keep still. She run on, and never noticed I had put in at all:

"The nigger run off the very night Huck Finn was killed. So there's a reward out for him—three hundred dollars. And there's a reward out for old Finn, too—two hundred dollars. You see, he come to town the morning after the murder and told about it, and was out with 'em on the ferryboat hunt, and right away after he up and left. Before night they wanted to lynch him but he was gone, you see. Well, next day they found out the nigger was gone; they found out he hadn't ben seen sence ten o'clock the night the murder was done. So then they put it on him, you see; and while they was full of it, next day, back comes old Finn, and went boo-hooing to Judge Thatcher to get money to hunt for the nigger all over Illinois with. The judge give him some, and that evening he got drunk and was around till after midnight with a couple of mighty hard-looking strangers, and then went off with them. Well, he hain't come back sence and they ain't looking for him back till this thing blows over a little, for people thinks now that he killed his boy and fixed things so folks would think robbers done it, and then he'd get Huck's money without having to bother a long time with a lawsuit. People do say he warn't any too good to do it. Oh, he's sly, I reckon. If he don't come back for a year he'll be all right. You can't prove anything on him, you know; everything will be quieted down then, and he'll walk into Huck's money as easy as nothing."

"Yes, I reckon so, 'm. I don't see nothing in the way of it. Has everybody quit thinking the nigger done it?"

"Oh, no, not everybody. A good many thinks he done it. But they'll get the nigger pretty soon now, and maybe they can scare it out of him."

"Why, are they after him yet?"

"Well, you're innocent, ain't you! Does three hundred dollars lay around every day for people to pick up? Some folks think the nigger ain't far from here. I'm one of them—but I hain't talked it around. A few days ago I was talking with an old couple that lives next door in the log shanty, and they happened to say hardly anybody ever goes to that island over yonder that they call Jackson's Island. Don't anybody live there? says I. No, nobody, says they. I didn't say any more but I done some thinking. I was pretty near certain I'd seen smoke over there, about the head of the island, a day or two before that, so I says to myself, like as not that nigger's hiding over there; anyway, says I, it's worth the trouble to give the place a hunt. I hain't seen any smoke sence, so I reckon maybe he's gone, if it was him; but husband's going over to see—him and another man. He was gone up the river; but he got back to-day, and I told him as soon as he got here two hours ago."

I had got so uneasy I couldn't set still. I had to do something

with my hands; so I took up a needle off of the table and went to
threading it. My hands shook and I was making a bad job of it.
When the woman stopped talking I looked up, and she was looking
at me pretty curious and smiling a little. I put down the needle
and thread and let on to be interested—and I was, too—and says:

"Three hundred dollars is a power of money. I wish my mother
could get it. Is your husband going over there to-night?"

"Oh, yes, He went up-town with the man I was telling you of,
to get a boat and see if they could borrow another gun. They'll
go over after midnight."

"Couldn't they see better if they was to wait till daytime?"

"Yes. And couldn't the nigger see better, too? After midnight
he'll likely be asleep and they can slip around through the woods
and hunt up his camp-fire all the better for the dark, if he's got
one."

"I didn't think of that."

The woman kept looking at me pretty curious, and I didn't feel
a bit comfortable. Pretty soon she says:

"What did you say your name was, honey?"

"M—Mary Williams."

Somehow it didn't seem to me that I said it was Mary before, so
I didn't look up—seemed to me I said it was Sarah; so I felt sort
of cornered and was afeard maybe I was looking it, too. I wished
the woman would say something more; the longer she set still the
uneasier I was. But now she says:

"Honey, I thought you said it was Sarah when you first come
in?"

"Oh, yes'm, I did. Sarah Mary Williams. Sarah's my first name.
Some calls me Sarah, some calls me Mary."

"Oh, that's the way of it?"

"Yes'm."

I was feeling better then but I wished I was out of there, anyway.
I couldn't look up yet.

Well, the woman fell to talking about how hard times was, and
how poor they had to live, and how the rats was as free as if they
owned the place, and so forth and so on, and then I got easy again.
She was right about the rats. You'd see one stick his nose out of
a hole in the corner every little while. She said she had to have
things handy to throw at them when she was alone, or they
wouldn't give her no peace. She showed me a bar of lead twisted
up into a knot and said she was a good shot with it generly, but
she'd wrenched her arm a day or two ago and didn't know whether
she could throw true now. But she watched for a chance and di-

rectly banged away at a rat, but she missed him wide and said, "Ouch!" it hurt her arm so. Then she told me to try for the next one. I wanted to be getting away before the old man got back, but of course I didn't let on. I got the thing, and the first rat that showed his nose I let drive, and if he'd 'a' stayed where he was he'd 'a' been a tolerable sick rat. She said that was first-rate and she reckoned I would hive the next one. She went and got the lump of lead and fetched it back, and brought along a hank of yarn which she wanted me to help her with. I held up my two hands and she put the hank over them, and went on talking about her and her husband's matters. But she broke off to say:

"Keep your eye on the rats. You better have the lead in your lap, handy."

So she dropped the lump into my lap just at that moment, and I clapped my legs together on it and she went on talking. But only about a minute. Then she took off the hank and looked me straight in the face, but very pleasant, and says:

"Come, now, what's your real name?"

"Wh-what, mum?"

"What's your real name? Is it Bill, or Tom, or Bob?—or what is it?"

I reckon I shook like a leaf and I didn't know hardly what to do. But I says:

"Please to don't poke fun at a poor girl like me, mum. If I'm in the way here, I'll—"

"No, you won't. Set down and stay where you are. I ain't going to hurt you and I ain't going to tell on you, nuther. You just tell me your secret, and trust me. I'll keep it; and, what's more, I'll help you. So'll my old man if you want him to. You see, you're a runaway 'prentice, that's all. It ain't anything. There ain't no harm in it. You've been treated bad and you made up your mind to cut. Bless you, child, I wouldn't tell on you. Tell me all about it now, that's a good boy."

So I said it wouldn't be no use to try to play it any longer, and I would just make a clean breast and tell her everything but she mustn't go back on her promise. Then I told her my father and mother was dead and the law had bound me out to a mean old farmer in the country thirty mile back from the river, and he treated me so bad I couldn't stand it no longer; he went away to be gone a couple of days and so I took my chance and stole some of his daughter's old clothes and cleared out, and I had been three nights coming the thirty miles. I traveled nights and hid daytimes and slept, and the bag of bread and meat I carried from home lasted me all the way, and I had a-plenty. I said I believed my uncle Abner Moore would take care of me, and so that was why I struck out for this town of Goshen.

"Goshen, child? This ain't Goshen. This is St. Petersburg. Goshen's ten mile further up the river. Who told you this was Goshen?"

"Why, a man I met at daybreak this morning, just as I was going to turn into the woods for my regular sleep. He told me when the roads forked I must take the right hand, and five mile would fetch me to Goshen."

"He was drunk, I reckon. He told you just exactly wrong."

"Well, he did act like he was drunk but it ain't no matter now. I got to be moving along. I'll fetch Goshen before daylight."

"Hold on a minute. I'll put you up a snack to eat. You might want it."

So she put me up a snack, and says:

"Say, when a cow's laying down, which end of her gets up first? Answer up prompt now—don't stop to study over it. Which end gets up first?"

"The hind end, mum."

"Well, then, a horse?"

"The for'rard end, mum."

"Which side of a tree does the moss grow on?"

"North side."

"If fifteen cows is browsing on a hillside, how many of them eats with their heads pointed the same direction?"

"The whole fifteen, mum."

"Well, I reckon you *have* lived in the country. I thought maybe you was trying to hocus me again. What's your real name, now?"

"George Peters, mum."

"Well, try to remember it, George. Don't forget and tell me it's Elexander before you go, and then get out by saying it's George Elexander when I catch you. And don't go about women in that old calico. You do a girl tolerable poor but you might fool men, maybe. Bless you, child, when you set out to thread a needle don't hold the thread still and fetch the needle up to it; hold the needle still and poke the thread at it; that's the way a woman most always does but a man always does t'other way. And when you throw at a rat or anything, hitch yourself up a-tiptoe and fetch your hand up over your head as awkward as you can and miss your rat about six or seven foot. Throw stiffarmed from the shoulder, like there was a pivot there for it to turn on, like a girl, not from the wrist and elbow, with your arm out to one side, like a boy. And, mind you, when a girl tries to catch anything in her lap she throws her knees apart; she don't clap them together, the way you did when you catched the lump of lead. Why, I spotted you for a boy when you was threading the needle and I contrived the other things just to make certain. Now trot along to your uncle, Sarah Mary Williams George Elexander Peters, and if you get into trouble you send word to Mrs. Judith Loftus, which is me, and I'll do what I can to get you out of it. Keep the river road all the way and next time you tramp take shoes and socks with you. The river road's a rocky one, and your feet'll be in a condition when you get to Goshen, I reckon."

I went up the bank about fifty yards, and then I doubled on my tracks and slipped back to where my canoe was, a good piece below the house. I jumped in and was off in a hurry. I went upstream far enough to make the head of the island, and then started across. I took off the sun-bonnet, for I didn't want no blinders on then. When I was about the middle I heard the clock begin to strike, so I stops and listens; the sound come faint over the water but clear—eleven. When I struck the head of the island I never waited to blow, though I was most winded, but I shoved right into the timber where my old camp used to be, and started a good fire there on a high and dry spot.

Then I jumped in the canoe and dug out for our place, a mile and a half below, as hard as I could go. I landed, and slopped through the timber and up the ridge and into the cavern. There Jim laid, sound asleep on the ground. I roused him out and says:

"Git up and hump yourself, Jim! There ain't a minute to lose. They're after us!"

PUDD'NHEAD WILSON'S CALENDAR

• Adam was but human—this explains it all. He did not want the apple for the apple's sake; he wanted it only because it was forbidden. The mistake was in not forbidding the serpent. Then he would have eaten the serpent.

• Training is everything. The peach was once a bitter almond; cauliflower is nothing but cabbage with a college education.

• Let us endeavor to live that when we come to die even the undertaker will be sorry.

• The holy passion of friendship is of so sweet and steady and loyal a nature that it will last through a whole lifetime, if not asked to lend money.

• When angry, count four; when very angry, swear.

• Behold the fool saith, "Put not all thine eggs in one basket." But the wise man saith, "Put all your eggs in one basket—*and watch that basket!"*

• If you pick up a starving dog and make him prosperous, he will not bite you. That is the principal difference between a dog and a man.

• Few things are harder to put up with than the annoyance of a good example.

• When in doubt, tell the truth.

• Noise proves nothing. Often a hen who has merely laid an egg cackles as if she had laid an asteroid.

• It could probably be shown by facts and figures that there is no native American criminal class except Congress.

• There is a Moral Sense and there is an Immoral Sense. History shows us that the Moral Sense enables us to perceive morality and how to avoid it, and that the Immoral Sense enables us to perceive immorality and how to enjoy it.

• It is by the goodness of God that in our country we have those three unspeakably precious things: freedom of speech, freedom of conscience, and the prudence never to practice either of them.

• The man with a new idea is a Crank until the idea succeeds.

• Prosperity is the best protector of principle.

• By trying we can easily learn to endure adversity. Another man's, that is.

• There are two times in a man's life when he should not speculate: when he can't afford it, and when he can.

• In the first place God made idiots. This was for practice. Then He made School Boards.

• Cats are the most lovable and most intelligent of creatures. It would be wonderful if we could cross the cat with man. It would elevate man, although it would debase the cat.

• Man is the only animal that blushes. Or needs to.

Paul Bunyan

The Paul Bunyan folk tale is a triumph of reckless hyperbole. Except in the saga of Gargantua (see page 154), never has exaggeration been so willfully expanded. In the Paul Bunyan country the trees grow so tall that it takes two men and a boy to see the top branches, mosquitoes are so big that they kill oxen, fogs are so heavy that barns are shingled six feet out on the fog, cyclones pick up wagon tracks in one county and drop them in the next, and Bunyan's Blue Ox, Babe, measures exactly forty-two and a half ax-handles and a box of tobacco between the eyes.

The soil of England produced Jack, the boy who became the Giant Killer; Scandinavian streams quickened the blood of Beowulf; German forests spoke through Siegfried, the hero who knew no fear. Paul Bunyan was born in the days when the woods of the American northwest were dark and immense, and the men who lived in them were few and lonely. The trees dwarfed the men; the men had to make themselves big, if only in imagination.

Bunyan is the brawling, bragging frontiersman glorified, the pioneer's dream, the last of the legendary supermen. A semi-epical figure in the evolution of the American tall tale, he swaggers across the nation, colossal and comic, a symbol of its youth, its high spirits, and its boundless energy.

The following excerpts are the second and third chapters of *The Wonderful Adventures of Paul Bunyan*, retold by Louis Untermeyer.

THE WONDERFUL ADVENTURES OF
PAUL BUNYAN
PAUL'S TIMBER

Stories about Paul Bunyan began to float back East. He was growing up and doing amazing things in Michigan. He was seen wandering across Wisconsin, lifting a team of horses over the Mississippi. He was building himself a house in Minnesota, a house that was so high that the last five stories had to be put on hinges to let the moon go by.

This was the country for Paul. Trees and trees and trees. Pines and maples and oaks for thousands of miles, from the Great Lakes clear through the Northwest right out to the Pacific Ocean. Here were trees so wide you'd get tired walking around their trunks, trees so high it took an ordinary man a whole week to see to the top of them.

"Here is where I make my home," said Paul. "This is a country to grow up in. But what am I going to do for a living?"

He wandered under the trees looking for an answer. But the trees whispered among themselves, mocking the young giant. The heavy branches seemed to gossip spitefully when he went by; there was always laughter in the leaves, and it seemed to Paul that they were laughing at him.

So Paul left the woods and went up to the Mesabi iron range and dug up some metal. Then he heated and hammered it into two bars. Then he welded the bars together, and sharpened them into an axe. Then he walked back into the forest and picked out the tallest tree.

"Now let's see what this axe can do"—and it seemed to Paul that all the trees stopped talking and only the little leaves kept up a sort of frightened whispering.

Paul swung his axe, and the first stroke made a wedge wide enough for a table. The second stroke made a gash deep enough for a man to lie down in. Then Paul walked around the tree to even up the strokes. He walked so fast it took him only half an hour— and there on the other side were six men chopping away as if their lives depended on getting the tree down. They were bigger than average—a mixture of Swedes and Finns and Irish—but they had made scarcely a dent in that gigantic tree.

"Hi!" said Paul, shouldering his axe. "How long have you fellows been working here?"

"About three years, more or less."

"Three years on one tree? Why," said Paul, "let me help you."

Running back to where he had started—it took only fifteen minutes this time—he gave another hack at the tree. There was a crack like a cannon-shot. Paul struck again. This time it was like a thunderbolt on a dead-still summer day. Once more Paul swung his axe. And now with a noise like a dozen earthquakes, there was a roaring through the forest like a tidal wave, and the tree came crashing down.

"You're a wonder," cried the men. "You're the champion logger of all time. Tell you what, let's join together—we'll work for you, and we'll make all the other lumberjacks look as if they were cutting corn instead of trees. Would you tell us your name?"

"You can call me Paul. And what will I call you?"

"Well," said the oldest of them, a loose-jointed fellow who wore a thinking look and a pair of spectacles, "my name's Johnny Inkslinger. I can keep accounts and do all the writing you'll ever need. And I can add up to a hundred without using my fingers. And I can make up jokes, too."

"Good," said Paul. "I like jokes. And it must be nice to be able to write. Some day I'll try it. And you?"

"Me?" This was a fat fellow with no hair on his head but a huge blanket of beard on his chin. "I'm called Hot Biscuit Slim and I'm the best all-weather cook that ever fried fish in the Northwest."

"And you?" Paul asked the next man.

"My name's Febold Feboldson," said the light-haired lean Swede with bright blue eyes. "I can't write and I can't cook; but I can make axe-helves and put a cutting edge on blades and fix all kinds of tools. What's more, I'll see that the pots and pans are kept in good shape. I'll keep everything sharp and shining if there's just somebody to bring in the food."

"That's where I come in," said the fourth, a young lad with a twisted laughing mouth, a pair of dark brown eyes with yellow lights in them, and a nose that had a lot of character because it had once been broken in a good fight. "I'm Thomas O'Meara, but everyone calls me Little Meery. When I'm not logging, I'm hunting—and there isn't anything that can get away from me. I can run as fast as a deer, climb as high as a raccoon, outswim a beaver and outwrestle a bear. No camp I've worked in has ever been without meat."

"That's fine, Little Meery. I can see where you'd be welcome anywhere," said Paul. "And you there, making that humming sound—who are you?"

"I'm a singer. I've never had a home, I've forgotten my real name, but I've always been called Shanty Boy. I can sing any song you ever knew, and I make up words and music you never heard in this world."

"That would be good entertainment for dull days," said Paul. "And you?"

This was a wiry Westerner wearing a bright orange shirt and wide leather trousers made out of cowhide.

"They call me the Galloping Kid. I used to be a cowboy, my home was on the range, and I always won first prize at the rodeo. One day I was thrown by a young bull, and I was so ashamed I swore I'd never rope another steer. But I can still ride. And if you ever need a horseman —"

Paul laughed. "Let's see. If I remember right, there's Johnny Inkslinger, and Hot Biscuit Slim, and Febold Feboldson, and Little Meery, and Shanty Boy, and the Galloping Kid. A writer, a cook, a mechanic, a hunter, a singer, and a cowboy—a queer crew."

"But we're all lumberjacks," they cried. "We know all there is to know about chopping down trees and trimming them and turning them into logs. With you for our leader we'd be the greatest logging outfit that ever went into the woods. What do you say?"

"It's a deal," said Paul. "We'll begin by giving Little Meery and Hot Biscuit Slim a chance to show what they can do. What would you like for supper, boys?"

"Ham and potatoes."

"Corned beef and cabbage."

"Apple pie."

"Sourdough doughnuts."

"Don't all shout at once," said Paul. "And Little Meery's got to do better than that. How long should it take, Little Meery, to hunt up something for us?"

"Oh, I guess I can rustle up enough for a snack in an hour," said Little Meery, picking up his gun.

He was back in thirty minutes with a burden so big that he seemed to be carrying a small mountain. Meanwhile, Hot Biscuit Slim had made a huge fire, and Febold Feboldson had sharpened a dozen enormous knives. Pots and pans appeared out of nowhere. All that they needed was a table.

"Here it is," said Paul. "The very thing!" With one sideswipe of his axe, he smoothed off the stump of the great tree. "You couldn't ask for anything better. And here," he said, lopping off seven pieces from one of the boughs, "here are seven seats. And now let's eat."

TALL TALES AROUND THE FIRE

It was a meal they never forgot. There was a great kettle of soup —Lumberjack Soup, Hot Biscuit Slim called it, for everyone had had a hand in it. Then there was wild turkey that Little Meery had shot on the wing. And, when that was gone, bear stew and venison chops and deer steaks and, just to make the food go down easier, lakes of gravy and a pile of biscuits big as the state capitol.

In half an hour there wasn't a crumb left. The men sprawled around the fire; there wasn't a sound except the snap of burning branches and the night-birds complaining softly in the woods.

"It's too early to sleep," said Paul. "And we ought to take one more look at the tree we chopped down. That tree isn't just lumber, it's history. Here," and he pointed to the stump they had been using for a table, "see this ring about a foot from the outside? That ring was formed when Lee surrendered to Grant at the end of the Civil War. And this one—" Paul's finger moved another few inches toward the center—"this one's much older; it must have formed itself when Washington was crossing the Delaware. And see this ring here? Well, that grew about the time Columbus was discovering America. And we're still so far from the center that I guess this tree must have been here when Adam and Eve took their first walk in the Garden of Eden. Yes, sir, there's history in that tree."

The men were silent for a while. Then Johnny Inkslinger spoke up.

"Talk about history," he said, "they make history out in Iowa. That's the state I come from, the greatest corn country in the world. The corn grows so high out there they have to climb ladders to gather the ears. Once, near a place called Gravity, a boy saw a green shoot of corn rising right up out of the black loam. When it was as high as his shoulder he mounted it just for fun. Before he could say 'Whoa!' the cornstalk gave a little shake and lifted itself. Up it went—high as the barn, higher than the silo. The boy's mother was frantic—there was the boy getting farther from the earth every second and beginning to disappear.

"'Call out the fire-engines!' cried his mother.

"'Twouldn't be no use,' said his father. 'They wouldn't get here in time, and the tallest hook-and-ladder couldn't reach him now.'

"They sent up a balloon to bring the boy down, but the cornstalk rose faster than the balloon could travel. Then they shot up biscuits to keep the boy from starving. Then it got beyond rifle range, and they had to drop food by airplane. They tried putting an axe to the root, but they might as well have tried to push over the Statue of Liberty with a toothpick."

"Whew!" whistled Little Meery. "Some cornstalk!"

"And how," asked the Galloping Kid, "did they get the boy down?"

"They didn't," answered Johnny Inkslinger. "He was never seen again. And if you don't believe it, just you go to Gravity, Iowa, and they'll show you the very place where the cornstalk grew."

The men looked at the Galloping Kid, but that wiry Westerner only shook his head. Then, taking a fresh chew of tobacco, he spoke.

"I don't know anything about Iowa, so I can't say what might or mightn't happen in such a state. But I know Montana. It's a high, wide and handsome state—the best sheepherding state in the country. And I've seen things out there that are hard to match.

"For one thing, if you want to hold on to your sheep in Montana, you've got to know how to count them. They tell about a famous sheep-counter who could size up a herd in a second, no matter how big it was. He never missed.

"One day a wealthy herder took this expert sheep-counter up a Montana hill and showed him a big flock of sheep grazing in the valley—ewes and rams and little lambs all mixed up. 'About how many would you say were there?' asked the herder.

"'I wouldn't say *about* how many,' answered the sheep-counter. 'I can tell you exactly. There are just nine hundred and seven sheep.'

"'That's right,' said the rancher. 'Exactly right. Now come on over to the other side of the hill, and see if you can guess how many sheep there are in the larger herd.'

"'I don't guess,' said the counter, 'I know.' He took a quick glance at the other valley. 'In that bunch yonder there are two thousand, six hundred and seventy-eight—no seventy-nine— sheep.'

"'Gosh!' said the rancher. 'That's wonderful! How do you do it?'

"'Nothing to it,' said the counter. 'It's easy. I just count their feet and divide by four.'"

The Galloping Kid was rewarded by a round of laughter and another plug of tobacco. "Bet you can't top that one," he grinned.

Hot Biscuit Slim took up the challenge. "Maybe I can't, maybe

I can," he said. "I've heard lots of tall stories traveling around the states. There's one they like to tell down in the Texas panhandle—that's the part of Texas that can't make up its mind whether to belong to the sultry South or to the woolly West. Iowa may be the state for corn, and Montana for sheep, but Texas is the place for temperature. Hot? Well, once you live in Texas you can't get warm any place in the world; spring in Iowa is like winter at the North Pole to a Texan.

"Anyway, this story tells about a man from Texas who came up to Michigan for work. Winter was over, but there were still a few flakes of snow left in the sky. The Texan shivered, fell to the sidewalk, and stiffened out. They tried to revive him. But he didn't respond. They poured whisky down his throat. But he didn't come to.

"'It's no use,' they said. 'He's dead. There's nothing more we can do except one thing: cremate him and send the ashes back home.'

"So they took his body to the crematory, stuck it in the oven, and stoked the fire.

"Two hours later they opened the door of the oven, and there was the man from Texas sitting bolt upright. He was shivering.

"'Hey, there!' he yelled, 'close that door! Do you want me to catch my death of cold in a draft like this!'"

A couple of whip-poor-wills were echoing each other, and a squirrel who had been quarrelling with a blue-jay lost the argument and ran scolding from bough to bough. The fire was dying; the moon went down.

"Getting late, men," said Paul. "But there's time for one more story, if anyone knows a good one. How about you, Febold Feboldson; you haven't said a word."

"There wasn't anything much to say," murmured Febold, trying out a blade against a finger-nail.

"Come on, now. Don't be so stubborn," said Paul. "Remember you're a man, not a mule."

Febold grunted and slid the sharpened blade along his thumb. Then he grinned. "All right," he said, "I'll talk about mules. Leastways I'll talk about one mule. Coal black. Name of Mabel. Wonderful worker. Couldn't be led and couldn't be licked; but she never knew when she had enough.

"One day Mabel was found with her heels up in the yard. They yelled and pulled her ears and punched her in the ribs. But nothing happened. Mabel just lay there and didn't move a muscle.

"'The life's gone out of the old mule,' they said. 'It just means more work, for now we'll have to get rid of the carcass. Poor old Mabel.'

"But, after all, mule-hide is mule-hide, and there's no use wasting anything. So they skinned her and went away.

"The next day when they came back to bury her, Mabel was standing on all fours, shaking a little because she was without hide or hair, but mostly good as ever. She just had been tired and had gone to sleep, and hadn't waked up during the skinning. You couldn't lick Mabel."

"And they left her like that?" asked Little Meery.

"Of course not," replied Febold. "They had been butchering sheep, and they got hold of a fine fat sheep skin. They spread it over Mabel. It slid around a little, for they had no thread to sew it on with. So they finally fastened it to the mule with blackberry thorns. You could hardly tell the difference — it was a black sheep skin just as black as Mabel."

"That's a pretty story," said Hot Biscuit Slim.

"And a pretty ending," said Johnny Inkslinger.

"That wasn't quite the ending," said Febold. "Come spring at shearing time Mabel had grown the thickest wool coat you ever saw. They sheared eighty pounds off her back. And, underneath the wool, where the blackberry thorns had gone through the sheep skin, they picked forty-five quarts of blackberries!"

The men gave a long whistle. No one cared to top that story. They began to take off their boots and turn in. Shanty Boy got out his guitar and ran his hands over the strings. Then he lifted his voice and sang:

We're tall tree-toppers,
Top the tall trees all the time;
We're goin' out to Michigan
To chop that tall jack-pine.

He kept on strumming for another minute or two. Then he, too, turned in. You couldn't hear a thing except the whip-poor-wills still echoing each other, and a deep breath that was maybe the men or maybe the forest yawning. Then the whip-poor-wills got tired and stopped. Even the earth stopped breathing. It was quieter than the Day before Creation.

W. S. Gilbert

Son of a forgotten novelist, William Schwenk Gilbert was born in 1836 in London. The most dramatic moment in his life was when, as a child with his parents in Italy, he was kidnapped by brigands and ransomed for twenty-five pounds. Educated at King's College, he received a commission in the militia, worked as a clerk in the Department of Education, and turning his attention to law, became a barrister at thirty.

Meanwhile, he had been contributing an unusual kind of light verse to *Fun* and *Punch*. The taunting stanzas that he wrote and illustrated were collected in the *Bab Ballads*, "Bab" being his boyhood nickname. A year after its publication, Gilbert met Arthur Sullivan and a famous partnership was formed. Sullivan was already well known as a composer of cantatas and oratorios; a series of comic operas resulted from the odd collaboration. Gilbert adapted several of the topsy-turvy plots from the *Bab Ballads*, while Sullivan turned his gift of hymnology into some of the most diverting English music ever written. Together they produced a dozen rapturously received operettas until they quarreled over a triviality— Gilbert fought over the price of a carpet installed in the newly built Savoy Theater.

Sullivan died in 1900. Seven years later Gilbert was knighted. By this time he was the owner of a theater, a magnificent mansion, an observatory, and an outdoor swimming pool. It was the swimming pool that ended his career. Rescuing a lady from drowning in the pool, he suffered heart failure and died in his seventy-fifth year.

Gilbert's librettos, like the best of his *Bab Ballads*, are masterpieces of whimsicality edged with satire. *H.M.S. Pinafore* is a gibing burlesque of political preferment and officialdom. *Iolanthe* uses its fairy paraphernalia to mock the pretentiousness of class, the arbitrary distinctions of rank, and the antics of politicians. *Patience* is an extended lampoon of Pre-Raphaelite limp, languorous ladies, with Oscar Wilde faintly disguised as the esthetic Bunthorne; it also exposes all preciosity. *The Pirates of Penzance* mocks sentimentality as well as absurd manifestations of law and order. The incongruous fusion of clowning and criticism, of delicacy and nonsense, has been the unaging delight of millions and the despair of countless imitators.

BAB BALLADS
GENTLE ALICE BROWN

It was a robber's daughter and her name was ALICE BROWN,
Her father was the terror of a small Italian town;
Her mother was a foolish, weak, but amiable old thing;
But it isn't of her parents that I'm going for to sing.

As ALICE was a-sitting at her window-sill one day,
A beautiful young gentleman, he chanced to pass that way;
She cast her eyes upon him, and he looked so good and true,
That she thought, "I could be happy with a gentleman like you."

And every morning passed her house this cream of gentlemen,
She knew she might expect him at a quarter unto ten,
A sorter in the Custom House, it was his daily road—
The Custom House was fifteen minutes walk from her abode.

But ALICE was a pious girl who knew it wasn't wise
To look at strange young sorters with expressive purple eyes;
So she sought the village priest to whom her family confessed,
The priest by whom their little sins were carefully assessed.

"Oh, holy father," ALICE said, "'twould grieve you, would it not?
To discover that I was a most disreputable lot!
Of all unhappy sinners I'm the most unhappy one!"
The padre said, "Whatever have you been and gone and done?"

"I have helped mamma to steal a little kiddy from its dad;
I've assisted dear papa in cutting up a little lad;
I've planned a little burglary and forged a little cheque,
And slain a little baby for the coral on its neck!"

The worthy pastor heaved a sigh, and dropped a silent tear —
And said, "You mustn't judge yourself too heavily, my dear —
It's wrong to murder babies, little corals for to fleece;
But sins like these one expiates at half-a-crown apiece.

"Girls will be girls — you're very young, and flighty in your mind;
Old heads upon young shoulders we must not expect to find:
We mustn't be too hard upon these little girlish tricks —
Let's see — five crimes at half-a-crown — exactly twelve-and-six."

"Oh, father," little ALICE cried, "your kindness makes me weep,
You do these little things for me so singularly cheap —
Your thoughtful liberality I never can forget;
But oh, there is another crime I haven't mentioned yet!

"A pleasant-looking gentleman, with pretty purple eyes,
I've noticed at my window, as I've sat a-catching flies;
He passes by it every day as certain as can be —
I blush to say I've winked at him, and he has winked at me!"

"For shame!" said FATHER PAUL, "my erring daughter! On my
        word,
This is the most distressing news that I have ever heard.
Why, naughty girl, your excellent papa has pledged your hand
To a promising young robber, the lieutenant of his band!

"This dreadful piece of news will pain your worthy parents so!
They are the most remunerative customers I know;
For many many years they've kept starvation from my doors:
I never knew so criminal a family as yours!

"The common country folk in this insipid neighbourhood
Have nothing to confess, they're so ridiculously good;
And if you marry any one respectable at all,
Why, you'll reform, and what will then become of FATHER
    PAUL?"

The worthy priest, he up and drew his cowl upon his crown,
And started off in haste to tell the news to ROBBER BROWN;
To tell him how his daughter, who was now for marriage fit,
Had winked upon a sorter, who reciprocated it.

Good ROBBER BROWN he muffled up his anger pretty well,
He said, "I have a notion, and that notion I will tell;
I will nab this gay young sorter, terrify him into fits,
And get my gentle wife to chop him into little bits.

"I've studied human nature, and I know a thing or two;
Though a girl may fondly love a living gent, as many do,
A feeling of disgust upon her senses there will fall
When she looks upon his body chopped particularly small."

He traced that gallant sorter to a still suburban square;
He watched his opportunity and seized him unaware;
He took a life-preserver and he hit him on the head,
And MRS. BROWN dissected him before she went to bed.

And pretty little ALICE grew more settled in her mind,
She never more was guilty of a weakness of the kind,
Until at length good ROBBER BROWN bestowed her pretty hand
On the promising young robber, the lieutenant of his band.

ETIQUETTE

The *Ballyshannon* foundered off the coast of Cariboo,
And down in fathoms many went the captain and the crew;
Down went the owners—greedy men whom hope of gain
    allured:
Oh, dry the starting tear, for they were heavily insured.

Besides the captain and the mate, the owners and the crew,
The passengers were also drowned excepting only two:

Young PETER GRAY, who tasted teas for BAKER, CROOP AND CO.,
And SOMERS, who from Eastern shores imported indigo.

These passengers, by reason of their clinging to a mast,
Upon a desert island were eventually cast.
They hunted for their meals, as ALEXANDER SELKIRK used,
But they couldn't chat together — they had not been introduced.

For PETER GRAY, and SOMERS, too, though certainly in trade,
Were properly particular about the friends they made;
And somehow thus they settled it without a word of mouth —
That GRAY should take the northern half, while SOMERS took the
    south.

On PETER'S portion oysters grew — a delicacy rare,
But oysters were a delicacy PETER couldn't bear.
On SOMERS' side was turtle, on the shingle lying thick,
Which SOMERS couldn't eat, because it always made him sick.

GRAY gnashed his teeth with envy as he saw a mighty store
Of turtle unmolested on his fellow-creature's shore:
The oysters at his feet aside impatiently he shoved,
For turtle and his mother were the only things he loved.

And SOMERS sighed in sorrow as he settled in the south,
For the thought of PETER'S oysters brought the water to his
    mouth.
He longed to lay him down upon the shelly bed, and stuff:
He had often eaten oysters, but had never had enough.

How they wished an introduction to each other they had had
When on board the *Ballyshannon!* And it drove them nearly
    mad
To think how very friendly with each other they might get,
If it wasn't for the arbitrary rule of etiquette!

One day, when out a-hunting for the *mus ridiculus,*
GRAY overheard his fellow-man soliloquising thus:
"I wonder how the playmates of my youth are getting on,
M'CONNELL, S. B. WALTERS, PADDY BYLES, and ROBINSON?"

These simple words made PETER as delighted as could be,
Old chummies at the Charterhouse were ROBINSON and he!
He walked straight up to SOMERS, then he turned extremely red,
Hesitated, hummed and hawed a bit, then cleared his throat,
      and said:

"I beg your pardon—pray forgive me if I seem too bold,
But you have breathed a name I knew familiarly of old.
You spoke aloud of ROBINSON—I happened to be by—
You know him?" "Yes, extremely well." "Allow me—so do I!"

It was enough: they felt they could more sociably get on,
For (ah, the magic of the fact!) they each knew ROBINSON!
And MR. SOMERS' turtle was at PETER's service quite,
And MR. SOMERS punished PETER's oyster-beds all night.

They soon became like brothers from community of wrongs;
They wrote each other little odes and sang each other songs;
They told each other anecdotes disparaging their wives;
On several occasions, too, they saved each other's lives.

They felt quite melancholy when they parted for the night,
And got up in the morning soon as ever it was light;
Each other's pleasant company they reckoned so upon,
And all because it happened that they both knew ROBINSON!

They lived for many years on that inhospitable shore,
And day by day they learned to love each other more and more.
At last, to their astonishment, on getting up one day,
They saw a vessel anchored in the offing of the bay!

To PETER an idea occurred. "Suppose we cross the main?
So good an opportunity may not occur again."
And SOMERS thought a minute, then ejaculated, "Done!
I wonder how my business in the City's getting on?"

"But stay," said MR. PETER: "when in England, as you know,
I earned a living tasting teas for BAKER, CROOP, AND CO.,
I may be superseded—my employers think me dead!"
"Then come with me," said SOMERS, "and taste indigo instead."

But all their plans were scattered in a moment when they found
The vessel was a convict ship from Portland, outward bound.
When a boat came off to fetch them, though they felt it very
    kind,
To go on board they firmly but respectfully declined.

As both the happy settlers roared with laughter at the joke,
They recognized an unattractive fellow pulling stroke.
'Twas ROBINSON—a convict, in an unbecoming frock,
Condemned to seven years for misappropriating stock!

They laughed no more, for SOMERS thought it had been rather
    rash
In knowing one whose friend had misappropriated cash;
And PETER thought a foolish tack he must have gone upon
In making the acquaintance of a friend of ROBINSON.

At first they didn't quarrel very openly, I've heard;
They nodded when they met, and now and then exchanged a
    word;
The word grew rare, and rarer still the nodding of the head,
And when they meet each other now, they cut each other dead.

To allocate the island they agreed by word of mouth,
And PETER takes the north again, and SOMERS takes the south;
And PETER has the oyster, which he loathes with horror grim,
And SOMERS has the turtle—turtle disagrees with him.

IOLANTHE

THE SENTRY'S SOLILOQUY

When all night long a chap remains
   On sentry-go, to chase monotony
He exercises of his brains,
   That is, assuming that he's got any.
Though never nurtured in the lap
   Of luxury, yet I admonish you,
I am an intellectual chap,
   And think of things that would astonish you.

I often think it's comical—Fal, lal, la!
How Nature always does contrive—Fal, lal, la!
That every boy and every gal
    That's born into the world alive
Is either a little Liberal
    Or else a little Conservative!
        Fal, lal, la!

When in that House M.P.'s divide,
  If they've a brain and cerebellum, too,
They've got to leave that brain outside,
  And vote just as their leaders tell 'em to.
But then the prospect of a lot
  Of dull M.P.'s in close proximity,
All thinking for themselves, is what
  No man can face with equanimity.
        Then let's rejoice with loud Fal la—Fal lal la!
        That Nature always does contrive—Fal lal la!
        That every boy and every gal
            That's born into the world alive
        Is either a little Liberal
            Or else a little Conservative!
                Fal lal la!

THE HOUSE OF LORDS

When Britain *really* ruled the waves
  (In good Queen Bess's time)
The House of Peers made no pretence
To intellectual eminence
  Or scholarship sublime;
Yet Britain won her proudest bays
In good Queen Bess's glorious days.

When Wellington thrashed Bonaparte,
  As every child can tell,
The House of Peers throughout the war
Did nothing in particu*lar*,
  And did it very well;
Yet Britain set the world ablaze
In good King George's glorious days.

And while the House of Peers withholds
   Its legislative hand,
And noble statesmen do not itch
To interfere with matters which
   They do not understand,
As bright will shine Great Britain's rays
As in King George's glorious days.

THE PIRATES OF PENZANCE

A POLICEMAN'S LOT

When a felon's not engaged in his employment,
   Or maturing his felonious little plans,
His capacity for innocent enjoyment
   Is just as great as any honest man's.
Our feelings we with difficulty smother
   When constabulary duty's to be done.
Ah, take one consideration with another,
   A policeman's lot is not a happy one.

When the enterprising burglar's not a-burgling,
   When the cut-throat isn't occupied in crime,
He loves to hear the little brook a-gurgling,
   And listen to the merry village chime.
When the coster's finished jumping on his mother,
   He loves to lie a-basking in the sun;
Ah, take one consideration with another,
   A policeman's lot is not a happy one.

THE YEOMEN OF THE GUARD

A PRIVATE BUFFOON

Oh! a private buffoon is a light-hearted loon,
   If you listen to popular rumour;
From the morn to the night he's so joyous and bright,
   And he bubbles with wit and good humour!
He's so quaint and so terse, both in prose and in verse;
   Yet though people forgive his transgression,

There are one or two rules that all family fools
  Must observe, if they love their profession.
          There are one or two rules,
              Half a dozen, may be,
          That all family fools,
              Of whatever degree,
      Must observe, if they love their profession.

If you wish to succeed as a jester, you'll need
  To consider each person's auricular:
What is all right for B would quite scandalise C
  (For C is so very particular);
And D may be dull, and E's very thick skull
  Is as empty of brains as a ladle;
While F is F sharp, and will cry with a carp
  That he's known your best joke from his cradle!
          When your humour they flout,
              You can't let yourself go;
          And it *does* put you out
              When a person says, "Oh,
      I have known that old joke from my cradle!"

If your master is surly, from getting up early
  (And tempers are short in the morning),
An inopportune joke is enough to provoke
  Him to give you, at once, a month's warning.
Then if you refrain, he is at you again,
  For he likes to get value for money;
He'll ask then and there, with an insolent stare,
  "If you know that you're paid to be funny?"
          It adds to the tasks
              Of a merryman's place,
          When your principal asks,
              With a scowl on his face,
      If you know that you're paid to be funny?

Though your head it may rack with a bilious attack,
  And your senses with toothache you're losing,
Don't be mopy and flat—they don't fine you for that,
  If you're properly quaint and amusing!
Though your wife ran away with a soldier that day,
  And took with her your trifle of money;

Bless your heart, they don't mind—they're exceedingly kind—
  They don't blame you—as long as you're funny!
          It's a comfort to feel,
            If your partner should flit,
          Though *you* suffer a deal,
            They don't mind it a bit—
  They don't blame you—so long as you're funny!

Ambrose Bierce

Beginning obscurely in an Ohio log cabin and ending mysteriously in the depths of Mexico, the career of Ambrose
Gwinnett Bierce was unlike that of any other American. Born
in 1842, youngest of nine children, Bierce suffered through
childhood and at the outbreak of the Civil War ran away to become a drummer-boy. Twice wounded, he was advanced to
lieutenant, and with a citation for bravery, to major. After the
war he went to San Francisco, where he became a night
watchman at the Sub-Treasury Building; temperamentally unfit to look after other people's money, he decided to make
money on his own. Journalism seemed an easy way of earning
a living, and in Bierce's case, it proved to be. After contributing
bits of flotsam and jetsam to various newspapers, he became
an editor.

At twenty-nine he married and moved to England. There,
after meeting W. S. Gilbert, he joined the staff of *Fun* and
published three books that were both frightening and funny.
The grimness of their humor was indicated by the titles: *The
Fiend's Delight, Nuggets and Dust Panned Out in California,*
and *Cobwebs from an Empty Skull.* Returning to San Francisco, he remained there twenty-five years, writing brusque
causeries, fantastic fiction, tireless prattle, and a vast amount
of slashing columns that made him the literary dictator of the
West Coast as "Bitter Bierce."

The bitterness was that of a man whom fate had made a confirmed misanthrope. Publishing misfortunes were followed by personal tragedies. His wife left him; one son was fatally shot in a sordid affair concerning a girl; another son died an alcoholic. In his sixties Bierce began to edit his *Collected Works*. There were twelve volumes of melodramatic writing ranging from Gothic horrors to morbid philosophizing, from the corrosive cynicism of *The Devil's Dictionary* to catch-as-catch-can verse.

At seventy-one a tired Bierce abjured his work, himself, and civilization. He headed for Mexico. Legends clustered about his disappearance. It was rumored that he had gone to join the revolutionists; it was also said that after having been reported killed on the battlefield, he was living in a remote village under an assumed name. The actual facts have never been established.

THE DEVIL'S DICTIONARY

A

Admiral: That part of a war-ship that does the talking while the figure-head does the thinking.

Admiration: Our polite recognition of another's resemblance to ourselves.

Alliance: In international politics the union of two thieves who have their hands so deeply inserted in each other's pocket that they cannot separately plunder a third.

Applause: The echo of a platitude.

B

Backbite: To speak of a man as you find him when he can't find you.

Belladonna: In Italian a beautiful lady; in English a deady poison. A striking example of the essential identity of the two tongues.

Bigot: One who is obstinately and zealously attached to an opinion you do not entertain.

Bore: A person who talks when you want him to listen.

Boundary: In political geography, an imaginary line between two nations separating the imaginary rights of one from the imaginary rights of the other.

Bride: A woman with a fine prospect of happiness behind her.

C

Callous: Gifted with great fortitude to bear the troubles afflicting another.

Circus: A place where horses, ponies, and elephants are permitted to watch men, women, and children acting the fool.

Commerce: A kind of transaction in which A plunders from B the goods of C, and for compensation B picks the pocket of D of money belonging to E.

Connoisseur: A specialist who knows everything about something and nothing about anything else.

Conservative: A statesman who is enamored of existing evils, as distinguished from the Liberal, who wishes to replace them with others.

Corporation: An ingenious device for obtaining individual profit without individual responsibility.

Cynic: A blackguard who sees things as they are instead of as they ought to be.

D

Debauchee: One who has so earnestly pursued pleasure that he has had the misfortune to overtake it.

Diary: A daily record of that part of one's life which one can relate to oneself without blushing.

Diplomacy: The patriotic art of lying for one's country.

Discussion: A method of confirming others in their errors.

E

Edible: Good to eat and wholesome to digest, as a worm to a toad, a toad to a snake, a snake to a pig, a pig to a man, and a man to a worm.

Education: That which discloses to the wise and disguises from the foolish their lack of understanding.

Egotist: A person of low taste, more interested in himself than in me.

Eulogy: Praise of a person who has either the advantages of wealth and power, or the consideration to be dead.

F

Faith: Belief without evidence in what is told by one who speaks without knowledge of things without parallel.

Fashion: A despot whom the wise ridicule—and obey.

Freedom: A political condition that every nation supposes itself to enjoy in virtual monopoly.

Friendship: A ship big enough to carry two in fair weather, but only one in foul.

G

Genealogy: An account of one's descent from an ancestor who did not particularly care to trace his own.

Gunpowder: An agency employed by civilized nations for the settlement of disputes which might become troublesome if left unadjusted.

H

Habit: A shackle for the free.

Happiness: An agreeable sensation arising from contemplating the misery of some other person.

Heaven: A place where the wicked cease from troubling you with talk of their personal affairs, and the good listen with attention while you expound your own.

History: An account mostly false, of events mostly unimportant, which are brought about by rulers mostly knaves, and soldiers mostly fools.

I

I: The first word of the language, the first thought of the mind, the first object of affection.

Immigrant: An unenlightened person who thinks one country better than another.

Immoral: Inexpedient.

Incompatibility: In matrimony a similarity of tastes, particularly the taste for domination.

Infancy: The period of our lives when according to Wordsworth, "heaven lies about us." The world begins lying about us soon afterward.

L

Lawyer: One skilled in circumventing the law.

Lecturer: One with his hand in your pocket, his tongue in your ear, and his faith in your patience.

Liberty: One of Imagination's most precious possessions.

Love: A temporary insanity curable by marriage.

M

Male: Commonly known to the female as Mere Man. The genus has two varieties: good providers and bad providers.

Marriage: The state or condition of a community consisting of a master, a mistress, and two slaves, making in all, two.

Mausoleum: The final and funniest folly of the rich.

Misfortune: The kind of fortune that never misses.

N

Neighbor: One whom we are commanded to love as ourselves, and who does all he can to make us disobey the command.

Notoriety: The fame of one's competitor for public honors. The kind of renown most accessible and most acceptable to mediocrities.

O

Once: Enough.

Optimist: A proponent of the doctrine that black is white.

P

Patience: A minor form of despair, disguised as a virtue.

Peace: In international affairs a period of cheating between two periods of fighting.

Philosophy: A route of many roads leading from Nowhere to Nothing.

Positive: Mistaken at the top of one's voice.

Prejudice: A vagrant opinion without visible means of support.

R

Radicalism: The conservatism of tomorrow injected into the affairs of today.

Reconsider: To seek a justification for a decision already made.

Resolute: Obstinate in a course of which we approve.

S

Saint: A dead sinner revised and edited.

Self-esteem: An erroneous appraisal.

Success: The one unpardonable sin against one's fellows.

T

Telephone: An invention of the devil which abrogates some of the advantages of making a disagreeable person keep his distance.

Twice: Once too often.

U

Un-American: Wicked and intolerable.

Uxoriousness: A perverted affection that has strayed to one's own wife.

W

War: A by-product of the arts of peace.

Weather: The climate of an hour. A permanent topic of conversation among persons whom it does not interest but who have inherited the tendency to chatter about it from naked aboreal ancestors whom it keenly concerned.

Wit: The salt with which the American humorist spoils his intellectual cookery by leaving it out.

Anatole France

Son of a bookseller into whose Paris shop writers came to discuss trends in politics and literature in general as well as books in particular, Anatole France, whose real name was Jacques Anatole Thibault, was born in 1844. With this background it was only natural that he should think of writing as the most desirable of occupations. He began by writing puffs for publishers and blurbs for book jackets. His first published volumes were in verse, but in his thirties he turned to prose, and for more than forty years issued pungent and sometimes profound novels, fables slightly disguised as fiction, plays, propaganda, histories, and philosophical satires. He died at eighty.

The intellectual heir of Voltaire, France became the alternately detached and angry conscience of his country. He delighted to portray not only what was absurd in mankind, but also what was self-defeating. A skeptical and mischievous mind shaped *The Opinions of Jerome Coignard, Penguin Island,* and *The Revolt of the Angels,* works that display a hatred of hypocrisy, oppression, and injustice and show them up with mordant yet gay mockery. A quiet impishness expresses such ironies as "The law in its majestic passion for equality forbids the rich as well as the poor to sleep under bridges," and "There are many honest people who do not think they have made a bargain unless they have cheated the merchant." Cynically clear, France's paradoxes compel the laugh.

Penguin Island is a model of what a parable should be. An extended and extremely funny skit on human progress, it mocks those who trace the course of history as a mounting evidence of man's achievements and his perfectibility. Maintaining the role of a stimulating skeptic, France demonstrates that humor rather than homilies can guide man toward reason — if anything can.

PENGUIN ISLAND

THE BAPTISM OF THE PENGUINS

After having drifted for an hour, the holy Maël approached a narrow strand, shut in by steep mountains. He went along the coast for a whole day and a night, passing around the reef which formed an insuperable barrier. He discovered in this way that it was a round island in the middle of which rose a mountain crowned with clouds. He joyfully breathed the fresh breath of the moist air. Rain fell, and this rain was so pleasant that the holy man said to the Lord:

"Lord, this is the island of tears, the island of contrition."

The strand was deserted. Worn out with fatigue and hunger, he sat down on a rock in the hollow of which there lay some yellow eggs, marked with black spots, and about as large as those of a swan. But he did not touch them, saying:

"Birds are the living praises of God. I should not like a single one of these praises to be lacking through me."

And he munched the lichens which he tore from the crannies of the rocks.

The holy man had gone almost entirely round the island without meeting any inhabitants, when he came to a vast amphitheatre formed of black and red rocks whose summits became tinged with blue as they rose towards the clouds, and they were filled with sonorous cascades.

The reflection from the polar ice had hurt the old man's eyes, but a feeble gleam of light still shone through his swollen eyelids. He distinguished animated forms which filled the rocks, in stages, like a crowd of men on the tiers of an amphitheatre. And at the same time, his ears, deafened by the continual noises of the sea, heard a feeble sound of voices. Thinking that what he saw were men living under the natural law, and that the Lord had sent him to teach them the Divine law, he preached the gospel to them.

Mounted on a lofty stone in the midst of the wild circus:

"Inhabitants of this island," said he, "although you be of small stature, you look less like a band of fishermen and mariners than like the senate of a judicious republic. By your gravity, your silence, your tranquil deportment, you form on this wild rock an assembly comparable to the Conscript Fathers at Rome deliberating in the temple of Victory, or rather, to the philosophers of Athens disputing on the benches of the Areopagus. Doubtless you possess neither their science nor their genius, but perhaps in the sight of God you are their superiors. I believe that you are simple and good. As I went round your island I saw no image of murder, no sign of carnage, no enemies' heads or scalps hung from a lofty pole or nailed to the doors of your villages. You appear to me to have no arts and not to work in metals. But your hearts are pure and your hands are innocent, and the truth will easily enter into your souls."

Now what he had taken for men of small stature but of grave bearing were penguins whom the spring had gathered together, and who were ranged in couples on the natural steps of the rock, erect in the majesty of their large white bellies. From moment to moment they moved their winglets like arms, and uttered peaceful cries. They did not fear men, for they did not know them, and had never received any harm from them; and there was in the monk a certain gentleness that reassured the most timid animals and that pleased these penguins extremely. With a friendly curiosity they turned towards him their little round eyes lengthened in front by a white oval spot that gave something odd and human to their appearance.

Touched by their attention, the holy man taught them the Gospel.

"Inhabitants of this island, the earthly day that has just risen over your rocks is the image of the heavenly day that rises in your souls. For I bring you the inner light; I bring you the light and heat of the soul. Just as the sun melts the ice of your mountains so Jesus Christ will melt the ice of your hearts."

Thus the old man spoke. As everywhere throughout nature voice calls to voice, as all which breathes in the light of day loves alternate strains, these penguins answered the old man by the sounds of their throats. And their voices were soft, for it was the season of their loves.

The holy man, persuaded that they belonged to some idolatrous people and that in their own language they gave adherence to the Christian faith, invited them to receive baptism.

"I think," said he to them, "that you bathe often, for all the hollows of the rocks are full of pure water, and as I came to your assembly I saw several of you plunging into these natural baths. Now purity of body is the image of spiritual purity."

And he taught them the origin, the nature, and the effects of baptism.

"Baptism," said he to them, "is Adoption, New Birth, Regeneration, Illumination."

And he explained each of these points to them in succession.

Then, having previously blessed the water that fell from the cascades and recited the exorcisms, he baptized those whom he had just taught, pouring on each of their heads a drop of pure water and pronouncing the sacred words.

And thus for three days and three nights he baptized the birds.

METAMORPHOSIS OF THE PENGUINS

The archangel, having gone down into the Island of the Penguins, found the holy man asleep in the hollow of a rock surrounded by his new disciples. He laid his hand on his shoulder and, having waked him, said in a gentle voice:

"Maël, fear not!"

The holy man, dazzled by a vivid light, inebriated by a delicious odour, recognised the angel of the Lord, and prostrated himself with his forehead on the ground.

The angel continued:

"Maël, know thy error, believing that thou wert baptizing children of Adam thou hast baptized birds; and it is through thee that penguins have entered into the Church of God."

At these words the old man remained stupefied.

And the angel resumed:

"Arise, Maël, arm thyself with the mighty Name of the Lord, and say to these birds, 'Be ye men!'"

And the holy Maël, having wept and prayed, armed himself with the mighty Name of the Lord and said to the birds:

"Be ye men!"

Immediately the penguins were transformed. Their foreheads enlarged and their heads grew round like the dome of St. Maria Rotunda in Rome. Their oval eyes opened more widely on the universe; a fleshy nose clothed the two clefts of their nostrils; their beaks were changed into mouths, and from their mouths went

forth speech; their necks grew short and thick; their wings became arms and their claws legs; a restless soul dwelt within the
breast of each of them.

However, there remained with them some traces of their first
nature. They were inclined to look sideways; they balanced themselves on their short thighs; their bodies were covered with fine
down.

And Maël gave thanks to the Lord, because he had incorporated
these penguins into the family of Abraham.

But he grieved at the thought that he would soon leave the island
to come back no more, and that perhaps when he was far away
the faith of the penguins would perish for want of care like a
young and tender plant.

And he formed the idea of transporting their island to the
coasts of Armorica.

"I know not the designs of eternal Wisdom," said he to himself.
"But if God wills that this island be transported, who could prevent it?"

And the holy man made a very fine cord about forty feet long
out of the flax of his stole. He fastened one end of the cord round
a point of rock that jutted up through the sand of the shore and,
holding the other end of the cord in his hand, he entered the stone
trough.

The trough glided over the sea and towed Penguin Island behind it; after nine days' sailing it approached the Breton coast,
bringing the island with it.

THE FIRST CLOTHES

One day St. Maël was sitting by the seashore on a warm stone
that he found. He thought it had been warmed by the sun and he
gave thanks to God for it, not knowing that the Devil had been
resting on it. The apostle was waiting for the monks of Yvern who
had been commissioned to bring a freight of skins and fabrics to
clothe the inhabitants of the island of Alca.

Soon he saw a monk called Magis coming ashore and carrying
a chest upon his back. This monk enjoyed a great reputation for
holiness.

When he had drawn near to the old man he laid the chest on the
ground and wiping his forehead with the back of his sleeve, he
said:

"Well, father, you wish then to clothe these penguins?"

"Nothing is more needful, my son," said the old man. "Since they have been incorporated into the family of Abraham these penguins share the curse of Eve, and they know that they are naked, a thing of which they were ignorant before. And it is high time to clothe them, for they are losing the down that remained on them after their metamorphosis."

"It is true," said Magis as he cast his eyes over the coast where the penguins were to be seen looking for shrimps, gathering mussels, singing, or sleeping, "they are naked. But do you not think, father, that it would be better to leave them naked? Why clothe them? When they wear clothes and are under the moral law they will assume an immense pride, a vile hypocrisy, and an excessive cruelty."

"Is it possible, my son," sighed the old man, "that you understand so badly the effects of the moral law to which even the heathen submit?"

"The moral law," answered Magis, "forces men who are beasts to live otherwise than beasts, a thing that doubtless puts a constraint upon them, but that also flatters and reassures them; and as they are proud, cowardly, and covetous of pleasure, they willingly submit to restraints that tickle their vanity and on which they found both their present security and the hope of their future happiness. That is the principle of all morality. . . . But let us not mislead ourselves. My companions are unloading their cargo of stuffs and skins on the island. Think, father, while there is still time! To clothe the penguins is a very serious business. At present when a penguin desires a penguin he knows precisely what he desires and his lust is limited by an exact knowledge of its object. At this moment two or three couples of penguins are making love on the beach. See with what simplicity! No one pays any attention and the actors themselves do not seem to be greatly preoccupied. But when the female penguins are clothed, the male penguin will not form so exact a notion of what it is that attracts him to them. His indeterminate desires will fly out into all sorts of dreams and illusions; in short, father, he will know love and its mad torments. And all the time the female penguins will cast down their eyes and bite their lips, and take on airs as if they kept a treasure under their clothes! . . . what a pity!

"The evil will be endurable as long as these people remain rude and poor; but only wait for a thousand years and you will see, father, with what powerful weapons you have endowed the daughters of Alca. If you will allow me, I can give you some idea of it beforehand. I have some old clothes in this chest. Let us take at hazard one of these female penguins to whom the male penguins give such little thought, and let us dress her as well as we can.

"Here is one coming towards us. She is neither more beautiful nor uglier than the others; she is young. No one looks at her. She strolls indolently along the shore, scratching her back and with her finger at her nose as she walks. You cannot help seeing, father, that she has narrow shoulders, clumsy breasts, a stout figure, and short legs. Her reddish knees pucker at every step she takes, and there is, at each of her joints, what looks like a little monkey's head. Her broad and sinewy feet cling to the rock with their four crooked toes, while the great toes stick up like the heads of two cunning serpents. She begins to walk, all her muscles are engaged in the task, and, when we see them working, we think of her as a machine intended for walking rather than as a machine intended for making love, although visibly she is both, and contains within herself several other pieces of machinery besides. Well, venerable apostle, you will see what I am going to make of her."

With these words the monk, Magis, reached the female penguin in three bounds, lifted her up, carried her in his arms with her hair trailing behind her, and threw her, overcome with fright, at the feet of the holy Maël.

And whilst she wept and begged him to do her no harm, he took a pair of sandals out of his chest and commanded her to put them on.

"Her feet," observed the old man, "will appear smaller when squeezed in by the woollen cords. The soles, being two fingers high, will give an elegant length to her legs and the weight they bear will seem magnified."

As the penguin tied on her sandals she threw a curious look towards the open coffer, and seeing that it was full of jewels and finery, she smiled through her tears.

The monk twisted her hair on the back of her head and covered it with a chaplet of flowers. He encircled her wrist with golden bracelets and making her stand upright, he passed a large linen band beneath her breasts, alleging that her bosom would thereby derive a new dignity and that her sides would be compressed to the greater glory of her hips.

He fixed this band with pins, taking them one by one out of his mouth.

"You can tighten it still more," said the penguin.

When he had, with much care and study, enclosed the soft parts of her bust in this way, he covered her whole body with a rose-coloured tunic which gently followed the lines of her figure.

"Does it hang well?" asked the penguin.

And bending forward with her head on one side and her chin on her shoulder, she kept looking attentively at the appearance of her toilet.

Magis asked her if she did not think the dress a little long, but she answered with assurance that it was not—she would hold it up.

Immediately, taking the back of her skirt in her left hand, she drew it obliquely across her hips, taking care to disclose a glimpse of her heels. Then she went away, walking with short steps and swinging her hips.

She did not turn her head, but as she passed near a stream she glanced out of the corner of her eye at her own reflection.

A male penguin, who met her by chance, stopped in surprise, and retracing his steps began to follow her. As she went along the shore, others coming back from fishing, went up to her, and after looking at her, walked behind her. Those who were lying on the sand got up and joined the rest.

Unceasingly, as she advanced, fresh penguins, descending from the paths of the mountain, coming out of clefts of the rocks, and emerging from the water, added to the size of her retinue.

And all of them, men of ripe age with vigorous shoulders and hairy breasts, agile youths, old men shaking the multitudinous wrinkles of their rosy, and white-haired skins, or dragging their legs thinner and drier than the juniper staff that served them as a third leg, hurried on, panting and emitting an acrid odour and hoarse gasps. Yet she went on peacefully and seemed to see nothing.

"Father," cried Magis, "notice how each one advances with his nose pointed towards the centre of gravity of that young damsel now that the centre is covered by a garment. The sphere inspires the meditations of geometers by the number of its properties. When it proceeds from a physical and living nature it acquires new qualities, and in order that the interest of that figure might be fully revealed to the penguins it was necessary that, ceasing to see it distinctly with their eyes, they should be led to represent it to themselves in their minds. I myself feel at this moment irresistibly attracted towards that penguin. Whether it be because her skirt gives more importance to her hips, and that in its simple

magnificence it invests them with a synthetic and general character and allows only the pure idea, the divine principle, of them to
be seen, whether this be the cause I cannot say, but I feel that if I
embraced her I would hold in my hands the heaven of human
pleasure. It is certain that modesty communicates an invincible
attraction to women. My uneasiness is so great that it would be
vain for me to try to conceal it."

He spoke, and, gathering up his habit, he rushed among the
crowd of penguins, pushing, jostling, trampling, and crushing,
until he reached the daughter of Alca, whom he seized and suddenly carried in his arms into a cave that had been hollowed out
by the sea.

Then the penguins felt as if the sun had gone out. And the holy
Maël knew that the Devil had taken the features of the monk,
Magis, in order that he might give clothes to the daughter of Alca.
He was troubled in spirit, and his soul was sad. As with slow steps
he went towards his hermitage he saw the little penguins of six
and seven years of age tightening their waists with belts made of
sea-weed and walking along the shore to see if anybody would
follow them.

THE FIRST CLOTHES—AFTERMATH

The holy Maël felt a profound sadness that the first clothes put
upon a daughter of Alca should have betrayed the penguin
modesty instead of helping it. He persisted, none the less, in his
design of giving clothes to the inhabitants of the miraculous
island. Assembling them on the shore, he distributed to them the
garments that the monks of Yvern had brought. The male penguins received short tunics and breeches, the female penguins
long robes. But these robes were far from creating the effect that
the former one had produced. They were not so beautiful, their
shape was uncouth and without art, and no attention was paid
to them since every woman had one. As they prepared the meals
and worked in the fields they soon had nothing but slovenly
bodices and soiled petticoats.

The male penguins loaded their unfortunate consorts with
work until they looked like beasts of burden. They knew nothing
of the troubles of the heart and the disorders of passion. Their
habits were innocent. Incest, though frequent, was a sign of rustic
simplicity and if drunkenness led a youth to commit some such
crime he thought nothing more about it the day afterwards.

THE ORIGIN OF PROPERTY

The island did not preserve the rugged appearance that it had formerly, when, in the midst of floating icebergs it sheltered a population of birds within its rocky amphitheatre. Its snow-clad peak had sunk down into a hill from the summit of which one could see the coasts of Armorica eternally covered with mist, and the ocean strewn with sullen reefs like monsters half raised out of its depths.

Its coasts were now very extensive and clearly defined and its shape reminded one of a mulberry leaf. It was suddenly covered with coarse grass, pleasing to the flocks, and with willows, ancient fig-trees, and mighty oaks. This fact is attested by the Venerable Bede and several other authors worthy of credence.

To the north the shore formed a deep bay that in after years became one of the most famous ports in the universe. To the east, along a rocky coast beaten by a foaming sea, there stretched a deserted and fragrant heath. It was the Beach of Shadows, and the inhabitants of the island never ventured on it for fear of the serpents that lodged in the hollows of the rocks and lest they might encounter the souls of the dead who resembled livid flames. To the south, orchards and woods bounded the languid Bay of Divers. On this fortunate shore old Maël built a wooden church and a monastery. To the west, two streams, the Clange and the Surelle, watered the fertile valleys of Dalles and Dombes.

Now one autumn morning, as the blessed Maël was walking in the valley of Clange in company with a monk of Yvern called Bulloch, he saw bands of fierce-looking men loaded with stones passing along the roads. At the same time he heard in all directions cries and complaints mounting up from the valley towards the tranquil sky.

And he said to Bulloch:

"I notice with sadness, my son, that since they became men the inhabitants of this island act with less wisdom than formerly. When they were birds they only quarrelled during the season of their love affairs. But now they dispute all the time; they pick quarrels with each other in summer as well as in winter. How greatly have they fallen from that peaceful majesty which made the assembly of the penguins look like the Senate of a wise republic!

"Look towards Surelle, Bulloch, my son. In yonder pleasant valley a dozen men penguins are busy knocking each other down with the spades and picks that they might employ better in tilling the ground. The women, still more cruel than the men, are tearing their opponents' faces with their nails. Alas! Bulloch, my son, why are they murdering each other in this way?"

"From a spirit of fellowship, father, and through forethought for the future," answered Bulloch. "For man is essentially provident and sociable. Such is his character and it is impossible to imagine it apart from a certain appropriation of things. Those penguins whom you see are dividing the ground among themselves."

"Could they not divide it with less violence?" asked the aged man. "As they fight they exchange invectives and threats. I do not distinguish their words, but they are angry ones, judging from the tone."

"They are accusing one another of theft and encroachment," answered Bulloch. "That is the general sense of their speech."

At that moment the holy Maël clasped his hands and sighed deeply.

"Do you see, my son," he exclaimed, "that madman who with his teeth is biting the nose of the adversary he has overthrown and that other one who is pounding a woman's head with a huge stone?"

"I see them," said Bulloch. "They are creating law; they are founding property; they are establishing the principles of civilization, the basis of society, and the foundations of the State."

"How is that?" asked old Maël.

"By setting bounds to their fields. That is the origin of all government. Your penguins, O Master, are performing the most august of functions. Throughout the ages their work will be consecrated by lawyers, and magistrates will confirm it."

Whilst the monk, Bulloch, was pronouncing these words a big penguin with a fair skin and red hair went down into the valley carrying a trunk of a tree upon his shoulder. He went up to a little penguin who was watering his vegetables in the heat of the sun, and shouted to him:

"Your field is mine!"

And having delivered himself of this stout utterance he brought down his club on the head of the little penguin, who fell dead upon the field that his own hands had tilled.

At this sight the holy Maël shuddered through his whole body and poured forth a flood of tears.

And in a voice stifled by horror and fear he addressed this prayer to heaven:

"O Lord, my God, O thou who didst receive young Abel's sacrifices, thou who didst curse Cain, avenge, O Lord, this innocent penguin sacrificed upon his own field and make the murderer feel the weight of thy arm. Is there a more odious crime, is there a graver offence against thy justice, O Lord, than this murder and this robbery?"

"Take care, father," said Bulloch gently, "that what you call murder and robbery may not really be war and conquest, those sacred foundations of empires, those sources of all human virtues and all human greatness. Reflect, above all, that in blaming the big penguin you are attacking property in its origin and in its source. I shall have no trouble in showing you how. To till the land is one thing, to possess it is another, and these two things must not be confused; as regards ownership the right of the first occupier is uncertain and badly founded. The right of conquest, on the other hand, rests on more solid foundations. It is the only right that receives respect since it is the only one that makes itself respected. The sole and proud origin of property is force. It is born and preserved by force. In that it is august and yields only to a greater force. This is why it is correct to say that he who possesses is noble. And that big red man, when he knocked down a labourer to get possession of his field, founded at that moment a very noble house upon this earth. I congratulate him upon it."

Oscar Wilde

The spoiled child of a profligate father and a pretentiously silly mother, Oscar Fingal O'Flahertie Wilde was born in Dublin in 1854. He was educated at Trinity College, Dublin, and Magdalen College, Oxford, where at twenty-one he won the Newdigate Prize for a poem, "Ravenna." Three years later he published his first book, *Poems,* and became the leader of an aesthetic cult whose credo was "Art for Art's sake." From that time on he was a controversial figure whose novels, criticisms, and plays glittered with epigrams that were platitudes turned upside down, startling disposals that delighted and shocked the society he both despised and adulated. *The Importance of Being Earnest* and *Lady Windermere's Fan* are composed of brilliant trivia, half-nonsensical, half-satirical sidelights on the established fox-hunting set, "the unspeakable in pursuit of the uneatable."

Wilde's career was a paradox of frivolity and pathos. He literally postured his way into notoriety. There was the languid decadent, preening himself in velvet jacket and knee breeches, apostrophizing the lily and carrying a sunflower, a flamboyant creature caricatured by Gilbert in *Patience.* There was the novelist who wrote a sensational damnation of himself in *The Picture of Dorian Gray,* and the fastidious stylist whose essays are a display of crackling fireworks and true fire. And there was the poet who wrote the *Ballad of Reading Gaol* in prison.

At forty, at the height of his reputation, Wilde was accused by the Marquis of Queensbury of having homosexual relations with his son, Lord Alfred Douglas. Wilde foolishly brought a libel action against the Marquis and lost the suit. The Crown then brought an action against Wilde for statutory offenses under the criminal law. He was found guilty and sentenced to two years hard labor. Three years later he came out of prison, fled to France, changed his name to Sebastian Melmoth, and supported by friends, barely survived. "It seems," he said, "I am dying beyond my means." A shabby derelict, he died at forty-six.

THE IMPORTANCE OF BEING EARNEST
ACT I, SCENE 1

SCENE—*Morning-room in* ALGERNON'S *flat in Half Moon Street. The room is luxuriously and artistically furnished. The sound of a piano is heard in the adjoining room.*

(LANE *is arranging afternoon tea on the table, and after the music has ceased,* ALGERNON *enters.*)

ALGERNON: Did you hear what I was playing, Lane?

LANE: I didn't think it polite to listen, sir.

ALGERNON: I'm sorry for that, for your sake. I don't play accurately —anyone can play accurately—but I play with wonderful expression. As far as the piano is concerned, sentiment is my forte. I keep science for Life.

LANE: Yes, sir.

ALGERNON: And, speaking of the science of Life, have you got the cucumber sandwiches cut for Lady Bracknell?

LANE: Yes sir. (*Hands them on a salver.*)

ALGERNON (*Inspects them, takes two, and sits down on the sofa*). Oh! . . . by the way, Lane, I see from your book that on Thursday night, when Lord Shoreman and Mr. Worthing were dining with me, eight bottles of champagne are entered as having been consumed.

LANE: Yes, sir; eight bottles and a pint.

ALGERNON: Why is it that at a bachelor's establishment the servants invariably drink the champagne? I ask merely for information.

LANE: I attribute it to the superior quality of the wine, sir. I have often observed that in married households the champagne is rarely of a first-rate brand.

ALGERNON: Good Heavens! Is marriage so demoralizing as that?

LANE: I believe it *is* a very pleasant state, sir. I have had very little experience of it myself up to the present. I have only been married once. That was in consequence of a misunderstanding between myself and a young person.

ALGERNON *(Languidly)*: I don't know that I am much interested in your family life, Lane.

LANE: No, sir; it is not a very interesting subject. I never think of it myself.

ALGERNON: Very natural, I am sure. That will do, Lane, thank you.

LANE: Thank you, sir.   (LANE *goes out.*)

ALGERNON: Lane's views on marriage seem somewhat lax. Really, if the lower orders don't set us a good example, what on earth is the use of them? They seem, as a class, to have absolutely no sense of moral responsibility.

(*Enter* LANE.)

LANE: Mr. Ernest Worthing.

(*Enter* JACK.)   (LANE *goes out.*)

ALGERNON: How are you, my dear Ernest? What brings you up to town?

JACK: Oh, pleasure, pleasure! What else should bring one anywhere? Eating as usual, I see, Algy!

ALGERNON *(Stiffly)*: I believe it is customary in good society to take some slight refreshment at five o'clock. Where have you been since last Thursday?

JACK *(Sitting down on the sofa)*: In the country.

ALGERNON: What on earth do you do there?

JACK (*Pulling off his gloves*): When one is in town one amuses oneself. When one is in the country one amuses other people. It is excessively boring.

ALGERNON: And who are the people you amuse?

JACK (*Airily*): Oh, neighbours, neighbours.

ALGERNON: Got nice neighbours in your part of Shropshire?

JACK: Perfectly horrid! Never speak to one of them.

ALGERNON: How immensely you must amuse them! (*Goes over and takes sandwich.*) By the way, Shropshire is your county, is it not?

JACK: Eh? Shropshire? Yes, of course. Hallo! Why all these cups? Why cucumber sandwiches? Why such reckless extravagance in one so young? Who is coming to tea?

ALGERNON: Oh! merely Aunt Augusta and Gwendolen.

JACK: How perfectly delightful!

ALGERNON: Yes, that is all very well; but I am afraid Aunt Augusta won't quite approve of your being here.

JACK: May I ask why?

ALGERNON: My dear fellow, the way you flirt with Gwendolen is perfectly disgraceful. It is almost as bad as the way Gwendolen flirts with you.

JACK: I am in love with Gwendolen. I have come up to town expressly to propose to her.

ALGERNON: I thought you had come up for pleasure? . . . I call that business.

JACK: How utterly unromantic you are!

ALGERNON: I really don't see anything romantic in proposing. It is very romantic to be in love. But there is nothing romantic about a definite proposal. Why, one may be accepted. One usually is, I believe. Then the excitement is all over. The very essence of romance is uncertainty. If ever I get married, I'll certainly try to forget the fact.

JACK: I have no doubt about that, dear Algy. The Divorce Court was specially invented for people whose memories are so curiously constituted.

ALGERNON: Oh! there is no use speculating on that subject. Divorces are made in Heaven——(JACK *puts out his hand to take a sandwich.* ALGERNON *at once interferes.*) Please don't touch the cucumber sandwiches. They are ordered specially for Aunt Augusta. *(Takes one and eats it.)*

JACK: Well, you have been eating them all the time.

ALGERNON: That is quite a different matter. She is my aunt. *(Takes plate from below.)* Have some bread and butter. The bread and butter is for Gwendolen. Gwendolen is devoted to bread and butter.

JACK *(Advancing to table and helping himself)*: And very good bread and butter it is too.

ALGERNON: Well, my dear fellow, you need not eat as if you were going to eat it all. You behave as if you were married to her already. You are not married to her already, and I don't think you ever will be.

JACK: Why on earth do you say that?

ALGERNON: Well, in the first place girls never marry the men they flirt with. Girls don't think it right.

JACK: Oh, that is nonsense!

ALGERNON: It isn't. It is a great truth. It accounts for the extraordinary number of bachelors that one sees all over the place. In the second place, I don't give my consent.

JACK: Your consent!

ALGERNON: My dear fellow, Gwendolen is my first cousin. And before I allow you to marry her, you will have to clear up the whole question of Cecily. *(Rings bell.)*

JACK: Cecily! What on earth do you mean? What do you mean, Algy, by Cecily? I don't know anyone of the name of Cecily.

(Enter LANE.)

ALGERNON: Bring me that cigarette case Mr. Worthing left in the smoking-room the last time he dined here.

LANE: Yes, sir.   (LANE *goes out.*)

JACK: Do you mean to say you have had my cigarette case all this time? I wish to goodness you had let me know. I have been writing frantic letters to Scotland Yard about it. I was very nearly offering a large reward.

ALGERNON: Well, I wish you would offer one. I happen to be more than usually hard up.

JACK: There is no good offering a large reward now that the thing is found.
(*Enter* LANE *with the cigarette case on a salver.* ALGERNON *takes it at once.* LANE *goes out.*)

ALGERNON: I think that is rather mean of you, Ernest, I must say. (*Opens case and examines it.*) However, it makes no matter, for, now that I look at the inscription inside, I find that the thing isn't yours after all.

JACK: Of course it's mine. (*Moving to him.*) You have seen me with it a hundred times, and you have no right whatsoever to read what is written inside. It is a very ungentlemanly thing to read a private cigarette case.

ALGERNON: Oh! it is absurd to have a hard-and-fast rule about what one should read and what one shouldn't. More than half of modern culture depends on what one shouldn't read.

JACK: I am quite aware of the fact, and I don't propose to discuss modern culture. It isn't the sort of thing one should talk of in private. I simply want my cigarette case back.

ALGERNON: Yes; but this isn't your cigarette case. This cigarette case is a present from someone of the name of Cecily, and you said you didn't know anyone of that name.

JACK: Well, if you want to know, Cecily happens to be my aunt.

ALGERNON: Your aunt!

JACK: Yes. Charming old lady she is, too. Lives at Tunbridge Wells. Just give it back to me, Algy.

ALGERNON (*Retreating to back of sofa*): But why does she call herself little Cecily if she is your aunt and lives at Tunbridge Wells? (*Reading.*) "From little Cecily with her fondest love."

JACK *(Moving to sofa and kneeling upon it)*: My dear fellow, what on earth is there in that? Some aunts are tall, some aunts are not tall. That is a matter that surely an aunt may be allowed to decide for herself. You seem to think that every aunt should be exactly like your aunt! That is absurd! For Heaven's sake give me back my cigarette case. *(Follows* ERNEST *round the room.)*

ALGERNON: Yes. But why does your aunt call you her uncle? "From little Cecily, with her fondest love to her dear Uncle Jack." There is no objection, I admit, to an aunt being a small aunt, but why an aunt, no matter what her size may be, should call her own nephew her uncle, I can't quite make out. Besides, your name isn't Jack at all; it is Ernest.

JACK: It isn't Ernest; it's Jack.

ALGERNON: You have always told me it was Ernest. I have introduced you to everyone as Ernest. You answer to the name of Ernest. You look as if your name was Ernest. You are the most earnest looking person I ever saw in my life. It is perfectly absurd your saying that your name isn't Ernest. It's on your cards. Here is one of them. *(Taking it from case.)* "Mr. Ernest Worthing, B 4, The Albany." I'll keep this as a proof your name is Ernest if ever you attempt to deny it to me, or to Gwendolen, or to anyone else. *(Puts the card in his pocket.)*

JACK: Well, my name is Ernest in town and Jack in the country, and the cigarette case was given to me in the country.

ALGERNON: Yes, but that does not account for the fact that your small Aunt Cecily, who lives at Tunbridge Wells, calls you her dear uncle. Come, old boy, you had much better have the thing out at once.

JACK: My dear Algy, you talk exactly as if you were a dentist. It is very vulgar to talk like a dentist when one isn't a dentist. It produces a false impression.

ALGERNON: Well, that is exactly what dentists always do. Now, go on! Tell me the whole thing. I may mention that I have always suspected you of being a confirmed and secret Bunburyist; and I am quite sure of it now.

JACK: Bunburyist? What on earth do you mean by a Bunburyist?

ALGERNON: I'll reveal to you the meaning of that incomparable expression as soon as you are kind enough to inform me why you are Ernest in town and Jack in the country.

JACK: Well, produce my cigarette case first.

ALGERNON: Here it is. *(Hands cigarette case.)* Now produce your explanation, and pray make it improbable. *(Sits on sofa.)*

JACK: My dear fellow, there is nothing improbable about my explanation at all. In fact it's perfectly ordinary. Old Mr. Thomas Cardew, who adopted me when I was a little boy, made me in his will guardian to his grand-daughter, Miss Cecily Cardew. Cecily, who addresses me as her uncle from motives of respect that you could not possibly appreciate, lives at my place in the country under the charge of her admirable governess, Miss Prism.

ALGERNON: Where is that place in the country, by the way?

JACK: That is nothing to you, dear boy. You are not going to be invited. . . . I may tell you candidly that the place is not in Shropshire.

ALGERNON: I suspected that, my dear fellow! I have Bunburyed all over Shropshire on two separate occasions. Now, go on. Why are you Ernest in town and Jack in the country?

JACK: My dear Algy, I don't know whether you will be able to understand my real motives. You are hardly serious enough. When one is placed in the position of guardian, one has to adopt a very high moral tone on all subjects. It's one's duty to do so. And as a high moral tone can hardly be said to conduce very much to either one's health or one's happiness, in order to get up to town I have always pretended to have a younger brother of the name of Ernest, who lives in the Albany, and gets into the most dreadful scrapes. That, my dear Algy, is the whole truth pure and simple.

ALGERNON: The truth is rarely pure and never simple. Modern life would be very tedious if it were either, and modern literature a complete impossibility!

JACK: That wouldn't be at all a bad thing.

ALGERNON: Literary criticism is not your forte, my dear fellow. Don't try it. You should leave that to people who haven't been at a University. They do it so well in the daily papers. What you really

are is a Bunburyist. I was quite right in saying you were a Bunburyist. You are one of the most advanced Bunburyists I know.

JACK: What on earth do you mean?

ALGERNON: You have invented a very useful younger brother
called Ernest, in order that you may be able to come up to town
as often as you like. I have invented an invaluable permanent invalid called Bunbury, in order that I may be able to go down into
the country whenever I choose. Bunbury is perfectly invaluable.
If it wasn't for Bunbury's extraordinary bad health, for instance,
I wouldn't be able to dine with you at Willis's to-night, for I have
been really engaged to Aunt Augusta for more than a week.

JACK: I haven't asked you to dine with me anywhere to-night.

ALGERNON: I know. You are absurdly careless about sending out
invitations. It is very foolish of you. Nothing annoys people so
much as not receiving invitations.

JACK: You had much better dine with your Aunt Augusta.

ALGERNON: I haven't the smallest intention of doing anything
of the kind. To begin with, I dined there on Monday, and once a
week is quite enough to dine with one's own relations. In the
second place, whenever I do dine there I am always treated as a
member of the family, and sent down with either no woman at all,
or two. In the third place, I know perfectly well whom she will
place me next to, to-night. She will place me next Mary Farquhar,
who always flirts with her own husband across the dinner-table.
That is not very pleasant. Indeed, it is not even decent . . . and
that sort of thing is enormously on the increase. The amount of
women in London who flirt with their own husbands is perfectly
scandalous. It looks so bad. It is simply washing one's clean linen
in public. Besides, now that I know you to be a confirmed Bunburyist I naturally want to talk to you about Bunburying. I want
to tell you the rules.

JACK: I'm not a Bunburyist at all. If Gwendolen accepts me, I am
going to kill my brother, indeed I think I'll kill him in any case.
Cecily is a little too much interested in him. It is rather a bore.
So I am going to get rid of Ernest. And I strongly advise you to do
the same with Mr. . . . with your invalid friend who has the absurd
name.

ALGERNON: Nothing will induce me to part with Bunbury, and if you ever get married, which seems to me extremely problematic, you will be very glad to know Bunbury. A man who marries without knowing Bunbury has a very tedious time of it.

JACK: That is nonsense. If I marry a charming girl like Gwendolen, and she is the only girl I ever saw in my life that I would marry, I certainly won't want to know Bunbury.

ALGERNON: Then you wife will. You don't seem to realize, that in married life three is company and two is none.

JACK *(Sententiously)*: That, my dear young friend, is the theory that the corrupt French Drama has been propounding for the last fifty years.

ALGERNON: Yes; and that the happy English home has proved in half the time.

JACK: For heaven's sake, don't try to be cynical. It's perfectly easy to be cynical.

ALGERNON: My dear fellow, it isn't easy to be anything now-a-days. There's such a lot of beastly competition about. *(The sound of an electric bell is heard.)* Ah! that must be Aunt Augusta. Only relatives, or creditors, ever ring in that Wagnerian manner. Now, if I get her out of the way for ten minutes, so that you can have an opportunity for proposing to Gwendolen, may I dine with you to-night at Willis's?

JACK: I suppose so, if you want to.

ALGERNON: Yes, but you must be serious about it. I hate people who are not serious about meals. It is so shallow of them.

THIRTY-THREE EPIGRAMS

• The Book of Books begins with a man and a woman in a garden. It ends with Revelations.

• There is one thing worse than being talked about. And that is not being talked about.

• Young men want to be faithful and are not. Old men want to be faithless and cannot.

• Men marry because they are tired, women because they are curious. Both are disappointed.

- When one is in love one begins by deceiving oneself; one ends by deceiving others. That is what the world calls romance.

- We live in an age when only unnecessary things are absolutely necessary to us.

- Fashion is that by which the fantastic becomes for the moment universal.

- One should always play fairly when one has the winning cards.

- To love oneself is the beginning of a lifelong romance.

- Books of poetry by young writers are usually promissory notes that are never met.

- Political corruption is the twin brother of political rhetoric.

- If one tells the truth, one is sure, sooner or later, to be found out.

- The old believe everything. The middle-aged suspect everything. The young know everything.

- I can resist everything except temptation.

- A cynic is a man who knows the price of everything and the value of nothing.

- In this world there are only two tragedies. One is not getting what one wants; the other is getting it.

- The amount of women who flirt with their own husbands is scandalous. It is simply washing one's clean linen in public.

- By persistently remaining single a man converts himself into a permanent public temptation.

- All women become like their mothers. That is their tragedy. No man does. That is his.

- In married life three is company and two is none.

- Twenty years of romance make a woman look like a ruin; but twenty years of marriage make her something like a public building.

- The youth of America is their oldest tradition. It has been going on now for three hundred years.

- Women as a sex are sphinxes without secrets.

- Men always want to be a woman's first love. Women like to be a man's last romance.

• The history of woman is the history of the worst form of tyranny the world has ever known: the tyranny of the weak over the strong. It is the only tyranny that lasts.

• The happiness of a married man depends on the people he has not married.

• The only difference between a saint and a sinner is that every saint has a past and every sinner has a future.

• Moderation is a fatal thing; nothing succeeds like excess.

• Life imitates Art far more than Art imitates Life.

• The public is wonderfully tolerant. It forgives everything except genius.

• There is no such thing as a moral or an immoral book. Books are well written or badly written. That is all.

• The nineteenth-century dislike of Realism is the rage of Caliban at seeing his own face in the glass. The nineteenth-century dislike of Romanticism is the rage of Caliban at not seeing his own face in the glass.

• There are three kinds of despots. There is the despot who tyrannizes over the body. There is the despot who tyrannizes over the soul. There is the despot who tyrannizes over both body and soul. The first is called the Prince. The second is called the Pope. The third is called the People.

A. E. Housman

Known chiefly because of a single volume of verse, Alfred
Edward Housman was born In 1859 in Fockbury, a Worcester
village, but it was nearby Shropshire county that became the
background of his poetry. Educated at St. John's College, Oxford, he served ten dreary years as clerk in the Patent Office
before he was appointed Professor of Latin at University College, London. A classical scholar, he was a bad-tempered
critic, not merely caustic but scathing concerning the work of
other scholars.

It was not until Housman was thirty-seven that *A Shropshire
Lad* was published. After a twenty-year silence he issued *Last
Poems*, a misleading title because fourteen years later the book
was followed by *More Poems*. The only popular one of the
three small volumes, *A Shropshire Lad* presents a queer paradox. In the blithest measures the enigmatic Housman assures
us that the world is treacherous: men betray and girls are unfaithful; people struggle to no purpose; Nature is only a little
more inhuman than human nature; heaven and earth "ail from
the prime foundation." "Luck's a chance, but trouble's sure,"
and men are noble only when, frustrated, they fight against
futility. Train for ill and not for good, he warns us to the tune
of bright and frequently humorous rhymes.

In spite of the outspoken tone of his poems, Housman was an
inordinately shy man. Withdrawn from the world, he spent
nearly thirty years on the text of Manilius, a minor Latin poet,

nursed a secret love for a college friend, Moses Jackson (the
"Terence" of *A Shropshire Lad*), and died in his seventy-
seventh year.

A SHROPSHIRE LAD
WHEN I WAS ONE-AND-TWENTY

When I was one-and-twenty
  I heard a wise man say,
"Give crowns and pounds and guineas
  But not your heart away;
Give pearls away and rubies
  But keep your fancy free."
But I was one-and-twenty,
  No use to talk to me.

When I was one-and-twenty
  I heard him say again,
"The heart out of the bosom
  Was never given in vain;
'Tis paid with sighs a plenty
  And sold for endless rue."
And I am two-and-twenty,
  And oh, 'tis true, 'tis true.

OH, WHEN I WAS IN LOVE WITH YOU

Oh, when I was in love with you,
  Then I was clean and brave,
And miles around the wonder grew
  How well I did behave.

But now the fancy passes by,
  And nothing will remain,
And miles around they'll say that I
  Am quite myself again.

OH, SEE HOW THICK THE GOLDCUP FLOWERS

Oh, see how thick the goldcup flowers
  Are lying in field and lane,

With dandelions to tell the hours
  That never are told again.
Oh, may I squire you round the meads
  And pick you posies gay?
—'Twill do no harm to take my arm.
  "You may, young man, you may."

Ah, spring was sent for lass and lad,
  'Tis now the blood runs gold,
And man and maid had best be glad
  Before the world is old.
What flowers to-day may flower to-morrow,
  But never as good as new.
—Suppose I wound my arm right round—
  "'Tis true, young man, 'tis true."

Some lads there are, 'tis shame to say,
  That only court to thieve,
And once they bear the bloom away
  'Tis little enough they leave.
Then keep your heart for men like me
  And safe from trustless chaps.
My love is true and all for you.
  "Perhaps, young man, perhaps."

Oh, look in my eyes, then, can you doubt?
  —Why, 'tis a mile from town.
How green the grass is all about!
  We might as well sit down.
—Ah, life, what is it but a flower?
  Why must true lovers sigh?
Be kind, have pity, my own, my pretty—
  "Good-bye, young man, good-bye."

TERENCE, THIS IS STUPID STUFF

  Terence, this is stupid stuff:
You eat your victuals fast enough;
There can't be much amiss, 'tis clear,
To see the rate you drink your beer.
But oh, good Lord, the verse you make,
It gives a chap the belly-ache.
The cow, the old cow, she is dead;

It sleeps well, the horned head:
We poor lads, 'tis our turn now
To hear such tunes as killed the cow.
Pretty friendship 'tis to rhyme
Your friends to death before their time
Moping melancholy mad:
Come, pipe a tune to dance to, lad.

Why, if 'tis dancing you would be,
There's brisker pipes than poetry.
Say, for what were hop-yards meant,
Or why was Burton built on Trent?
Oh many a peer of England brews
Livelier liquor than the Muse,
And malt does more than Milton can
To justify God's ways to man.
Ale, man, ale's the stuff to drink
For fellows whom it hurts to think:
Look into the pewter pot
To see the world as the world's not.
And faith, 'tis pleasant till 'tis past:
The mischief is that 'twill not last.
Oh I have been to Ludlow fair
And left my necktie God knows where,
And carried half-way home, or near,
Pints and quarts of Ludlow beer:
Then the world seemed none so bad,
And I myself a sterling lad;
And down in lovely muck I've lain,
Happy till I woke again.
Then I saw the morning sky.
Heigho, the tale was all a lie;
The world, it was the old world yet,
I was I, my things were wet,
And nothing now remained to do
But to begin the game anew.

Therefore, since the world has still
Much good, but much less good than ill,
And while the sun and moon endure
Luck's a chance, but trouble's sure,
I'd face it as a wise man would,

And train for ill and not for good.
'Tis true the stuff I bring for sale
Is not so brisk a brew as ale:
Out of a stem that scored the hand
I wrung it in a weary land.
But take it: if the smack is sour,
The better for the embittered hour;
It should do good to heart and head
When your soul is in my soul's stead;
And I will friend you, if I may,
In the dark and cloudy day.

    There was a king reigned in the East:
There, when kings will sit to feast,
They get their fill before they think
With poisoned meat and poisoned drink.
He gathered all that springs to birth
From the many-venomed earth;
First a little, thence to more,
He sampled all her killing store;
And easy, smiling, seasoned sound,
Sat the king when healths went round.
They put arsenic in his meat
And stared aghast to watch him eat;
They poured strychnine in his cup
And shook to see him drink it up:
They shook, they stared as white's their shirt.
Them it was their poison hurt.
—I tell the tale that I heard told.
Mithridates, he died old.

Stephen Leacock

A dual personality, Stephen Leacock was born in 1869 in Hampshire, England. When he was seven his parents emigrated to Canada, where his father had a hard time keeping up a run-down farm. Leacock recalled that there were nine chunk stoves that needed ceaseless woodchopping and that he and his brother did their studying by the light of a lone tallow candle. Somehow enough money was saved to send him to the University of Toronto, and after further study at the University of Chicago, he became a teacher. Teaching, he concluded, was "an experience which left me with a profound sympathy for those compelled to spend their lives in the most dreary, most thankless, and the worst paid profession in the world." Head of the department of economics at McGill University, he began his double life when he published *Elements of Political Science*, which became a standard textbook, and also the burlesques in *Literary Lapses*, which started him on the career of a popular humorist. The duality increased with the appearance of such disparate works as *Moonbeams from the Larger Lunacy* and *The Unsolved Riddle of Social Justice*, *Nonsense Novels* and critical biographies of Mark Twain and Dickens. Author of such solemn tomes as *Economic Prosperity in the British Empire*, Leacock never deprecated his pastiches and parodies. On the contrary, he said that he would rather have written *Alice in Wonderland* than the entire *Encyclopaedia Britannica*.

Leacock died at seventy-five. His uncompleted autobiography, *The Boy I Left Behind Me*, appeared two years after his death.

MY FINANCIAL CAREER

When I go into a bank I get rattled. The clerks rattle me; the wickets rattle me; the sight of the money rattles me; everything rattles me.

The moment I cross the threshold of a bank and attempt to transact business there, I become an irresponsible idiot.

I knew this beforehand, but my salary had been raised to fifty dollars a month and I felt that the bank was the only place for it.

So I shambled in and looked timidly round at the clerks. I had an idea that a person about to open an account must needs consult the manager.

I went up to a wicket marked "Accountant." The accountant was a tall, cool devil. The very sight of him rattled me. My voice was sepulchral.

"Can I see the manager?" I said, and added solemnly, "alone." I don't know why I said "alone."

"Certainly," said the accountant, and fetched him.

The manager was a grave, calm man. I held my fifty-six dollars clutched in a crumpled ball in my pocket.

"Are you the manager?" I said. God knows I didn't doubt it. "Yes," he said.

"Can I see you," I asked, "alone?" I didn't want to say "alone" again, but without it the thing seemed self-evident.

The manager looked at me in some alarm. He felt that I had an awful secret to reveal.

"Come in here," he said, and led the way to a private room. He turned the key in the lock.

"We are safe from interruption here," he said; "sit down."

We both sat down and looked at each other. I found no voice to speak.

"You are one of Pinkerton's men, I presume," he said.

He had gathered from my mysterious manner that I was a detective. I knew what he was thinking, and it made me worse.

"No, not from Pinkerton's," I said, seeming to imply that I came from a rival agency.

"To tell the truth," I went on, as if I had been prompted to lie about it, "I am not a detective at all. I have come to open an account. I intend to keep all my money in this bank."

The manager looked relieved but still serious; he concluded now that I was a son of Baron Rothschild or a young Gould.

"A large account, I suppose," he said.

"Fairly large," I whispered. "I propose to deposit fifty-six dollars now and fifty dollars a month regularly."

The manager got up and opened the door. He called to the accountant.

"Mr Montgomery," he said unkindly loud, "this gentleman is opening an account, he will deposit fifty-six dollars. Good morning."

I rose.

A big iron door stood open at the side of the room.

"Good morning," I said, and stepped into the safe.

"Come out," said the manager coldly, and showed me the other way.

I went up to the accountant's wicket and poked the ball of money at him with a quick convulsive movement as if I were doing a conjuring trick.

My face was ghastly pale.

"Here," I said, "deposit it." The tone of the words seemed to mean, "Let us do this painful thing while the fit is on us."

He took the money and gave it to another clerk.

He made me write the sum on a slip and sign my name in a book. I no longer knew what I was doing. The bank swam before my eyes.

"Is it deposited?" I asked in a hollow, vibrating voice.

"It is," said the accountant.

"Then I want to draw a cheque."

My idea was to draw out six dollars of it for present use. Someone gave me a cheque-book through a wicket and someone else began telling me how to write it out. The people in the bank had the impression that I was an invalid millionaire. I wrote something on the cheque and thrust it in at the clerk. He looked at it.

"What! are you drawing it all out again?" he asked in surprise. Then I realized that I had written fifty-six instead of six. I was too far gone to reason now. I had a feeling that it was impossible to explain the thing. All the clerks had stopped writing to look at me.

Reckless with misery, I made a plunge.

"Yes, the whole thing."

"You withdraw your money from the bank?"

"Every cent of it."

"Are you not going to deposit any more?" said the clerk, astonished.

"Never."

An idiot hope struck me that they might think something had insulted me while I was writing the cheque and that I had changed my mind. I made a wretched attempt to look like a man with a fearfully quick temper.

The clerk prepared to pay the money.

"How will you have it?" he said.

"What?"

"How will you have it?"

"Oh"—I caught his meaning and answered without even trying to think—"in fifties."

He gave me a fifty-dollar bill.

"And the six?" he asked dryly.

"In sixes," I said.

He gave it me and I rushed out.

As the big door swung behind me I caught the echo of a roar of laughter that went up to the ceiling of the bank. Since then I bank no more. I keep my money in cash in my trousers pocket and my savings in silver dollars in a sock.

H. H. Munro (Saki)

Son of a police inspector of Scottish descent, Hector Hugh Munro was born in 1870 in Akyab, Burma, and was brought up by aunts in Devon. He traveled with his father through Europe until at twenty-five he received an appointment with the police department in Burma. The climate was bad for his health; after several attacks of fever he returned to England and became a journalist. In his thirties he served as a foreign correspondent and turned to political and social satire, mainly of the upper-class Edwardians, as well as to odd short stories. These he signed with the pen name "Saki," the cupbearer in *The Rubáiyát of Omar Khayyám*. In the First World War he enlisted as a private with the Royal Fusiliers, having refused several offers of a commission, and was killed in France in 1916.

Saki has a way of twisting humor around horror. At one moment he dispenses trivialities across the tea table; at the next he transforms a polite country house into a jungle of cynically talking cats, with women turned into werewolves and otters, and boys converted into primitive woodlawn fauns. Above all, he has the gift of casually presenting the reader with a mixture of the mockingly macabre and the blandly absurd.

THE RETICENCE OF LADY ANNE

Egbert came into the large, dimly lit drawing-room with the air of a man who is not certain whether he is entering a dovecote or a bomb factory, and is prepared for either eventuality. The little domestic quarrel over the luncheon-table had not been fought to a definite finish, and the question was how far Lady Anne was in a mood to renew or forgo hostilities. Her pose in the arm-chair by the tea-table was rather elaborately rigid; in the gloom of a December afternoon Egbert's pince-nez did not materially help him to discern the expression of her face.

By way of breaking whatever ice might be floating on the surface he made a remark about a dim religious light. He or Lady Anne were accustomed to make that remark between 4.30 and 6 on winter and late autumn evenings; it was a part of their married life. There was no recognized rejoinder to it, and Lady Anne made none.

Don Tarquinio lay astretch on the Persian rug, basking in the firelight with superb indifference to the possible ill-humour of Lady Anne. His pedigree was as flawlessly Persian as the rug, and his ruff was coming into the glory of its second winter. The page-boy, who had Renaissance tendencies, had christened him Don Tarquinio. Left to themselves, Egbert and Lady Anne would unfailingly have called him Fluff, but they were not obstinate.

Egbert poured himself out some tea. As the silence gave no sign of breaking on Lady Anne's initiative, he braced himself for another Yermak effort.

"My remark at lunch had a purely academic application," he announced; "you seem to put an unnecessarily personal significance into it."

Lady Anne maintained her defensive barrier of silence. The bullfinch lazily filled in the interval with an air from *Iphigénie en Tauride*. Egbert recognized it immediately, because it was the only air the bullfinch whistled, and he had come to them with the reputation for whistling it. Both Egbert and Lady Anne would have preferred something from *The Yeoman of the Guard*, which was their favourite opera. In matters artistic they had a similarity of taste. They leaned towards the honest and explicit in art, a picture, for instance, that told its own story, with generous assistance from its title. A riderless warhorse with harness in obvious disarray, staggering into a courtyard full of pale swooning women, and marginally noted "Bad News," suggested to their minds a distinct interpretation of some military catastrophe. They could see what it was meant to convey, and explain it to friends of duller intelligence.

The silence continued. As a rule Lady Anne's displeasure became articulate and markedly voluble after four minutes of introductory muteness. Egbert seized the milk-jug and poured some of its contents into Don Tarquinio's saucer; as the saucer was already full to the brim an unsightly overflow was the result. Don Tarquinio looked on with a surprised interest that evanesced into elaborate unconsciousness when he was appealed to by Egbert to come and drink up some of the spilt matter. Don Tarquinio was prepared to play many rôles in life, but a vacuum carpet-cleaner was not one of them.

"Don't you think we're being rather foolish?" said Egbert cheerfully.

If Lady Anne thought so she didn't say so.

"I darcsay the fault has been partly on my side," continued Egbert, with evaporating cheerfulness. "After all, I'm only human, you know. You seem to forget that I'm only human."

He insisted on the point, as if there had been unfounded suggestions that he was built on Satyr lines, with goat continuations where the human left off.

The bullfinch recommenced its air from *Iphigénie en Tauride*. Egbert began to feel depressed. Lady Anne was not drinking her tea. Perhaps she was feeling unwell. But when Lady Anne felt unwell she was not wont to be reticent on the subject. "No one knows what I suffer from indigestion" was one of her favourite statements; but the lack of knowledge can only have been caused by defective listening; the amount of information available on the subject would have supplied material for a monograph.

Evidently Lady Anne was not feeling unwell.

Egbert began to think he was being unreasonably dealt with; naturally he began to make concessions.

"I daresay," he observed, taking as central a position on the hearth-rug as Don Tarquinio could be persuaded to concede him, "I may have been to blame. I am willing, if I can thereby restore things to a happier standpoint, to undertake to lead a better life."

He wondered vaguely how it would be possible. Temptations came to him, in middle age, tentatively and without insistence, like a neglected butcher-boy who asks for a Christmas box in February for no more hopeful reason than that he didn't get one in December. He had no more idea of succumbing to them than he had of purchasing the fish-knives and fur boas that ladies are impelled to sacrifice through the medium of advertisement columns during twelve months of the year. Still, there was something impressive in this unasked-for renunciation of possibly latent enormities.

Lady Anne show no sign of being impressed.

Egbert looked at her nervously through his glasses. To get the worst of an argument with her was no new experience. To get the worst of a monologue was a humiliating novelty.

"I shall go and dress for dinner," he announced in a voice into which he intended some shade of sternness to creep.

At the door a final access of weakness impelled him to make a further appeal.

"Aren't we being very silly?"

"A fool," was Don Tarquinio's mental comment as the door closed on Egbert's retreat. Then he lifted his velvet forepaws in the air and leapt lightly on to a bookshelf immediately under the bullfinch's cage. It was the first time he had seemed to notice the bird's existence, but he was carrying out a long-formed theory of action with the precision of mature deliberation. The bullfinch, who had fancied himself something of a despot, depressed himself of a sudden into a third of his normal displacement; then he fell to a helpless wing-beating and shrill cheeping. He had cost twenty-seven shillings without the cage, but Lady Anne made no sign of interfering. She had been dead for two hours.

THE OPEN WINDOW

"My aunt will be down presently, Mr. Nuttel," said a very self-possessed young lady of fifteen; "in the meantime you must try and put up with me."

Framton Nuttel endeavoured to say the correct something which should duly flatter the niece of the moment without unduly discounting the aunt that was to come. Privately he doubted more than ever whether these formal visits on a succession of total strangers would do much towards helping the nerve cure which he was supposed to be undergoing.

"I know how it will be," his sister had said when he was preparing to migrate to this rural retreat; "you will bury yourself down there and not speak to a living soul, and your nerves will be worse than ever from moping. I shall just give you letters of introduction to all the people I know there. Some of them, as far as I can remember, were quite nice."

Framton wondered whether Mrs. Sappleton, the lady to whom he was presenting one of the letters of introduction, came into the nice division.

"Do you know many of the people round here?" asked the niece, when she judged that they had had sufficient silent communion.

"Hardly a soul," said Framton. "My sister was staying here, at the rectory, you know, some four years ago, and she gave me letters of introduction to some of the people here."

He made the last statement in a tone of distinct regret.

"Then you know practically nothing about my aunt?" pursued the self-possessed young lady.

"Only her name and address," admitted the caller. He was wondering whether Mrs. Sappleton was in the married or widowed state. An undefinable something about the room seemed to suggest masculine habitation.

"Her great tragedy happened just three years ago," said the child; "that would be since your sister's time."

"Her tragedy?" asked Framton; somehow in this restful country spot tragedies seemed out of place.

"You may wonder why we keep that window wide open on an October afternoon," said the niece, indicating a large French window that opened on to a lawn.

"It is quite warm for the time of the year," said Framton; "but has that window got anything to do with the tragedy?"

"Out through that window, three years ago to a day, her husband and her two young brothers went off for their day's shooting. They never came back. In crossing the moor to their favourite snipe-shooting ground they were all three engulfed in a treacherous piece of bog. It had been that dreadful wet summer, you know, and places that were safe in other years gave way suddenly without warning. Their bodies were never recovered. That was the dreadful part of it." Here the child's voice lost its self-possessed note and became falteringly human. "Poor aunt always thinks that they will come back some day, they and the little brown spaniel that was lost with them, and walk in at that window just as they used to do. That is why the window is kept open every evening till it is quite dusk. Poor dear aunt, she has often told me how they went out, her husband with his white waterproof coat over his arm, and Ronnie, her youngest brother, singing, 'Bertie, why do you bound?' as he always did to tease her, because she said

it got on her nerves. Do you know, sometimes on still, quiet evenings like this, I almost get a creepy feeling that they will all walk
in through that window—"

She broke off with a little shudder. It was a relief to Framton
when the aunt bustled into the room with a whirl of apologies for
being later in making her appearance.

"I hope Vera has been amusing you?" she said.

"She has been very interesting," said Framton.

"I hope you don't mind the open window," said Mrs. Sappleton
briskly; "my husband and brothers will be home directly from
shooting, and they always come in this way. They've been out for
snipe in the marshes today, so they'll make a fine mess over my
poor carpets. So like you men-folk, isn't it?"

She rattled on cheerfully about the shooting and the scarcity
of birds, and the prospects for duck in the winter. To Framton
it was all purely horrible. He made a desperate but only partially
successful effort to turn the talk on to a less ghastly topic; he was
conscious that his hostess was giving him only a fragment of her
attention, and her eyes were constantly straying past him to the
open window and the lawn beyond. It was certainly an unfortunate
coincidence that he should have paid his visit on this tragic
anniversary.

"The doctors agree in ordering me complete rest, an absence
of mental excitement, and avoidance of anything in the nature
of violent physical exercise," announced Framton, who laboured
under the tolerably wide-spread delusion that total strangers and
chance acquaintances are hungry for the least detail of one's
ailments and infirmities, their cause and cure. "On the matter of
diet they are not so much in agreement," he continued.

"No?" said Mrs. Sappleton, in a voice which only replaced a
yawn at the last moment. Then she suddenly brightened into
alert attention—but not to what Framton was saying.

"Here they are at last!" she cried. "Just in time for tea, and don't
they look as if they were muddy up to the eyes!"

Framton shivered slightly and turned towards the niece with
a look intended to convey sympathetic comprehension. The
child was staring out through the open window with dazed horror
in her eyes. In a chill shock of nameless fear Framton swung
round in his seat and looked in the same direction.

In the deepening twilight three figures were walking across
the lawn towards the window; they all carried guns under their
arms, and one of them was additionally burdened with a white

coat hung over his shoulders. A tired brown spaniel kept close at their heels. Noiselessly they neared the house, and then a hoarse young voice chanted out of the dusk: "I said, Bertie, why do you bound?"

Framton grabbed wildly at his stick and hat; the hall-door, the gravel-drive, and the front gate were dimly noted stages in his headlong retreat. A cyclist coming along the road had to run into the hedge to avoid imminent collision.

"Here we are, my dear," said the bearer of the white mackintosh, coming in through the window; "fairly muddy, but most of it's dry. Who was that who bolted out as we came up?"

"A most extraordinary man, a Mr. Nuttel," said Mrs. Sappleton; "could only talk about his illnesses, and dashed off without a word of good-bye or apology when you arrived. One would think he had seen a ghost."

"I expect it was the spaniel," said the niece calmly; "he told me he had a horror of dogs. He was once hunted into a cemetery somewhere on the banks of the Ganges by a pack of pariah dogs, and had to spend the night in a newly dug grave with the creatures snarling and grinning and foaming just above him. Enough to make any one lose their nerve."

Romance at short notice was her speciality.

Max Beerbohm

Max Beerbohm was born in London on August 24, 1872. Educated at Charterhouse and Oxford, he made a name for himself as an undergraduate with his caricatures of noted personalities accompanied by acid commentaries. Descending upon the London of the nineties, he soon became one of the highly sophisticated *fin de siècle* group centered about *The Yellow Book*. George Bernard Shaw's successor as dramatic critic of *The Saturday Review*, Beerbohm became an institution, a mirror of "the irrepressible, the inimitable, the insouciant, and the impertinent." *Zuleika Dobson*, an ironic takeoff on Gothic romances, and *The Happy Hypocrite: A Fairy Tale for Tired Men* combine the trivial and the touching, the ultrafastidious and the unexpectedly sentimental.

Nearing forty, Beerbohm married Florence Kahn of Memphis, Tennessee; after 1911 they made their home in Rapallo, on the Italian Riviera. By this time he was famous for his critical and flashing essays as well as for his audacious wit. At twenty-four he had published his first small volume and had blandly called it *The Works of Max Beerbohm*. He continued to delight his readers with a succession of volumes entitled *More, Yet Again, And Even Now*. He was knighted in 1938 and died in 1956 at the age of eighty-four.

Beerbohm's humor is both light and lambent; it seems precious but it is penetrating. His gift for pictorial caricature extended into verbal parody. Called the inimitable Max, he had, said E. F. Benson, "the quality of sympathetic ridicule," a quality that "purifies the mind not by pity and terror but by laughter."

A. V. LAIDER

I unpacked my things and went down to await luncheon.

It was good to be here again in this little old sleepy hostel by the sea. Hostel I say, though it spelt itself without an s and even placed a circumflex above the o. It made no other pretension. It was very cosy indeed.

I had been here just a year before, in mid-February, after an attack of influenza. And now I had returned, after an attack of influenza. Nothing was changed. It had been raining when I left, and the waiter—there was but a single, a very old waiter—had told me it was only a shower. That waiter was still here, not a day older. And the shower had not ceased.

Steadfastly it fell on to the sands, steadfastly into the iron-grey sea. I stood looking out at it from the windows of the hall, admiring it very much. There seemed to be little else to do. What little there was I did. I mastered the contents of a blue hand-bill which, pinned to the wall just beneath the framed engraving of Queen Victoria's Coronation, gave token of a concert that was to be held—or rather, was to have been held some weeks ago—in the Town Hall, for the benefit of the Life-Boat Fund. I looked at the barometer, tapped it, was not the wiser. I glanced at a pamphlet about Our Dying Industries (a theme on which Mr. Joseph Chamberlain was at that time trying to alarm us). I wandered to the letter-board.

These letter-boards always fascinate me. Usually some two or three of the envelopes stuck into the cross-garterings have a certain newness and freshness. They seem sure they will yet be claimed. Why not? Why *shouldn't* John Doe, Esq., or Mrs. Richard Roe, turn up at any moment? I do not know. I can only say that nothing in the world seems to me more unlikely. Thus it is that these young bright envelopes touch my heart even more than do their dusty and sallow seniors. Sour resignation is less touching than impatience for what will not be, than the eagerness that has to wane and wither. Soured beyond measure these old envelopes are. They are not nearly so nice as they should be to the young ones. They lose no chance of sneering and discouraging. Such dialogues as this are only too frequent:

A VERY YOUNG ENVELOPE. Something in me whispers that he will come to-day!

A VERY OLD ENVELOPE. He? Well, that's good! Ha, ha, ha! Why didn't he come last week, when *you* came? What reason have you for supposing he'll ever come *now*? It isn't as if he were a frequenter of the place. He's never been here. His name is utterly unknown here. You don't suppose he's coming on the chance of finding *you*?

A V. Y. E. It may seem silly, but—something in me whispers—

A V. O. E. Something in *you*? One has only to look at you to see there's nothing in you but a note scribbled to him by a cousin. Look at *me!* There are three sheets, closely written, in *me*. The lady to whom I am addressed—

A V. Y. E. Yes, sir, yes; you told me all about her yesterday.

A V. O. E. And I shall do so to-day and to-morrow and every day and all day long. That young lady was a widow. She stayed here many times. She was delicate, and the air suited her. She was poor, and the tariff was just within her means. She was lonely, and had need of love. I have in me for her a passionate avowal and strictly honourable proposal, written to her, after many rough copies, by a gentleman who had made her acquaintance under this very roof. He was rich, he was charming, he was in the prime of life. He had asked if he might write to her. She had flutteringly granted his request. He posted me to her the day after his return to London. I looked forward to being torn open by her. I was very sure she would wear me and my contents next to her bosom. She was gone. She had left no address. She never returned. . . This I tell you, and shall continue to tell you, not because I want any of your callow sympathy,—no, *thank* you!—but that you may judge how much less than slight are the chances that you yourself—

But my reader has overheard these dialogues as often as I. He wants to know what was odd about this particular letter-board before which I was standing. At first glance I saw nothing odd about it. But presently I distinguished a handwriting that was vaguely familiar. It was mine. I stared, I wondered. There is always a slight shock in seeing an envelope of one's own after it has gone through the post. It looks as if it had gone through so much. But this was the first time I had ever seen an envelope of mine eating its heart out in bondage on a letter-board. This was outrageous. This was hardly to be believed. Sheer kindness had impelled me to write to 'A. V. Laider, Esq.', and this was the result! I hadn't minded receiving no answer. Only now, indeed, did I remember that I hadn't received one. In multitudinous London the memory of A. V. Laider and his trouble had soon passed from my mind. But—well, what a lesson not to go out of one's way to write to casual acquaintances!

My envelope seemed not to recognise me as its writer. Its gaze was the more piteous for being blank. Even so had I once been gazed at by a dog that I had lost and, after many days, found in the Battersea Home. "I don't know who you are, but whoever you are, claim me, take me out of this!" That was my dog's appeal. This was the appeal of my envelope.

I raised my hand to the letter-board, meaning to effect a swift and lawless rescue, but paused at sound of a footstep behind me. The old waiter had come to tell me that my luncheon was ready. I followed him out of the hall, not, however, without a bright glance across my shoulder to reassure the little captive that I should come back.

I had the sharp appetite of the convalescent, and this the sea-air had whetted already to a finer edge. In touch with a dozen oysters, and with stout, I soon shed away the unreasoning anger I had felt against A. V. Laider. I became merely sorry for him that he had not received a letter which might perhaps have comforted him. In touch with cutlets, I felt how sorely he had needed comfort. And anon, by the big bright fireside of that small dark smoking-room where, a year ago, on the last evening of my stay here, he and I had at length spoken to each other, I reviewed in detail the tragic experience he had told me; and I fairly revelled in reminiscent sympathy with him. . . .

A. V. LAIDER—I had looked him up in the visitors' book on the night of his arrival. I myself had arrived the day before, and had been rather sorry there was no one else staying here. A convalescent by the sea likes to have some one to observe, to wonder about, at meal-time. I was glad when, on my second evening, I found seated at the table opposite to mine another guest. I was the gladder because he was just the right kind of guest. He was enigmatic. By this I mean that he did not look soldierly nor financial nor artistic nor anything definite at all. He offered a clean slate for speculation. And thank heaven! he evidently wasn't going to spoil the fun by engaging me in conversation later on. A decently unsociable man, anxious to be left alone.

The heartiness of his appetite, in contrast with his extreme fragility of aspect and limpness of demeanour, assured me that he, too, had just had influenza. I liked him for that. Now and again our eyes met and were instantly parted. We managed, as a rule, to observe each other indirectly. I was sure it was not merely because he had been ill that he looked interesting. Nor did it seem to me that a spiritual melancholy, though I imagined him sad at the best of times, was his sole asset. I conjectured that he was clever. I thought he might also be imaginative. At first glance I had mistrusted him. A shock of white hair, combined with a young face and dark eyebrows, does somehow make a man look like a charlatan. But it is foolish to be guided by an accident of colour. I had soon rejected my first impression of my fellow-diner. I found him very sympathetic.

Anywhere but in England it would be impossible for two solitary men, howsoever much reduced by influenza, to spend five or six days in the same hostel and not exchange a single word. That is one of the charms of England. Had Laider and I been born and bred in any other land we should have become acquainted before the end of our first evening in the small smoking-room, and have found ourselves irrevocably committed to go on talking to each other throughout the rest of our visit. We might, it is true, have happened to like each other more than any one we had ever met. This off-chance may have occurred to us both. But it counted for nothing as against the certain surrender of quietude and liberty. We slightly bowed to each other as we entered or left the dining-room or smoking-room, and as we met on the widespread sands or in the shop that had a small and faded circulating library. That was all. Our mutual aloofness was a positive bond between us.

Had he been much older than I, the responsibility for our silence would of course have been his alone. But he was not, I judged, more than five or six years ahead of me, and thus I might without impropriety have taken it on myself to perform that hard and perilous feat which English people call, with a shiver, "breaking the ice." He had reason, therefore, to be as grateful to me as I to him. Each of us, not the less frankly because silently, recognised his obligation to the other. And when, on the last evening of my stay, the ice actually was broken no ill-will rose between us; neither of us was to blame.

It was a Sunday evening. I had been out for a long last walk and had come in very late to dinner. Laider left his table almost immediately after I sat down to mine. When I entered the smoking-room I found him reading a weekly review which I had bought the day before. It was a crisis. He could not silently offer, nor could I have silently accepted, sixpence. It was a crisis. We faced it like men. He made, by word of mouth, a graceful apology. Verbally, not by signs, I besought him to go on reading. But this, of course, was a vain counsel of perfection. The social code forced us to talk now. We obeyed it like men. To reassure him that our position was not so desperate as it might seem, I took the earliest opportunity to mention that I was going away early next morning. In the tone of his "Oh, are you?" he tried bravely to imply that he was sorry, even now, to hear that. In a way, perhaps, he really was sorry. We had got on so well together, he and I. Nothing could efface the memory of that. Nay, we seemed to be hitting it off even now. Influenza was not our sole theme. We passed from that to the aforesaid weekly review, and to a correspondence that was raging therein on Faith and Reason.

This correspondence had now reached its fourth and penultimate stage — its Australian stage. It is hard to see why these correspondences spring up; one only knows that they do spring up, suddenly, like street crowds. There comes, it would seem, a moment when the whole English-speaking race is unconsciously bursting to have its say about some one thing — the split infinitive, or the habits of migratory birds, or faith and reason, or what-not. Whatever weekly review happens at such a moment to contain a reference, however remote, to the theme in question reaps the storm. Gusts of letters blow in from all corners of the British Isles. These are presently reinforced by Canada in full blast. A few weeks later the Anglo-Indians weigh in. In due course we have the help of our Australian cousins. By that time, however, we of the Mother Country have got our second wind, and so determined are we to make the most of it that at last even the Editor suddenly loses patience and says "This correspondence must now cease. — Ed." and wonders why on earth he ever allowed anything so tedious and idiotic to begin.

I pointed out to Laider one of the Australian letters that had especially pleased me in the current issue. It was from "A Melbourne Man," and was of the abrupt kind which declares that "all your correspondents have been groping in the dark" and then settles the whole matter in one short sharp flash. The flash

in this instance was "Reason is faith, faith reason—that is all we
know on earth and all we need to know." The writer then inclosed his card and was, etc., "A Melbourne Man." I said to Laider
how very restful it was, after influenza, to read anything that
meant nothing whatsoever. Laider was inclined to take the letter
more seriously than I, and to be mildly metaphysical. I said that
for me faith and reason were two separate things, and (as I am no
good at metaphysics, however mild) I offered a definite example,
to coax the talk on to ground where I should be safer. "Palmistry,
for example," I said. "Deep down in my heart I believe in palmistry."

Laider turned in his chair. "You believe in palmistry?"

I hesitated. "Yes, somehow I do. Why? I haven't the slightest
notion. I can give myself all sorts of reasons for laughing it to
scorn. My common sense utterly rejects it. Of course the shape
of the hand means something—is more or less an index of character. But the idea that my past and future are neatly mapped out
on my palms——" I shrugged my shoulders.

"You don't like that idea?" asked Laider in his gentle, rather
academic voice.

"I only say it's a grotesque idea."

"Yet you do believe in it?"

"I've a grotesque belief in it, yes."

"Are you sure your reason for calling this idea 'grotesque' isn't
merely that you dislike it?"

"Well," I said, with the thrilling hope that he was a companion
in absurdity, "doesn't it seem grotesque to *you?*"

"It seems strange."

"You believe in it?"

"Oh, absolutely."

"Hurrah!"

He smiled at my pleasure, and I, at the risk of re-entanglement
in metaphysics, claimed him as standing shoulder to shoulder
with me against "A Melbourne Man." This claim he gently dis-
puted. "You may think me very prosaic," he said, "but I can't
believe without evidence."

"Well, I'm equally prosaic and equally at a disadvantage: I can't
take my own belief as evidence, and I've no other evidence to go
on."

He asked me if I had ever made a study of palmistry. I said I
had read one of Desbarolles' books years ago, and one of Heron-
Allen's. But, he asked, had I tried to test them by the lines on my

own hands or on the hands of my friends? I confessed that my actual practice in palmistry had been of a merely passive kind — the prompt extension of my palm to any one who would be so good as to "read" it and truckle for a few minutes to my egoism. (I hoped Laider might do this.)

"Then I almost wonder," he said, with his sad smile, "that you haven't lost your belief, after all the nonsense you must have heard. There are so many young girls who go in for palmistry. I am sure all the five foolish virgins were 'awfully keen on it' and used to say 'You can be led, but not driven,' and 'You are likely to have a serious illness between the ages of forty and forty-five,' and 'You are by nature rather lazy, but can be very energetic by fits and starts.' And most of the professionals, I'm told, are as silly as the young girls."

For the honour of the profession, I named three practitioners whom I had found really good at reading character. He asked whether any of them had been right about past events. I confessed that, as a matter of fact, all three of them had been right in the main. This seemed to amuse him. He asked whether any of them had predicted anything which had since come true. I confessed that all three had predicted that I should do several things which I had since done rather unexpectedly. He asked if I didn't accept this as at any rate a scrap of evidence. I said I could only regard it as a fluke — a rather remarkable fluke.

The superiority of his sad smile was beginning to get on my nerves. I wanted him to see that he was as absurd as I. "Suppose," I said, "suppose for sake of argument that you and I are nothing but helpless automata created to do just this and that, and to have just that and this done to us. Suppose, in fact, we *haven't* any free will whatsoever. Is it likely or conceivable that the Power that fashioned us would take the trouble to jot down in cipher on our hands just what was in store for us?"

Laider did not answer this question, he did but annoyingly ask me another. "You believe in free will?"

"Yes, of course. I'll be hanged if I'm an automaton."

"And you believe in free will just as in palmistry — without any reason?"

"Oh, no. Everything points to our having free will."

"Everything? What, for instance?"

This rather cornered me. I dodged out, as lightly as I could, by saying "I suppose *you* would say it was written in my hand that I should be a believer in free will."

"Ah, I've no doubt it is."

I held out my palms. But, to my great disappointment, he looked quickly away from them. He had ceased to smile. There was agitation in his voice as he explained that he never looked at people's hands now. "Never now—never again." He shook his head as though to beat off some memory.

I was much embarrassed by my indiscretion. I hastened to tide over the awkward moment by saying that if *I* could read hands I wouldn't, for fear of the awful things I might see there.

"Awful things, yes," he whispered, nodding at the fire.

"Not," I said in self-defence, "that there's anything very awful, so far as I know, to be read in *my* hands."

He turned his gaze from the fire to me. "You aren't a murderer, for example?"

"Oh, no," I replied, with a nervous laugh.

"*I* am."

This was a more than awkward, it was a painful, moment for me; and I am afraid I must have started or winced, for he instantly begged my pardon. "I don't know," he exclaimed, "why I said it. I'm usually a very reticent man. But sometimes—" He pressed his brow. "What you must think of me!"

I begged him to dismiss the matter from his mind.

"It's very good of you to say that; but—I've placed myself as well as you in a false position. I ask you to believe that I'm not the sort of man who is 'wanted' or ever was 'wanted' by the police. I should be bowed out of any police-station at which I gave myself up. I'm not a murderer in any bald sense of the word. No,"

My face must have perceptibly brightened, for "Ah," he said, "don't imagine I'm not a murderer at all. Morally, I am." He looked at the clock. I pointed out that the night was young. He assured me that his story was not a long one. I assured him that I hoped it was. He said I was very kind. I denied this. He warned me that what he had to tell might rather tend to stiffen my unwilling faith in palmistry, and to shake my opposite and cherished faith in free will. I said "Never mind." He stretched his hands pensively toward the fire. I settled myself back in my chair.

"My hands," he said, staring at the backs of them, "are the hands of a very weak man. I dare say you know enough of palmistry to see that for yourself. You notice the slightness of the thumbs and of the two 'little' fingers. They are the hands of a weak and over-sensitive man—a man without confidence, a man who would certainly waver in an emergency. Rather Hamlet-ish hands," he mused. "And I'm like Hamlet in other respects, too: I'm no fool, and I've rather a noble disposition, and I'm unlucky. But Hamlet was luckier than I in one thing: he was a murderer by accident, whereas the murders that I committed one day fourteen years ago—for I must tell you it wasn't one murder, but many murders that I committed—were all of them due to the wretched inherent weakness of my own wretched self.

"I was twenty-six—no, twenty-seven years old, and rather a nondescript person, as I am now. I was supposed to have been called to the Bar. In fact, I believe I *had* been called to the Bar. I hadn't listened to the call. I never intended to practise, and I never did practise. I only wanted an excuse in the eyes of the world for existing. I suppose the nearest I have ever come to practising is now at this moment: I am defending a murderer. My father had left me well enough provided with money. I was able to go my own desultory way, riding my hobbies where I would. I had a good stableful of hobbies. Palmistry was one of them. I was rather ashamed of this one. It seemed to me absurd, as it seems to you. Like you, though, I believed in it. Unlike you, I had done more than merely read a book or so about it. I had read innumerable books about it. I had taken casts of all my friends' hands. I had tested and tested again the points at which Desbarolles dissented from the gypsies, and—well, enough that I had gone into it all rather thoroughly, and was as sound a palmist as a man may be without giving his whole life to palmistry.

"One of the first things I had seen in my own hand, as soon as I had learned to read it, was that at about the age of twenty-six I should have a narrow escape from death—from a violent death. There was a clean break in the life-line, and a square joining it —the protective square, you know. The markings were precisely the same in both hands. It was to be the narrowest escape possible. And I wasn't going to escape without injury, either. That is what bothered me. There was a faint line connecting the break in the life-line with a star on the line of health. Against that star was another square. I was to recover from the injury, whatever it might be. Still, I didn't exactly look forward to it. Soon after I had reached the age of twenty-five, I began to feel uncomfortable. The thing might be going to happen at any moment. In palmistry, you know, it is impossible to pin an event down hard and fast to one year. This particular event was to be when I was *about* twenty-six; it mightn't be till I was twenty-seven; it might be while I was only twenty-five.

"And I used to tell myself that it mightn't be at all. My reason rebelled against the whole notion of palmistry, just as yours does. I despised my faith in the thing, just as you despise yours. I used to try not to be so ridiculously careful as I was whenever I crossed a street. I lived in London at that time. Motor-cars had not yet come in, but—what hours, all told, I must have spent standing on curbs, very circumspect, very lamentable! It was a pity, I suppose, that I had no definite occupation—something to take me out of myself. I was one of the victims of private means. There came a time when I drove in four-wheelers rather than in hansoms, and was doubtful of four-wheelers. Oh, I assure you, I was very lamentable indeed.

"If a railway-journey could be avoided, I avoided it. My uncle had a place in Hampshire. I was very fond of him and of his wife. Theirs was the only house I ever went to stay in now. I was there for a week in November, not long after my twenty-seventh birthday. There were other people staying there, and at the end of the week we all travelled back to London together. There were six of us in the carriage: Colonel Elbourn and his wife and their daughter, a girl of seventeen; and another married couple, the Blakes. I had been at Winchester with Blake, but had hardly seen him since that time. He was in the Indian Civil, and was home on leave. He was sailing for India next week. His wife was to remain in England for some months, and then join him out there. They had been married five years. She was now just twenty-four years old. He told me that this was her age.

"The Elbourns I had never met before. They were charming people. We had all been very happy together. The only trouble had been that on the last night, at dinner, my uncle asked me if I still went in for 'the gypsy business,' as he always called it; and of course the three ladies were immensely excited, and implored me to 'do' their hands. I told them it was all nonsense, I said I had forgotten all I once knew, I made various excuses; and the matter dropped. It was quite true that I had given up reading hands. I avoided anything that might remind me of what was in my own hands. And so, next morning, it was a great bore to me when, soon after the train started, Mrs. Elbourn said it would be 'too cruel' of me if I refused to do their hands now. Her daughter and Mrs. Blake also said it would be 'brutal'; and they were all taking off their gloves, and—well, of course I had to give in.

"I went to work methodically on Mrs. Elbourn's hands, in the usual way, you know, first sketching the character from the backs of them; and there was the usual hush, broken by the usual little noises—grunts of assent from the husband, cooings of recognition from the daughter. Presently I asked to see the palms, and from them I filled in the details of Mrs. Elbourn's character before going on to the events in her life. But while I talked I was calculating how old Mrs. Elbourn might be. In my first glance at her palms I had seen that she could not have been less than twenty-five when she married. The daughter was seventeen. Suppose the daughter had been born a year later—how old would the mother be? Forty-three, yes, Not less than that, poor woman!"

Laider looked at me. "Why 'poor woman,' you wonder? Well, in that first glance I had seen other things than her marriage-line. I had seen a very complete break in the lines of life and of fate. I had seen violent death there. At what age? Not later, not possibly *later*, than forty-three. While I talked to her about the things that had happened in her girlhood, the back of my brain was hard at work on those marks of catastrophe. I was horribly wondering that she was still alive. It was impossible that between her and that catastrophe there could be more than a few short months. And all the time I was talking; and I suppose I acquitted myself well, for I remember that when I ceased I had a sort of ovation from the Elbourns.

"It was a relief to turn to another pair of hands. Mrs. Blake was an amusing young creature, and her hands were very characteristic, and prettily odd in form. I allowed myself to be rather whimsical about her nature, and, having begun in that vein, I went on in it—somehow—even after she had turned her palms. In those palms were reduplicated the signs I had seen in Mrs. Elbourn's. It was as though they had been copied neatly out. The only difference was in the placing of them; and it was this difference that was the most horrible point. The fatal age in Mrs. Blake's hands was—not past, no, for here *she* was. But she might have died when she was twenty-one. Twenty-three seemed to be the utmost span. She was twenty-four, you know.

"I have said that I am a weak man. And you will have good proof of that directly. Yet I showed a certain amount of strength that day—yes, even on that day which has humiliated and saddened the rest of my life. Neither my face nor my voice betrayed me when in the palms of Dorothy Elbourn I was again confronted with those same signs. She was all for knowing the future, poor child! I believe I told her all manner of things that were to be. And she had no future—none, none in *this* world—except—

"And then, while I talked, there came to me suddenly a suspicion. I wondered it hadn't come before. You guess what it was?
It made me feel very cold and strange. I went on talking. But, also,
I went on—quite separately—thinking. The suspicion wasn't a
certainty. This mother and daughter were always together. What
was to befall the one might anywhere—anywhere—befall the
other. But a like fate, in an equally near future, was in store for
that other lady. The coincidence was curious, very. Here we all
were together—here, they and I—I who was narrowly to escape,
so soon now, what they, so soon now, were to suffer. Oh, there
was an inference to be drawn. Not a *sure* inference, I told myself.
And always I was talking, talking, and the train was swinging and
swaying noisily along—to what? It was a fast train. Our carriage
was near the engine. I was talking loudly. Full well I had known
what I should see in the Colonel's hands. I told myself I had not
known. I told myself that even now the thing I dreaded was not
sure to be. Don't think I was dreading it for myself. I wasn't so
'lamentable' as all that—now. It was only of them that I thought—
only for them. I hurried over the Colonel's character and career;
I was perfunctory. It was Blake's hands that I wanted. *They* were
the hands that mattered. If *they* had the marks— Remember,
Blake was to start for India in the coming week, his wife was to
remain in England. They would be apart. Therefore—

"And the marks were there. And I did nothing—nothing but
hold forth on the subtleties of Blake's character. There was a
thing for me to do. I wanted to do it. I wanted to spring to the
window and pull the communication-cord. Quite a simple thing
to do. Nothing easier than to stop a train. You just give a sharp
pull, and the train slows down, comes to a standstill. And the
Guard appears at your window. You explain to the Guard.

"Nothing easier than to tell him there is going to be a collision.
Nothing easier than to insist that you and your friends and every
other passenger in the train must get out at once. . . . There *are*
easier things than this? Things that need less courage than this?
Some of *them* I could have done, I daresay. This thing I was going
to do. Oh, I was determined that I would do it—directly.

"I had said all I had to say about Blake's hands. I had brought
my entertainment to an end. I had been thanked and complimented all round. I was quite at liberty. I was going to do what I
had to do. I was determined, yes.

"We were near the outskirts of London. The air was grey,
thickening; and Dorothy Elbourn had said, 'Oh, this horrible

old London! I suppose there's the same old fog!' And presently
I heard her father saying something about 'prevention' and 'a
short act of Parliament' and 'anthracite.' And I sat and listened
and agreed and——'

Laider closed his eyes. He passed his hands slowly through
the air.

"I had a racking headache. And when I said so, I was told not to
talk. I was in bed, and the nurses were always telling me not to
talk. I was in a hospital. I knew that. But I didn't know why I was
there. One day I thought I should like to know why, and so I asked.
I was feeling much better now. They told me, by degrees, that I
had had concussion of the brain. I had been brought there unconscious, and had remained unconscious for forty-eight hours.
I had been in an accident—a railway accident. This seemed to me
odd. I had arrived quite safely at my uncle's place, and I had no
memory of any journey since that. In cases of concussion, you
know, it's not uncommon for the patient to forget all that happened just before the accident; there may be a blank of several
hours. So it was in my case. One day my uncle was allowed to
come and see me. And somehow, suddenly, at sight of him, the
blank was filled in. I remembered, in a flash, everything. I was
quite calm, though. Or I made myself seem so, for I wanted to
know how the collision had happened. My uncle told me that the
engine-driver had failed to see a signal because of the fog, and
our train had crashed into a goods-train. I didn't ask him about
the people who were with me. You see, there was no need to ask.
Very gently my uncle began to tell me, but—I had begun to talk
strangely, I suppose. I remember the frightened look of my uncle's
face, and the nurse scolding him in whispers.

"After that, all a blur. It seems that I became very ill indeed,
wasn't expected to live. However, I live."

There was a long silence. Laider did not look at me, nor I at him.
The fire was burning low, and he watched it.

At length he spoke. "You despise me. Naturally. I despise myself."

"No, I don't despise you; but——"

"You blame me." I did not meet his gaze. "You blame me,"
he repeated.

"Yes."

"And there, if I may say so, you are a little unjust. It isn't my
fault that I was born weak."

"But a man may conquer weakness."

"Yes, if he is endowed with the strength for that."

His fatalism drew from me a gesture of disgust. "Do you really mean," I asked, "that because you didn't pull that cord, you *couldn't* have pulled it?"

"Yes."

"And it's written in your hands that you couldn't?"

He looked at the palms of his hands. "They are the hands of a very weak man," he said.

"A man so weak that he cannot believe in the possibility of free will for himself or for any one?"

"They are the hands of an intelligent man, who can weigh evidence and see things as they are."

"But answer me: Was it fore-ordained that you should not pull that cord?"

"It was fore-ordained."

"And was it actually marked in your hands that you were not going to pull it?"

"Ah, well, you see, it is rather the things one *is* going to do that are actually marked. The things one *isn't* going to do,—the innumerable negative things,—how could one expect *them* to be marked?"

"But the consequences of what one leaves undone may be positive?"

"Horribly positive," he winced. "My hand is the hand of a man who has suffered a great deal in later life."

"And was it the hand of a man *destined* to suffer?"

"Oh, yes. I thought I told you that."

There was a pause.

"Well," I said, with awkward sympathy, "I suppose all hands are the hands of people destined to suffer."

"Not of people destined to suffer so much as *I* have suffered— as I still suffer."

The insistence of his self-pity chilled me, and I harked back to a question he had not straightly answered. "Tell me: Was it marked in your hands that you were not going to pull that cord?"

Again he looked at his hands, and then, having pressed them for a moment to his face, "It was marked very clearly," he answered, "in *their* hands."

Two or three days after this colloquy there had occurred to me in London an idea—an ingenious and comfortable doubt.

How was Laider to be sure that his brain, recovering from concussion, had *remembered* what happened in the course of that railway-journey? How was he to know that his brain hadn't simply, in its abeyance, *invented* all this for him? It might be that he had never seen those signs in those hands. Assuredly, here was a bright loop-hole. I had forthwith written to Laider, pointing it out.

This was the letter which now, at my second visit, I had found miserably pent on the letter-board. I remembered my promise to rescue it. I arose from the retaining fireside, stretched my arms, yawned, and went forth to fulfil my Christian purpose. There was no one in the hall. The "shower" had at length ceased. The sun had positively come out, and the front door had been thrown open in its honour. Everything along the sea-front was beautifully gleaming, drying, shimmering. But I was not to be diverted from my errand. I went to the letter-board. And—my letter was not there! Resourceful and plucky little thing—it had escaped! I did hope it would not be captured and brought back. Perhaps the alarm had already been raised by the tolling of that great bell which warns the inhabitants for miles around that a letter has broken loose from the letter-board. I had a vision of my envelope skimming wildly along the coastline, pursued by the old but active waiter and a breathless pack of local worthies. I saw it out-distancing them all, dodging past coast-guards, doubling on its tracks, leaping breakwaters, unluckily injuring itself, losing speed, and at last, in a splendour of desperation, taking to the open sea. But suddenly I had another idea. Perhaps Laider had returned?

He had. I espied afar on the sands a form that was recognisably, by the listless droop of it, his. I was glad and sorry—rather glad, because he completed the scene of last year; and very sorry, because this time we should be at each other's mercy: no restful silence and liberty, for either of us, this time. Perhaps he had been told I was here, and had gone out to avoid me while he yet could. Oh weak, weak! Why palter? I put on my hat and coat, and marched out to meet him.

"Influenza, of course?" we asked simultaneously.

There is a limit to the time which one man may spend in talking to another about his own influenza; and presently, as we paced the sands, I felt that Laider had passed this limit. I wondered that he didn't break off and thank me now for my letter.

He must have read it. He ought to have thanked me for it at once. It was a very good letter, a remarkable letter. But surely he wasn't waiting to answer it by post? His silence about it gave me the absurd sense of having taken a liberty, confound him! He was evidently ill at ease while he talked. But it wasn't for me to help him out of his difficulty, whatever that might be. It was for him to remove the strain imposed on myself.

Abruptly, after a long pause, he did now manage to say, "It was—very good of you to—to write me that letter." He told me he had only just got it, and he drifted away into otiose explanations of this fact. I thought he might at least say it was a remarkable letter; and you can imagine my annoyance when he said, after another interval, "I was very much touched indeed." I had wished to be convincing, not touching. I can't bear to be called touching.

"Don't you," I asked, "think it *is* quite possible that your brain invented all those memories of what—what happened before that accident?"

He drew a sharp sigh. "You make me feel very guilty."

"That's exactly what I tried to make you *not* feel!"

"I know, yes. That's why I feel so guilty."

We had paused in our walk. He stood nervously prodding the hard wet sand with his walking-stick. "In a way," he said, "your theory was quite right. But—it didn't go far enough. It's not only possible, it's a fact, that I didn't see those signs in those hands. I never examined those hands. They weren't there. *I* wasn't there. I haven't an uncle in Hampshire, even. I never had."

I, too, prodded the sand. "Well," I said at length, "I do feel rather a fool."

"I've no right even to beg your pardon, but——"

"Oh, I'm not vexed. Only—I rather wish you hadn't told me this."

"I wish I hadn't had to. It was your kindness, you see, that forced me. By trying to take an imaginary load off my conscience, you laid a very real one on it."

"I'm sorry. But you, of your own free will, you know, exposed your conscience to me last year. I don't yet quite understand why you did that."

"No, of course not. I don't deserve that you should. But I think you will. May I explain? I'm afraid I've talked a great deal already about my influenza, and I shan't be able to keep it out of my explanation. Well, my weakest point—I told you this last year, but it happens to be perfectly true that my weakest point—is my will. Influenza, as you know, fastens unerringly on one's weakest point. It doesn't attempt to undermine my imagination. That would be a forlorn hope. I have, alas! a very strong imagination. At ordinary times my imagination allows itself to be governed by my will. My will keeps it in check by constant nagging. But when my will isn't strong enough even to nag, then my imagination stampedes. I become even as a little child. I tell myself the most preposterous fables, and—the trouble is—I can't help telling them to my friends. Until I've thoroughly shaken off influenza, I'm not fit company for any one. I perfectly realise this, and I have the good sense to go right away till I'm quite well again. I come here usually. It seems absurd, but I must confess I was sorry last year when we fell into conversation. I knew I should very soon be letting myself go, or rather, very soon be swept away. Perhaps I ought to have warned you; but—I'm a rather shy man. And then you mentioned the subject of palmistry. You said you believed in it. I wondered at that. I had once read Desbarolles' book about it, but I am bound to say I thought the whole thing very great nonsense indeed."

"Then," I gasped, "it isn't even true that you believe in palmistry?"

"Oh, no. But I wasn't able to tell you that. You had begun by saying that you believed in palmistry, and then you proceeded to scoff at it. While you scoffed I saw myself as a man with a terribly good reason for *not* scoffing; and in a flash I saw the terribly good reason; I had the whole story—at least I had the broad outlines of it—clear before me."

"You hadn't ever thought of it before?" He shook his head. My eyes beamed. "The whole thing was a sheer improvisation?"

"Yes," said Laider, humbly, "I am as bad as all that. I don't say that all the details of the story I told you that evening were filled in at the very instant of its conception. I was filling them in while we talked about palmistry in general, and while I was waiting for the moment when the story would come in most effectively. And I've no doubt I added some extra touches in the course of the actual telling. Don't imagine that I took the slightest pleasure in deceiving you. It's only my will, not my conscience, that is weakened after influenza. I simply can't help telling what I've made up, and telling it to the best of my ability. But I'm thoroughly ashamed all the time."

"Not of your ability, surely?"

"Yes, of that, too," he said with his sad smile. "I always feel that I'm not doing justice to my idea."

"You are too stern a critic, believe me."

"It is very kind of you to say that. You are very kind altogether. Had I known that you were so essentially a man of the world — in the best sense of that term — I shouldn't have so much dreaded seeing you just now and having to confess to you. But I'm not going to take advantage of your urbanity and your easy-going ways. I hope that some day we may meet somewhere when I haven't had influenza and am a not wholly undesirable acquaintance. As it is, I refuse to let you associate with me. I am an older man than you, and so I may without impertinence warn you against having anything to do with me."

I deprecated this advice, of course; but, for a man of weakened will, he showed great firmness. "You," he said, "in your heart of hearts don't want to have to walk and talk continually with a person who might at any moment try to bamboozle you with some ridiculous tale. And I, for my part, don't want to degrade myself by trying to bamboozle any one — especially one whom I have taught to see through me. Let the two talks we have had be as though they had not been. Let us bow to each other, as last year, but let that be all. Let us follow in all things the precedent of last year."

With a smile that was almost gay he turned on his heel, and moved away with a step that was almost brisk. I was a little disconcerted. But I was also more than a little glad. The restfulness of silence, the charm of liberty — these things were not, after all, forfeit. My heart thanked Laider for that; and throughout the week I loyally seconded him in the system he had laid down for us. All was as it had been last year. We did not smile to each other, we merely bowed, when we entered or left the dining-room or smoking-room, and when we met on the widespread sands or in that shop which had a small and faded, but circulating, library.

Once or twice in the course of the week it did occur to me that perhaps Laider had told the simple truth at our first interview and an ingenious lie at our second. I frowned at this possibility. The idea of any one wishing to be quit of *me* was most distasteful. However, I was to find reassurance. On the last evening of my stay, I suggested, in the small smoking-room, that he and I should, as sticklers for precedent, converse. We did so, very pleasantly. And after a while I happened to say that I had seen this afternoon a great number of sea-gulls flying close to the shore.

"Sea-gulls?" said Laider, turning in his chair.

"Yes. And I don't think I had ever realised how extraordinarily beautiful they are when their wings catch the light."

"Beautiful?" Laider threw a quick glance at me and away from me. "You think them beautiful?"

"Surely."

"Well, perhaps they are, yes; I suppose they are. But—I don't like seeing them. They always remind me of something—rather an awful thing—that once happened to me." . . .

It was a very awful thing indeed.

Guy Wetmore Carryl

Guy Wetmore Carryl, born in 1873 in New York City, inherited from his father, Charles Edward Carryl, the ability to contort legends, fables, and fairy tales into fantastic rhymes. His novels, short stories, and serious poetry received little attention; it was his virtuosity in light verse that brought him acclaim. Anthologists continue to rifle his perversions of the parables of Aesop *(Fables for the Frivolous),* the topsy-turvy interpretations of nursery doggerel *(Mother Goose for Grownups),* and the strange variations of household stories *(Grimm Tales Made Gay),* all of them with punning morals attached. Even those who belittle the gymnastics of most light verse succumb to the way Carryl turns the fable of the fox and the raven into a rhyme-leaping jest.

Practically all of Carryl's writing—some nine volumes—was done during his twenties. He died at thirty-one.

THE SYCOPHANTIC FOX AND THE GULLIBLE RAVEN

A raven sat upon a tree,
    And not a word he spoke, for
His beak contained a piece of Brie,
    Or, maybe, it was Roquefort.

We'll make it any kind you please —
At all events it was a cheese.

Beneath the tree's umbrageous limb
    A hungry fox sat smiling;
He saw the raven watching him,
    And spoke in words beguiling:
        "J'admire," said he, "ton beau plumage,"
        (The which was simply persiflage.)

Two things there are, no doubt you know,
    To which a fox is used:
A rooster that is bound to crow,
    A crow that's bound to roost;
        And whichsoever he espies
        He tells the most unblushing lies.

"Sweet fowl," he said, "I understand
    You're more than merely natty,
I hear you sing to beat the band
    And Adelina Patti.
        Pray render with your liquid tongue
        A bit from 'Götterdämmerung.'"

This subtle speech was aimed to please
    The crow, and it succeeded;
He thought no bird in all the trees
    Could sing as well as he did.
        In flattery completely doused,
        He gave the "Jewel Song" from "Faust."

But gravitation's law, of course,
    As Isaac Newton showed it,
Exerted on the cheese its force,
    And elsewhere soon bestowed it.
        In fact, there is no need to tell
        What happened when to earth it fell.

I blush to add that when the bird
    Took in the situation
He said one brief, emphatic word,
    Unfit for publication.

The fox was greatly startled, but
He only sighed and answered "Tut."

The Moral is: A fox is bound
To be a shameless sinner.
And also: When the cheese comes round
You know it's after dinner.
But (what is only known to few)
The fox is after dinner, too.

William Somerset Maugham

Born in 1874 in Paris, where his father was solicitor to the British Embassy, William Somerset Maugham spoke French before he learned English; many of his stories are turned with a Gallic twist. An orphan at nine, he was educated at King's School, Canterbury, studied philosophy at Heidelberg, and after six years in St. Thomas's Hospital qualified as a surgeon. Because of a bad stammer, he never practiced except briefly in the slums, an experience that prompted his first novel, the pathological *Liza of Lambeth*. The background material was extended in *Of Human Bondage*, an autobiography in the form of a novel, which many consider his finest work. Determined to be a dramatist, Maugham had to wait some time before his plays were accepted. However, after the success of *Lady Frederick* in his thirty-third year, four of his plays ran simultaneously in London.

During the First World War Maugham became a secret agent; *Ashenden*, a more-fact-than-fiction spy story, was the result. He traveled extensively; his voyages in the South Seas inspired *The Moon and Sixpence*, the saga of an English Gaugin. Settling in the south of France, he wrote the astringent *Cakes and Ale, or the Skeleton in the Cupboard*, a pseudo portrait of Thomas Hardy, which many resented as a malicious caricature.

By the time Maugham was sixty-five he had published more than fifty volumes. New collections—reprinted, dramatized for the stage and television—enlarged his audience, enhanced his reputation, and swelled his increasing fortune. With the growing demand for his work, the critics grew more and more patronizing. On his seventy-fifth birthday Maugham summed up their attitude: "In my twenties the critics said I was brutal; in my thirties they said I was flippant; in my forties they said I was cynical; in my fifties they said I was competent; and in my sixties they concluded I was superficial." By the time he was seventy-five he had written some of the most sardonic, sensational, and most often anthologized short stories of the period. Whatever his final status as an artist may be, Maugham is in the direct line of those who entertained countless crowds as an observer and recorder of the vagaries of human conduct: the traditional and ever-popular teller of tales.

He was ninety-one when he died in a hospital in Nice, France. Shortly before his death he was asked whether he would like to live his life over again. "On the whole," Maugham replied, "it has been a pretty good life, perhaps better than most people's. But I should see no point in repeating it."

THE COLONEL'S LADY

All this happened two or three years before the outbreak of the war.

The Peregrines were having breakfast. Though they were alone and the table was long they sat at opposite ends of it. From the walls George Peregrine's ancestors, painted by the fashionable painters of the day, looked down upon them. The butler brought in the morning post. There were several letters for the Colonel, business letters, the *Times* and a small parcel for his wife Evie. He looked at his letters and then, opening the *Times,* began to read it. They finished breakfast and rose from the table. He noticed that his wife hadn't opened the parcel.

"What's that?" he asked.

"Only some books."

"Shall I open it for you?"

"If you like."

He hated to cut string and so with some difficulty untied the knots.

"But they're all the same," he said when he had unwrapped the parcel. "What on earth d'you want six copies of the same book for?" He open one of them. "Poetry." Then he looked at the

title page. *When Pyramids Decay,* he read, by E. K. Hamilton.
Eva Katherine Hamilton: that was his wife's maiden name. He
looked at her with smiling surprise. "Have you written a book,
Evie? You are a slyboots."

"I didn't think it would interest you very much. Would you like
a copy?"

"Well, you know poetry isn't much in my line, but—yes, I'd like
a copy; I'll read it. I'll take it along to my study. I've got a lot to do
this morning."

He gathered up the *Times,* his letters and the book and went
out. His study was a large and comfortable room, with a big desk,
leather armchairs and what he called "trophies of the chase" on
the walls. In the bookshelves were works of reference, books on
farming, gardening, fishing and shooting, and books on the last
war, in which he had won an M.C. and a D.S.O. For before his
marriage he had been in the Welsh Guards. At the end of the war
he retired and settled down to the life of a country gentleman in
the spacious house, some twenty miles from Sheffield, which one
of his forebears had built in the reign of George II. George Peregrine had an estate of some fifteen hundred acres which he managed with ability; he was a justice of the peace and performed
his duties conscientiously. During the season he rode to hounds
two days a week. He was a good shot, a golfer and though now a
little over fifty could still play a hard game of tennis. He could
describe himself with propriety as an all-round sportsman.

He had been putting on weight lately, but was still a fine figure
of a man; tall, with gray curly hair, only just beginning to grow
thin on the crown, frank blue eyes, good features and a high
colour. He was a public-spirited man, chairman of any number
of local organizations and, as became his class and station, a
loyal member of the Conservative party. He looked upon it as his
duty to see the welfare of the people on his estate and it was a
satisfaction to him to know that Evie could be trusted to tend the
sick and succour the poor. He had built a cottage hospital on the
outskirts of the village and paid the wages of a nurse out of his
own pocket. All he asked of the recipients of his bounty was that
at elections, county or general, they should vote for his candidate.
He was a friendly man, affable to his inferiors, considerate with
his tenants and popular with the neighbouring gentry. He would
have been pleased and at the same time slightly embarrassed if
someone had told him he was a jolly good fellow. That was what
he wanted to be. He desired no higher praise.

It was hard luck that he had no children. He would have been an excellent father, kindly but strict, and would have brought up his sons as a gentleman's sons should be brought up, sent them to Eton, you know, taught them to fish, shoot and ride. As it was, his heir was a nephew, son of his brother killed in a motor accident, not a bad boy, but not a chip off the old block, no, sir, far from it; and would you believe it, his fool of a mother was sending him to a co-educational school. Evie had been a sad disappointment to him. Of course she was a lady, and she had a bit of money of her own; she managed the house uncommonly well and she was a good hostess. The village people adored her. She had been a pretty little thing when he married her, with a creamy skin, light brown hair and a trim figure, healthy too and not a bad tennis player; he couldn't understand why she'd had no children; of course she was faded now, she must be getting on for five and forty; her skin was drab, her hair had lost its sheen and she was as thin as a rail. She was always neat and suitably dressed, but she didn't seem to bother how she looked, she wore no make-up and didn't even use lipstick; sometimes at night when she dolled herself up for a party you could tell that once she'd been quite attractive, but ordinarily she was—well, the sort of woman you simply didn't notice. A nice woman, of course, a good wife, and it wasn't her fault if she was barren, but it was tough on a fellow who wanted an heir of his own loins; she hadn't any vitality, that's what was the matter with her. He supposed he'd been in love with her when he asked her to marry him, at least sufficiently in love for a man who wanted to marry and settle down, but with time he discovered that they had nothing much in common. She didn't care about hunting, and fishing bored her. Naturally they'd drifted apart. He had to do her the justice to admit that she'd never bothered him. There'd been no scenes. They had no quarrels. She seemed to take it for granted that he should go his own way. When he went up to London now and then she never wanted to come with him. He had a girl there, well, she wasn't exactly a girl, she was thirty-five if she was a day, but she was blonde and luscious and he only had to wire ahead of time and they'd dine, do a show and spend the night together. Well, a man, a healthy normal man had to have some fun in his life. The thought crossed his mind that if Evie hadn't been such a good woman she'd have been a better wife; but it was not the sort of thought that he welcomed and he put it away from him.

George Peregrine finished his *Times* and being a considerate fellow rang the bell and told the butler to take the paper to Evie.

Then he looked at his watch. It was half-past ten and at eleven he had an appointment with one of his tenants. He had half an hour to spare.

"I'd better have a look at Evie's book," he said to himself.

He took it up with a smile. Evie had a lot of highbrow books in her sitting room, not the sort of books that interested him, but if they amused her he had no objection to her reading them. He noticed that the volume he now held in his hands contained no more than ninety pages. That was all to the good. He shared Edgar Allan Poe's opinion that poems should be short. But as he turned the pages he noticed that several of Evie's had long lines of irregular length and didn't rhyme. He didn't like that. At his first school, when he was a little boy, he remembered learning a poem that began: *The boy stood on the burning deck* and later, at Eton, one that started: *Ruin seize thee, ruthless king;* and then there was Henry V; they'd had to take that one half. He stared at Evie's pages with consternation.

"That's not what I call poetry," he said.

Fortunately it wasn't all like that. Interspersed with the pieces that looked so odd, lines of three or four words and then a line of ten or fifteen, there were little poems, quite short, that rhymed, thank God, with the lines all the same length. Several of the pages were just headed with the word *Sonnet,* and out of curiosity he counted the lines; there were fourteen of them. He read them. They seemed all right, but he didn't quite know what they were all about. He repeated to himself: *Ruin seize thee, ruthless king.*

"Poor Evie," he sighed.

At that moment the farmer he was expecting was ushered into the study, and putting the book down he made him welcome. They embarked on their business.

"I read your book, Evie," he said as they sat down to lunch. "Jolly good. Did it cost you a packet to have it printed?"

"No, I was lucky. I sent it to a publisher and he took it."

"Not much money in poetry, my dear," he said in his good-natured, hearty way.

"No, I don't suppose there is. What did Bannock want to see you about this morning?"

Bannock was the tenant who had interrupted his reading of Evie's poems.

"He's asked me to advance the money for a pedigree bull he wants to buy. He's a good man and I've half a mind to do it."

George Peregrine saw that Evie didn't want to talk about her book and he was not sorry to change the subject. He was glad she had used her maiden name on the title page; he didn't suppose anyone would ever hear about the book, but he was proud of his own unusual name and he wouldn't have liked it if some damned penny-a-liner had made fun of Evie's effort in one of the papers.

During the few weeks that followed he thought it tactful not to ask Evie any questions about her venture into verse and she never referred to it. It might have been a discreditable incident that they had silently agreed not to mention. But then a strange thing happened. He had to go to London on business and he took Daphne out to dinner. That was the name of the girl with whom he was in the habit of passing a few agreeable hours whenever he went to town.

"Oh, George," she said, "is that your wife who's written a book they're all talking about?"

"What on earth d'you mean?"

"Well, there's a fellow I know who's a critic. He took me out to dinner the other night and he had a book with him. 'Got anything for me to read?' I said. 'What's that?' 'Oh, I don't think that's your cup of tea,' he said. 'It's poetry. I've just been reviewing it.' 'No poetry for me,' I said. 'It's about the hottest stuff I ever read,' he said. 'Selling like hot cakes. And it's damned good.'"

"Who's the book by?" asked George.

"A woman called Hamilton. My friend told me that wasn't her real name. He said her real name was Peregrine. 'Funny,' I said, 'I know a fellow called Peregrine.' 'Colonel in the army,' he said. 'Lives near Sheffield.'"

"I'd just as soon you didn't talk about me to your friends," said George with a frown of vexation.

"Keep your shirt on, dearie. Who'd you take me for? I just said, 'It's not the same one.'" Daphne giggled. "My friend said: 'They say he's a regular Colonel Blimp.'"

George had a keen sense of humour.

"You could tell them better than that," he laughed. "If my wife had written a book I'd be the first to know about it, wouldn't I?"

"I suppose you would."

Anyhow the matter didn't interest her and when the Colonel began to talk of other things she forgot about it. He put it out of his mind too. There was nothing to it, he decided, and that silly fool of a critic had just been pulling Daphne's leg. He was amused at the thought of her tackling that book because she had been told it was hot stuff and then finding it just a lot of stuff cut up into unequal lines.

He was a member of several clubs and next day he thought he'd lunch at one in St. James's Street. He was catching a train back to Sheffield early in the afternoon. He was sitting in a comfortable armchair having a glass of sherry before going into the dining-room when an old friend came up to him.

"Well, old boy, how's life?" he said. "How d'you like being the husband of a celebrity?"

George Peregrine looked at his friend. He thought he saw an amused twinkle in his eyes.

"I don't know what you're talking about," he answered.

"Come off it, George. Everyone knows E. K. Hamilton is your wife. Not often a book of verse has a success like that. Look here, Henry Dashwood is lunching with me. He'd like to meet you."

"Who the devil is Henry Dashwood and why should he want to meet me?"

"Oh, my dear fellow, what do you do with yourself all the time in the country? Henry's about the best critic we've got. He wrote a wonderful review of Evie's book. D'you mean to say she didn't show it you?"

Before George could answer his friend had called a man over. A tall, thin man, with a high forehead, a beard, a long nose and a stoop, just the sort of man whom George was prepared to dislike at first sight. Introductions were effected. Henry Dashwood sat down.

"Is Mrs. Peregrine in London by any chance? I should very much like to meet her," he said.

"No, my wife doesn't like London. She prefers the country," said George stiffly.

"She wrote me a very nice letter about my review. I was pleased. You know, we critics get more kicks than halfpence. I was simply bowled over by her book. It's so fresh and original, very modern without being obscure. She seems to be as much at her ease in free verse as in the classical metres." Then because he was a critic he thought he should criticize. "Sometimes her ear is a trifle at fault, but you can say the same of Emily Dickinson. There are several of those short lyrics of hers that might have been written by Landor."

All this was gibberish to George Peregrine. The man was nothing but a disgusting highbrow. But the Colonel had good manners and he answered with proper civility: Henry Dashwood went on as though he hadn't spoken.

"But what makes the book so outstanding is the passion that

throbs in every line. So many of these young poets are so anaemic, cold, bloodless, dully intellectual, but here you have real naked, earthy passion; of course deep, sincere emotion like that is tragic — ah, my dear Colonel, how right Heine was when he said that the poet makes little songs out of his great sorrows. You know, now and then, as I read and reread those heart-rending pages I thought of Sappho."

This was too much for George Peregrine and he got up.

"Well, it's jolly nice of you to say such nice things about my wife's little book. I'm sure she'll be delighted. But I must bolt, I've got to catch a train and I want to get a bit of lunch."

"Damned fool," he said irritably to himself as he walked up-stairs to the dining-room.

He got home in time for dinner and after Evie had gone to bed he went into his study and looked for her book. He thought he'd just glance through it again to see for himself what they were making such a fuss about, but he couldn't find it. Evie must have taken it away.

"Silly," he muttered.

He'd told her he thought it jolly good. What more could a fellow be expected to say? Well, it didn't matter. He lit his pipe and read the *Field* till he felt sleepy. But a week or so later it happened that he had to go into Sheffield for the day. He lunched there at his club. He had nearly finished when the Duke of Haverel came in. This was the great local magnate and of course the Colonel knew him, but only to say how d'you do to; and he was surprised when the Duke stopped at his table.

"We're so sorry your wife couldn't come to us for the week end," he said, with a sort of shy cordiality. "We're expecting rather a nice lot of people."

George was taken aback. He guessed that the Haverels had asked him and Evie over for the week end and Evie, without saying a word to him about it, had refused. He had the presence of mind to say he was sorry too.

"Better luck next time," said the Duke pleasantly and moved on.

Colonel Peregrine was very angry and when he got home he said to his wife:

"Look here, what's this about our being asked over to Haverel? Why on earth did you say we couldn't go? We've never been asked before and it's the best shooting in the county."

"I didn't think of that. I thought it would only bore you."

"Damn it all, you might at least have asked me if I wanted to go."

"I'm sorry."

He looked at her closely. There was something in her expression that he didn't quite understand. He frowned.

"I suppose *I* was asked?" he barked.

Evie flushed a little.

"Well, in point of fact you weren't."

"I call it damned rude of them to ask you without asking me."

"I suppose they thought it wasn't your sort of party. The Duchess is rather fond of writers and people like that, you know. She's having Henry Dashwood, the critic, and for some reason he wants to meet me."

"It was damned nice of you to refuse, Evie."

"It's the least I could do," she smiled. She hesitated a moment. "George, my publishers want to give a little dinner party for me one day towards the end of the month and of course they want you to come too."

"Oh, I don't think that's quite my mark. I'll come up to London with you if you like. I'll find someone to dine with."

Daphne.

"I expect it'll be very dull, but they're making rather a point of it. And the day after, the American publisher who's taken my book is giving a cocktail party at Claridge's. I'd like you to come to that if you wouldn't mind."

"Sounds like a crashing bore, but if you really want me to come I'll come."

"It would be sweet of you."

George Peregrine was dazed by the cocktail party. There were a lot of people. Some of them didn't look so bad, a few of the women were decently turned out, but the men seemed to him pretty awful. He was introduced to everybody as Colonel Peregrine, E. K. Hamilton's husband, you know. The men didn't seem to have anything to say to him, but the women gushed.

"You *must* be proud of your wife. Isn't it *wonderful?* You know, I read it right through at a sitting, I simply couldn't put it down, and when I'd finished I started again at the beginning and read it right through a second time. I was simply *thrilled.*"

The English publisher said to him:

"We've not had a success like this with a book of verse for twenty years. I've never seen such reviews."

The American publisher said to him:

"It's swell. It'll be a smash hit in America. You wait and see."

The American publisher had sent Evie a great spray of orchids. Damned ridiculous, thought George. As they came in, people were taken up to Evie and it was evident that they said flattering things to her, which she took with a pleasant smile and a word or two of thanks. She was a trifle flushed with the excitement, but seemed quite at her ease. Though he thought the whole thing a lot of stuff and nonsense George noted with approval that his wife was carrying it off in just the right way.

"Well, there's one thing," he said to himself, "you can see she's a lady and that's a damned sight more than you can say of anyone else here."

He drank a good many cocktails. But there was one thing that bothered him. He had a notion that some of the people he was introduced to looked at him in rather a funny sort of way, he couldn't quite make out what it meant, and once when he strolled by two women who were sitting together on a sofa he had the impression that they were talking about him and after he passed he was almost certain they tittered. He was very glad when the party came to an end.

In the taxi on their way back to their hotel Evie said to him: "You were wonderful, dear. You made quite a hit. The girls simply raved about you; they thought you so handsome."

"Girls," he said bitterly. "Old hags."

"Were you bored, dear?"

"Stiff."

She pressed his hand in a gesture of sympathy.

"I hope you won't mind if we wait and go down by the afternoon train. I've got some things to do in the morning."

"No, that's all right. Shopping?"

"I do want to buy one or two things, but I've got to go and be photographed. I hate the idea, but they think I ought to be. For America, you know."

He said nothing. But he thought. He thought it would be a shock to the American public when they saw the portrait of the homely, desiccated little woman who was his wife. He'd always been under the impression that they liked glamour in America.

He went on thinking and next morning when Evie had gone out he went to his club and up to the library. There he looked up recent numbers of the *Times Literary Supplement,* the *New Statesman* and the *Spectator.* Presently he found reviews of Evie's book. He didn't read them very carefully, but enough to see that they were extremely favourable. Then he went to the bookseller's in Piccadilly where he occasionally bought books. He'd made up his mind that he had to read this damned thing of Evie's properly, but he didn't want to ask her what she'd done with the copy she'd given him. He'd buy one for himself. Before going in he looked in the window and the first thing he saw was a display of *When Pyramids Decay*. Damned silly title! He went in. A young man came forward and asked if he could help him.

"No, I'm just having a look round." It embarrassed him to ask for Evie's book and he thought he'd find it for himself and then take it to the salesman. But he couldn't see it anywhere and at last, finding the young man near him, he said in a carefully casual tone: "By the way, have you got a book called *When Pyramids Decay?*"

"The new edition came in this morning. I'll get a copy."

In a moment the young man returned with it. He was a short, rather stout young man, with a shock of untidy carroty hair and spectacles. George Peregrine, tall, upstanding, very military, towered over him.

"Is this a new edition then?" he asked.

"Yes, sir. The fifth. It might be a novel the way it's selling."

George Peregrine hesitated a moment.

"Why d'you suppose it's such a success? I've always been told no one reads poetry."

"Well, it's good, you know. I've read it meself." The young man, though obviously cultured, had a slight Cockney accent, and George quite instinctively adopted a patronizing attitude. "It's the story they like. Sexy, you know, but tragic."

George frowned a little. He was coming to the conclusion that the young man was rather impertinent. No one had told him anything about there being a story in the damned book and he had not gathered that from reading the reviews. The young man went on.

"Of course it's only a flash in the pan, if you know what I mean. The way I look at it, she was sort of inspired like by a personal experience, like Housman was with *The Shropshire Lad.* She'll never write anything else."

"How much is the book?" said George coldly to stop his chatter. "You needn't wrap it up, I'll just slip it in my pocket."

The November morning was raw and he was wearing a great-coat.

At the station he bought the evening papers and magazines

and he and Evie settled themselves comfortably in opposite
corners of a first-class carriage and read. At five o'clock they went
along to the restaurant car to have tea and chatted a little. They
arrived. They drove home in the car which was waiting for them.
They bathed, dressed for dinner, and after dinner Evie, saying she
was tired out, went to bed. She kissed him, as was her habit, on
the forehead. Then he went into the hall, took Evie's book out of
his greatcoat pocket and going into the study began to read it.
He didn't read verse very easily and though he read with attention,
every word of it, the impression he received was far from clear.
Then he began at the beginning again and read it a second time.
He read with increasing malaise, but he was not a stupid man
and when he had finished he had a distinct understanding of what
it was all about. Part of the book was in free verse, part in conventional metres, but the story it related was coherent and plain
to the meanest intelligence. It was the story of a passionate love
affair between an older woman, married, and a young man. George
Peregrine made out the steps of it as easily as if he had been doing
a sum in simple addition.

Written in the first person, it began with the tremulous surprise of the woman, past her youth, when it dawned upon her
that the young man was in love with her. She hesitated to believe
it. She thought she must be deceiving herself. And she was terrified when on a sudden she discovered that she was passionately
in love with him. She told herself it was absurd; with the disparity
of age between them nothing but unhappiness could come to her
if she yielded to her emotion. She tried to prevent him from speaking, but the day came when he told her that he loved her and
forced her to tell him that she loved him too. He begged her to run
away with him. She couldn't leave her husband, her home; and
what life could they look forward to, she an ageing woman, he
so young? How could she expect his love to last? She begged him
to have mercy on her. But his love was impetuous. He wanted her,
he wanted her with all his heart, and at last trembling, afraid,
desirous, she yielded to him. Then there was a period of ecstatic
happiness. The world, the dull, humdrum world of every day,
blazed with glory. Love songs flowed from her pen. The woman
worshipped the young, virile body of her lover. George flushed
darkly when she praised his broad chest and slim flanks, the
beauty of his legs and the flatness of his belly.

Hot stuff, Daphne's friend had said. It was that all right. Disgusting.

There were sad little pieces in which she lamented the emptiness of her life when as must happen he left her, but they ended with a cry that all she had to suffer would be worth it for the bliss that for a while had been hers. She wrote of the long, tremulous nights they passed together and the languor that lulled them to sleep in one another's arms. She wrote of the rapture of brief stolen moments when, braving all danger, their passion overwhelmed them and they surrendered to its call.

She thought it would be an affair of a few weeks, but miraculously it lasted. One of the poems referred to three years having gone by without lessening the love that filled their hearts. It looked as though he continued to press her to go away with him, far away, to a hill town in Italy, a Greek island, a walled city in Tunisia, so that they could be together always, for in another of the poems she besought him to let things be as they were. Their happiness was precarious. Perhaps it was owing to the difficulties they had to encounter and the rarity of their meetings that their love had retained for so long its first enchanting ardour. Then on a sudden the young man died. How, when or where, George could not discover. There followed a long, heartbroken cry of bitter grief, grief she could not indulge in, grief that had to be hidden. She had to be cheerful, give dinner parties and go out to dinner, behave as she had always behaved, though the light had gone out of her life and she was bowed down with anguish. The last poem of all was a set of four short stanzas in which the writer, sadly resigned to her loss, thanked the dark powers that rule man's destiny that she had been privileged at least for a while to enjoy the greatest happiness that we poor human beings can ever hope to know.

It was three o'clock in the morning when George Peregrine finally put the book down. It had seemed to him that he heard Evie's voice in every line, over and over again he came upon turns of phrase he had heard her use, there were details that were as familiar to him as to her: there was no doubt about it; it was her own story she had told, and it was as plain as anything could be that she had had a lover and her lover had died. It was not anger so much that he felt, nor horror or dismay, though he was dismayed and he was horrified, but amazement. It was as inconceivable that Evie should have had a love affair, and a wildly passionate one at that, as that the trout in a glass case over the chimney piece in his study, the finest he had ever caught, should suddenly wag its tail. He understood now the meaning of the amused look he had seen in the eyes of that man he had spoken with at the club, he understood why Daphne when she was talking about the book had seemed to be enjoying a private joke, and why those two women at the cocktail party had tittered when he strolled past them.

He broke out into a sweat. Then on a sudden he was seized with fury and he jumped up to go and awake Evie and ask her sternly for an explanation. But he stopped at the door. After all what proof had he? A book. He remembered that he'd told Evie he thought it jolly good. True, he hadn't read it, but he'd pretended he had. He would look a perfect fool if he had to admit that.

"I must watch my step," he muttered.

He made up his mind to wait for two or three days and think it all over. Then he'd decide what to do. He went to bed, but he couldn't sleep for a long time.

"Evie," he kept on saying to himself. "Evie, of all people."

They met at breakfast next morning as usual. Evie was as she always was, quiet, demure and self-possessed, a middle-aged woman, who made no effort to look younger than she was, a woman who had nothing of what he still called It. He looked at her as he hadn't looked at her for years. She had her usual placid serenity. Her pale blue eyes were untroubled. There was no sign of guilt on her candid brow. She made the same little casual remarks she always made.

"It's nice to get back to the country again after those two hectic days in London. What are you going to do this morning?"

It was incomprehensible.

Three days later he went to see his solicitor. Henry Blane was an old friend of George's as well as his lawyer. He had a place not far from Peregrine's and for years they had shot over one another's preserves. For two days a week he was a country gentleman and for the other five a busy lawyer in Sheffield. He was a tall, robust fellow, with a boisterous manner and a jovial laugh, which suggested that he liked to be looked upon essentially as a sportsman and a good fellow and only incidentally as a lawyer. But he was shrewd and worldly-wise.

"Well, George, what's brought you here today?" he boomed as the Colonel was shown into his office. "Have a good time in London? I'm taking my missus up for a few days next week. How's Evie?"

"It's about Evie I've come to see you," said Peregrine, giving him a suspicious look. "Have you read her book?"

His sensitivity had been sharpened during those last days of troubled thought and he was conscious of a faint change in the lawyer's expression. It was as though he were suddenly on his guard.

"Yes, I've read it. Great success, isn't it? Fancy Evie breaking out into poetry. Wonders will never cease."

George Peregrine was inclined to lose his temper.

"It's made me look a perfect damned fool."

"Oh, what nonsense, George! There's no harm in Evie's writing a book. You ought to be jolly proud of her."

"Don't talk such rot. It's her own story. You know it and everyone else knows it. I suppose I'm the only one who doesn't know who her lover was."

"There is such a thing as imagination, old boy. There's no reason to suppose the whole thing isn't just made up."

"Look here, Henry, we've known one another all our lives. We've had all sorts of good times together. Be honest with me. Can you look me in the face and tell me you believe it's a made-up story?"

Henry Blane moved uneasily in his chair. He was disturbed by the distress in old George's voice.

"You've got no right to ask me a question like that. Ask Evie."

"I daren't," George answered after an anguished pause. "I'm afraid she'd tell me the truth."

There was an uncomfortable silence.

"Who was the chap?"

Henry Blane looked at him straight in the eye.

"I don't know, and if I did I wouldn't tell you."

"You swine. Don't you see what a position I'm in? Do you think it's very pleasant to be made absolutely ridiculous?"

The lawyer lit a cigarette and for some moments silently puffed it.

"I don't see what I can do for you," he said at last.

"You've got private detectives you employ, I suppose. I want you to put them on the job and let them find everything out."

"It's not very pretty to put detectives on one's wife, old boy; and besides, taking for granted for a moment that Evie had an affair, it was a good many years ago and I don't suppose it would be possible to find out a thing. They seem to have covered their tracks pretty carefully."

"I don't care. You put the detectives on. I want to know the truth."

"I won't, George. If you're determined to do that you'd better consult someone else. And look here, even if you got evidence that Evie had been unfaithful to you what would you do with it? You'd look rather silly divorcing your wife because she'd committed adultery ten years ago."

"At all events I could have it out with her."

"You can do that now, but you know just as well as I do, that if you do she'll leave you. D'you want her to do that?"

George gave him an unhappy look.

"I don't know. I always thought she'd been a damned good wife to me. She runs the house perfectly, we never have any servant trouble; she's done wonders with the garden and she's splendid with all the village people. But damn it, I have my self-respect to think of. How can I go on living with her when I know that she was grossly unfaithful to me?"

"Have you always been faithful to her?"

"More or less, you know. After all we've been married for nearly twenty-four years and Evie was never much for bed."

The solicitor slightly raised his eyebrows, but George was too intent on what he was saying to notice.

"I don't deny that I've had a bit of fun now and then. A man wants it. Women are different."

"We only have men's word for that," said Henry Blane, with a faint smile.

"Evie's absolutely the last woman I'd have suspected of kicking over the traces. I mean, she's a very fastidious, reticent woman. What on earth made her write the damned book?"

"I suppose it was a very poignant experience and perhaps it was a relief to her to get it off her chest like that."

"Well, if she had to write it why the devil didn't she write it under an assumed name?"

"She used her maiden name. I suppose she thought that was enough and it would have been if the book hadn't had this amazing boom."

George Peregrine and the lawyer were sitting opposite one another with a desk between them. George, his elbow on the desk, his cheek resting on his hand, frowned at his thought.

"It's so rotten not to know what sort of a chap he was. One can't even tell if he was by way of being a gentleman. I mean, for all I know he may have been a farmhand or a clerk in a lawyer's office."

Henry Blane did not permit himself to smile and when he answered there was in his eyes a kindly, tolerant look.

"Knowing Evie so well I think the probabilities are that he was all right. Anyhow I'm sure he wasn't a clerk in my office."

"It's been such a shock to me," the Colonel sighed. "I thought she was fond of me. She couldn't have written that book unless she hated me."

"Oh, I don't believe that. I don't think she's capable of hatred."

"You're not going to pretend that she loves me."

"No."

"Well, what does she feel for me?"

Henry Blane leaned back in his swivel chair and looked at George reflectively.

"Indifference, I should say."

The Colonel gave a little shudder and reddened.

"After all, you're not in love with her, are you?"

George Peregrine did not answer directly.

"It's been a great blow to me not to have any children, but I've never let her see that I think she's let me down. I've always been kind to her. Within reasonable limits I've tried to do my duty by her."

The lawyer passed a large hand over his mouth to conceal the smile that trembled on his lips.

"It's been such an awful shock to me," Peregrine went on. "Damn it all, even ten years ago Evie was no chicken and God knows, she wasn't much to look at. It's so ugly." He sighed deeply. "What would you do in my place?"

"Nothing."

George Peregrine drew himself bolt upright in his chair and he looked at Henry with the stern set face that he must have worn when he inspected his regiment.

"I can't overlook a think like this. I've been made a laughing-stock. I can never hold up my head again."

"Nonsense," said the lawyer sharply, and then in a pleasant, kindly manner: "Listen, old boy: the man's dead; it all happened a long while back. Forget it. Talk to people about Evie's book; rave about it, tell 'em how proud you are of her. Behave as though you had so much confidence in her, you *knew* she could never have been unfaithful to you. The world moves so quickly and people's memories are so short. They'll forget."

"I shan't forget."

"You're both middle-aged people. She probably does a great deal more for you than you think and you'd be awfully lonely without her. I don't think it matters if you don't forget. It'll be all to the good if you can get it into that thick head of yours that there's a lot more in Evie than you ever had the gumption to see."

"Damn it all, you talk as if *I* was to blame."

"No, I don't think you were to blame, but I'm not so sure that Evie was either. I don't suppose she wanted to fall in love with this boy. D'you remember those verses right at the end? The impression they gave me was that though she was shattered by his death, in a strange sort of way she welcomed it. All through she'd been aware of the fragility of the tie that bound them. He died in the full flush of his first love and had never known that love so seldom endures; he'd only known its bliss and beauty. In her own bitter grief she found solace in the thought that he'd been spared all sorrow."

"All that's a bit above my head, old boy. I see more or less what you mean."

George Peregrine stared unhappily at the inkstand on the desk. He was silent and the lawyer looked at him with curious, yet sympathetic eyes.

"Do you realize what courage she must have had never by a sign to show how dreadfully unhappy she was?" he said gently.

Colonel Peregrine sighed.

"I'm broken. I suppose you're right; it's no good crying over spilt milk and it would only make things worse if I made a fuss."

"Well?"

George Peregrine gave a pitiful little smile.

"I'll take your advice. I'll do nothing. Let them think me a damned fool and to hell with them. The truth is, I don't know what I'd do without Evie. But I'll tell you what, there's one thing I shall never understand till my dying day: What in the name of heaven did the fellow ever see in her?"

P. G. Wodehouse

Pelham (pronounced "Plum") Grenville Wodehouse, whose full name sounds like that of one of his more eccentric characters, was born in Guildford, England, in 1881. Educated at Dulwich College, he gave no indication in his early writings of the humorist he was to become. On the contrary, be began by writing serious articles and stories for boys. His first book, *The Pothunters*, appeared when Wodehouse was not quite twenty-one; after that time he kept on publishing an average of a book a year. He wrote random pieces under such pseudonyms as "P. Brookhaven," "C. P. West," and "Pelham Grenville," as well as scenarios for motion pictures, plays, and parts of musical comedies—the lyric for "Bill" from *Show Boat* was one of his more popular songs.

At twenty-eight Wodehouse went to New York for a three-week vacation. He had been making five pounds a week as an assistant editor, selling an occasional story for ten pounds. While in New York he sent a short story to *Cosmopolitan* and another to *Collier's*. Both were accepted. *Cosmopolitan* offered him $200 and *Collier's* $300. Wodehouse decided to stay. He sold a serial for $3,500 and collaborated with the playwright Guy Bolton and the composer Jerome Kern. Sixty books and forty-fours years later he became an American citizen. His prankish energy never waned; nearing ninety and the author of some eighty-six volumes, he wrote *No Nudes Is Good Nudes*.

Wodehouse surprises not by any novelty in plot or personages but by the continuing high spirits of his performance. His stories deal with practically the same cast of characters: idle young nincompoops floundering between insolvency and matrimony, who are attended by perfect valets and surrounded by formidable aunts and slightly mad uncles. Like many of his countless extravaganzas, "Strychnine in the Soup" is a tongue-in-cheek love story that is also an outrageous "tour de farce."

STRYCHNINE IN THE SOUP

From the moment the Draught Stout entered the bar parlor of the Angler's Rest, it had been obvious that he was not his usual cheery self. His face was drawn and twisted, and he sat with bowed head in a distant corner by the window, contributing nothing to the conversation which, with Mr. Mulliner as its center, was in progress around the fire. From time to time he heaved a hollow sigh.

A sympathetic Lemonade and Angostura, putting down his glass, went across and laid a kindly hand on the sufferer's shoulder.

"What is it, old man?" he asked. "Lost a friend?"

"Worse," said the Draught Stout. "A mystery novel. Got halfway through it on the journey down here, and left it in the train."

"My nephew Cyril, the interior decorator," said Mr. Mulliner, "once did the very same thing. These mental lapses are not infrequent."

"And now," proceeded the Draught Stout, "I'm going to have a sleepless night, wondering who poisoned Sir Geoffrey Tuttle, Bart."

"The bart. was poisoned, was he?"

"You never said a truer word. Personally, I think it was the vicar who did him in. He was known to be interested in strange poisons."

Mr. Mulliner smiled indulgently.

"It was not the vicar," he said. "I happen to have read *The Murglow Manor Mystery*. The guilty man was the plumber."

"What plumber?"

"The one who comes in Chapter Two to mend the shower bath. Sir Geoffrey had wronged his aunt in the year '96, so he fastened a snake in the nozzle of the shower bath with glue, and when Sir

Geoffrey turned on the stream the hot water melted the glue. This released the snake, which dropped through one of the holes, bit the baronet in the leg, and disappeared down the waste pipe."

"But that can't be right," said the Draught Stout. "Between Chapter Two and the murder there was an interval of several days."

"The plumber forgot his snake and had to go back for it," explained Mr. Mulliner. "I trust that this revelation will prove sedative."

"I feel a new man," said the Draught Stout. "I'd have lain awake worrying about that murder all night."

"I suppose you would. My nephew Cyril was just the same. Nothing in this modern life of ours," said Mr. Mulliner, taking a sip of his hot Scotch and lemon, "is more remarkable than the way in which the mystery novel has gripped the public. Your true enthusiast, deprived of his favorite reading, will stop at nothing in order to get it. He is like a victim of the drug habit when withheld from cocaine. My nephew Cyri—"

"Amazing the things people will leave in trains," said a Small Lager. "Bags . . . umbrellas . . . even stuffed chimpanzees, occasionally, I've been told. I heard a story the other day. . . ."

My nephew Cyril (said Mr. Mulliner) had a greater passion for mystery stories than anyone I have ever met. I attribute this to the fact that, like so many interior decorators, he was a fragile, delicate young fellow, extraordinarily vulnerable to any ailment that happened to be going the rounds. Every time he caught mumps or influenza or German measles or the like, he occupied the period of convalescence in reading mystery stories. And, as the appetite grows by what it feeds on, he had become, at the time at which this narrative opens, a confirmed addict. Not only did he devour every volume of this type on which he could lay his hands, but he was also to be found at any theater which was offering the kind of drama where skinny arms come unexpectedly out of the chiffonier and the audience feels a mild surprise if the lights stay on for ten consecutive minutes.

And it was during a performance of *The Gray Vampire* at the St. James's that he found himself sitting next to Amelia Bassett, the girl whom he was to love with all the stored-up fervor of a man who hitherto had been inclined rather to edge away when in the presence of the other sex.

He did not know her name was Amelia Bassett. He had never seen her before. All he knew was that at last he had met his fate, and for the whole of the first act he was pondering the problem of how he was to make her acquaintance.

It was as the lights went up for the first intermission that he was aroused from his thoughts by a sharp pain in the right leg. He was just wondering whether it was gout or sciatica when, glancing down, he perceived that what had happened was that his neighbor, absorbed by the drama, had absent-mindedly collected a handful of his flesh and was twisting it in an ecstasy of excitement.

It seemed to Cyril a good *point d'appui.*

"Excuse me," he said.

The girl turned. Her eyes were glowing, and the tip of her nose still quivered.

"I beg your pardon?"

"My leg," said Cyril. "Might I have it back, if you've finished with it?"

The girl looked down. She started visibly.

"I'm awfully sorry," she gasped.

"Not at all," said Cyril. "Only too glad to have been of assistance."

"I got carried away."

"You are evidently fond of mystery plays."

"I love them."

"So do I. And mystery novels?"

"Oh, yes!"

"Have you read *Blood on the Banisters?*"

"Oh, *yes!* I thought it was better than *Severed Throats!*"

"So did I," said Cyril. "Much better. Brighter murders, subtler detectives, crisper clues . . . better in every way."

The two twin souls gazed into each other's eyes. There is no surer foundation for a beautiful friendship than a mutual taste in literature.

"My name is Amelia Bassett," said the girl.

"Mine is Cyril Mulliner. Bassett?" He frowned thoughtfully. "The name seems familiar."

"Perhaps you have heard of my mother. Lady Bassett. She's rather a well-known big-game hunter and explorer. She tramps through jungles and things. She's gone out to the lobby for a smoke. By the way"—she hesitated—"if she finds us talking, will you remember that we met at the Polterwoods'?"

"I quite understand."

"You see, Mother doesn't like people who talk to me without a formal introduction. And when Mother doesn't like anyone, she is so apt to hit them over the head with some hard instrument."

"I see," said Cyril. "Like the Human Ape in *Gore by the Gallon.*"

"Exactly. Tell me." said the girl, changing the subject, "if you were a millionaire, would you rather be stabbed in the back with a paper knife or found dead without a mark on you, staring with blank eyes at some appalling sight?"

Cyril was about to reply when, looking past her, he found himself virtually in the latter position. A woman of extraordinary formidableness had lowered herself into the seat beyond and was scrutinizing him keenly through a tortoise-shell lorgnette. She reminded Cyril of Wallace Beery.

"Friend of yours, Amelia?" she said.

"This is Mr. Mulliner, Mother. We met at the Polterwoods'."

"Ah?" said Lady Bassett.

She inspected Cyril through her lorgnette.

"Mr. Mulliner," she said, "is a little like the chief of the Lower Isisi—though, of course, he was darker and had a ring through his nose. A dear, good fellow," she continued reminiscently, "but inclined to become familiar under the influence of trade gin. I shot him in the leg."

"Er—why?" asked Cyril.

"He was not behaving like a gentleman," said Lady Bassett primly.

"After taking your treatment," said Cyril, awed, "I'll bet he could have written a Book of Etiquette."

"I believe he did," said Lady Bassett carelessly. "You must come and call on us some afternoon, Mr. Mulliner. I am in the telephone book. If you are interested in man-eating pumas, I can show you some nice heads."

The curtain rose on Act Two, and Cyril returned to his thoughts. Love, he felt joyously, had come into his life at last. But then so, he had to admit, had Lady Bassett. There is, he reflected, always something.

I will pass lightly over the period of Cyril's wooing. Suffice it to say that his progress was rapid. From the moment he told Amelia that he had once met Dorothy Sayers, he never looked back. And one afternoon, calling and finding that Lady Bassett was away in the country, he took the girl's hand in his and told his love.

For a while all was well. Amelia's reactions proved satisfactory to a degree. She checked up enthusiastically on his proposition. Falling into his arms, she admitted specifically that he was her Dream Man.

Then came the jarring note.

"But it's no use," she said, her lovely eyes filling with tears. "Mother will never give her consent."

"Why not?" said Cyril, stunned. "What is it she objects to about me?"

"I don't know. But she generally alludes to you as 'that pipsqueak.'"

"Pipsqueak?" said Cyril. "What *is* a pipsqueak?"

"I'm not quite sure, but it's something Mother doesn't like very much. It's a pity she ever found out that you are an interior decorator."

"An honorable profession," said Cyril, a little stiffly.

"I know; but what she admires are men who have to do with the great open spaces."

"Well, I also design ornamental gardens."

"Yes," said the girl doubtfully, "but still—"

"And, dash it," said Cyril indignantly, "this isn't the Victorian age. All that business of Mother's Consent went out twenty years ago."

"Yes, but no one told Mother."

"It's preposterous!" cried Cyril. "I never heard such rot. Let's just slip off and get married quietly and send her a picture postcard from Venice or somewhere, with a cross and a 'This is our room. Wish you were with us' on it."

The girl shuddered.

"She would be with us," she said. "You don't know Mother. The moment she got that picture postcard, she would come over to wherever we were and put you across her knee and spank you with a hairbrush. I don't think I could ever feel the same toward you if I saw you lying across Mother's knee, being spanked with a hairbrush. It would spoil the honeymoon."

Cyril frowned. But a man who has spent most of his life trying out a series of patent medicines is always an optimist.

"There is only one thing to be done," he said. "I shall see your mother and try to make her listen to reason. Where is she now?"

"She left this morning for a visit to the Winghams in Sussex."

"Excellent! I know the Winghams. In fact, I have a standing

invitation to go and stay with them whenever I like. I'll send them a wire and push down this evening. I will oil up to your mother sedulously and try to correct her present unfavorable impression of me. Then, choosing my moment, I will shoot her the news. It may work. It may not work. But at any rate I consider it a fair sporting venture."

"But you are so diffident, Cyril. So shrinking. So retiring and shy. How can you carry through such a task?"

"Love will nerve me."

"Enough, do you think? Remember what Mother is. Wouldn't a good, strong drink be more help?"

Cyril looked doubtful.

"My doctor has always forbidden me alcoholic stimulants. He says they increase the blood pressure."

"Well, when you meet Mother, you will need all the blood pressure you can get. I really do advise you to fuel up a little before you see her."

"Yes," agreed Cyril, nodding thoughtfully. "I think you're right. It shall be as you say. Good-bye, my angel one."

"Good-bye, Cyril, darling. You will think of me every minute while you're gone?"

"Every single minute. Well, practically every single minute. You see, I have just got Horatio Slingsby's latest book, *Strychnine in the Soup,* and I shall be dipping into that from time to time. But all the rest of the while . . . Have you read it, by the way?"

"Not yet. I had a copy, but Mother took it with her."

"Ah? Well, if I am to catch a train that will get me to Barkley for dinner, I must be going. Good-bye, sweetheart, and never forget that Gilbert Glendale in *The Missing Toe* won the girl he loved in spite of being up against two mysterious stranglers and the entire Black Mustache gang."

He kissed her fondly, and went off to pack.

Barkley Towers, the country seat of Sir Mortimer and Lady Wingham, was two hours from London by rail. Thinking of Amelia and reading the opening chapters of Horatio Slingsby's powerful story, Cyril found the journey pass rapidly. In fact, so preoccupied was he that it was only as the train started to draw out of Barkley Regis station that he realized where he was. He managed to hurl himself onto the platform just in time.

As he had taken the five-seven express, stopping only at Glue-bury Peveril, he arrived at Barkley Towers at an hour which enabled him not only to be on hand for dinner but also to take part in the life-giving distribution of cocktails which preceded the meal.

The house party, he perceived on entering the drawing room, was a small one. Besides Lady Bassett and himself, the only visitors were a nondescript couple of the name of Simpson, and a tall, bronzed, handsome man with flashing eyes who, his hostess informed him in a whispered aside, was Lester Mapledurham (pronounced Mum), the explorer and big-game hunter.

Perhaps it was the oppressive sensation of being in the same room with two explorers and big-game hunters that brought home to Cyril the need for following Amelia's advice as quickly as possible. But probably the mere sight of Lady Bassett alone would have been enough to make him break a lifelong abstinence. To her normal resemblance to Wallace Beery she appeared now to have added a distinct suggestion of Victor McLaglen, and the spectacle was sufficient to send Cyril leaping toward the cocktail tray.

After three rapid glasses he felt a better and a braver man. And so lavishly did he irrigate the ensuing dinner with hock, sherry, champagne, old brandy, and port that at the conclusion of the meal he was pleased to find that his diffidence had completely vanished. He rose from the table feeling equal to asking a dozen Lady Bassetts for their consent to marry a dozen daughters.

In fact, as he confided to the butler, prodding him genially in the ribs as he spoke, if Lady Bassett attempted to high-hat *him,* he would know what to do about it. He made no threats, he explained to the butler; he simply stated that he would know what to do about it. The butler said "Very good, sir. Thank you, sir," and the incident closed.

It had been Cyril's intention—feeling, as he did, in this singularly uplifted and dominant frame of mind—to get hold of Amelia's mother and start oiling up to her immediately after dinner. But, what with falling into a doze in the smoking room and then getting into an argument on theology with one of the underfootmen whom he met in the hall, he did not reach the drawing room until nearly half past ten. And he was annoyed, on walking in with a merry cry of "Lady Bassett! Call for Lady Bassett!" on his lips, to discover that she had retired to her room.

Had Cyril's mood been even slightly less elevated, this news might have acted as a check on his enthusiasm. So generous, however, had been Sir Mortimer's hospitality that he merely nodded eleven times, to indicate comprehension, and then, having ascertained that his quarry was roosting in the Blue Room, sped thither with a brief "Tallyho!"

Arriving at the Blue Room, he banged heartily on the door and breezed in. He found Lady Bassett propped up with pillows. She was smoking a cigar and reading a book. And that book, Cyril saw with intense surprise and resentment, was none other than Horatio Slingsby's *Strychnine in the Soup.*

The spectacle brought him to an abrupt halt.

"Well, I'm dashed!" he cried. "Well, I'm blowed! What do you mean by pinching my book?"

Lady Bassett had lowered her cigar. She now raised her eyebrows.

"What are you doing in my room, Mr. Mulliner?"

"It's a little hard," said Cyril, trembling with self-pity. "I go to enormous expense to buy detective stories, and no sooner is my back turned than people rush about the place sneaking them."

"This book belongs to my daughter Amelia."

"Good old Amelia!" said Cyril cordially. "One of the best."

"I borrowed it to read in the train. Now will you kindly tell me what you are doing in my room, Mr. Mulliner?"

Cyril smote his forehead.

"Of course. I remember now. It all comes back to me. She told me you had taken it. And, what's more, I've suddenly recollected something which clears you completely. I was hustled and bustled at the end of the journey. I sprang to my feet, hurled bags onto the platform—in a word, lost my head. And, like a chump, I went and left my copy of *Strychnine in the Soup* in the train. Well, I can only apologize."

"You can not only apologize. You can also tell me what you are doing in my room."

"What I am doing in your room?"

"Exactly."

"Ah!" said Cyril, sitting down on the bed. "You may well ask."

"I *have* asked. Three times."

Cyril closed his eyes. For some reason, his mind seemed cloudy and not at its best.

"If you are proposing to go to sleep here, Mr. Mulliner," said Lady Bassett, "tell me, and I shall know what to do about it."

The phrase touched a chord in Cyril's memory. He recollected now his reasons for being where he was. Opening his eyes, he fixed them on her.

"Lady Bassett," he said, "you are, I believe, an explorer?"

"I am."

"In the course of your explorations, you have wandered through many a jungle in many a distant land?"

"I have."

"Tell me, Lady Bassett," said Cyril keenly, "while making a pest of yourself to the denizens of those jungles, did you notice one thing? I allude to the fact that Love is everywhere—aye, even in the jungle. Love, independent of bounds and frontiers, of nationality and species, works its spell on every living thing. So that, no matter whether an individual be a Congo native, an American song writer, a jaguar, an armadillo, a bespoke tailor, or a tsetse-tsetse fly, he will infallibly seek his mate. So why shouldn't an interior decorator and designer of ornamental gardens? I put this to you, Lady Bassett."

"Mr. Mulliner," said his roommate, "you are blotto!"

Cyril waved his hand in a spacious gesture, and fell off the bed.

"Blotto I may be," he said, resuming his seat, "but, none the less, argue as you will, you can't get away from the fact that I love your daughter Amelia."

There was a tense pause.

"What did you say?" cried Lady Bassett.

"When?" said Cyril absently, for he had fallen into a daydream and, as far as the intervening blankets would permit, was playing This Little Pig Went to Market with his companion's toes.

"Did I hear you say . . . my daughter Amelia?"

"Gray-eyed girl, medium height, sort of browny red hair," said Cyril, to assist her memory. "Dash it, you *must* know Amelia. She goes everywhere. And let me tell you something, Mrs.—I've forgotten your name. We're going to be married, if I can obtain her foul mother's consent. Speaking as an old friend, what would you say the chances were?"

"Extremely slight."

"Eh?"

"Seeing that I *am* Amelia's mother. . . ."

Cyril blinked, genuinely surprised.

"Why, so you are! I didn't recognize you. Have you been there all the time?"

"I have."

Suddenly Cyril's gaze hardened. He drew himself up stiffly.
"What are you doing in my bed?" he demanded.
"This is not your bed."
"Then whose is it?"
"Mine."
Cyril shrugged his shoulders helplessly.
"Well, it all looks very funny to me," he said. "I suppose I must believe your story, but, I repeat, I consider the whole thing odd, and I propose to institute very strict inquiries. I may tell you that I happen to know the ringleaders. I wish you a very hearty good night."

It was perhaps an hour later that Cyril, who had been walking on the terrace in deep thought, repaired once more to the Blue Room in quest of information. Running over the details of the recent interview in his head, he had suddenly discovered that there was a point which had not been satisfactorily cleared up.
"I say," he said.
Lady Bassett looked up from her book, plainly annoyed.
"Have you no bedroom of your own, Mr. Mulliner?"
"Oh, yes," said Cyril. "They've bedded me out in the Moat Room. But there was something I wanted you to tell me."
"Well?"
"Did you say I might or mightn't?"
"Might or mightn't what?"
"Marry Amelia?"
"No, You may not."
"No?"
"No!"
"Oh!" said Cyril. "Well, pip-pip once more."

It was a moody Cyril Mulliner who withdrew to the Moat Room. He now realized the position of affairs. The mother of the girl he loved refused to accept him as an eligible suitor. A dickens of a situation to be in, felt Cyril, somberly unshoeing himself.
Then he brightened a little. His life, he reflected, might be wrecked, but he still had two thirds of *Strychnine in the Soup* to read.
At the moment when the train reached Barkley Regis station, Cyril had just got to the bit where Detective Inspector Mould looks through the half-open cellar door and, drawing in his breath

with a sharp hissing sound, recoils in horror. It was obviously going to be good. He was just about to proceed to the dressing table where, he presumed, the footman had placed the book on unpacking his bag, when an icy stream seemed to flow down the center of his spine and the room and its contents danced before him.

Once more he had remembered that he had left the volume in the train.

He uttered an animal cry and tottered to a chair.

The subject of bereavement is one that has often been treated powerfully by poets, who have run the whole gamut of the emotions while laying bare for us the agony of those who have lost parents, wives, children, gazelles, money, fame, dogs, cats, doves, sweethearts, horses, and even collar studs. But no poet has yet treated of the most poignant bereavement of all—that of the man halfway through a detective story who finds himself at bedtime without the book.

Cyril did not care to think of the night that lay before him. Already his brain was lashing itself from side to side like a wounded snake as it sought for some explanation of Inspector Mould's strange behavior. Horatio Slingsby was an author who could be relied on to keep faith with his public. He was not the sort of man to fob the reader off in the next chapter with the statement that what had made Inspector Mould look horrified was the fact that he had suddenly remembered that he had forgotten all about the letter his wife had given him to post. If looking through cellar doors disturbed a Slingsby detective, it was because a dismembered corpse lay there, or at least a severed hand.

A soft moan, as of something in torment, escaped Cyril. What to do? What to do? Even a makeshift substitute for *Strychnine in the Soup* was beyond his reach. He knew so well what he would find if he went to the library in search of something to read. Sir Mortimer Wingham was heavy and county-squire-ish. His wife affected strange religions. Their literature was in keeping with their tastes. In the library there would be books on Bahai-ism, volumes in old leather of the *Rural Encyclopedia, My Two Years in Sunny Ceylon,* by the Rev. Orlo Waterbury . . . but of anything that would interest Scotland Yard, of anything with a bit of blood in it and a corpse or two into which a fellow could get his teeth, not a trace.

What, then, coming right back to it, to do?

And suddenly, as if in answer to the question, came the solution. Electrified, he saw the way out.

The hour was now well advanced. By this time Lady Bassett must surely be asleep. *Strychnine in the Soup* would be lying on the table beside her bed. All he had to do was to creep in and grab it.

The more he considered the idea, the better it looked. It was not as if he did not know the way to Lady Bassett's room or the topography of it when he got there. It seemed to him as if most of his later life had been spent in Lady Bassett's room. He could find his way about it with his eyes shut.

He hesitated no longer. Donning a dressing gown, he left his room and hurried along the passage.

Pushing open the door of the Blue Room and closing it softly behind him, Cyril stood for a moment full of all those emotions which come to man revisiting some long-familiar spot. There the dear old room was, just the same as ever. How it all came back to him! The place was in darkness, but that did not deter him. He knew where the bed table was, and he made for it with stealthy steps.

In the manner in which Cyril Mulliner advanced toward the bed table there was much which would have reminded Lady Bassett, had she been an eyewitness, of the furtive prowl of the Lesser Iguanodon tracking its prey. In only one respect did Cyril and this creature of the wild differ in their technique. Iguanodons—and this applies not only to the Lesser but to the Larger Iguanodon— seldom, if ever, trip over cords on the floor and bring the lamps to which they are attached crashing to the ground like a ton of bricks.

Cyril did. Scarcely had he snatched up the book and placed it in the pocket of his dressing gown, when his foot became entangled in the trailing cord and the lamp on the table leaped nimbly into the air and, to the accompaniment of a sound not unlike that made by a hundred plates coming apart simultaneously in the hands of a hundred scullery maids, nose-dived to the floor and became a total loss.

At the same moment, Lady Bassett, who had been chasing a bat out of the window, stepped in from the balcony and switched on the lights.

To say that Cyril Mulliner was taken aback would be to understate the facts. Nothing like his recent misadventure had happened to him since his eleventh year, when, going surreptitiously to his mother's cupboard for jam, he had jerked three shelves down on his head, containing milk, butter, homemade preserves, pickles, cheese, eggs, cakes, and potted meat. His feelings on the present occasion closely paralleled that boyhood thrill.

Lady Bassett also appeared somewhat discomposed.

"You!" she said.

Cyril nodded, endeavoring the while to smile in a reassuring manner.

"Hullo!" he said.

His hostess's manner was now one of unmistakable displeasure.

"Am I not to have a moment of privacy, Mr. Mulliner?" she asked severely. "I am, I trust, a broad-minded woman, but I cannot approve of this idea of communal bedrooms."

Cyril made an effort to be conciliatory.

"I do keep coming in, don't I?" he said.

"You do," agreed Lady Bassett. "Sir Mortimer informed me, on learning that I had been given this room, that it was supposed to be haunted. Had I known that it was haunted by you, Mr. Mulliner, I should have packed up and gone to the local inn."

Cyril bowed his head. The censure, he could not but feel, was deserved.

"I admit," he said, "that my conduct has been open to criticism. In extenuation, I can but plead my great love. This is no idle social call, Lady Bassett. I looked in because I wished to take up again this matter of my marrying your daughter Amelia. You say I can't. Why can't I? Answer me that, Lady Bassett."

"I have other views for Amelia," said Lady Bassett stiffly. "When my daughter gets married it will not be to a spineless, invertebrate product of our modern hothouse civilization, but to a strong, upstanding, keen-eyed, two-fisted he-man of the open spaces. I have no wish to hurt your feelings, Mr. Mulliner," she continued, more kindly, "but you must admit that you are, when all is said and done, a pipsqueak."

"I deny it," cried Cyril warmly. "I don't even know what a pipsqueak is."

"A pipsqueak is a man who has never seen the sun rise beyond the reaches of the Lower Zambezi; who would not know what to do if faced by a charging rhinoceros. What, pray, would you do if faced by a charging rhinoceros, Mr. Mulliner?"

"I am not likely," said Cyril, "to move in the same social circles as charging rhinoceri."

"Or take another simple case, such as happens every day. Suppose you are crossing a rude bridge over a stream in Equatorial Africa. You have been thinking of a hundred trifles and are in a

reverie. From this you wake to discover that in the branches overhead a python is extending its fangs toward you. At the same time,
you observe that at one end of the bridge is a crouching puma; at
the other are two head-hunters—call them Pat and Mike—with
poisoned blowpipes to their lips. Below, half hidden in the stream,
is an alligator. What would you do in such a case, Mr. Mulliner?"

Cyril weighed the point.

"I should feel embarrassed," he had to admit. "I shouldn't know
where to look."

Lady Bassett laughed an amused, scornful little laugh.

"Precisely. Such a situation would not, however, disturb Lester
Mapledurham."

"Lester Mapledurham!"

"The man who is to marry my daughter Amelia. He asked me
for her hand shortly after dinner."

Cyril reeled. The blow, falling so suddenly and unexpectedly,
had made him feel boneless. And yet, he felt, he might have expected this. These explorers and big-game hunters stick together.

"In a situation such as I have outlined, Lester Mapledurham
would simply drop from the bridge, wait till the alligator made its
rush, insert a stout stick between its jaws, and then hit it in the
eye with a spear, being careful to avoid its lashing tail. He would
then drift downstream and land at some safer spot. This is the
type of man I wish for as a son-in-law."

Cyril left the room without a word. Not even the fact that he now
had *Strychnine in the Soup* in his possession could cheer his
mood of unrelieved blackness. Back in his room, he tossed the
book moodily onto the bed and began to pace the floor. And he had
scarcely completed two laps when the door opened.

For an instant, when he heard the click of the latch, Cyril supposed that his visitor must be Lady Bassett, who, having put
two and two together on discovering her loss, had come to demand
her property back. And he cursed the rashness which had led him
to fling it so carelessly upon the bed, in full view.

But it was not Lady Bassett. The intruder was Lester Mapledurham. Clad in a suit of pajamas which in their general color
scheme reminded Cyril of a boudoir he had recently decorated for
a society poetess, he stood with folded arms, his keen eyes fixed
menacingly on the young man.

"Give me those jewels!" said Lester Mapledurham.

Cyril was at a loss.

"Jewels?"

"Jewels!"

"What jewels?"

Lester Mapledurham tossed his head impatiently.

"I don't know what jewels. They may be the Wingham Pearls or the Bassett Diamonds or the Simpson Sapphires. I'm not sure which room it was I saw you coming out of."

Cyril began to understand.

"Oh, did you see me coming out of a room?"

"I did. I heard a crash and, when I looked out, you were hurrying along the corridor."

"I can explain everything," said Cyril. "I had just been having a chat with Lady Bassett on a personal matter. Nothing to do with diamonds."

"You're sure?" said Mapledurham.

"Oh, rather," said Cyril. "We talked about rhinoceri and pythons and her daughter Amelia and alligators and all that sort of thing, and then I came away."

Lester Mapledurham seemed only half convinced.

"H'm!" he said. "Well, if anything is missing in the morning, I shall know what to do about it." His eye fell on the bed. "Hullo!" he went on, with sudden animation. "Slingsby's latest? Well, well! I've been wanting to get hold of this. I hear it's good. The Leeds *Mercury* says: 'These gripping pages . . .'"

He turned to the door, and with a hideous pang of agony Cyril perceived that it was plainly his intention to take the book with him. It was swinging lightly from a bronzed hand about the size of a medium ham.

"Here!" he cried vehemently.

Lester Mapledurham turned.

"Well?"

"Oh, nothing," said Cyril, "Just good night."

He flung himself face downwards on the bed as the door closed, cursing himself for the craven cowardice which had kept him from snatching the book from the explorer. There had been a moment when he had almost nerved himself to the deed, but it was followed by another moment in which he had caught the other's eye. And it was as if he had found himself exchanging glances with Lady Bassett's charging rhinoceros.

And now, thanks to this pusillanimity, he was once more *Strychnine in the Soup* -less.

How long Cyril lay there, a prey to the gloomiest thoughts, he could not have said. He was aroused from his meditations by the sound of the door opening again.

Lady Bassett stood before him. It was plain that she was deeply moved. In addition to resembling Wallace Beery and Victor Mc-Laglen, she now had a distinct look of George Bancroft.

She pointed a quivering finger at Cyril.

"You hound!" she cried. "Give me that book!"

Cyril maintained his poise with a strong effort.

"What book?"

"The book you sneaked out of my room."

"Has someone sneaked a book out of your room?" Cyril struck his forehead. "Great heavens!" he cried.

"Mr. Mulliner," said Lady Bassett coldly, "more book and less gibbering!"

Cyril raised a hand.

"I know who's got your book. Lester Mapledurham!"

"Don't be absurd."

"He has, I tell you. As I was on my way to your room just now, I saw him coming out, carrying something in a furtive manner. I remember wondering a bit at the time. He's in the Clock Room. If we pop along there now, we shall just catch him red-handed."

Lady Bassett reflected.

"It is impossible," she said at length. "He is incapable of such an act. Lester Mapledurham is a man who once killed a lion with a sardine opener."

"The very worst sort," said Cyril. "Ask anyone."

"And he is engaged to my daughter." Lady Bassett paused. "Well, he won't be long, if I find that what you say is true. Come, Mr. Mulliner!"

Together the two passed down the silent passage. At the door of the Clock Room they paused. A light streamed from beneath it. Cyril pointed silently to this sinister evidence of reading in bed, and noted that his companion stiffened and said something to herself in an undertone in what appeared to be some sort of native dialect.

The next moment she had flung the door open and, with a spring like that of a crouching zebu, had leaped to the bed and wrenched the book from Lester Mapledurham's hands.

"So!" said Lady Bassett.

"So!" said Cyril, feeling that he could not do better than follow the lead of such a woman.

"Hullo!" said Lester Mapledurham, surprised. "Something the matter?"

"So it was you who stole my book!"

"Your book?" said Lester Mapledurham. "I borrowed this from Mr. Mulliner there."

"A likely story!" said Cyril. "Lady Bassett is aware that I left my copy of *Strychnine in the Soup* in the train."

"Certainly," said Lady Bassett. "It's no use talking, young man, I have caught you with the goods. And let me tell you one thing that may be of interest. If you think that, after a dastardly act like this, you are going to marry Amelia, forget it!"

"Wipe it right out of your mind," said Cyril.

"But listen—"

"I will not listen. Come, Mr. Mulliner."

She left the room, followed by Cyril. For some moments they walked in silence.

"A merciful escape," said Cyril.

"For whom?"

"For Amelia. My gosh, think of her tied to a man like that. Must be a relief to you to feel that she's going to marry a respectable interior decorator."

Lady Bassett halted. They were standing outside the Moat Room now. She looked at Cyril, her eyebrows raised.

"Are you under the impression, Mr. Mulliner," she said, "that, on the strength of what has happened, I intend to accept you as a son-in-law?"

Cyril reeled.

"Don't you?"

"Certainly not."

Something inside Cyril seemed to snap. Recklessness descended upon him. He became for a space a thing of courage and fire, like the African leopard in the mating season.

"Oh!" he said.

And, deftly whisking *Strychnine in the Soup* from his companion's hand, he darted into his room, banged the door, and bolted it.

"Mr. Mulliner!"

It was Lady Bassett's voice, coming pleadingly through the woodwork. It was plain that she was shaken to the core, and Cyril smiled sardonically. He was in a position to dictate terms.

"Give me that book, Mr. Mulliner!"

"Certainly not," said Cyril. "I intend to read it myself. I hear good reports of it on every side. The Peebles *Intelligencer* says: 'Vigorous and absorbing.'"

A low wail from the other side of the door answered him.

"Of course," said Cyril suggestively, "if it were my future mother-in-law who was speaking, her word would naturally be law."

There was a silence outside.

"Very well," said Lady Bassett.

"I may marry Amelia?"

"You may."

Cyril unbolted the door.

"Come — Mother," he said, in a soft, kindly voice. "We will read it together, down in the library."

Lady Bassett was still shaken.

"I hope I have acted for the best," she said.

"You have," said Cyril.

"You will make Amelia a good husband?"

"Grade A," Cyril assured her.

"Well, even if you don't," said Lady Bassett resignedly, "I can't go to bed without that book. I had just got to the bit where Inspector Mould is trapped in the underground den of the Faceless Fiend."

Cyril quivered.

"*Is* there a Faceless Fiend?" he cried.

"There are two Faceless Fiends," said Lady Bassett.

"My gosh!" said Cyril. "Let's hurry."

Damon Runyon

Alfred Damon Runyon emigrated from one Manhattan to become the racy chronicler of another. Born in 1884, he left Manhattan, Kansas, at the age of fourteen to serve in the Spanish-American War—he had managed to convince the recruiting officer that he was eighteen. After that experience he became a reporter, a war correspondent, a columnist, and a feature writer. His first published volumes were volumes of verse, but he soon found himself at home in the world of Broadway's crapshooters, racketeers, actors waiting to act, slangsters and gangsters, all of whom were hard-boiled sports with a liberal streak of sentimentality. The short stories in Runyon's *Guys and Dolls* (also the title of an enormously popular musical comedy) are enlivened by characters who answer to such names as Nicely-Nicely Jones, Nathan Detroit, Izzy Cheesecake, Harry the Horse, Joe the Joker, Frankie Ferocious, Ropes McGonnigle, Hymie Banjo-Eyes, Madame La Gimp, Cold Cuts, Big Butch, and Little Isadore. Runyon renders their wisecracking speech to the slightest inflection, so exactly that when his books were published in England a glossary had to be furnished so that the readers could follow Runyon's rapid-fire Broadwayese.

In his fifties Runyon tried film-producing, but the venture was not successful. He died a few years later, in 1946.

THE HOTTEST GUY IN THE WORLD

I wish to say I am very nervous indeed when Big Jule pops into my hotel room one afternoon, because anybody will tell you that Big Jule is the hottest guy in the whole world at the time I am speaking about.

In fact, it is really surprising how hot he is. They wish to see him in Pittsburgh, Pa., about a matter of a mail truck being robbed, and there is gossip about him in Minneapolis, Minn., where somebody takes a fifty G pay roll off a messenger in cash money, and slugs the messenger around somewhat for not holding still.

Furthermore, the Bankers' Association is willing to pay good dough to talk to Big Jule out in Kansas City, Mo., where a jug is knocked off by a stranger, and in the confusion the paying teller, and the cashier, and the second vice president are clouted about, and the day watchman is hurt, and two coppers are badly bruised, and over fifteen G's is removed from the counters, and never returned.

Then there is something about a department store in Canton, O., and a flour mill safe in Toledo, and a grocery in Spokane, Wash., and a branch postoffice in San Francisco, and also something about a shooting match in Chicago, but of course this does not count so much, as only one party is fatally injured. However, you can see that Big Jule is really very hot, what with the coppers all over the country looking for him high and low. In fact, he is practically on fire.

Of course I do not believe Big Jule does all the things the coppers say, because coppers always blame everything no matter where it happens on the most prominent guy they can think of, and Big Jule is quite prominent all over the U.S.A. The chances are he does not do more than half these things, and he probably has a good alibi for the half he does do, at that, but he is certainly hot, and I do not care to have hot guys around me, or even guys who are only just a little bit warm.

But naturally I am not going to say this to Big Jule when he pops in on me, because he may think I am inhospitable, and I do not care to have such a rap going around and about on me, and furthermore Jule may become indignant if he thinks I am inhospitable, and knock me on my potato, because Big Jule is quick to take offense.

So I say hello to Big Jule, very pleasant, and ask him to have a chair by the window where he can see the citizens walking to and fro down in Eighth Avenue and watch the circus wagons moving into Madison Square Garden by way of the Forty-ninth Street side, for the circus always shows in the Garden in the spring before going out on the road. It is a little warm, and Big Jule takes off his coat, and I can see he has one automatic slung under his arm, and another sticking down in the waistband of his pants, and I hope and trust that no copper steps into the room while Big Jule is there because it is very much against the law for guys to go around rodded up this way in New York City.

"Well, Jule," I say, "this is indeed a very large surprise to me, and I am glad to see you, but I am thinking maybe it is very foolish for you to be popping into New York just now, what with all the heat around here, and the coppers looking to arrest people for very little."

"I know," Jule says. "I know. But they do not have so very much on me around here, no matter what people say, and a guy gets homesick for his old home town, especially a guy who is stuck away where I am for the past few months. I get homesick for the lights and the crowds on Broadway, and for the old neighborhood. Furthermore, I wish to see my Maw. I hear she is sick and may not live, and I wish to see her before she goes."

Well, naturally anybody will wish to see their Maw under such circumstances, but Big Jule's Maw lives over in West Forty-ninth Street near Eleventh Avenue, and who is living in the very same block but Johnny Brannigan, the strong arm copper, and it is a hundred to one if Big Jule goes nosing around his old neighborhood, Johnny Brannigan will hear of it, and if there is one guy Johnny Brannigan does not care for, it is Big Jule, although they are kids together.

But it seems that even when they are kids they have very little use for each other, and after they grow up and Johnny gets on the strong arm squad, he never misses a chance to push Big Jule around, and sometimes trying to boff Big Jule with his blackjack, and it is well known to one and all that before Big Jule leaves town the last time, he takes a punch at Johnny Brannigan, and Johnny swears he will never rest until he puts Big Jule where he belongs, although where Big Jule belongs, Johnny does not say.

So I speak of Johnny living in the same block with Big Jule's Maw to Big Jule, but it only makes him mad.

"I am not afraid of Johnny Brannigan," he says. "In fact," he says, "I am thinking for some time lately that maybe I will clip

Johnny Brannigan good while I am here. I owe Johnny Brannigan a clipping. But I wish to see my Maw first, and then I will
go around and see Miss Kitty Clancy. I guess maybe she will be
much surprised to see me, and no doubt very glad."

Well, I figure it is a sure thing Miss Kitty Clancy will be surprised to see Big Jule, but I am not so sure about her being glad,
because very often when a guy is away from a doll for a year or
more, no matter how ever-loving she may be, she may get to thinking of someone else, for this is the way dolls are, whether they
live on Eleventh Avenue or over on Park. Still, I remember hearing that this Miss Kitty Clancy once thinks very well of Big Jule,
although her old man, Jack Clancy, who runs a speakeasy, always
claims it is a big knock to the Clancy family to have such a character as Big Jule hanging around.

"I often think of Miss Kitty Clancy the past year or so," Big Jule
says, as he sits there by the window, watching the circus wagons,
and the crowds. "I especially think of her the past few months.
In fact," he says, "thinking of Miss Kitty Clancy is about all I have
to do where I am at, which is in an old warehouse on the Bay of
Fundy outside of a town that is called St. Johns, or some such,
up in Canada, and thinking of Miss Kitty Clancy all this time,
I find out I love her very much indeed.

"I go to this warehouse," Big Jule says, "after somebody takes a
jewelry store in the town, and the coppers start in blaming me.
This warehouse is not such a place as I will choose myself if I am
doing the choosing, because it is an old fur warehouse, and full
of strange smells, but in the excitement around the jewelry store,
somebody puts a slug in my hip, and Leon Pierre carries me to the
old warehouse, and there I am until I get well.

"It is very lonesome," Big Jule says. "In fact, you will be surprised how lonesome it is, and it is very, very cold, and all I have
for company is a lot of rats. Personally, I never care for rats under
any circumstances because they carry disease germs, and are apt
to bite a guy when he is asleep, if they are hungry, which is what
these rats try to do to me.

"The warehouse is away off by itself," Jule says, "and nobody
ever comes around there except Leon Pierre to bring me grub and
dress my hip, and at night it is very still, and all you can hear is
the wind howling around outside, and the rats running here and
there. Some of them are very, very large rats. In fact, some of them
seem about the size of rabbits, and they are pretty fresh, at that.
At first I am willing to make friends with these rats, but they seem

very hostile, and after they take a few nips at me I can see there is no use trying to be nice to them, so I have Leon Pierre bring me a lot of ammunition for my rods every day and I practice shooting at the rats.

"The warehouse is so far off there is no danger of anybody hearing the shooting," Big Jule says, "and it helps me pass the time away. I get so I can hit a rat sitting, or running, or even flying through the air, because these warehouse rats often leap from place to place like mountain sheep, their idea being generally to take a good nab at me as they fly past.

"Well, sir," Jule says, "I keep score on myself one day, and I hit fifty rats hand running without a miss, which I claim makes me the champion rat shooter of the world with a .45 automatic, although of course," he says, "if anybody wishes to challenge me to a rat shooting match I am willing to take them on for a side bet. I get so I can call my shots on the rats, and in fact several times I say to myself, I will hit this one in the right eye, and this one in the left eye, and it always turns out just as I say, although sometimes when you hit a rat with a .45 up close it is not always possible to tell afterwards just where you hit him, because you seem to hit him all over.

"By and by," Jule says, "I seem to discourage the rats somewhat, and they get so they play the chill for me, and do not try to nab me even when I am asleep. They find out that no rat dast poke his whiskers out at me or he will get a very close shave. So I have to look around for other amusement, but there is not much doing in such a place, although I finally find a bunch of doctors' books which turn out to be very interesting reading. It seems these books are left there by some croaker who retires there to think things over after experimenting on his ever-loving wife with a knife. In fact, it seems he cuts his ever-loving wife's head off, and she does not continue living, so he takes his books and goes to the warehouse and remains there until the law finds him, and hangs him up very high, indeed.

"Well, the books are a great comfort to me, and I learn many astonishing things about surgery, but after I read all the books there is nothing for me to do but think, and what I think about is Miss Kitty Clancy, and how much pleasure we have together walking around and about and seeing movie shows, and all this and that, until her old man gets so tough with me. Yes, I will be very glad to see Miss Kitty Clancy, and the old neighborhood, and my Maw again."

Well, finally nothing will do Big Jule but he must take a stroll over into his old neighborhood, and see if he cannot see Miss Kitty Clancy, and also drop in on his Maw, and he asks me to go along with him. I can think of a million things I will rather do than take a stroll with Big Jule, but I do not wish him to think I am snobbish, because as I say, Big Jule is quick to take offense. Furthermore, I figure that at such an hour of the day he is less likely to run into Johnny Brannigan or any other coppers who know him than at any other time, so I say I will go with him, but as we start out, Big Jule puts on his rods.

"Jule," I say, "do not take any rods with you on a stroll, because somebody may happen to see them, such as a copper, and you know they will pick you up for carrying a rod in this town quicker than you can say Jack Robinson, whether they know who you are or not. You know the Sullivan law is very strong against guys carrying rods in this town."

But Big Jule says he is afraid he will catch cold if he goes out without his rods, so we go down into Forty-ninth Street and start west toward Madison Square Garden, and just as we reach Eighth Avenue and are standing there waiting for the traffic to stop, so we can cross the street, I see there is quite some excitement around the Garden on the Forty-ninth Street side, with people running every which way, and yelling no little, and looking up in the air.

So I look up myself, and what do I see sitting up there on the edge of the Garden roof but a big ugly faced monkey. At first I do not recognize it as a monkey, because it is so big I figure maybe it is just one of the prize fight managers who stand around on this side of the Garden all afternoon waiting to get a match for their fighters, and while I am somewhat astonished to see a prize fight manager in such a position, I figure maybe he is doing it on a bet. But when I take a second look I see that it is indeed a big monk, and an exceptionally homely monk at that, although personally I never see any monks I consider so very handsome, anyway.

Well, this big monk is holding something in its arms, and what it is I am not able to make out at first, but then Big Jule and I cross the street to the side opposite the Garden, and now I can see that the monk has a baby in its arms. Naturally I figure it is some kind of advertising dodge put on by the Garden to ballyhoo the circus, or maybe the fight between Sharkey and Risko which is coming off after the circus, but guys are still yelling and running up and down, and dolls are screaming until finally I realize that a most surprising situation prevails.

It seems that the big monk up on the roof is nobody but Bongo, who is a gorilla belonging to the circus, and one of the very few gorillas of any account in this country, or anywhere else, as far as this goes, because good gorillas are very scarce, indeed. Well, it seems that while they are shoving Bongo's cage into the Garden, the door becomes unfastened, and the first thing anybody knows, out pops Bongo, and goes bouncing along the street where a lot of the neighbors' children are playing games on the sidewalk, and a lot of Mammas are sitting out in the sun alongside baby buggies containing their young. This is a very common sight in side streets such as West Forty-ninth on nice days, and by no means unpleasant, if you like Mammas and their young.

Now what does this Bongo do but reach into a baby buggy which a Mamma is pushing past on the sidewalk on the Garden side of the street, and snatch out a baby, though what Bongo wants with this baby nobody knows to this day. It is a very young baby, and not such a baby as is fit to give a gorilla the size of Bongo any kind of struggle, so Bongo has no trouble whatever in handling it. Anyway, I always hear a gorilla will make a sucker out of a grown man in a battle, though I wish to say I never see a battle between a gorilla and a grown man. It ought to be a first class drawing card, at that.

Well, naturally the baby's Mamma puts up quite a squawk about Bongo grabbing her baby, because no Mamma wishes her baby to keep company with a gorilla, and this Mamma starts in screaming very loud, and trying to take the baby away from Bongo, so what does Bongo do but run right up on the roof of the Garden by way of a big electric sign which hangs down on the Forty-ninth Street side. And there old Bongo sits on the edge of the roof with the baby in his arms, and the baby is squalling quite some, and Bongo is making funny noises, and showing his teeth as the folks commence gathering in the street below.

There is a big guy in his shirt sleeves running through the crowd waving his hands, and trying to shush everybody, and saying "quiet, please" over and over, but nobody pays any attention to him. I figure this guy has something to do with the circus, and maybe with Bongo, too. A traffic copper takes a peek at the situation, and calls for the reserves from the Forty-seventh Street station, and somebody else sends for the fire truck down the street, and pretty soon cops are running from every direction, and the fire engines are coming, and the big guy in his shirt sleeves is more excited than ever.

"Quiet, please," he says. "Everybody keep quite, because if Bongo becomes disturbed by the noise he will throw the baby down in the street. He throws everything he gets his hands on," the guy says. "He acquires this habit from throwing coconuts back in his old home country. Let us get a life net, and if you all keep quiet we may be able to save the baby before Bongo starts heaving it like a coconut."

Well, Bongo is sitting up there on the edge of the roof about seven stories above the ground peeking down with the baby in his arms, and he is holding this baby just like a Mamma would, but anybody can see that Bongo does not care for the row below, and once he lifts the baby high above his head as if to bean somebody with it. I see Big Nig, the crap shooter, in the mob, and afterwards I hear he is around offering to lay 7 to 5 against the baby, but everybody is too excited to bet on such a proposition, although it is not a bad price, at that.

I see one doll in the crowd on the sidewalk on the side of the street opposite the Garden who is standing perfectly still staring up at the monk and the baby with a very strange expression on her face, and the way she is looking makes me take a second gander at her, and who is it but Miss Kitty Clancy. Her lips are moving as she stands there staring up, and something tells me Miss Kitty Clancy is saying prayers to herself, because she is such a doll as will know how to say prayers on an occasion like this.

Big Jule sees her about the same time I do, and Big Jule steps up beside Miss Kitty Clancy, and says hello to her, and though it is over a year since Miss Kitty Clancy sees Big Jule she turns to him and speaks to him as if she is talking to him just a minute before. It is very strange indeed the way Miss Kitty Clancy speaks to Big Jule as if he has never been away at all.

"Do something, Julie," she says. "You are always the one to do something. Oh, please do something, Julie."

Well, Big Jule never answers a word, but steps back in the clear of the crowd and reaches for the waistband of his pants, when I grab him by the arm and say to him like this:

"My goodness, Jule," I say, "what are you going to do?"

"Why," Jule says, "I am going to shoot this thieving monk before he takes a notion to heave the baby on somebody down here.

For all I know," Jule says, "he may hit me with it, and I do not care to be hit with anybody's baby."

"Jule," I say, very earnestly, "do not pull a rod in front of all these coppers, because if you do they will nail you sure, if only for having the rod, and if you are nailed you are in a very tough spot, indeed, what with being wanted here and there. Jule," I say, "you are hotter than a forty-five all over this country, and I do not wish to see you nailed. Anyway," I say, "you may shoot the baby instead of the monk, because anybody can see it will be very diffi- cult to hit the monk up there without hitting the baby. Further- more, even if you do hit the monk it will fall into the street, and bring the baby with it."

"You speak great foolishness," Jule says. "I never miss what I shoot at. I will shoot the monk right between the eyes, and this will make him fall backwards, not forwards, and the baby will not be hurt because anybody can see it is no fall at all from the ledge to the roof behind. I make a study of such propositions," Jule says, "and I know if a guy is in such a position as this monk sitting on a ledge looking down from a high spot his defensive reflexes tend backwards, so this is the way he is bound to fall if anything un- expected comes up on him such as a bullet between the eyes. I read all about it in the doctors' books," Jule says.

Then all of a sudden up comes his hand, and in his hand is one of his rods, and I hear a sound like ker-bap. When I come to think about it afterwards, I do not remember Big Jule even taking aim like a guy will generally do if he is shooting at something sitting, but old Bongo seems to lift up a little bit off the ledge at the crack of the gun and then he keels over backwards, the baby still in his arms, and squalling more than somewhat, and Big Jule says to me like this:

"Right between the eyes, and I will bet on it," he says, "although it is not much of a target, at that."

Well, nobody can figure what happens for a minute, and there is much silence except from the guy in his shirt sleeves who is expressing much indignation with Big Jule and saying the circus people will sue him for damages sure if he has hurt Bongo because the monk is worth $100,000, or some such. I see Miss Kitty Clancy kneeling on the sidewalk with her hands clasped, and looking up- wards, and Big Jule is sticking his rod back in his waistband again.

By this time some guys are out on the roof getting through from the inside of the building with the idea of heading Bongo off from that direction, and they let out a yell, and pretty soon I see one of them holding the baby up so everyone in the street can see it. A couple of others guys get down near the edge of the roof and pick up Bongo and show him to the crowd, as dead as a mackerel, and one of the guys puts a finger between Bongo's eyes to show where the bullet hits the monk, and Miss Kitty Clancy walks over to Big Jule and tries to say something to him, but only busts out crying very loud.

Well, I figure this is a good time for Big Jule and me to take a walk, because everybody is interested in what is going on up on the roof, and I do not wish the circus people to get a chance to serve a summons in a damage suit on Big Jule for shooting the valuable monk. Furthermore, a couple of coppers in harness are looking Big Jule over very critically, and I figure they are apt to put the old sleeve on Jule any second.

All of a sudden a slim young guy steps up to Big Jule and says to him like this:

"Jule," he says, "I want to see you," and who is it but Johnny Brannigan. Naturally Big Jule starts reaching for a rod, but Johnny starts him walking down the street so fast Big Jule does not have time to get in action just then.

"No use getting it out, Jule," Johnny Brannigan says. "No use, and no need. Come with me, and hurry."

Well, Big Jule is somewhat puzzled because Johnny Brannigan is not acting like a copper making a collar, so he goes along with Johnny, and I follow after them, and half way down the block Johnny stops a Yellow short, and hustles us into it and tells the driver to keep shoving down Eighth Avenue.

"I am trailing you ever since you get in town, Jule," Johnny Brannigan says. "You never have a chance around here. I was going over to your Maw's house to put the arm on you figuring you are sure to go there, when the thing over by the Garden comes off. Now I am getting out of this cab at the next corner, and you go on and see your Maw, and then screw out of town as quick as you can, because you are red hot around here, Jule.

"By the way," Johnny Brannigan says, "do you know it is my kid you save, Jule? Mine and Kitty Clancy's? We are married a year ago today."

Well, Big Jule looks very much surprised for a moment, and then he laughs, and says like this: "Well, I never know it is Kitty

Clancy's but I figure it for yours the minute I see it because it looks like you."

"Yes," Johnny Brannigan says, very proud. "Everybody says he does."

"I can see the resemblance even from a distance," Big Jule says. "In fact," he says, "it is remarkable how much you look alike. But," he says, "for a minute, Johnny, I am afraid I will not be able to pick out the right face between the two on the roof because it is very hard to tell the monk and your baby apart."

Edith Sitwell

Edith Sitwell was born in 1887 at Scarborough, England, the only daughter of Sir George Sitwell and Lady Ida Emily Denison, daughter of the Earl of Londesborough. Hers was an unhappy childhood—"my parents were strangers to me from the moment of my birth." Unattractive and lonely, she protected herself with compensating self-adulation. When asked what she planned to be when she grew up, she unhesitantly answered, "A genius."

A sensationalist, if not a genius, she became. Her poems ranged from the startingly surrealistic to the somewhat self-consciously pathetic, from the patently autobiographical to the entertainingly eccentric—she recited her *Façade,* accompanied by the music of William Walton, through a megaphone. Eccentricity was natural to her. She always wore richly archaic robes; her fingers were covered with huge gemmed rings; her headdress was both regal and absurd. Although she published some fifteen volumes of poetry, she took particular pleasure in *English Eccentrics,* a witty excursion into a world where she was thoroughly at home. She delighted to chronicle the foibles and oddities of scarcely believable characters: the squire who set fire to his nightgown to frighten away his hiccups, the cannibal chief who turned out to be a onetime butler, the member of the Royal Society who sported an iron wig, the gentleman who married for the first time at eighty, marriage after that becoming a habit with him, "though there was an occasion when, owing no doubt to an oversight, he was made to do public penance at the age of one hundred and five for omitting this ceremony."

Edith Sitwell was created a Dame Commander of the Order of the British Empire in 1954. Ten years later, upon the completion of her autobiography, *Taken Care Of*, she died of heart failure at the age of seventy-seven.

PORTRAIT OF A LEARNED LADY

On a foggy evening in the month of October, 1846, had we peered through a window into the dining-room of a certain house in Chelsea, which was filled always with a shaggy Highland-cattle-like odour of homespun materials and by a Scotch mist of tobacco smoke, we might have seen a successful dinner-party in full blast. The host was Thomas Carlyle, the guest of honour an American lady of thirty-six, Miss Margaret Fuller, the author of *Woman in the Nineteenth Century* and the first editor of *The Dial.*

This chaste, passionate, and high-principled woman, at once splendid and ridiculous, was the direct outcome of the movement towards the Emancipation of Women, a movement in which learned, trousered and vivacious ladies like George Sand made presents of themselves with the same frequency, cheapness and indiscrimination as that with which other ladies present Christmas cards. This caused them to be collected with great eagerness by sex-snobs, who, unlike all other snobs, or collectors, prefer the ubiquitous to the rare.

Miss Fuller's principles, but not her behaviour, were derived from ladies such as these, and her friend Mr. Emerson tells us that Margaret "was always a most earnest, devoted champion of the Emancipation of Women, from their past and present condition of inferiority, to an independence on men. She demanded for them the fullest recognition of Social and Political Equality with the rougher sex; the freest access to all stations, professions, employments, which are open to men. To this demand I heartily acceded. It seemed to me however that her clear perceptions of abstract right were often overborne in practice by the influence of education and habit; that while she demanded absolute equality for women, she exacted a deference and courtesy from men to women, as women, which was entirely inconsistent with that requirement.

"So long as a lady shall deem herself in need of some gentleman's arm to conduct her properly out of a dining-room or ballroom, so long as she shall consider it dangerous or unbecoming to walk half a mile alone by night, I cannot see how the Woman's Rights theory is ever to be more than a logically defensible abstraction. . . . Whenever she (Margaret) said or did anything implying the usual demands of woman on the courtesy and protection of manhood, I was apt, before complying, to look her in the face and exclaim with marked emphasis—quoting from her *Woman in the Nineteenth Century*—'Let them be Sea-Captains if they will.'"

However, according to Mr. Emerson's letter introducing her to Mr. Carlyle, she was "a wise, sincere and accomplished, and one of the most entertaining of women, one of the noblest of women," although her appearance, according to the same gentleman's memoirs of her published after her death, "had nothing prepossessing. Her extreme plainness," he continued, "a trick of incessantly opening and shutting her eyelids, the nasal tone of her voice, all repelled. It is to be said that Margaret made a disagreeable first impression on most persons, including those who afterwards became her best friends, to such an extent that they did not wish to remain in the same room with her. This was partly the effect of her manners, which expressed an overweening sense of power and slight esteem of others."

Mr. Emerson, however, admired Miss Fuller's "severity of truth," for "I have known her," he wrote, "mow down the crop of evil, like the angel of retribution itself, and could not sufficiently admire her courage. My friends told me of a verdict, pronounced upon Mr. —— at Paris, which they said was perfectly tremendous. They themselves sat breathless; Mr. —— was struck dumb; his eyes fixed on her with wonder and amazement, yet gazing too with an attention which seemed like fascination. When she had done, he still looked to see if she was to say more, and when he found she had really finished, he arose, took his hat, said faintly 'I thank you,' and left the room." Miss Fuller was in no doubt as to her own mental attainments, and Mr. Emerson tells us that "she would let slip, with all the innocence imaginable, some phrase betraying the presence of a rather mountainous ME, in a way to surprise those who knew her great sense."

Mr. Emerson was however grateful to her for he, owing to his years of arduous mental toil, had almost lost the "capacity to laugh," and Mrs. Emerson, deciding that he must make a new and thorough study of this useful accomplishment under the careful tutorship of Margaret Fuller, had invited that lady for a fortnight's visit, and had insisted that the two sages should take a daily walk together, with the result that the lessons were, after a while, crowned with comparative success. I can imagine the happy chatter, the gay badinage about metempsychosis and Goethe, Locke, English metaphysics, Racine, Körner, Truth, Liberty for Woman, Carlyle and Liberty for Man, the Christian religion, Plato, Socrates, Bigelow's Elements, Jacob's Letters to Fichte, which constituted those Lessons in Laughter. I can imagine too the spell of ordinariness which came over the Emerson household during these brief respites from Wisdom.

At first Mr. Emerson did not find the lessons easy, for he tells us that he "was, at that time, an eager scholar of ethics, and had tasted the sweets of solitude and stoicism, and I found something profane in the hours of amusing gossip into which she drew me." Hollow sounds, as from an owl in a metaphysical holly-bush, an owl imprisoned in the mausoleum of Goethe, were heard floating over the woodlands. Then the sounds grew lighter, took on a more shrill and batlike note. In the end, however, though slowly and painfully, the accomplishment to which I have referred was restored to Mr. Emerson through the tutelage of Margaret, and now he had passed his teacher on to his friend Carlyle, in the hope perhaps that he also might derive some benefit of the same kind.

Mr. Carlyle however would not allow himself to receive any instruction of any kind, and Miss Fuller tells us that "it is the usual misfortune of such marked men, happily not one invariable or inevitable, that they cannot allow other minds room to breathe, and show themselves in their atmosphere, and thus miss the refreshment and instruction which the greatest never cease to need from the experience of the humblest. Carlyle allows no one a chance, but bears down all opposition, not only by his wit, and onset of words, resistless as so many bayonets, but by actual physical superiority, raising his voice, and rushing on his opponent with a torrent of sound. This is not in the least from unwillingness to allow freedom to others. On the contrary, no man would more enjoy a manly resistance to his thought." Still, Mr. Carlyle would not allow Miss Fuller to speak, and Miss Fuller was used to talking uninterrupted and to interrupting others. "The worst of hearing Carlyle," she assured her correspondent, "is that you cannot interrupt him. I understand the habit of haranguing has increased very much upon him, so that you are a perfect prisoner when he has once got hold of you. To interrupt him is a physical impossibility. If you get a chance to remonstrate for a moment, he raises his voice and bears you down. True, he does you no injustice, and, with his admirable penetration sees the disclaimer in your mind, so that you are not morally delinquent; but it is not pleasant to be unable to utter it."

Another guest at this dinner-party, was "a witty French, flippant sort of man, author of a *History of Philosophy*, and now writing a *Life of Goethe*, a task for which he must be as unfit as irreligion and sparkling shallowness can make him. But he told stories admirably, and was allowed sometimes to interrupt Carlyle for a little." This irreligious sparkling shallowness caused the witty flippant sort of man, whose name was George Henry Lewes, to enter into a ménage with that monument of lightness, George Eliot.

The inability to interrupt seems to have been a great problem in literary circles, in the year 1846. For Miss Martineau, immediately before Miss Fuller's meeting with Wordsworth, which took place a month or so before her inability to interrupt Carlyle, warned her that "He does all the talking, and never knows the name of the person he is addressing. He talks mostly about his poems and he is pretty sure to take the visitor to see the terrace where he has composed so many." But then Miss Martineau did not entirely approve of her neighbours. She could, and did, give Margaret other and equally important information about the author of the *Ode on the Intimations of Immortality*. In the winter he wore a long cloak, a Scotch bonnet and great goggles. Usually a score of children ran along after him, coaxing him to cut switches out of the hedge for them. A curious combination of economy and generosity he was. If you dropped in to tea you were likely not to have enough cream to put into it, and yet Wordsworth gave away all the milk the household did not want to cottagers perfectly well able to buy their own. If you dropped in for any other meal, you were greeted with "You are very well welcome to have a cup of tea with us, but if you want any meat you must pay for it."

Others of Miss Martineau's neighbours were hardly respectable, but like a comfortable Christian woman Miss Martineau said no more about them than would destroy their reputation for respectability and enhance her own. Take the Coleridges, for example. The poet's son, Hartley, had died of drink. De Quincey was not only on the verge of starvation, but, according to his virtuous neighbour, was in such a state that "when he lived at Keswick he drank five or six wineglasses of laudanum a night. Coleridge was to blame for that of course, for De Quincey ran across him shortly after he came down from Oxford, and Coleridge was then drinking his tumblerful a day."

After these revelations, we cannot for a moment doubt that Miss Martineau, with her striking virtues, was a more valuable inhabitant of the world than the authors of the *Ode on the Intimations of Immortality*, the *Ancient Mariner* and *Kubla Khan*, and the *Confessions of an Opium Eater*.

Margaret Fuller however was not as critical of these benighted beings as was Miss Martineau, and she was glad to be in Europe, because her life in Boston must remind her of the imaginary being, clothed in actual flesh, whom she had lost.

Two years before Margaret Fuller's journey to Europe she had fallen passionately in love with a young gentleman named James Nathan, who came from Hamburg. Mr. Nathan was younger than Miss Fuller, was pale, had long dark hair, played the guitar, spent his days in the City, and talked about the Soul. He was consistently and profitably misunderstood, as we shall see. "His was no plebeian mind," Miss Bell informs us in her book on Margaret Fuller. "Not for him the utilitarian life, where leisure was considered a waste of time, and graceful indolence the pastime of fools and women. He felt a little out of place in the world of lower Broadway."

The work-shy and superior Mr. Nathan spent a good deal of time in being melancholy with the aid of Margaret, and between them developed one of those innocently incestuous brother-and-sister relationships which are always so grateful and convenient to the gentleman, so shattering to the nerves and dignity of the lady.

At first the nature of Mr. Nathan's behaviour had not allowed Margaret to guess that she was his sister. Do gentlemen, she wondered, when the nature of the relationship had been made abundantly clear, pour blackberry blossoms into the laps of their sisters? She fancied not. Blackberry blossoms, though they are frail, seem to hold in them some promise of fruition, however cold, belated and hard. However, Mr. Nathan proved to her that she was wrong; for after some time he discovered that she had no money, and this fact made their relationship clearer than ever. They had, he said, a *spiritual* affinity. He proposed that it should be recognized, that their relationship came from *within*, although

I imagine that this high spirtual life was interspersed, even then, by interludes of a distressing tenderness.

At last, owing partly to overwork, partly to the wrack and worry and general wear and tear of this inhibited incest, Miss Fuller's face began to show increased signs of her age, and these signs were noted by Mr. Nathan with distress and a profound distaste for the misunderstanding which had caused them. He meanwhile had been giving a good deal of time to the contemplation of himself, his prospects, his outlook, etc. . . . and the result was that, in Miss Fuller's eyes, his face was sicklied o'er with the pale cast of thought, though a prejudiced observer might have said that he was suffering from an enlarged liver. His curls, too, were less luxuriant than formerly. But these signs of mental pain only made the woman who loved him move more closely to him, with a deeper, more foolish, phœnix-like love.

The disillusioned Mr. Nathan began to pick quarrels with Miss Fuller, but she replied only: "You shall upbraid me to the stars, and I feel sure that you will not find me incompetent." This irritated Mr. Nathan so much that he found more and more faults in her.

At last, he wrote and told her that he was about to leave America and return to Europe, and this drove Margaret to despair, for she did not know what this might mean, or if he would ever return. Then, as she read his long and extremely noble letter, at last, at the very end of that letter, she found the heart which had inspired it. Mr. Nathan needed money because he wished to explore the East, and be the first to navigate the Dead Sea. Also, he wanted to go to Jerusalem. Margaret, he felt, might ask her rich and influential friends for some money which would make these aspirations possible. He would be glad, too, if she would take charge of his Newfoundland pup Josey, and the irresistible guitar.

The money was, of course, forthcoming; Margaret saw to that; and for some time Mr. Nathan was too busy packing and making arrangements for the explorations to pay her a visit. But at last, just a week before he sailed, he found time to come and see her, bringing Josey and the guitar, and explaining that he would carry her letters with him wherever he went.

When he had gone, Margaret, in her loneliness and sadness, wrote: "I have lost my dear companion, the first I ever had who could feel every better side of life and beauty as exquisitely as myself."

Other sides of life and beauty, however, were occupying the thoughts of Mr. Nathan, and, although Margaret wrote often, two months passed before a letter reached her in return. But then how noble was the letter, and how long! "Let me lie down and die," exclaimed Mr. Nathan, "rather than my presence abet falsehood." It was not till the end of that long letter, that the unpractical and unworldly Mr. Nathan enquired if his correspondent would secure for him a letter of introduction from Mr. George Bancroft, the Minister of Marine, and place Mr. Nathan's articles on travel under the editorship of Mr. Greeley.

The months passed and Mr. Nathan's letters grew fewer and fewer: her heart knew that the tone of those rare letters had changed. Perhaps, she might have broken the bond that held her, but although Mr. Nathan felt himself as free as air, it would have injured his high ideals to see any signs of such a frailty on the part of Woman, whose legendary fidelity is her birthright, bestowed upon her by heaven. What an inspiration is this fidelity to Man, supporting as it does his belief in human nature on those many occasions when he is weighed down by the disillusionment brought about by the contemplation of his own lack of fidelity. Besides, any shadow cast on Mr. Nathan's belief in Woman would have been particularly tragic at this moment, since— although Margaret did not know this—he was about to marry another and a younger woman. Margaret wrote to him, "You will love me as much, as long, and as carefully as you can, will you not?"

The months dragged on, and it was only a fortnight before Margaret sailed for Europe that she received his reply to this letter. He had arrived in Hamburg, where he was the centre of attention, the guest of honour at dinner-parties and receptions . . . but his funds were exhausted. Where could he get a book published? Would Margaret see to it that Mr. Greeley published this? . . . Then comes this sublime and characteristic touch, showing all Mr. Nathan's childlike and beautiful gift for casting other people's bread upon the waters: "As for Josey" (his Newfoundland pup), "if he is too much trouble and if Mr. March cannot keep him for me and you know of no other person that will, just have him sold at auction, *or run loose away, or what he may do, a kind Providence will have a care of him.*"

When Margaret was in Edinburgh, she received another letter from this childlike believer. She too might run loose away, or do what she might do, and a kind Providence would have a care of her, for Mr. Nathan was soon to be married to the younger lady.

But Mr. Nathan would not entrust the letters that the celebrated older lady had written him, to the care of Providence. They might, he thought, prove valuable yet. In answer to her request that he would return these pledges of her affection, he wrote, "My loving regard is and was too sincere and earnest and holy as to change with any new ties or external events. . . . And to permit me to part with things so dear, so suddenly. Let me entreat you to let the spiritual offspring of our friendship remain in the home they were born to and intended for, until on our return to New York we will talk the matter over more fully and fairly. In the meantime, let me assure you, they enjoy the sacredness and privacy of this uninterrupted and uninterfered with from any foreign alliance or relationship, and that at our meeting there I shall do nothing but what is right, manly and honourable." Anxious to add one further incitement to madness, he proclaimed that he felt "a deep admiration for your great, superior well-stored mind, an equally true regard for the integrity, profundity, and holiness of your character and for the many womanly virtues and sentiments of your capacious heart and true love for the purity of your soul, from which noble source I have drawn many deep inspirations."

It may be that the thought of these letters written to the unworldly Mr. Nathan, gnawed into Miss Fuller's mind as she sat, listening to the thunder of Carlyle's talk, and being allowed, once an hour or so, to speak, "enough to free my lungs and change my position, so that I did not get tired." Or perhaps she thought of the difference between her repressed childhood and youth, and the freedom that had come to her by way of her friendship with such people as the Emersons, and Horace Greeley and his wife. She was in many ways a remarkable woman, and we find ourselves agreeing with Emerson's verdict that, although "Margaret often loses herself in sentimentalism, here was a head so creative of new colours, of wonderful gleams, so iridescent that it piqued curiosity and stimulated thought and communicated mental activity to all who approached her; though her perceptions were not to be compared to her fancy, and she made numerous mistakes. Her integrity was perfect, and she was led and followed by love, and was really bent on truth, but was too indulgent to the meteors of her fancy."

She lived, indeed, a life full of noble ideals, backfisch nonsense

and moonshine, silly cloying over-emotionalized friendships
and repressed loves, (friendship being often disguised as love,
and love as friendship), extreme mental and moral courage, and
magnificent loyalty to her ideals, friends, and loves.

Miss Fuller's life was one mass of symbolism; even the magnificent and tragic shipwreck with which her life, together with
those of her young Italian husband and her baby boy ended, was
symbolic. It is impossible not to feel an embarrassed sympathy,
and a kind of affection for her, since the whole record of her life
leaves us with the impression of a certain nobility and upright-
ness, blurred over by an overheated nervous sensibility mas-
querading as imagination. She had a certain non-productive
intellect, and considerable rectitude, but these qualities were
balanced, to some degree, by her almost incomparable silliness.
As in the case of nearly all remarkable women, opinions were
strongly divided about her, and one hostile biographer exclaimed
that her writing was "a striking illustration of the propensity of
all strong-minded ladies to Monster Nothings." Miss Fuller took
an untiring interest in everything and everybody, including herself, and wrote that "mine is a large, rich, but unclarified nature.
My history presents much superficial temporary tragedy. The
woman in me kneels and weeps in tender rapture, the man in me
rushes forth, but only to be baffled."

Alas, this was only too true, and when Miss Fuller enquired of
herself and of others: "Who may understand me?" the answer was
"None."

Robert Benchley

Robert Charles Benchley was born in 1889 in Worcester, Massachusetts, and attended Phillips Exeter Academy, where he enlivened a course in English composition by his essay "How to Embalm a Corpse." His career as a professional zany began at Harvard when he edited *Lampoon*. Writing for a variety of newspapers and magazines, he won an academy award for a short film, "How to Sleep," and was featured in motion picture and radio series.

Benchley was a specialist in absurd situations that he made increasingly ridiculous; he talked his way in and out of a subject—any subject—with a kind of insane logic. It was said that he would be remembered as the supreme champion of the pricelessly nonsensical, a statement corroborated by the titles of most of his books: *My Ten Years in a Quandary, and How They Grew; From Bed to Worse, or Comforting Thoughts about the Bison; No Poems, or Around the World Backwards and Sideways; The Treasurer's Report, and Other Aspects of Community Singing*. His death and the publication of his last book, *One Minute Please*, occurred in his fifty-sixth year.

THE MURDER WITHOUT INTEREST

People interested in murders (and who, aside possibly from the victims themselves, is not interested in murders?) have been re-

minded by the recent strange killings in the little French town of
Messy-sur-Saône of a famous case twenty-five years ago in the
same neighborhood, which, up until now, has remained unsolved.
One of the reasons why it has remained unsolved is probably that
nobody gave much of a hang. It was known as the Murder Case
Without Interest.

In the early spring of 1907, the little French village of Ouilly-
Oise, fifteen kilometers from Messy-sur-Saône, was asleep among
its apple blossoms and Cinzano signs, little dreaming that it was
soon to become the center of activity for one of the dullest murders on record. In fact, immediately after the murder had been
committed, and all during the long months of the investigation
and subsequent trial, Ouilly-Oise (and its neighbor, Oisey-Ouille,
which lies directly across the little river) still continued to sleep.
Even the oldest inhabitant of the town, when confronted today
with a request for the details of the crime, does not remember
that any crime ever took place. And this, please remember, in spite
of the fact that he himself was one of the murderers.

It was late in April (still 1907) that the murder occurred, although it was not discovered until the first two weeks in June,
and even then only half-heartedly. Old Lucien Delabriex and his
daughter, Anisette, lived together under the schoolhouse, in the
place where all the old algebra books were stored, and this kept
them more or less out of the social life of the town, as nobody
liked algebra. (Alegbra in English is silly enough. You can imagine
what it is in French.) The young girl, however, did not care
whether or not she and her father were accepted socially, for she
had a young and handsome lover in Pierre Vineuille, cadet at the
local *épicerie,* and her father gave her little or no trouble as he
was murdered most of the time. So life went on at its quiet pace
in Ouilly-Oise, with the drums of the Great War still seven years
in the future.

Every night Pierre used to come to the hedge in front of the
schoolhouse and whistle: *"The French they are a funny race —
parlay-voo!"* and every night Anisette would creep out from under
the schoolhouse, go to the gate, and tell him (in French) for
Heaven's sake to cut out that incessant whistling and go home.
Then she would go back to bed, for she had to get up very early
in the morning and drive the geese down the village street in
rehearsal for *The Big Parade* and *What Price Glory?* and all the
other war pictures which were scheduled to come. (It has been
estimated that those French geese cleaned up over $250,000 from
Metro-Goldwyn alone during the post-war period.)

This routine began finally to get on the nerves of the cadet Pierre, and one night he didn't whistle at all, which so irritated Anisette that she went off to the village movies with him. The next morning the geese ran through their act alone. Pierre and Anisette were never seen again. With this, the mystery, such as it is, begins. And from now on the story begins to lose interest.

On the morning of the eighth, the town barber, making his daily rounds to collect old mustaches (the French even then were a thrifty race and saved everything, just in case), knocked at the door of the schoolhouse, and receiving no answer thought nothing of it and went on to the next house. So the barber cannot possibly be under suspicion, although he later claimed to have committed the murder. It was not until the following week that it was discovered that old Lucien Delabriex was no more.

We use the phrase "was no more," not as a euphemism for "was dead," but as a literal translation of the French *"etait non plus."* This seems to be about the only way to describe what the old gentleman was. For some algebra agents, on a search for contraband algebra books, on forcing an entrance to the cellar of the schoolhouse found that not only was the octogenarian not there, but that he seemed never to have been there. There was an octogenarian suit hanging in the closet and evidences of an octogenarian debauch (beaver hats, carpet slippers, and spilled oatmeal) scattered about the room, but on the mantelpiece was a note, written in a round schoolgirl hand (round schoolgirls write with difficulty, owing to being so round) which read:

To Whom It Probably Will Not Concern: You are just making a monkey of yourself looking for Lucien Delabriex. What do you care?

This was a question which nobody seemed able to answer, but the law made a coroner's inquest obligatory, so a coroner's inquest there was. The coroner couldn't be there himself, but he sent flowers and saw to it that everybody had plenty of rice and old shoes. There was nobody to question, but, as there were no questions to be asked except "How are you?" and "Did you have a pleasant vacation?" the lack of testimony did not seem so glaring. One of the villagers who had crashed the gate, Emu Vandouze by name, offered to pose as a witness, and we have been able to salvage a transcript of his testimony. It follows:

Q. Did you know the deceased personally?

A. How did you ever come to ask me that question?

Q. Oh, I don't know. It just popped into my head. Why?

A. Well, it's very funny — almost spooky. I was just about to ask you the same question myself.

Q. Mental telepathy, I guess. It happens to me all the time.

A. You can kid all you like, but I think there is a great deal more to this mental telepathy than we think.

Q. *You* think there is more to it than we think? What are you talking about? Make up your mind who you are.

A. I'm Bon-Bon Buddie, the Chocolate Drop——

Q. *(Joining in)* — the Chocolate Drop, that's me-e-e!

A. What else do you know?

Q. Don't ask me — I might tell you.

A. Witness excused.

Q. Where do you get off to excuse the witness? You *are* the witness.

COUNSEL FOR THE DEFENSE: I move to have that last remark stricken from the record as irrelevant, irrelevant, and irrelevant.

THE COURT: Motion denied, but thought awfully well of.

COUNSEL FOR THE DEFENSE: That's cold comfort. Thank you for nothing.

Q. Court adjourned.

This sort of thing dragged on for days, until finally it got so that nobody went into the court room at all, not even the Court. Another family moved into the courthouse and changed all the furniture around so that the room where the trial was being held became the baby's room and before long was all cluttered up with broken toys and picture books. Every once in a while some one connected with the trial would drop in to see how things were going and they would be shushed up for fear they would wake the baby. This more or less made a mockery of the law, and, after a year or two, the citizens of the town took the matter into their own hands (known as the Lynch Law in America) and stopped the whole thing for good.

Thus ended one of the strangest murder mysteries in the annals of French jurisprudence, ending where it had begun — in a deadlock. And yet some people hold that Truth is stranger than Fiction!

Dorothy Parker

She was born Dorothy Rothschild at West End, New Jersey, in 1893. Terrified of her Jewish father, she hated her Gentile stepmother. "If I wrote about my childhood," she said, "you wouldn't sit in the same room with me." At twenty-four she married Edwin Parker, and after a divorce she married a film actor, Alan Campbell, divorced and then remarried him. He died of an overdose of sleeping pills. An embittered woman, bitter not only about what she despised in a Philistine world but also about herself, she died in 1967.

Writing was both a release and a torture for her—"I write five words and erase seven"—but the writing itself was both fierce and funny. "She can no more help being amusing than a peach tree can help bearing peaches," wrote Somerset Maugham. "She seems to carry a hammer in her handbag to hit the appropriate nail on the head." Her curt, usually cruel, disposals were continually quoted. "She [a certain actress] ran the gamut of emotions from A to B." "I take issue with Hemingway, and there is nothing better for that morning headache than taking a little issue." "She spoke eighteen languages and couldn't say 'no' in any of them." "You can lead a horticulture but you can't make her think." To a snob who dismissed all humorists because he couldn't bear fools, she said, "That's odd. Your mother could."

Her facile quips did her a disservice. They spoiled much of her prose and twisted most of her poetry (she published three volumes of verse) into self-conscious archness and last lines that were patently contrived. Nevertheless, she could turn from punch lines to pathos—the sad and sordid "Big Blonde" won the O. Henry Prize in 1929—and in such virtuoso performances as "The Waltz" she distilled a mixture of persiflage and poison.

THE WALTZ

Why, thank you so much. I'd adore to.

I don't want to dance with him. I don't want to dance with anybody. And even if I did, it wouldn't be him. He'd be well down among the last ten. I've seen the way he dances; it looks like something you do on Saint Walpurgis Night. Just think, not a quarter of an hour ago, here I was sitting, feeling so sorry for the poor girl he was dancing with. And now *I'm* going to be the poor girl. Well, well. Isn't it a small world?

And a peach of a world, too. A true little corker. Its events are so fascinatingly unpredictable, are not they? Here I was, minding my own business, not doing a stitch of harm to any living soul. And then he comes into my life, all smiles and city manners, to sue me for the favor of one memorable mazurka. Why, he scarcely knows my name, let alone what it stands for. It stands for Despair, Bewilderment, Futility, Degradation, and Premeditated Murder, but little does he wot. I don't wot his name, either; I haven't any idea what it is. Jukes, would be my guess from the look in his eyes. How do you do, Mr. Jukes? And how is that dear little brother of yours, with the two heads?

Ah, now why did he have to come around me, with his low requests? Why can't he let me lead my own life? I ask so little—just to be left alone in my quiet corner of the table, to do my evening brooding over all my sorrows. And he must come, with his bows and his scrapes and his may-I-have-this-ones. And I had to go and tell him that I'd adore to dance with him. I cannot understand why I wasn't struck right down dead. Yes, and being struck dead would look like a day in the country, compared to struggling out a dance with this boy. But what could I do? Everyone else at the table had got up to dance, except him and me. There was I, trapped. Trapped like a trap in a trap.

What can you say, when a man asks you to dance with him? I

most certainly will *not* dance with you, I'll see you in hell first. Why, thank you, I'd like to awfully, but I'm having labor pains. Oh, yes, *do* let's dance together—it's so nice to meet a man who isn't a scaredy-cat about catching my beri-beri. No. There was nothing for me to do, but say I'd adore to. Well, we might as well get it over with. All right, Cannonball, let's run out on the field. You won the toss; you can lead.

Why, I think it's more of a waltz, really. Isn't it? We might just listen to the music a second. Shall we? Oh, yes, it's a waltz. Mind? Why, I'm simply thrilled. I'd love to waltz with you.

I'd love to waltz with you. I'd love to waltz with you. I'd love to have my tonsils out, I'd love to be in a midnight fire at sea. Well, it's too late now. We're getting under way. *Oh.* Oh, dear. Oh, dear, dear, dear. Oh, this is even worse than I thought it would be. I suppose that's the one dependable law of life—everything is always worse than you thought it was going to be. Oh, if I had any real grasp of what this dance would be like, I'd have held out for sitting it out. Well, it will probably amount to the same thing in the end. We'll be sitting it out on the floor in a minute, if he keeps this up.

I'm so glad I brought it to his attention that this is a waltz they're playing. Heaven knows what might have happened, if he had thought it was something fast; we'd have blown the sides right out of the building. Why does he always want to be somewhere that he isn't? Why can't we stay in one place just long enough to get acclimated? It's this constant rush, rush, rush, that's the curse of American life. That's the reason that we're all of us so— *Ow!* For God's sake, don't *kick,* you idiot; this is only second down. Oh, my shin. My poor, poor shin, that I've had ever since I was a little girl!

Oh, no, no, no. Goodness, no. It didn't hurt the least little bit. And anyway it was my fault. Really it was. Truly. Well, you're just being sweet, to say that. It really was all my fault.

I wonder what I'd better do—kill him this instant, with my naked hands, or wait and let him drop in his traces. Maybe it's best not to make a scene. I guess I'll just lie low, and watch the pace get him. He can't keep this up indefinitely—he's only flesh and blood. Die he must, and die he shall, for what he did to me. I don't want to be of the over-sensitive type, but you can't tell me that kick was unpremeditated. Freud says there are no accidents. I've led no cloistered life, I've known dancing partners who have spoiled my slippers and torn my dress; but when it comes to kicking, I am Outraged Womanhood. When you kick me in the shin, *smile.*

Maybe he didn't do it maliciously. Maybe it's just his way of showing his high spirits. I suppose I ought to be glad that one of us is having such a good time. I suppose I ought to think myself lucky if he brings me back alive. Maybe it's captious to demand of a practically strange man that he leave your shins as he found them. After all, the poor boy's doing the best he can. Probably he grew up in the hill country, and never had no larnin'. I bet they had to throw him on his back to get shoes on him.

Yes, it's lovely, isn't it? It's simply lovely. It's the loveliest waltz. Isn't it? Oh, I think it's lovely, too.

Why, I'm getting positively drawn to the Triple Threat here. He's my hero. He has the heart of a lion, and the sinews of a buffalo. Look at him—never a thought of the consequences, never afraid of his face, hurling himself into every scrimmage, eyes shining, cheeks ablaze. And shall it be said that I hung back? No, a thousand times no. What's it to me if I have to spend the next couple of years in a plaster cast? Come on, Butch, right through them! Who wants to live forever?

Oh. Oh, dear. Oh, he's all right, thank goodness. For a while I thought they'd have to carry him off the field. Ah, I couldn't bear to have anything happen to him. I love him. I love him better than anybody in the world. Look at the spirit he gets into a dreary, commonplace waltz; how effete the other dancers seem, beside him. He is youth and vigor and courage, he is strength and gaiety and—*Ow!* Get off my instep, you hulking peasant! What do you think I am, anyway—a gangplank? *Ow!*

No, of course it didn't hurt. Why, it didn't a bit. Honestly. And it was all my fault. You see, that little step of yours—well, it's perfectly lovely, but it's just a tiny bit tricky to follow at first. Oh, did you work it up yourself? You really did? Well, aren't you amazing! Oh, now I think I've got it. Oh, I think it's lovely. I was watching you do it when you were dancing before. It's awfully effective when you look at it.

It's awfully effective when you look at it. I bet I'm awfully effective when you look at me. My hair is hanging along my cheeks, my skirt is swaddling about me, I can feel the cold damp of my brow. I must look like something out of the "Fall of the House of Usher." This sort of thing takes a fearful toll of a woman my age. And he worked up his little step himself, he with his degenerate

cunning. And it was just a tiny bit tricky at first, but now I think
I've got it. Two stumbles, slip, and a twenty-yard dash; yes. I've
got it. I've got several others things, too, including a split shin and
a bitter heart. I hate this creature I'm chained to. I hated him the
moment I saw his leering, bestial face. And here I've been locked
in his noxious embrace for the thirty-five years this waltz has
lasted. Is that orchestra never going to stop playing? Or must this
obscene travesty of a dance go on until hell burns out?

*Oh, they're going to play another encore. Oh, goody. Oh, that's
lovely. Tired? I should say I'm not tired. I'd like to go on like this
forever.*

I should say I'm not tired. I'm dead, that's all I am. Dead, and
in what a cause! And the music is never going to stop playing,
and we're going on like this, Double-Time Charlie and I, throughout eternity. I suppose I won't care any more, after the first hundred thousand years. I suppose nothing will matter then, not
heat nor pain nor broken heart nor cruel, aching weariness. Well.
It can't come too soon for me.

I wonder why I didn't tell him I was tired. I wonder why I didn't
suggest going back to the table. I could have said let's just listen
to the music. Yes, and if he would, that would be the first bit of
attention he has given it all evening. George Jean Nathan said that
the lovely rhythms of the waltz should be listened to in stillness
and not be accompanied by strange gyrations of the human body.
I think that's what he said. I think it was George Jean Nathan.
Anyhow, whatever he said and whoever he was and whatever he's
doing now, he's better off than I am. That's safe. Anybody who
isn't waltzing with this Mrs. O'Leary's cow I've got here is having
a good time.

Still if we were back at the table, I'd probably have to talk to him.
Look at him — what could you say to a thing like that! Did you go
to the circus this year, what's your favorite kind of ice cream,
how do you spell cat? I guess I'm as well off here. As well off as if
I were in a cement mixer in full action.

I'm past all feeling now. The only way I can tell when he steps
on me is that I can hear the splintering of bones. And all the events
of my life are passing before my eyes. There was the time I was in
a hurricane in the West Indies, there was the day I got my head
cut open in the taxi smash, there was the night the drunken lady
threw a bronze ash-tray at her own true love and got me instead,
there was that summer that the sailboat kept capsizing. Ah, what
an easy, peaceful time was mine, until I fell in with Swifty, here.

I didn't know what trouble was, before I got drawn into this *danse macabre.* I think my mind is beginning to wander. It almost seems to me as if the orchestra were stopping. It couldn't be, of course; it could never, never be. And yet in my ears there is a silence like the sound of angel voices. . . .

Oh, they've stopped, the mean things. They're not going to play any more. Oh, darn. Oh, do you think they would? Do you really think so, if you gave them twenty dollars? Oh, that would be lovely. And look, do tell them to play this same thing. I'd simply adore to go on waltzing.

James Thurber

James Grover Thurber was born in 1894 in Columbus, Ohio. His boyhood, he said in an unassuming third-person monologue, "was pretty well devoid of significance. He fell down a great deal during this period because of a trick he had of walking into himself, and his gold-rimmed glasses forever needed straightening, which gave him the appearance of a person who hears somebody calling but can't make out where the sound is coming from." Actually he had lost the sight of one eye in a childhood bow-and-arrow accident; as he grew older he saw imperfectly from the remaining eye and became almost totally blind.

At Ohio State University Thurber edited the humor magazine; after the First World War he became a reporter and was on the Paris staff of the Chicago *Tribune;* at thirty-three he became the life and soul of *The New Yorker* and collaborated with E. B. White on his first book, *Is Sex Necessary?* On his own, Thurber published some twenty volumes—collections of eerie whimsicalities and stories as provocative as *The Owl in the Attic and Other Perplexities; The Seal in the Bedroom and Other Predicaments; My World—and Welcome to it*—before his death at sixty-seven.

Chronicler of man's quiet desperations, Thurber was also a cartoonist who drew a fantastic world of frustrated little men, monolithic women, and thoughtful dogs. As a writer he gave significance to what seemed inconsequential—"The Secret

Life of Walter Mitty" is a saga of all browbeaten, dream-compensating, helpless husbands. He defined humor, at least his own half-mad, half-sad humor, as "a kind of emotional chaos told about calmly and quietly in retrospect."

THE SECRET LIFE OF WALTER MITTY

"We're going through!" The Commander's voice was like thin ice breaking. He wore his full-dress uniform, with the heavily braided white cap pulled down rakishly over one cold gray eye. "We can't make it, sir. It's spoiling for a hurricane, if you ask me." "I'm not asking you, Lieutenant Berg," said the Commander. "Throw on the power lights! Rev her up to 8,500! We're going through!" The pounding of the cylinders increased: ta-pocketa-pocketa-pocketa-*pocketa-pocketa*. The Commander stared at the ice forming on the pilot window. He walked over and twisted a row of complicated dials. "Switch on No. 8 auxiliary!" he shouted. "Switch on No. 8 auxiliary!" repeated Lieutenant Berg. "Full strength in No. 3 turret!" shouted the Commander. "Full strength in No. 3 turret!" The crew, bending to their various tasks in the huge, hurtling eight-engined Navy hydroplane, looked at each other and grinned. "The Old Man'll get us through," they said to one another. "The Old Man ain't afraid of Hell!" . . .

"Not so fast! You're driving too fast!" said Mrs. Mitty. "What are you driving so fast for?"

"Hmm?" said Walter Mitty. He looked at his wife, in the seat beside him, with shocked astonishment. She seemed grossly unfamiliar, like a strange woman who had yelled at him in a crowd. "You were up to fifty-five," she said. "You know I don't like to go more than forty. You were up to fifty-five." Walter Mitty drove on toward Waterbury in silence, the roaring of the SN202 through the worst storm in twenty years of Navy flying fading in the remote, intimate airways of his mind. "You're tensed up again," said Mrs. Mitty. "It's one of your days. I wish you'd let Dr. Renshaw look you over."

Walter Mitty stopped the car in front of the building where his wife went to have her hair done. "Remember to get those overshoes while I'm having my hair done," she said. "I don't need overshoes," said Mitty. She put her mirror back into her bag. "We've been all through that," she said, getting out of the car. "You're not a young man any longer." He raced the engine a little. "Why don't you wear your gloves? Have you lost your gloves?" Walter Mitty reached in a pocket and brought out the gloves. He put them on, but after she had turned and gone into the building and he had driven on to a red light, he took them off again. "Pick it up, brother!" snapped a cop as the light changed, and Mitty hastily pulled on his gloves and lurched ahead. He drove around the streets aimlessly for a time, and then he drove past the hospital on his way to the parking lot.

. . . "It's the millionaire banker, Wellington McMillan," said the pretty nurse. "Yes?" said Walter Mitty, removing his gloves slowly. "Who has the case?" "Dr. Renshaw and Dr. Benbow, but there are two specialists here, Dr. Remington from New York and Mr. Pritchard-Mitford from London. He flew over." A door opened down a long, cool corridor and Dr. Renshaw came out. He looked distraught and haggard. "Hello, Mitty," he said. "We're having the devil's own time with McMillan, the millionaire banker and close personal friend of Roosevelt. Obstreosis of the ductal tract. Tertiary. Wish you'd take a look at him." "Glad to," said Mitty.

In the operating room there were whispered introductions: "Dr. Remington, Dr. Mitty. Mr. Pritchard-Mitford, Dr. Mitty." "I've read your book on streptothricosis," said Pritchard-Mitford, shaking hands. "A brilliant performance, sir." "Thank you," said Walter Mitty. "Didn't know you were in the States, Mitty," grumbled Remington. "Coals to Newcastle, bringing Mitford and me up here for a tertiary." "You are very kind," said Mitty. A huge, complicated machine, connected to the operating table, with many tubes and wires, began at this moment to go pocketa-pocketa-pocketa. "The new anesthetizer is giving way!" shouted an interne. "There is no one in the East who knows how to fix it!" "Quiet, man!" said Mitty, in a low, cool voice. He sprang to the machine, which was now going pocketa-pocketa-queep-pocketa-queep. He began fingering delicately a row of glistening dials. "Give me a fountain pen!" he snapped. Someone handed him a fountain pen. He pulled a faulty piston out of the machine and inserted the pen in its place. "That will hold for ten minutes," he said. "Get on with the operation." A nurse hurried over and whispered to Renshaw, and Mitty saw the man turn pale. "Coreopsis has set in," said Renshaw nervously. "If you would take over, Mitty?" Mitty looked at him and at the craven figure of Benbow, who drank, and at the grave, uncertain faces of the two great specialists. "If you wish," he said. They slipped a white gown on him; he adjusted a mask and drew on thin gloves, nurses handed him shining . . .

"Back it up, Mac! Look out for that Buick!" Walter Mitty jammed on the brakes. "Wrong lane, Mac," said the parking-lot attendant, looking at Mitty closely. "Gee. Yeh," muttered Mitty. He began cautiously to back out of the lane marked "Exit Only." "Leave her sit there," said the attendant. "I'll put her away." Mitty got out of the car. "Hey, better leave the key." "Oh," said Mitty, handing the man the ignition key. The attendant vaulted into the car, backed it up with insolent skill, and put it where it belonged.

They're so damn cocky, thought Walter Mitty, walking along Main Street; they think they know everything. Once he had tried to take his chains off, outside New Milford, and he had got them wound around the axles. A man had had to come out in a wrecking car and unwind them, a young, grinning garageman. Since then Mrs. Mitty always made him drive to a garage to have the chains taken off. The next time, he thought, I'll wear my right arm in a sling; they won't grin at me then. I'll have my right arm in a sling and they'll see I couldn't possibly take the chains off myself. He kicked at the slush on the sidewalk. "Overshoes," he said to himself, and he began looking for a shoe store.

When he came out into the street again, with the overshoes in a box under his arm, Walter Mitty began to wonder what the other thing was his wife had told him to get. She had told him twice, before they set out from their house for Waterbury. In a way he hated these weekly trips to town—he was always getting something wrong. Kleenex, he thought, Squibb's, razor blades? No. Toothpaste, toothbrush, bicarbonate, carborundum, initiative and referendum? He gave it up. But she would remember it. "Where's the what's-its-name?" she would ask. "Don't tell me you forgot the what's-its-name." A newsboy went by shouting something about the Waterbury trial.

. . . "Perhaps this will refresh your memory." The District Attorney suddenly thrust a heavy automatic at the quiet figure on the witness stand. "Have you ever seen this before?" Walter Mitty took the gun and examined it expertly. "This is my Webley-Vickers 50.80," he said calmly. An excited buzz ran around the courtroom. The judge rapped for order. "You are a crack shot with any sort of firearms, I believe?" said the District Attorney, insinuatingly. "Objection!" shouted Mitty's attorney. "We have shown that the defendant could not have fired the shot. We have shown that he wore his right arm in a sling on the night of the fourteenth of July." Walter Mitty raised his hand briefly and the bickering attorneys were stilled. "With any known make of gun," he said evenly, "I could have killed Gregory Fitzhurst at three hundred feet *with my left hand.*" Pandemonium broke loose in the courtroom. A woman's scream rose above the bedlam and suddenly a lovely, dark-haired girl was in Walter Mitty's arms. The District Attorney struck at her savagely. Without rising from his chair, Mitty let the man have it on the point of the chin. "You miserable cur!" . . .

"Puppy biscuit," said Walter Mitty. He stopped walking and the buildings of Waterbury rose up out of the misty courtroom and surrounded him again. A woman who was passing laughed. "He said 'Puppy biscuit,'" she said to her companion. "That man said 'Puppy biscuit' to himself." Walter Mitty hurried on. He went into an A. & P., not the first one he came to but a smaller one farther up the street. "I want some biscuit for small, young dogs," he said to the clerk. "Any special brand, sir?" The greatest pistol shot in the world thought a moment. "It says 'Puppies Bark for It' on the box," said Walter Mitty.

His wife would be through at the hairdresser's in fifteen minutes, Mitty saw in looking at his watch, unless they had trouble drying it; sometimes they had trouble drying it. She didn't like to get to the hotel first; she would want him to be there waiting for her as usual. He found a big leather chair in the lobby, facing a window, and he put the overshoes and the puppy biscuit on the floor beside it. He picked up an old copy of *Liberty* and sank down into the chair. "Can Germany Conquer the World Through the Air?" Walter Mitty looked at the pictures of bombing planes and of ruined streets.

. . . "The cannonading has got the wind up in young Raleigh, sir," said the sergeant. Captain Mitty looked up at him through tousled hair. "Get him to bed," he said wearily. "With the others. I'll fly alone." "But you can't, sir," said the sergeant anxiously. "It takes two men to handle that bomber and the Archies are pounding hell out of the air. Von Richtman's circus is between here and Saulier." "Somebody's got to get that ammunition dump," said Mitty. "I'm going over. Spot of brandy?" he poured a drink for the sergeant and one for himself. War thundered and whined around the dugout and battered at the door. There was a rending of wood and splinters flew through the room. "A bit of a near thing," said Captain Mitty carelessly. "The box barrage is closing in," said the sergeant. "We only live once, Sergeant," said Mitty, with his faint, fleeting smile. "Or do we?" He poured another brandy and tossed it off. "I never see a man could hold his brandy like you, sir," said the sergeant. "Begging your pardon, sir." Captain Mitty stood up and strapped on his huge Webley-Vickers automatic. "It's forty kilometers through hell, sir," said the sergeant. Mitty finished one last brandy. "After all," he said softly, "what isn't?" The pounding of the cannon increased; there was the rat-tat-tatting of machine guns, and from somewhere came the menacing pocketa-pocketa-pocketa of the new flame-throwers. Walter Mitty walked to the door of the dugout humming "Auprès de Ma Blonde." He turned and waved to the sergeant. "Cheerio!" he said. . . .

Something struck his shoulder. "I've been looking all over this hotel for you," said Mrs. Mitty. "Why do you have to hide in this old chair? How did you expect me to find you?" "Things close in," said Walter Mitty vaguely. "What?" Mrs. Mitty said. "Did you get the what's-its-name? The puppy biscuit? What's in that box?" "Overshoes," said Mitty. "Couldn't you have put them on in the store?" "I was thinking," said Walter Mitty. "Does it ever occur to you that I am sometimes thinking?" She looked at him. "I'm going to take your temperature when I get you home," she said.

They went out through the revolving doors that made a faintly derisive whistling sound when you pushed them. It was two blocks to the parking lot. At the drugstore on the corner she said, "Wait here for me. I forgot something. I won't be a minute." She was more than a minute. Walter Mitty lighted a cigarette. It began to rain, rain with sleet in it. He stood up against the wall of the drugstore, smoking. . . . He put his shoulders back and his heels together. "To hell with the handkerchief," said Walter Mitty scornfully. He took one last drag on his cigarette and snapped it away. Then, with that faint, fleeting smile playing about his lips, he faced the firing squad; erect and motionless, proud and disdainful, Walter Mitty the Undefeated, inscrutable to the last.

FILE AND FORGET

I want to thank my secretary, Miss Ellen Bagley, for putting the following letters in order. I was not up to the task myself, for reasons that will, I think, become clear to the reader.   J. T.

WEST CORNWALL, CONN.
NOVEMBER 2, 1949

Miss Alma Winege,
The Charteriss Publishing Co.,
132 East What Street,
New York, N.Y.

DEAR MISS WINEGE:
    Your letter of October 25th, which you sent to me in care of
The Homestead, Hot Springs, Ark., has been forwarded to my
home in West Cornwall, Conn., by The Homestead, Hot Springs,
Va. As you know, Mrs. Thurber and I sometimes visit this Virginia resort, but we haven't been there for more than a year. Your
company, in the great tradition of publishers, has sent so many
letters to me at Hot Springs, Ark., that the postmaster there has
simply taken to sending them on to the right address, or what
would be the right address if I were there. I explained to Mr. Cluffman, and also to Miss Lexy, when I last called at your offices,
that all mail was to be sent to me at West Cornwall until further
notice. If and when I go to The Homestead, I will let you know in
advance. Meanwhile, I suggest that you remove from your files
all addresses of mine except the West Cornwall one. Another
publishing firm recently sent a letter to me at 65 West 11th Street,
an address I vacated in the summer of 1930. It would not come as
a surprise to me if your firm, or some other publishers, wrote me
in care of my mother at 568 Oak Street, Columbus, Ohio. I was
thirteen years old when we lived there, back in 1908.
    As for the contents of your letter of the 25th, I did *not* order
thirty-six copies of Peggy Peckham's book, "Grandma Was a
Nudist." I trust that you have not shipped these books to me in
care of The Homestead, Hot Springs, Ark., or anywhere else.

Sincerely yours,
J. THURBER

    P.S. Margaret Peckham, by the way, is not the author of this
book. She is the distinguished New York psychiatrist whose "The
Implications of Nudism" was published a couple of years ago.
She never calls herself Peggy.   J. T.

WEST CORNWALL, CONN.
NOVEMBER 3, 1949

Miss Alma Winege
The Charteriss Publishing Co.,
132 East What Street,
New York, N.Y.

DEAR MISS WINEGE:

In this morning's mail I received a card from the Grand Central branch of the New York Post Office informing me that a package of books had been delivered to me at 410 East 57th Street. The branch office is holding the package for further postage, which runs to a considerable amount. I am enclosing the notification card, since these must be the thirty-six copies of "Grandma Was a Nudist." I have not lived at 410 East 57th Street since the fall of 1944. Please see to it that this address is removed from your files, along with The Homestead address.

Whoever ordered those books, if anyone actually did, probably wonders where they are.

Sincerely yours,
J. THURBER

THE CHARTERISS PUBLISHING COMPANY
NEW YORK, N.Y.

November 5, 1949

Mr. James M. Thurber,
West Cornwall, Conn.

DEAR MR. THURBER:

I am dreadfully sorry about the mixup over Miss Peckham's book. We have been pretty much upset around here since the departure of Mr. Peterson and Mr. West, and several new girls came to us with the advent of Mr. Jordan. They have not yet got their "sea legs," I am afraid, but I still cannot understand from what file our shipping department got your address as 165 West 11th Street. I have removed the 57th Street address from the files and also the Arkansas address and I trust that we will not disturb your tranquillity further up there in Cornwall. It must be lovely this time of year in Virginia and I envy you and Mrs. Thurber. Have a lovely time at The Homestead.

Sincerely yours,
ALMA WINEGE

P.S. What you had to say about "Grandma" amused us all. A. W.

COLUMBUS, OHIO
NOVEMBER 16, 1949

DEAR MR. THURBER:

I have decided to come right out with the little problem that was accidentally dumped in my lap yesterday. I hope you will forgive me for what happened, and perhaps you can suggest what I should do with the books. There are three dozen of them and, unfortunately, they arrived when my little son Donald was alone downstairs. By the time I found out about the books, he had torn off the wrappings and had built a cute little house out of them. I have placed them all on a shelf out of his reach while awaiting word as to where to send them. I presume I could ship them to you C.O.D. if I can get somebody to wrap them properly.

I heard from old Mrs. Winston next door that you and your family once lived here at 568 Oak Street. She remembers you and your brothers as cute little tykes who were very noisy and raised rabbits and guinea pigs. She says your mother was a wonderful cook. I am sorry about Donald opening the books and I hope you will forgive him.

Sincerely yours,
CLARA EDWARDS
(Mrs. J. C.)

WEST CORNWALL, CONN.
NOVEMBER 19, 1949

Mr. Leon Charteriss,
The Charteriss Publishing Co.,
132 East What Street,
New York, N.Y.
DEAR MR. CHARTERISS:

I am enclosing a letter from a Mrs. J. C. Edwards, of Columbus, Ohio, in the fervent hope that you will do something to stop this insane flux of books. I never ordered these books. I have not read "Grandma Was a Nudist." I do not intend to read it. I want something done to get these volumes off my trail and cut out of my consciousness.

I have written Miss Winege about the situation, but I am afraid to take it up with her again, because she might send them to me in care of the Department of Journalism at Ohio State University, where I was a student more than thirty years ago.

Sincerely yours,

J. THURBER

P.S. I never use my middle initial, but your firm seems to think it is "M." It is not.   J. T.

THE CHARTERISS PUBLISHING COMPANY
NEW YORK, N.Y.

NOVEMBER 23, 1949

Mr. James M. Thurber,
West Cornwall, Conn.

DEAR MR. THURBER:

Mr. Charteriss has flown to California on a business trip and will be gone for several weeks. His secretary has turned your letter of the 19th over to me. I have asked Mr. Cluffman to write to Miss Clara Edwards in Columbus and arrange for the reshipment of the thirty-six copies of "Grandma Was a Nudist."

I find, in consulting the records, that you have three times ordered copies of your own book, "Thurber's Ark," to be shipped to you at West Cornwall, at the usual discount rate of forty per cent. I take it that what you really wanted was thirty-six copies of your own book and they are being sent out to you today with our regrets for the discomfit we have caused you. I hope you will be a little patient with us during this so trying period of reorganization.

Cordially yours,

JEANNETTE GAINES

Stock Order Dept.

P.S. You will be happy to know that we have traced down the gentleman who ordered those copies of "Grandma."

WEST CORNWALL, CONN.
NOVEMBER 25, 1949

Mr. Henry Johnson,
The Charteriss Pub. Co.,
New York, N.Y.

DEAR HARRY:

Since the reorganization at Charteriss, I have the forlorn and depressing feeling that I no longer know anybody down there except you. I know that this immediate problem of mine is not in your field, but I turn to you as a last resource. What I want, or rather what I don't want, is simple enough, Harry. God knows it is simple.

I don't want any more copies of my book. I don't want any more copies of my book. I don't want any more copies of my book.

As ever,

Jim

P.S. It has just occurred to me that I haven't seen you for more than two years. Let's have a drink one of these days. I'll give you a ring the next time I'm in the city.   J. T.

The Charteriss Publishing Company

New York,N.Y.

November 26, 1949

Mr. James Grover Thurber,
Cornwall, Conn.
Dear Jim Thurber:

I haven't had the pleasure of meeting you since I had the great good luck to join forces with Charteriss, but I look forward to our meeting with a high heart. Please let me know the next time you are in the city, as I should like to wine and dine you and perhaps discuss the new book that I feel confident you have in you. If you don't want to talk shop, we can discuss the record of our mutual football team. You were at Northwestern some years ahead of my time, I believe, but I want you to know that they still talk about Jimmy Thurber out there.

Your letter to Harry Johnson has just come to my attention, and I regret to say that Harry is no longer with us. He went to Simon and Schuster in the summer of 1948. I want you to feel, however, that every single one of us here is your friend, willing and eager to drop everything to do your slightest bidding. All of us feel very deeply about your having turned against your book "Thurber's Ark." I note that in your present mood you have the feeling that you never want to see it again. Well, Jim, let me assure you that this is just a passing fancy, derived from a moment of depression. When you put in your last order for thirty-six copies, you must surely have had some definite use in mind for them, and I am banking on twenty years' experience in the book-publishing game when I take the liberty of sending these twenty books off to you today. There is one thing I am something of an expert at, if I do say so myself, and that is the understanding of the "creative spirit."

We have a new system here, which is to send our authors not ten free copies, as of old, but fifteen. Therefore, five of the thirty-six copies will reach you with our compliments. The proper deductions will be made on the record.

Don't forget our dinner date.

Cordially,

CLINT JORDAN

P.S. I approve of your decision to resume the use of your middle name. It gives a book dignity and flavor to use all three names. I think it was old Willa Cather who started the new trend, when she dropped the Seibert.   C. J.

THE CHARTERISS PUBLISHING COMPANY
NEW YORK, N.Y.
DECEMBER 13, 1949

DEAR THURBER:

Just back at the old desk after a trip to California and a visit with my mother, who is eighty-nine now but as chipper as ever. She would make a swell Profile. Ask me about her someday.

Need I say I was delighted to hear from the staff when I got back about your keen interest in "Grandma Was a Nudist"? The book has been moving beautifully and its ceiling has gone sky-high. We're planning a brief new advertising campaign and I'd be tickled pink if you would be good enough to bat out a blurb for us.

Yours,

LEON

THE CHARTERISS PUBLISHING COMPANY
NEW YORK, N.Y.
DECEMBER 15, 1949

Mr. James M. Thurber,
West Cornwall, Conn.
DEAR MR. THURBER:

I hope you will forgive me—indeed, all of us—for having inexcusably mislaid the address of the lady to whom the thirty-six copies of "Grandma Was a Nudist" were sent by mistake. I understand that we have already dispatched to you at your home another thirty-six volumes of that book.

My apologies again.

Sincerely yours,
H. F. CLUFFMAN

WEST CORNWALL, CONN.
DECEMBER 19, 1949

Mr. H. F. Cluffman,
The Charteriss Publishing Co.,
132 East What Street,
New York, N.Y.
DEAR MR. CLUFFMAN:

The lady's name is Mrs. J. C. Edwards, and she lives at 568 Oak Street, Columbus, Ohio.

I have explained as clearly as I could in previous letters that I did not order thirty-six copies of "Grandma Was a Nudist." If you have actually shipped to me another thirty-six copies of this book, it will make a total of seventy-two copies, none of which I will pay for. The thirty-six copies of "Thurber's Ark" that Mr. Jordan has written me he intends to send to West Cornwall would bring up to one hundred and eight the total number of books that your firm, by a conspiracy of confusion unique even in the case of publishers, has mistakenly charged to my account. You may advise Mr. Jordan that I do not wish to receive the five free copies he mentioned in his letter.

If your entire staff of employees went back to *Leslie's Weekly,* where they belong, it would set my mind at rest.

Sincerely yours,
J. THURBER

P.S. I notice that you use only my middle initial, "M." Mr. Jordan and I — or was it Mr. Charteriss? — have decided to resume the use of the full name, which is Murfreesboro.   J. T.

WEST CORNWALL, CONN.
DECEMBER 27, 1949

Mr. Leon Charteriss,
The Charteriss Publishing Co.,
132 East What Street,
New York, N.Y.

DEAR MR. CHARTERISS:

I am sure you will be sorry to learn that Mr. Thurber has had one of his spells as a result of the multiplication of books and misunderstanding that began with Miss Alma Winege's letter of October 25, 1949. Those of us around Mr. Thurber are greatly disturbed by the unfortunate circumstances that have caused him to give up writing, at least temporarily, just after he had resumed work following a long fallow period.

Thirty-six copies of Mr. Thurber's book and thirty-six copies of "Grandma Was a Nudist" have arrived at his home here, and he has asked me to advise you that he intends to burn all seventy-two. West Cornwall is scarcely the community for such a demonstration—he proposes to burn them in the middle of U.S. Highway No. 7—since the town regards with a certain suspicion any writer who has not won a Pulitzer Prize. I am enclosing copies of all the correspondence between your company and Mr. Thurber, in the hope that someone connected with your firm will read it with proper care and intelligence and straighten out this deplorable and inexcusable situation.

Mr. Thurber wishes me to tell you that he does not want to hear from any of you again.

Sincerely yours,
ELLEN BAGLEY
Secretary to Mr. Thurber

THE CHARTERISS PUBLISHING COMPANY
NEW YORK, N.Y.

DECEMBER 28, 1949

Mr. James Murfreesboro Thurber,
72 West,
Cornwall, Conn.
DEAR MR. THURBER:

I have at hand your letter of December 19th, the opening paragraph of which puzzles me. You send me the following name and address—Mrs. J. C. Edwards, 568 Oak Street, Columbus, Ohio—but it is not clear what use you wish me to make of this. I would greatly appreciate it if you would clear up this small matter for me.

Sincerely yours,
H. F. CLUFFMAN

P.S. *Leslie's Weekly* ceased publication many years ago. I could obtain the exact date if you so desire.   H. F. C.

THE CHARTERISS PUBLISHING COMPANY
NEW YORK, N.Y.
DECEMBER 29, 1949

Mr. James M. Thurber,
West Cornwall, Conn.
DEAR MR. THURBER:

You will be sorry to hear that Mr. Charteriss was taken suddenly ill with a virus infection. His doctor believes that he lost his immunity during his visit to the West Coast. He is now in the hospital, but his condition is not serious.

Since the departure of Miss Gaines, who was married last week, I have taken over the Stock Order Department for the time being. I did not take the liberty of reading your enclosures in the letter to Mr. Charteriss, but sent them directly to him at the hospital. I am sure that he will be greatly cheered up by them when he is well enough to read. Meanwhile, I want you to know that you can repose all confidence in the Stock Order Department to look after your needs, whatever they may be.

Sincerely yours,

GLADYS MACLEAN

P.S. I learned from Mr. Jordan that you were a friend of Willa Cather's. Exciting!

COLUMBUS, OHIO
JANUARY 3, 1950

DEAR JAMIE:

I don't understand the clipping from the Lakeville *Journal* Helen's mother sent me, about someone burning all those books of yours in the street. I never heard of such a thing, and don't understand how they could have taken the books without your knowing it, or what you were doing with so many copies of the novel about the naked grandmother. Imagine, at her age! She couldn't carry on like that in Columbus, let me tell you. Why, when I was a girl, you didn't dare walk with a man after sunset, unless he was your husband, and even then there was talk.

It's a good thing that state policeman came along in time to save most of the books from being completely ruined, and you must be thankful for the note Mr. Jordan put in one of the books, for the policeman would never have known who they belonged to if he hadn't found it.

A Mrs. Edwards phoned this morning and said that her son Donald collects your books and wants to send them to you—to be autographed, I suppose. Her son has dozens of your books and I told her you simply wouldn't have time to sign all of them, and she said she didn't care what you did with them. And then she said they weren't your books at all, and so I just hung up on her.

Be sure to bundle up when you go out.

With love,
MOTHER

P.S. This Mrs. Edwards says she lives at 568 Oak Street. I told her we used to live there and she said God knows she was aware of that. I don't know what she meant. I was afraid this little boy would send you all those books to sign and so I told his mother that you and Helen were at The Homestead, in Hot Springs. You don't suppose he would send them there, do you?

And here, gentle reader, I know you will be glad to leave all of us.

Isaac Bashevis Singer

Isaac Bashevis Singer was born in 1904 in the Polish town of Radzymin. Son and grandson of rabbis, he attended the Rabbinical Seminary Warsaw, but decided against overseeing a congregation. Instead he went to work for the Yiddish press in Poland. At thirty he came to the United States and wrote for the New York *Jewish Daily Forward*. Articles and book reviews were followed by stories written in Yiddish, translated into English, and published in national magazines as culturally far apart as *Commentary* and *Esquire*. In his mid-sixties Singer's published works in English included half a dozen novels, five collections of short stories, four books for children, and a memoir, *In My Father's Court*. All of them received an immediate and enthusiastic response.

Inexhaustibly inventive, Singer is a natural teller of tales. He is a Yiddish Maupassant: his stories escape categories. They are gay and grotesque, pious and skeptical, macabre and metaphysical, and always sensitive to the nuances of everyday speech. Writing in a special tongue, Singer holds his readers with universal understanding.

COCKADOODLEDOO

Cockadoodledoo! In your language this means good morning, time to get up, day is breaking in Pinchev. What a lot of words you people use! For us chickens, cockadoodledoo says everything. And how much it can mean! It all depends on the melody, the accent, the tone.

I am a great-grandson of the rooster who perched on King Solomon's chair and I know languages. Therefore I tell you that one cockadoodledoo is worth more than a hundred words. It's not so much a matter of voice as it is of the flap of the wings, the way the comb quivers, the eye tilts, the neck feathers ruffle.

We even have what you call dialects. A Litvak rooster crows cookerikoo, a Polish rooster crows cookerikee, and there are some who can even manage cockerikko. Each has a style inherited from generations of roosters. Even the same chicken will never crow the same way twice. But for such distinctions you need a good ear.

On my mother's side I have blood of the Ancient Prophetic Woodcock. If you put me in a dark cage, I can tell by the pitch of the roosters' crowing and the hens clucking whether it is day-break or twilight, clear or cloudy, whether it is mild or a frost is coming, if it's raining, snowing, or hailing. My ear tells me that the moon is full, half full, or new. I even can tell an eclipse of the sun. I know a thousand things that don't even occur to you. You talk too much, you drown in your own words. All truth lies hidden in one word: cockadoodledoo.

I wasn't born yesterday. A world of hens and roosters has passed before my eyes. I have seen a rooster castrated and force-fed. I know the end all too well: death. Whether they'll make a sacrifice of me for Yom Kippur, whether they'll put me aside until Passover, Succoth or for the Sabbath of Moses' Song of the Red Sea, the slaughterer waits, the knife is sharp, everything is prepared: the tub for soaking, the salting board, the gravy bowl, the stew pot, or maybe the roasting oven.

The garbage dump is crammed with our heads and entrails. Every good-for-nothing housewife carries around one of our wings for a whisk broom. Even if by some chance I should miss the slaughterer's knife, I still can't last indefinitely. I might get a nail in my gizzard. I might catch the pip. I might have—may it not happen to you—pox in my bowels. I might gulp down a wire, a pebble, a needle, a little snake. Every fowl ends up in the bowl.

So then what? Cockadoodledoo resolves all questions, solves all riddles. The rooster may die but not the cockadoodledoo. We were crowing long before Adam and, God willing, we'll go on crowing long after all slaughterers and chicken-gluttons have been laid low. What is rooster, then, and what is hen? Nothing more than a nesting place for the cockadoodledoo. No butcher in the world can destroy that.

There exists a heavenly rooster—his image is our own; and there is a heavenly Cockadoodledoo. The Rooster on High crows through our windpipes, he performs the midnight services through us, gets up with us for prayers when the morning stars sing together. You people pore over the Cabala and rack your brains. But for us the Cabala is in the marrow of our bones. What is cockadoodledoo? A magical name.

Maybe I'm betraying secrets. But to whom am I talking? To deaf ears. Your ancestors were never able to find out the secret of the cockadoodledoo; it is certain that you won't either. It is said that in distant countries there are machines where they hatch out hens by the millions and pull them out by the shelfful. The slaughterhouse is as big as our marketplace. One butcher boy ties, one cuts, one plucks. Tubs fill up with blood. Feathers fly. Every moment a thousand fowl give up their souls. And yet, can they really finish us this way?

Right now, while I'm talking, the under side of my wing begins to itch. I want to hold myself back, but I can't. My throat tickles, my tongue trembles, my beak itches, my comb burns. The quill of every feather tingles. It must come out! Cockadoodledoo!

2

Apropos of what you say about hens: you mustn't take them too lightly. When I was a young rooster, a hen was less than nothing to me. What is a hen? No comb, no spurs, no color in her tail, no strength in her claws. She cackles her few years away, lays eggs, hatches them, rubs her what-do-you-call-it in the dirt, puts on pious airs.

At an early age I began to see the hypocrisy of hens. They bow down to every big shot. Among themselves, in their own yard, whoever is stronger picks on the others. I have a hatred of gossip and a hen just can't hold her tongue. Cluck-cluck and cluck-cluck. My rule is: don't talk too much with a chicken. It is true that you can't get along without them. Everybody has a mother. But what of it? You can't stay stuck in the eggshell forever.

But that's the conceit of young roosters. With age I found that it must be this way. In all lands and in all the heavens there is male and female. Everything is paired, from the fly to the elephant, from the Rooster on High to the ordinary cock. It is true that cluck-cluck is just not the same as cockadoodledoo, but a hen, too, is not to be sneezed at.

Your so-called philosophers love to ask: which came first, the chicken or the egg? Garrulous chickens argue endlessly: which came first, the cockadoodledoo or the cluck-cluck? But all this is empty chatter. My opinion is that there was no first egg and there's not going to be any last egg. First is last and last is first. You don't understand? The answer is: cockadoodledoo.

I have five wives and each one is a tale in herself. Kara is a princess. Where she got her pedigree, I couldn't say. She is fat, easygoing, has golden eyes and a tranquil heart. She does not hobnob with the other hens. When the mistress scatters a handful of millet, the rabble run to grab it, but Kara has both patience and faith. The kernel destined for her will reach her. She keeps herself clean, doesn't look at other cocks, avoids bickering. She has the right to peck at all her competitors but considers it beneath her dignity to start up with every silly hen. She clucks less than the others and the eggs that she lays are big and white.

I have no great passion for her nor she for me, but I have more chicks by her than by any of the others. Every year she hatches two dozen eggs and without complaint she does everything that a hen should. When she's through with her laying, they'll put her away and she'll make a rich soup. I suspect that she doesn't even know that there's such a thing as death, because she likes to play around with the guts of her sisters. That's Kara.

Tsip is the exact opposite: red, thin, bony, a screecher, a glutton, and jealous—fire and flame. She picks on all the hens, but loves me terribly. Just let her see me coming and down she plops and spreads her wings. In your language you would say she is oversexed, but I forgive her everything. She twitches, every limb quivers. Her eggs are tiny, with bloody specks. In all the time I've known her she's never stopped screaming. She runs around the yard as though she were possessed. She complains and complains. This one pecked her, that one bit her, the third one pulled some down from her breast, the fourth grabbed a crumb from under her beak. Lays eggs and doesn't remember where. Tries to fly and almost breaks a leg. Suddenly she's in a tree and then on a roof. At night in the coop she doesn't close an eye. Fidgets, cackles, can't find any place for herself. A witch with an itch. They would have slaughtered her long ago if she were not so skinny, eating herself up alive—and for what? That's Tsip.

Chip is completely white, a hen without any meanness in her, as good as a sunny day, quiet as a dove. She runs from quarrels as from fire. At the least hubbub she stops laying. She loves me with a chaste love, considers me a hen-chaser, but keeps everything to herself. She clucks with a soft-tongued cluck and gets fatter every day.

If she feels like sitting on eggs and there are none to sit on, she might sit on a little white stone; she isn't very bright. The other day she hatched out three duck eggs. As long as the ducklings didn't crawl into the water, Chip thought they were chicks; but as soon as they began to swim in the pond, she almost dropped dead. Chip stood by the bank, her mother's heart close to bursting. I tried to explain to her what a bastard is, but try to talk to a frightened mother.

For some strange reason, Chip loves Tsip and does everything to please her. But Tsip is her blood enemy. Anyone else in Chip's place would have scratched her eyes out long ago; but Chip is good and asks for no reward. She's full of the mercy which comes from the Heavenly Chicken. That's Chip.

Pre-pre is the lowest hen I've ever met. Has all the vices a hen can have: black as coal, thin as a stick, a thief, a tattletale, a scrapper, and blind in one eye from a fight with her first husband, may the dunghill rest lightly on him. She carries on with strange roosters, slips into other people's yards, rummages in all kinds of garbage. She has the comb of a rooster and the voice of a rooster. When the moon is full, she starts to crow as though possessed by a dybbuk.

She lays an egg and devours it herself or cracks it open from sheer meanness. I hate her, that Black Daughter of a Black Mother. How many times I've sworn to have no dealings with the slut, but when she wants what's coming to her, she begins to fawn, flatter, gaze into my eyes like a beggar.

I'm no fighter by nature, but Pre-pre has a bad effect on me. I grab her by the head feathers and chase her all over the yard. My other wives avoid her like the plague. Many times our mistress wanted to catch her and send her to the slaughterer, but just when she's wanted she's not at home, that gadabout, that dog of a hen. That's Pre-pre.

Cluckele is my own little daughter, Kara is her mother, and a father doesn't gossip about his daughter even when she's his wife. I look at her and I don't believe my own eyes: when did she grow up? Only yesterday, it seems, this was a tiny little chick, just out of the eggshell, hardly covered with down. But she's already coquettish, already knows hennish wiles and lays eggs, although they're small. Very soon I'll be the father of my own grandchildren.

I love her, but I suspect that her little heart belongs to another rooster, that cross-eyed idiot on the other side of the fence. What she sees in that sloppy tramp, I have no idea. But how can a rooster know what a hen sees in another rooster? Her head could be turned by a feather in the tail, a tooth in the comb, a side spur, or even the way he shuffles his feet in the sand and stirs up the dust.

I'm good to her, but she doesn't appreciate it. I give her advice, but she doesn't listen. I guard her like the apple of my eye, but she's always looking for excitement. . . . The new generation is completely spoiled, but what can I do? One thing I want: as long as I live, may she live too. What happens afterward is not up to me.

3

Your experts in the Cabala know that cockadoodledoo is based on sheer faith. What else, logic? But faith itself has different degrees. A rooster's little faith may give out and he will become crestfallen. His wings droop, his comb turns white, his eyes glaze over and his crow sticks in his gullet. Why crow? For whom and for how long? Roosters have been crowing since ancient times and for what? When one begins to think about time, it's no good. Occasionally a rooster will even weep. Yes, roosters are capable of weeping. Listen sometime to the roosters crowing the night before Yom Kippur when you people are reciting the midnight prayers. If your human ears could hear our weeping, you would throw away all your slaughtering knives.

But let me tell you something that happened.

The night was dark. The chickens dozed or pretended to doze. It was during the Ten Days of Repentance before the Yom Kippur sacrifice of fowls. All day long it was oppressively hot. At night the sky clouded over, hiding a sliver of moon. The air was warm and humid like the mud in the duck pond. There was lightning, but no thunder, no rain. People closed their shutters and snored under their feather comforters. The grass stood motionless; the leaves on the apple trees were still; even the grasshoppers fell asleep. The frogs in the swamp were voiceless. The moles rested in their molehills.

Everything was silent, everything held its breath. It seemed as if the world had asked the ultimate question and was waiting for an answer: yes or no, one way or another. Things cannot go on like this. If a clear answer does not come, creation will return to primeval chaos. I did not move. My heart didn't beat, my blood didn't flow, nothing stirred. It was midnight, but I had no urge to crow. Had the end come?

Suddenly a flap of wings and from somewhere close at hand: cockadoodledoo! I trembled. I became all ears. It was the old cockadoodledoo, but with a new meaning. No, not the old one, but a brand-new one: a new style, another approach, a different melody. I didn't know what it was saying, but suddenly everything was light, I felt rejuvenated. Is it possible? I asked myself. Millions of generations of roosters had crowed, but no one before had ever crowed like that. It opened doors in my brain, it cheered my heart. It spilled over with hope and happiness. Could it really be? I asked. And I, fool that I was, had doubted! I felt both shame and joy. I, too, wanted to crow, but I was shy. What could I say after him? Tsip woke up and asked, "What's that?"

"A new voice, a new word," I said. "Chickens, let us join in a blessing. We have not lived in vain."

"Who is he, where is he?" asked Chip.

"What difference does it make who he is? The power lies in the crowing, not in the rooster."

"Still—"

I didn't answer her. I closed my eyes. The crowing had stopped, but its sound still echoed in the silence from trees, roofs, chimneys, birdhouses. It sang like a fiddle, rang like a bell, resounded like a ram's horn. It sang and didn't stop singing.

The dog in the kennel awoke and barked once. The pig in his sty uttered a grunt; the horse in the stable thumped the ground with his hoof. The clouds parted in the sky and a moon appeared, white as chalk. For a while I thought: who knows, perhaps I only imagined it. True, the hens heard it too, but perhaps it was a dream, perhaps it was only the wind. Perhaps it was a wolf howling, the sound of a trumpet, a hunter's call, a drunkard's shout.

Even though fowl wait all their lives for a miracle, still, when it happens, they can't believe it. I expected the other roosters to answer him as usual, but I didn't hear a sound. Had all the roosters been slaughtered, with only this one left? Perhaps I myself was already slaughtered and the voice I heard was only the dream of a chopped-off head? The stillness was not of this world. I stuck my beak in my feathers and pinched my own skin to see if it hurt.

Suddenly: cockadoodledoo! It was the same rooster and the same crow. No, not the same, already different: a song which rent the soul and then revived it; a melody lifting a rooster's heart into heights where no eagle ever flew, above all towers, all clouds, into a brightness that made the stars seem dark.

Everything I know I learned that night. I can't reveal secrets — my tongue is tied — but there is a cockadoodledoo which rights every wrong, forgives every sin, straightens all crookedness. Everything is cockadoodledoo: butcher and fowl; knife and throat; feathers and plucker; the blood in the veins and the blood in the ditch. Crow, rooster, and ask no questions! We must accept all: the crow of the rooster, the cluck of the hen, the egg which is hatched, the egg which is eaten, the egg which is stepped upon, and the egg with the splotch of blood in it.

Sing, rooster, praise God, love your hens, don't fight with other roosters unless they attack you. Eat your grain, drink your water, stand on the rooftop and crow as if the whole world — all four corners of it — were waiting for your crowing. It is really waiting. Without your crowing, something would be missing. You don't understand? God willing, you will understand. You have eternity behind you and eternity before you. You will go through many lives. If you knew what awaits you, you would die of joy. But that wouldn't do. As long as you live, you must live. . . .

All night long that rooster crowed and not a single rooster dared answer him. He was a cantor without a choir. Just at daybreak, when it began to redden in the East, he let out his last crow — the loudest, the loveliest, the most divine.

The next day there was a furor among the neighboring roosters. Some swore by their comb and spurs that they had heard nothing. Others admitted they had heard something, but it wasn't a rooster. As for the hens, every one of them had forgotten. What will chickens not do to avoid the truth? They fear the truth more than the knife, and this is in itself a mystery.

But since that rooster crowed — exalted be his name — and I had the privilege to hear and to remember, I have wanted to spread the word, especially since tomorrow is the day before Yom Kippur. Happy is he who believes. A time will come when all will see and hear, and the cockadoodledoo of the Rooster on High will ring throughout heaven and earth.

Cockadoodledoo!

Translated by Ruth Whitman

S. J. Perelman

Sidney Joseph Perelman was born in Brooklyn in 1904 and immediately after graduating from Brown University began writing burlesques of current clichés for various weeklies. His first book, *Dawn Ginsbergh's Revenge*, was published when he was twenty-five, and he was immediately whisked off to Hollywood. There he wrote screenplays for the Marx Brothers —*Monkey Business* and *Horse Feathers* rank as film classics that are *sui generis* to a fault. From then on, according to Robert Benchley, who furnished an introduction to Perelman's *Strictly from Hunger,* "It was just a matter of time before Perelman took over the *dementia praecox* field."

In his late twenties he and his brother-in-law, the late Nathanael West, bought a farm in Bucks County, Pennsylvania, but in his mid-sixties he found himself disaffected by the political climate of the United States and moved to London. "The news in my own country," he explained, "is so filled with insanity and violence that the newspapers from which I derive many of my ideas have scant room for the sort of thing that turns me on—the bizarre, the unusual, the eccentric. In Britain they still have a taste for eccentricity."

At first glance such volumes as *The Dream Department, Crazy Like a Fox, Acres and Pains,* and *The Ill-Tempered Clavichord* look like mere nonsense. Actually they are furious, though hilarious, protests against the nonsense that clutters the world of lushly advertised products from bargain cruises to breakfast foods. Perelman's estimate is more modest. In an introduction to *The Best of S. J. Perelman,* his alter ego "Sidney Namlerep" wrote: "In any consideration of S. J. Perelman—and S. J. Perelman certainly deserves the same consideration one accords old ladies on street cars, babies traveling unescorted on planes, and the feeble-minded generally—it is important to remember the crushing, the well-nigh intolerable odds under which the man has struggled to produce what may well be the most picayune prose ever produced in America. The damage he has done to the language is incalculable." His admirers, however, maintain that his verbal lunacies—such as "I have Bright's disease and he has mine," "I had gone into the Corn Exchange bank to exchange some corn"—have enriched the language with effervescent word-plays and mad but penetrating parodies.

INSERT FLAP "A" AND THROW AWAY

One stifling summer afternoon last August, in the attic of a tiny stone house in Pennsylvania, I made a most interesting discovery: the shortest, cheapest method of inducing a nervous breakdown ever perfected. In this technique (eventually adopted by the psychology department of Duke University, which will adopt anything), the subject is placed in a sharply sloping attic heated to 340° F. and given a mothproof closet known as the Jiffy-Cloz to assemble. The Jiffy-Cloz, procurable at any department store or neighborhood insane asylum, consists of half a dozen gigantic sheets of red cardboard, two plywood doors, a clothes rack, and a packet of staples. With these is included a set of instructions mimeographed in pale-violet ink, fruity with phrases like "Pass Section F through Slot AA, taking care not to fold tabs behind washers (see Fig. 9)." The cardboard is so processed that as the subject struggles convulsively to force the staple through, it suddenly buckles, plunging the staple deep into his thumb. He thereupon springs up with a dolorous cry and smites his knob (Section K) on the rafters (RR). As a final demonic touch, the Jiffy-Cloz people cunningly omit four of the staples necessary to finish the job, so that after indescribable purgatory, the best the subject can possibly achieve is a sleazy, capricious structure which would reduce any self-respecting moth to helpless laughter. The cumulative frustration, the tropical heat, and the soft, ghostly chuckling of the moths are calculated to unseat the strongest mentality.

In a period of rapid technological change, however, it was inevitable that a method as cumbersome as the Jiffy-Cloz would be superseded. It was superseded at exactly nine-thirty Christmas morning by a device called the Self-Running 10-Inch Scale-Model Delivery-Truck Kit Powered by Magic Motor, costing twenty-nine cents. About nine on that particular morning, I was spread-eagled on my bed, indulging in my favorite sport of mouth-breathing, when a cork fired from a child's air gun mysteriously lodged in my throat. The pellet proved awkward for a while, but I finally ejected it by flailing the little marksman (and his sister, for good measure) until their welkins rang, and sauntered in to breakfast. Before I could choke down a healing fruit juice, my consort, a tall, regal creature indistinguishable from Cornelia, the Mother of the Gracchi, except that her foot was entangled in a roller skate, swept in. She extended a large, unmistakable box covered with diagrams.

"Now don't start making excuses," she whined. "It's just a simple cardboard toy. The directions are on the back —"

"Look, dear," I interrupted, rising hurriedly and pulling on my overcoat, "it clean slipped my mind. I'm supposed to take a lesson in crosshatching at Zim's School of Cartooning today."

"On Christmas?" she asked suspiciously.

"Yes, it's the only time they could fit me in," I countered glibly. "This is the big week for crosshatching, you know, between Christmas and New Year's."

"Do you think you ought to go in your pajamas?" she asked.

"Oh, that's O.K.," I smiled. "We often work in our pajamas up at Zim's. Well, goodbye now. If I'm not home by Thursday, you'll find a cold snack in the safe-deposit box." My subterfuge, unluckily, went for naught, and in a trice I was sprawled on the nursery floor, surrounded by two lambkins and ninety-eight segments of the Self-Running 10-Inch Scale-Model Delivery-Truck Construction Kit.

The theory of the kit was simplicity itself, easily intelligible to Kettering of General Motors, Professor Millikan, or any first-rate physicist. Taking as my starting point the only sentence I could comprehend, "Fold down on all lines marked 'fold down;' fold up on all lines marked 'fold up,'" I set the children to work and myself folded up with an album of views of Chili Williams. In a few moments, my skin was suffused with a delightful tingling sensation and I was ready for the second phase, lightly referred to in the directions as "Preparing the Spring Motor Unit." As nearly as I could determine after twenty minutes of mumbling, the Magic Motor ("No Electricity—No Batteries—Nothing to Wind—Motor Never Wears Out") was an accordion-pleated affair operating by torsion, attached to the axles. "It is necessary," said the text, "to cut a slight notch in each of the axles with a knife (see Fig. C.). To find the exact place to cut this notch, lay one of the axles over diagram at bottom of page."

"Well, *now* we're getting some place!" I boomed, with a false gusto that deceived nobody. "Here, Buster, run in and get Daddy a knife."

"I dowanna," quavered the boy, backing away. "You always cut yourself at this stage." I gave the wee fellow an indulgent pat on the head that flattened it slightly, to teach him civility, and commandeered a long, serrated bread knife from the kitchen. "Now watch me closely, children," I ordered. "We place the axle on the diagram as in Fig. C, applying a strong downward pressure on the knife handle at all times." The axle must have been a factory second, because an instant later I was in the bathroom grinding my teeth in agony and attempting to stanch the flow of blood. Ultimately, I succeeded in contriving a rough bandage and slipped back into the nursery without awaking the children's suspicions. An agreeable surprise awaited me. Displaying a mechanical aptitude clearly inherited from their sire, the rascals had put together the chassis of the delivery truck.

"Very good indeed," I complimented (naturally, one has to exaggerate praise to develop a child's self-confidence). "Let's see — what's the next step? Ah, yes. 'Lock into box shape by inserting tabs C, D, E, F, G, H, J, K, and L into slots C, D, E, F, G, H, J, K, and L. Ends of front axle should be pushed through holes A and B.'" While marshalling the indicated parts in their proper order, I emphasized to my rapt listeners the necessity of patience and perseverance. "Haste makes waste, you know," I reminded them. "Rome wasn't built in a day. Remember, your daddy isn't always going to be here to show you."

"Where *are* you going to be?" they demanded.

"In the movies, if I can arrange it," I snarled. Poising tabs C, D, E, F, G, H, J, K, and L in one hand and the corresponding slots in the other, I essayed a union of the two, but in vain. The moment I made one set fast and tackled another, tab and slot would part company, thumbing their noses at me. Although the children were too immature to understand. I saw in a flash where the trouble lay. Some idiotic employee at the factory had punched out the wrong design, probably out of sheer spite. So that was his game, eh? I set my lips in a grim line and, throwing one hundred and fifty-seven pounds of fighting fat into the effort, pounded the component parts into a homogeneous mass.

"There," I said with a gasp, "that's close enough. Now then, who wants candy? One, two, three—everybody off to the candy store!"

"We wanna finish the delivery truck!" they wailed. "Mummy, he won't let us finish the delivery truck!" Threats, cajolery, bribes were of no avail. In their jungle code, a twenty-nine-cent gew-gaw bulked larger than a parent's love. Realizing that I was dealing with a pair of monomaniacs, I determined to show them who was master and wildly began locking the cardboard units helter-skelter, without any regard for the directions. When sections refused to fit, I gouged them with my nails and forced them together, cack-ling shrilly. The side panels collapsed; with a bestial oath, I drove a safety pin through them and lashed them to the roof. I used paper clips, bobby pins, anything I could lay my hands on. My fingers fairly flew and my breath whistled in my throat. "You want a delivery truck, do you?" I panted. "All right, I'll show you!" As merciful blackness closed in, I was on my hands and knees, bunting the infernal thing along with my nose and whinnying, "Roll, confound you, roll!"

"Absolute quiet," a carefully modulated voice was saying, "and fifteen of the white tablets every four hours." I opened my eyes carefully in the darkened room. Dimly I picked out a knifelike character actor in a Vandyke beard and pencil-striped pants fold-ing a stethoscope into his bag. "Yes," he added thoughtfully, "if we play our cards right, this ought to be a long, expensive re-covery." From far away, I could hear my wife's voice bravely trying to control her anxiety.

"What if he becomes restless, Doctor?"

"Get him a detective story," returned the leech. "Or better still, a nice, soothing picture puzzle—something he can do with his hands."

Joseph Heller

Joseph Heller was born in Brooklyn in 1923 and served in the United States Air Force during the Second World War. After his discharge he completed his education, receiving his B.A. at Columbia in 1948 and his M.A. at Columbia the following year. A Fulbright scholar at Oxford, he returned to America at twenty-seven to become instructor at Pennsylvania State University for two years, after which he was advertising writer and promotion manager for various periodicals.

On his first mission in World War II he was assigned as a wing bombardier. His subsequent experiences furnished the material for his first book, *Catch-22*, a madly comic novel that is also a violent antiwar indictment. A sensational success, it was translated into more than a dozen languages. The author obviously regarded society as something organized by idiots, and war as something run by madmen — "the enemy is anybody who's going to get you killed, no matter which side he's on." He implied that the military bureaucracy is, by its very nature, insane. Yossarian, the central figure of *Catch-22*, just wants to survive and tries to escape from the prevailing madness by feigning insanity. That is the catch. Since it is normal to want to stop killing and getting one's self killed, Yossarian is considered sane, and therefore cannot escape.

Compounded of horror and gallows humor, *Catch-22* is the kind of book that Swift might have written in collaboration with Kafka.

CATCH-22

CHIEF WHITE HALFOAT

Doc Daneeka lived in a splotched gray tent with Chief White Halfoat, whom he feared and despised.

"I can just picture his liver," Doc Daneeka grumbled.

"Picture my liver," Yossarian advised him.

"There's nothing wrong with your liver."

"That shows how much you don't know," Yossarian bluffed, and told Doc Daneeka about the troublesome pain in his liver that had troubled Nurse Duckett and Nurse Cramer and all the doctors in the hospital because it wouldn't become jaundice and wouldn't go away.

Doc Daneeka wasn't interested. "You think you've got troubles?" he wanted to know. "What about me? You should've been in my office the day those newlyweds walked in."

"What newlyweds?"

"Those newlyweds that walked into my office one day. Didn't I ever tell you about them? She was lovely."

So was Doc Daneeka's office. He had decorated his waiting room with goldfish and one of the finest suites of cheap furniture. Whatever he could he bought on credit, even the goldfish. For the rest, he obtained money from greedy relatives in exchange for shares of the profits. His office was in Staten Island in a two-family firetrap just four blocks away from the ferry stop and only one block south of a supermarket, three beauty parlors, and two corrupt druggists. It was a corner location, but nothing helped. Population turnover was small, and people clung through habit to the same physicians they had been doing business with for years. Bills piled up rapidly, and he was soon faced with the loss of his most precious medical instruments: his adding machine was repossessed, and then his typewriter. The goldfish died. Fortunately, just when things were blackest, the war broke out.

"It was a godsend," Doc Daneeka confessed solemnly. "Most of the other doctors were soon in the service, and things picked up overnight. The corner location really started paying off, and I soon found myself handling more patients than I could handle competently. I upped my kickback fee with those two drugstores. The beauty parlors were good for two, three abortions a week. Things couldn't have been better, and then look what happened. They had to send a guy from the draft board around to look me

over. I was Four-F. I had examined myself pretty thoroughly and
discovered that I was unfit for military service. You'd think my
word would be enough, wouldn't you, since I was a doctor in good
standing with my county medical society and with my local Better
Business Bureau. But no, it wasn't, and they sent this guy around
just to make sure I really did have one leg amputated at the hip
and was helplessly bedridden with incurable rheumatoid arthritis.
Yossarian, we live in an age of distrust and deteriorating spiritual
values. It's a terrible thing," Doc Daneeka protested in a voice
quavering with strong emotion. "It's a terrible thing when even
the word of a licensed physician is suspected by the country he
loves."

Doc Daneeka had been drafted and shipped to Pianosa as a
flight surgeon, even though he was terrified of flying.

"I don't have to go looking for trouble in an airplane," he noted,
blinking his beady, brown, offended eyes myopically. "It comes
looking for me. Like that virgin I'm telling you about that couldn't
have a baby."

"What virgin?" Yossarian asked. "I thought you were telling me
about some newlyweds."

"That's the virgin I'm telling you about. They were just a couple
of young kids, and they'd been married, oh, a little over a year
when they came walking into my office without an appointment.
You should have seen her. She was so sweet and young and pretty.
She even blushed when I asked about her periods. I don't think
I'll ever stop loving that girl. She was built like a dream and wore
a chain around her neck with a medal of Saint Anthony hanging
down inside the most beautiful bosom I never saw. 'It must be a
terrible temptation for Saint Anthony,' I joked—just to put her at
ease, you know. 'Saint Anthony?' her husband said. 'Who's Saint
Anthony?' 'Ask your wife,' I told him. 'She can tell you who Saint
Anthony is.' 'Who is Saint Anthony?' he asked her. 'Who?' she
wanted to know. 'Saint Anthony,' he told her. 'Saint Anthony?'
she said. 'Who's Saint Anthony?' When I got a good look at her
inside my examination room I found she was still a virgin. I spoke
to her husband alone while she was pulling her girdle back on and
hooking it onto her stockings. 'Every night,' he boasted. A real
wise guy, you know. 'I never miss a night,' he boasted. He meant
it, too. 'I even been puttin' it to her mornings before the breakfasts she makes me before we go to work,' he boasted. There was
only one explanation. When I had them both together again I gave
them a demonstration of intercourse with the rubber models I've

got in my office. I've got these rubber models in my office with all the reproductive organs of both sexes that I keep locked up in separate cabinets to avoid a scandal. I mean I used to have them. I don't have anything any more, not even a practice. The only thing I have now is this low temperature that I'm really starting to worry about. Those two kids I've got working for me in the medical tent aren't worth a damn as diagnosticians. All they know how to do is complain. They think they've got troubles? What about me? They should have been in my office that day with those two newlyweds looking at me as though I were telling them something nobody'd every heard of before. You never saw anybody so interested. 'You mean like this?' he asked me, and worked the models for himself awhile. You know, I can see where a certain type of person might get a big kick out of doing just that. 'That's it,' I told him. 'Now, you go home and try it my way for a few months and see what happens. Okay?' 'Okay,' they said, and paid me in cash without any argument. 'Have a good time,' I told them, and they thanked me and walked out together. He had his arm around her waist as though he couldn't wait to get her home and put it to her again. A few days later he came back all by himself and told my nurse he had to see me right away. As soon as we were alone, he punched me in the nose."

"He did what?"

"He called me a wise guy and punched me in the nose. 'What are you, a wise guy?' he said, and knocked me flat on my ass. Pow! Just like that. I'm not kidding."

"I know you're not kidding," Yossarian said. "But why did he do it?"

"How should I know why he did it?" Doc Daneeka retorted with annoyance.

"Maybe it had something to do with Saint Anthony?"

Doc Daneeka looked at Yossarian blankly. "Saint Anthony?" he asked with astonishment. "Who's Saint Anthony?"

"How should I know?" answered Chief White Halfoat, staggering inside the tent just then with a bottle of whiskey cradled in his arm and sitting himself down pugnaciously between the two of them.

Doc Daneeka rose without a word and moved his chair outside the tent, his back bowed by the compact kit of injustices that was his perpetual burden. He could not bear the company of his roommate.

Chief White Halfoat thought he was crazy. "I don't know what's the matter with that guy," he observed reproachfully. "He's got no brains, that's what's the matter with him. If he had any brains he'd grab a shovel and start digging. Right here in the tent, he'd start digging, right under my cot. He'd strike oil in no time. Don't he know how that enlisted man struck oil with a shovel back in the States? Didn't he ever hear what happened to that kid — what was the name of that rotten rat bastard pimp of a snotnose back in Colorado?"

"Wintergreen."

"Wintergreen."

"He's afraid," Yossarian explained.

"Oh, no. Not Wintergreen." Chief White Halfoat shook his head with undisguised admiration. "That stinking little punk wise-guy son of a bitch ain't afraid of nobody."

"Doc Daneeka's afraid. That's what's the matter with him."

"What's he afraid of?"

"He's afraid of you," Yossarian said. "He's afraid you're going to die of pneumonia."

"He'd *better* be afraid," Chicf White Halfoat said. A deep, low laugh rumbled through his massive chest. "I will, too, the first chance I get. You just wait and see."

Chief White Halfoat was a handsome, swarthy Indian from Oklahoma with a heavy, hard-boned face and tousled black hair, a half-blooded Creek from Enid who, for occult reasons of his own, had made up his mind to die of pneumonia. He was a glowering, vengeful, disillusioned Indian who hated foreigners with names like Cathcart, Korn, Black and Havermeyer and wished they'd all go back to where their lousy ancestors had come from.

"You wouldn't believe it, Yossarian," he ruminated, raising his voice deliberately to bait Doc Daneeka, "but this used to be a pretty good country to live in before they loused it up with their goddam piety."

Chief White Halfoat was out to revenge himself upon the white man. He could barely read or write and had been assigned to Captain Black as assistant intelligence officer.

"How could I learn to read or write?" Chief White Halfoat demanded with simulated belligerence, raising his voice again so that Doc Daneeka would hear. "Every place we pitched our tent, they sank an oil well. Every time they sank a well, they hit oil. And every time they hit oil, they made us pack up our tent and go someplace else. We were human divining rods. Our whole family had a natural affinity for petroleum deposits, and soon every oil company in the world had technicians chasing us around. We were always on the move. It was one hell of a way to bring a child up, I can tell you. I don't think I ever spent more than a week in one place."

His earliest memory was of a geologist.

"Every time another White Halfoat was born," he continued, "the stock market turned bullish. Soon whole drilling crews were following us around with all their equipment just to get the jump on each other. Companies began to merge just so they could cut down on the number of people they had to assign to us. But the crowd in back of us kept growing. We never got a good night's sleep. When we stopped, they stopped. When we moved, they moved, chuckwagons, bulldozers, derricks, generators. We were a walking business boom, and we began to receive invitations from some of the best hotels just for the amount of business we would drag into town with us. Some of those invitations were mighty generous, but we couldn't accept any because we were Indians and all the best hotels that were inviting us wouldn't accept Indians as guests. Racial prejudice is a terrible thing, Yossarian. It really is. It's a terrible thing to treat a decent, loyal Indian like a nigger, kike, wop, or spic." Chief White Halfoat nodded slowly with conviction.

"Then, Yossarian, it finally happened—the beginning of the end. They began to follow us around from in front. They would try to guess where we were going to stop next and would begin drilling before we even got there, so we couldn't even stop. As soon as we'd begin to unroll our blankets, they would kick us off. They had confidence in us. They wouldn't even wait to strike oil before they kicked us off. We were so tired we almost didn't care the day our time ran out. One morning we found ourselves completely surrounded by oilmen waiting for us to come their way so they could kick us off. Everywhere you looked there was an oilman on a ridge, waiting there like Indians getting ready to attack. It was the end. We couldn't stay where we were because we had just been kicked off. And there was no place left for us to go. Only the Army saved me. Luckily, the war broke out just in the nick of time, and a draft board picked me right up out of the middle and put me down safely in Lowery Field, Colorado. I was the only survivor."

Yossarian knew he was lying, but did not interrupt as Chief White Halfoat went on to claim that he had never heard from his parents again. That didn't bother him too much, though, for he had only their word for it that they were his parents, and since they had lied to him about so many other things, they could just as well have been lying to him about that too. He was much better acquainted with the fate of a tribe of first cousins who had wandered away north in a diversionary movement and pushed inadvertently into Canada. When they tried to return, they were stopped at the border by American immigration authorities who would not let them back into the country. They could not come back in because they were red.

It was a horrible joke, but Doc Daneeka didn't laugh until Yossarian came to him one mission later and pleaded again, without any real expectation of success, to be grounded. Doc Daneeka snickered once and was soon immersed in problems of his own, which included Chief White Halfoat, who had been challenging him all that morning to Indian wrestle, and Yossarian, who decided right then and there to go crazy.

"You're wasting your time," Doc Daneeka was forced to tell him.

"Can't you ground someone who's crazy?"

"Oh, sure. I have to. There's a rule saying I have to ground anyone who's crazy."

"Then why don't you ground me? I'm crazy. Ask Clevinger."

"Clevinger? Where *is* Clevinger? You find Clevinger and I'll ask him."

"Then ask any of the others. They'll tell you how crazy I am."

"They're crazy."

"Then why don't you ground them?"

"Why don't they ask me to ground them?"

"Because they're crazy, that's why."

"Of course they're crazy," Doc Daneeka replied. "I just told you they're crazy, didn't I? And you can't let crazy people decide whether you're crazy or not, can you?"

Yossarian looked at him soberly and tried another approach. "Is Orr crazy?"

"He sure is," Doc Daneeka said.

"Can you ground him?"

"I sure can. But first he has to ask me to. That's part of the rule."

"Then why doesn't he ask you to?"

"Because he's crazy," Doc Daneeka said. "He has to be crazy to keep flying combat missions after all the close calls he's had. Sure, I can ground Orr. But first he has to ask me to."

"That's all he has to do to be grounded?"

"That's all. Let him ask me."

"And then you can ground him?" Yossarian asked.

"No. Then I can't ground him."

"You mean there's a catch?"

"Sure there's a catch," Doc Daneeka replied. "Catch-22. Anyone who wants to get out of combat duty isn't really crazy."

There was only one catch and that was Catch-22, which specified that a concern for one's own safety in the face of dangers that were real and immediate was the process of a rational mind. Orr was crazy and could be grounded. All he had to do was ask; and as soon as he did, he would no longer be crazy and would have to fly more missions. Orr would be crazy to fly more missions and sane if he didn't, but if he was sane he had to fly them. If he flew them he was crazy and didn't have to; but if he didn't want to he was sane and had to. Yossarian was moved very deeply by the absolute simplicity of this clause of Catch-22 and let out a respectful whistle.

"That's some catch, that Catch-22," he observed.

"It's the best there is," Doc Daneeka agreed.

Appendix A

ANECDOTES, JESTS, AND JOKES

No sharp line separates the anecdote from the jest or the jest from the joke. An anecdote is often nothing more than an extended jest, and a joke, according to Freud, "passes from person to person like news of the latest conquest." Compilers were busy gathering and circulating broad jokes and other gay intimacies ten years before the first complete English Bible was issued in 1535. *C Mery Tales* appeared in 1526. Even before the hundred laugh-provokers were assembled, England's first printer, William Caxton, added eleven humorous tales by "Poge the Florentyn" to his translation of Aesop in 1484. "Poge, or Poggio Bracciolini, born in 1380, put together *Liber Facetiarum* and justified his collection by saying that "our forefathers, men of the greatest discretion and learning, took delight in jests, jokes, and tales. . . . It is, moreover, a worthy and indeed a necessary thing to comfort the mind when it is weighed down by troubles and study, and to restore its gaiety by means of light recreation."

Caxton's innovation was widely imitated. Compilers stole from each other; anecdotes and jokes were amplified, revised, and reworded to suit the changing tastes of the times. In his introduction to *Humour, Wit, & Satire of the Seventeenth Century*, published in 1883, John Ashton wryly remarked that most of the jokes of the period lacked refinement "and cannot be reproduced at the present day, and much of the book suffers therefrom." Reissued in 1968, it presented a coy and curious contrast to *Jest Upon Jest* (1970), a sprightly and uninhibited selection from jestbooks and collections of merry tales from the reign of Richard III to George III. Among the early collections were those entitled *Wits, Fits, and Fancies* (1595), *Tarlton's Jests* (1570), *A Nest of Ninnies* (1608), *Mirth in Abundance* (1659), *Archie's Jests* (1639), *A Choice Banquet of Witty Jests* (1660), *Westminster Drollery* (1672), *The Sack-full of News* (1673), and *Pinkethman's Jests: or Wit Refined* (1720).

All of these were rifled for jokes about quarreling couples, nagging wives, cuckolded husbands, and mothers-in-law, jokes that became hardy perennials and are the stock in trade of today's "standup comics." Nothing was too serious or too sacred for the jest collector. Every human activity was covered, or uncovered, from bed to board as well as from bawd to bed. The compilations varied with the years; they flourished and proliferated widely in the twentieth century. Ranging from the innocuous to the scatological, they included *The Thesaurus of Anecdotes*, which contained more than 2,600 entries. Evan Esar's *Comic Dictionary*, Leo Rosten's *The Joys of Yiddish*, G. Legman's 800-page *Rationale of the Dirty Joke*, and that extraordinary compendium of classic jokes, Freud's *Wit and Its Relation to the Unconscious*.

It was apparent that the place, time, and tone of the anecdote shifted in the retelling; the central figures changed, and one famous name was substituted for another. But the twist, the "tag" line, the point of the joke remained constant. Over the centuries they varied only in style and idiom. Here, modernized in spelling, is a prime favorite.

A company of neighbors that dwelt on one side of a street said, "It is reported that all those who dwell on our side of the street are cuckolds—all except one."

When one of the husbands asked why his wife was so pensive, she replied, "I am studying which of our neighbors can it be that is not cuckold."

This appeared in *Wit and Mirth*, published in 1630 by John Taylor, the Water-Poet. The following is the way it is retold today:

A husband comes home greatly perturbed. He says to his wife, "They tell me the janitor boasts he has slept with every woman in this apartment except one."

"Hm," says his wife. "It must be that stuck-up Mrs. Nussbaum on the seventh floor."

Still extant are varied versions of the following ancient jokes, anecdotes, and repartees. Many of them are ascribed to Joe Miller, a comedian whose name was used to promote a jest-book assembled from other joke books by a hack writer, John Mottley. First published in 1739, it was entitled *Joe Miller's Jests: or The Wit's Vade-Mecum*. The book went into edition after edition until the original 247 jokes grew to more than 1,500. It was said that during the eighteenth and nineteenth centuries *Joe Miller's Jests* had more readers than Chaucer, Milton, and *Pilgrim's Progress* combined.

A young lady who had been married but a short time, seeing her husband arising quite early one morning, said, "My dear, why are you getting up so early? Come back to bed and rest yourself."

"No, my dear," replied the husband. "I will rest myself by getting up."

A man was praising a woman's chastity when a bystander questioned him. "Is she truly chaste? Has she never had a baby?"

"Well," replied the man, "she did happen to have a baby. But it was such a *little* one."

I had a love and she was chaste;
    Alack, the more's the pity.
For wot you how my love was chaste:
    She was chaste right through the city.

A certain man died and when he came to heaven-gates Saint Peter asked him what he was. "A married man," he replied.

"Come in," said Saint Peter. "You deserve a crown of glory."

Another dead man came to heaven-gate and in answer to Saint Peter's question said he had been married twice. "Come in," said the Saint, "for you have had double trouble and are worthy of a double crown of glory."

A third came claiming heaven and told Saint Peter he had had three wives. "Away with you!" cried the Saint. "Twice you were delivered from trouble, but you entered willingly in trouble a third time. Therefore, go your way to hell. You are unworthy of heaven."

When the Emperor Augustus saw a noble-looking young Greek who resembled him, he asked the young man if his mother had not been in Rome.

"No, your majesty," said the youth. "But my father has."

A young fellow had been having an affair with a maiden when her father found out what had been going on. When he learned that the young man was about to marry another maid, he demanded and obtained a sum of money because the young man refused to wed his unchaste daughter. The bride wheedled the facts from her husband and laughed. "That girl was a fool to tell her father," she said. "I carried on with a man-servant for a whole year. But you are the first person to know anything about it."

A man he did say
To his friend t'other day
That his sow had lost her life.
Said one Mister Howes,
"Speaking of sows,
Pray, neighbor, how does your wife?"

A young gentleman playing at Questions and Commands with some pretty young ladies was commanded to take off the garter from one of them. But she, as soon as he had laid hold of her petticoats, ran into the next room.

"Now, madam," said the young gentleman, tripping up her heels, "I bar squealing."

"Bar the door, you fool!" cried she.

A scholar meeting a person said to him, "I am surprised to see you. I was told you were dead."

To which the person replied, "Now you see I am alive."

The scholar thought a moment, then he said, "Perhaps so. But the man who told me has a better reputation than you for telling the truth."

A gentleman that bore a spleen to another met him in the street and boxed his ears. The struck man asked, "Was that a jest or were you in earnest?"

The gentleman replied, "It was in earnest."

"I am glad of that," said the other man, "for if it had been done in jest, I would have been very angry."

Scylla is toothless. Yet when she was young
She had both tooth enough and too much tongue.
What should I now of toothless Scylla say?
Just that her tongue has worn her teeth away.

A poor scholar traveling without money came to an alehouse and asked for a penny loaf of bread. Instead of eating it he gave it back to the hostess for a pot of ale. Having drunk it, he started to go away, when the woman said, "Give me the penny."

"For what?" said he.

"For the ale," said she.

"I gave you a loaf of bread for the ale," said he.

"Then pay for the loaf," said she.

"Why should I pay for the loaf?" he said. "You've got it, haven't you?" and he went his way.

A parson, seeing his son play roguish tricks, said, "Look! Did you ever see me do things like that when I was a boy?"

A company of friends, including the witty comedian Samuel Foote, were discussing a happily married lady who had indulged in a variety of love affairs before her marriage. They mentioned that she had told her husband all about her previous amours.

"What frankness!" said one.

"What honesty!" said another.

"And *what* a memory!" said Foote.

John-a-Noaks was driving his cart toward Croydon, and growing tired, he fell asleep in it. While he was sleeping someone unhitched his two horses and went away with them. When he awoke and found his horses missing, he exclaimed, "Either I am John-a-Noaks or I am not John-a-Noaks. If I am John-a-Noaks, then I have lost two horses. If I am not John-a-Noaks, then I have found a cart."

An amorous fellow hotly wooed a pretty young wife. "Pray cease," said she. "I have a husband that won't thank you for making him a cuckold."

"No, madam," replied the young fellow, "but you will, I hope."

A miller had wooed many girls and did lie with them and then refused to marry any of them. One girl whom he solicited declined. Whereupon he married her, and on the wedding night said to her, "If you would have let me do as I did with the rest I would not have married you."

"That is what I thought," said she, "for I was served so by half a dozen before."

Two persons who had been formerly acquainted but had not seen each other in a great while met on the road and one asked the other how he did.

"I've been married since I saw you," said the first.

"That is well," said the second.

"Not so well either," said the first, "for I married a shrew."

"That is ill," said the second.

"Not so ill either," said the first, "for she brought me two thousand pounds."

"That is well," said the second.

"No so well either," said the first, "for I spent it all on sheep, and they died of the rot."

"That is ill indeed," said the second.

"Not so ill either," said the first, "for I sold the skins for more money than the sheep cost."

"That was well indeed," said the second.

"Not so well either," said the first, "for I spent the money on a house and it burned down."

"That was very ill," said the second.

"Not so ill either," said the first, "for my wife was in it."

Two men fought a duel. One overcame the other and disarmed him. "Ask for your life," said he.

"I'll die first," said the other.

"Well," said the first, "if it's not worth your asking, it's not worth my taking."

At a trial for assault a carpenter was being browbeaten by a counselor. "What distance were you from the parties when you saw the defendant strike the plaintiff?" he was asked.

"Exactly four feet, five and a half inches," replied the carpenter.

"How is it possible," asked the counsel, "for you to be so very exact as to the distance?"

"To tell the truth," said the carpenter, "I thought perhaps some fool would ask me, and so I measured the distance."

A gentleman, having lent a guinea for two or three days to a person whose promises he had not much faith in, was very surprised to find he very punctually kept his word with him. The same person later desired to borrow a like sum. "No," said the gentleman, "you deceived me once, and I am resolved you shan't do it a second time."

A lady's age happening to be questioned, she affirmed she was only forty and called upon a gentleman for his agreement. "Cousin," said she, "do you not believe I am in the right when I say I am but forty?"

"I cannot dispute it," said he, "for I have heard you say so for the last ten years."

An Irish lawyer, having occasion to go to dinner, left these directions written and put in the keyhole of his chamber door: "I am gone to the *Elephant and Castle,* where you shall find me. If you can't read this note, carry it to the stationer's and he will read it for you."

A country farmer going across his grounds in the dusk spied a young fellow and a lass very busy near a five-bar gate. When the farmer called to them to know what they were about, the young man said, "No harm, farmer. We are just going to prop-a-gate."

Mr. G———n, the surgeon, being sent for by a gentleman who had received a slight wound, gave order to his servant to go home with all haste imaginable and fetch a certain plaster. The patient turned a little pale. "Sir," said he, "is there any danger?"

"Indeed there is," answered the surgeon. "If the fellow doesn't hurry, the wound will heal before he returns."

A gentlewoman, growing big with child, had two gallants, one of them with a wooden leg. The question was put: which of the two would father the child? He who had the wood leg offered to decide it thus: "If the child," said he, "comes into the world with a wooden leg, I will father it. If it doesn't, it must be yours."

A melting sermon being preached in a country church, all fell a-weeping — all but one. When he was asked why he did not weep with the rest, he replied, "I belong to another parish."

A famous teacher had long been married but had no child. Someone said to the wife, "Madam, your husband is an advanced mathematician."

"Yes," she replied, "but he doesn't know how to multiply."

A woman once prosecuted a gentleman for a rape. At the trial the judge asked if she had made any resistance.

"I cried out loud!" said she.

"Aye," said one of the witnesses. "But that was nine months after."

A soldier was bragging before Caesar about the many wounds he had received in the face. Caesar, knowing him to be a coward, said, "Better take heed the next time you run away. Don't look back."

A gentleman, turning against a house to make water, did not see two young ladies looking out till he heard them giggling. "What makes you so merry?" he asked.

"O sir," said one of them, "a very little thing will make us laugh."

A lap dog belonging to a fashionable lady bit a piece out of a male visitor's leg. "Oh, dear," said the lady. "I hope it doesn't make the poor creature sick."

Sydney Smith hated dogs. Therefore he was embarrassed when a lady patron asked him to name one of her new dogs. "Mind you," said she, "I want something out of the ordinary. None of your commonplace names."

"I have just the right name for your dog," said Smith. "Call him Spot."

"But," demurred the lady, "Spot is a most commonplace name."

"Not if you think of him as a dog out of Shakespeare," said Smith.

"Shakespeare?" she asked.

"Macbeth, fifth act," said Smith. "*Out*, damned Spot!"

"I am glad to see you better," said his surgeon to the actor Samuel Foote. "You followed my prescription, of course."

"On the contrary," said Foote. "Had I followed your prescription I would have broken my neck."

"Broken your neck?" exclaimed the surgeon. "How so?"

"Absolutely," said Foote. "I threw the prescription out of my third-story window."

At a dinner table where there were a large number of guests, Charles Lamb was mistaken for a clergyman and was called on to say grace.

"Is there no cl-cl-clergyman pr-pr-present?" stuttered Lamb.

"No," said a guest.

"Then," said Lamb, bowing his head, "l-l-let us thank God."

Lady C—— and her two daughters had taken lodgings at a leather-breeches-maker's in Piccadilly. The lodgings were comfortable, but she was always put to the blush when she had to give anyone direction to her lodgings, for the sign said "The Cock and Leather Breeches." Finally the lady told her landlord, a jolly young fellow, that she liked him and his lodgings very well, but she must quit them on account of his sign.

"O madam," said the young fellow, "I would do anything rather than lose such good lodgers. I can easily alter the sign."

"That is what I thought," said the lady. "I'll tell you how you may satisfy both me and my daughters. Take down your Leather Breeches and let your Cock stand."

On a time Scoggin was jesting with the queen and said, "Madam, riches—gold, silver, precious stones—do tempt men, and especially women, and cause women to fall to lechery and folly."

The queen said a good woman would never be tempted with gold or silver or other riches.

"I pray you, madam," said Scoggin the jester, "if there were a goodly lord that would give you forty thousand pounds to dally with you, what would you say to it?"

The queen said, "If any man would give a hundred thousand pounds, I would not lose my virtue for it."

Then said Scoggin, "What if a man should offer a hundred thousand thousand pounds, what would you do?"

"I would," said the queen, "do no folly for such."

Then said Scoggin, "What if a man did give you a house full of gold?"

"Well," said the queen, "a woman might do much for that."

"Lo!" said Scoggin. "If a man had goods enough, he might have the most sovereign lady." For which words the queen took a high displeasure with Scoggin. Wherefore it doth appear that it is not good jesting with lords and ladies, for if a man be plain he shall be ruined for his labor.

The piece of repartee above is from a sixteenth-century joke-book, *The Jests of Scoggin*, but the story is borrowed from a fourteenth-century Italian jest about the Duchess of Ferrara.

This is the way it has been twisted to fit the taste of the twentieth century:

At a gala cocktail party an out-of-town businessman is flirting with a leader of high society. After the third martini he says to her, "I am a man of few words. I am taking a plane in the morning. Will you spend the night with me for fifty dollars?"

She laughs. "You're quite a joker."

"I mean it," he says. "How about a hundred dollars?"

"You can't be serious," she replies. "But if you are, of course it's out of the question."

"I *am* serious. What about five hundred?" he persists. "Five hundred dollars for a couple of hours."

"Well," she says, "for five hundred, perhaps. . . ."

"Good," he says. "Now that we've established the principle, let's haggle about the price."

Appendix B

THE PUN

Universally ridiculed, punning (like poetry) is something everyone belittles and almost everyone attempts. A pun is pro-
verbially "the lowest form of wit," and "he who will make a
pun will pick a pocket." Oliver Wendell Holmes deprecated
the punning habit, but he himself was not only a New England
pundit but also a punster. He began his medical career by
announcing that "small fevers would be thankfully received,"
and his house was a unique sort of pun exchange; it was observed that there was no place like Holmes'.

It seems that no one enjoys any puns except his own. A word
—any word—with punning possibilities drops into a conversation, and someone seizes on the sound, twists it, and gives it
another sense. Whereupon the other, usually slower-minded
members turn upon the punster, emit unpleasant noises, and
threaten to sever his jocular vein.

Actually the pun is a poetic device, which is why poets have
excelled as punsters. Poetry is essentially a form of play—a
play of metaphor, a play of imagery, a play of rhyme. The pun
is, like certain forms of verse, a form of verbal dexterity, a
syllabic matching of sounds that, like rhymes, are similar yet
not quite the same. Whatever change it assumes, searching or
silly, the pun springs from the same combination of wit and
imagination that speeds the poetic process.

The best puns depend on spontaneity—a printed, annotated anthology of puns is unreadable. Remove the momentary time-liness that gives rise to them, and they become virtually mean-ingless. One must recall the Spanish Civil War to appreciate the remark that when the Barcelonians were moving through a dangerous corridor, someone said it was foolish to put all the Basques in one exit, and that in any case Spain was a snare Andalusian.

In spite of its detractors, punning has had a long and honor-able lineage. Shakespeare was one of its chief exponents. He used puns constantly to intensify the light and shade of almost overpowering dramas. The tragic-lyrical *Romeo and Juliet* opens with rude and bawdy banter as two of Capulet's servants play with words.

SAMPSON: Gregory, o' my word, we'll not carry coals.
GREGORY: No, for then we should be colliers.
SAMPSON: I mean, an we be in choler, we'll draw.
GREGORY: Ay, while you live, draw your neck out o' the collar.
SAMPSON: I strike quickly being moved.
GREGORY: But thou art not quickly moved to strike.
SAMPSON: A dog of the Montague house moves me.
GREGORY: To move is to stir, and to be valiant is to stand. Therefore if thou art moved, thou run'st away.
SAMPSON: A dog of that house shall move me to stand. I will take the wall of any man or maid of Montague's.
GREGORY: That shows thee a weak slave, for the weakest goes to the wall.
SAMPSON: 'Tis true, and therefore women, being the weaker vessels, are ever thrust to the wall. Therefore I will push Montague's men from the wall, and thrust his maids to the wall. . . .
When I have fought with the men, I will be cruel with the maids. I will cut off their heads.
GREGORY: The heads of the maids?
SAMPSON: Ay, the heads of the maids, or their maidenheads. Take it in what sense thou wilt.
GREGORY: They must take it in sense that feel it.
SAMPSON: Me they shall feel while I am able to stand. And 'tis known I am a pretty piece of flesh.

In the first scene of *Julius Caesar*, the Roman tribune Mar-cellus asks a commoner his trade, and the man, who happens to be a shoemaker, replies: "A trade, sir, that I hope I may use with a safe conscience; which is, indeed, sir, a mender of bad soles."

Shakespeare employed such verbal bandyings not merely to amuse the groundlings but to provide a contrast, a comic relief to ease the tension. He knew that even a small flash of wit would be welcome against the murky violence of death and disaster. The greatest of poets and playwrights put his puns not only in the mouths of clowns and fools, but also on the lips of noble souls. After Mercutio has been stabbed, Romeo tries to assure him that the hurt cannot be much; and the dying hero—one of the most short-lived yet one of the most endearing of Shakespeare's characters—expires with a pun: "No, 'tis not so deep as a well, nor so wide as a church-door, but 'tis enough, 'twill serve. Ask for me to-morrow, and you shall find me a grave man."

It is no accident that the best punsters have been poets, for there is a natural affinity between the two. A pun is for the ear as well as for the eye; a good pun, like a good rhyme, seems both accidental and inevitable. The poets were forever punning, even on their own names. The seventeenth-century George Wither wrote:

> *I Grow and Wither*
> *Both together.*

When reproached for not writing more serious poetry, Thomas Hood replied:

> *If I would earn my livelihood*
> *I have to be a lively Hood.*

And it was probably Hood—although the lines are sometimes attributed to Samuel Johnson, an avowed enemy of punning—who excused his passion for punning by saying:

> *If I were ever punishéd*
> *For every little pun I shed,*
> *I'd hie me to a puny shed*
> *And there I'd hang my punnish head.*

Joyce's *Finnegans Wake* is a book-length frolic of puns. The nonrational logic of the many-level parable (or parody) of the life of everyman embodies more than a thousand surrealist word-plays. In a long labyrinth in which even scholars lose their way, Joyce, the most riotous punster since Shakespeare, misleads the careless reader with such ploys as "There's no plagues like Rome," "Wring out the clothes! Wring in the new!" and "Ibscenest nanscence." His gargantuan characters eat with the utmost joviality, but in Joyce's nightmare language, they indulge with "eatmost boviality." His common fellows are "abelboobied," humanity is "danzzling on the age of a vulcano," and a famous watering place is "Aches-les-Pains." Attempting to combine two senses simultaneously, Joyce joins the words "melody" and "odorous." This results in "melo-dorous," the opposite of "malodorous." But Joyce wants it still sweeter. Remembering the French word for honey *(miel)*, he incorporates this, writes "mielodorous"—and a new word has been coined from a bilingual pun.

Robert Frost was another poet who knew that the pun was Pierian, that it sprang from the same soil as the Muse. He insisted that the most American trait was a combination of patriotism and shrewdness; he called it Americanniness. He made fun of the liberal-lugubrious lyrics of Conrad Aiken by referring to the poet as "Comrade Aching." "T. S. Eliot and I have our similarities and our differences," he once wrote. "We are both poets and we both like to play. That's the similarity. The difference is this: I like to play euchre; he liked to play Eucharist."

The best puns are those that embody not only a twist in meaning, but a trick of idea. No one ever surpassed the remark by Eugene Field, who criticized John McCullough's performance of King Richard III: "He played the king as if he were afraid somebody else might play the ace." And no article on puns dares face the public unless it includes Artemus Ward's appraisal of Brigham Young and his ever-growing collection of Mormon wives. "Pretty girls in Utah," said the humorist, "mostly marry Young."

It was in Hollywood that a maturing glamour girl complained she was not her former sylph, and a writer decided to change her features that were markedly Semitic. "Ah," said one of her friends when the plastic surgeon had finished his reconstruction, "I see you've cut off your nose to spite your race." "Yes," replied the writer imperturbably, "now I'm a thing of beauty and a *goy* forever." One does not have to know the line from Keats's "Endymion" or the Jewish word for Gentile to appreciate the double twist of the pun. Likewise one does not have to be a French scholar to relish the story of the exchange of courtesies between two of the world's great department stores. When the head of Macy's visited Paris, he went to the Galeries Lafayette, where a committee received him. As he entered, the American said, "Galeries Lafayette, we are here!" Whereupon his French colleague, not to be outdone, murmured, "Macy beaucoup."

The apotheosis of the pun may well be the one about the jester who punned on every subject except his royal master. When commanded to do so, he replied that the king was not a subject, whereupon the monarch ordered his execution. As the poor fellow stood on the gallows, a messenger arrived with news that the king would pardon him on condition that he would never commit another pun. Looking at the rope coiled about his neck, the jester said, "No noose is good noose," and was hanged.

Index of Authors

Index of Titles

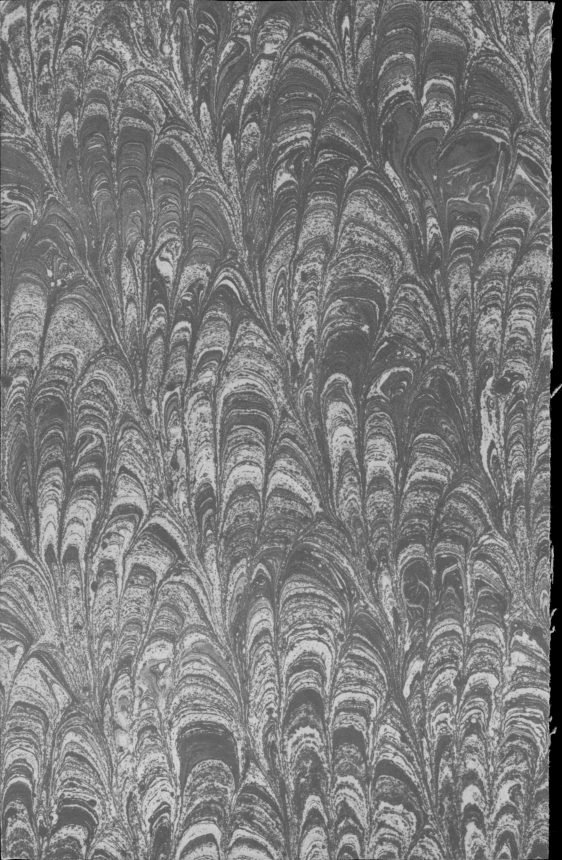